BRITISH FAMILY NAMES

THEIR ORIGIN AND MEANING

BRITISH FAMILY NAMES

Their Origin and Meaning

WITH

LISTS OF SCANDINAVIAN, FRISIAN, ANGLO-SAXON AND NORMAN NAMES

BY

Rev. HENRY BARBER, M.D., F.S.A.

AUTHOR OF

'FURNESS AND CARTMEL NOTES,' 'THE CISTERCIAN ABBEY OF MAULBRONN,' 'SOME QUEER NAMES,' 'THE SHRINE OF ST BONIFACE AT FULDA,' ETC.

'What's in a name?'—*Romeo and Juliet.*

'I believe now, there is some secret power and virtue in a name.'
BURTON'S *Anatomy of Melancholy.*

SECOND EDITION, ENLARGED

LONDON
ELLIOT STOCK, 62 PATERNOSTER ROW, E.C.
1903

REPUBLISHED BY GALE RESEARCH COMPANY, BOOK TOWER, DETROIT, 1968

Library of Congress Catalog Card Number 68–17914

CONTENTS

PREFACE TO THE FIRST EDITION

THE following pages are offered to the public in the belief that they will be found useful to those interested in the study of names or engaged in compiling family histories.

Although the vast catalogue of British surnames may not have been exhausted, yet by many years' labour more than eight thousand representative modern names, extracted from directories, newspapers, voting lists, etc., have been traced to their source, and when it is remembered that this includes the numerous variations and ramifications of these patronymics, the extensive scope of this work will then be appreciated.

The utility of the lists of ancient names to the student of local etymology must at once be apparent, whilst to the genealogist (whether British, Colonial, or American) the revelations as to the transformation of family names will be of the utmost service.

H. B.

RAVENSTONE,
ASHBY-DE-LA-ZOUCH.

vii

PREFACE TO THE SECOND EDITION

ANOTHER edition being demanded, an effort has been made to present it in a cheap and popular form.

The book has been revised, enlarged, and improved; and, besides additional information in the introductory part, the number of family names has been brought up to over ten thousand.

Many errors have been rectified, but the writer is conscious of defects still existing, which time, experience, and further research may help to overcome.

He takes this opportunity of thanking his numerous correspondents, in all parts of the world, for their kind and encouraging communications.

BOOKS CONSULTED

Abel, H. F. Otto. Die deutschen Personen-Namen. Berlin, 1889.

Bailey, N. German and English Dictionary. 2 vols. 8vo. Jena, 1810.

Bartholomew, J. Gazetteer of Great Britain. Edin. 1887.

Bosworth, Rev. J. Anglo-Saxon Dictionary. Lond. 1868.

Buchanan, W. Scottish Surnames. 8vo. Glasgow, 1820.

Burke's Peerage and Baronetage.

Camden Society. Lists of Foreign Protestants and Aliens. 1862.

Chambers's Etymological Dictionary. Lond. 1868.

Charnock, R. S. Patronymica Cornu-Britannica. 8vo. 1870.

Cleasby and Vigfusson's Icelandic-English Dictionary. Oxf. 1874.

Directories of Belgium, Denmark, Germany, Holland, Normandy, Norway, Sweden.

Domesday Book.

Edmunds, F. Names of Places. Lond. 1869.

Ellis, Sir H. Introduction to the Study of Domesday Book. 2 vols. 8vo. Lond. 1833.

Ferguson, R. Surnames as a Science. 8vo. Lond. 1884.

Finlayson, J. Surnames and Sirenames. 8vo. Lond.

Fishwick, H., F.S.A. Rochdale Surnames.

Frey, A. B. Names, Nicknames, and Sobriquets. 8vo. 1888.

Guppy, H. B. Homes of Family Names. 8vo. Lond. 1890.

Halliwell, J. O. Dictionary of Archaic Terms. 2 vols. Lond. 1868.

Hardy, T. D. Rotuli de Oblatis et Finibus, *temp*. Regis Johannis. 8vo. Lond. 1835.

Hardy, T. D. Rotuli Normanniæ. 8vo. Lond. 1835.

Innes, C. Some Scotch Surnames. 4to. Edin. 1860.

Islands Landnáma-bók.

Joyce, P. W. Irish Names of Places. 2 vols. 1883.

Kelly's County Directories of England.

Kemble, J. M. The Names, Surnames, and Nicknames of the Anglo-Saxons. 8vo. Lond. 1846.

Koolmann, T. D. Wörterbuch der Ostfrieschen Sprache. 3 vols. Norden, 1882.

Long, H. A. Personal and Family Names. 8vo. Lond. 1883.

Lower, M. A. Patronymica Britannica. Lond. 1860.

Matheson, R. E. Surnames in Ireland. Dublin, 1894.

Matheson, R. E. Synomyms of Irish Surnames. Dublin, 1890.

Moisy, H. Glossaire comparatif Anglo-Normand. Caen, 1889.

Moisy, H. Noms de famille Normands. Paris, 1875.

Moore, A. W. Surnames and Place-names of the Isle of Man. 8vo. Lond. 1890.

Morris, T. E., LL.M. Welsh Surnames, " Bygones." Oswestry, 1899-1900.

Murray's Handbook of Normandy, with Maps. 8vo. Lond. 1854.

O'Hart, J. Irish Pedigrees. 8vo. Dublin, 1876.

Palgrave, Sir F. Normandy and England. 4 vols. 8vo. Lond. 1851-64.

Planché, J. R. The Conqueror and his Companions. 2 vols. Lond. 1874.

Registrar-General's Reports, England and Scotland, 1890-94.

Rotuli Hundredorum. 2 vols. fol. A.D. 1273.

Round, J. H. Calendar of Documents in France, A.D. 918-1206, vol. i. 8vo. Lond. 1899.

Searle, W. G. Onomasticon Anglo-Saxonicum. Camb. 1897.

Sharpe, R. R. Calendar of Wills, Court of Husting, 1258 to 1688. 2 vols. 8vo. Lond. 1889.

Sims, C. S. Scottish Surnames. 1862.

Taylor, Rev. I. Words and Places. Lond. 1865.

The Norman People. 8vo. Lond. 1874.

Vigfusson, Dr G. Sturlinga Saga. Index of Names in vol. ii. 8vo. 1878.

Worsaae, J. J. A. Danes in England. 8vo. Lond. 1852.

Yonge, C. M. History of Christian Names. 8vo. Lond. 1884.

INTRODUCTION

'A painful work it is and more than difficult, wherein what toyle hath been taken, as no man thinketh, so no man believeth, but he that hath made the trial.'—ANTHONY A WOOD.

D URING a lengthened research in studying the place-names of the Danelagh, the writer accumulated a great number of names from ancient sources necessary for unravelling the tangled skein of local etymology.

It occurred to him that these might be utilised in the treatment of British surnames, and his first idea was to publish the lists with an introductory chapter on the origin of surnames, for the use of students of this branch of archæology, who were in need of such things, for easy reference.

With this view the author wrote an article in the *Antiquary* (September 1891), in order to draw attention to the subject, as Lower's 'English Surnames' is both out of date and altogether unreliable.

After this he met with, for the first time, the last-mentioned author's 'Patronymica Britannica,' a more ambitious work, and a great improvement upon the previous attempt, but still deficient in precise information and investigation.

The dictionary form, however, seemed to be the best for ready reference, and he thought a few examples, to show the way in which he had wrought out the names, would be of service to those who are interested in this important study. Hence it came about that this work has gradually grown until it assumes its present proportions.

The chief object has been, as far as possible, to avoid anything like guess-work or fancy interpretation, and to seek for a definition among such sources as seemed likely to supply it; so that, when a word could not be referred to any reasonable origin, it was put on the shelf until time, experience, and discovery should verify it.

Besides the works of reference which he consulted, he found it necessary to prepare, for his own use, the lists of names already mentioned, and these have been of so much service that he trusts they will be found equally available for all those who wish to enter upon this arduous but fascinating task.

In addition to these he has examined directories and maps of Great Britain, Norway, Sweden, Denmark, Holland, Flanders, Germany, Normandy, etc.

Many a name that seemed to defy all explanation was found to be that of some obscure village, so disguised as to be almost past

A

recognition.   Who, for instance, would expect to see Sevenoaks in Snooks, St Olave's Street in Tooley Street, St Etheldreda in Tawdry, D'Eagles in Diggles, Wilburgham in Wilbraham, Tuberville in Trouble-field, Longueville in Longfellow, Longchamps in Longshanks, Blondeville in Blomfield, Adburgham in Abraham and Abram, Renshaw in Wrencher and Wrinch, Wymondham in Wyndham?

Indeed, as Mr Lower truly says :

'Corruptions which many family names have undergone tend to baffle alike the genealogical and etymological inquirer.'

The following will serve as illustrations of the corruption to which names are liable.   The family name of Weewall occurs frequently in the parish register of Peckleton, Leicestershire, and between 1735 and 1750 there are many variations of the spelling, scarcely two entries being alike.   It appears as Whewaugh, Whewvaugh, Wheevaw, Weway, Weewaa, Wheewhal, Whewwhaw, Whealwhal, Weewal, Wheelwall.   In the North of England it took the form of Whewell.

The name of the great English dramatist is generally spelt Shakes-peare, but there are many ways of spelling the name according to English orthography.   Here are a few of them as appearing in old documents :   Shakspere, Shaxpere, Shakspire, Shaxspere, Schaksper, Shakespere, Shakspeare, Schakespeyr, Shaxespeare, Shagspere, Shax-pur, Shaxsper, Shaksper, Shackspeare, Saxpere, Shakespire, Shakespeire, Shackespeare, Shakaspear, Shaxper, Shakspear, Shaxpeare, Shakspeere, Shaxbure, Shackspeyr, Shakespear, Schakesper, etc.

Goodwin is found in ancient documents as Godewyn, Godin, Godwin, Godwyn, Goodwen, Goodwin, Goodwyn, Goodwyne.

Bugge as Buci, de Bougy, de Bucy, Bugi, Boci, Bogge, Busse, Boge, Bouche, Boughe, Buggey, Bussey, Bogg, Boag, Boake, Bogue, Beucy, Beucey, Boogie, Bugey, Buggy, Buggie, Bukie, Bouky, Boog, etc.*

Yule appears as Yovele, Youhill, Youille, Youle, Yowell, Yewell, Youell, Yuell, Yewle, Yeule, Jouel, Jowel, Jewell, Jule, Yull, Juler, etc.

Applethwaite as Ablewhite, Ablett, Ebblethwaite, Hebblethwaite, Hepplewhite, etc.

Job as Jopp, Jupp, Jubb, Juby, Jubey, Chubb, Chope, Jupp, Jupe.

Mr W. P. Phillimore, M.A., B.C.L., in 'Notes on Finnimore, Phillimore, and their Allied Surnames,' gives fifty-nine different ways of spelling the former, and thirty-four of the latter surname.

---

* The arms of Bugge, Bouge, Bugey, or de Bougy, are :—Or on a fesse sable three water bougets ar.   This is a play upon the name, but it gives the early pronunciation.

BRITISH SURNAMES

'This is a subject which involves many curious questions of antiquarian interest, bearing upon the language, habits and pursuits of our countrymen in bygone days. It is one, also, that immediately concerns every man who feels an honest pride in being called by his father's name.'—*Notes and Queries*, vi. 201.
'To find out the true originall of surnames is full of difficulty.'—CAMDEN.

MUCH speculation has arisen as to the date when surnames were first used in this country. It is now pretty well admitted that they began to be adopted about A.D. 1000.

According to Lower, the practice commenced in Normandy, and gradually extended itself to this country; but the use of surnames was occasionally hereditary among the Anglo-Saxons before the Conquest, and the general adoption of family designations.

In the time of King Edward the Confessor there was among the Saxon tenants in Suffolk one Leuric Hobbesune. Suert Magno or Manni, Godric Poinc, Tedricus Pointel, Siuuard Rufus, Stigand Soror also occur.

At the time of the Domesday Survey they were becoming more numerous, for both the tenants in chief and the under-tenants possessed them. Thus we find Alwin Dodesune, Godric Cratel, William Goizenboded, William Hosed, Hugo Lasne, Walter Achet, Osmund Angevin, Roger Arundel, Bernard Barb, Walter Bec, Hugo Bolebec, William Bonvaslet, Aluin Coc (bedellus), William Denomore, Roger Deramis, etc.

Various writers have treated the subject of British surnames in different ways, from Camden and Lower downwards. Some have produced very amusing articles by grouping the most extraordinary names they could find together, as the names of birds, beasts, flowers, objects in common use, trades, etc.

A few have made some attempts to give the derivations of well-known names according to their own classification, ignoring altogether the possibility of many being traced to extremely ancient sources.

Names which betoken association with territorial possession and occupations, and Christian names also, are not difficult to distinguish; but the oldest names of all are those which belong to the Norse or Frisian settlers, except such as are probably of Celtic or British origin.

It is a well-known fact that many family names are peculiar to certain localities, where they have remained for many generations, as can be proved from the old church registers. The spread of railways and the increased facilities for locomotion in every way are fast altering the old state of things, however, especially where there is a sudden development of one or more local industries, causing a great influx of strangers.

In remote country places, and particularly in agricultural districts, many of the old family names still remain—some, indeed, are seldom found in any other part of England.

In one district in England a marked peculiarity in the names of the people exists. This is known as the Danish Settlement (Danelagh), already referred to.

Here, as might be expected, is a strong Norse element, and this distinction is more clearly marked the farther east one goes, as the names have not undergone the modification so often found in the west, since in many cases the original Scandinavian form prevails.

The family nomenclature of this part of the country undoubtedly requires particular treatment. It is not surprising, therefore, to discover many personal names, either of pure Norse families or of places or qualities.

In East Anglia a large proportion of the family names are mono-syllabic. This singularity is so striking that it forces itself upon the most casual observer. Perhaps it is owing to the large infusion of names of Dutch and Flemish origin.

Moreover, strangely enough, the local pronunciation of names of persons and places has long outlived the many orthographical changes which took place in our written language while men spelt words phonetic-ally, or as fancy dictated. Accordingly, we find in old records, from Anglo-Saxon charters and Domesday Book to later times, strange varia-tions, in some cases making the derivation from the original source by no means easy.

All this is very interesting to the student of British surnames, who looks at the subject, not on the humorous side only, but in its historical, etymological, ethnological, and topographical aspect.

The language—dialect if preferred—of the North of England is to this day full of words and expressions which can only be explained by the help of the Icelandic, as the representative of the old Northern languages spoken by the Scandinavian settlers in England. The colonization of Iceland was included in that stream of emigration which began to leave Norway A.D. 852, and spread along the coasts of Normandy, England, Ireland, and Scotland up to the end of the eleventh century. For about four hundred years afterwards the old Norse tongue was locked up in that remarkable Northern island, and preserved almost incorrupt, while the mother-country became affected, and its original language considerably modified, by contact with other European nations.

In a sort of Domesday Book, compiled by the authorities in Iceland (Islands Landnámá-bók), there was, among other matters recorded and deposited in the cathedral of Reykyavik, a roll of the names of the original settlers (of which perhaps a third are women) and the lands they occupied, making about five thousand proper names.

This remarkable document, which has been preserved, throws great light upon the derivation of many personal and local names in Scotland and Northern England hitherto considered to be obscure, and it is as necessary to the antiquary as the so-called 'Roll of Battell Abbey' or the Domesday Book of the Conqueror. It is, in fact, the chief storehouse for genealogical knowledge.

The study of the Icelandic, in its relation to old and provincial English and its comparison with Swedish, Norwegian, Danish, Frisian, Flemish, and German, has opened out a wonderful field of never-ending interest, and made us acquainted with things we never before dreamed of in connection with this subject.

In the course of his researches the writer has picked up a few odds and ends of information which may perhaps be useful to others. It is possible to derive some instruction and to extract no little amusement from the carrying out of a train of speculation on the origin of names, so, if these details appear somewhat dry, it is to be hoped they will be set down as a humble effort to deal as carefully with a special and difficult subject as the nature of the materials within reach and limited qualifications for the task will permit of. It may appear to some, possibly, that the importance of the old Norse has been over-estimated, and not enough credit given to the Anglo-Saxon.

Perhaps it is so; but, besides the names of places, it must be admitted that very many modern English words show early Northern influence, and even in Anglo-Saxon times the language was so blended with Scandinavian words that there were often double expressions for the same thing.

It seems clear that the Frisian dialect of the Low German gives the best idea of the original so-called Anglo-Saxon, for it is the modern representative of the language of old Dutch Friesland, whence so many of those who settled in England (after the departure of the Romans) came.

This appears to be borne out by the fact that the early English missionaries (notably St. Boniface) made their way to that country because it was the home of their fathers, and there was no more difficulty with the language than in the case of a citizen of the United States visiting Britain.

It will be seen that even at this early period names were derived from localities, occupations, personal and mental qualities and peculiarities as nicknames, social relations, etc. Further, in common with the Teutonic races, the Norse used diminutives, or pet names, which afterwards stuck to the individuals so designated and became family names.

The terminations ing, kin, and son, so common in English names, are derived from the Norse, *ingr, kyn,* and *sonr,* the *r* being dropped in compounds. The Danish make the last *sen.* Also *kyn* must not be confounded with the diminutive-endings: Germ., *chen;* Fris., *ken* and *ke;* Flem., *kin;* which have quite a different meaning and are used in pet names chiefly.

The diminutives, Frisian, ken, ke, ock, and cock;* Norman French,

* There has been much controversy over the termination 'cock.' It appears to be derived from the Frisian *gök* or *kök,* a foolish, silly, awkward person, hence the Scotch *gowk.* The Fris. *Jankök* (Johncock) is equivalent to the German *Hans Wurst.* At first applied to children as a check to thoughtlessness, it would become gradually used as a diminutive. *Cock* and *ock* are akin to *ke.* In some cases cock is a corruption of *cot* found in local names.

et, ette, let, ot, otte, ell; Old Norse, i, a, ki, ka, gi, ga, ungr, ingr, lingr, should be noted.

It will be useful to apply the test of the old world sources to the family names of this country, comparing them in the first instance with those of the Northern nations, the Scandinavians (Danes so called), the Frisians (*i.e.* Saxons), the Old English (Anglo-Saxon) in Domesday Book, and, in the second place, with existing names in Northern Germany, Sweden, Denmark, Normandy, Holland, and Flanders.

In addition to these quarries, which the writer will endeavour to work, it may be mentioned that there are many names which clearly bear the stamp of foreign origin, and have not yet been so entirely metamorphosed but that their Continental source may be discovered. An Act of the Irish Parliament (5 Edw. IV., c. 3, A.D. 1465) ordained that every Irishman dwelling betwixt or amongst Englishmen in the counties of Dublin, Myeth, Vriel, and Kildare, should dress like Englishmen and take an English surname, of a town (as Sutton, Chester, etc.), or colour (as white, black), or art (as smith, carpenter, etc.), or office (as cook or butler), and he and his issue should use the same under a specified penalty. Thus, O'Gowan became Smith and MacIntyre Carpenter, etc. Most surnames will be found to come under one or other of the following heads :

1. Nicknames.
2. Clan or tribal names.
3. Place-names.
4. Official names.

5. Trade names.
6. Christian names.
7. Foreign names.
8. Foundling names.

I.—NICKNAMES

' You had not your name for nothing.'—Old Proverb.

Unquestionably the oldest names of all are those derived from by-names, given on account of a strong peculiarity of figure, feature, or character, deed of prowess, eccentricity of dress, speech, or carriage.

Among primitive nations the slightest deviation from the ordinary course of life or difference among his fellows was enough to mark a man, especially where a striking cognomen was readily applied. Fleet-ness of foot, a mighty hunter, skill in the use of a particular weapon, or the very opposite, gave rise to a name implying praise or contempt. Indeed, the most trifling cause served to invent a title by which a man was distinguished from his contemporaries. When King Magnus assumed the Highland dress he become known as Berbeinn (Bareleg) among his followers, and this is preserved to us in the modern though Puritan-sounding Barebones.

A man became notorious on account of a fearful scar upon his leg, hence he was called Orra-beinn (Scar-leg), which we see in Horrabin to this day.

In the Orkneys the Norse Earl Einar gained the *soubriquet* of

'Turf-Einar' (Torf-Einarr) from having taught the Norsemen to dig peat, he having probably learnt it himself from the Gaelic tribes in Scotland.

Blund and Blunt (Blunðr, dozing, slumber), Brock (Bróki), Hannay (Hani, a cock), Hacker and Harker (Hákr), Harfoot (Héra-fotr, a Danish king), Read, Reader (Hreðr), Rell (Hrella), Rooke (Hrúkr), Root (Hrútr), Hook (Húkr), Catt (Köttr, a cat), Kemp, Camp (Kampi, a champion), Capps, Capper (Kappi), Kimber (Kimbi), Cropper (Kroppr), Maxey (Maxi), Masey, Macey (Mási), Monk (Munki), Orry (Orri, a moor fowl), Peak, Pick (Pík), Payne (Peini), Ramm (Ramr, strong), Spurr (Spörr, a sparrow), Stott (Stoti, foolish), Sandys (Sandi), Sellers, Sell (Selr, a seal), Silver (Silfri), Strong (Strangi), Scarth (Scarði, hare-lip), Skinner (Skinni), Scory (Skorri), Skeat, Skett (Skyti, a marksman, a shooter), Stubbs (Stubbi), Syers, Siers (Syr), Young (Ungi), Horrocks (Örrek) are familiar names derived from old Norse nicknames.

Among these also may be classed pet names. In girls Sigga from Sig-riðr, Gunna from Guð-run, Inga from Ing-unn, Imba from Ingi-björg, Gudda from Guð-riðr, etc.

In boys Siggi from Sig-urðr, Gvendr from Guð-mundr, Simbi from Sigmundr, Brynki from Bryn-jólfr, Steinki from Stein-grimr, Mangi from Magnus, etc.

A list of these will be found in the appendix to the Norse names.

The Anglo-Saxons also had their nicknames. In Codex Dipl. are Godwine Rust (rustiness), Toui hwita (white), Towi reâda (red), Brihtric geonga (younger), Þurcyl hwita, Þurcyl blâca, Godwine reâda, Eâdgyfu swanhals (Edith the swan-necked), Æðelflœd hwite, Harald Hâranfôt (harefoot), Þurcyl myranheâfod (mareshead) Eâdrîc streôna (the acquirer), from streôn (treasure), Eâdberht Pren (priest), Oda se gôda (the good), Ælfgâr se gyldena (the golden) Ælfrîc Prœt (ingenious), Anfrid ceocesfôt (cocksfoot). Also Mol or Mûl (mule), Leofing (dearling, darling), hwœde (gentle), Tâte (tender), Enede (duck), Crâwe (crow), Coifi, Coefe, Coefig, Cêfig (the bold or active one), Dun (dark), Mucel (big), Brorda (swordsman), Cnebba (with a beak), Stefna (with a stem or prow—a ship-owner), Pâda (with a tunic), Buc (stag), and even Bucge and Bycge were used as by-names.

Of pet-names or diminutives there are Totta for Torthelm, Sicgga for Sigiberd, Æti for Eâdsige, Ælle for Ælfwine, Odda for Ordgâr, Podda, Dudda, Bubba, Tudda, Obe, Offa, Ibe, Beda, Becca, Beonna, Acca, Heca, Lulla, may have had a similar origin.

Of later date may be mentioned that of Fortescue, said to have been bestowed on Sir Richard le Fort, one of the leaders of the Conqueror's army at the Battle of Hastings, who had the good fortune to protect his chief by bearing before him the *escue*, or shield.

The name of Plantagenet, borne by eight successive kings of England, originated with Fulke or Foulques, Count of Anjou, about the twelfth century, who went on a pilgrimage to Jerusalem, and wore in his helmet, as a mark of his humility, a piece of *planta genista*, or broom. Armstrong and Strongitharm arose from some feat of strength; Santerer was one who had been to the Holy Land (Saint Terre); Romer, one who had been to Rome; Palmer, a pilgrim, etc.

Again, Applejohn, Brownjohn, Littlejohn, Micklejohn, Prettyjohn, Properjohn, Upjohn, etc., are probably of this class. The French have Beaujean, Bonjean, Grandjean, Grosjean, Henryjean, Klinjean, Mallejean, Neujean, Petitjean.

II.—CLAN OR TRIBAL NAMES

'My foot is on my native heath and my name is MacGregor.'—SCOTT.

According to the Rev. Dr. Todd:

'Clan signifies children or descendants. The tribe being descended from a common ancestor, the chieftain, as the representative of that ancestor, was regarded as the common father of the clan, and they as his children.'

The Gaelic *Mac*, the Irish *O*, the British *Ap*, the Norse *ungar*, the Frisian *ingar* and *en*, the Anglo-Saxon *ing*, the Norman *Fitz*,* are all indications of a family name.

'By Mac and O you'll always know
    True Irishmen, they say;
But if they lack both "O" and "Mac,"
    No Irishmen are they.'

The ancient tribe of Waring or Wearing, the Vœringi or Veringen, originally from what is still called the Vœringifjord in Norway, formed the celebrated Varangian Guard of the Byzantine Emperors, which was afterwards recruited largely from the North, and especially from Britain.

The following list, compiled from 'Words and Places,' by the Rev. Isaac Taylor, and from 'Surnames as a Science,' by Mr R. Ferguson, will be found to contain ancient Scandinavian and Frisian family names, with the Old English or Anglo-Saxon suffix.

A reference to and comparison with the Icelandic names of the Landnámabók and the Saxon tenants of Domesday Book will prove of great assistance to the reader.

Mr Taylor points out settlements of these families in England, Normandy, and Germany. Some of these are corruptions of the genitive *an*, as Pœccing for Pœccan.

A

Ading	Arring	Æcling	Ælping
Alding	Arting	Æfing	Æscing
Aldring	Æbing	Ælcing	Æscling
Anning	Æbling	Æling	Æsling
Anting	Æcering	Ælfing	Æting
Arling			

* Verstegan is of opinion that the prefix Fitz originated in Flanders. It is remarkable that it is now unknown in France, and that it does not occur in the ancient chronicles of that country (Noble).

The generally accepted idea is that it is derived from the Latin *filius*, Fr. *fils*, old Norman Fr. *filz, fiz, fitz*. It has been used to distinguish the illegitimate children of kings and princes of royal blood. Many Irish families substituted Fitz for Mac in ～ ～ times

B

Bæbing
Bæding
Bædling
Bæling
Bafing
Basing
Beccing
Belling
Belting
Benning
Beofing
Beoring
Beorling

Beorning
Beorhting
Berling
Bermaring
Berring
Bessing
Billing
Bing
Binning
Birling
Bitering
Blœcing
Bobbing

Bocing
Bofing
Boling
Bonding
Bonning
Bosing
Brahcing
Branting
Bressing
Bridling
Brihtling
Brimming
Brining

Brisling
Briting
Bruning
Bryding
Bucing
Buding
Bulling
Burring
Busling
Bydeling
Byrting
Bytting

C

Cæding
Cæging
Cæssing
Calling
Camering
Ceading
Ceadling
Ceaning

Cearling
Cenesing
Cenning
Centing
Cerring
Cifing
Cnotting

Cnudling
Cocing
Coding
Cofing
Colling
Coping
Coring

Coting
Cressing
Cridling
Cubing
Culling
Cylling
Cyrtling

D

Dæfing
Dælling
Darting
Dedding
Deming

Denning
Deorling
Diceling
Didding
Dilling

Dinning
Dinting
Dissing
Docing
Doding

Doring
Dunning
During
Dycing

E

Eadling
Eagling
Eardling
Earming
Eastring
Eberding

Ecging
Ecling
Eding
Efing
Elcing
Elling

Elming
Elring
Elsing
Emming
Eoring
Eorping

Epping
Ercensing
Essing
Etting
Evering

F

Fearing
Fearning
Ferring. *See*
    Wæring

Feorming
Fincing
Finning
Folcing

Freling
Frescing
Fresting
Frilling

Fring
Froding
Fyling

G

Gæging	Geofening	Gilling	Gisling
Garing	Gerling	Ging	Golding
Gealding	Gestinge	Gipping	Gystling
Gedding			

H

Hæcing	Halling	Hensing	Horing
Hæding	Hanesing	Heoring	Horning
Hæfering	Haning	Hereling	Hucing
Hægling	Hearding	Hiceling	Huding
Hæsling	Hearing	Hilling	Hunding
Hæssing	Helling	Hocing	Huning
Hæsting	Helveling	Honing	Hunting
Hafocing	Heming	Hopping	

I

Iceling	Illing	Ipping	Ising
Ifing	Imming	Iring	Isling

L

Læcing	Leasing	Lidling	Loding
Læfering	Leding	Ling	Lofing
Leafing	Ledring	Locing	Lulling

M

Mading	Mæting	Merling	Motting
Mæding	Malling	Milling	Mundling
Mægling	Manning	Mincing	Mutling
Mæring	Mecing	Minting	Mycging
Mæssing	Melling	Molling	Myrcing

N

Næcing	Nolling	Notting	Nyding
Nedding			

O

Ofing	Ossing

P

Pæccing	Pætring	Petling	Poling
Pæfing	Paling	Pipering	Porning
Pælling	Peging	Piting	Puning
Pæting	Penning	Pocling	

R

Ræding	Ricling	Ripling	Rossing
Ræfning	Riding	Rising	Rowing
Ratling	Rifing	Rocing	Rucing
Renning	Rilling	Roding	Ruscing
Ricing	Rimming	Rolling	Rusting

S

Sæling	Scearding	Sepping	Stufing
Sandling	Scearing	Serring	Sulling
Sandring	Sceding	Sinning	Surling
Sceacling	Scyrling	Snoring	Swanning
Sceading	Scyting	Snoting	Swefeling
Sceafing	Seafing	Specing	Sycling
Sceafling	Sealfing	Stæning	Sydling
Scealing	Seaxling	Stelling	Syfing
Sceaning	Secging		

T

Tæding	Terring	Toding	Trumping
Tæling	Thorning	Torting	Tucing
Tæting	Tilling	Tring	Tutling
Teorling	Ting		

U

Uffing	Uling	Upping

V

Veorling (Feorling)

W

Wacering	Wealcing	Wendling	Wiscing
Wading	Wealcring	Weording	Witling
Wælsing	Wealding	Wiccing	Witting
Wæpling	Wealdring	Wickling	Wræning
Wæring	Wealing	Wiging	Wrihting
Wasing	Wearning	Willing	Wylfing
Wating	Wedering	Wining	Wylring
Watring	Welling	Wipping	

III.—PLACE-NAMES

'A local habitation and a name.'—*Midsummer-Night's Dream.*

It was the custom of the Norsemen and the Saxons to give their names to the lands upon which they settled.

Hence it is that so many towns and villages in England as well as in Normandy show the name of the original occupier who appropriated the soil by right of conquest, and the prefix is generally found in the possessive case common to all Teutonic nations.

After the Norman Conquest the followers of William, among whom the land was divided, adopted the title of the manor or estate granted to them by the king.

These afterwards became their family names.

Ivo de Taillebois was made Baron of Kendal, but his descendant, William, assumed the style of de Lancaster. Robert de Tours became Robert de Lowick from his English estate, as, in like manner, William le Fleming was William de Aldingham from his lordship of that manor, and Nigel, younger son of Robert de Statford, inheriting the manor of Gresley, in the county of Derby, took the name and was known as Nigel de Gresley. This last family is one of the very few remaining of those who have retained their lands since the Conquest.

In the reign of Henry VIII., Welsh gentlemen, who had not done so in Norman times, adopted the name of their estates. It is very likely that in after-years change of residence was usually the cause of the bestowal of the original abode as a surname.

About the thirteenth century another way of adopting place-names sprung up, as is seen from the registers of wills in the Court of Husting, London, A.D. 1258 to 1358, at Lincoln and other cities.

The word 'atte,' as implying residence, if not possession, crept in, and thereby arose such names as Atte Boure, Atte Brig, Atte Hash, Atte Hay, Atte Kirkstile, Atte Lane, Atte Maydens, Atte Stile, Atte Well. Indeed, this custom may be traced back to Anglo-Saxon times, for in a charter, No. 775 of the Codex Dip., there occurs Eâdmar æt Burhâm, and in No. 492, dated about 960, we have Godwine æt Fechâm, Eâdric æt Hô, Ælfgâr æt Meâpahâm.

William Atwater was Bishop of Lincoln in 1574.

In course of time the *de* and the *atte* were dropped, as the persons using them lost their estates or changed their place of abode; but retaining the surname, they wandered into various parts of the country as fancy or necessity led them.

Hence it happens that many extraordinary surnames, which have been a puzzle to investigators hitherto, and almost defy derivation, are found to be traceable to some obscure spot in Great Britain or France.

Richard Verstegan wrote in 1673

> 'In Foord, in Ham, in Ley, in Tun
> The most of English surnames run.'

But it is only a partial statement, as we know. Also, as Camden says,

> 'By Tre, Ros, Lan, Car, Pol, and Pen,
> Ye shall know the most Cornishmen,'

is true as far as it goes, for many other local names in that county have given names to families.

Names derived from localities are more common in England and Scotland than in Wales and Ireland.

IV.—Official Names

'I am become a name.'—Tennyson.

When the country became settled under Edward the Confessor, and the Norsemen, Saxon, and Welsh lived together with something like a suspension of their international feuds, the land was brought into a semblance of law and order, and, consequently, offices of influence and responsibility arose.

Bright, Steward, and Despencer are names of this period. They all mean the same thing. *Bryti* is the Norse and Dispensator the Latin equivalent of Steward.

Lagman (lawgiver), Fawcett (Forseti, judge), Alderman, Reeve, Sheriff, Tabberer (Tabarðr, a Tabard), Chamberlain (Camerarius), Chancellor (Canceler), Chaplain (Capellanus), Clerk (Clericus), Deacon (Diaconus), Beadle (Bedellus), Latimer (Latinarius, or interpreter), Miles (Miles, a soldier), Marshall (Marescal), Redman (Radman), Sumner or Somner (Chaucer's Sompnoure, a summoner or apparitor), Poynder (a bailiff), Parker (Park-keeper), Palliser (Park-pailings keeper), Franklin (a free-holder), Vavasour or Valvasour * (an office or dignity below a baron and above a knight), Arblaster (Balistarius), Botiler (Butler), etc.

Some, such as Abbot, Bishop, and Scripture-names, may have originally been given to play-actors who took the parts in mediæval times, as people now speak of the Ober-Ammergau actors by their stage names.

V.—Trade Names

'A rose by any other name would smell as sweet.'—*Romeo and Juliet.*

As might be expected, a man's occupation gave him notoriety, especially if he were skilled in his handicraft.

Even among primitive nations there seems to have been a tendency to adopt this mode of distinguishing an artificer by his calling.

The Norse *Skapti*, originally a shaft-maker, became a nickname, and afterwards a personal name as Scapti and Scafti, the Scotch form of which is Shafto. *Sneypir* (a snipper), gives us Snapper ; *Dengir* (one who whets), Denger ; *Kembir* (a comber), Kimber ; *Smið* (a smith), etc.

The Anglo-Saxon *Bæc-ere* (baker), *Cu-hyrde* (cowherd), *Feormere* (farmer), *Fiscere* (fisher), *Fugelere* (fowler), *Fullere* (bleacher), *Sceáphyrde* (shepherd), *Scìpere* (sailor), *Webere* (weaver), etc.

In Domesday Book occur Arbalistarius (a crossbowman), Aurifaber (goldsmith), Arcuarius (bowyer), Artifex (workman), Accipitrarius (fal-coner), Cocus (cook), Carpentarius, Censorius, Cubicularius (groom of the chamber), Dapifer (a server), Faber (smith), Forestarius, Harparius, Ingeniator, Joculator, Larderius, Lorimarius (bridle-maker), Monialis, Machinator, Medicus, Ostiarius (usher), Porcarius (swineherd), Piscator

* The Norman kings had an officer who kept ward at the entrances and borders of the realm, *ad valvas Regni.*

(fisher), Pincerna (butler), Portarius (porter), Stalrus, Staller (groom), Stirman, Scutularius (page), Scriba, Tonsor, Venator (huntsman).

In middle English times we find, according to Lower, Massinger (Fr., Massager, a messenger), Pottinger (apothecary), Brownsmith (a maker of 'brown bills'?), Nasmith (nail-smith?), Ferrier and Farrier (horse-shoer), Jenner (joiner), Furner (Fr., Fournier, a baker), Lavender (Fr., Lavandier, a washerman), Pullinger (Fr., Boulanger, a baker), Pointer (a maker of 'points,' an obsolete article of dress), Pilcher (a maker of pilches, the great coat of the fourteenth century), Shearman and Sharman (one who shears worsteds, fustians, etc.). They sheared the roughest off the nap of cloth before it was done by machinery. Caird (a travelling tinker), Maunder (a beggar), Kidder and Kidman (a pedlar; N., *kyta*, to hawk, deal), Crowther (one who plays upon the crowd; Welsh, *crwth*, a rude sort of violin), Polter and Pulter (poulterer), etc.

It is open to question, however, whether some of the names popularly ascribed to occupations, such as Arkwright, Baker, Barber, Beadle, Botwright, Butcher, Carter, Cartwright, Cooper, Carver, Collier, Driver, Dyer, Fidler, Fuller, Glaisher, Iremonger, Leadbeater, Packer, Painter, Pinder, Pointer, Plummer, Potter, Poulter, Plowright, Nailer, Osler, Sawyer, Seaman, Shearer, Sharman, Shearman, Sheppard, Skinner, Tanner, Tinker, Tucker, Turner, Tyler, Walker, Wheeler, Warrener, etc., will not bear a different interpretation. The reader is invited to study these names in their proper places.

In England there is one Smith in every seventy-three persons, in Scotland one in sixty-eight.

VI.—CHRISTIAN NAMES

'What is your name?'—Tempest, Act iii. Sc. 1.

When Christianity spread among the northern nations in the eleventh century, a baptismal name followed as a matter of course, and for a long time was the only one possessed by the individual upon whom it was conferred. Thus John, Peter, and Paul were great favourites, and those who were named in this way transmitted the Christian name to their descendants, who became known as Janson, Johnson, Peterson, Patterson, Polson, etc. (N. *sonr*, pl. *synir*). In Wales and Cornwall, as well as in Denmark, Friesland, and the Netherlands, the final *s* alone served to mark the fact that it had become a patronymic. Indeed, it is remarkable that a large proportion of the family names of Wales should be those of Teutonic, Christian, and other names, and is difficult to account for, as there is no evidence of a special legislative enactment (as was the case in Ireland) requiring the inhabitants of the Principality to adopt such designations as would be understood by the English. Mr T. E. Morris thinks 'there are sufficient grounds for believing that the Teutonic names of the (Norman) invaders were gradually adopted, first by the large landowners of Wales, a class which included noblemen and gentry, then by their retainers and tenants, and finally by the ordinary common people.'

Whether the final *s* indicates the family name or not, it makes the plural, even if it does not represent *synir*, *son*, or *sen*, and it seems quite natural for us, in these days, to speak of the Whites, the Browns, the Smiths, the Robinsons, and even the Joneses, the Edwardses and Thomases.

In some instances the Christian name is undoubtedly a contraction of the Latin form in use in early English times, for it is very common to find in old documents John's for Johannes, Will's for Willelmus, Ricard's for Ricardus, Edward's for Edwardus, Phillip's for Philippus, Jacob's for Jacobus, etc.

Of these names there are also many diminutives and modifications, as Jon, Ion, Jan, Jane, Jennis, Jenner, Jenkin, Jinks. In like manner we find Pete, Peet, Pate, Pett, Pitt, Pittar. Also Paul, Spaull, Powell, Pull, Pulley, Powley, Pollyn, Poll, Pole, Pullein, Pulleyne, Poole, etc.

Jones is the second most common name in England.

VII.—FOREIGN NAMES

' I cannot tell what the dickens his name is.'—*Merry Wives of Windsor*, Act iii. Sc. 2.

Some of these are undoubtedly Norman, others are more recent, and may presumably be set down to Huguenot and other refugee emigrants, or to the influx of followers of the Orange or Hanoverian Dynasties.

Edward III. was the first to promote woollen manufacture in England. He brought seventy families of Walloons for the purpose in 1331. A colony of Flemings was established in Pembrokeshire in the reign of Henry I. There is a list of the names of 'Foreigners' in the town and county of Cambridge in the year 1440, including French, Dutch, Flemish, Irish and Scotch. French and Flemish names came into N.-W. Lincolnshire and S.-E. Yorkshire with Vermuyden and the draining of 'The Levels' in the seventeenth century. The Irish Parliament in 1674 passed an Act granting letters of naturalisation to French and Flemish Huguenot refugees. Colonies were founded at Dublin, Kilkenny, Portarlington, Waterford, Cork, and Lisburn. In 1709 a fleet was sent to Rotterdam by Queen Anne, which brought over about 7000 German emigrants from the Palatinate of the Rhine. About 3000 were sent to North America, the remainder, except a few families which remained in England, settled principally in the County of Limerick.

It is well known, moreover, that many French prisoners of war during the reign of George III. married or formed other ties during their captivity, and when peace was restored, remained in this country. To these may be added those who have been attracted to Great Britain by greater facilities of trade, or more political or individual liberty than they found at home.

Many names bear a close resemblance to such as are at present existing in the North of Germany and in the Low Countries—a large number, indeed, being very little changed.

The question arises, Are they direct importations, or are they derived through Frisian sources?

There is no doubt about many Frisian names having spread along the southern shore of the Baltic, for the prevalence of the diminutive 'ke,' in contradistinction to the German 'chen,' is transparently obvious. Nevertheless, many of them are difficult to trace, either through the Frisian, or those of ancient Scandinavia as found in Iceland.

Further research may possibly throw more light upon this interesting but complicated subject.

Of these foreign names many have become naturalised in this country. The earliest instances occur among the Norman tenants in chief in Domesday Book.

Those of more recent times will be readily distinguished as Aufrere, Beauchamp, Caux, Drew, Durrant, Frere, Grand, Jacques, Le Neve, Motte, Pettit, Roche, Sant, Vipond, etc.

Sir W. Russell brought over settlers from Holland to drain the Cambridgeshire Fens. At Thorney there is a French Register of Baptisms, 1653 to 1727.

The intimate relationship between Scotland, France, and the Netherlands, which existed before and after the time of the ill-fated Queen Mary, will account for the presence of names in Scotland which are clearly derived from the latter countries.

VIII.—FOUNDLING NAMES

' Phœbus, what a name ! '—BYRON.

There is every reason to believe that we are indebted to the parish beadle and the workhouse officials for many extraordinary and even ridiculous names which cannot be derived from any known sources. They have been evolved from the imagination of the Bumbles of a past generation, as Charles Dickens shows us in 'Oliver Twist,' and they remain a puzzle to all who would attempt to clear them up, unless they are classed in this section.

Indeed, it is a convenience to have a receptacle of this sort in which to stow away, until further research comes to our aid, such names as philologists cannot yet account for, except upon the supposition that the ingenuity of the public servants has suggested them. Some of those which have been a source of wonder to many for a long time, and were supposed to be foundling names, can now be shown to possess a real historical signification.

Possibly, by-and-by, more may be rescued, but in the meantime they must be classified somehow, and it is better to put them on the unknown list rather than invent a fanciful origin which may be, after all, mere guess-work.

According to Burns' 'History of Parish Registers,' p. 80, an Act was passed in the second year of George III., 1761-2, specially directing that children received in a workhouse were, in cases where their names were unknown, to have surnames given them by the overseers and churchwardens.

That there was a custom of naming foundling children after the parishes where they have been picked up is proved by the entries in the registers of several of the London City churches. The Registers of the

Temple, London, show that in that district alone, between 1728 and 1755, no less than 104 foundlings were christened, all of whom were surnamed Temple or Templer. Nicholas Acons, after the parish of that name, and Benetfink, Orgar, Sherehog, with many others, exist as surnames which may be all traced to this source. Other stray children have been named from the circumstances under which they were found.

Over the signature of 'Peter Lombard,' a writer in the *Church Times* has recently drawn attention to the registers of St Mary Woolnoth where are these entries: 'A male child was found in our parish with a penny in his hand, and was named accordingly Henry Penny.' 'A child found in the alley between the church and the stocks on the morning of St John's Day was named John Before Day.'

A girl who was so picked up was christened Anne Monday, after the day of the week, and a boy who was laid 'atte Mr Garrett's dore' was christened 'John Bynight.' Such names as Christmas, Easter, Lammas, Paske, etc., may have been suggested by the season when a child was found.

Lower gives, among other instances, Jack Parish, Tom Among-us, and Napkin Brooker as the names bestowed by the parish authorities on foundlings. The last-mentioned, it is stated, was found by the side of a brook, tied up in a napkin.

Allbone (from Holborn?) and such names as Lilywhite and Sweet-apple may belong perhaps to this category.

At the baptism of the children first taken into the Foundling Hospital, which was on the 29th March 1741, it is recorded that 'there was at the ceremony a fine appearance of persóns of quality and distinction. His Grace the Duke of Bedford, our President, their Graces the Duke and Duchess of Richmond, the Countess of Pembroke, and several others, honouring the children with their names and being their sponsors.' For long after this it was the fashion to come down to the Foundling on a Sunday morning to be sponsor to a child, and to give it a name quite incongruous with its station and fortune. A child was left with a £50 note pinned to its clothes, and it was called Japhet Newland from the name of the governor of the Bank of England, Abraham Newland, on the note. The last child taken in when the parliamentary control ceased was named Kitty Finis!

A lady sends that of a family named Haycock. She was told that the father was found as an infant deserted under a haycock. The name is not uncommoἀ, and may be otherwise accounted for. There is a hill in Cumberland called Haycock, and Hayo and Heie are Frisian personal names, to which may be added the diminutive 'cock.'

Indeed, Heij-Koch is a Dutch proper name.

ABBREVIATIONS

N. Old Norse (Icelandic), S. Swedish, D. Danish, F. Frisian, Dch. Dutch, Fl. Flemish, Fr. French, G. German, A.S. Anglo-Saxon, N.-Fr. Norman-French, D.B. Domesday Book, p.n. personal name, n.n. nickname, loc. n. local name.

OLD NORSE PERSONAL NAMES

FROM ISLANDS LANDNÁMA-BÓK (THE ICELANDIC BOOK OF SETTLEMENT) AND OTHER SOURCES

(Revised by Professor Hjalmer Petersen of Christiania)

A

Abraham (Bp.)	Are (Ari)	Arnórr	Áslaug (f.)
Adam	Arinbjörn	Arnriðr	Ásleif (f.)
Aðisl	Armoðr	Arnsteinn	Ásleikr
Aðrianus	Arnaldr	Arnþjófr	Ásmóðr
Afvaldr	Arnbjörg	Arnþóra. See	Ásmundr
Agnar	Arnbjörn	Arnóra	Ásný (f.)
Agni	Arndis (f.)	Arnþórr. See	Ásolfr
Aistein	Arneiðr (f.)	Arnórr	Ásrauðr
Albert	Arnfinnr	Arnðruðr (f.)	Ásta (f.)
Aldis (f.)	Arnfriðr (f.)	Arun	Ástriðr (f.)
Alexius	Arngeirr	Ása. See Æsa	Ásvaldr
Álfarekkar or	Arngerðr (f.)	Ásbera (f.)	Ásvarðr
Halfrekkar	Arngrimr	Ásbjarnarsynir	Ásvör (f.)
Álfarinn	Arngunnr	Ásbjörg (f.)	Atli
Álfdis (f.)	Arnhaldr. See	Ásbjörn	Audolfr
Álfeiðr (f.)	Arnaldr	Ásborg (Asbjörg)	Audr (f.)
Álfgeirr	Árni	Ásbrandr	Auðunn
Álfgerðr (f.)	Arnis	Ásdis (f.)	Aun
Álfjótr or Ulfjótr	Arnkatla (f.)	Ásgautr	Aungull
Álfr	Arnkel	Ásgeirr	Aunundr. See
Áli	Arnlaug (f.)	Ásgerðr (f.)	Önundr
Álrekr	Arnlaugr	Ásgrimr	Aurlyger. See
Álöf (f.)	Arnleif	Áshildr (f.)	Örlygr
Ámundi	Arnljótr	Ási	Auzor. See Özurr
Án	Arnmoðr	Áskell, n.n.	Ásvaldi
Áni	Arnoddr	Askr	Ávaldr
Anti-cristr	Arnóra (f.)	Áslákr, n.n.	Ávangr

18

From other sources

Aðils.   *A.S.* Eadgils (a king)
Akra-carl, cogn.
Akra-spillir, cogn.
Ali-karl, n.n.
Amb-höfði, n.n.   *See* Hjart-höfði
Amloði (Hamlet),

Angan-tyr, p.n.   *A.S.* Ongentheow
Aska-spillir, cogn.
Auðr (f.), p.n.
Auðunn, p.n.   *A.S.* Eâðvin
Aust-rænn, n.n.

B

Baldvini
Bálki
Barbara
Bardi
Bardr
Bárekr
Barna, n.n.
Baugr, n.n.
Beda
Beinir
Beiskaldi
Bekan (Gaelic)
Bera (f.)
Berðlu, n.n.
Bergðis (f.)
Bergljót (f.)
Bergr
Bergþora (f.)
Bergþor
Bersi
Bjaðmakr
  (Gaelic)
Bjálfi

Bjargey (f.)
Bjarnaðr
Bjarneyja
Bjarnharðr
Bjarnheðin
Bjarni
Bjarnvarðr. *See*
  Bjarnharðr
Bjartmarr
Bifra, n.n.
Bjolan (Gaelic)
Bjólfr
Bjollok (f.),
  (Gaelic)
Birna (f.)
Birningr
Birtingr
Bitru, n.n.
Björg
Björn
Björnolfr
Bla-kinn
Blígr

Blót-mar
Blund-Ketill
Blundr, n.n.
Blæingr
Bogi
Bolli
Borgillðr (f.)
Bót
Bótey (f.)
Bótolf
Bragi
Brandax
Brandi
Brandr
Brandönundr
Brattr
Braut-Önundr
  (Svia-Konungr)
Breidar-Skeggi
Breidr
Brennu-Kári
Bresasynir
Bresi

Briann or Brann
  (Gaelic)
Bryngerðr
Brynhildr (f.)
Brynjólfr
Brodd-Helgi
Broddi
Broddr
Brunda-Bjalfi
Bruni
Brunólfr
Brúsi
Bröndólfr
Budli
Burislafr
Bægifótr
Bödmóðr
Bódólfr
Bödvarr
Böggvir
Bölverkr
Börkr

From other sources

Bak-skiki, cogn.
Barka-bazi, cogn.
Berbeinn, cogn.
Beiskaldi, n.n.
Beit-stokkr, cogn.
Beli, cogn.
Berserkr, n.n.
Bersi, p.n.
Bifr, cogn.
Birtingr, n.n.
Bitra, cogn.

Blá-ber, cogn.
Blá-hattr, cogn.
Blá-siða, cogn.
Blá-tönn, cogn.
Blígr, cogn.
Blunðr, cogn.
Bog-sveigr, cogn.
Bófi, n.n.
Bragi
Brák, n.n.
Brikar-nef, n.n.

Brimstein, n.n.
Bróki, n.n.
Bryti
Bullu-fótr
Buttr
Buttraldi
Bui. *D.* Boye
Bægi-fótr, cogn.
Boðvildr
Böggull, n.n.
Böl-viss, n.n.

D

Dadi	Dalkr	Dómarr	Duf-þakr (Gaelic)
Dagr	Dalla (f.)	Drafdritr (Gaelic)	= Dofnakr
Dagrun	Darri	Drafli	Dugfus (Gaelic
Dagstyggr	Digr-Ormr	Drumb-Oddr	Dygvi [Dufgus)
Dala-alfr	Dís. *See* Dýs	Dufan (Gaelic)	Dýrfinnr (f.)
Dala-kollr = Hof-	Dofnakr	Dufnall (Gaelic)	Dýri
kolli (?)	Dómaldr	Dufniall (Gaelic)	Dýs (f.)

From other sources

Dampr	Drettingr, cogn.	Dyntill, cogn.
Dapi, n.n.	Dyðrill or Dyrðill, n.n.	Dytta, cogn.
Dengir, cogn.		

E

Eadmund. *See*	Eldjárn	Erný (Eirný)	Eyja (f.)
Jatmundr	Elfraðr	Erplingar	Eyjarr
Edna (f.)	Elina (f.)	Erpr	Eyjolfr
Egill	Elliðagrimr	Errubeinn	Eylaugr
Eiðr	Endridi	Evarr. *See* Ævarr	Eymundr
Eilifir	Enoc	Exna-Þorir. *See*	Eyrný (f.)
Einarr	Erlendr	Yxna-Þorir	Eysteinn
Eindriði	Erlingr (dim. of	Eydis (f.)	Eyvindr (a jarl)
Eiríkr	Jarl)	Eyfreyðr	Eyvör (f.)
Eirný	Erlygr	Eygerðr (f.)	Eyþjófr
Eldgrímr			

From other sources

Eysill, n.n.

F

Falgerðr (f.)	Finnbjörn	Flosi	Freysteinn
Falki	Finnbogi	Flugu-Grimr	Freyviðr
Fastný (f.)	Finngeirr	Foka	Frið-Froði (Dana-
Faxa-Brandr	Finni	Fostolfr	Konungr)
Faxi	Finnr	Frayr (Freyr)	Friðgerðr
Feilan (Gaelic)	Finnvarðr	Freygerðr (f.)	Friðleifr = Odd-
Fenkell	Fiska-Finnr	Freyja. *See* Fraija	leifr
Fjarska = Fiska(?)	Fjölnir	Freyleif. *See*	Friðmundr
Fiðr	Fjörleif (f.)	Fjörleif	Friðrekr (Frith-
Filippus	Fleinn	Freyer	recr)
Finna (f.)	Flóki	Freysgyðlingr	Fróði

From other sources

Fasi, n.n.	Fola-fótr, n.n.	Fuð-hundr, n.n.
Fisk-reki, n.n.	Freys-goði, n.n.	Fugl

G

Galmi	Gerpir	Goðmundr =	Guðleif (f.)
Galti	Gestr (f.)	Guðmundr	Guðmund
Gamli	Gjaflaug	Goðröphr	Guðný (f.)
Garðar, or	Gjafvaldr	Grafar-leifr	Guðriðr (f.)
Garðarr	Gils	Granni	Guðrikr
Garða-Snorri	Gisl	Graut	Guðrun (f.)
Gaukr	Gisli	Greipr. *See* Gripr	Guðröðr
Gautr	Gisroðr	Grelöd(f., Gaelic)	Guðormr
Gautrekr	Gizur	Grenjaðr	Gufa (Gaelic)
Geirbjörg (f.)	Glædir	Grettir. *See* Ófeigr	Gufi
Geirhildr = Geir-	Glámr, or Glam-	Grima (f.)	Gull-Þorir
riðr (f.)	maðr, n.n.	Grímkell	Gunnarr
Geiri	Gleðill, n.n.	Grímólfr	Gunnbjörn
Geirlaug (f.)	Gljómall (Gaelic)	Grímr	Gunnhildr (f.)
Geirleifr	Glíru-Halli	Grimssynr	Gunnlaugr
Geirmundr	Glúmr	Grjótgarðr	Gunnólfr
Geirný (f.)	Gnupa	Gripr	Gunnsteinn
Geirolfr	Góa (f.)	Gris	Gunnvaldr
Geirr	Goðormr-Goddi	Gróa (f.)	Gunnvör
Geirriðr (f.)	Goðrun (f.)	Guðbjörg (f.)	Gunn-Þjólfr
Geirröðr	Godun. *See* Jódis	Guðbrandr	Guttormr = Guð-
Geirsteinn	Gollnir	Guðhormr. *See*	hormr
Geirþjofr	Gormr	Guttormr	Gyða (kona)
Geitir	Gorr	Guðiskolkr. *See*	Gyðja
Gellir (Gaelic)	Goti	Goðiscolkr	Gyða
Gerdr (f.)	Goðiscolkr (Bp.)	Guðlaug (f.)	Göngu-Hrólfr

From other sources

Galli and Gallaðr, n.n.	Goddi, n.n.
Galpin, n.n.	Gormr, contr. of Goð-ormr.
Gapa-muðr, n.n.	*A.S.* Guthrum
Geit-heðinn	Grá-barði, cogn.
Geit-skór, n.n.	Graut-nefr, n.n.
Gellini, n.n.	Greifi, n.n.
Gestr	Gríss, n.n.
Gisl, Gisli, p.n. by metathesis ; Gils	Gull-hjálmr, n.n.
—as Þor-gils, Auð-gils, Spá-gils,	Gull-höttr, n.n.
Her-gils	Gull-knapper, n.n.
Gleðill, n.n.	Gull-kroppr, n.n.
Glenna, n.n.	Gull-skeggr, n.n.
Gloppa, n.n.	Gull-tanni, n.n.
Glúmr, n.n.	Gurpr, n.n.
Gnúpa = Gnufa	

H

Hafgrimr	Haukr (berserkr)	Hildi-björn	Hreinn
Hafliði	Hávaror	Hildi-brandr	Hrifla
Hafljótr	Hávarr	Hildi-grimmr	Hringr
Hafnar-Ormr	Heðin	Hildigunnr (f.)	Hríseyjar
Hafr, n.n.	Heggr	Hildir	Hrisi, n.n.
Hafrsteinn	Heiðr	Hildiriðr (f.)	Hróaldr-hryggr
Hafsteinn	Heimir (jarl)	Hildi-tannr, n.n.	Hróarr
Hafþora (f.)	Heimlaug (f.)	Hild-ólfr	Hróðgeirr
Hafþorr	Heimrekr (Bp.)	Hildr	Hróðmarr
Hagbaror	Helga (f.)	Hjörleifr	Hróðný (f.)
Haki	Helgi	Hjörr	Hróðólfr (Bp.)
Hákon	Helgu-Steinnarr	Hjörtr	Hroi
Háleygar	Helias	Hlenni	Hrojn, n.n.
Hálfdan (King)	Hella-Björn	Hlif	Hrólfr
Hálfr (K.)	Hellu-Narfi	Hlödverr	Hrollaugr
Hallaðr (jarl)	Herborg (f.)	Hnaki	Hrolleifr
Hallbera (f.)	Herdis (f.)	Hnokan (Gaelic)	Hrómundr
Hallbjörg (f.)	Herbrandr	Hofgarða	Hrónarr
Hallbjörn (f.)	Herfinnr	Hof-Kolli	Hrossbjörn
Halldis (f.)	Hergils	Holbarki, n.n.	Hrosskell
Halldora (f.)	Hergrimr	Hólmfastr	Hrútr
Halldórr	Hergunnr (f.)	Hólmfriðr (f.)	Hrærekr
Hallfreðr	Herjólfr	Holmgöngu-	Hudar-Steinarr
Hallfriðr (f.)	Herlaugr	Hrafn	Húnbogi
Hallgerðr (f.)	Herleifr	Holmgöngu-	Hundi
Hallgils	Hermoðr	Máni	Hundólfr (jarl)
Hallgrima (f.)	Hermundr	Holmgöngu-	Hungerð (f.)
Hallgrimr	Herrauðr	Starri	Hunrauðr
Halli	Herriðr	Hólmkell	Hvati
Hallkatla	Hersteinn	Holm-Starri	Hvítserkr
Hallkell	Hervaror	Holmsteinn	Hyrna, n.n.
Hallormr	Hertili	Holta-Þorir	Hyrningr
Hallr	Hervör (f.)	Holti, n.n.	Hý-nefr, n.n.
Hallsteinn	Her-Þjólfr	Hraði	Hækingr
Hallvaror	Her-Þruðr (f.)	Hrafn	Hængr, n.n.
Hallveig	Hesta-Gellir	Hrafna-Floki	Hæringr
Hallvör	Heyjángrs-Björn	Hrafnhilðr (f.)	Hofða-Þórðr
Háls	Heyjángs-Björn	Hrafnkell	Höggvandi, n.n.
Hamall	Hjaldr (K.)	Hrafsi	Höggvin - Kinni,
Hamundr	Hjallkárr	Hramn	n.n.
Haraldr (K.)	Hjalmgerðr (f.)	Hrani	Högni
Hardrefr	Hjalmólfr	Hrappr	Hörða-Kari
Hárekr	Hjálmun-Gautr	Hrefna (f.)	Höror
Harri	Hjálp (kona)	Hreiðarr	Höskuldr
Hásteinn	Hjalti		

From other sources

Haddinja-skati, n.n.	Herj-ólfr. *A.S.* Here-	Hreimr, n.n.
Hak-langr, n.n.	wolf	Hrella, n.n.
Hali, n.n.	Hiði	Hrókr
Hamðir	Hildingr	Hrúga, n.n.
Hani, n.n.	Himaldi, n.n.	Hrúkr, n.n.
Harð-beinn, n.n.	Hjálmr	Hugi, p.n.
Harð-jaxl, n.n.	Hjálmgeirr	Hundingi
Harð-magi, n.n.	Hjálgrimr	Hundsfótr, n.n.
Hausa-Kljúfr, n.n.	Hjálmgunnr	Húkr, n.n.
Hákr, n.n.	Hjálm-týr	Hvitr. *D.* Hvid.
Hálfr, n.n.	Hjalm-gerðr	Hvit-beinn, n.n.
Hálfs-rekkr, n.n.	Hjörr	Hvita-skald, n.n.
Há-fæta, n.n.	Hjörtr	Hvita-ský, n.n.
Há-nefr, n.n.	Hlöðr	Hvita-kollr, n.n.
Heikil-nefr, n.n.	Hnúfa, n.n.	Hvita-leðr, n.n.
Heið-rekr (King)	Hol-muðr, n.n.	Hækill, n.n.
Hein, n.n. *D.* King	Horti, n.n.	Hænsa-Þorir, n.n.
Hemingr	Hrani	Hæru-kollr, n.n.
Hera-fótr, n.n. *D.* King	Hreða, n.n.	Höd-broddr, n.n.
Herjan	Hregg-viðr	Höttr

I

Idunn (f.)	Íngi-marr	Íngunn (f.)	Íngyoldr. *See*
Illugi	Íngi-mundr	Íngunnr (f.)	Inguðr
Indriði	Íngimundarsynr	Íngvarr. *See*	Ísgerðr (f.)
Íngjaldr	Íngiriðr (f.)	Yngvarr	Ísleifr (Bp.)
Íngibjörg (f.)	Íngolfr	Íngvildr. *See*	Ísólfr
Íngigerðr (f.)	Inguðr (f.), or	Yngvildr	Ísrauðr
Íngileif (f.)	Ingvoldr		Ivarr

From other sources

Imi	Isja, n.n.	Ístru-magi, n.n.	Ísungr, n.n.

J

Jakob	Jóan. *See* Jón	Jólgeirr	Josteinn
Jarngerðr (f.)	Jódis (f.)	Jón	Jökull
Jatmundr. *See*	Jófreiðr	Jóra (f.)	Jörundr
Eadmund	Jófriðr (f.)	Jóreiðr (f.)	Jösurr
Játvarðr (Edward).	Jóhann (Bp.)	Jórunn (f.)	Jötun-Björn
K. of Eng.			

From other sources

Jarn-hauss, n.n.	Jarn-saxa, n.n.	Jólfr (a name of Odin)
Jarn-hryggr, n.n.	Jarn-skjöldr, n.n.	

K

Kaðall (Gaelic)	Kjarran (Gaelic)	Knöttr	Korni
Kaðlin (f., Gaelic)	Kjarfalr (Gaelic)	Koðrán	Krafla
Kálfr	Kjartan (Gaelic)	Kolbeinn	Krákneflingar
Kald-munnr, n.n.	Kjarvalr	Kolbjörn	Kraku-Hreiðarr
Kali (Gaelic)	Kimbi, n.n.	Kolbrún	Kristofórus
Kalman (Gaelic)	(Gaelic)	Kolfinna (f.)	Krókr, n.n.
Kamban, n.n.	Kjöl-fari, n.n.	Kolgrima (f.)	Kroppa, n.n.
(Gaelic)	Kjölvör (f.)	Kolgrimr	Krumr
Kampa-Grímr	Kjötvi	Kolka, n.n.	Kymlingar
Kári	Klaufi	Kolli (Gaelic)	Kræklingar
Karl	Kleppjarn	Kollr	Krömu-Oddr
Karli	Kleykir, n.n.	Kollsveinn	Kúgaldi
Karlsefui	Klyppr	Kolr (Bp.)	Kuggi
Kárr	Klæingr	Kolskeggr	Kveld
Katla	Klöku	Kolssynir	Kvistr
Kaun	Knappi, n.n.	Koltherna	Kýlan (Gaelic)
Ketilbjörn	Kneif, n.n.	Kolumba	Kögurr, n.n.
Ketill	Knútr	Konáll (Gaelic)	Körmlöð (Gaelic)
Ketilriðr (f.)	Knýtr, n.n.	Kori (Gaelic)	Körtr, n.n. (Karta)
Kjallakr (Gaelic)	Knörr	Kórmakr (Gaelic)	Köttr, n.n. (a cat)
Kjallæklingar			

From other sources

Kaggi, n.n.	Kerling	Kolbeinn, n.n.
Kakali, n.n.	Kesja, n.n.	Konr
Kambari, n.n.	Kiðlingr, n.n.	Kráka, n.n.
Kamb-höttr, n.n.	Kiðlings-munnr, n.n.	Kráka-nef, n.n.
Kampi, n.n.	Kikini, n.n.	Kregð, n.n.
Kappi, n.n.	Kikr, n.n.	Krepp-hendr, n.n.
Karls-ungi, n.n.	Kirjalax	Krista, n.n.
Kastan-razi, n.n.	Kisi, n.n.	Kristin (f.), Christina
Katrin (f.)	Kjötvi, n.n.	Krist-röðr
Kauða (f.) n.n.	Klaka	Krist-rún
Kaupungr, n.n.	Klápr = Kláfr, n.n.	Kroppr, n.n.
Kausi, n.n.	Klemus	Kumbi, n.n.
Ká-beinn, n.n.	(Clements)	Kussa, n.n.
Kárhöfðaðr, n.n.	Kliningr, n.n.	Kutiza, n.n.
Kegill, n.n.	Kló, n.n.	Kúgaðr, n.n.
Keikan, n.n.	Knerra, n.n.	Kúgi, n.n.
Keis, n.n.	Knúi, n.n.	Kúla-nefr
Kekkja = Kökkr, n.n.	Knarra-bringa, n.n.	Kveld-úlfr, n.n.
Kembir, n.n.	Kobbi, pet n. Jacob	Kylli-nef, n.n.
Keppr, n.n.		

L

Lambi	Leik-goði, n.n.	Ljúfina (f.)	Lunan (Gaelic)
Laugarbrekku,	Leó (Keisari)	Ljoðhattr	Lunda-Steinarr
n.n.	Lina (f.)	Ljoðinn	(jarl)
Lecný (Lækný),	Ljódarkeptr	Ljoðmundr	Lýtingr
or Leikny	Ljót (f.)	Loka-senna, n.n.	Lækný. *See*
Leðrháls	Ljótólfr	Loki, n.n.	Lecný
Leggjaldi, n.n.	Ljótr	Lón-Einarr	Lög-Skapti
Leiðolfr	Ljótunn	Lopþæna (f.)	Löngu-bak, n.n.
Leifr	Ljúfa (Kona)	Loptr (Bp.)	

From other sources

Lafranz (Laurence)	Leggr	Lygra, n.n.
Laf-skeggr, n.n.	Leira, n.n.	Lyngvi
Lang-beinn, n.n.	Lindi-áss, n.n.	Lyrgr, n.n.
Langa-spjöt, n.n.	Lín-seyma, n.n.	Lyrtr, n.n. (lurtr)
Lang-brók, n.n.	Líri, n.n.	Lyst-Knappr, n.n.
Lang-höfði, n.n.	Ljóð-horn, n.n.	Lysu-Knappr, n.n
Lang-nefr, n.n.	Ljómi, n.n.	Lög-maðr
Láfi, pet n. (Oláfr)	Lúndi, n.n.	Lömbungr, n.n.
Láki, pet n. (Þrolákr)	Lúfa, n.n.	

M

Mábil (f.)	Maria (f.)	Melpatrekr	Mos-hals, n.n.
Maddaðr (K.,	Markús	(Gaelic)	Munnr, n.n.
Gaelic)	Martein (Bp.)	Miðfjarðr, n.n.	Myra-Knjukr
Magnús	Má-scári, n.n.	Mjöll (f.)	Myrgjol (f.,
Magr-Helgi	Mein-frettr	Módólfr	Gaelic)
Mág-Snorri	Mela-Snorri	Moð-skegg	Myrkjartan (K.,
Mána-Ljotr	Melkorka (f.,	Moeiðr (f.)	Gaelic)
Máni. *See* Menni	Gaelic)	Molda-Gnúpr	Mýrun
Már	Meldun (jarl	Moldi, n.n.	
Margret (f.)	Scot., Gaelic)		

From other sources

Magni	Málga, n.n.	Mundi, pet n.
Magr, n.n.	Mál-spakr, n.n.	Murta, n.n.
Manar-menn (Manx-	Mási, n.n.	Munki, n.n.
men)	Mein-akr, n.n.	Myntari, n.n.
Mangi (Magnus)	Mein-fretr, n.n.	Mögr, p.n. *See*
Manni, n.n.	Menni, n.n.	Mágr
Mar-drap, n.n.	Mikill	Mör-landi, n.n.
Mat-Krákr, n.n.	Mikla, n.n.	Mör-nefr, n.n.
Maull, n.n.	Mildi, n.n.	Mör-strútr, n.n.
Maxi, n.n.	Mjo-beinn, n.n.	Möttull, p.n.
Mág (Mac, Mc)	Mjóvi, n.n.	(Finnish King)

N

Naððoðr	Náttfari	Nesja-Knjukr	Njáll (Gaelic)
Nafar-Helgi	Nefsteinn	Niðbjörg (f.)	Njörðr
Nagli	Nereiðr (jarl)	Nikolás	Norr (K.)
Narfi			

From other sources

Nef, n.n.	Nes-konungr, p.n.	Næfra-maðr, n.n.
Nefja (f.), n.n.	Njosnar-helgi, n.n.	Nörtr, n.n.

O

Oblauðr	Oddleifr	Orð-lokarr, n.n.	Órækja
Oddbjörg (f.)	Oddmarr	Ormarr	Ósk
Oddbjörn	Oddný	Ormhildr (f.)	Ósku (f.)
Oddfriðr (f.)	Oddr	Orms-tunga, n.n.	Óspakr
Oddgeirr	Ófeigr	Ormr	Ósvaldr (K.)
Oddi	Óláfr	Orny (f.)	Ósvífr (Osyfr)
Oddkatla	Óleifr	Orrabeinn	Otryggr
Oddlaug	Óli	Orra-skáld, n.n.	Óttarr
Oddleif (f.)	Ólöf		

From other sources

Opin-sjoðr, n.n.	Orri, n.n.	Oxi, p.n.

P

Páll	Parak, n.n.	Patrekr (Gaelic)	Pétr
Papar (Gaelic)	Paschalis	Petrus	Philippus

From other sources

Paktin, n.n.	Pitlor, n.n.	Prest-mágr, n.n.
Pálnir, p.n.	Pík, n.n.	Prúði, n.n.
Peini, n.n.	Plógr, p.n. (*D.*)	Pung-elta, n.n.
Petarr	Plytr, n.n.	

R

Ráðormr	Rannveig (f.)	Refr (a fox)	Rodolfr. *See*
Rafn	Ráðormr	Ref-skeggr, n.n.	Hródólfr
Rafnkell	Rauða-Björn	Reginleif	Roðrekr
Rafsi	Rauð-bekri, n.n.	Reidarr. *See*	Rólf. *See* Hrólfr
Raförta (f.,	Rauð-feldr, n.n.	Hreidarr	Rotinn, n.n.
Gaelic)	Rauðr	Reistr	Rudolphus
Raga-broðir, n.n.	Rauð-skeggr, n.n.	Reyðr-siða, n.n.	Ruðu-Ulfr (Bp.)
Ragi	Rauðúlfr	Reyni-björn	Ruggi, n.n.
Ragnarr (K.)	Rauðum-skjaldi,	Reyr-Ketill	Runolfr
Ragnheiðr (f.)	n.n. (red shield)	Rifla	Rútr. *See* Hrútr
Ragnhildr (f.)	Raumr	Rjúpa (f.)	Rögnvoldr (jarl)
Rang-látr, n.n.	Raunguðr		

From other sources

Rafa-Kollr, n.n.	Rand-verr	Remba, n.n.
Ramr, n.n.	Regg-búss, n.n. (Wen-	Ruza, n.n.
Rand-eiðr (f.)	dish)	Rykill, n.n.
Rang-muðr, n.n.	Reikall, p.n.	Rympill, n.n.
Ranka (Ragnheiðr)		

S

Salbjörg (f.)	Skjaldbjörn	Spak-Böðvarr	Svana (f.)
Salgerðr (f.)	Skálgr	Spana (f.)	Svanlaug (f.)
Samr	Skiði	Spörr, n.n.	Svanr
Saurr, n.n.	Skinna-Björn	Stafngrimr	Svart-höfði
Saxi	Skjöldólfr	Starkaðr	Svarðkell
Sela-Kálfr	Skolmr	Starri	Svarta-þurs, n.n.
Sel-Þórir	Skopti	Steigar-Þorir	Svartr
Semingr	Skorargeirr	Steinbjörn	Svasi
Sigarr (K.)	Skorri	Steinfirðr	Svavarr
Sigfastr	Skota-Kollr, n.n.	Steingrimr	Svegðir
Sigfús	Skrof-Skrofi	Steini	Sveinbjörn
Sighvatr	Skrof-uðr, n.n.	Steinmóðr	Sveinn
Sigmundr	Skuli	Steinn	Sveinúngar
Signý	Skúmr	Steinnar (jarl)	Svertingr. A.S.
Sigriðr (f.)	Skútaðar-Skeggi	Steinólfr	Swerthing
Sigtryggr	Skæringr	Steinrauðr	Svið-balki
Sigurðr (Bp.)	Sleitu-Helgi	Steinuðr. See	Sviðu-Kári
Sigvaldi	Slettu-Björn	Steinunn	Svigna-Kappi, n.n.
Sigvatr	Smiðkell	Steinvör	Svína-Böðvarr
Sigvör	Smiðr	Steinþórr	Svinhaga-Björn
Símon	Smiðskeggi	Stephanus (Bp.)	Svörfuðr
Sjóni, n.n.	Snar-fari, n.n.	Stigandi, n.n.	Sæbjörn
Skagi	Snepill	Stórólfr	Sæhildr (f.)
Skáld-Helgi	Snertlingar	Stoti, n.n.	Sælingr, n.n.
Skáldhrafn	Snjallr. D.	Strangi, n.n.	Sæmundr
Skáld-Refr	Snolde	Stúfr	Sæuðr (Sæunn)
Skalla-Grimr	Snjallsteinn	Sturla	(f.)
Skálp-hæna, n.n.	Snorri	Styrbjörn	Sæ-úlfr (Sjólfr)
Skamkell	Snæbjörn	Styrkárr	Sökkólfr
Skapti	Snækollr	Styrmir	Sölgi (K.)
Skarpheðinn	Snælaug (f.)	Styrr	Sölmundr
Skati	Snörtr	Sulki (K.)	Solverr (Sölvarr)
Skefill = Skemill	Sokki, n.n.	Sumarliði	(K.)
Skegg-ávaldi	Solveig (f.)	Sunnólfr	Sölvi
Skegg-broddi	Sólvör	Súrr	Sörkvir-Svarkr
Skeggi, n.n.	Sóti	Surtr	Söxólfr
Skjalda-Björn	Spá-Kona, n.n.		

From other sources

Salt-eyða, n.n.	Sandi, n.n.	Sel-byggr, n.n.
Samr, n.n.	Saup-ruðr, n.n.	Selr, n.n.

Sepill, n.n.
Sið-nefr, n.n.
Siggi (Sigurðr)
Signjótr
Silfri, n.n.
Sjaundi
Skakki, n.n.
Skam-fótr, n.n.
Skam-háls, n.n.
Skammi, n.n.
Skarði, n.n.
Skati, n.n.
Skat-Kaupendi, n.n.
Skála-glam, n.n.
Skáldi, n.n.
Skálf
Skálgr, n.n.
Skári, n.n.
Skemill = Skefill
Skeið-Kollr, n.n.
Skeifr, n.n.
Skekill, n.n.
Sker-auki, n.n.
Skerðingr, n.n.
Skerja-blesi, n.n.
Skin-hringr, n.n.
Skinni, n.n.
Skinn-vefja, n.n.
Skirvill, n.n.
Skíðungar (the descendants of Skíði)
Skífa, n.n.
Skjómi, n.n.
Skjöldr
Skol-beinn, n.n.
Skoppr, n.n.
Skorpa, n.n.
Skorri, n.n.
Skota, n.n.
Skota-Kollr, n.n.

Skotti, n.n.
Skógungar, n.n.
Skólmr, n.n.
Skrafari, n.n.
Skratt-hanki, n.n.
Skrauti, n.n.
Skrápi, n.n.
Skreyja, n.n. *D.*
Skryde
Skrill, n.n.
Skrukka, n.n. *D.*
Skrog
Skrúð-hyrna, n.n.
Skúma (f.), n.n.
Skúmr, n.n.
Skvaðra, n.n.
Skvaldri, n.n. *S.*
squallia
Skúli
Skyti, n.n. *D.* Skytte
Skæla, n.n.
Slafsi, n.n.
Slaga-Kollr, n.n.
Slakki, n.n.
Slandri, n.n.
Slappi, n.n.
Slefa, n.n.
Sleggja, n.n.
Sleppi, n.n.
Slinkr, n.n.
Slókr, n.n.
Slyngr, n.n.
Smetta, n.n. *D.*
Smutte
Snákr, n.n.
Snati, n.n.
Sneypir, n.n.
Snjólfr (Snæ-úlfr)
Snoppa-langr, n.n.
Snókr, n.n. *See* Snákr

Snuin-bruni, n.n.
Snæ-þryma, n.n.
Soddi, n.n.
Sopi, n.n.
Spá-Kona, n.n.
Spraka-leggr, n.n. *D.*
Sprade
Spýtu-leggr, n.n.
Stag-brellr, n.n.
Stag-nál (f.), n.n.
Standali, n.n.
Stand-eykr, n.n.
Steðja-Kollr, n.n.
Steypir, n.n.
Stigandi, n.n.
Stigr, n.n.
Stiku-bligr, n.n.
Storgr, n.n.
Storka, n.n.
Stoti, n.n.
Strangr, n.n.
Stri-nefr, n.n.
Strylltr, n.n.
Stubbi, n.n.
Stangar-högg, n.n.
Stöpuðr
Súrr, n.n.
Svaði, p.n.
Svagi, n.n.
Sveiði, n. of a sea king
Sveimr, n.n.
Sveinki (Sveinungr)
Sveltir, n.n.
Sverrir
Sviðr-balki, n.n.
Sviðandi = Sviðingr, n.n.
Svín-höfði, n.n.
Syrja (f.) n.n. (sori)
Sýr, n.n.

T

Talkni
Tanni
Tasaldi, n.n.
Teitr
Tindr
Tinforni
Tjörfi

Tófa (f.)
Tófi
Torf-Einarr (jarl)
Torfi
Torráðr
Tor-tryggr
Trandill, n.n.

Trefill, n.n.
Trolli, n.n.
Trumbu-beinn, n.n.
Tryggvi (K.)
Tumi
Túngu-Kári

Túngu-Oddr
Túngu-Steinn
Tunhani
Tvennum-brúni, n.n.
Tyrfingr

From other sources

Tabarðr, n.n.	Tosti
Tölu-sveinn, n.n.	Toti
Tandri, n.n.	Tottr, n.n. *D.* Tommel-tot
Tann-gnjóstr, n.n.	Tóki. *D.* Tyge, *Lat.* Tycho
Tann-grisnir, n.n.	Tónn, n.n.
Tann-refill, n.n.	Trausti
Tann-skári, n.n.	Tré-bót, n.n.
Tálgi, n.n.	Tre-telja, n.n.
Táta	Trúðr, n.n.
Tin-forni, n.n.	Trú-fast, n.n. of K. Athelstan
Tin-teinn, n.n.	Tronu-beinn, n.n.
Titlingr, n.n.	Tulkari, n.n.
Tiðinda-Skopti, n.n.	Tungu-goði, n.n.
Tjörn-skinn, n.n.	Tunni, n.n.
Tjúgu-skegg, n.n.	Tysti = Tosti, n.n.
Todda (f.), n.n.	Tyza, n.n.

U

Uggi	Úlf-heiðr (f.)	Úlfrun (f.)	Úrækja
Úlfarr	Úlf-hildr (f.)	Una (f.)	Úspakr
Úlfeiðr	Úlf-Kell	Uni	Útryggr
Úlf-hamr	Úlfljótr	Unnr	
Úlf-heðinn	Úlfr		

From other sources

Ubbi. *A.S.* Ubba, Uffa	Ungi, n.n.
Uðr	Urðar-Köttr, n.n. = Hreysi-Köttr
Ull-höttr, n.n.	Urðar-steinn, n.n.
Ulli, dim. of Erlendr	Urka, n.n.
Ull-serkr, n.n.	Úrr, n.n.
Ull-strengr, n.n.	

V

Vaði	Vand-raðr	Végestr	Véþörn
Valbrandr	Vanlandi (K.)	Vékell	Viðarr
Valdis (f.)	Vápni	Vélaug (f.)	Vífill
Valgarðr	Vatnarr (K.)	Véleifr	Víga-Barði
Valgautr	Vebjörn	Vémundr	Víga-Bjarni
Valgerðr (f.)	Vébrandr	Vèný (f.)	Víga-Glumr
Vali	Védis (f.)	Vermundr	Víga-Hrappr
Valla-Brandr	Véðormr. *See*	Vestarr	Víga-Skuta
Valla-Ljótr	Veþormr	Vesteinn	Viga-Sturla
Valþjoflingar	Veðra-grimr	Vestliði	Víga-Styrr
Valþófr	Veðr, n.n.	Vestmaðr	Vígbjoðr
Valþýflingar	Véfreyðr	Vetrliði	Vigdis (f.)
(Valþýfingr)	Végeirr	Véþormr	Vígfús

Viglundr	Vilbaldr	Vilmundr	Vorsar
Vigsterkr	Vilburg (f.)	Vilraðr	Vorsa-Úlfr
Vikarr	Vilgeirr	Visburr (K.)	Væpnlingar
Vikinga-Kari	Vilgerðr (f.)	Vívill	Völu-steinn
Víkingr	Vilhjálmr		

From other sources

Vaggaldi, n.n.	Veljungr = Vælungr,	Við-leggr, n.n.
Vagn	n.n.	Viggjar-skalli, n.n.
Val-frekr, n.n.	Vendill	Vippa (f.), n.n.
Vandill	Vendill-Kráka, n.n.	Víg-ólfr
Vágr	Vesall, n.n.	Væringi (the Warings)
Vei	Vettir, n.n.	Vörsa-Krákr, n.n.
Veðr, n.n.	Við-finnr	Vöttr, p.n.
Veili, n.n.		

Y

Ýnglingar	Ýngvi	Ýr (Yri), (f.)	Ysja (f.), n.n.
Ýngvarr	Ýngvildr (f.)	Yxna-Þorir	

Þ

Þángbrandr	Þorbjörn	Þórhildr (f.)	Þórormr
Þengill	Þorbrandr	Þórhrolfr	Þorsteinn
Þiðrandi	Þórdis (f.)	Þóriðr. *See*	Þorsteinnsbjörn
Þjóðarr	Þórðr	Þuriðr	Þórunn
Þjóðgerðr (f.)	Þórelfr (f.)	Þórir	Þorvaldr
Þjóðhildr (f.)	Þórey (f.)	Þorkatla (f.)	Þorvarðr
Þjóð-mar. *G.*	Þorfiðr (Máni)	Þorkell	Þór-vé (Þor-veig)
Ditmar	Þorfinna (f.)	Þorketill	Þorviðr
Þjóðrekr. *G.*	Þorfinnr	Þorlakr	Þórvör (f.)
Deitrich	Þorgautr	Þorlaug (f.)	Þráin
Þjökka (f.), n.n.	Þorgeirr	Þorleif (f.)	Þrándr
Þjóstarr	Þorgerðr (f.)	Þorleifr	Þrasi
Þjóstólfr	Þorgestr	Þorleikr	Þraslaug (f.)
Þóra (f.)	Þorgils	Þorljót (f.)	Þróndr. *See*
Þórálfr	Þorgnýr	Þorljótr	Þrándr
Þóralldr. *See*	Þorgrima (f.)	Þormoðr	Þröstr
Þórhallr	Þorgrímr	Þornjótr	Þuriðr (f.)
Þórarinn	Þórhaddr	Þórný (f.)	Þussasprengir, n.n.
Þórarna (f.)	Þórhalla (f.)	Þórodda (f.)	Þyna (f.), n.n.
Þorbergr	Þórhalli	Þoroddr	Þöngull, n.n.
Þorbjörg (f.)	Þórhallr	Þórólfr	

From other sources

Þak-raðr = Þakk-raðr, p.n. *G.* Tancred

Þas-ramr, n.n.

Þausnir, n.n.

Þegjandi, n.n.

Þenja, n.n.

Þing-bitr, n.n.
Þing-höttr, n.n.
Þjálfi
Þjóri, n.n. *D.* tyr
Þjóti, n.n.
Þórðr
Þrjúgr. *D.* Tryge
Þruma, n.n.

Þrúða, Sig-Þruðr (f.)
Þumli, n.n.
Þura, Þuriðr (f.)
Þurs, n.n (a giant). *D.* Tosse
Þvari, n.n.
Þveit, p.n. (Thwaite). *D.* Tvæde
Þyrni-fótr, n.n.
Þömb, n.n.

Æ

Æði-Kollr, n.n.
Ægileif (f.)

Æsa (f.)
Ævarr

O

Ögmundr
Ögurr
Ögvaldr. *See*
  Afvaldr
Ölfuss, n.n.
Ölmóðr
Ölmæðlingar
Ölver

Ön. *See* Aun
Ondott (f.)
Ondottr-Kraka
Öngr
Öngull. *See*
  Aungull
Önn

Önundr
Örlygr
Örn
Örnólfr
Örrek, n.n.
Örv-öndr, or
  Örvhendr, n.n.

Ösyfr. *See*
  Ósvifr
Öxna-megn, n.n.
Öxna-Þorir. *See*
  Yxna-Þorir
Özurr
Öþr. *See* Auðr

From other sources

Ölbogi, n.n.
Örðigr, n.n.

Örðig-skeggi
Ör-eiðr, n.n.

Örkn-höfði, n.n.
Ör-nefni

Örra-beinn, n.n.

PET NAMES—GIRLS

Ása, from Ás-laug
Ásta, from Ás-triðr
Disa, from Val-dís, Vig-dís, Her-dís
Dóra, from Hall-dóra
Friða, from Holm-friðr
Geira, from Geir-laug
Gudda, from Guð-riðr
Gunna, from Guð-rún
Imba, from Ingi-björg
Inga, from Ing-unn, Ingveldr
Jóka, from Jó-hanna

Jóra, from Jóreiðr
Kata, from Katrin
Lauga, from Guð-laug
Manga, from Margrét
Ranka, from Ragn-eiðr, Ragn-hildr
Sigga, from Sig-riðr
Sissa, from Sig-þruðr
Tobba, from Þor-björg
Valka, from Val-gerðr
Þrúða, from Jar-þrúðr, Sig-þruðr
Þura, from Þur-iðr

PET NAMES—BOYS

Arni (Arne), from Örn
Ási, from Ás-mundr
Atli, from Attila
Bensi, from Benedikt

Bersi, from Björn
Bjarni, from Björn
Björsi, from Björn
Brynki, from Bryn-jólfr

Daði, from David
Erli, from Erl-indr (Erlingr)
Eyvi, from Eyj-ólfr
Fusi, from Víg-fús
Gamli, from Gamel
Goddi, from compounds in Guð
Grimsi, from Grímr
Gutti, from Guðormr
Gvendr, from Guð-mundr
Helgi, from Há-leygr
Ingi, from compounds in Ing
Jónsi, from Jon
Karli, from Karl
Keli, from Þor-kel
Kobbi, from Jacob

Láfi, from Óláfr
Láki, from Þor-lákr
Laugi, from Gunn-laugr
Mangi, from Magnus
Mundi, from Ás-mundr
Ragni, from compounds in Ragn
Runki, from Rún-ólfr
Sebbi, from Sig-björn
Siggi, from Sig-urðr
Simbi, from Sig-mund
Snorri, from Snerrir
Steinki, from Stein-grímr
Sveinki, from Sveinn
Tumi, from Thomas
Valdi, from Þor-valdr

FRISIAN PERSONAL AND FAMILY NAMES

A

Abbo, m.; fam. n., Abben, Abena
Adde, m.; Adda, f.; fam. n., Adden
Ade, m.; fam. n., Aden, Adena
Afke, f. dimin. *See* Efke, Eveke, from Eva
Agatha, f.
Agge, m.; fam. n., Aggen
Agt, Agte, f. dimin. of Agatha
Aisso, Aisse, Eisse, m.; fam. n., Aissen, Eissen
Albert, Albarts, Albardus, Albertus (Albrecht), m.; fam. n., Alberts, Albers; f. Albertje
Alerk (Alarich, contraction of Athalarich), m.; fam. n., Alerks, Alers, Ahlers
Alle, m.; fam. n., Allen, Allena

Almôd, Almôth, Almt, f. (Allmuth)
Alt, m.; fam. n., Alts
Amel, m.; fam. n., Amels. Comp. Amala, Amalia, Amalung, etc.
Amke, m. and fam. n. *See* Hamke
Anke, f. (Antje), from Anna, as also Anken, Aennchen, Annechin
Anna, f.
Arend, Arnd, Arndt, m. (Arnold); fam. n., Arends
Arjen or Arien, m.; fam. n., Arjens, Ariens, Arjes
Arkonâ, Arkenâ, fam. n., from Arko
Arrel, Arl. *See* Harrel
Athe, m.; fam. n., Athen. *See* Ade, Atte
Atte, Atto, m.; fam. n., Attena

B

Baino, Beino, m.; fam. n., Bainen, Beinen
Bantje, m.; fam. n., Bantjes, dimin. of Banno
Bärend, Bêrend, Bernd, m.; fam. n., Bärends, Berend, a contraction of Bernhard

Bauke, Bâwke, Bâfke or Bâvke, f. dimin. of Old *F.* Bavo; fam. n., Bavink
Beelke, Belke, dimin. of Bele
Beino. *See* Baino
Bela, f.
Bele, Behl, Beil, Bill, m.

Belemar, Biletrud
Bêner, m. ; fam. n., Bêners
Benge, m. ; fam. n., Bengen
Bêninga, Bênenga, fam. n.
Benno, m. ; Benna, f.
Berend. *See* Bärend
Bôdewîn, m. Comp. Bouduin,
    Balduin, Boldewin
Boko, m. *N.* Baugr
Boldewîn

Bôle, Boele, m. ; fam. n., Bôlen,
    Bolema
Bôleke, Bôlke, Bolkes, dimin.
Bonno, m. ; fam. n., Bonnen
Boys, Boye, Boy, m. ; dimin. Boyke ;
    fam. n., Boyen, Boyinga, Boyink,
    Boyunga
Brûno, m. ; Brûnke and Brûntje, f. ;
    and fam. n., Brûninga, Brûns,
    Bronsema, and Brûnken

D

Datter, m.
Dedde, m. ; fam. n., Dedden
Dêtlêf, m.
Detmer, m.
Dever. *Dch.* Dieven
Deverke, dimin. f.
Dîderik, Dîdrîk, Dîdrîch, Dîderk,
    Dierk, Dirk, m. (Dietrich)
Dîko or Dyko, m. ; fam. n., Dîken,
    Dyken, Dikena, Dykena

Dîle, Diele, m. ; fam. n., Dielen
    (Dil.)
Dirk, Dierk, m. ; f. Dirktje, Dirtje ;
    fam. n., Dirks, Dirksen, Dirken,
    Dierken
Djure, m. ; fam. n., Djuren ; f.
    Djurke, Jurke
Djurelt and Durelt, m.
Dodo, m. ; f. Doda ; fam. n., Doden,
    Dodens, Dodena

E

Ebbe, m.
Ebbo, m.
Ebo, Ebbo, Ebe, Eppo, Eve, m. ;
    f. Ebbe, Eveke ; fam. n., Eben,
    Even, Eppen, Ebeling
Edde, m. ; fam. n., Edden
Edo, m. ; dimin. Edje ; fam. n.,
    Eden, Edinga
Edsard (Esdert ?), m. ; fam. n.,
    Edsards, Edzards, Esderts
Egbert, Ebbert, m. ; fam. n., Egberts,
    Egbers
Egge, m. ; fam. n., Eggen
Eibo, Eibe, m. ; fam. n., Eiben
Eiko, Eike, m.
Eilert, Eilt, m. ; fam. n., Eilerts,
    Eilers, Eilts, Eils (contraction of
    Egilhardt, Ailhardt)

Eimo, Eime, m. ; fam. n., Eimers
Eint, Eent, m. ; fam. n., Eints
    (Aginhardt ?)
Eka, Eke, Ekea, Eckea, f.
Ele, Ehle, m. ; fam. n., Ehlen
Elle, m. ; Ella, f. ; Ellen, fam. n.
Eme, Emo, Ehme, and Eimo, m. ;
    fam. n., Emen, Ehmen, Em-
    minga ; dimin. Emke ; fam. n.,
    Emken
Emminga, Emmius, fam. n.
Emmo, Emme, m. ; Emma, f.
Eppo, m. ; Eppen, fam. n.
Ernst, m.
Esdert. *See* Edsard
Eta, Etta, f. dimin. Ettje
Eve, Ewe, Aeve, m.

F

Fauke, m.
Fekko, Fêko, Feyko, Fekke, m. ;
    fam. n., Fekken, Feyken, Fei-
    kena

Feyen, fam. n.
Feyke, m. ; Feyken, fam. n.
Fia, dimin. of Sophia, dimin. Fiake,
    Fîke

c

Fimmo, Fimme, m.; fam. n., Fimmen
Flamê, Flâm, a Fleming
Fôke, Fauke, m.; Fôken, fam. n.
Fokke, Fokko, m.; Fokka, f.; Fokken, Fokkena, fam. n.
Folerk. *See* Folrick
Foletta, f.
Fôlke, f.
Folkerd, m. (Folk-ward); Folkerds, Folkers, fam. n.
Folkmar, m.
Folpmer, m.

Folpt, Fulpt, m.; Folpts, fam. n.
Folrâd, Fulrâd, m. (Vollrath, Folkrâd)
Fôlrîk, Fôlrîch, Fôlerk, m.; Folrichs, Fôlerks, Fôlers, fam. n.
Frërk, Frêrk, m.; Frërksen, fam. n., from Frêrik, Frederik
Frese or Frêse, a *F.*
Fulbrand, m.
Fulf, m.
Fulke, f., or Fulka, Fulleke, from Fulla, Folla
Fulko, m., from Fullo

G

Gaiko. *See* Geiko
Galt, m.
Gâlt, m., contraction of Garrelt, Garlt, Gerlt
Garbrand, Garbert, m.
Garrelt, Gerrelt, m.; Garrelts, Garrels, Gerrelts, Gerrels, fam. n. (Garhold, Gerhold)
Geiko, Gaiko, Gayko, Geike, m.; Geiken, fam. n., from Geio, Gayo
Gerd, m.; dimin. f. Gerdtje; fam. n., Gerdes, contraction of Ger-

hard. Also Gerjet, Gêjert, Gert, and Gerriet
Gerdrût, Gädrût, f. (Gertrude)
Gerke, m.; Gerken, fam. n.
Gërman, old fam. n.
Gêske, f. dimin. of Gêso, Gêsa, Giso (Gîsbert)
Grendel, Grennel; f. dimin. Grendelke, Grennelke
Greta (Margaretha), dimin. Gretje
Grôn, fam. n.
Grönefeld, Grönfeld, fam. n.
Gronewold, Gronwold, fam. n.

H

Habbo, m.; Habben and Habbinga, fam. n.
Haddo (Hatto), m.; Haddinga, fam. n. *See* Heddo
Hagen, m.; Hagena, fam. n.
Hamke, dimin. of Hamo; fam. n. Haming
Harm, m. (contraction of Hermann); f. dimin. Harmke; fam. n., Harms, Harmens
Hâro, Hâre, m.; Hâren, Haringa, Harringa, fam. n.
Harrell, Harle, m.
Hayo, m.; Hayung, Heyungs, Hayunga, fam. n.
Hebe, f. dimin. Hebeke, Hêbke, Hëpke

Heddo, Hedde, m.; Hedden, Heddinga, fam. n.; Heddo, *A.S.* Bishop, A.D. 676
Heie, Hei, m. *See* Hayo
Heiko or Haiko, m.; Heikens, Heiken, Heikena, Haiken, Hayken
Hein, m.; Heine, Heinen, fam. n. (from Heinrich)
Heini
Heink, m. *See* Hein
Heite, Heit, m.; Heits, fam. n,
Helmer, m.; Helmers, fam. n.
Herman, m.
Hêro, Hêre, Herre, m.; Hêren, Herren, fam. n.
Hester (Esther)

Hibbo, Hibbe, m.; Hibben, fam. n.
Hidde. *See* Hiddo
Hiddo, m.; Hidden, fam. n.
Hilke, f. dimin. of Hille, Hilla, Hilda
Hillerd, Hillerk. *See* Hillrich
Hillmer, Hilmer, m.; Hillmers, fam. n.
Hillrîch, Hillrik, Hillerk, Hillerd, m.; Hillrichs, Hillerks, Hillers, Hillern, fam. n.

Hima, f.
Himke, dimin. of Hima
Hinderk. *See* Hinrich
Hinrich, m.; Hinrichs, Hinnerks, Hinners, Hinnerssen, Hünerssen, fam. n.
Hiske, f.
Hoot, m.; Hoots, Hôting, Hooting (from Hotbert)

I

Ibo, Ibe, Ihbe, m.; Iben, Ibben, Ibeling, fam. n.
Ide
Idje, Itje, f. dimin. of Ida
Idse, Itse, Idze, m.; Idsen, Itzen, Idsinga, fam. n.
Igge, m.; Iggen, Iggena, fam. n.
Ikke, Ikka, Ika, f.
Iko, Ike, m.; Iken, Ikena, fam. n.
Imel, m.; Imels, fam. n.

Imke, f., also Immeke, dimin. of Imme
Imme, Immo, m.; Immen, fam. n.
Ine. *See* Ino
Ing, Ingo, Inguio, m.
Inka, f.
Ino, Ine, Ihno, m.; dimin. Inke, Ihnke; fam. n., Inen, Ihnen; Ino, *A.S.* King, A.D. 727
Ippo, Ippe, m.; Ippen, fam. n.

J

Jabbo, Jabbe, Jabe, m.; Jabben, fam. n.
Jak, m., also fam. n.; dim. Jäkchen
Jakub, Jakup, m.
Jan, m.; Janna, Jantje, f.; Jansen, Janssen, Jenssen, fam. n.
Jasper, m.; Jaspers, fam. n.
Jelle, m.; Jellen, Jellena, fam. n. (from Jellrich?)
Jellrich, Jellrik, Jellerk, m.

Jetta, f. dimin. Jettchen
Jibbo, m.; Jibben, fam. n.
Jimme, m.; Jimmen, fam. n.
Jochem, Jofen, m. (Joachim)
Juist. *See* Jûst
Jürgen, Jürjen, contraction of Jürn, m. (Görgen), also Jörg; fam. n. Jürgens, Jürjens, Jürns
Jurke, f.
Just, loc. and fam. n.

K

Karsten, Kersten, Karsen, Kassen, Kasjen, from Kristjan (Christian); fam. n., Karstens, Karsens, Kassens, Kasjens
Kasper, m.

Kâtje, f. dimin. of Kate, Catherina
Kês, m., contraction of Cornelius
Klâs (Klaus), Niklâs, m.
Klûn, Kluin, fam. n.

L

Lambert, Lampert, Lambrecht, m.
Lanbert, Lanpert, Lantpert, m.

Lübbert, m.; Lubberts, Lübbers, fam. n.

Lübbo, m.; Lübben, Lübbena, fam. n.; dimin. Lübke; fam. n., Lübkes
Lûdowig, Lûdewig, Lûdwig, m.; Lûdowigs, Lûdewigs, Lûdwigs, fam. n.
Lûdo, m.
Lüitje, m.; Luitjens, fam. n.

Lüke, m.; Lüken, fam. n., contraction of Lüdeke, Ludeke, Liudeke, dimin. of Ludo, Lindo, etc.
Lükke, f. *See* Lüke
Lûks, m. (Lucas)
Lüppo, Lübbo, m.; dim. Lüpke; fam. n., Lüpkes
Lûth, m. (Lütet); Lûitje, f.

M

Machelt, f. (Machtild)
Machtild, Mechtild, f.
Magrêta, f. (Margrêta)
Maike. *See* Marê
Mammo, Mamme, m.; Mammen, Memmen, Mamminga, Memminga, fam. n.
Manno, Manne, m.; Manninga, fam. n.
Marê (Maria), dimin. Marêken, Marêke, Maike
Margrêta, Margrêt, Magrêta, Magrêt, Megrêt, Mergrêt, contraction Grêta; dimin. Grêtje
Meinert, Mênert, contraction Meint, Meent, m. (Meinhard); Meinerts, Meiners, Meints, Meents, fam. n.
Meino, m. (Magino, Megino)
Memke, Mêmke. *See* Memmo. Memkes, Mêmkes, Mimkes, fam. n.

Memmo, Mémo, Méme, m.; Memmen, Memminga, fam. n.
Mêne, m.; Mênen, fam. n.
Menje, f. dimin. of Menna
Menko, Menke, m.; Menken, fam. n.
Menno, Menne, m.; f. Menna; Mennen, Menninga, fam. n.
Mense, Mens, m.; Mensen, Mensinga, fam. n.
Mês or Mêwes, contraction of Bartolomaeus
Meta, Metta, f. dimin. Metje
Mêwes. *See* Mês
Mia, f. (Maria); dimin. Mîke, Mîtje
Michel, m.
Mimke, Mimmke, m. (Mimeken, Mimmeken)
Mimste, m.

N

Nanno, Nanne, m.; Nannen, Nan ninga, fam. n.

Nâtje, f., contraction of Annatje, dimin. of Anna
Nôme, Nôm, m.

O

Ode, Odo, m.; Odens, Odenga, Odinga
Okko, Ocko, Okke, m.; Okka, f.; Okken, Okkinga
Ommo, m.; Ommen, Omkes, fam. n.
Onke, Onneke, dimin. of Onno; fam. n., Onkes, Onnekes

Onno, m.; Onna, f.; Onnen, fam. n.
Ontje, m.; Ontjes, fam. n., from Onno
Ordgîs, Ortgîs, Oortgies, Oorthgies, Oordgiese, m.
Ortwin, Oorthwin, Ooordwin, m.
Otte, Otto, m.; Otten, fam. n.

P

Paul, m. ; Pauls, Paulsen, fam. n.
Peta, f.
Peter, m. ; dimin. Peterke, f. ; Peters, Petersen, fam. n.

Poppe, m. ; Poppen, Poppinga, fam. n. ; dimin. Popke, Popken
Poppe, Duke of Friesland, was slain in battle by Charles Martel in 734

R

Reent, m. ; Reents, fam. n.
Reimer, m. (Regimar) ; Reimers, fam. n.
Reiner, m. (Reinhard) ; Reiners, fam. n.
Reinhard, m.
Reint, m. ; Reints, fam. n.
Rembold, m.
Remmer, m. ; Remmers, Remmersen, fam. n.

Rewert, m. ; Rewerts, fam. n.
Rikkerd, Rikkert, m. (Richard) ; Rikkerts, Rikkers, fam. n.
Rôlf. (Rodolf), m.; Rôlfs, fam. n.
Rötger, m. (Hrodgar) ; Rötgers, fam. n.
Rumke, m., contraction of Rumo or Hrom ; Rumkes, fam. n.
Rummert, m. ; Rummerts, Rummers, fam. n.

S

Sebo, m. ; Seba, Sebens, fam. n.
Sibet, m.
Sibo, m.; Siebens, fam. n.
Sikko, Sikke, m.; Sikkens, Sikkinga, fam. n.

Swêerd, Swêert, m. ; Swêerds, Swêerts, Swêers, fam. n.
Swîthert, Swittert, Switer, m. ; Switers, Switters, fam. n.

T

Tado, Tade. *See* Thado and Tjado
Tako, m. ; Takes, fam. n., contraction Tâks, Takens
Tale, Talea, f. dimin. Tâlke
Taletta, f.
Tammo, Tamme, m. ; Tammen, Tamminga, fam. n.
Tanno, m. ; Tannen, fam. n.
Tâtje, f.
Tebbo, Tebbe, m.; Tebben, fam. n.
Tetta, f. dimin. Tetje

Têwes, m., contraction of Matheus. Comp. Mes
Thado, Tado, Thade, Tade, m. ; Thaden, Taden, fam. n.
Tjado, Tjade, m.; Tjaden, fam. n.
Tjârd, Tjard, Tjârt, m. ; Tjârds, Tjards, Tjârts, fam. n.
Tjarko, m.; Tjarks, fam. n.
Tjetmer, m. ; Tjetmers, fam. n. (Dietmar)
Tönjes, m. (Antonius)

U

Ubbo, Ubbe, m. ; Ubben, Ubbinga, fam. n.
Udo, Ude, m.; Uden, fam. n.

Ufo, Ufe, Uvo, Uffo, Uffe, m.; Ufen, Uven, Uffen, fam. n.; dimin. Ufke ; Ufkes, fam. n.

Uko, Üko, Uke, m.; Uken, Ukena, fam. n.

Ulerk (Ulrich), m. ; Ulerks, Ulers, fam. n.

Ulferd, Ulfert, m.; Ulferds, Ulferts, Ulfers. The Dutch form is Olferd, Ulferd, Ulverd, Ulverdus Ulrîk. *See* Ulerk

W

Warner, m. (Werner); dimin. Warntje; Warners and Warntjes, fam. n.

Wêert, m. ; Wêerts, Wêers, Weiers, fam. n.

Wêrda, Wiarda, fam. n.

Wêt, m. ; Wêts, fam. n.

Wilbert, m. ; Wilberts, Wilbers, fam. n.

Wildert, contraction Wilt, m.

Wilhelm, contraction Wilm, m. ; Wilms, fam. n.

Wilko, Wilke, m. ; Wilken, fam. n.

Wît, Wiet, dimin. Witje, Wietje, m.; Wîts, Wiets, Wîtjes, Wietjes, fam. n.

Wîterd, Wîtherd, Wîthert, m.

Wobbo, Wobbe, Wobbi, m.; dimin. f. Wobbeke, Wobke; fam. n., Wobbena, Wobben.

Wolbrecht, m. ; Wolbrechts, Wolbergs, fam. n.

Wübbo, m. ; Wübbens, Wubbena, fam. n. ; Wübke, dimin. f.

NAMES OF PERSONS ENTERED IN DOMESDAY BOOK AS HOLDING LANDS *TEMP.* KING ED. CONFR.

A

Aben	Adeluuald	Ægduuardus	Ælfleda
Abet	Adelwoldus	Æileua	Ælfric
Abo	Ademar	Æilmar	Ælgar
Achebranni	Adestan	Æilmer	Ælger
Achestanus	Adjuuar	Æilmund	Ælget
Achi	Adret	Æilric	Æli
Achil	Adstan	Ællard	Ælmar
Achins	Adstanus	Ældeua	Ælmer
Acolf	Adulf	Ældid	Ælmund
Acum	Æchebrand	Ældiet	Ælnod
Acun	Ædelflete	Ældit	Ælric
Adam	Ædeldreda	Ældred	Ælsi
Adeldreda	Ædgeua	Ældreda	Ælstanus
Adelmus	Ædi	Ældret	Æluert
Adelid	Ædmundus	Ælfag	Ælueua
Adelinge	Ædricus	Ælfec	Æluin
Adeliz	Æduinus	Ælfelm	Æluric
Adelo	Ædwardus	Ælfer	Æluuacre
Adeold	Æduui	Ælfeth	Æluuard
Adelric	Ædwoldus	Ælfled	Æluui

Æluuin
Ælwius
Æluuold
Ærefast
Ærgrim
Æstanus
Ætheldreda
Æthericus
Æthesi
Ætmarus
Ætnod
Agelmarus
Agebred
Agelricus
Ageluuard
Agemund
Agenulfi
Aghemundus
Aghete (Linc.)
Aieluert
Aifride
Ailad
Ailardus
Ailbernus
Ailbric
Ailbriht
Aildeig
Ailet
Aileua
Ailhalle
Ailid
Ailida
Ailiet
Ailith
Ailm
Ailmar
Ailmer
Ailmundus
Ailof
Ailred
Ailric
Ailsi
Ailuerd
Ailuert
Ailueua
Ailuuard
Ailward
Ailwi
Aimar

Ainar
Aiolf
Airaf
Airet
Aischil
Aisil
Aiulf
Aki
Ala
Alanus
Albani
Alberic
Albernus
Albertus
Albricht
Albus
Alcerl
Alchel
Alchemont
Alchen
Alcher
Alcheris
Alcherl
Alchetel
Alchil
Alcolm
Alcot
Alcude
Aldebert
Alded
Alden
Aldene
Aldeuuif
Aldgid (f.)
Aldi
Aldid
Aldiet
Adolfus
Aldred
Aldreman
  (Linc.)
Aldret
Aldvi
Alduin
Aldulf
Alebric
Alebrix
Alestan
Aluesdef

Alfa (Notts)
Alfac
Alfag
Alfah
Alfeg
Alfeih
Alfer
Alferd
Alfgerus
Alfhilla
Alfidis
Alfit
Alfled
Alfleda
Alflet
Alfnod
Alfric
Alfriz
Alfsi
Alfuuinus
Algar
Algerus
Algod
Algrim
Alham
Alid
Aliet
Alli
Allic
Allric
Almær
Almar
Almer
Almund
Almunt
Alnod
Alnoht
Alnold
Alnot
Alnoth
Alous
Alrebot
Alredi
Alreforda de
Alret
Alric
Alris
Alselmus
Alsi

Alsicus
Alsius
Alstan
Altei
Altet
Alti
Altor
Alwardus
Alued
Aluena
Aluene
Aluer
Aluerd
Aluerle
Alueron
Aluert
Aluet
Aluied
Aluiet
Aluin
Alun
Alunold
Aluol
Aluold
Aluort
Alur
Alured
Aluret
Aluric
Aluuacre
Aluuald
Aluuard
Aluuart
Aluuen
Aluui
Aluuid
Aluuin
Aluuol
Aluuold
Aluuric
Amod
Amund
Anand
Anant
Anaut
Ancholfus
Andrac
Andreæ
Andreas

Angarus
Angerus
Angot
Anschil
Anscot
Ansculf
Ansfrid
Ansfrig
Ansgar
Ansger
Ansgot
Ansketill
Anund
Anunt
Ape (Som.)
Appe (Wilts)
Arcebald
Arcenbald
Archel
Archetel
Archii
Archilbar

Archisti
Ardegrip
Arduin
Ardul
Ardulf
Aregri
Aregrim
Aret
Arfastus
Aric
Arich
Arling
Arnebrand
Arnegrim
Arnenger
Arnui
Arnul
Artor
Arulf
Asa
Ascer
Ascha

Aschi
Aschil
Aschilbar
Asci
Ascored
Aseloc
Asford
Asfort
Asgar
Asgot
Asi
Aslac
Asli
Assemann
Assorin
Asul
Asulf
Athelwold
Atilie
Atserus
Atsur
Attile

Atules
Audoen
Auduid
Audulf
Auegrin
Auelin
Aueue
Augustinus
Auic
Auitius
Aured
Ausgar
Austin
Autbert
Auti
Avigi
Awart
Azelinus
Azer
Azor
Azur

B

Baco (Linc.)
Bada (Derb.)
Bade
Bain
Balchi
Baldeuin
Baldric
Balduin
Bar
Barch
Bardi
Bared
Baret
Barn
Barne
Basin (Yorks)
Basine (Yorks)
Batoc
Batsuen
Bedel
Bedling
Belam
Belehorne

Belrap
Benedict
Benne
Benz
Beorus
Ber
Berchinges de
Bercsi
Bere
Berguluer
Bern
Bernac
Bernard
Berne
Bernolt
Bernalf
Berrnar
Bers
Bertor
Bertunt
Besi
Beso
Besy

Beteslau
Bettice
Biche (Devon)
Biga
Bil
Bisi
Blac
Blach
Blache
Blacheman
Blachemer
Blacre
Blacsune
Blacuin
Blacun
Blacus
Blakeman
Blancar
Blund
Boche
Boda
Boddus
Bode

Bodin
Boding
Boi
Boia
Bole
Bolest
Bolla
Bolle
Bollo
Boln
Bolne
Bonde
Bondi
Bondo
Bondus
Borda
Boret
Borgered
Borgeret
Borred
Borret
Boso
Bosteinn

Bot	Brictmer	Bristui	Bruning
Boti	Brictolf	Bristuin	Bruno
Botild	Brictred	Bristuoldus	Brunus
Botius	Brictric	Bristuuard	Brunwin
Botiz	Brictsuin	Briteua	Bu (Yorks)
Bou	Brictuald	Britfleda (f.)	Bubba
Boui	Brictuard	Britheue	Buge (Notts)
Brand	Brictui	Brithmar	Bugered
Brandulf	Brictuid	Brithwold	Bughered
Branduna	Brictuin	Britmar	Bugo (Notts,
Branting	Brictuold	Britnod	Yorks)
Branuuine	Brictuolt	Britric	Bului
Breme	Brictuuard	Brixe	Bunda
Bresibalt	Bricxtric	Brixi	Bunde
Bretel	Brideuuold	Brixtuin	Bundi
Bricfrid	Briford	Brocles	Bundo
Brichtmar	Brihferd	Brode	Burc
Bricmar	Brihmar	Broder	Burcard
Bricmær	Briht	Brodo	Burch de
Bricnod	Brihtman	Brodor	Burchard
Bricsi	Brihtmar	Brodre	Burchart
Bricsic	Brihtnoth	Bruhise	Burchric
Bricsmar	Brihtnot	Brumage	Burkart
Bricstan	Brihtric	(Northants)	Burgel
Bricstec	Brihtuold	Bruman	Burgered
Bricsteg	Brihtwald	Brumanbeard	(Devon)
Bricstouuard (Som.)	Brinot	Brumann	Burli
Bricstual	Brisid	Brumar	Burnes
Bricstuard	Brismar	Brun	Burnod
Bricstuin	Brisnod	Brune	Burred
Bricstul	Bristec	Brunesune	Burrer
Brictere	Bristei	Brungar	Burret
Bricteua	Bristeuuard	Brungart	Burric
Brictic	Bristoaldus	Brunier	Burro
Brictmar	(Devon)	Bruniht	Busch (Herts)

C

Cabe	Cana	Capellanus	Caron
Cadiand	Canceler	Capin	Caschin
Caduualent	Candovre	Capus	Cassa
Cædd	Cane	Carentoch	Caua
Caflo	Canistre	Cari	Cauua
Calpus	Cano	Carle	Cecus
Camerarius	Cantuin	Carlesone	Cedd
Camp	Canud	Carleunda	Cedde
Campa	Canus	Carlo	Celcott
Campo	Canut	Carman	Celeinus

Celestan
Cellinc
Celmar
Celred
Celric
Cerret
Certesyg
Ceruel
Cestre
Ceterith
Chelbertus
Chenegar
Chenestan
Cheneue
Cheneuuard
Chenias
Chenicte
Chening
Chenisi
Chenistre
Chenna
Chenp
Chenric
Chentis
Chentiscus
Chentuinus
Chenuard

Chenui
Chenuicelle
Chenvichelle
Chenvin
Chenut
Chepin
Cheping
Cheric
Cheteber
Chetel
Chetelbar
Chetelbern
Chetelbert
Chilbert
Chiluert
Chinesi
Chinestan
Chinias
Chiping
Chit
Chitel
Cild
Cille
Cilleham de
Cilt
Clac
Claman

Clarebold
Cliber
Clibert
Cloch
Cnud
Cnut
Cobbe
Coc
Code
Codolf
Codricus
Coduius
Cofsi
Cola
Colben
Colbert
Colbrand
Cole
Colebran
Coleg
Colegrim
Coleman
Colgrim
Colgrin
Colibertus
Colle
Collnic

Colne
Colo
Colocar
Coloen
Cols
Colsegc
Colsuan
Colsuein
Coluin
Colvin
Commend
Constabularius
Coolf
Coolle
Copsi
Corbun
Costellin
Couta
Crac
Crin
Croc
Crucan
Cubold
Cudulf
Cunlf
Cutbert

D

Dachelin
Dacus
Dagobertus
Dainz
Dane
Danemund
Dedol
Dedou
Deincora
Delfin
Dena
Dene
Depekin
Derch

Derinc
Dering
Derolfus
Derstanus
Deule
Doda
Dode
Doding
Dodo
Dolesuuif
Dolfin
Domne
Domniz
Domno

Don
Done
Donne
Donning
Donno
Dons
Dore
Dot
Doth
Dotus
Dringlel
Drogo
Drondus
Duglei

Dunestan
Dunne
Dunniht
Dunninc
Dunning
Dunno
Duns
Dunstan
Durand
Durilda
Dustan
Duna (f.)
Dunen

E

Eadmund
Eaduin
Ealgar

Earne
Ebrard
Eburg

Ecchebrand
Ecchefrid
Eculf

Edded
Eddeua
Eddeva

Eddid	Eilaf	Elsi	Ernuin
Eddied	Eilsberie	Elstan	Ernuit
Eddiet	Eileua	Elsuid	Ernulf
Edduin	Eilmer	Eltor	Ertein
Eddulf	Eilric	Eluena	Eruastus
Edeldreda	Eingar	Eluin	Esber
Edelmund	Einulf	Eluine	Esbern
Edelric	Eiric	Eluolt	Escelf
Edeluuold	Eiulf	Eluret	Eschet
Edena	Elaf	Eluric	Escul
Ederic	Elded	Elurilde	Escule
Edestan	Eldeua	Eluuacre	Esgar
Edeulf	Eldid	Eluuar	Esket
Edgar	Eldildæ	Eluuard	Eskmeld
Edged	Eldit	Eluui	Esmoda
Edgida	Eldred	Eluuin	Esnar
Edic	Eldret	Eluuold	Esneburn
Edid	Elduif	Engelri	Essocher
Ediet	Elduin	Engelric	Essul
Edilt	Eleua	Enisan	Estan
Edina	Elfac	Epy	Estarcher
Edlouedief	Elfag	Erchebrand	Estmunt
Edmær	Elfeg	Erding	Estori
Edmar	Elfelm	Erfast	Estorp de
Edmer	Elfelt	Ergrim	Estred
Edmund	Elfer	Eric	Etgar
Ednod	Elfgiva	Erich	Etmar
Ednoth	Elfin	Erlebald	Etnod
Edred	Elflet	Erlechin	Etone
Edric	Elfric	Erlenc	Etsius
Eduin	Elgar	Erne	Euchill
Eduuard (Cild,	Elget	Erneber	Eudo
Cilt.)	Eli	Ernebold	Euing
Eduui	Eliard	Ernebrand	Eur
Edwin	Eliert	Erneburne	Eureuu-
Eduunus	Eliet	Ernegrin	acre
Eduuold	Elintone	Erneis	(Devon)
Eduuolt	Elmær	Ernesi	Euroac
Edzi	Elmar	Erneuin	Eustachius
Egbert	Elmer	Erneuui	Eustan
Egbrand	Elmund	Erni	Euuacre
Egilfride	Elnoc	Erniet	Ewen
Egfride	Elnod	Ernold	Ewicman
Eghebrand	Elous	Ernu	Ezi
Eglesham, Abbatia	Elric	Ernui	Ezui
de (Glouc.)			

F

Faber
Fader
Fanchel
Fardan
Fardein
Fargrim
Fastolf
Fech
Feche
Feg
Fegarus
Felaga
Fenchel
Fenisc
Fin
Fin (danus)

Finegal
Fisc
Fitel
Fitheus
Floteman
Forn
Forne
Forst
Fot
Fradre
Frambolt
Fran
Frane
Frano
Franpalt
Franpold

Frauuin
Frebertus
Fredebern
Frederic
Fredghis
Fredgis
Fredgist
Fredregis
Fredri
Fregis
Fregist
Freowin
Freuuin
Fridebert
Friebern
Friebert

Frodo
Frogerus
Fuglo
Fulbert
Fulcard
Fulcher
Fulcheric
Fulchi
Fulchri
Fulcoi
Fulcui
Fulghel
Furcard
Fursa
Fyach

G

Galterus
Gam
Game
Gamebar
Gamel
Gamelbar
Gamelcarle
Gangemere
Gardulf
Garle
Gellinge
Genret
Genuis
Genust
Genut
Gerinus
Gerling
Germund
Gernan
Gerneber
Gernebern
Gerold
Gert
Gest
Getda
Gethe (f.)
Gethne
Gheri

Ghida
Ghil (Yorks)
Ghilander
Ghile
Ghilebrid
Ghilemicel
Ghilepatric
Ghille
Gida
Gilemichel
Giraldus
Girardus
Giroldus
Gislebertus
Giso
Gitda
Gladewin
Gladuin
Gladuine
Gleuuin
Glouuec
Glunier
God
Goda
Godbold
Goddua
Gode
Goded

Godefrid
Godel
Godelent
Godeman
Godere
Goderic
Goderus
Godessa
Godestan
Godet
Godeua
Godeurt
Godeva
Godgeua
Godhit
Godid
Godil
Godinc
Goding
Godiva (Countess Warwick)
Godman
Godmar
Godmund
Godo
Godred
Godric
Godrid

Godton
Godtovi
Goduin
Goerth
Gogan
Gola
Golde
Golderon
Goldinus
Goldstan
Goldus
Golegrim
Golleue
Golnil
Golstan
Goltoui
Goluin
Gonchel
Gonchetel
Gondrede
Gonhard
Gonnar
Gonneu-
  uate
Gonni
Gonnil
Gonuerd
Gort

Gos	Griketel	Grutt	Gunner
Gosfrid	Grim	Guda (f.)	Gunneuuate
Gosp	Grimbald	Gudda	Gunni
Gospatric	Grimber	Gudeta	Gunnild
Gotil	Grimbert	Gudmund	Gunning
Gotild	Grimbold	Gudmunt	Gunnor
Gotius	Grimchel	Gudret	Gunnulf
Gotlac	Grimchil	Gueda	Gunre
Gotone	Grimmus	Guerd	Gunuer
Gotra	Grimolfus	Guert	Gunuert
Gouti	Grimulf	Gueth	Gunuuar
Gozelin	Grimus	Guiolf	Gunward
Grene	Grinchel	Gulbert	Gurert
Greslet	Grino	Guluert	Guret
Greue	Grossus	Gunchil	Gurt
Gribol	Grud	Gundulf	Guthac
Grichetel	Grunulf	Guneuuare	Gutmund
Grifin	Grut	Gunnar	

H

Hache	Hardechin	Herc	Horim
Haco	Hardecnut	Heremannus	Horling
Hacon	Hardewin	Hereuuard	Horne
Hacun	Harding	(Linc.)	Horolf
Hademar	Hardul	Hereuuoldus	Hosmund
Hadeuui	Hardulf	Herfast	Houden
Hadimar	Haregrim	Herfrid	Hugo
Haduic	Haregrin	Herfrind	Humman
Hadulf	Harold	Herleng	Huna
Haduuin	Harparius(Camb.	Hermann	Hunchil
Haemar	Aluui)	Hernetoc	Hundic
Hagana	Hasten	Herold	Hundin
Hagane	Hauuard	Herolf	Hunding
Hagris	Hauuart	Herueus	Hundulp
Haimer	Heche	Herulfus	Hune
Haiminc	Hedned	Hildeuert	Hunef
Hairand	Hedul	Hobbesune Leu-	Hunepot
Hakena	Helewis	ricus (Suff.).	Huni
Haldan	Helga	*See* Obbesune	Huning
Haldein	Helge	Hoch	Hunneue
Halden	Helghi	Hofward	Hunni
Haltor	Helghin	Hoga	Hunnic
Hambe	Helins	Holangar	Hunnit
Haminc	Helmelea	Holchetel	Hunnith
Haming	Heltor	Holefest	Hunta
Handone	Henricus	Holmo	Hunus
Hannart	Her	Holt	Husteman
Hapra	Herald	Holund	Huthtrad
Har	Herbert	Homdai	Huthtret
Hard	Herch	Honeuain	Hveche

I AND J

Jadulfus	Ingefrid	Inguare	Judichel
Jalt	Ingelric	Ingulf	Juin
Jaul	Ingemund	Johannes (danus)	Juing
Ilbert	Ingeuuar	Joseph	Juo
Ineuuar	Ingolf	Jouin	Justan
Ingar	Ingrede	Iric	Justin

K

Kee (Norf.)	Kerinc	Ketelbern	Keueua
Keneuuard	Ketel	Ketelbert	Kochaga
Kenoldus	Ketelber	Keteluua	Kochagana
Kenric			

L

Ladulf	Lefquena	Leuard	Leustan
Lag	Lefric	Leue	Leuuard
Laghemann	Lefriz	Leuecild	Leuuare
Lagman	Lefsi	Leueclai	Leuui
Lambe	Lefsida	Leuecol	Leuuin
Lambecarl	Lefsinus	Leuedai	Leuuold
Lambertur	Lefsius	Leuefa	Leuuord
Lanbecarl	Lefstan	Leuegar	Leuuric
Lanc	Lefsune	Leuget	Ligul
Lancfer	Leftan	Leueno	Ligulf
Lanch	Lefwin	Leuenod	Lihtwin
Lanchei	Leimar	Leueric	Linbald
Lang	Leising	Leueron	Linxi
Langabein	Leisini	Leuestan	Liseman
Lange	Leit	Leuesuna	Lisius
Langfer	Leman	Leuesunas	Liuing
Langfere	Lemar	Leuet	Liuric
Lant	Lemer	Leuetuna	Liuuard
Lasciuus	Leodmer	Leueua	Lochi
Ledi	Leofleda	Leuid	Locre
Ledman	Leofric	Leuiet	Lodric
Ledmar	Leofsi	Leuiget	Lofe
Ledmer	Leofstan	Leuild	Longus
Ledric	Leofsun	Leuinc	Lord
Leduui	Leomer	Leuin	Loten
Leduuin	Leonestan	Leuing	Ludi
Lefchil	Lepsi	Leuolt	Ludri
Lefcill	Lesinc	Leured	Lufchel
Lefelm	Lesing	Leuret	Lurc
Leffcilt	Lesius	Leuric	Lustuin
Lefflet	Lestan	(Leofric, the last	Luttin
Lefled	Leswin	Bp. of Crediton,	Luuare
Leflet	Let	transferred his seat	Luuede
Lefmer	Letfled	to Exeter by per-	Luuet
Lefolt	Leua (f.)	mission of K. Ed.	Luuetote
		Confr., 1050.)	

M

Maban
Machel (Yorks, 332)
Machern
Machus
Macus
Madoch
Magbanec
Magne
Magno (Suert)
Mainard
Maino
Mal
Malet
Malf
Malgrim
Malgrin
Man (Yorks)
Mancus
Manegot
Manesuna
Manna

Mannicus
Mannig
Mannius (Swert)
Manno
Manstan
Mansuna
Mapesone
Marculf
Martinus
Maruaen
Maruuen
Matheld
   (Devon)
Mathila
   (Devon)
Mauna
Melc
Meldona
Melduna
Mellessam de
   (Suff., 409)
Melmidoc

Menleua
Merde
Merdo
Merefin
Meresuuet
Mereuin
Merken
Merlesuain
Merlesuen
Meruen
Meruin
Meurdoch
Micelenie
Michaelis
Michahel
Milda
Milegrim
Milnegrim
Modephefe (f.)
Modeva
Modgeva
Modinc

Moding
Moduin
Moithar
Molleve
Monulf
Morcar
Moregrim
Morewin
Morfar
Morganau
Moruant
Morulf
Mule (Yorks)
Mulo
Munding (Suff.)
Mundret
Munulf
Murdac
Murdoc
Muscham
Musla

N

Nicholaus
Nigell

Niuelig
Niuelin

Noriolt
Norman

Novi

O

Obbesune. *See*
   Hobbesune
Ocsen
Oda
Ode
Odeman
Oderus
Odeua
Odfrid
Odil
Odincar
Odincarl
Odo
Odulfus
Ofchetel
Offa
Offels
Offerd

Offers
Offo
Offram
Ofl
Oghe
Oin
Oiranti
Olbolt
Olf
Olgrim
Olketel
Olvva (f.)
Oluius
Oluuard
Oluuin
Olviet
Orde
Ordec

Ordgar
Ordin
Ording
Ordinc
Ordmær
Ordmar
Ordmer
Ordoff
Ordric
Ordui
Ordulf
Orduuold
Orgar
Orgrim
Orm
Ormar
Ormchetel
Orme

Ormer
Ornod
Orthi
Oruenot
Orulf
Osber
Osbern
Osbert
Oschete
Oschil
Osfert
Osford
Osgar
Osgod
Osgot
Osiar
Osier
Osiet

Osketel
Oslac
Osmar
Osmer
Osmund
Ostebrand
Ostula
Osul
Osulf
Osuuald

Oswar
Osuuard
Osui
Osuid
Osuuol
Oswald
Otbert
Otburuilla
Ote
Othen

Otho
Othon
Otre
Otro
Otti
Oualet
Oudencar
Oudfride
Oudgrim

Oudon
Oudulf
Ouen
Ouiet
Oune
Outbert
Outi
Ouu
Ouuine

P

Padda
Pagan
Pagen
Pallinus
Pat (Ches.)

Paulin
Pauli
Pbochestan
Perci
Perlo

Peurel
Phin
Pic
Pileuuin
Pin

Pinchengi
Pinslan
Poinc Godricus
Pointel Tedricus
Pur

R

Rachenild
Rada
Radboda
Radolf
Radulf
Rænold
Rafrid
Rafuuin
Ragenal
Ragenald
Ragenalt
Ragenild
Ragenot
Rainald
Rainbald
Rainer
Ram
Ramechil
Rannulf
Rasrid

Ratho
Rauan
Rauecate
Rauechel
Rauechet
Rauechetel
Rauechil
Ravelin
Raven
Rauen
Rauenchil
Rauene
Rauengar
Rauensuar
Rauensuard
Raues
Rauesard
Rauesue
Raulfus

Rausnar
Rauuen
Rayner
Reder
Redulf
Rees (Ches.)
Regifer
Reider
Reimbald
Reinbald
Rembald
Renold
Restef
Restelf
Reuensuard
Reuer
Ricard
Rinbold
Ringul

Ringulf
Robert
Roc
Roches
Roger
Rold
Rolf
Rolft
Roschel
Roschet
Roschil
Rot
Rotbert
Rotlesc
Roulf
Rozo
Rufus Siuuard
Ruillic
Ruschil

S

Sac
Sæmar
Sagar
Sagera
Sagrim
Saiard
Saied

Saiet
Sailt
Saisi
Saisil
Salecoe
Salomon
Salpus

Salvage
Samar
Saolf
Sared
Saric
Sarpo
Sauard

Sauin
Saul
Saulf
Sauord
Sauuard
Sauuata
Sauuin

Sauuold	Seuuard	Sorches	Stergar
Saxa	Seuuart	Sorchoued	Sterr
Saxi	Seuuen	Soror Stigandi	Sterre
Saxo	Seuui	Sort	Stichehare
Saxulf	Seuuin	Sorte	Stigand
Saxwin	Seward	Sortebrand	Stikestac
Sbern	Sexi	Sortocol	Stilla
Scaldefort	Sibe	Sota	Stille
Scalpi	Sichet	Soteman	Stingand
Scanchel	Sidgar	Sotinz	Stori
Scapius	Sigar	Sparhauoc	Stou
Scelfride	Sighet	Sperhauoc	Strami
Scemund	Sigred	Sperri	Stramun
Scet	Simon	Sperun	Strang
Sceua	Simond	Spieta	Strangulf
Scheit (Norf.)	Simund	Spille	Stric
Scipti	Sinod	Spirites	Strui
Scireuold	Sired	Spirtes	Struostun
Scirold	Siret	Sport	Stubart
Sclula	Sireuuald	Spretman	Stur
Scotcol	Sireuuold	Sprot	Suain
Scotecol	Siric	Sprotulf	Suan
Scotel	Sirof	Spuda	Suardcol
Scoua	Sistain	Spur	Suart
Scroti	Sistric	Staigrim	Suartcol
Scrotin	Siuard	Stainulf	Suartin
Scula	Siuargent	Stam	Suartric
Scule	Siuerd	Stanard	Suaue
Sech	Siuert	Stanart	Sudan
Seduin	Siulf	Stanchil	Suein
Segar	Siuuard	Stanfled	Suert
Segrida	Siuuart	Stangrim	Suerting
Seiar	Siuuin	Stanhard	Suet
Selecolf	Siuuold	Stanhart	Sueteman
Seleuuin	Siuurad	Stankar	Sueting
Selua	Smail	Stanmar	Suetman
Semær	Smalo	Stannechetel	Suetth
Seman	Smer	Stanuin	Suga
Semar	Smert	Stapleuin	Suglo
Semer	Smeuuin	Stari	Sumersul
Sendi	Snellinc	Starling	Summerde
Sercar	Snerri	Stauhart	Summerled
Seric	Snoch	Stein	Suneman
Serlo	Snode	Steinchetel	Suuain
Sessi	Snot	Steinulf	Suuarger
Seubar	Soartin	Stepi	Suuen
Seuen	Sol	Stepiot	Suwart
Seulf	Sonneua	Ster	Swert
Seuuar	Sonulf	Stercher	Syric

D

T

Taini, Teini, Teigni	Tochi	Tormord	Tunne
Taldus	Tochil	Torn	Turber
Tallgebosc	Tocho	Toroi	Turbern
Tarmoht	Tof	Torol	Turbert
Tedgar	Toiswald	Torolf	Turbran
Tedric	Toka	Torp	Turbrant
Tedricus	Toke	Torsus	Turch
Teit	Tokesone	Tort	Turchel
Tela (f.)	Tol	Toruerd	Turchetel
Tenus	Tolf	Toruert	Turchil
Teodric	Toli	Torulf	Tureuert
Teolf	Tona	Tosti	Turgar
Teos	Tone	Tostil	Turgis
Tepechin	Tonna	Toti	Turgisle
Tepekin	Tonne	Tou	Turgod
Terus	Tono	Toue	Turgot
Thol	Tope	Touet	Turgrim
Thole	Topi	Toui	Turi
Tholi	Topic	Touilda	Turketel
Thor	Tor	Toul	Turkil
Thoret	Toradre	Toulf	Turlog
Thori	Torber	Touni	Turmod
Thouus	Torbern	Toxus	Turmund
Thuinam	Torbert	Trasemund	Turold
Thurbern	Torbrand	Trasmund	Turolf
Thure	Torbrant	Trauuin	Turorne
Thuri	Torchel	Trec	Turot
Thurmer	Torchetel	Trumin	Turstan
Thurmot	Torchil	Tube	Turstin
Tidulf	Tord	Tuffa	Turtin
Tihell	Tored	Tuini	Turued
Tisellin	Toret	Tumi	Turuer
Toc	Toreth	Tumme	Turuerd
Tocha	Torfin	Tunbi	Turuert
Tochæ	Tori	Tuneman	Turuet
Toche	Torif	Tunna	Turulf

V

Vbe	Vital	Vlchil	Vlfeg
Vctebrand	Vitel	Vlestan	Vlfeih
Vctred	Viulf	Vlf	Vlfelm
Vdebrun	Vlbert	Vlfac	Vlfenisc
Vdeman	Vlbold	Vlfah	Vlfer
Vgelbert	Vlchel	Vlfar	Vlfert
Vgheta	Vlchet	Vlfchetel	Vlfenisc
Vibald	Vlchetel	Vlfech	Vlfiet

Vlfketel	Vlmer	Vluert	Vluuin
Vlflet	Vlnod	Vluerun	Vluuinchil
Vlfmer	Vlnoth	Vlueua	Vluuold
Vlfon (Sussex)	Vlric	Vluied	Vluured
Vlfra	Ulsi	Vluiet	Vlvi
Vlfret	Vlsiet	Vluin	Vnban
Vlfric	Vlstan	Vluoi	Vnfac
Ulfriz	Vlsuin	Vluret	Unlot
Vlfstan	Vlsy	Vluric	Vnspac
Vlfus	Vltain	Ulwar	Vntani
Vlfwin	Vltan	Vluuard	Vntan
Vlgar	Vluara	Vluuen	Vnton
Vlgrim	Vluard	Vluui	Vrleuuine
Vlketel	Vluer	Vluuic	Vstred
Vlmar	Vlueron	Vluuiet	Uthtret
Vlmær			

W

Wacra	Weghe	Widard	Wine
Wada	Weinhou	Widegrip	Winegod
Wade	Weleret	Widenesci	Winemar
Wadel	Welgrim	Wider	Winestan
Wadelo	Welland	Widuis	Winge
Wadels	Welle	Wiet	Winterled
Wado	Uuelp	Wifare	Wintrelet
Waga	Welp	Wifle	Wintremelc
Waih	Welrauen	Wiflet	(Alricus)
Wailoff	Wenesi	Wig	Wirelmus
Walduin	Wenestan	Wiga	Wiscar
Walle	Wenhou	Wigar	Wisg
Wallef	Weniet	Wige	Wisgar
Walleus	Wenning	Wigha	Wislac
Wallo (Ches.)	Vuenoit	Wighe	Wistan
Walraue	Wenric	Wiglac	Wistric
Walræuen	Werden	Wigod	Wit
Walt	Wester	Wigot	Uuit
Waltef	Westre	Wihenoc	Uuite
Walteif	Wetman	Wihtgar	Witg
Walter	Wgulafra	Wightmar	Witgar
Walteu	Whita	Wihtred	Wither
Wana	Wiber	Wihtric	Withgar
Wand	Wibert	Wiking (Suff.)	Withmer
Wants	Wichigus	Wilac	Withri
Wardham	Wichin	Wilaf	Witlac
Warrena, Will de	Wicling	Wilde	Witric
Waso	Wicnod	Wilegrip	Wiuar
Wateman	Wicolf	Willa	Wiuara
Wdebrun	Wicstric	Wimarc	Wiuelac
Wege	Wictric	Wimer	Wiulf

Wlbald	Wlmer	Wleua	Wluuen
Wlf	Wlnod	Wlui	Wluui
Wlfah	Wlsi	Wluin	Wlwi
Wlfric	Wlsin	Wlured	Wluuin
Wlgar	Wlstan	Wluric	Wnulf
Wlmær	Wluard	Wluuar	Wordron
Wlmar	Wluar	Wluuard	

NAMES OF TENANTS IN CHIEF IN DOMESDAY BOOK

A

Abetot de	Albamarla de	Almund	Ansger
Achebranni	Albani	Alnod	Ansgot
Adam	Alberic	Alric	Arches de
Adeldreda	Albert	Alselin	Archil
Adeling	Albingi de	Alsi	Arcis de
Adeliz	Albus	Alverd	Aregrin
Adobod	Alden	Aluers	Areti
Adrecide	Aldit	Aluena	Artor
Ældeva	Aldred	Alvied	Arundel
Ældred	Aldvi	Aluiet	Aschil
Agebric	Alestan	Alured	Ascuit
Agemund	Alfhilla	Aluric	Asinus
Ailmar	Alfildis	Alward	Asne
Ailrun	Alfred	Alwi	Audoen
Ailunard	Algar	Alwin	Autbert
Aincurt de	Alis	Alwold	Azelina
Aiulf	Almar	Andeli	Azor
Alan	Almer	Anschetil	

B

Bade de	Belet	Bernard	Bolle
Badpalmas de	Bella Fago de	Berneres de	Bollo
Baignard	(Beaufoy)	Bernerus	Bomene de
Balduin	Belmont de	Bersers de	Bonvalest
Balgiole	Belot	Bertone de	Bosch de
Bangiard	Belvaco de	Bertram de	Boscnorman de
Bano de	Benz	Bevrere de	Breteville de
Barbatus Hugo	Benzelin	Bigot	Bricteua
Bastard	Berchelai de	Bituricensis	Brictoward
Batailge de la	Berchingis de	Blunders	Brictric
Bech de	Bereville de	Boci de	Brictuin
Bedford de	Bernai de (Nor-	Bohun de	Brimor de
Belcamp de	mandy)	Bolebec de	Brismar

Brito	Bruning	Buenvaslet de	Burun de
Bruis Robertus	Bucfestre de	Buge (Notts)	Buruolt
de (Yorks)	Buci de	Buiville de	Busli de
Brun	Budi de	Burci de	

C

Cadomo de	Ceterith de	Clibert	Crass, Norman
(Caen)	Chana, Lewin	Coci de	Cratel, Godric
Cahainges de	Chelbert	Cola	Credun, Wido de
Cailgi	Chenvin	Colebern	Creneburne de
Cambrai de	Cheping	Colegrim	Crispin, Milo
Canut	Chetel	Collinc	Christina (f.)
Carbonel	Chetelbern	Colsvain	Croc
Carentoch de	Chetelbert	Colsuen	Croiland de
Carle	Chievre, Wm.	Colsuin	Cudulf
Carnot	Chilbert	Columbels de	Cvenild
Cedda, S.	Cicestre de	Colvin	Curbespine de
Cernel de	Croches de	Corcelles de	Curci de
Certesyg de	Claville de	Cormelies de	Cutbert
Cestre de	Clec, Godwin	Corniole, Wm.	

D

Dalari de	Doai de	Donne	Dreimes de
David	Dodesone, Alwin	Donno	Drogo
Derman	Dodid	Dons	Dunning
Dispensator	Dodo	Dovre de	Durand
Dive de	Dolfin	Dowai de	Dwai de

E

Eadmund	Edred	Eldred	Ernald
Ebrard	Edric	Elfain	Ernebern
Ebrulf	Eduin	Elmer	Erneis
Eddeva	Eduard	Elnod	Ernui
Eddid	Edwi	Elric	Ernuin
Eddiet	Edwin	Elsi	Ertald
Eddulf	Eglesham de	Elward	Esnebern
Edeua	(Eynsham, in	Equarius	Eudo
Edgar	Oxfordshire)	Erchenger	Eustachius
Ediet	Eldild	Eric	Exesse de
Edmund	Eldit	Erleching	

F

Fafiton	Ferendon de	Forne	Fresle, Richard
Faleise de	Flamme	Fossard	Frodo
Feireres de, or	Flanbard	Fossart, Nigel	Fulcher
Ferieres	Flandren	Fouuer, Ansger	Fulcred
Fenisc, Ulf	Flavus	Framen, Rudulf	

G

Galterus	Girold	Goizenboded,	Greno or Grenon.
Game	Giselbert	Wm.	*See* Gernon
Gamel	Goda (f.)	Goismer	Grentebrige de
Gand de	Gode	Golde	Grestain de
Gant de	Godebold	Gonduin	Gretuilla de
Gerin	Godefrid	Gosbert, Hugo	Griffin
Gernio	Godescal	Goscelmus	Grimbald
Gernon	Godeua	Gospatric	Grim
Ghilo	Godmund	Gozelin	Gudmund
Gifard	Godric	Granetarius	Gunduin
Gilo	Goduin	Greistein de	Gunfrid
Girard	Goisfrid	(France)	Gurnai
Girbert			

H

Hagheburn	Hardulf	Herald	Hispaniensis,
Hago	Haregrin	Herbert	Alured
Haimeric	Harold	Herbrand	Holmo de
Haldein	Hascoit	Hereford de	Hortone de
Haluille de	Hascoith	Herion de	Hosed, Wm.
Hamelin	Hascolf	Hermer	Hugo
Hamo	Helion, Her-	Herveus	Hugolin
Handone de	veus de	Hesding	Humfrid
Hardinc	Henricus	Hghbern	Hunfrid
Harding	Heppo		Hunger

I AND J

Ida (Countess	Illinge	Insula de	Iveri de
of Bologne	Ingald	Johannes	Ivichel
Jeanio	Ingania de	Isac	Ivikel
Ilbert	(Engaine)	Iseldis	Justen
Ilbodo	Ingulf	Judhel de Tote-	
		nais (Totness)	

K

Ketel

L

Laci de	Lawirce. *See*	Leuric	Loges de
Lanchei de	Wirce	Leutfrid	Lorz de
Landri	Leduin	Leuuin	Losward
Landric	Lefstan	Ligult	Lovet
Lanfranc	Legat	Limesi de	Loveth
Lanheie de	Leuena	Liof	Luith
Lasne, Hugo	Leviet	Lira de	Luri de
Latimarus	Levild	Liseman	Lusorüs de
Launire de	Leving		

M

Madoc	Maldrith	Medehal de	Molebec de
Magnavilla	Malet	Melchisan de	Monneuile de
(Mannwille)	Malf	Mellend de	Montagud de
Maigno	Maminot	Merde de	Monteburg de
Maino. *See*	Mantel	Mereuuin	Montfort de
Manno	Mappesone	Merleberge de	Montgomery de
Mal. *See* Malf	Martin	Mert	Morin
Malaopa	Matheus	Micelenie de	Mortemer de
Malcolun	Mathild	Moduin	Mucelgros de
Maldoith	Mauric	Moion de	Musard
Maldred	Mauritaniensis		

N

Nicolaus	Nigel	Niger	Norman

O

Oaura	Oilgi de	Osbern	Oswold
Obarvilla de	Oirant de	Osgot	Otha
Odard	Olaf	Osiet	Otho
Odburville de	Ordgar	Oslac	Otto
Ode	Ordric	Osmer	Ou de
Odin	Ordui	Osmund	Outi
Odo	Orlatelle	Ostreham de	Ouus
Odolin	Orm	Osward	Ow de
Oger			

P

Pagen	Peret	Pilardintone de	Pointel de
Pagenel	Persore de	*Pincerna*	Pomerei de
Pancevolt	Peverel	Pinel	Porth de
Parcher, An-	Picot	Piperellus. *See*	Pugnant
schitil	Pictavensis	Peverel	Puingiant
Percehaie	Pierani de	Poillgi de	Puintel
Perci			

Q

Quintin, S. de

R

Rabellus	Rames de	Rayner	Roelent
Radulf	Ramesy de	Reinbald	Roger
Ragenald	Ramis de	Restold	Rolf
Rainald	Rannalf	Ricard	Romenel de
Rainbald	Ravelin	Riueire	Rotbert
Rainburgis	Raven	Robert	Rothais (f.)
Reinbuedcurt de	Ravenchil	Rodmund	Ruald
Ramechil			

S

Saiet
Saieva
Saisselin
Salceid de
Salceit de
Salebi de
Salmur de
S. Quintin de
Sanson
Saric
Sariz
Sasford
Sasselin
Saulf

Saward
Sawin
Sawold
Sbern
Scalers de (or d'Echallers)
Schelin
Scohies de
Scrope
Scudet
Sedret
Seric
Seuard

Sibold
Sigar de Cioches
Siric
Siuard
Soartin
Sortebrand
Spech (or Espec?)
Sperri
Stanard
Starcolf
Stefan
Steinulf

Stigand
Stirman
Stratfort de
Sturmid
Suain
Suarding
Suarting
Suen
Sueno
Surdeual de
Suuen
Svain
Swan

T

Tailgebosch
Tedfort de
Tehell
Teodric
Tetbald
Tezelin
Theodric

Thomas
Tison
Tisun
Tochi
Todeni de
Toenio de
Tona

Tor
Torber
Torbern
Torchil
Tored
Tornyg de (Thomey)

Totenais de
Tovi
Turbern
Turbert
Turchil
Turstui
Turstun

U AND V

Valbadon de
Valonges de
Valonis de
Vctred
Vdi
Veci de

Ver de
Verdun de
Verli de
Vernon de
Vis de Lew

Vlbert
Vlchel
Vlf
Vlfric
Vlgar

Vlmar
Vlnod
Ulsi
Vluiet
Vluui

W

Wadard
Wado
Walchelin
Waldin
Waleram
Waleran
Waleric
Walter

Wanz
Warene de
Warwell de
Wateman
Wateuille de
Waula
Wibert

Widuile de
Wielard
Wigar
Willelm
Wiltune
Winemar
Wintremelc

Wirce de
Wislac
Wit
Wlmar
Wluin
Wlwi
Wrehantune de

NAMES OF UNDER-TENANTS OF LANDS AT THE TIME OF THE DOMESDAY SURVEY

A

Aba (Northts.)	Ailuuacre	Alnulf	Anger
Abba (Norf.)	Aincurt de	Alred	Ansger
Abel (Kent)	Airard	Alric	Ansgered
Abernon de	Aistan	Alselin	Ansgot
Abetot de	Aitard	Alsi	Anslepe de
Abraham	Aiulf	Altet	(Northampt.)
Acard	Alam	Aluerad	Ansleuile
Achet, Walterus	Alan	Aluered	Appeuile
Acun	Albengi de	Aluena	Archil
Adam	Alberi	Aluiet	Archis
Adelard	Alberic	Alulf	Arcis de
Adeledmus	Albert	Alured	Arda de
Adelelmus	Albin'	Aluric	Ardulf
Adelina	Albold	Aluuard	Arling
Adelold	Albus	Alward	Armenteres
Adelolf	Alcher	Alwart	Arnald
Adelulf	Alde	Alwewe	Arnegrim
Adelwin	Alded	Aluui	Arni
Adeluuold	Aldelin	Aluuin	Arnuf
Adestan	Alden	Aluuold	Artur
Adolf	Aldi	Amalric	Arundel, Roger
Adret	Aldred	Ambrose	Asc' (Ascelin)
Ældeua	Aldrie	Amelfrid	Aschil
Ældred	Alelm	Amelger	Ascolf
Ælfelm	Alencun	Amerland	Aselin
Ælgot	Alestan	Aman	Asford
Ælmer	Alflet	Amund	Asfort
Aelons	Alfred	Anchitill	Aslac
Ælric	Alfric	Andeli de	Aslen
Ælueue	Alfrid	Andreas (Cornw.)	Asne
Æluuard	Algar	Anger	Asso
Ærnold	Alger	Angevin, Osmund	Asuert
Agemund	Alich	Anschetill	Avenel
Aguet	Allic	Anschill	Auesgot
Agenulf	Almær	Anschitil	Ausgustin
Aghemund	Almar	Ansegis	Avigi
Agnes	Almer	Ansel	Auigi
Ailbold	Almfrid	Anseredus	Auti
Ailmar	Almod	Ansfred	Azelin
Ailric	Alno	Ansfrid	Azo
Ailuard	Alnod	Ansgar	Azor

B

Baderon	Berengarius	Bono	Brisard
Bagod	Bereuuold	Bonuaslet, Willm.	Brismer
Baignar	Berger	Borci	Bristeua
Baignard	Bernai de	Bordin	Bristist
Bainard	Bernar	Borel	Bristoald
Baingiard	Bernard	Boret	Bristoard
Bainiard	Berner	Borghill	Brito
Baldeuin	Bernulf	Bosc de	Brixi
Baldric	Berold	Boscroard de	Brodo
Balduin	Berruarius	Boselin	Bruman
Balt	Bertran	Boso	Brun
Barb, Bernard	Beruold	Boteric	Brunard
(Heref.)	Beuerde	Boter	Brunel
Barbes de	Beulf	Boti	Brungar
Baret	Big	Botild	Bruning
Baro	Bigot	Braiboue de	Brunnuin
Basset	Blach	Braiose de	Bruno
Basuin	Blacheman	Brant	Bucard
Beatrix	Blancard	Bretel	Buci de
Bec, Walter	Blancus	Breteuile de	Buerd
Bech de	Blechu	Bricmær	Bueret
Belcamp de	Bleio	Brictmar	Buissel
Belencun' de	Blize	Brictmer	Bundo
Belet	Blohin	Brictolf	Burci de
Belfago	Bloiet	Brictred	Burdet
Belfou	Blon	Brictric	Burghard
Bellafago	Blond	Brichelf	Burnard
Beluard	Blosseuille de	Brictuin	Burnart
Benedict	Blund	Brictuuard	Burneuill de
Benthelm	Bodin	Brien	Bursigni de
Benzelin	Bolebec, Hugo	Briend	Busch
Berard	Bollo	Brienz	Busli de
Berchelai de	Bondi	Brion	Buter
Berdic			

C

Cada' de (de	Candos de	Chemarhnec	Clarebald
Cadamo)	Cardon	Chenesis	Clarenbald
Cadio	Cardun	Chenret	Claron
Cadomi	Carnot'	Cheping	Clauile de
Cadomo de	Caron de	Chernet de	Clavilla de
Caflo	Carun de	Chetel	Clodoan
Cahainges de	Cedde	Chetelbar	Coc, Aluuin
Caisned de	Celric	Chetelbern	(bedellus)
Calpus	Celsi de	Chetelburn	Coci de
Caluus	Cepe	Cheure	Cola
Calvus	Chacepol	Cioches de	Colbert

Colegrim	Coluin	Corbun	Cruel
Colevil de	Colvin	Corcel de	Cudhen
Colgrim	Conded	Co'rp	Culling
Collo	Constantin	Credun, Wido	Curcan de
Colo	Corbelin	de	Curci de
Colsuain	Corbet	Crispin, Milo	Cus
Colsuan	Corbin	Croc	

D

Daniel, Roger	Derinc	Dodesone, Alu-	Douuai de
(Suss.)	Derisbou, W.	uin (Herts.)	Dreuues, Amal-
Dauid	Derman	Dodin	ric de (Wilts)
David	Deuais, Robt.	Dodo	Drogo
Denomore, Wm.	Deuernu' (De	Dolfin	Dudeman
Denuers, Wm.	Vernon)	Domnic	Dunning
Depeiz, Guerno	Doda	Donecan	Dunstan
Deramis, Roger	Doddus	Doneuuald	Dur'
Dereman	Dodeman	Donno	Durand
Dereuuen	Dodemund	Douenold	Dynechaie

E

Eadvuun	Egbriht	Elsi	Ernald
Ebrard	Ehelo	Eluard	Ernegis
Ecchebrand	Eideua	Elward	Erneis
Eddeua	Eileua	Eluui	Ernold
Eddid	Eiluuard	Eluunin	Ernolf
Eddiet	Einbold	Engelbric	Ernucion
Eddille	Elbert	Engeler	Ernui
Eddulf	Eldeid	Engenold	Ernuin
Edelo	Eldred	Engelulf	Ernulf
Ederic	Elduin	Enisan	Ernuzen
Edgar	Elfin	Enisant	Ertein
Edied	Elfric	Er (Ermen-	Escalers de
Edmar	Elfrid	hald)	Ettard
Edmund	Eli	Erchebrand	Eudo
Ednod	Elinant	Erchenbald	Euen
Edred	Elmar	Erenburgis	Euerwin
Edric	Elmer	Erfast	Eurard
Eduin	Elmui	Erluin	Eurold
Eduuard	Elmund	Ermenhald	Euruin
Eduui	Elnod	Ermenfrid	Eustachius
Egbert	Elric	Erm'iot	

F

Fabri	Faeicon	Farman	Fech
Faderlin	Faeto	Fastrad	Feggo
Fadrelin	Falcus	Fatat	Felcher

Felger	Floc de	Frodo	Fulco
Ferme	Folcheran	Froger	Fulcoin
Ferron	Folcran	Froissart, Wm.	Fulcold
Firmat	Folet	Frumond	Fulcran
Fla'bard	Forist	Fulbert	Fulcred
Fla'mart	Fragrin	Fulbric	Fulcui
Fla'mens	Frane	Fulcard	Fulcuin
Flanbard	Franco	Fulche	Fulkered
Flandr'	Frano	Fulcher	Fulo
Flavus	Fredgis	Fulchered	Furic
Flint	Fredo	Fulcho	

G

Gadinc	Gifart	Goisfrid	Grichetel
Gadio	Gildre	Goislan	Grifin
Gadomo de	Gingom	Goislen	Griketel
Galicer	Girald	Goismer	Grim
Galt'	Girande	Goldwin	Grimbald
Galterus	Girard	Goleman	Grinon
Gamas	Girold	Gollam	Gros
Game	Giron	Golstan	Gualter
Gamel	Gisbert	Gondran	Guarin
Gamelin	Gislebert	Gonfrid	Gudhen. *See*
Gand de	Gislold	Gonther	Cudhen
Gaosfrid	Giso	Gosbert	Gudmund
Garenger	Glauill	Goscelin	Gueri
Garin	Gleduin (Leic.)	Goscelm	Gveric
Garmund	Gleu (Bedf.)	Goselin	Guerlin
Garner	Glodoen	Gosfrid	Guert
Gatelea	Godard	Goslin	Guibert
Gaufrid	Godebold	Gospatric	Gvihu'mar
Gaurinc	Godefrid	Gotwin	Gulaffra
Gausfrid	Goderet	Goze	Gulbert
Gerald	Goderun	Gozel	Gulfer
Gerard	Godescal	Gozet	Gulfered
Gerbodo	Godeue	Grai de	Gummar
Gerelm	Godid	Grando	Gunduin
German	Godinc	Grantcurt	Gundulf
Germund	Goding	Grapinel	Gunequata
Gerneber	Godman	Greno	Gunfrid
Gernon	Godmund	Grentmaisnil	Gvnhar
Gerold	Godric	de	Gunner
Geron	Goduin	Grento	Guntard
Gherui	Godzelin	Greslet	Gunter
Gifard	Goisbert	Grichel	Gutbert

H

Hacun	Heldered	Herion, Tihell	Hosed
Hadeuuin	Heldred	de	Hotot de
Hadulf	Heldret	Herlebald	Houard
Hagebert	Heldric	Herlebold	Huard
Haimard	Helduin	Herleuin	Hubald
Haimer	Helgod	Herman	Hubb'
Haiming	Helgot	Hermenfrid	Hubert
Haimo	Helio	Hermer	Hubold
Halanant	Helmer	Hernold	Hveche
Halsard	Helto	Herold	Hugo
Hame	Hengebald	Herolf	Hugol'
Hamelin	Henric	Herpul	Hugolin
Haminc	Herold	Heruen	Hunald
Hamo	Herbert	Hesdinc	Hunfrid
Hamon	Herbrand	Hesding	Hunger
Hardeuuin	Herding	Hezelm	Hunnit
Harding	Hereberd	Hildebrand	Hunulf
Harold	Hereuuard	Hosdena de	Hurant
Hato	Herfrid	Hosdenc de	Huscarle

I AND J

Jacob	Inganie	Johannes	Junain
Jagelin	Ingelbald	Jouin	Junan
James	Ingelbert	Iric	Junen
Jarnacot	Ingelram	Isac	Iuo
Idhel	Ingelran	Iseldis	Ivo
Ilbert	Ingelric	Isenbard	Iuran
Ilbod	Ingenulf	Iseuuard	Iurei
Ildebert	Ingrann	Ispania de	Iuri
Ilduin	Ingulf	Judhell	Ivri
Ingald	Johais	Judichel	Iward
Ingelra'n	Joh's	Juhell	Iuuein
Ilgerus			

K

Keresburg de

L

Lacei de	Langetot de	Laurentius	Leftan
Lachelin	Langhetot de	Ledman	Lemar
Laci de	Lanzelin	Ledmar	Lemei
Lambert	*Lardarius*	Leflet	Lepsi
Lanbert	Latin	Lefric	Lestan
Landri	*Latinarius*	Lefsi	Letard
Landric	Latinus	Lefsun	Lethelin

Letmar	Leuuard	Lira de	Losoard
Leucilt	Lewes	Liseman	Losuard
Leuegar	Leuui	Lisoisus	Louel
Leuenot	Leuuine	Locels de	Louet
Leueua	Leuuric	Loder	Ludichel
Leuiet	Liboret	Lodouuin	Ludo
Leuinc	Ligulf	Loeruic	Lundonie de
Leuing	Limesi de	Lof	Lunen
Leuric	Lincole de	Loges de	Lungus
Leusin	Liof	Loher	Lusorio de

M

Machar	Manasses	Mellend de	Moriland
Machinator	Manbodo	Melling de	Morin
Machus	Manneuille de	Merc de	Moriton de
Maci	Mara de	Merde de	Mortemer de
Madoc	Marcher	Mereuin	Mortuing
Maigno	Marci de	Merlebey	Morua
Mainard	Marcud	*Miles*	Moruant
Mainfrid	*Marescal*	Modbert	Moruuin
Maino	Martel	Moion de	Mosters de
Maiulf	Mascerel	Molebec	Motbert
Malauill	Mascherell	Monetar	Moyses
Malbedeng	Mater	Monfort de	Mucedent de
Maldoit	Mathild	Monulf	Mucelgros de
Malet	Matheus	Moran	Muceull
Malf	Mechenta	Morcar	Mundret
Malger	*Medicus*	More de	Murdac
Malus Vicinus	Meinard	Morel	Musard
Maminot	Meinfrid		

N

Nardred	Nicolaus	Nogiold	Norun
Nauuen	Nigel	Norgiot	Noui
Nemore	Noiers de	Norgot	Nouuers de
Nepos	Noies de	Norman	Nubold
Nicol			

O

Oburuilla de	Odo	Oilgi de	Oluu'
Odard	Odon	Oismelin	Orbec de
Odarus	Offa	Olaf	Ordmær
Odbert	Offels	Olbald	Ordmar
Odburcuilla de	Offran	Ole de	Ordric
Oddo	Oger	Olf	Ordulf
Odelin	Ogis	Olgi de	Orduui
Odin	Oidelard	Oliuer	Orenet
Odmus	Oilard	Olnei de	Orenge de

Orgar
Orger
Orm
Ormar
Orme
Ornod
Osbern
Osbert

Osgot
Oslach
Osmund
Osulf
Oswald
Oswar
Osuuard
Osuuic

Osuuold
Otbert
Otbold
Otburville de
Othelin
Othem
Othingar

Otho
Otto
Oudchel
Ouethel
Outi
Ow de
Ou

P

Pagan
Pagen
Paisfor
Paisforere
Pancefold
Pantul
Pantulf
Papald
Parisiac
Parisiacenis
Parler
Passaq'

Peccatu'
Perapund de
Perci de
Periton de
Pertenai de
Pesserara
Peteuin
Petrus
Peverel
Peurel
Phanexon

Picot
Pictavensis
Pincerna
Pinchengi de
Pinc'u'n'
Pinel
Pipe (Som.)
Piperell
Pipin
Pirot
Piscator

Pistor
Pleines
Poingiant
Pointel
Polchehard
Pomerei de
Ponther
Ponz
Port de
Pugnant
Pungiant

Q
Quintin

R

Rabboda
Rabel
Rademar
Rademer
Radfred
Radman
Radulf
Radus
Rafri
Raimar
Raimund
Rainald
Rainalm
Rainbald
Rainbert
Rainbold
Rainelm
Rainer
Rainfrid
Rainold

Ramis de
Randulf
Rannulf
Rardulf
Rasrid
Ratho
Rauemer
Rauen
Rauengar
Rauenot
Raynald
Rayner
Raynold
Raynouuard
Reduers de
Reger
Reimund
Reinbald
Reinbert
Reiner

Reinfrid
Reinold
Remir
Renald
Renbald
Renelm
Reneuuald
Renold
Renuuar
Restald
Restold
Restolt
Ret
Ribald
Ricaiard
Ricar
Ricard
Richer
Ricoard
Ricolf

Rictan
Ricuard
Riculf
Rippe
Risboil de
Riset de
Riuold
Riuualo
Roald
Robert
Rodbert
Rodeland de
Roder
Rodulf
Rog'e
Roger
Rogo
Rogus
Rohard
Roic

Rold	Ros de	Rozelin	Rumald
Rolf	Rotbert	Ruallon	Rumbold
Rolland	Rotroc	Rualon	Rumold
Romenel de	Rozel'	Rufus	Runeuille
Roric			

S

Sacheuilla de	Schelin	Silua de	Stenulf
Sæfrid	Schelm	Silvester	Stirman
Safrid	Scohies de	Simon	Stoches
Sagar	Scolland	Simond	Sturm'
Sagrim	Scoua	Simund	Sturmid
Saiet	*Scriba*	Sinod	Sturstan
Saieua	Scudet	Sired	Suain
Sais de	Scutet	Sireuuold	Suan
Salmur de	Sedred	Siric	Suarting
Salo	Segrim	Siuert	Suartric
Salomon	Seibert	Siuuard	Suausey de
Sanson	Seifrid	Siuuate	Suauis
Sasfrid	Semar	Smalavill de	Suen
Sasgar	Semer	Soies de	Suertin
Sasuualo	Sencler de	Sotus	Suerting
Sasuuard	Sent Cler de	Spec	Suetin
S. Leger	Sentebor de	Spech	Sueting
S. Quintin	Seolf	Sprottulf	Suetman
S. Sansone de	Septniuels de	Stable	Sufreint
Saucnie de	Seric	Stanard	Suin
Sauigneio de	Serlo	Stanart	Sumeri de
Sauigni de	Sessibert	Stannechetel	Surd've
Saulf	Seward	Stantone de	Suttuna
Sauuard	Seuuen	Stauhart	Suuan
Sauuold	Seuui	Stefan	Suuen
Saxlef	Sigar		

T

Taccham de	Tedbold	Tham de	Toka
Tædald	Tedric	Thochi	Toli
Tailgebosc	Tehel	Tidbald	Tonne
Taissel de	Teher	Tiger	Tor
Talebot	Teodbald	Tinel	Torchill
Talliebosc	Teoderic	Tirel de	Tored
Tame de	Teodric	Tirus	Toret
Tascelin	Teodulf	Toche	Torgis
T'chetel	Terbert	Tochi	Tornai
Tebald	Tetbald	Tochil	Torold
Tedald	Tetbaud	Todeni de	Torstin
Tedbert	Tezelin	Toeni de	Tosard

Tosti	Troarz de	Turbern	Turlauillade
Toui	Tual	Turchetil	Turmit
Touilt	Tuder	Turchil	Turold
Traillgi de	Tumbi	Turgar	Turstan
Tralgi de	Tur	Turgis	Tursten
Trauers	Turald	Turi	Turstin
Troard de	Turbat		

U AND V

Vagan	Verley de	Vlf	Vlueua
Valbadon de	Verli de	Vlfac	Vluiet
Vallibus de	Vernon de	Vlfchetel	Vluric
Valonges	Vill'o de	Vlketel	Vluuard
Valongies de	Vinitor	Vlmar	Vlwart
Valonis de	Uis de Leun	Vlmer	Vluui
Vals de	Uisdelups	Vlnod	Vluuin
Uctebrand	Visolupi	Vloi	Vnifrid
Vctred	Vitalis	Vlric	Vrfer
Veci	Vitard	Vlsi	Vrso
Venables de	Vlchel	Vlstan	Vruoi
Venator	Vlchetel	Vltbert	Uttal
Ver de	Vlestan	Vluard	Uual' de

W

Wachelin	Walo de	Wateuile de	Widelard
Wadard	Walscin	Wazelin	Wido
Wal' de	Walter	Wazo	Widr
Wala	Waluille de	Wenelinc	Wielard
Walbert	Wanceio de	Weneuc	Wigar
Walchel	Wanz	Wenric	Wigemore
Walchelin	War' de	Werelc	Wiger
Walcher	Waras de	Werenc	Wighen
Walcin	Wareger	Werestan	Wigot
Waldin	Warene de	Wert	Wihanoc
Walen	Wareng'	Wesman	Wihomarc
Walenn	Warenger	Westone	Wihtmar
Walenses	Warenna de	Wgulafra	Wihuene c
Waler'	Wares de	(W. Gulafra)	Wihumar
Waleram	Waribold	Wiard	Wihvmarc
Waleran	Warin	Wibald	Wilard
Walicher	Warinbold	Wiberg	Willac
Walifrid	Warinc	Wibert	Willelm
Wallef	Warmund	Wicard	Wimarcæ
Walo	Warner	Wichin	Wimerus
Walon' de	Wast	Widald	Wimund
Waloniencis de	Wasunic	Widard	Wineman

E

Winemar	Witbert	Wizo	Wluuard
Wintrehard	Witburg	Wlb'tus	Wluui
Wiscand de	Witsand de	Wlric	Wluuold
Wisgar	Wituile de	Wlsi	Wodeman
Wissand de	Hugo	Wlueua	

Y

Ymfrid (Humfrid)

NORMAN NAMES

A GREAT deal has been written about the Roll of Battell Abbey and the companions of the Conqueror, which is doubtless of great interest to those who claim to be descendants of the persons therein recorded.

There was such a roll suspended in the great hall of the building, and it bore the names of 645 knights, but it has disappeared long ago, as well as the other relics of the battle, which were removed to Cowdray, and perished in the great fire there in 1793.

There are several copies more or less imperfect. The lists which appear to be the most authentic are: Duchesne's list, taken from the abbey charter, containing 405 names; Leland's collection, with 498 names; Magny's catalogue, with 425 names; Delisle's, with 485 names. These are all of a much later date than the Conquest, probably *temp.* Ed. I.

Of the great array of time-honoured names very few are now borne by direct representatives. They exist rather among the old gentry than in the peerage. In the majority of cases the later descendants of illustrious families have sunk into poverty and obscurity unconscious of their origin, and this was more likely to be the case with the younger branches, since the name or title of the family went with the elder line that inherited the estates.

The following names have been collected from the lists above mentioned. Many of them will be found in Domesday Book, and where such is the case they may be considered to be genuine followers of the Conqueror. It is obvious that those which compare favourably with Domesday Book are the most reliable, and others which do not stand that test may be looked upon as of later date. The names of some of the Flemings who accompanied William are also included in this list.

Much doubt has long existed as to the authenticity of the several versions which have appeared at different times, claiming to be a roll of the names of the Norman invaders who survived the battle of Hastings, but it is manifest that many of those recorded, even if they were ever upon the original document deposited with the monks of Battell Abbey, are not found to correspond with either the tenants-in-chief or the under-tenants of Domesday Book at the time of the Survey (A.D. 1086). On the other hand, the last mentioned—of whom there is a great number —have hardly a place upon the roll.

It is well known that the heralds of the fourteenth and fifteenth centuries were not scrupulous in adding names to the list.

Queen Isabella of France, the consort of Edward II., introduced in her train many personages bearing surnames previously unknown in England.

The Rotuli Normanniæ, R. Hundredorum, and R. de Oblatis et Finibus, *temp.* Regis Johannis, Testa de Neville, Pipe Rolls, etc., are valuable evidence as to Norman names. The place-names of Normandy have been added.

The asterisk denotes a tenant-in-chief.

A

Abbeville. Appeville; a loc. n. *D.B.* Appeuile, de Oburvilla

Abell. *D.B.* Abeel, loc. n., Belg.

Aimeris. *D.B.* Haimeric*

Aincourt. *D.B.* de Aincurt.* Agincourt; a loc. n.

Akeny. *D.B.* Acun (?). Acquigny, Aucun, loc. n.

Albeny. *D.B.* Albani*

Amay (Johannes Ame). Amécourt (?), loc. n.

Amerenges

Amouerduile, Aumarill, Amundeville, loc. n.

Angenoun. Angennes; a loc. n.

Angers, Aunwers. *D.B.* Anger. Angers; a loc. n.

Angewyne. *D.B.* Angevin Osmund

Angilliam, Aungeloun. Angoulême; a loc. n.

Anuay. Aunay, loc. n.

Archere. *D.B.* de Arcis,* de Arques, loc. n. France

Arcy, D'Arcie, Darcy,* from de Ardreci. *D.B.*, T.C. (Lincs.)

Argentoune. David de Argentomo in *D.B.* Reginald de A., Sheriff of Camb. 5 Rich. I., Argentan; a loc. n.

Arundel. *D.B.*

Arwerne

Aspermound

Aspervile

Audeley. *D.B.* Andeli* (?). Andelys; a loc. n.

Audeville or Adryelle (?). Adervielle; a loc. n.

Auenant, Avenele. *D.B.* Avenel

Aumarle. *D.B.* de Albamarle*

Avereris. *D.B.* de Iveri*

Aybeuare (John Aubry). Aubevoye, loc. n.

B

Bagott. *D.B.* Bagod

Bailif. Le Bailli

Baillol. *D.B.* Balgiole.* Bailleul; a loc. n.

Bainard, Byngard. *D.B.* Bangiard*

Baious, or Baus. Bayeux; a loc. n.

Baloun. Bâlines, loc. n.

Banastre, Banestre; a loc. n.

Banet or Benny. *D.B.* de Bano * (?)

Barchampe. Beauchamp, loc. n.

Bardolfe

Barduedor

Barnivale, Berenvile, Burneville, Burinell. *D.B.* de Burneuill. Barneville; a loc. n.

Barrett, Baret. *D.B.* Baret
Bary, Barre, Barry. Berry; a loc. n.
Bascoun. *D.B.* Basuin (?)
Baskerville, Bacqueville; a loc. n.
Basset or Bassey. *D.B.* Basset
Bastard. *D.B.**
Baudewin, Baudin, Baldwin. *D.B.* Balduin,* Count of Flanders
Baupere. Beauport; a loc. n.
Beauchamp. *D.B.* de Belcamp
Beaumont. *D.B.* de Belmont (?), de Bomene*; a loc. n.
Beauvise or Bevers. Beauvais; a loc. n.
Beelhelme, Beakum. Bellême; a loc. n.
Beisin. Bessin; a loc. n. *D.B.* Basuin (?)
Beke. *D.B.* de Bech.* Bec-Hellouin; a loc. n. or Beeck, Belg.
Belefroun. Beauvron; a loc. n.
Belesur. Bellecourt; a loc. n.
Beleuers, Belliéres; a loc. n.
Bellet. *D.B.* Will. Belet (Hants). Harvey Belet lived *temp.* K. Steph.
Bellew. *D.B.* Belot.* Bellou, loc. n.
Bellire. Balleroy; a loc. n.
Berners. *D.B.* de Berners.* Bernières; a loc. n.
Bernon. *D.B.* Bernar (?)
Berteuilay. Berthouville (?), loc. n.
Bertin. *D.B.* de Bertone.* St Bertin; a loc. n.
Bertram. *D.B.* de Bertram,* Robert Vicomte, 1047
Beteruile or Breteville. *D.B.* de Breteville. Bretteville; a loc. n.
Beurey or Bevery. *D.B.* de Bevrere* (a Fleming)
Bevill, Belevile. Belleville; a loc. n.
Bigot. *D.B.**
Bikard, Bekard. *D.B.* Brictoward.* Briquesart; a loc. n.

Biroune. *D.B.* de Burun.* Biron; a loc. n.
Blondell or Blundel. *D.B.* Blunders* or Blond (?)
Bluet. *D.B.* Bloiet. Briqueville la Blouette; a loc. n.
Blunt, Blundet, or Blounte. *D.B.* Blunders.* Blandain; a loc. n.
Bodin, Bidin. *D.B.* Bodin. Beaudéan; a loc. n.
Boels. Bouelles, loc. n.
Bohun. Bohon; a loc. n. *D.B.* de Bohun*
Bois. *D.B.* de Bosch* (*Fl.*), Busch, or Bois, loc. n., Belg.
Bondeville. Bonneville; a loc. n. *D.B.*
Bonett. Bonnat; a loc. n., *Fr.*
Bonrett. Bonnart; a loc. n., Belg.
Bonueier. Bonnières; a loc. n.
Boranvile. Bérengeville (?), loc. n.
Botelere, a loc. n., Belg.
Botevile or Boyville. *D.B.* Botild(?). Bouille; a loc. n. (?)
Boundes. *D.B.* Bondi (?) or Bundo (?)
Bounilaine
Bourcher. *D.B.* Borci (?) Boursières; a loc. n., Burgund.
Brabason or Brabaion. *D.B.* de Braibone. Brabençon (Brabant)
Bracy. Brecy; a loc. n.
Braibuf. *D.B.* de Braiboue
Braine. *D.B.* Brien. Brionne; a loc. n., or Braine, Belg.
Brand. *D.B.* Brant
Braunch. St Denisde Branche; a loc. n.
Bray, loc. n., also Belg.
Brazard. Brassehaet; a loc. n., Belg. *D.B.* Suss., Hants, Berks, Wilts, Dors.
Brebus
Brent. *D.B.* Brant
Breton. *D.B.* Brito*
Brette. Bretteville (?); a loc. n.
Broilem. Breuilpont (?), loc. n.
Broleuy. Broglie; a loc. n.

Brouce, Brus, Brutz, Bruys. *D.B.* Robertus de Bruis* (Yorks). Breux, loc. n., now Brix.

Browe, Broy. Breux, loc. n.

Bryan. *D.B.* Brion. Brionne; a loc. n.

Buffard. Bouffey; a loc. n. Or Beaufour

Burdett. *D.B.* Burdet

Burdon. *D.B.* Buerd (?). Beaudoin, loc. n.

Bures. *D.B.* Buret (?). Bures; a loc. n.

Burgh, Bourg; a loc. n.

Busard. *D.B.* Bucard. Buzet; a loc. n., Fland.

Bushell. *D.B.* Buissel. Buscel; a loc. n.

Bushy or Bussey. *D.B.* de Buci. * Bougy, Buchy, loc. n.

Busseuille, Boseville. *D.B.* de Buiville.* Boscherville, Beuzeville, loc. n.

Buttecourt. *D.B.* Buter. Butot, loc. n.

Bysey. *D.B.* de Buci.* Buzy; a loc. n.

C

Cammile. *D.B.* de Cormelies.* Cormeilles; a loc. n.

Camois, Camoys. Camous; a loc. n.

Camvile, Cameville; a loc. n.

Caperoun. Rad. Capron, 1180

Carbonelle. Chabannes; a loc. n. *D.B.* Carbonel

Carevile, Coruyele. Courville; a loc. n.

Cateray, Cartrait. *D.B.* de Ceterith.* Cauterêts; a loc. n.

Cauncy, Chauncy. Canchy; a loc. n.

Chaiters, Chartres. Chartres; a loc. n.

Challouns. Challones; a loc. n.

Chamberay. Chambrais; a loc. n.

Chamberlain (Camerarius)

Chambernoun or Chaumberoun. Cambernon; a loc. n.

Champney, Champnais, Chawnes. Champigny, loc. n.

Chanduit, Chaudut. Chanday; a loc. n.

Chantelow (Cantelupe?), Cauntelow. Canteloupe; a loc. n.

Charles, Chaleys. Chalais; a loc. n.

Chaumont, a loc. n.

Chaundos. Chanday; a loc. n. *D.B.* de Candos

Chaward, Chaworth. Chauvincourt (?), loc. n.

Chawent, Chauunt. Chaumont (?); a loc. n.

Cheine, Cheines, Cheyni. *D.B.* Chenesis. Chênée and Chiny, Flanders. Chaignes, Le Chesne, loc. n., *Fr.*

Chereberge. Cherbourg; a loc. n. Cherecourt

Cholmeloy. Chamblac, loc. n.

Chopis, Chapes; a loc. n.

Clarell. *D.B.* de Claville (?). Clavelle, Cléville, loc. n.

Cleremaus, Clerevals; a loc. n. Clerenay

Clifford. *D.B.* Clibert (?) Clinels

Coinvile. Cornouailles (?); a loc. n.

Columber. *D.B.* de Columbels.* Colomby; a loc. n.

Colvile. *D.B.* de Colevil. Colleville; a loc. n.

Comin, Comeyn. Comines; a loc. n.

Conderay. Connerré; a loc. n. (?)

Conestable (De Gand)

Corbett, Corbet. *D.B.* Corbet

Corbine, Corby. *D.B.* Corbin. Corbie; a loc. n., Corbais, Belg.

Coville. Couville; a loc. n.
Cressy, Crescy. Crécy; a loc. n.
Creuquere, Crevecuer. Crevecœur;
a loc. n.
Cribett

Cuily; a loc. n.
Curly, de Curleio; a loc. n.
Curson, Courson. *D.B.* de
Curcan
Curtenay, Courteny, loc. n.

D

Dabernoune. *D.B.* de Abernon
Dabitott. *D.B.* de Abetot *
Dakeny. Acquigny; a loc. n.
Dalseny
Dambleton
Damnot, Damot. Motteville (?),
loc. n.
Damry, Damary. Amory, near Caen,
loc. n.
Daniel. *D.B.* Roger Daniel (Suss.)
Danway. Hanouard (?), loc. n.
Darell. Airel, near St Lo, loc. n.
Daubeney. *D.B.* de Albingi.*
Aubigné; a loc. n.
Daueros, Deveroys
Dauntre, Dautry
Dauonge, Daverenge. Avranches;
a loc. n.
Davers. *D.B.* Denvers (?); Anvers,
la Manche, loc. n.
Deheuse, De la Huse. Héas and
La Hisse, loc. n.
De la Bere. Labouheyre (?); a
loc. n.
De la Hill
De la Hoid, De la Hay. La Haye;
a loc. n.
De la Linde, Lindebeuf, loc. n.
De la Planche. Planquery; a
loc. n.
De la Pole. St Pol de Léon; a
loc. n.
De la Vache, De Wake. La
Vacherie, loc. n.

De la Vere. *D.B.* de Ver.* Ver;
a loc. n.
De la Ware. Wierre; a loc. n.
Delaund. La Londe, loc. n.
Delaward. *D.B.* de War'
Delee, Del Isle. Ille; a loc. n.
Denaville. Dénestanville, loc. n.
Derey. *D.B.* Derinc (Fleming)
Desny, Diseny. Isigny; a loc. n.
Devaus. Vaux; a loc. n.
Deverelle. Vireville; a loc. n.
Devereux. Évreux; a loc. n.
Devile, Deyville. Déville; a
loc. n.
Devise. *D.B.* Devais. Vaacey,
loc. n.
Disard, Disart. Deserte; a loc. n.
Dispencere, Dispenser. *D.B.* Dis-
pensator *
Dive. Dives; a loc. n. *D.B.* de
Dive *
Dodingsels, Dodingle. *D.B.* Do-
did * (?)
Doiville. Ouville, loc. n.
Druel. Ruelle; a loc. n.
Drury. Rouray; a loc. n.
Duilly, Duylly. *D.B.* de Oilgi (?).
Ailly; a loc. n.
Dulce. Dolcé; a loc. n.
Dunchamp. Encamp; a loc. n.
Dunstervile. Dénestanville, loc. n.
Durand, Durant. *D.B.* Durand.*
Douvrend (?), loc. n.
Durange

E

Engaine. Enghien; a loc. n. *D.B.*.*
Estrange, Destranges (Breton)
Estriels

Esturney
Estuteville, Estoteville. Etréville (?),
loc. n.

F

Facunburge. Fauquembergues, loc. n.

Fauecourt. Fallencourt, loc. n.

Fenes. *D.B.* Fenisc Ulf.* Fains, Fiennes, loc. n.

Fermbaud. *D.B.* Ferme (?)

Ferrerers. *D.B.* de Ferieres.* Ferrère; a loc. n.

Fichet, Fichent

Filberd, Filebert. St Philbert; a loc. n.

Finere

Fingez

Fitz Aleyn. *D.B.* Alan *

Fitz Auger. De Agou (?) *D.B.* Aguet

Fitz Browne. *D.B.* Brun *

Fitz Eustach. *D.B.* Eustachius *

Fitz Fitz

Fitz Fouk. *D.B.* Fulche

Fitz Geffrey. *D.B.* Gaufrid

Fitz Henrie. *D.B.* Henricus *

Fitz Herbert. *D.B.* Herbert *

Fitz Hugh. *D.B.* Hugo *

Fitz John. *D.B.* Johannes *

Fitz Laurence. *D.B.* Laurentius

Fitz Marmaduke

Fitz Morice. *D.B.* Mauric *

Fitz Otes. *D.B.* Otho (?) *

Fitz Pain. *D.B.* Pagen *

Fitz Peres. *D.B.* Peret *

Fitz Philip

Fitz Rainold. *D.B.* Rainald *

Fitz Rauf, Rafe. *D.B.* Rolf *

Fitz Rewes. *D.B.* Rufus (?)

Fitz Roand. *D.B.* Rohard (?)

Fitz Robert. *D.B.* *

Fitz Roger. *D.B.* *

Fitz Simon. *D.B.*

Fitz Thomas. *D.B.* *

Fitz Walter. *D.B.* Walter *

Fitz Waren. *D.B.* Warin

Fitz William. *D.B.* Willelm *

Flamville. *D.B.* Flamme.* Flamanville; a loc. n.

Fleschampe

Fleuez or Flevez. *D.B.* Flavus *

Folioll, Filiol. Folleville (?), loc. n.

Foliot, Filiot. *D.B.* Folet

Folville. Folleville; a loc. n.

Formay. Formerie; a loc. n.

Formibaud. *See* Fermbaud

Forz, Forges (?), Belgium

Fouke. *D.B.* Fulche

Fourbeville

Freville, Fryville. Fréville, loc. n.

Frisell, Fresell. *D.B.* Fresle, Richard.* Fresville; a loc. n.

Frisound, Frisoun

Front de Bœf. Daubeuf (?), loc. n.

Furnieueus, Forneux. Furnaux, Belgium

Furnival, Furnivaus; a loc. n.

G

Gamages. *D.B.* Gamas (?). Gamaches; a loc. n.

Garre, Karre. Gare; a loc. n.

Gaugy, Gorgeise, Georges, Gourges Gaunson

Gaunt, Kaunt. *D.B.* de Gand,* *Fl.* Gand; a loc. n.

Gernoun. *D.B.* Gernon.* Gernon de Montfichet

Giffard, Gifard. *D.B.* Gifard *

Glateuile. *D.B.* Glauill

Goband, Gobaude. *D.B.* Godebold * (?)

Gobion, Gubioun; a loc. n., Britt.

Golofre, Galofer. *D.B.* Gulaffra, Gulfer. Goulafrière, loc. n.

Gower, Goher; a loc. n.

Grammori, Grymward (?)

Graunson. Grandchain (?), loc. n.

Graunt. *D.B.* Grando. Le Grand

Gray. *D.B.* de Grai; a loc. n.

Greile, Greilly. Gresillé, Anjou
Grendon, Graundyn
Grenet. *D.B.* Granetarius. Grenade ; a loc. n.
Greneuile, Geneville. Granville ; a loc. n.
Grensy
Gressy, Gracy. Graçay ; a loc. n.

Griuel. Greuville, loc. n.
Guines, a loc. n.
Gurdon, Gerdoun ; a loc. n.
Gurley. *See* Curly
Gurnay, Gurney. *D.B.* Gurnai, Gournay. Gurney, loc. n.
Gurry. ·Gueures, loc. n.

H

Haket. *D.B.* Walter Achet. Achiet ; a loc. n.
Hamelin. *D.B.**
Hamound. *D.B.* Amund, Hamont(?), loc. n., Belgiuh
Hanlay, Haulley. Aulnay (?), loc. n.
Hanville. Anneville, loc. n.
Hardell
Harecourt, Harcord. Harcourt ; a loc. n.
Harewell, Hareville. Ardouval (?), loc. n.
Hastings. Hastingues ; a loc. n., island in the river near Bayonne

Haunsard. Hanouard, loc. n.
Haurell, Hurel. Eurville (?), loc. n.
Hauteny, Hautein. Autigny, loc. n.
Hayward. Hauwaert, loc. n., Belgium
Henoure
Hercy, Herey. Herseaux (?), Belgium, or Hericy, Norm.
Herioun, Heroun. *D.B.* de Herion.* Héron le, loc. n.
Herne. Hern, loc. n., Belgium
Heryce. Heriz ; a loc. n.
Houell. Houville, loc. n., *Fr.*
Husee. Useé, or Houssaye ; a loc. n.

J

Januile
Jarden, Jardyn (De Gardino), 1189
Jasperuile

Jay (De Gaio or Gai)
Jeniels
Jerconuise

K

Kancey
Karrowe
Keine, Kanæs. Kain, loc. n., Belgium. Cahaignes, Norm.

Kenelre
Keveters
Kimaronne, Kymarays
Kiriell (De Criol)

L

Lacy, Lascy. *D.B.* de Laci.* Laissey or Lessay ; a loc. n.
Lane, Lenias. Lens ; a loc. n.
Lascales, Lascels. Lacella ; a loc. n.
Latomer, Latymer (Latinarius)
Laumale, La Muile. Lamballe (?) ; a p. n.
Leded

Lemare, Lymers (?). *D.B.* Lemar. Limours ; a loc. n.
Liffard
Limers, Limesey, Limousin ; a loc. n. *D.B.* de Limesi.* Limours ; a loc. n.
Linnebey. Lindebeuf, loc. n.
Lisours. Lisieux (?) ; a loc. n., *Fr.*

Loious. De Loe (?)
Longechampe. Longchamps ; a loc. n., Belgium
Longespes
Longueuale, Longville, Logevile. Longueville ; a loc. n.
Lorancourt. Loraine (?) ; a loc. n.
Loriage
Loterell. Loudervielle ; a loc. n., *Fr.* (?)
Loueney, Loveyne, Lovein, Lovan.

D.B. Leuuin.* Lieuvin ; a loc. n., *Fr.* Louvain, loc. n., Belgium
Louerace, Loverak. Louvres ; a loc. n. Leuric *
Loveday, Leuetot, Lovetot. *D.B.* Leviet * (?), Loudet and Louvetot, loc. n., France
Lovell. *D.B.* Laval ; a loc. n.
Lownay. Luynes ; a loc. n. (?)
Loy, Loif. Louye, loc. n.
Lucy, Luse. Lucy ; a loc. n.

M

Maiell. *D.B.* de Medehal*
Maine, Maoun. *D.B.* Maino.* Mayne ; a loc. n.
Mainell. Ménilles, loc. n.
Maingun (?). *D.B.* Maigno
Mainwaring, Mesnil-Warin, loc. n.
Malebranch, Malebys (?). Malbise
Maleheire. Mellier ; a loc. n., Belg.
Maleherbe, Maleberge. Malesherbes ; a loc. n.
Maleluse. Malause ; a loc. n.
Malemaine, Maumasin. Malmaison ; a loc. n.
Malemis. Malines (?), Fland.
Malet. *D.B.* Malet.* Melet ; a loc. n., Fland.
Maleuile. Maleville ; a loc. n. *D.B.* Malauill
Malevere. Maulévrier ; a loc. n.
Mallony. Malaunay ; a loc. n.
Mallop. *D.B.* Mala opa
Mandut, Maudiet (?). Mauduit, loc. n.
Mangisere
Maniard, Mainard. *D.B.*
Manlay
Manse, Monceus (?). *D.B* Manasses (?). Manage ; a loc. n., Belg.
Manteuenant. Mainenon ; a loc. n.
Mantolet, Montelent. *D.B.* Mantel.* Manthelon, loc. n.
Manuile, Meneville. *D.B.* de Manneuille. Manneville, loc. n.

Marceaus. *D.B.* de Marci.* Marsous ; a loc. n.
Mare, Marre. *D.B.* de Mara. St Maure ; a loc. n. (?)
Marmilon, Marmion ; a loc. n.
Marny. Mauny, loc. n.
Marteine. *D.B.* Martin.* St Martin ; a loc. n.
Martinaste. Martinvaast ; a loc. n.
Massey. *D.B.* Maci. Massay ; a loc. n.
Matelay. Madeleine - de - Nonacourt (?), loc. n.
Mauches. Monchaux (?), loc. n.
Mauclerke
Maularde
Maulay, Maule, Morley. Marley ; a loc. n.
Maulicerer. Mauleverer (?), loc. n.
Maunchenell, Mauncel. Mansel, loc. n.
Maundervile, Maundeville. *D.B.* de Manneville.* Mondeville ; a loc. n.
Maurewarde
Mauveysin. Mauvezin ; a loc. n.
Meintenore
Meletak. Melite ; a loc. n.
Meller. Le Meillur
Melun. *D.B.* de Mellend.* Melen, loc. n., Belgium
Menere, Maners (?). Le Manoir, loc. n.
Menpincoy, Mounpinson

Merke, Merkenfell. *D.B.* de Merc.
Marques (?), loc. n.
Miriel. Mirville ; a loc. n.
Mohant. Moen (?) ; a loc. n., Belg.
Moion, Norm.
Monchenesey, Mountheusey
Monhout. Manéhouville (?), loc. n.
Montfichet. *See* Muschet, Mussett
Monthermon, Maihermer
Montrauers, Mountravers. Montaure (?), loc. n.
Morell. *D.B.* ; a loc. n.
Moren. *D.B.* Morin.* Morainville, loc. n.
Moribray, Mowbray. Moutbray ; a loc. n. Maubray, loc. n., Belgium. Moubrai, Norm.
Morleian. *D. B.* Moriland (?). Morillon ; a loc. n.
Morreis, Mourreis, Murres. *D.B.* Mauric.* St Maurice, loc. n.
Mortimere. *D.B.* de Mortemer ; a loc. n.
Mortiuale, Mortivaus. Motteville(?); a loc. n.
Morville ; a loc. n.

Mouett, Movet. Mouettes, loc. n.
Mouncey. Monchy (?), loc. n.
Mountagu. *D.B.* de Montagud.*
Montaigu ; a loc. n., Belg.
Mountbother. *D.B.* Manbodo
Mountford. Montfort ; a loc. n. *D.B.* de Montfort*
Mountgomerie. *D.B.* de Montgomery. Monte Goumeril, loc. n.
Mountlovel, Maulovel. Malleville(?), loc. n.
Mountmarten, Mortimaine. Montmain, loc. n.
Mountsoler, Mounsorel (?). Moncello
Mourteney, Morteyn. *D.B.* Mortuing. Mortain ; a loc. n.
Mowne, Mooun, Moine, or Mohun. Moyon ; a loc. n. *D.B.* de Moion
Musarde. *D.B.* Musard.* Bretagne
Muse. *D.B.* Musard.* Moux (?) ; a loc. n., *Fr.*
Musegros. *D.B.* de Mucelgros
Musett, Muschet. Mozet (?), loc. n., Fland.

N

Navimere. *D.B.* Nemore (?)
Nefmarch, Newmarch. Neufmarché, loc. n.
Neile, Fitz-Nele. *D.B.* Nigel. Nagel, loc. n.
Neiremet
Nembrutz
Nermitz. Neumarché (?) ; a loc. n.
Neville, Nereville. Neuille and Néville, loc. n.

Newborough, Newburgh. Neubourg ; a loc. n.
Noers, Neuers. Noyers; a loc. n. (?). *D.B.* de Noiers
Norbet, Newbet. *D.B.* Nubold (?)
Norice. Norrey ; a loc. n.
Normaville. Normanville, loc. n.
Nusetys

O

Oisell. Oissel ; a loc. n.
Olenel, Otinel (?). *D.B.* de Olney (?). Aulnay (?), loc. n.
Olibef. Elbœuf ; a loc. n.

Olifard, Olifant. *D.B.* Oliver
Orioll. Orival (?), loc. n.
Otevell. Octeville, loc. n.
Ounall. Ouainville, loc. n.

P

Paifrere. *D.B.* Paisforere

Paignel or Panel. *D.B.* Pagenel* Paiteny

Pampilium. Papillon, Pavillon, loc. n.

Pantolf. *D.B.* Pantulf

Patefine, Parthenay ; a loc. n.

Pauey. Poey le Houn ; a loc. n.

Pavley, Paveley. Pavilly ; a loc. n. Peccell

Peche. *D.B.* Pecchaie. Le Pecq ; a loc. n. and Belg.

Peito. Poitou ; a loc. n.

Pekeny. Picquigny ; a loc. n.

Penecord. Piencourt, loc. n.

Percelay, Perechay. *D.B.* Percehaie.* Perche, loc. n.

Percivale. Puisenval (?), loc. n.

Percy. *D.B.* Perci.* Percy ; a loc. n.

Perepound, Pierrepoint. *D.B.* de Perapund

Perere, Perrers. Perrières, loc. n. Pershale

Perot, *D.B.* Peret,* Pirot

Pery, Perier, Bretagne

Petiuoll. Petiville, loc. n.

Pevrell. *D.B.* Peverel.* Pierreval (?), loc. n.

Phuars, Fours, loc. n.

Picard. Picardy ; a loc. n.

Pigot, Pygot. *D.B.* Picot.* Picot Avenel

Pinchard, Punchardoun, Pinkadoun. Punchardon or Pincherdoun, loc. n.

Pinel. *D.B.** Pinterville (?), loc. n.

Pinkenie. *D.B.* de Pinchengi

Placy, Place. Plessis ; a loc. n.

Plukenet. Plangenoit,loc.n., Belgium

Pomeray. *D.B.* De Pomerie.* Pommeraie ; a loc. n.

Poterell. La Poterie (?), loc. n.

Pounce, Poynce. *D.B.* Ponz. Pontoise (?) ; a loc. n.

Power, Poer. *D.B.* de Porth * (?). Portes, loc. n., or Puers, Belg.

Preaus. Preaux, loc. n.

Preulirlegast

Pugoy, Pugoys. *D.B.* Pugnant (?). Puchay (?), loc. n.

Putrill. Futerel (?)

Q

Quinci, Quyncy, Quincé, Maine, loc. n.

Quintini. *D.B.* de St Quintin.* St Quintin ; a loc. n.

R

Raband. *D.B.* Rabbada

Raimond. *D.B.* Raimund

Rait. *D.B.* Ret. Reeth ; a loc. n., Belg.

Randvile. Ranville ; a loc. n.

Rastoke. Rusticus (?)

Richmound. Richemont, loc. n. Ridell

Rie, Ry. Rhuys, loc. n. Rigny

Rinuill, Reynevile. Regneville, loc. n.

Ripere, Ripers. *D.B.* Rippe

Risers, Rysers. *D.B.* de Riset

Rivell. *D.B.* Rivvuls. Riville, loc. n.

Rivers. Reviers, loc. n. *D.B.* Riveire.* Rivière, Belg.

Rochford. Roquefort, loc. n.

Rokell. Rocheville ; a loc. n.

Romilly ; a loc. n.

Ronde. De Rotundo, Norm.

Ros. *D.B.* de Ros. Rosay (?), loc. n.

Roselin. *D.B.* Roselent,* Rozelin. Rouisillon ; a loc. n.

Rougere. *D.B.* Roger. Rochers; a loc. n.

Rous, Rothais (?) or Roic (Roys). Roux, loc. n., Belg.

Rushell, Rozel, Russell. Risle; a loc. n. *D.B.* Rozel

Ryan. Royan, loc. n. Ruyen, Belg.

S

Saluin. *D.B.* Sawin* (?). Silvanus

Sanctes, Sainct Tesc. St Eustache (?), loc. n.

Sandvile. Sandouville, loc. n.

Sanford. Sancourt (?), loc. n.

Sauay. *D.B.* de Sais (?), or de Soies (?)

Saulay, Souley. Soule ; a loc. n.

Saunay. *D.B.* de Sauigni. Savigny ; a loc. n.

Sauncey. *D.B.* de St Sansone

Saunsouerre. *D.B.* de Saucnei. St Saire (?), loc. n.

Say. Sées or Saie ; a loc. n.

Seffe. *D.B.* Seifrid (?)

Seguin, Sengryn. Serquigny, loc. n.

Senclere. *D.B.* de Sencler. St Clair ; a loc. n.

Sent Albin. St Aubin ; a loc. n.

Sent Amond. St Amand, loc. n.

Sent Barbe. *D.B.* de Barbes. St Barbe-sur-Gaillon : a loc. n.

Sent Cheveroll, Soucheville. *D.B.* de Sacheuilla. Sacquenville, loc. n.

Sent George. St Georges-sur-Fontaine, loc. n.

Sent John, St Jean. St Jouin, loc. n. ; Sent Jean, Flanders

Sent Legere, St Ligiere. St Léger, loc. n.

Sent Les. Lez ; a loc. n.

Sent Martin ; a loc. n.

Sent More. *D.B.* de More. St Maur, loc. n.

Sent Omere. St Omer, loc. n.

Sent Quintin. *D.B.* de St Quintin*

Sent Scudemore. Escudemore, loc. n.

Sent Vile. Sainneville, loc. n.

Sheuile. Seuilly (?) ; a loc. n.

Sieward. *D.B.* Siuuard

Sirewast

Snylly. St Helier (?), loc. n.

Somerey, Someray. *D.B.* de Sumeri. Somery ; a loc. n.

Somerville ; a loc. n., Caen

Soreglise

Sorell. Surville (?), loc. n.

Souch. Sauchay (?), loc. n.

Sourdemale, Surdevale. *D.B.* Sourdeval ; a loc. n.

Sucheus

Sules, Soules, Solers. Selles (?), loc. n.

Suremounte. Saumont, loc. n.

T

Talbot. *D.B.* Talebot

Taket or Takel. Tocqueville (?), loc. n.

Tankervile. Tancarville ; a loc. n.

Tanny, Tany

Tardevile

Tarteray

Tavernez. Le Tavernier

Tenwis

Tercy. Tessé (?) ; a loc. n.

Thorney. *D.B.* Tornai. Tournay ; a loc. n.

Thornille. R. Tornelvie

Tibtote, Thibtot ; a loc. n.

Tinel. *D.B.* Tinel

Tinevile

Tirell. *D.B.* Tirelde

Tisoun. *D.B.* Tisun.* Dison, Belg.

Toget, Tuchet. Touchet ; a loc. n.

Tolet. De Toleta, Norm.

Tollemach, Tolimer. Tolemer ; a loc. n.
Tolous. Toulouse ; a loc. n.
Tomy. De Thelomeio (?)
Torell. *D.B.* Torchill (?). Tocqueville (?), loc. n.
Tortechappell
Totelles
Touke, Tuk. *D.B.* Tochi.*
Touques ; a loc. n.
Touny, Tony. *D.B.* Tona.* Tonnay ; a loc. n.
Tracy ; a loc. n.
Traies, Thays
Trainell

Travers. *D.B.* Trevieres, loc. n.
Travile. Trouville, loc. n.
Tregos. Tregoz ; a loc. n.
Trenchevile
Trenchilion
Treverell, Treville (?)
Trison
Trivet
Trousbut
Trussell
Trylly. *D.B.* de Traillgi
Turbevile. *D.B.* Turberv, loc. n.
Turley
Turvile. Tourville ; a loc. n.
Tyriet. Turretot (?), loc. n.

V

Vaberon
Valence ; a loc. n.
Valenger, Valenges. *See* Wallangy, Valognes ; a loc. n.
Valers ; a loc. n.
Valingford
Valiue. Valliquerville (?), loc. n.
Vanay. Vannes ; a loc. n.
Vancorde, Venecorde
Vasderol
Vauuruile. Varaville ; a loc. n.
Vaux, loc. n.
Vavasour. Vavassor, Norm., 1180
Veirny. Vernet ; a loc. n.
Venables, loc. n.
Vendore, Venour. Vendres ; a loc. n., or Venator
Veniels. Vénesville (?), loc. n.
Verdeire, Verders, Verdour
Verdoune. Verdon ; a loc. n.
Vere. Ver ; a loc. n.
Verland. Verlaine, loc. n., Flanders

Verlay, Werlay. Verlée, loc. n., Flanders
Vernoun. Vernon ; a loc. n.
Vernoys. Vernai ; a loc. n.
Veroun. Verune ; a loc. n.
Verrere. *See* Ferrer
Vesey, Vessay. *D.B.* de Vesci *
Vian. Vienne ; river
Viez. *D.B.* de Uis (?). Wieze, Belg.
Vilan. Vilaine ; a river. Villainville, loc. n.
Vinoun. Veinions ; a loc. n.
Vipont. Veteriponte ; a loc. n.
Viville, Wyville, Wivell. Virville (?), loc. n.
Umfravile. Amfreville, loc. n.
Vnket
Vrnaful
Vrnall. Verneuil ; a loc. n.
Vschere. Le Huissier, Ostarius

W

Wacely, Wely. Vesly (?), loc. n.
Wafre. Wavre, loc. n., Belgium
Walangy, Valenger. *D.B.* de Valonges.* Valognes ; a loc. n.

Waloys, Valers (?). *D.B.* de Wals. Valailles (?), loc. n.
Wake, Wace (?). Wace ; a loc. n.
Wamerville

Ward. *D. B.* Wiard. Weerd, Belg.

Wardebois, Warroys (?)

Wareine, Warrene. *D.B.* de Warene,* Warenger. Varenge-ville, loc. n.

Wate. Le Waite, 1180

Watelin

Watevil, Waterville. *D.B.* de Wateuile.* Vatteville ; a loc. n.

Werdonell

Wermelay

Wespaile. Wespelaer, loc. n., Flanders

ALPHABETICAL LIST OF BRITISH SURNAMES

A

ABBISS. *N.-Fr.* De Abbacia; a p.n.
1198, R. de A.; 1272, Rot. Hund.

ABBOTT. Dimin. of Abb.; or *see* official names.

ABBS. *F.* Abbo; *D.B.* Api, Appe, Aba, Abba, Abo; *G.* Aber, Ahber, Haber; *Dch.* Abas, Abbing, Appij; *Fl.* Abas, Abs, Abts; p.n. (mighty). From a Gothic stem *aban* (to have power). *See* Abbiss

ABDALE. From Abbeydale; a loc. n., Yorks

A'BECKETT. From Beckett; a loc. n., Berks; Atte-Beckett

ABELL. F. om Abeele; a loc. n., Belg., or *D.S.G.* Abel; *Fl.* Abbeele, Abeels; *Dch.* Abels, Eble; *G.* Abel, Ebel; *D.B.* Abel; p.n.
Abell is on the Roll of Battell Abbey. Abel, tenant in *D.B.* (Kent); *A.S. abal* (?) (strength)

ABERCORN. A loc. n., Linlithgow

ABERCROMBIE. A loc. n., Fife

ABERNETHY. A loc. n., Elgin, Fife, Moray, Perths.

ABIGAIL. *A.S.* Abagisl (?) (mighty hostage)

ABLE. *See* Abell

ABLETT. *N.-Fr.* De Abelot; a p.n.; Camb. Rot. Hund., 1274; or *see* Ablewhite

ABLEWHITE. From Applethwaite; a loc. n., Cumb., Westmd.

ABLEY. From Abberley; a loc. n., Worcest.

ABNEY. A loc. n., Derbysh.; *D.B.* Habenai

ABRAHALL. From Aberhale; a loc. n., Mongomeryshire

ABRAM. A loc. n., Lancs., formerly Adburgham

ABSELL. *Fl.* Absil; a p.n. *See* Abbs

ABY. A loc. n., Lincs.

ACHESON. *See* Atkinson

ACHMUTY. From Auchtermuchty; a loc. n., Fife

ACKERS. *A.S.* Acca, Æcca; p.n. (edge, point); *Fl.* Hakkars; fam. n.

ACKMAN, AIKMAN. *N.* Ögmundr (sharp, terrible director); *A.S.* Agemund; *G.* Egmond; *D.* Hageman; *Dch.* Haagman; *Fl.* Haakman; p.n.

ACLAM. A loc. n., Yorks; *D.B.* Aclun, Achelum
Roger de Aclum in Rot. Obl. et Fin. K. John

ACLAND. A loc. n., Devon
De Acland was settled there *temp.* Hen. II. Also de Accalen

ACORNS. *Dch.* Akens; a p.n.

ACRES. *See* Ackers

ACTON. A loc. n., Chesh., Middlx., etc.; *N.-Fr.* Burnell, 1086

ADAIR. From Adare (?); a loc. n., Limerick

ADAMS. *A.S. Fr.* Adam; *Fl.* Adams; p.n.

ADCOCK. *A.S.* Adda, Hadda; *F.* Adde; *G.* Hädicke; p.n. Dim. of Adda; or *see* Addicott Atte-Cocke, Court of Husting, 1258

ADCROFT. From Addiscroft; a loc. n., Cornw.

ADDERLEY. A loc. n., Salop. De Dunstanville held it Hen. I.

ADDERTON. From Atherton; a loc. n., Lancs. Or Edderton, Ross

ADDICOTT. From Adcott; a loc. n., Salop

ADDINGTON. A loc. n., Kent, Northants., Surrey. De Abernon, 1086

ADDISON. *See* Addy

ADDLEY. *See* Adderley

ADDY, ADE, ADEY. *F.* Ade; *A.S.* Ada, Æddi, Eada; *S.* Adde; *Dch.* Ade, Adee; p.n. (father's ancestor). Welsh form of Adam

ADEANE. From Atte-Dean. Dean; a loc. n., Glost., Hants, etc.; or *F.* Adde, Adden; p.n. *See* Dean

ADENEY. *See* Adney

ADLAM. *See* Headlam; or *A.S.* Adhelm, Eadhelm, Ealdhelm, Æthelhelm; p.n. (noble helm)

ADLINGTON. A loc. n., Lancs.

ADNEY. A loc. n., Salop

ADSHEAD. From Adsett; a loc. n., Glost.

AFFECTION. *Fr.* Afchain; *A.S.* Æfic (Ælfic), p.n. Dim. of Elf

AFFLECK. A loc. corruption of Auchinleck, Ayrshire

AGACE. *See* Aggs

AGATE. *G.* Agath; a p.n. *Old G.* Achgoz (Goth); or *see* Hackett

AGGAS, AGGS, AGGIS, AGGUS. *A.S.* Aga, Agis; *F.* Agge;, *D.* Ager, Acker; *G.* Hakus; p.n. Perhaps from *Old G.* Hadgis (war hostage); or *ac, ag, ecg* (edge, point, as of a weapon)

AGG. *N.-Fr.* Auge; a p.n. De Augo, Norm., 1200; Eng., 1199; Oxfd., 1249

AGGER, AGAR. *See* Egarr

AGNEW. From Aigneaux, near Bayeux. *N.-Fr.* Agneau; *Fl.* Agnier; p.n., Winchester, 1148; Wigtown, Scotl.

AGUTTER. *A.S.* Agatho, Ægteard, Agtard; p.n. *ag* (point, edge); *hard* (strong)

AHEARNE. *See* Heron

AIKEN. *See* Eykin

AILSBY. From Aylesby; a loc. n., Lincs.

AINGER. *See* Angier

AINSLIE. *Dch.* Enslie; a p.n. or *see* Ansley

AINSWORTH. A loc. n., Lancs.

AIREY. From the Castle of Airey, Norm.

AISHFORD. *See* Ashford

AISTROP. From Aisthorpe; a loc. n., Lincs.

AITCHISON. *See* Atkinson

AKEHURST. *See* Akhurst

AKENHEAD. From Aikenhead; a loc. n., Lanark

AKERS. *See* Ackers and Aggs

AKHURST. From Hawkhurst; a loc. n., Kent

AKISTER. From Acaster; a loc. n., Yorks

ALABASTER. Albastre, Court of Husting, 1258. *See* Arblaster

ALAN. Scot. p.n. (cheerful)

ALBAN. *D.* Allbahn; *D.B.* Alban; p.n. *See* St. Aubyn

ALBIN. *A.S.* Albuin; *Fl.* Albouin; p.n. (elf-friend); or *see* Alban

ALBISTON. From Albaston; a loc. n., Devon

ALBRIGHT. *A.S.* Æthelbeorht, Alberct, Albert; *Dch.* Albregt; *G.* Albrecht; p.n. *œl-beorht* (noble, illustrious)

ALBRIGHTON. A loc. n., Salop

ALDERDISE. *See* Allardyce

ALDERTON. A loc. n., Northants, Wilts

ALDHAM. A loc. n., Ess., Suff., Yorks

ALDINGTON. A loc. n., Kent

ALDIS. *N.* Aldis (Alfdis), elf-goddess. Or *see* Allardyce

ALDOM. *See* Aldham

ALDRED. From Aldreth; a loc. n., Camb. Or *A.S.* Ealdred; a p.n., *eald-ræd* (aged counsellor)

ALDRICH. *A.S.* Alderich, Ealdric; p.n. (old ruler). Or *see* Aldridge

ALDRIDGE. A loc. n., Staff., Suff.

ALDWINCKLE. A loc. n., Northants

ALDWORTH. A loc. n., Berks

ALECOCK. *A.S.* Ail, Æthel (noble); *F.* Alle; *G.* Alker; *D.* Halck; *Dch.* Alchen; *D.B.* Alchen, Alcher, Alcot; p.n., dimin.

ALESBURY. *See* Aylesbury

ALEXANDER. *Dch.*, *G.* p.n.; *Fr.* Alexandre; a p.n.

ALFORD. A loc. n., Lincs, Somers.

ALFRED. *N.* Elfraðr; *A.S.* Ælfrede (fairy counsellor); *D.B.* Alured, or Alvred; *D.* Allert; p.n.

ALFREE. *N.-Fr.* Alveré, Caen, 1195; *A.S.* Ælffrith; a p.n. (peaceful elf)

ALGAR, ALGER. *N.* Álf-geirr; *Dch.* Algie, Allgäuer; *A.S.* Algar, Ælfgar, Elfgar, Elgar; *G.* Allger; p.n. (Elfspear)

ALINGTON. A loc. n., N. Wales, Wilts

ALKER. From Altcar; a loc. n., Lancs

ALLAN. *See* Allen

ALLANBY. *See* Allonby

ALLARD. *A.S.* Alhard, Ealheard (all strong); p.n.; *N.-Fr.* Aelart. *See* Allott

ALLARDYCE. A loc. n., Kincardineshire

ALLBERRY. From Alderbury; a loc. n., Wilts

ALLBON. *See* Alban

ALLBROOK. A loc. n., Hants

F

ALLBUTT. *A.S.* Ælbeorht; *Fl.* Albert, Albot; p.n., Alburtt, a Fl. Prot. ref., Lond. 1618. *See* Albright

ALLCARD. *See* Allgood

ALLCHIN. From Haulchin; a loc. n., Fland. Or *Fl.* Halkin; *Dch.* Halk; *D.B.* Alchen; p.n. Dimin. of *N.* Halli; a p.n.

ALLCHURCH. From Alvechurch; a loc. n., Worcest.

ALLCOCK. *See* Alecock

ALLCORN. From Alchorne; a loc. n., Suss. (?)

ALLDAY. *A.S.* Alda, Ealda (old); p.n. Or *see* Halliday

ALLDIN. From Halden; a loc. n., Kent; *N.-Fr.* Alden, 1195. Or Irish McAldin

ALLDRITT. *See* Aldred

ALLEN. *A.S.* Al, Æthel (noble); *F.* Alle, Allen; *Dch.* Alink; *D.B.* Alan; *Fr.* Allain; a fam. n.

ALLENGAME. *See* Allingham

ALLERTON. A loc. n., Yorks

ALLERY. *See* Elleray

ALLETT. *See* Allott

ALLEYNE. Welsh Aluyen; Irish Allwin, Alain; Gaelic Aluinn; Manx Aalin; *S.* Alin; p.n. (fair, beautiful). Or *see* Elvin

ALLFLAT, ALLFAT. *A.S.* Ælffet, Ælfrith, Alvert; *Fl.* Aelvoet; *Dch.* Alphert; p.n. (peaceful elf)

ALLGOOD. *A.S.* Ælfgod, Algod; p.n. (elf Goth); a Fl. Prot. ref. n., Lond. 1618

ALLINGHAM. A loc. n., Kent

ALLINGTON. A loc. n., Devon, Dorset, Lincs, Salop, Hants, Wilts

ALLISON. *See* Allen

ALLKIN. From Alken; a loc. n., Belg.; Halkyn, N. Wales. Or *see* Allchin

ALLMAN. From Allemagne, near Caen. *Norm.* or *A.S.* Ælfman, Ællman (elfman); *D.S.* Ahlman; *Fl.* Aleman; *G.* Hallman; p.n.; Prot. ref., Lond. 1618

ALLMARK. *See* Almack

ALLNATT, ALLNUTT. *A.S.* Ælnoth, Ælfnoth (elfbold) ; *D.B.* Alnod ; p.n.

ALLONBY. A loc. n., Cumb.

ALLOTT. *N.* Hallaðr ; *S.* Allart ; *D.* Allert ; *Dch.* Allot ; *Fl.* Allard, Allart, Hallart ; *N.-Fr.* Hallet ; p.n. ; a Hugt. n., Norwich, 1622, Lond. 1688. *See* Allard

ALLOWAY. A loc. n., Ayrshire

ALLPASS, ALLPRESS. Fam. n. of Alpe ; *D.* Alpers ; a p.n.

ALLSHORN. A loc. n.

ALLUM. From Hallam ; a loc. n., Derbysh.

ALLWARD. *N.* Hallvarðr ; a p.n. (hill-warder, watchman) ; or *A.S.* Ælfweard, Alward (elf warden)

ALLWAY. *See* Alloway or Holloway.

ALLWIN. *See* Alwyn

ALLWOOD. *See* Allward

ALLWORK. From Aldwark ; a loc. n., Yorks

ALLWORTH, ALLWORTHY. *See* Aldworth

ALLWRIGHT. *See* Alldritt

ALMACK. From Almeneches (?) ; a loc. n., Normandy

> There is a tradition that a Scotchman, coming to London, changed his name from MacAll to Allmack ! It may be so.

ALMENT, ALMOND. *A.S.* Almund, Ealhmund (Hall protector)

ALNWICK. A loc. n., Northbd.

ALPE. *N.* Hjálpr (a helper, saviour); *Fl.* Alpen ; *Dch.* Alphen ; *G.* Hallop, Hallup ; p.n.

ALPIN. Scot. (elf)

ALPORT. A loc. n., Derbysh.

ALSFORD. *See* Aylesford

ALSOP. A loc. n., Derbysh. ; *D.B.* Elleshope

ALSTON. A loc. n., Cumb. ; or *N.* Hallstein ; *Fl.* Alsteens ; *A.S.* Alstan, Alestan, Ealhstan (Hall the firm) ; p.n.

ALTHORP. A loc. n., Lincs, Northants

ALTMAN. *A.S.* Ealdman (old man) ; *G.* Altmann ; a p.n.

ALTON. A loc. n., Staffs.

ALTY. *A.S.* Alt, Alti, Eald ; *F.* Alt ; p.n. (old)

ALURED. *See* Alfred

ALVEN. *A.S.* Æthelwine, Ailwin (noble friend) ; or Ælfwine, Alwin (elf friend) ; *Fl.* Alvin ; p.n. *See* Elven

ALVEY. *N.* Halveig ; *A.S.* Ealhwig ; *Dch.* Halfweeg ; *G.* Hallwig ; p.n. (Hall-war)

ALVIS. From Alves ; a loc. n., Elgin

ALWYN. From Halluin ; a loc. n., France. Prot. ref., Lond. 1618. Or *see* Alven

AMAS. *See* Ames

AMBLER. *A.S.* Amalhere ; a p.n. (old warrior)

AMEN. *Dch.* p.n. Or from Amagne ; a loc. n., France. *See* Ames

AMER. *See* Hamer

AMERY. *Fl.* Emery ; *G.* Emerich ; p.n. (work rule)

AMES, AMESS, AMIES, AMIS, AMISS. From Hamois ; a loc. n., Fland. Or Hiesmes, Normandy; *A.S.* Am, Em, Haim, Ham ; *F.* Emo, Eme ; *Dch.* Ameaz, Amsen, Emous, Amen ; *Fl.* Ameys ; *D.* Ham, Hemme ; *G.* Ameis, Emmes, Hems, Hemme ; p.n. (active); Hameus, a Flem. ref., Lond. 1618 De Hames in Rot. Obl. et Fin. De Amias, Amyas, Amys, Court of Husting, 1288.

AMHERST. A loc. n., Kent

AMMAND, AMMON. From St Amand ; a loc. n., Norm. Or *see* Hammond

AMOORE, AMOR. From Atte-Moor

AMOOTY. *See* Achmuty

AMOS. *See* Ames

AMPHLETT. From Amflete ; a loc. n., Normandy

AMPS. *A.S.* Imper, Ingwar ; *Dch.* Ampers, Hampe ; p.n. (Frey's defence)

AMYS. *See* Ames

ANCIENT. *See* Innocent

ANDERTON. A loc. n., Cornw., Yorks

ANGEL. *D.*, *Dch.* p.n. *See* Inglis

ANGIER, ANGRE. A loc. n., Belg.; *Fr.* Anger; *D.* Anger; *D.B.* Anger; p.n.
> Angers in Roll of Battell Abbey; Anger or Auinger (venator) in Rot. Obl. et Fin., K. John.

ANGLE. From Les Angles; a loc. n., Norm. Or *see* Angel
> G. de Angle in Rot. Obl. et Fin. A.D. 1199, Ireland.

ANGLER. From Angleur; a loc. n., Belg. Or *A.S.* Engelhere, Engeler; p.n. (a warrior of the Angles)

ANGRAVE. From Hengrave; a loc. n., Suff.

ANGUIN. *N.-Fr.* Angevin in *D.B.* From Anjou

ANGUS. Irish Aenghas; a p.n. (excellent virtue)

ANKER. *D.* Anker; *G.* Anke; *Dch.* Hankart; p.n. *See* Hanks

ANLEY. From Hanley; a loc. n., Staffs. Or Andely, Norm.

ANLEZARK. From Anglezark; a loc. n. (manor), Bolton, Lancs
> John Anglezargh, Duxbury, 1598; Robert Anzleark, 1680; John Anleyzargh, 1681.—*Chester Wills.* In Estham Register, Cheshire, are twenty-seven entries under Anglizer.

ANNABLE. *See* Hunnibell

ANNAN. A loc. n., Scotl.

ANNES, ANNESS, ANNIS, ANNISON. *A.S.* Anna, Enna (defender); *F.* Enno; *D.B.* Enisan; *Dch.* Annes; *Fl.* Hanes, Hanneson, Anhes, Annez; *D.* Hanisch, Annise; p.n. Ennis, a Prot. ref., Lond. 1618

ANNESLEY. A loc. n., Notts
> Rd. le Breton held it, 1079. Ralph de A., with Reg. his son, founded Felley Abbey, 1152. From them descended Visct. Valentia, Jas. I., and Earls of Angelesey, Annesley, Mt. Norris.

ANSAR. *See* Ensor

ANSELL. *Old G.* Ansilor; *Dch.* Ansel; or *N.-Fr.* Ancelle; p.n. (a servant)

ANSLEY. *See* Annesley

ANSON. *See* Hanson

ANSTEAD. From Henstead (?); a loc. n., Suff.

ANSTEY. A loc. n., Devon, Hants, Herts, Warw., Wilts

ANSTRUTHER. A loc. n., Fife
> Held by De Candel, formerly Malherbe.

ANTHONY. From St Antoine; a loc. n., Norm.
> In Rot. Hund., 1272.

ANTILL. From Ampthill; a loc. n., Beds. Or *Fr.* Antieul, Antil; p.n.

ANTROBUS. A loc. n., Chesh.

ANYON. *See* Onions; a Hugt. n., Lond. 1618

ANWYL. Welsh (beloved); or from Anneville; a loc. n., Normandy

APLIN. *Dch.* Abeelen; *Old G.* Abbilin; p.n. Dim. of Abbo. *See* Abbs. Or *N.-Fr.* de Abelon, 1180

APPERLEY. A loc. n., Glost., Yorks

APPLEBEE. *See* Appleby

APPLEBY. A loc. n., Leicest., Lincs, Westmd.

APPLEGARTH. A loc. n., Dumfries

APPLEGATE. *See* Applegarth

APPLETON. A loc. n., Lancs, Norf., Yorks

APPLEYARD. *See* Applegarth

APPS. *See* Abbs

APRILE. *Fl.* April; a p.n.

APTHORPE. A loc. n., Northants, Notts

AQUS. *See* Ackers

ARBER. From Arbre; a loc. n., Belg. Or *see* Harbard

ARBLASTER. *D.B.* Arbalistarius (an officer of cross-bowmen)

ARBOURN. From Harborne; a loc. n., Worcs.

ARBUCKLE. A loc. n., Lanark

ARBUTHNOT. A loc. n., Kincardineshire; anciently de Arberbothenoth, a barony

ARCH. From Arches; a loc. n., France. *N.-Fr.* Arques; *D.B.* de Arches, de Arcis; p.n.

> In Roll of Battell Abbey. Tenant in chief in *D.B.* Henry de Arches held land in Yorks *temp.* K. John. A Hugt. n., Lond. 1618.

ARCHARD. *N.-Fr.* Achard *A.S.* Archeard (Domfront, Norm. 1020); p.n. (strong hero)

ARCHBELL, ARCHBOLD. From Archibald; a p.n. *D.B.* Arcebald (a bold hero)

ARCHDALL. From Arkendale; a loc. n., Yorks

ARCHDEACON. From the office

ARCHER. *N.-Fr.* L'Archer; a p.n.

> Richard le Archer and Nicholas Archer in Rot. Obl. et Fin., K. John.

ARCHIBALD. *A.S.* Eorcenbeald, Arcenbald; *G.* Erchanbald; p.n. (sacred prince)

ARDA. *A.S.* Ard, Eard, Heard; p.n. (hard, strong)

ARDEN. A loc. n., Lanark, Yorks

ARDILL. From Ardle; a river, Perth (?). Or Hartell, Worcs.

ARDLEY. A loc. n., Herts

ARGLES. *Dch.* Arkels; a fam. n. *See* Arkle. Arcklus; a loc. n., Holland

ARGYLE. A loc. n., Scotl.

ARKCOLL, ARKELL, ARKILL, ARKLE. *A.S.* Arcytel, Arkil; *Dch.* Arkel (noble Ketel); p.n.

ARKWRIGHT. *Old G.* Archarat (hero - counsellor); or *A.S.* Archeard, Arch-hart (strong hero); p.n.

ARLESEY. From Arlsey; a loc. n., Beds

ARLIDGE. From Arley; a loc. n., Warw. *D.B.* Arlege (?)

ARLINGTON. A loc. n., Suss.

ARLOSH. From Harlosh; a loc. n., Skye

ARMER. *G.* Armer, Hermer; *Fl.* Harmer; p.n. *See* Harmer

ARMES, ARMIS. *D.* Harms; *Dch.* Armes; p.n. *See* Armer

ARMFIELD. *S.* Armfelt; a p.n. Or Amfield; a loc. n., Hants

ARMITAGE. A loc. n., Staff.

ARMON. *N.* Hermundr; *A.S.* Arimund (warrior - protector); *Fr.* Armand; p.n.

ARMSBY. *See* Ormsby

ARMSTEAD. *See* Hampstead

ARMSTRONG. From Armston (?); a loc. n., Northants. Or from the Irish Lamb Laidir (strong arm); a n.n.

ARMSWORTH. A loc. n., Hants

ARNALL, ARNELL. *See* Arnold

ARNE. A loc. n., Dorset; or *A.S., D.* p.n. (eagle)

ARNOLD. A loc. n., Notts, Wilts, Yorks; *D.B.* Ernehale. Or *N.* Arnhaldr (eagle - holder); *A.S.* Earnweald; p.n. A Prot. ref., Lond. 1618

ARNOTT. *Fr.* Arnaud; a Hugt. n., Lond. 1687

ARRAND. *A.S.* Arnold, Earnweald; *F., Dch., G.* Arend; p.n. (eagle ruler)

ARRINDELL. *See* Arundell

ARROWSMITH. *See* Athersmith

ARSCOTT. A loc. n., Salop

ARSTON. *See* Harston

ARTER, ARTHY, ARTHEY. *N.* Arnpórr; *A.S.* Arthur, Earnthor; *Fl.* Artur; p.n. (eagle Thor)

ARTIS. *N.* Hjörtr (a stag); *A.S.* Hart; *G.* Harter, Hart, Harte; *Fl.* Art, Arts, Artus; *D.* Hartig; *Dch.* Arts; p.n. Or *A.S. heard* (hard, strong)

ARUNDELL. A loc. n., Suss. R. Hirendale, Norm. 1198; also Fr. Hugt. n., Lond. 1618

ASBURY. From Ashbury; a loc. n., Berks, Devon. Or *see* Astbury

ASCOITH. *See* Askew

ASCOTT. A loc. n., Cornw.

ASH. *See* Dash

ASHBEE. *See* Ashby

ASHBRIDGE. From Agbridge; a loc. n., Yorks

ASHBURNER. *See* Ashburnham. Or *A.S.* Æscbeorn; a p.n. (spear bear)

ASHBURNHAM. A loc. n., Suss.; *D.B.* Esseborne
Held by de Criol, 1086.

ASHBY. A freq. loc. n.

ASHCROFT. A loc. n., Yorks

ASHDOWN. From Ashdon; a loc. n., Ess.

ASHENDEN. A loc. n., Herts

ASHFIELD. A loc. n., Suff.

ASHFORD. A loc. n., Derbys., Devon, Hants, etc.

ASHLEY. A loc. n., Hants, Wilts

ASHMAN. *N.* Ásmundr; *D.* Asmund; *G.* Assman; *Dch.* Asman; *A.S.* Asman, Osmund; p.n. *See* Osmund

ASHMORE. A loc. n., Dorset, Wilts

ASHPITEL. From Ashbrittle (?); a loc. n., Somers.

ASHPLANT. *See* Aspland

ASHPOLE. From Aspull; a loc. n., Lancs

ASHTON. A loc. n., Lancs, Hants, Herts, Glos., Wilts

ASHURST. A loc. n., Kent, Lancs, Suss.

ASHWELL. A loc. n., Herts, Rutl., Somers.

ASHWIN. *A.S.* Ascwine, Æscwine; p.n. (spear friend)

ASHWORTH. A loc. n., Lancs

ASKER. *N.* Askviðr (ash-pole or staff, spear); *D.* Askov; *S.* Asker; *Dch.* Asscher; *D.B.* Ascuit; p.n. Comp. Askew, Ascoith, etc.

ASKEW. A loc. n., Yorks; *D.B.* Ascwith, Hascoith; p.n. (Ashwood)
Held by Fitz-Akaris after 1086.

ASKHAM. A loc. n., Notts, Lancs

ASKIN. *See* Erskine

ASKWITH. *See* Askew

ASPDEN. From Aspenden; a loc. n., Herts

ASPINALL. *Fr.* Espagnol; a p.n. (a Spaniard); or a loc. n., Aspenhall (?)

ASPINWALL. *See* Aspinall

ASPLAND. *S.* Asplund, Espelund; a loc. and p.n.

ASPRAY. From Esperraye; a loc. n., Norm.

ASSHETON. A loc. n., Ess.

ASTBURY. A loc. n., Ches.

ASTELL. From Astwell; a loc. n., Northants

ASTLEY. A loc. n., Lancs, Salop, Warw., Worc.

ASTON. A loc. n., Glos., Hants, Heref., Salop

ASTOR. *N.-Fr.* Fitz-Estur; a p.n.
Wm. Fitz-Estur, Norm. 1180, And. Estor, 1198. Astor in Rot. Hund.

ASTPREY. *See* Aspray or Astbury

ASTROP. From Asthorpe; a loc. n., Herts; Astorp; a loc. n., Sweden

ATCHLEY. From Atcherley; a loc. n.
Sir Roger Atcherley, Lord Mayor of London, A.D. 1511.

ATCHIESON. *See* Atkinson

ATHAWES. From Atte-Hawes; a loc. n. Athus; a loc. n., Belg.

ATHERLEY. From Hatherleigh; a loc. n., Devon

ATHERSMITH. *F.* Athe; a p.n., and Schmid. Or *F.* Atteschmid, the obsolete form of Ritterschmid, an armourer, who belonged once to the lower orders of nobility

ATHERSTONE. A loc. n., Warw.

ATHERTON. A loc. n., Lancs
Robert de Atherton, Sheriff of Lancs, A.D. 1206.

ATHORNE. From Atte-Horn; a loc. n. Or Haythorne
Horn was a corner or triangular piece of land.

ATHORPE. From Authorpe; a loc. n., Lincs

ATHOW. From Hathow; a loc. n., Lincs. Or *see* Atto

ATKINS, ATKINSON. *See* Atto

ATLAY. *See* Attlee

ATTENBOROUGH. A loc. n., Notts

ATTERBURY. A loc. n., Devon

ATTERSLEY. *See* Haddesley

ATTFIELD. *See* Hatfield

ATTHEL, ATTLE. *A.S.* Æthel; a p.n. (noble)

ATTHILL. From Atte Hill
A surname adopted as early as the fourteenth century from place of residence (at the hill). Or *see* above.

ATTLEE. From Atterley; a loc. n., Salop. Or Hatley, Camb.
Atte-Lee, Court of Husting, 1258.

ATTMORE. From Atte-moor (at the moor)

ATTO, ATTOE. *N.* Höttr (Hattr) (a hood); *F.* Athe, Haddo, Hatto; *A.S.* Atto; *G.* Hatto; *Fl.* Athée, Attout; *D.* Hatting; *Dch.* Ates, Atten, Atkins; p.n. Or *see* Addy

ATTREE. Atte-tree; loc. n.

ATTRIDGE. Atte-ridge; loc. n. Or *A.S.* Ætheric, Æthelric (noble ruler)

ATTS. *See* Atto

ATTWATER. Atte-water; loc. n.

ATTWOOD. From Atte-wood

ATTY. From Athiès, near Amiens. *See* Atto.
John de Atie or Athy, custodian of Limerick, 1311.

ATWELL. From Atte-welle; a loc. n.
Court of Husting, London, 1258-1358.

ATYEO. *A.S.* æt-ea (at water); a loc. n. *See* Yeo

AUBREY. *N.-Fr.* De Alebrai
Norm. 1198. Sir Reg. A. held lands in Brecknock, 1088. *N.-Fr.* Aubraye, a place planted with elders.

AUCHINLECK. A loc. n., Ayr

AUCHMUTIE. *See* Achmuty

AUCOTT. From Hawcoat; a loc. n., Lancs (?)

AUDLAND. From Audlem (?); a loc. n., Ches.

AUDLEY. A loc. n., Ess., Staffs., formerly Aldithley

AUDSLEY. *See* Audley

AUGER. From Orgières (?); a loc. n., France; or pays d'Auge. *G.* Augar; a p.n.; *Fr.* Augier; a Hugt. n.

AUKER. *N.* Haukr (a hawk); *G.* Hauk, Hauke; *Fl.* Haucq; *Dch.* Aukes; *A.S.* Heafeca; p.n.

AUKLAND. A loc. n., Dur.

AUSTEN, AUSTIN. *D.* Augustin; *D.B.* Augustin, Austin; p.n.

AUSTWICK. A loc. n., Yorks

AVANT. From Havant; a loc. n., Hants

AVELEY, AVELING. From Aveline; a loc. n., Belg. *Fl.* Evely; *Dch.* Evelein; *D.B.* Avelin; p.n.

AVENELL. *N.-Fr.*; p.n.; *D.B.* Avenel (under tenant)
W. Avenel, in Rot. Obl. et Fin., K. John. Auneuil (?); a loc. n., France.

AVERELL. From Haverhill; a loc. n. Suff. Or Avril, Norm.

AVERY. From Evreux (?); a loc. n., Normandy. *See* Every
Cecil de Evereus in Rot. Obl. et Fin., K. John. Havery; Hugt. n., Norwich, 1622.

AWDRY. From Audrieu, near Caen, Norm.

AXFORD. A loc. n., Wilts

AXHAM. From Hexham; a loc. n., Northd.

AXON. From Auxonne; a loc. n., France

AYBEL. *See* Abell

AYERS, AYRES. *N.* Eyar; *N.-Fr.* Le Heres; *Fl.* Eyer, Eyers; p.n. (island warrior)

AYLESBURY. A loc. n., Bucks

AYLETT, AYLOTT. *D.*, *F.* Eilert; *D.B.* Ailet; *Fl.* Heylaert; *G.* Heilert; p.n. *See* Aylward

AYLIFFE. *N.* Eilífr (ever living); *D.B.* Ailof, Eilaf; p.n.

AYLING. From Eeelen, Belg.; a loc. n., Hants. Or *A.S.* Æling; a fam. n.; *Fl.* Elen, Eylen p.n.

AYLIVARD. *See* Aylward

AYLMER. *A.S.* Ælmer; a p.n. *See* Helm
Ailmar, a tenant in chief, *D.B.*

AYLWARD. *N.* Adelvardr; *A.S.* Æthelweard, Ailward (noble warden); *F.* Eilart; *D.* Eylard; *G.* Ehlert; p.n. *See* Aylett
Ailward in Rot. Obl. et Fin., K. John.

AYRTON. A loc. n. Yorks.

AYRE. From Ayr; a loc. n., Scotl.; Ere, Belg.; or Aire, France. *See* Ayers

AYSCOUGH. From Aysgarth; a loc. n., Yorks

AYSCUE. *See* Askew

AYTON. A loc. n., Berwick, Yorks

B

BAALAM, BAALHAM. From Baylham; a loc. n., Suff. Or Bellem; a loc. n., Fland; Bellème, France. *See* Bellamy
In Roll of Battell Abbey.

BAAS. *A.S.* Bass; *D.* Basse; *Dch.* Baas, Bas; *Fl.* Baes; p.n. (one in authority)
Le Bas in Rot. Obl. et Fin.

BABBAGE. *Fr.* Babiche; *G.* Babisch; p.n. (stranger)

BABBINGTON. A loc. n., Cornw., Northd., Notts, Somers.

BABBS. *A.S.* Babba (protector)
Babbe in Rot. Obl. et Fin.

BABER. A loc. n., Norf.

BACCHUS. *See* Backhouse

BACK. *A.S.* Bac; *Dch.* Bac, Bak; p.n. *See* Bagge. Or Welsh *bach* (little)

BACKHOUSE. *Dch.* Backhaus; a p.n.

BACON. *N.* Bekan (from the Gaelic); a p.n.
Bacun in Rot. Obl. et Fin., K. John.

BADCOCK. *A.S.* Bad, Bat, Beado; *D.* Badock; *G.* Badke, Batke; p.n. Dim. *beado* (war)

BADDELEY. From Baddiley; a loc. n., Ches.

BADGER. A loc. n., Salop. *D.B.* Beghesovre, Begesour, Bechesore

BADHAM. A loc. n., Cornw.

BADKIN. *Fl.* Batkin; a p.n. Dim. of Bad

BADLEY. A loc. n., Suff.

BADMAN. From Baudemont; a loc. n., Norm. Or *A.S.* Beadumund, Bademund; p.n. (war protector)

BAGGALLAY. *See* Baguley

BAGGE. *N.* Bögvir (a bag), or *bagga* (to hinder); *A.S.* Bag; *S.*, *Fl.*, *D.*, *Dch.* Bagge; *G.* Baake, Backe; p.n.
Bagge in Rot. Obl. et Fin., K. John.

BAGLEY. A loc. n., Berks, Salop, Somers.

BAGNALL. A loc. n., Staffs.

BAGOT. *Old G.* Badgad, Badgaut (battle Goth); *Fl.* Bygodt; *Fr.* Baguet; *D.B.* Baco, Bagod; p.n. *See* Bygod
Baggard, Bagod, Bagot, Bargard, Bigard, Bigod, Bigot, in Rot. Obl. et Fin., K. John.

BAGSHAW. From Bagshot; a loc. n., Surrey, Wilts

BAGULEY. A loc. n., Ches.

BAGWELL. *See* Bakewell

BAIGENT. *See* Bezant

BAILEY. From Belley, France. Or Beeleigh; a loc. n., Ess.; or *G.* Behlau; *Fl.* Beeli; p.n.; *Fr.* Baillé; a Hugt. n., Lond. 1688
Or it may be derived from the office of "bailiff," a title formerly applied to many feudal, municipal, and executive appointments. It also may have been "atte Bailey," the name given to the outworks of a castle.

BAIN. From Beyne; a loc. n., Belg. Prot. ref., Norwich, 1622. Or *see* Baines

BAINBRIDGE. A loc. n., Yorks

BAINES. From Baynes, near Bayeux, Norm. Or *N.* Beinir (legs, tall (?)); *F.* Baino, Beino; *D.* Behn; *S.* Been; *Fl.* Bayens, Beine, Beyns; *Dch.* Beens; *G.* Bens; *D.B.* Bain, Benz; p.n.

BAIRD. *N.-Fr.* Baiart; a p.n.
  Godf. Baiard, Northbd. 1165. Bard,
  Visct. Bellamont, Chas. I., Scotl.,
  12th cent.
BAKE. *See* Beck
BAKER. *A.S.* Becca; a p.n. (mat-
  tock). Or *Fl.* Becker; *G.* Becher;
  Dch. Becker, Beeke; p.n. *See*
  Beck, Becke, a Prot. ref. n.,
  Norwich, 1622.
    It may be from *Dch.* Bakker; a p.n.;
    A.S. bœcere (a baker). Le Baker
    in Rot. Hund., vols. i. ii.
BAKEWELL. A loc. n., Derbysh.
BALCHIN. *D.* Balchen; *Fl.* Bal-
  caen; *N.* Bálki (a beam); *D.B.*
  Balchi; *G.* Balcke; p.n.; or dim.
  of Baldr
BALCOMBE. A loc. n., Suss.
BALDCOCK. *See* Balchin
BALDERS. *N.* Baldr; *A.S.* Bald,
  Bold (foremost, bold); *G.* Balder;
  D. Bald, Balle, Boldt; *Dch.*
  Balder, Bols, Bolt; p.n.
BALDERSON, BALDERSTON. From
  Balderstone; a loc. n., Lancs
BALDING. *D., Dch.* Bolding; fam.
  n. of Bald. *See* Baldwin
BALDOCK. A loc. n., Beds
BALDRY. *A.S.* Baldric; a p.n.
  (bold ruler)
BALDWIN. *N.* Baldvinni (friend
  of the god Baldr); *A.S.* Beald-
  wine; *G.* Baldin; *Fl.* Bauduin,
  Boldewin (bold friend)
    The name of the Counts of Flanders.
    Bawdwin is on the Roll of Battell
    Abbey, and Baldwin among the
    tenants in chief in *D.B.*
BALE. A loc. n., Norf.; also Besle,
  France. *See* Bell
BALFOUR. A loc. n., Fife
BALLANTYNE. *See* Bannatyne
BALLARD. *A.S.* Bealdheard; a
  p.n. (strong)
BALLENGER, BALLINGER. *Fl.* Bel-
  langer; a p.n. Prot. ref. n.,
  Lond. 1688
BALLOCH. Irish *ballagh* (the
  freckled)

BALLS. *See* Balders
BALMER. From Balmire; a loc. n.,
  Cumb.
BAMBER. *See* Bambury
BAMBRIDGE. From Bembridge; a
  loc. n., Camb., Hants. Also
  Bambrugge, Flanders
BAMBURY. From Bamburgh; a
  loc. n., Lincs, Northd.
BAMFORD. A loc. n., Lancs;
  Derbysh.
BAMFYLDE. A loc. n., Somers.
BAMPTON. A loc. n., Cumb., Devon,
  Oxf., Westmd.
BANBURY. A loc. n., Oxon
BANCROFT. From Brancroft; a
  loc. n., Ches., Yorks. *See* Butler
    Held by Boteler.
BANE, BANEY. *See* Bain
BANFATHER. *N.* Bjarnvardr (bear-
  ward). Or *see* Pennefeather
BANGER, BANGERT. *Dch.* Bangert;
  A.S. Bangeard (death-guard); p.n.
BANGHAM. *See* Banham
BANGS. From Banc, near Hon-
  fleur. W. Bancs, Camb. 1203;
  or *D.* Bang; *G.* Banke; *Dch.*
  Bank; p.n. *See* Banger
BANHAM. A loc. n., Norf.
BANISTER, BANNISTER. From Ban-
  astre, now Beneter, near Etampes,
  Norm.
    In Roll of Battell Abbey. Warin B.,
    baron of Newton, Lancs, *temp.*
    Wm. I. Adam B. in Rot. Obl. et
    Fin.
BANNING. *A.S.* Baningas; a tribal
  n. *Bana* (a slayer)
BANKS. A loc. n., Yorks. Or *see*
  Bangs
BANNATYNE. From Ballindean; a
  loc. n., Perth. Or *see* Valentine
BANNER. *Dch., A.S.* Bana (a
  slayer); p.n.
BANNERMAN. *Dch.* Bonnerman; a
  p.n. *See* Banner
BANTHORPE. A loc. n.
BANTIN, BANTING. *Dch.*; p.n.;
  G. Bantein; a loc. n. *See* Pantin

BANYARD. *See* Banger
BARADALE. A loc. n., Ayrsh.
BARBEN. *See* Barbon.
BARBER, BARBOUR. From St Barbe sur Gaillon; a loc. n., Norm., where was the celebrated abbey of St Barbara; Barber or Barbour, a hamlet in Dumbartonshire. Or *Fr.* Barbe, Barbier, Barbare, Barberie, Barbry; *G.* Barber; p.n.
Bernard Barb and de Barbes, tenants in *D.B.* St Barbe is on the Roll of Battell Abbey. William de St Barbara, Bishop of Durham, A.D. 1143. Le Barbier, Court of Husting, Lond. 1258.

BARBEY. *Fr.* Barbé, Barbet, Barbey; p.n. (bearded)
Hugo Barbatus in *D.B.* (Hugh with the beard.)

BARBON. A loc. n., Westmd.
BARCLAY. *See* Berkeley
BARDELL, BARDILL. *See* Bardwell
BARDRICK. *D.B.* Baldric (foremost ruler); a p.n. Or *see* Brodrick
BARDSEY. A loc. n., Lancs
Anciently de Berdesey, Byrdeseey.
BARDSLEY. A loc. n., Lancs
BARDWELL. A loc. n., Suff.
BARE. *See* Bear
BAREFOOT. *See* Barfoot
BARFF. A loc. n., Lincs
BARFITT, BARFOOT. *D.* Barfod; *N.-Fr.* Barfot; p.n.
Norm. 1180, Rot. Hund.
BARGE. *Dch.*, *G.* Berg (a hill); p.n.
BARGMAN. *Dch.*, *G.* Bergmann (a miner); p.n.
BARHAM. A loc. n., Kent, Suff.
BARING. *A.S.* Beoring, Berring; fam. n. *See* Bear
BARKER. *N.* Börkr (bark); *S.* Barck; *Dch.* Barger; *Fl.* Barker; *G.* Barche; *N.-Fr.* Le Bercher; *D.B.* Barch; p.n.
BARKLEY. *See* Berkeley
BARKSHIRE. From Berkshire; the county

BARKUS. From Bargus; a loc. n., Cornw.
BARKWAY. A loc. n., Herts
BARKWORTH. From Barkwith; a loc. n., Lincs
BARLEE, BARLEY. A loc. n., Herts
BARLOW. A loc. n., Derbysh., Yorks
BARNABY. *See* Barnby. Or from Barnabas (?)
BARNACKLE. *N.* Bjornkell (bearkettle)
BARNARD. *N.* Bjarnarðr (strong bear); *Fl.* Barnard; *D.B.* Bernard; p.n.
BARNBY. A loc. n., Suff., Yorks
BARNES. From Berners or Bernieres; a loc. n., Norm. Also a loc. n., Surr.
BARNETT. From Barnet; a loc. n., Herts; or *G.* Barnatt, Barnert; *Fl.* Bernert; p.n. *See* Barnard
BARNEWALL. *See* Barnwell
BARNEY. From Bernai, Norm.; loc. n., Norf.; or *N.* Bjárni, a p.n.
BARNICLE. *See* Barnackle
BARNSDALE. A loc. n., Yorks
BARNSLEY. A loc. n., Dorset, Yorks
BARNWELL. From Barneville; a loc. n., Normandy
BARON. A loc. n., Normandy
BARR. La Barre, Norm.; a loc. n., Ayrshire, Staffs; or *A.S.* Bar (a bear). *D.* Barr; *Fl.* Bar; *N.-Fr.* de la Barre; p.n.
The Norman, de Dreux, assumed the name of de Barre from his manor of Great Barr. De la Barr, Hugt. n., Lond. 1618. Barre in Rot. Obl. et Fin.

BARRADALE. From Borrodale; a loc. n., Cumb.
BARRELL. *Fl.* Barel, Bareel; *D.* Baruël; *Fr.* Barill; p.n.; dim. of Bear. A Hugt. n., Cant. 1622
BARRET. *A.S.* Barath, Bared, Baret; *Fr.* Barette; p.n.; *A.S.* beor-ræd (bear counsel); *N.-Fr.* barette, a measure of corn; seems unlikely

BARRIE. A loc. n., Forfar
BARRINGTON. A loc. n., Camb., Lincs, Somers. Or from Barenton; a loc. n., Normandy
BARROW. A freq. loc. n. Or *D.* Barroe; *Dch.* Barrau; *Fl.* Baro; p.n.
BARRY. A loc. n., Belg. Or *see* Barrie
    In Roll of Battell Abbey.
BARSBY. A loc. n., Leics.
BARSTOW. From Barstone; a loc. n., Kent
BARTER. *See* Barth
BARTH. *D.*, *Dch.*, *Fl.*, *G.*; p.n.; a contr. of Bartholomew
BARTHORP, BARTHROPP, BARTROP, From Barthorp; a loc. n., Lincs
BARTINGTON. *See* Partington
BARTLETT. *G.* Bartelt; *Fr.* Bartalot; p.n.; dimin. of Bartholomew
BARTLEY. A loc. n., Hants, Worcs.
BARTON. A freq. loc. n.
BARWELL. From Berville, Norm. Also a loc. n., Leics.
BARWIS, BARWISE. *A.S.* Beornwig (war-bear); *Fr.* Barvais; *G.* Barwisch; p.n.
BASAN. *See* Bezant
BASCOMB, BASCUM. From Boscombe; a loc. n., Hants, Wilts
BASE. *See* Bayes
BASEY. *See* Beazer
BASHALL. A loc. n., Yorks
BASHAM. From Barsham; a loc. n., Norf.
BASHFORD. From Bassford; a loc. n., Staffs.
BASIN, BASSIN. *See* Bass
BASKETT. From the *Fr.* Bassecourt; a loc. n. Or Bosquet; a p.n.
BASS. A loc. n., Invury, Haddington. Or *see* Baas
BASSANT. *See* Bezant
BASSETT. *N.-Fr.* (a dwarf); dimin. of Bass. Under tenant in *D.B.* Also Hugt. n., Sandwich, 1622
BASTABLE. From Barnstaple; a loc. n., Devon. Or *N.-Fr.* Wasteble; a p.n.

BASTARD. *Dch.* Bastert; *Fl.* Batard; p.n.
    In Roll of Battell Abbey and in *D.B.* (baron), Devon. Wm. le Bastard held lands in Yorks *temp.* K. John.
BASTIN, BASTING. *Fr.* Bastien; *Fl.* Bastin; *Dch.* Basting; *D.* Bastian; p.n.; contr. of Sebastian
BASTOW. From Baston; a loc. n., Lincs
BATCHELDER, BATCHELOR. From Becelaere; a loc. n., Fland.; *Dch.* Baggelaar; *Fr.* Bachelier; *G.* Bachaly; p.n. Or *N.-Fr.* Bachlier, Bacheler (bachelor, esquire).
    Lewis Batchelier, Hugt. n., Lond. 1682.
BATE, BATES. *D.* Betz; *Dch.* Beets; *Fl.* Bette, Beths, Beetz, Bets; p.n.; Beez; a loc. n., Belg.
BATELEY. *See* Batley
BATEMAN. *S.* Betjeman; *Dch.* Betman; p.n. *See* Badman
BATGER. *See* Badger
BATH. A loc. n., Somers
BATHE. *A.S.* Bath, Beada; *Dch.* Bethe, Beth; p.n. (war)
BATHURST. A loc. n., Suss.
BATHY. From La Bathie, Norm. Or Welsh, Ab Adde (Adam)
BATLEY. A loc. n., Yorks
BATSFORD. A loc. n., Glost., Suff.
BATSON. *See* Bathy
BATT, BATTY, BATTYE. *See* Bathy
BATTAM. *See* Batterham or Badham
BATTCOCK. *See* Badcock
BATTELL, BATTLE. A loc. n., S. Wales, Suss. Or *N.-Fr.* Battaille; a p.n.
BATTEN. *N.-Fr.* Bethune or de Bethune; a p.n.
BATTERHAM. *See* Buttram
BATTERSBURY. From Battlesbury (?); a loc. n., Wilts
BATTERSBY. A loc. n., Yorks
BATTERSHALL. From Patishull (?); a loc. n., Staffs
BATTISCOMBE. From Bettiscombe; a loc. n., Dorset

BATTOCK. *See* Badcock
BATTRUM. *See* Buttrum
BAULY. From Beoley (?) ; a loc. n., Worcest. Or *see* Bowley
BAVE. *Fr.* Bavay ; a loc. and p.n.
BAVEN, BAVIN. From Bavent; a loc. n., Normandy ; *Fl.* Bawin ; a p.n.
BAWDEN. A loc n., Cornw. Or *see* Baldwin
BAWN. *D.* Baun ; *Fl.* Bauwen ; p.n. Or Irish *ban* (white)
BAWTREE. From Bawtry ; a loc. n., Yorks
BAXENDALE. A loc. n.
BAXENDEN. A loc. n., Lancs
BAXTER. The Scot. and N. Engl. form of Baker. *A.S. bæc-estre,* a f. baker
BAYES, BAYS. *Fl.* Baye ; *D.* Beyer ; *Dch.* Bes, Bey, Bies; p.n. *See* Bee
BAYLISS. *Fl.* Bellis ; a p.n. Or Welsh ab Elis
BAYNES. *See* Baines
BAYNHAM. *See* Banham
BAYNTON. A loc. n., Northants, Oxf., Yorks
BAZELEY. *See* Beasley
BEACH. *N.-Fr.* De la Beche ; a p.n. ; Goisfrid de Bech, t. in chief, Hertfd, 1086. *See* Beck
BEACHAM. From Beauchamp ; a loc. n. in the Cotentin, France
BEACOM. *Dch.* Becküm, Beekum ; p.n. Or *see* Beacham
BEADLE. From Bedale ; a loc. n., Yorks ; or *N.-Fr.* Bedel, a p.n., Bucks, 1086
BEADMAN. *See* Badman
BEADSMORE. From Birdsmoor; a loc. n., Dorset. De Berdesmor, 1327
BEAMAND, BEMAND. Welsh Ap Edmund ; a p.n.
BEAK. *See* Bick
BEAL. A loc. n., Yorks
BEALE. A loc. n., Dur.
BEALES. From Bealings ; a loc. n., Suff.
BEALEY. From Beeley ; a loc. n., Derbysh.

BEAMENT. *See* Beaumont
BEAMES. *See* Beamish
BEAMISH. A loc. n., Dur.
BEAN. From Bienne ; a loc. n., Belg. ; *D., Dch.* Biene ; a p.n. (a bee). Prot. ref., Norwich, 1622
BEANHAM. *See* Baynham
BEANLANDS. A loc. n., Cumb.
BEAR. *N.* Bera (a bear); *A.S.* Beor; *D.* Bjerre ; *D.B.* Bere ; *Dch., Fl.* Beer, Behr ; *G.* Behr ; p.n. Or Baer; a loc. n., Belg. ; Fl. ref., Lond. 1618
BEARCHELL. From Bircholt (?) ; a loc. n., Kent
BEARCROFT. A loc. n.
BEARD. *See* Baird. *Fl.* Baert ; a Hugt. n. ; Lond. 1618
BEARDMORE. *See* Beadsmore
BEARDSHAW. A loc. n.
BEARDSLEY. From Buwardsley, Ches. Or *see* Bardsley
BEARDSWORTH. From Beardswood ; a loc. n., Lancs
BEARDWELL. From Bardwell ; a loc. n., Suff.
BEASANT. *See* Bezant
BEASEY. *See* Bessey
BEASLEY. From Beazley ; a loc. n., Warw.
BEASTON. *See* Beeston
BEATON. From Bethune in Artois ; *Fr.* Bethune ; a p.n. Or from Beighton; a loc. n., Derbys., Norf., Suff.
BEATTIE or BEATTY. From the Irish Betagh (biadhtach), a public victualler ; p.n. Or *A.S.* Betti ; a p.n. *See* Bathy
BEAUMONT. A loc. n., Belg. and Normandy.
> In Roll of Battell Abbey. *D.B.* De Belmont, Bomene. Rot. Obl. et Fin., K. John.

BEAVEN, BEAVIN, BEAVON. *See* Bevan
BEAZER. From Baisy ; a loc. n., France. Or *Fr.* Bisez ; a p.n.
> Bisi or Bysey in the Roll of Battell Abbey. *See* Bessey

BEBELL. *A.S.* Babel; a p.n. Dim. of Babba

BECCLES. A loc. n., Suff.

BECK. From Beeck; a loc. n., Belg.; *D.*, *S.*, *G.*, *Dch.* Beck; *Fl.* Baeck; p.n. Atte Becke, 1327
Beke on the Roll of Battell Abbey. De Bec, a tenant in chief, Walter Bec at the time of the Survey, in *D.B.* Bec and Bek in Rot. Obl. et Fin., K. John. Also Prot. ref., Lond., 1618; Norwich, 1622.

BECKETT. *A.S.* Beagheard; *Dch.* Beket; *Fl.* Beckaert, Becquart, Becquet; *N.-Fr.* Bechet, Béquet; p.n. (strong crown)

BECKFORD. A loc. n., Hants

BECKHAM. A loc. n., Norf.

BECKLEY. A loc. n., Hants, Suss.

BECKWITH. A loc. n., Yorks

BED. *N.*, *A.S.* Beda; *Fr.* Béde; *Fl.* Bette; *G.*, *Dch.* Beth; p.n. *See* Bathe

BEDALL. From Bedale; a loc. n., Yorks. Or *A.S.* *bidel*, a beadle

BEDDOE. *A.S.* Beada; *G.* Beddau; *Fr.* Bidaut; p.n. Or Welsh Ab Edward. *See* Bathe

BEDFORD. A loc. n., the county town

BEDINGFIELD. A loc. n., Suff.

BEDSON. From Bedstone; a loc. n., Salop

BEDWARD. Welsh, Ab Edward; a p.n.

BEDWELL. A loc. n., Beds

BEE. *D.*, *Dch.* Bie, Bye; *N.* Bui; p.n. *See* Bye (a neighbour)

BEEBEE. From Beeby; a loc. n., Leics.

BEECH. *See* Beach

BEECHEY. *See* Beeching

BEECHING. A loc. n., Suss., Wilts

BEECROFT. *See* Bearcroft

BEEDELL. *See* Bedall

BEEDEN. A loc. n., Berks or Bidon, Burgundy

BEEFORTH. From Beaford; a loc. n., Devon

BEEL. *A.S.* Bil; *Old G.* Bilo; *G.* Bill, Biel; *Fl.* Beel; p.n. (gentle)

BEER. A loc. n., Devon. Or *see* Bear

BEESLEY, BESLEY. *See* Beasley

BEESTON. A loc. n., Norf., Notts

BEETHAM. *See* Betham

BEETLES. *See* Bedall

BEETON. *See* Beaton

BEETS. *See* Bates

BEEVER. *A.S.* Beffa; *Fl.* Bevers; *Fr.* Biver; p.n. (a beaver)

BEGBIE. From Bigby; a loc. n.; Lincs

BEGG. *A.S.* Beg; a p.n. *See* Bigg. Or Irish p.n. (little)

BEHAG. *N.* Baugr; a n.n. (ring of a shield, also money); *A.S.* Beag; a p.n.; *Fl.* Behagel; p.n.; dim. Hugt. n., Sandwich, 1622

BEILBY. From Belby; a loc. n., Yorks

BEITH. A loc. n., Ayr, Renfrew. Or *G.* Bieth; a p.n.

BELCHAM. From Belchamp; a loc. n., Ess. *D.B.* De Belchamp; p.n. Or *Fr.* Beljambe; a p.n.

BELCHER. From Bellecourt; a loc. n., Normandy, near Perrone, and in Belg.

Bellesur in Roll of Battell Abbey.

BELDAN, BELDEN, BELDING. From Beltinge; a loc. n., Kent

BELFRAGE. From the Norman-French Beaufoy, Latinised into de Bella Fago. *D.B.* Belvaco, Belvou; p.n.

BELHAM, BELHOMME. *See* Baalam

BELL. *N.* Beli (obese); *F.* Bela, Bêl, Bele; *S.* Bell; *A.S.*, *Dch.* Bel; *Fl.*, *N.-Fr.* Baele, Beli; p.n. Le Bel in Rot. Obl. et Fin. (the handsome)

BELLAIRS. *See* Bellares

BELLAMY. A *Fr.* p.n. from Bellème; a loc. n. in Normandy. *D.B.* Belam; *D.* Beilum; *Fl.* Belemme; *Dch.* Bellm; p.n.; *Fl.* ref., Lond. 1618

Beelhelme in Roll of Battell Abbey.

BELLARS, BELLARES. From Bellaires; a loc. n., Belg.; *Fl.* Bellers; a p.n.
Beleuers in Roll of Battell Abbey. Hamon Bellars was a hostage to K. John, A.D. 1216 (Whitwick, Leics.). De Belhus and De Bello in Rot. Obl. et Fin.

BELLASIS. A loc. n., Cornw., Northbd., Yorks; *Fr.* de Belassize; a loc. n., Norm.
Ballisise in Roll of Battell Abbey.

BELLCHAMBER. From Bellencombre Castle, near Dieppe. Bernd. de B. Suff. 1086, Ess. 1272. Rot. Hund.

BELLEW. *Fr.* Bellot; a p.n. From Belleau; a loc. n., Norm.
Bellew in Roll of Battell Abbey; Belot, a tenant in chief in *D.B.* Gaufrid Belewe and Robt. de Baleewe in Rot. Obl. et Fin., K. John.

BELLIN. *A.S.* Bæling; *Fl.* Belin, Bellen, Belyn; p.n. *See* Bell. A Hugt. n., Lond. 1685

BELLINGHAM. A loc. n., Northbd.

BELLIS. Welsh Ab Ellis. *See* Bayliss

BELLOE. *See* Bellew

BELLOWS. *See* Bellew

BELSCHES. *See* Bellasis

BELSHAM. *See* Belchamp

BELSHAW. *See* Belcher

BELSTEN. *See* Belston

BELSTON. A loc. n., Devon

BELTON. A loc. n., Leics.

BELWARD. *A.S.* Belweard, Beluuard; p.n. (gentle guard)

BEMROSE. From Penrhôs(?); a loc. n., Wales. Or Penrose, Cornwall

BENBOW. From Benningborough; a loc. n., Yorks

BENCE. In Rot. Hund. 1272. *See* Benson, Benns. A Hugt. n., Sandwich, 1662

BENDALL. *D.* Bendahl, Bendal; *Dch.* Bendel; p.n. A loc. n. (?)

BENDELOW. *Dch.* Bentelaar; a p.n. (one from Bendal)

BENDER. *D.*, *Dch.*, *Fl.*, *G.*; p.n.

BENDING. *D.* Benthin; *Dch.* Bendien, Bentinck; p.n. *See* Benn

BENDON. From Benton; a loc. n., Northmbd. Or Benden; a Hugt. n., Lond. 1618.

BENDY. *G.* Bendig; a p.n. (Benedict (?))

BENFIELD. From Benefield; a loc n., Northants

BENFORD. From Bainsford; a loc. n., Stirling

BENHAM. From Benholme; a loc. n., Kincardine

BENINGFIELD. *See* Benfield

BENN, BENNETT, BENNY. Dimin. of Benedict. Hugt. n., Lond. 1688

BENNION. Welsh, Apwenwyn (ap Einion), *eynon* (just); a p.n. *See* Beynon

BENNINGTON. A loc. n., Lincs

BENNISON. *See* Benson

BENSLEY. A loc. n., Ayr

BENSON. *N.* Benni and Bensi; *F.* Benne (dimin. of Benedict); *S.* Benzon; *D.* Bengtsen, Bendsen, Benzen; *Dch.* Bense; *D.B.* Benz; p.n.

BENSTED, BENSTEAD. From Binstead; a loc. n., Hants, Suss.

BENT. *D.* Bendt; a p.n. *See* Benn

BENTHALL. A loc. n., Salop

BENTHAM. A loc. n., Staffs.

BENTLEY. A loc. n., Yorks

BENWELL. A loc. n., Northbd.

BENYON. *See* Bennion

BERBIDGE. *See* Burbage

BERGAN, BERGEN. *See* Burgoyne

BERGIN. *See* Burgoyne

BERKELEY. A loc. n., Glos.

BERRALL. *See* Burrell

BERRETT. *See* Barret
Barrett in Roll of Battell Abbey.

BERRICK. *See* Berwick

BERRIDGE. From Berwich; a loc. n., Ess.

BERRY. A loc. n., Devon and Normandy; or from the Irish O'Beara; a p.n.

BERWICK. A loc. n., Ess., Northbd., Wilts

BESANT. *See* Bezant

BESFORD. A loc. n., Worc.

BESSELL. *A.S.* Besel. Dim. of Besa. *D.* Bestle; a p.n.

BESSEY. *A.S.* Besi; a p.n.

BEST. A loc. n., Holl. *D.*, *Dch.*, *Fl.*, *G.* p.n. De Best; *Fl.* ref., Lond. 1618

BESTOW. *See* Bastow

BESWICK. A loc. n., Yorks

BETHAM. A loc. n., Westmd.
Ralph de Betham was a benefactor to Furness Abbey, Hen. II.

BETHELL. *G.* Bethel; *Fl.* Beethel; p.n. Dim. *See* Bathe. Or Welsh Ab Ithell

BETSWORTH, BETTESWORTH. From Betchworth; a loc. n., Surrey

BETT. *Fl.* Bette; *Dch.*, *G.* Beth; p.n. *See* Bathe

BETTELEY. From Betley; a loc. n., Staffs.

BETTERIDGE. From Pettridge; a a loc. n., Kent. Or *A.S.* Beaduric; a p.n. (battle ruler)

BETTERTON. A loc. n., Berks

BETTS. *See* Bates

BETTY. *See* Beattie

BEVAN. From Bièvène; a loc. n., Belg. Or Welsh ab Evan
Bevan and Bevin occur in Rot. Obl. et Fin., K. John.

BEVERIDGE. *See* Berridge

BEVINGTON. A loc. n., Lancs

BEVINS. *A.S.* Bafing, Beofing; *Fl.* Beving; p.n.; fam. n. of Beever

BEVIS. From Beauvais; a loc. n., France
In Roll of Battell Abbey. W. Beaufiz de Rya in Rot. Obl. et Fin., K. John.

BEW. *See* Pugh or Boow

BEWICK. A loc. n., Yorks

BEWLEY. A loc. n., Westmd.

BEWSHER. *See* Butcher

BEX. *Fl.* Bex; *D.* Becks; p.n. *See* Beck

BEYNON. *See* Bennion

BEZANT. From Beausaint; a loc. n., Belg. Or *Fr.* Baisant; a Hugt. p.n. A Byzantine coin. In heraldry a disc without impress

BIBBINGTON. From Bebington; a loc. n., Ches.

BIBBY. *See* Beebee

BICHENS. *A.S.* Bic, Big; p.n. *See* Bigg

BICK. *A.S.* Bic, Big (a crown), chaplet; *Fr.* Bické, Bicqué; *G.* Bick; p.n.

BICKELL, BICKLE. *Fr.*, *Dch.* Bickel, Bichel; p.n. Dim. of Bic

BICKER. A loc. n., Lincs. *See* Bick

BICKERDYKE. A loc. n.

BICKERSTETH. From Bickerstaffe; a loc. n., Lancs; anciently Bykyrstath, Bekerstath

BICKERTON. A loc. n., Norf.

BICKFORD. A loc. n., Staffs.

BICKLEY. A loc. n., Kent, Worcest. Or Bickleigh, Devon

BICKMORE. From Bicknor; a loc. n., Glos., Heref., Kent

BICKNELL. From Bickenhall; a loc. n., Somers. Or Bickenhill, Warw.

BICKTON. From Bickton; a loc. n., Cornw., Devon, Hants

BIDDLE. *See* Biddulph or Bedall

BIDDLECOMBE. A loc. n.

BIDDULPH. A loc. n., Staffs.

BIDGOOD. From Bidacott (?); a loc. n., Devon

BIDMEAD. A loc. n.

BIDWELL. A loc. n., Beds

BIGG. *A.S.* *D.* Big; *G.* Bick; *Dch.* Bicker; a p.n. *See* Bick

BIGGADIKE. *See* Bickerdyke

BIGGAR. A loc. n., Lanarks

BIGGEN. A loc. n., Dur.

BIGGINS. A loc. n., Derbysh.

BIGGS. A loc. n. (?). Peter de Bixe in Rot. Obl. et Fin., K. John. *See* Bigg

BIGHAM. *See* Bingham

BIGNALL, BIGNELL. A loc. n., Staffs.

BIGSBY, BIXBY. From Bigby; a loc. n., Lincs

BILBOROUGH. A loc. n., Notts, Yorks

BILBY. A loc. n., Notts. Or Beilby, Yorks

BILL. *A.S.* Bil, Bill; *D.*, *G.*, *Fr.*, *Dch.* Bille; p.n. (a sword)

BILLETT. *N.-Fr.* Belet; p.n.

BILLING. A loc. n., Lancs, Northants, Yorks (contr. of Billingham); or *D.S.* Billing; *Fl.* Billen; p.n.
Billing, an ancient noble northern clan.

BILLINGTON. A loc. n., Staffs.

BILLYARD. *A.S.* Bilgeard; *Fr.* Billiard; p.n. A Hugt. n., Dover, 1622 (gentle protection)

BILTON. From Bilston; a loc. n., Staffs.

BINDLEY. A loc. n., Hants

BINDLOSS. *G.* Bindlos; a p.n. (bandless)

BINDON. A loc. n., Hants

BINGHAM. A loc. n., Notts. Held by De Buisli
Hugo and Robert de Bingeham in Rot. Obl. et Fin., K. John (Notts).

BINGLEY. A loc. n., Yorks

BINKS. *D.* Bing, Bink; *A.S.* Bing; *Fr.* Binne; *S.* Bing; *G.* Bieneck; *Dch.* Bing, Binger, Bink; p.n.
This patronymic gives the names to Bing (Suff.), Bingham (Notts), Bingley (Yorks), Bingen (Rhine), Binges (Burgundy).

BINLESS. *See* Bindloss

BINNEY. From Binnie; a loc. n., Linlithgow

BINNS. A loc. n., Roxburgh. Or from Binche; a loc. n., Belg.; *Dch.*, *Fl.* Bins; *G.* Binas; p.n.

BINSTEAD. A loc. n., Hants, Suss.

BINYON. *See* Bennion

BIRCH. A loc. n., Ess., Lancs, Salop, Yorks. Or *see* Burch

BIRCHALL. From Bircholt; a loc. n., Kent

BIRCHAM. A loc. n., Norf. Or Berchem, Belg.

BIRCHENOUGH. *A.S.* Burchenoth, Burgnoth; p.n. (courageous protector). Or *Dch.* Berkenhoff; a loc. and p.n. *A.S. birchenhóf* (birch house)

BIRCHINGTON. A loc. n., Kent

BIRCHMORE. A loc. n., Warw.

BIRD, BIRT. *A.S.* Birht, Beorht; *D.* Bird; *Fl.* Burdo, Burth; *G.* Burde, Berto, Berdie; *Fr.* Bert; p.n. (bright)

BIRDSEYE. *See* Bardsey

BIRKENSHAW. A loc. n., Yorks

BIRKETT. *See* Borret

BIRKIN. A loc. n., Yorks
De Birchinges, a tenant in chief in *D.B.* John de Birkin held land in Yorks *temp.* K. John.

BIRKLE. From Birkhall; a loc. n., Aberdeen. Or Birkhill, Fife

BIRLEY. A loc. n., Heref.

BIRMINGHAM. A loc. n.
Held by Fulco Paynel *temp.* Hen. I. Peter de B. went to Ireland and was ancestor of the Earls of Louth.

BIRNIE. A loc. n., Elgin

BIRRELL. *See* Burrell

BIRTHWRIGHT. From Birthwaite; a loc. n., Westmd.

BISPHAM. A loc. n., Lancs

BISS. From La Bisse; a loc. n., Norm. Or *A.S.* Byssa, *bisi* (?) (busy); *S.* Bishe; p.n.

BISSELL. *N.-Fr.* Bichell; a p.n. (a hind). Or dim. of Biss. *See* Buscall

BISSETT. *Fr.* Bissot; *G.* Bissert; p.n. A Hugt. n., Lond. 1618
Biset in Rot. Obl. et Fin.

BISSICKS. Welsh Ab Isaac (?)

BISSMIRE. *G.* Bessemer; *Fl.* Pessemier; *A.S.* Bisimær; p.n. (Besi the famous)

BITTLESTON. From Biddlestone; a loc. n., Heref.

BIXBY. *See* Bigsby

BIZLEY. *See* Beasley

BIZZELL. *See* Bissell

BLABY. A loc. n., Leics.
BLACK. *A.S.* Blac, Blæc ; *D.* Black; *Fl.* Blake ; *Dch.* Blaak, Blak ; p.n. *See* Blake
BLACKABY. From Blackfordby; a loc. n., Leics.
BLACKADDER. A loc. n., Scotl.
BLACKALL. A loc. n., Devon
BLACKBORN. *See* Blackburn
BLACKBURN. A loc. n., Lancs, Linlithgow
BLACKFORD. A loc. n., Devon
BLACKGROVE. From Blagrave ; a loc. n., Berks
BLACKLEDGE. *See* Bleackley
BLACKLOCK. From Black Loch ; a loc. n., Lanark, Renfrew, Stirling
BLACKMORE. From Blackmoor ; a loc. n., Somers.
BLACKSTONE. A loc. n., Devon

Held by Alured le Breton, 1086.

BLACKTIN. From Blackden ; a loc. n., Ess.
BLACKWELL. A loc. n., Derbysh., Dur., Worc.
BLACRE. *Fr.* De Blacquiere ; a p.n.
BLADE. From Bleid ; a loc. n., Belg. Or *A.S.* Blæd ; *D.* Blad, Bladt ; *S.* Blad ; *Fl.* Bled ; *Dch.* Blad, Blatt ; *Scot.* Blate ; *G.* Blöde (blade of a sword) ; p.n.
BLADES. A loc. n., Yorks
BLADON. From Bladen ; a loc. n., Dorset
BLAGBURN. *See* Blackburn
BLAGDEN. *See* Blagdon
BLAGDON. A loc. n., Devon
BLAGG. *See* Black
BLAGROVE. From Blagrave ; a loc. n., Berks
BLAIR. A loc. n., Perth
BLAKE. *Dch.* Bleek ; *Fl.* Blieck ; *N. bleikr* ; p.n. (pale). *See* Black

Walter Blacke. Rot. Hund. 1273.
Le Blake in Rot. Obl. et Fin.

BLAKEMORE. From Blakemere ; a loc. n., Heref.
BLAKENEY. A loc. n., Glos., Norf.
BLAKESLEY. A loc. n., Northants
BLAKISTON. A loc. n., Dur.
BLAMIRE. *D.* Blumer ; *Dch.* Bloemer ; *Fl.* Bloemart ; a p.n. Or *N.* blá-mœr (blue moor), a poetical name for the sea
BLAND. *A.S.* Bland ; *Fr.* Blandre ; p.n. (blend, mixture, perhaps racial)
BLANDFORD. A loc. n., Dorset
BLANKLEY. From Blankney ; a loc. n., Lincs
BLATCH. *D.* Blache ; *G.* Blach, Blasche ; p.n. *See* Black
BLATCHLEY. From Bletchley ; a loc. n., Oxon, Salop
BLATHERWAYT, BLATHWAYT. From Bleathwaite ; a loc. n., Cumb.
BLATHERWICK. A loc. n., Northants
BLAXALL. A loc. n., Suff.
BLAXLAND. From Blackland ; a loc. n., Suff.
BLAY, BLEY. *See* Bly
BLAYDON. *See* Bladon
BLAYNEY. From Blaney ; a loc. n., Fermanagh
BLAZY. From St Blazey ; a loc. n., Cornw. and France. *Fr.* Blaise ; *Dch.* Blaze, Blazer, Bles ; *Fl.* Blaes, Blazy ; *D.B.* Blize ; p.n.
BLEACKLEY. From Blakeley ; a loc. n., Lancs
BLEANEY. *See* Blayney
BLEASBY. A loc. n., Lincs
BLEASDALE. A loc. n., Lancs
BLEASDELL. *See* Bleasdale
BLEASE. *See* Bliss
BLEBY. *See* Blaby
BLECHYNDEN. A loc. n., Hants
BLENCOE. From Blencow; a loc. n., Cumb.
BLENKARNE. From Blencarn ; a loc. n., Cumb.
BLENKIN. *See* Blenkarne
BLENKINSOPP. A loc. n., Northbd.

BLENNERHASSET. A loc. n., Cumb. Held by De Tilliol *temp.* Hen. I.

BLESSLEY. *See* Blatchley

BLEW, BLOW. *G.* Blüh; a p.n.

BLEWITT. From Briqueville la Blouette; a loc. n., Norm. *Fr.* Bluet; *D.B.* Bloiet; p.n. (cornflower)
Bluat in Roll of Battell Abbey. Robert Bloet, Bishop of Lincoln. 1093. Robert Bloet held land in Wilts *temp.* K. John, 1201.

BLEZARD. *See* Blizard

BLICK. *N.* Blígr (shy); *S.* Blix; *D.* Blicker; *Fl.* Blieck; *G.* Blicke; *Dch.* Bliek; p.n.

BLIGH. *See* Blick or Bly. *N.* *bljúgr*; *S.* *blyg*; *D.* *bly* (bashful, shy)

BLIGHT. *A.S.* Blith; *D.* Blyt; p.n. (joyful)

BLISS. From Blois; a loc. n., Norm.
W. de Bleys, Worcs., Rot. Hund. 1272.

BLIZARD. *A.S.* Blic, Plec, Plegheard; *D.* Blichert; p.n. (strong sword player)

BLOCK. *A.S.* Bloc; *D.* Blok; *Dch.*, *Fl.* Block; *Fr.* Bloc; p.n. (a block; one who lived in a log hut)

BLOCKIN. *See* Block; fam. n.

BLOCKLEY. A loc. n., Worcest.

BLOGG. *Dch.* Blog; a p.n. *See* Block

BLOMEFIELD. From Blomville, near Caen

BLOOD. *G.* Blöde; *Dch.* Blöte; p.n. *See* Blade

BLOOM. *S.* Blom; *D.* and *Fl.* Blom, Blum; *Dch.* Bloem, Blom, Blum; *G.* Bluhm, Blum, Blume; p.n. (a flower)

BLORE. A loc. n., Staffs.

BLOSS. *See* Blowers

BLOSSOM. *See* Bloxham

BLOTT. *A.S.* Blœdda; *S.* Blad; *Dch.* Blöte; p.n. *See* Blade

BLOUNT. *See* Blunt

BLOWERS. *D.* Bloes; a p.n. (naked)

BLOWEY. *See* Bloye

BLOXAM. From Bloxham; a loc. n., Lincs

BLOY, BLOYE. From Blois; a loc. n., Normandy

BLUDWORTH. From Blidworth; a loc. n., Notts

BLUETT. *See* Blewitt

BLUNDELL. *Fr.* Blondel; a p.n. Dim. of blonde (fair)
Robert Blundel in Rot. Obl. et Fin., K. John.

BLUNT. *N.* Blundr (sleepy); a n.n.; *D.B.* Blund; a p.n.
Blund in Rot. Obl. et Fin., K. John.

BLY. From Blaye; a loc. n., France. *G.* Blei, Bloy; *Dch.* Bleij; *D.B.* Bleio; p.n.

BLYTH. A loc. n., Northbd., Notts

BOAG, BOAK. *N.* Bogi (a bow, or bowshaped); *D.B.* Boche; *D.* Boeck, Booek; *Dch.* Bock, Boeg, Bok; *G.* Bock, Böge; p.n. Or *see* Bugg

BOARBANK. *See* Bowerbank

BOARD, BOORD. *A.S.* Bord, Brord (a sword); *Dch.* Bordes; p.n.

BOAREE. *Dch.* Boeree; *G.* Boerey; p.n. (rustic, countryman)

BOASE, BOAZ. *D.* Boas, Boese, Bohse; *Dch.* Boas; *Fl.* Boes; *Fr.* Bous; *G.* Boas, Boos; *A.S.* Boso; p.n.

BOAST. *Fr.* Bost, Boust; p.n.

BOATWRIGHT. *See* Botwright

BOBBIT. *Dch.* Bobbert; a p.n.

BOBBY. *A.S.* Bobba, Bubba; *G.* Bube, Bober, Bobisch; *D.* Bobe; *Dch.* Bobbe; *Fr.* Bobée; p.n. (a boy)

BOCOCK. *See* Boocock

BODDINGTON. A loc. n., Glos., Northants

BODENHAM. A loc. n., Wilts and Heref.

BODGER, BOGER. *N.-Fr.* Boschier; *G.* Böger; p.n.
W. le Boghier, Rot. Hund. 1272.

G

BODGINER. *Fr.* Bodinier; a p.n. *boudinier* (a pudding maker)

BODILLY. A loc. n., Cornwall. *See* Baddeley

BODKIN. *D.* Bodecker; *Dch.* Boddeke; p.n. Dim. of Bode Bodkint in Rot. Obl. et Fin., K. John.

BODLE. *See* Boodle

BODLEY. *See* Badley

BODY. *N.* Boddi. Dimin. of Bödvarr (wary in battle). Or *A.S.* Boda, Boter, Boti, Bot; *Fr.* Bodé; *D.* Bodi, Bodin, Bott; *Fl.* Bodhy, Body; *G.* Bods, Bode, Böde; *S.* Bode, Bodin; *Dch.* Boddé, Bode, Bodt, Botter, Bott; p.n. (a messenger)

BOFFAY. From Beaufay; a loc. n., Norm.

BOFFIN. From Bovignes; a loc. n., Belg. Or *N.* Bófi; a p.n.; *A.S.* Bofing; a fam. n.; *Fr.* Boffin; a p.n.; Bovin, a Hugt. n., Lond. 1685

BOGERT. *Dch.*, *Fl.* Bogaert; *Fr.* Boygard; *Dch.* Bogaardt; p.n. (bow guard). Hugt. n., Lond. 1681

BOGG. *See* Boag

BOGGERS, BOGGIS. A p.n.

BOGGS, BOGGERS, BOGGIS. *N.-Fr.* De Bogis or De Boges; p.n., 1180

BOGUE. *See* Boag

BOHANAN. *See* Buchanan

BOLDERS. *See* Balders

BOLES. *See* Bowles

BOLITHO. A loc. n., Cornw.

BOLIVER. Welsh Ab Oliver

BOLLAND. A loc. n., Yorks, Belg.; Boilantes, Norm.

BOLLARD. *A.S.* Baldred, Boldred; *Fr.* Boulard; a p.n. *See* Pollard

BOLLINGTON. A loc. n., Ess.

BOLSHAW. From Balsham; a loc. n., Camb.

BOLSOVER. A loc. n., Derbys.

BOLSTER. *See* Alabaster

BOLT. From Bolt or Bout, Norm. *N.-Fr.* De Boalt; *D.*, *Dch.*; p.n.

BOLTON. A freq. loc. n.

BOLUS. *See* Bowles

BOMPAS. From Bonpas, near Perpignan

BONALLACK. From Banhaglog; a loc. n., Montgomeryshire

BONAR. A loc. n., Sutherland

BONCHER, BONSHER. *N.-Fr.* Bonnechière (bon visage); a p.n.

BOND. *N.* Bondi (a yeoman); *D.* Bond; *S.* Bonde; *Fl.* Bondue; *A.S.* Bonde, Bondi, Bundi; p.n.

BONE. From Bohon; loc. n., Normandy. Or *Fr.* Bouhon; *Dch.* Boon; *G.* Bohn; *D.*, *Fl.* Bon; p.n. A Hugt. n., Lond. 1621 De Buun in Rot. Obl. et Fin.

BONEHILL. A loc. n., Staff.; or Bonhill, Dumbarton. Or *N.-Fr.* Bonnel; *Dch.* Bonel; p.n. A Hugt. n., Lond. 1618

BONFIELD. *See* Bonville

BONHAM. A loc. n., Somerset

BONIFACE. *Dch.*, *G.* Bonifacius; *Fr.* Boniface; p.n. (well-doer)

BONIWELL. *See* Bonville

BONNER. From Bonnard; a loc. n., France. *Fr.* Bonnard, Bonneau, Bonheur; p.n. Hugt., Lond. 1618. Or *N.-Fr.* Bonnaire (courteous); a p.n. *See* Bunner

BONNETT. *Fr.* Bonnet; p.n. Bonnat and St Bonnet; loc. n., France Bonet in Rot. Obl. et Fin.

BONNEY, BONNY. *Fr.* Bonné; a p.n. (capped). Or *see* above

BONSALL. From Boncelles; a loc. n., Belg. Or Bonsall, Derbys.

BONVILLE. A loc. n., near Rouen, Normandy

BOOBY, BOOBYER. A loc. n. From *N.* Búibýr. *See* Boow

BOOCOCK. *Dch.* Boock; *D.*, *S.* Book; p.n. Dimin. of *N.* Búi; p.n. *See* Boow

BOODLE. From Bootle; a loc. n.,
Lancs, Cumb.; *D.B.* Bodele
BOOKER. *See* Boucher
BOOL. *Fr.* Boulle; a p.n. *See* Bull
BOOME. From Boom; a loc. n.,
Belg. *Dch.* Boom; a p.n.
BOON. *Dch.*; p.n. *See* Bone
BOORMAN. *See* Borman
BOORN. *See* Bourne
BOOSEY. From Bussey; a loc. n.,
Norm. *Fr.* Bussy, Buzi; *D.B.*
Buci; p.n. A Hugt. n., Lond.
1684
De Busey in Rot. Obl. et Fin., K.
John.
BOOT. From Buat, a castle near
Falaise, Norm. Or *see* Butter
BOOTH. A loc. n., Derbysh. Or
D., Dch., Fl. Bude, Budde; p.n.
BOOTHBY. A loc. n., Lincs
Held by de Tateshall, 13th century.
BOOTHROYD. From Bodewryd; a
loc. n., Anglesey
BOOTON. *See* Button
BOOTY. From Bothey; a loc. n.,
Belg. Or *G.* Buthy; *Fr.* Boutez
(straight-legged); p.n.
BOOW. From Bow; a loc. n.,
Devon. Or *N.* Búi (a neigh-
bour); *D.* Boye; *F.* Boyo; *Fl.*
Boey, Bohy; *G.* Boy; *D.B.*
Boui, Boi, Bou, Bu; p.n.
BOOY. *See* Boow
BORHAM. From Boreham; a loc. n.,
Wilts, Ess., Suss.
BORKING. From Barking; a loc. n.,
Surr.
BORLAND. From Burland; a loc. n.,
Yorks
BORLAND. A loc. n., Perth
BORLASE. From Borlez; a loc. n.,
Belg.
BORMAN. *A.S.* Beorhtman; *Dch.*
Boerman, Borman; p.n. (illus-
trious man)
BORN. A loc. n., Germ. Or *N.* Björn
(a bear); *D., Dch., G.* Born; *N.-Fr.*
Le Borne; p.n. Or *see* Bourne
BORNER. *Fr.* Borné; a p.n.

BORRADAILE. *See* Barradale
BORRET. *N.* Berg-harðr (?) (hard
as a rock); *D.B.* Borgeret, Bor-
gret, Borret, Burghard, Burred,
Burret, Borred; *D.* Borregaard;
Fl. Boret, Burkard; *G.* Bur-
chardt, Burghardt; *Fr.* Bourret;
Dch. Berkhout; p.n.
BORRINGTON. *See* Barrington
BORRIS. *See* Burrows
BORTHWICK. A loc. n., Edinburgh
BORWELL. *See* Barwell
BORWICK. A loc. n., Lancs
BOSCAWEN. A loc. n., Cornw.
BOSHIER. *A.S.* Boshere, Bossa;
G. Boscher; p.n. (stall warrior)
BOSS. *A.S.* Bos, Bosa (stall
keeper (?)); *Fr.* Bosse; *D.* Boss;
G., Dch. Bos; p.n.
In Rot. Obl. et Fin.
BOSSEY. *Fr.* Bossis; a p.n. *See*
above
BOSSOM. From Bosham; a loc. n.,
Suss.
BOSTEN. *See* Boston
BOSTOCK. A loc. n., Ches.
BOSTON. A loc. n., Lincs
BOSWELL. *Fr.* Bosseville; a p.n.
Bosville; a loc. n., Normandy
BOSWORTH. A loc. n., Leics.
BOTFIELD. A loc. n., Salop
BOTHAM. From Bodham; a loc. n.,
Norf.
BOTHAMLEY. From Barthomley; a
loc. n., Ches.
BOTHERWAY. *Dch.* Botterweg; a
p.n.
BOTHWELL. A loc. n., Lanark. Or
Botwell, Middlx.
BOTT. *N.-Fr.* Bot; a p.n., 1195.
See Body
Brien Bot in Rot. Obl. et Fin.,
K. John.
BOTTEN, BOTTING. A loc. n., Lancs.
N.-Fr. Botin; a p.n., 1180
BOTTENHAM. From Bodenham; a
loc. n., Wilts

BOTTERIL. From Bottereaux ; a loc. n., Norm. *Fr.* Bottrel ; a p.n.

De Boterell in Rot. Obl. et Fin.

BOTWRIGHT. *See* Bootheroyd. Or *A.S.* Botred ; a p.n. (riding messenger)

BOUCHER. From Boursières ; a loc. n., Burgund.

BOUGEN, BOUGHEN. From Bouchain ; a loc. n., France. Or *see* Buggins

BOUGHAL. *See* Arbuckle

BOUGHEY. *See* Boag, Bugg

BOULT. *See* Balders

BOULTBEE. From Boulby ; a loc. n., Yorks

BOULTER. *A.S.* Bealdhere (bold warrior) ; *Fr.* Bolté ; a p.n. *See* Balders

W. Bulder, York, 1272. Rot. Hund.

BOULTON. From Bolton ; a freq. loc. n., Lancs, etc.

BOUND, BOWN. *See* Bone

BOUNDY. From Bondy ; a loc. n., France. Or *D.* Bonde ; a p.n. *See* Bond

BOURKE, BURKE. *Fr.* de Burgo ; a p.n. ; Bourg ; a loc. n., Normandy

Burgh in Roll of Battell Abbey ; *D.B.* Burc, de Burck, tenants in chief

BOURNE. A loc. n., Devon, Lincs, Norf., Somers., Suff.

BOUSFIELD. From Bousville ; a loc. n., near Pavilly, Norm.

BOUSTEAD. A loc. n., Cumb.

BOUTTELL. *Fr.* Boutel, Bouteille ; a p.n.

Boteville in Roll of Battell Abbey.

BOVER. From Beauvais ; a loc. n., France. *Fl.* Bouvier ; *Dch.* Bouwer, Boeve ; p.n. Or *Fr.* Beaufour (Beaufort) ; p.n.

BOVILL. From Bowell ; a loc. n., Belg. Or *see* Boswell

De Bovill in Rot. Obl. et Fin., K. John.

BOWCH. From Buce ; a loc. n., Norm. *Fr.* Bouche; a p.n.; *N.-Fr.* de Buce, 1180

BOWCHER. Hugt., Lond. 1685. *See* Boucher

BOWDEN. A loc. n., Ches., Leics., Northants, Roxburgh

BOWEN. Bovignes ; a loc. n., Belg. *Fl.* Boen ; *Dch.* Bowen ; p.n. Or Welsh Ab Owen. *See* Boy

BOWERBANK. A freq. loc. n.

BOWERS. A loc. n., Staffs.

BOWES. From Boves ; a loc. n., Norm.

J. de Bowes, 1180 ; Hugh de B., Notts, Willm. I.

BOWGEN, BOWGIN. *See* Bougen

BOWHILL. *See* Bovill

BOWKER. From Beaucaire ; a loc. n., France. Or *G.* Bauke ; a p.n. *See* Bowcher

BOWLER. *Fr.* Boulard ; a p.n.

BOWLES. From Baulers ; a loc. n., Belg. *F., Dch., Fl.* Boels ; *D.B.* Bollers ; p.n.

BOWLEY. A loc. n., Heref. Or *Fr.* Beaulieu

BOWMAR. *See* Beaumont

BOWRING. From Beauraing ; a loc. n., Belg. *Fl.* Bauraing ; a p.n.

BOWSER. *See* Boucher

BOWSKELL. From Bouskall ; a loc. n., Cumb.

BOWSTEAD. *N.* Bú-stað (a dwelling) ; *S.* Bostad, Bystedt ; *G.* Baustatte ; loc. and p.n. *See* Boustead

BOWYEAR, BOWYER. *N.-Fr.* Bouvier, 1180 ; Le Boyer, Kent, 1250 ; *Dch.* Bowier ; p.n.

BOX. A loc. n., Wilts. Or *D., Fl.* Bock ; *G.* Bochs ; *Dch.* Box ; p.n.

De Boxe in Rot. Obl. et Fin., K. John.

BOXALL. A loc. n., Herts

BOY. *N.* Búi (a dweller, neighbour); *A.S.* Boia; *S.* Boye; *D.* Boye; *F.* Boyo, Boye, Boy; *G.* Bühr, Böer, Böhr; *Fl.* Boes, Bour, Bues; *Dch.* Boh, Boeje, Buys, Buys; p.n.

BOYACK. *F.* Boyke (dimin. of Boy); *D.* Boëck; *Fl.* Boek; *D.B.* Boche (?); p.n.

BOYCE. *D.*, *Fl.* Boyes; a p.n. *See* Boy

BOYCOTT. A loc. n., Salop

BOYD. *Fr.* Boyard; a p.n. Or Gaelic *boidh* (fair-haired). Hugt. n., Lond. 1687

BOYDELL. *G.* Beudell; a p.n.

BOYER. *Fr.*; p.n. *See* Bowyer

BOYLE. From the Irish O'Baoighill; a p.n. Or Boelles (now La Buille, Norm.)

BOYLING. *Fl.* Boelin; a p.n.

BOYNES. *Fl.* Boyen; *Dch.* Bouwens; p.n.; fam. n. of Boy

BOYNTON. A loc. n., Yorks.
De Bruce held it 1129.

BOYS. *See* Boyce

BRABAZON. From Barbançon; a loc. n., Fland.

BRABBS. *Dch.* Braber; *Fl.* Brabandt; *G.* Brab, Brabender; p.n. (a native of Brabant)

BRABY. From Brawby; a loc. n., Yorks

BRACEBRIDGE. A loc. n., Lincs
De Arden held it 13th century.

BRACEY. *See* Brassey

BRACHER. *See* Brasier

BRACKENBURY. A loc. n., Lincs

BRACKETT. *Fl.* Brachert; *Fr.* Braquet; p.n. Dimin. of Bragg

BRACKLEY. A loc. n., Northants

BRADBEER. *See* Bradby

BRADBROOK. From Bradbridge; a loc. n., Suss.

BRADBURY. A loc. n., Durham

BRADBY. A loc. n., Derbysh., now Bretby

BRADDOCK, BRADOCK. From Broadoak; a loc. n., Cornw., Ess.

BRADDON. From Bradden; a loc. n., Northants, Somers.

BRADDYLL. From Bradwall; a loc. n., Ches. Or Bradwell (?); a loc. n., Derbysh.
Radulph de Bradel held land in Lincs *temp.* K. John.

BRADE. From Breda, a loc. n., Holland. *G.* Breede; *Fl.* Breda, Bret; *D.* Breede, Brede, Bret; *Dch.* Brade, Brat, Breda; p.n.
Prot. ref., Lond. 1688

BRADING. A loc. n., Isle of Wight

BRADLAUGH. From Bradley; a loc. n., Lincs; *D.B.* Bredlow. Also Broadlaw, a mountain in Peebles

BRADLEY. A loc. n., Glost., Lincs, Wilts, Staffs., Yorks

BRADNAM. From Braddenham; a loc. n., Norf.

BRADRIDGE. *See* Brodrick

BRADSELL. From Breadsall; a loc. n., Derbysh.

BRADSHAW. A loc. n., Lancs

BRADSTOCK. A loc. n., Dorset

BRADWELL. A loc. n., Derbysh., Ess., Suff.

BRADY. From the Irish O'Braidaigh; a p.n.

BRAGG. *N.* Bragi (a hero); *S.* Brag; *D.* Bracker; *Dch.* Brakke; *Fl.* Brack; *Fr.* Bracq; *A.S.* Breg; p.n.

BRAHAM. A loc. n., Camb.

BRAIDLEY. A loc. n., Yorks

BRAIDWOOD. *See* Broadwood

BRAIKENRIDGE. From Brackenrigg; a loc. n., Cumb.

BRAILEY. From Breuillet; a loc. n., France

BRAILSFORD. A loc. n., Derbysh.

BRAIN. From Braisnes; a loc. n., France. Or Braine; a loc. n., Belg. *Fr.* Breyne; p.n.; Breon, a Hugt. n., Lond. 1688
In Roll of Battell Abbey. Matt. de Brain, Yorks, 1199.

BRAITHWAITE. A loc. n., Yorks

BRAKE. *N.-Fr.* De Brac, 1180. *Fl.* Braecke; p.n.

R. de la Brache, Bedf. 1199.

BRAKSPEAR. From Bran-spée or Branc-spée; a *N.-Fr.* term for a long sword used by the northern nations. Or Braceby (?); a loc. n., Lincs. *See* Shakespeare and Winspear

BRAMALL. A loc. n., Ches.

BRAMBLE. From Brambeley; a loc. n., Middlx. Or *see* Brimble

BRAME. *A.S.* Breme (renowned); *D.* Bram; *S.* Brehm; *Fl.* Brame, Brems; *Dch.* Brehm, Brem; *Fr.* Brame; p.n. Or *see* Braham

BRAMLEY. A loc. n., Yorks

BRAMMER. *G.* Bramer; *F.* Bremer; *D.* Brammer; p.n. *See* Brame

BRAMWELL. *See* Bramall

BRAN. *A.S.* Bren, Beorn (bear); *G.* Brann; p.n.

BRANCH. From St Denis de Branche; a loc. n., Norm. *Dch.* Branse; *Fl.* Branche; p.n. Branchon; a loc. n., Belg.

Braunch in Roll of Battell Abbey.

BRANCHFLOWER. *Fr.* Blanchfleur; a p.n. (white flower)

BRAND, BRANDER. *N.* Brandr; *D.* Brandt; *S.* Brander; *Dch.*, *G.* Brand; p.n. (a sword-blade); *N.-Fr.*; Norf. 1086

Brand in Roll of Battell Abbey and *D.B.* G. Prot. ref., Lond. 1618.

BRANDON. A loc. n., Norf., Suff.

BRANDRAM. From Brandrum; a loc. n., Monaghan. *N.-Fr.* 1198

BRANDRETH. A loc. n., Cumb.

BRANDUM. From Brantham; a loc. n., Suff.

BRANFORD. A loc. n., Worcest.

BRANSCOMBE. A loc. n., Devon

BRANSGROVE. From Bromsgrove(?); Worc.

BRANSTON. A loc. n., Hants, Leics, Lincs, Staffs.

BRANWHITE. From Brandthwaite; a loc. n., Cumb.

BRAS. A loc. n., Belg. *Dch.* Bras, Brass; *Fr.* Brasse; p.n.

BRASH. From Brages (?); a loc. n., Belg.

BRASIER, BRAZIER. From Bressuire; a loc. n., France. Or *G.* Breyesser; *Fr.* Brasseur; p.n. A Hugt. n., Norwich, 1622

BRASSEY. From Brachy or Brécy; loc. n., Normandy

Bracy in Roll of Battell Abbey. Robert de Brasey in Rot. Obl. et Fin., K. John.

BRATBY. *See* Bradby

BRATT. *See* Brade

BRATTLE. From Braithwell; a loc. n., Yorks. Or *see* Braddyll

BRATTON. A loc. n., Devon, Somers

BRAUNSTON. A loc. n., Leics, Northants

BRAY. A loc. n., Norm., Belg., Berks. *N.-Fr.* de Bray; *Dch.*, *G.* Bree; p.n.

Bray in Roll of Battell Abbey. Radulph de Bray in Rot. Obl. et Fin., K. John.

BRAYBROOK. A loc. n., Northants

BRAYSHAW. *See* Brasier

BRAZENDALE. From Braystonedale; a loc. n., Cumb.

BREACH. *A.S.* Brich (Beorht); *Fr.* Briche; p.n. (bright)

De Briche in Rot. Obl. et Fin., K. John.

BREAM, BREAME. A loc. n., Glost.

BREARLEY. A loc. n., Yorks

BREDDY. *See* Brady

BREE. *Dch.*; p.n.; Brye; a loc. n., Belg.; *Fr.* Briey. Or *A.S.* Bri (bright)

BREEDEN. *See* Breedon

BREEDON. A loc. n., Glost., Leics, Worc. Or Bridon. A Hugt. n., Lond. 1681

BREEKS. *See* Briggs

BREESE. *N.* Bresi; *S.* Braise; *D.* Bræs; *Fl.* Brees; *Dch.* Bres, Breys; *G.* Briese; p.n. Or *see* Brice (fire (?))

BREHENY. From the Irish Breathamh (a judge)

BRELY. From Brilley; a loc. n., Hunts

BRENCHLEY. A loc. n., Kent

BRERETON. A loc. n., Ches., Staffs.

BRETHERTON. A loc. n., Lancs

BRETT. *Fr.* Bret; a p.n.
Le Bret in Rot. Obl. et Fin., K. John.
Le Breton (?)

BRETTON. A loc. n., Yorks. Or *see* Britton

BREWER. From Brueria, now Breviere, near Caen, Norm. *Fr.* Bruyère; a p.n.
William Briwere, a favourite of Hen. II., descended from Drogo de Bevreire, a Fleming, who held lands in Northants, Leics., Lincs, Norf., Suff., Yorks, *D.B.* Briwer in Rot. Obl. et Fin., K. John. Or *see* Bryer.

BREWIN. *A.S.* Bregwin, Archbp. Cant. 765; *Fl.* Bruin; p.n. (a ruler friend). Or *see* Brown

BREWSTER. The Scot. and N. Engl. form of Brewer

BRICE. From St Brice; a loc. n., Norm. Or *A.S.* Bris; *Fl.* Brys; a p.n. (bright). Or Welsh Ab Rhys; a p.n.

BRICKDALE. From Briquedale; a loc. n., Norm.

BRICKNELL. *See* Brignall

BRICKSTOCK. *See* Brigstocke

BRICKWOOD. From Bricket Wood(?); a loc. n., Herts.

BRIDE. *N.* Breidr; *D.* Bryde; *A.S.* Brada; *G.* Breit; p.n. (broad)

BRIDGES. An old way of spelling Bruges. *See* Briggs

BRIDGEWATER. A loc. n., Somers.

BRIDLE. From Bridell; a loc. n., Pembroke. Or *A.S.* Brithwall, Beorhfweald (bright ruler); *Fl.* Breydel; a p.n.

BRIERLEY. A loc. n., Glost., Yorks

BRIGGS. From Bruges; a loc. n., Belgium. *S.* Brügge; *Dch.* Brigg; *Fl.* Bruges; p.n. A Hugt. n., Lond. 1618. Atte Brigge, 1327
Brig and de Brug occur in Rot. Obl. et Fin., K. John.

BRIGHT. *A.S.* Beorht, Brict; p.n. (bright, illustrious)

BRIGHTING. Fam. n.; descendant of Bright

BRIGHTWELL. A loc. n., Suff.

BRIGNALL. A loc. n., Yorks

BRIGSTOCK. A loc. n., Northants

BRILEY. From Broilly; a loc. n. Norm.

BRILL. A loc. n., Bucks., Cornw. Or Brielle, Holl.; *D.* Brill; *Fl.* Brille; *Dch.* Briel; *G.* Briehl; p.n. Prot. ref., Sandwich, 1622

BRIMBLE. From Bremble; a loc n., Wilts

BRINE. From Brin; a loc. n., France. *See* Brain. Or *A.S.* Brine, Beorn; a p.n. (bear)

BRINKHURST. From Bringhurst; a loc. n., Leics.

BRINKLEY. From Brinklow; a loc. n., Warw.

BRINSLEY. A loc. n., Notts

BRISCOE. A loc. n., Yorks. Also de Birkskeugh, Cumb.

BRISCOMBE. From Brinscombe; a loc. n., Somers.

BRISLEY. A loc. n., Norf.

BRISTOW. From Bristow, the ancient name of Bristol

BRITCHER. *Fl.* Brichard, Brichart; *A.S.* Brictuard; *G.* Brichta, Brieger; *Fr.* Briche; p.n. (illustrious guard)

BRITTON. *Fr.* Breton, Britton, le Breton; *D.* Bretton; *Fl.* Breting; *D.B.* Brito; p.n.
Breton in Roll of Battell Abbey. Brito, Briton, le Briton in Rot. Obl. et Fin., K. John.

BROAD. *A.S.* Brod, Brorda; a p.n. (a sword)

BROADHEAD. From Broadheath; a loc. n., Lancs, Worcest.

BROADHURST. A loc. n., Lincs

BROADWAY. A loc. n., Dorset, Heref., Somers., Worcest.

BROADWOOD. A loc. n., Devon, Lanark

BROCK. From Broc; a loc. n., Norm. Or *N.* Broki; a n.n. (a badger); *S.* Brock; *D.*, *Dch.* Broch, Brock; *Fl.* Brockx, Bruch; *D.B.* Broc; p.n.

> Robert le Broc and Ranulph de Broc in Rot. Obl. et Fin., K. John.

BROCKBANK, BROCKLEBANK. A loc. n., Cumb.

BROCKLEHURST. From Brockenhurst; a loc. n., Hants

BROCKLESBY. A loc. n., Lincs

BROCKLEY. A loc. n., Suff.

BROCKSOPP. From Brockthrop (?); a loc. n., Glost.

BROCKWELL. A loc. n.

BRODICK. A loc. n., Bute

BRODIE. A loc. n., Nairn

BRODRIBB. From Bawdrip; a loc. n., Somers

BRODRICK. From the Welsh Ab Roderic. *See* Phrydderch

BRODY. From the Irish *brodach* (proud). Or *see* Brodie

BROGDEN. A loc. n., Yorks

BROMAGE, BROMEDGE. *See* Bromwich

BROMLEY. A loc. n., Staffs.

BROMMELL. From Broomhill; a loc. n., Norf.

BROMWICH. A loc. n., Staffs.

BROOKE. A loc. n., Norf. Atte Broke

BROOKES, BROOKS. *A.S.* Bruc, Bruchyse; *Fl.* Broeckx; *G.* Brucks, Brucksch, Bruksch; *Dch.* Broeks; p.n. *See* Brock

BROOKHOUSE. A loc. n., Staffs., Yorks

BROOM. From Broome; a loc. n., Norf. Atte Brome, Court of Husting. Or *A.S.* Brum, contr. of Brunman; *D.* Brummer; *Dch.* Brom; *G.* Brumme; p.n. (brown man)

BROOMHALL. A loc. n., Worc.

BROOMHEAD. *See* Brummit

BROS. *N.-Fr.* Bros, 1180; Broche, 1198; p.n. *See* Brows

BROTHERHOOD. From Boughrood (?); a loc. n., Radnor

BROTHERIDGE. From Brodrick (?); a loc. n.

BROTHERS. *N.* Broddr (a spike, sword); *A.S.* Broder, Brother; *Fl.* Broothaers; *Dch.* Broeders; p.n. Prot. ref., Sandwich, 1622

BROTHERSTON. *See* Brotherton

BROTHERTON. A loc. n., Yorks

BROUGHAM. A loc. n., Westmd.

BROWN. *N.* Bruni (fire); *D.* Braun, Bruhn, Brun, Bruun; *A.S.* Brun; *F.* Brûno; *Dch.*, *Fl.* Brun, Brune, Brown; *G.* Braun, Brun, Bruno; *Fr.* Brune, Bruné; p.n.; *N.-Fr.* Le Brun

> Brun, Bruni, Brunus in Rot. Obl. et Fin., K. John.

BROWNING. *F.* Brûninga; a fam. n.; *D.* Breuning, Bryning; *D.B.* Bruning; *Dch.* Bruning; *Fl.* Brunin; *G.* Brünig, Brüning; p.n.

BROWNJOHN. From Brongwyn (?); a loc. n., Cardigan

BROWNLOW. A loc. n., Ches., Lancs

BROWNRIGG. A loc. n., Cumb.

BROWNSWORD. From Brownswood; a loc. n., Wexford. Or *A.S.* Brunswith; a p.n.

BROWS. *Fl.* Browaeys; *G.* Brause; *D.B.* de Braiose; *Fr.* Brousse; p.n. *See* Bruce

BROXHOLM. A loc. n., Lincs

BRUCE. From Breux; a loc. n., Normandy (?); probably derived from the original Norse owner. Or *N.* Brúsi (a buck, he-goat); *D.* Bruse, Bruus; *S.* Bruse, Bruze; *Fr.* Brousse, de Brouas; *Fl.* Broos, Brouez; *Dch.* Brus, Brusse; *G.* Brusch, Brysch; p.n.

> *D.B.* Robertus de Bruis, a tenant in chief (Yorks). The founder of the family of Brus of Skelton, from whom the Kings of Scotland and the family of Bruce, Earl of Ailesbury, are descended. His seal is engraved in the *Registrum Honoris de Richmond.* Bruys in Roll of Battell Abbey. Giles de Brewse, Bishop of Hereford, 1200. Adam, Peter, and William de Brus in Rot. Obl. et Fin., K. John.

BRUDENELL. From Bretignolles, near Alençon, Norm.

BRUFF. From Brough; a loc. n., Yorks

BRUMBRIDGE. From Broomridge; a loc., n., Northbd.

BRUMBY. *See* Bromby

BRUMMELL. *See* Brommell

B R U M M I T. *Dch.* Bromet; a p.n. Or Bramwith; a loc. n., Yorks

BRUNDRITH. *See* Brandreth

BRUNDSDEN. *See* Brundsdon

BRUNDSDON. From Brundon; a loc. n., Ess.

BRUNLEES. From Bronllys; a loc. n., Brecknock

BRUNT. From Brund; a loc. n., Staffs. Or *A.S.* Brunheard (Brown the strong); *Dch.* Brunt; *D.* Brund; *Fl.* Brunard; *Fr.* Brunet; p.n.

BRUNTON. A loc. n., Fife

BRUNYEE. *N.* Bruni (fire, burning); *Fr.* Bruné, Brunier; *Dch.* Brunje; *D.B.* Brune; p.n. Fl. ref., Lond. 1618

BRUSH. *G.* Brusch; a p.n. *See* Bruce

BRUTON. *See* Brereton

BRYAN. From Brionne; a loc. n., Normandy. Or *see* O'Brien

> Will. de Brion in Rot. Obl. et Fin., K. John, A.D. 1207.

BRYANT. From Breaunt; a loc. n., Norm. *Fr.* Briand, Briant; p.n.

BRYDGES. From de Bruges. *See* Bridges

BRYER. From Briar; a loc. n., France. *D.* Breyer; *Dch.* Bruijer; *Fl.* Breyer, Briers; *G.* Breier, Breyer; *Fr.* Brière, Bruyère; p.n. *See* Brewer

BUBB. *See* Bobby. Prot. ref., Sandwich, 1622

BUBBINGS. *See* Bobby

> Descendants of Bobe. Comp. Bobbinger, a loc. n., Ess.

BUBEAR. *See* Boobyer

BUCHANAN. A loc. n., Fife

BUCK. *A.S.* Buc, Buga; *S., D.* Buck; *N.-Fr.* De Boc and Le Buc; p.n. *See* Bugge

> Herlewin Buc in Rot. Obl. et Fin., K. John. Prot. ref., Lond. 1618.

BUCKBY. A loc. n., Northants

BUCKENHAM. A loc. n., Norf.

BUCKETT. *Fr.* Bouquet, Buchet; p.n. Dim. of Buck

> Richard Bucket in Rot. Obl. et Fin., K. John. Also Hugt. n., Lond. 1685.

BUCKHURST. A loc. n., Ess., Lancs

BUCKINGHAM. The county town

BUCKLAND. A loc. n., Berks, Bucks, Devon, Hants, Herts, Kent, Surr., Wilts

BUCKLE. From Boucle; a loc. n., Fland. *G.* Buchal, Buckol; p.n. *See* Arbuckle

BUCKLEY. A loc. n., Bucks

BUCKNELL. A loc. n., Salop, Staffs.

BUCKTON. A loc. n., Yorks

BUCKWELL. A loc. n.

BUCKWORTH. A loc. n., Yorks

BUDD. *D., Dch.* Budde; *G.* Bude; p.n. *See* Body

> Simon Bude in Rot. Obl. et Fin., K. John.

BUDDELL. From Budel; a loc. n., Belg.

BUDDEN. *Fr.* Boudain, Boudin; *G.* Budan; p.n.

BUDDERY. *Fr.* Butré; a p.n. *See* Butter

BUDDLE. A loc. n., Northbd.

BUDGEN. *See* Buggins

BUDGETT. *Fr.* Bugat; a p.n. Dim. of Bugg

BUDICOMB. *See* Puddicombe

BUGG. From Bouge; a loc. n., Belg. Or Bougy, Buchy, Normandy. *Fr.* Bougy, Bugué. Or *S., D.* Bugge; *G.* Böger, Büge, Bugge, Buke; *Dch.* Boggia, Boeg, Büger, Bugers, Buggers (a bow); p.n.
> Bushy on Roll of Battell Abbey. *D.B.* De Buci and Bugg, tenants in chief (Notts). Buge, Bugo, Saxon tenants. W. Bugge in Rot. Obl. et Fin., K. John.
> The N.-Fr. forms are local; the rest may be possibly derived from the Danish as a n.n. *N. bygan; D. bugne,* to bend; *A.S. búgan,* to bow. In the dialect of the Midlands *bug* is used in the sense of set up, proud. *See* p. 2.

BUGGINS. *N.-Fr.* Bogin; *Fl.* Buchin, Bughin, Buyghens; p.n. *See* Bugg

BUIST. *N.-Fr.* Boiste or Buiste, 1198; *Fr.* Buisset; p.n.

BULBECK, BULBICK. From Bolbec; a loc. n., Normandy
> *D.B.* de Bolebec, a tenant in chief. In Rot. Obl. et Fin., K. John.

BULCAMP. From Bulscamp; a loc. n., Flanders

BULCRAIG. A loc. n., Cumb.

BULFORD. A loc. n., Wilts

BULKLEY. From Bulkeley; a loc. n., Ches.

BULL. From Bulles; a loc. n., Belg. and Fr. Or *A.S.* Bul; *N.* Bolli; *F.* Bóle, Boele; *G.* Buhl, Bulla; *S.* Bolle; *Fl.* Bully, Buls, Boel; *Dch.* Boll, Boel, Bull; *D.* Bull, Bollé, Boelle; p.n. (a bull)
> Richard Bole and Radulph Bule in Rot. Obl. et Fin., K. John. Prot. ref. n., Lond. 1618.

BULLEN. From Bologne. *Fr., N.-Fr.* De Buliun, de Bolein, Boleyn; p.n. Or *F.* Bólen; *S.* Bollin; *Fl.* Bulens; *Dch.* Boelen; p.n.; Bolinnes; a loc. n., Belg.; *A.S.* Bolling, the fam. or tribal name of Bolli. Bollen, Prot. ref., Lond. 1618

BULLER. From Boulaere; a loc. n., Fland. *G.* Buller; a p.n.
> Baldwin de Buller in Rot. Obl. et Fin., K. John.

BULLETT. *N.-Fr.* Bulete, Bolet; *Fr.* Boullet; p.n. Dim. of Bull

BULLIFANT. *See* Bullivant

BULLIMORE. From Bulmore; a loc. n., Wilts

BULLINGBROOK. From Bolingbroke; a loc. n., Lincs

BULLIVANT. From Polliphant; a loc. n., Cornw. Or *N.-Fr.* Beleffant (good-looking); *Dch.* Belinfante; p.n.

BULLOCK. *G.* Bullok; p.n. Dim. of Bull

BULLWINKLE. *Dch.* Belwinkel; a p.n. (bell-corner)

BULPIT. From Bullapit; a loc. n., Devon

BULPORT. A loc. n.

BULSTRODE. A loc. n., Bucks

BULTITUDE. *A.S.* Bealdthryth, Baldetrude; *Dch.* Boldoot; *Fr.* Bultot; p.n. (bold—true)

BULWER. From Bouloire; a loc. n., Normandy. *D.B.* Bulvi (?)

BUMPUS. *See* Bompas

BUNBURY. A loc. n., Ches.

BUNCE. *Dch.* Bunge; p.n. Dim. *See* Bunn

BUNGEY. From Bungay; a loc. n., Suff.

BUNKALL, BUNCKLE. A loc. n., Scotl. Or dim. of Bunn. *G.* Bunkale; a p.n.

BUNN. *A.S.* Bun, Buna (gushing, spirited)

BUNNER. From the Welsh Ab Ynyr; a p.n. Or *see* Bonner

BUNNETT. *Fr.* p.n. (hedge-sparrow)

BUNNEY. From Bougnies (?) ; a loc. n., Belg. Or *see* Bunn

BUNNING. *A.S.* Buna; *Dch.* Buning; p.n. ; *N. buna* (to gush as water, brisk) son of Bun

BUNTER. *D.* Bunde; *Dch.* Bunte; p.n. *See* Bond

BUNTING. *Fl.* Buntinx; a p.n.
Unfrid Bunting in Rot. Obl. et Fin., K. John. Fam. n. from Bunte.

BUNYAN, BUNYON. *Fl.* Bonichon, Bundgen; *Fr.* Bonjean; p.n. Dim. of Bunn (?)

BURBIDGE, BURBRIDGE. From Burbage ; a loc. n., Derbysh., Leics., Wilts

BURCH. *See* Burdge

BURDASS. From Burdiehouse; a loc. n., Edinburgh

BURDEN. *Fr.* Bourdain, Bourdin, Bourdon ; p.n. From Burdinne ; a loc. n., Belg.
Burdon in Roll of Battell Abbey; *D.B.* Buerd (?). Bourdon in Rot. Obl. et Fin., K. John. *See* Bird.

BURDETT. *Fr.* Bourdet ; a p.n.
Burdet in Roll of Battell Abbey and in *D.B.* William Burdet in Rot. Obl. et Fin., K. John. Hugt. n., Lond. 1685. *N.-Fr. bourdet* (a border).

BURDGE, BURGE. *D.*, *G.*, *Dch.* Berg; p.n. Or *A.S.* Berch; a p.n. (bright)

BURFIELD. From Burghfield; a loc. n., Berks

BURFITT, BURFOOT. *See* Barfoot

BURFORD. A loc. n., Salop, Wilts

BURGESS, BURGIS. *Dch.* Burges, Burgess ; p.n. Burges is an old way of spelling Bruges
In Rot. Obl. et Fin.

BURGOYNE. *N.-Fr.* Bourgain, Bourgogne ; p.n.

BURGRAVE. A loc. n., Lincs

BURKET, BURKITT. *See* Birkett

BURLEY. A loc. n., Hants, Rutl.

BURNABY. *See* Burnby

BURNBY. A loc. n., Yorks

BURNESS. *See* Burns

BURNETT. *A.S.* Beornheard; *N.-Fr.* Burnard, Bernard ; p.n. (strong bear)

BURNHAM. A loc. n., Bucks, Ess., Lincs, Norf., Somers.

BURNINGHAM. From Briningham ; a loc. n., Norf. Or Birmingham

BURNS. A loc. n., Fife. Or *N.* Björn (a bear); *D.* Bjoern, Born ; *S.* Björn, Berns ; *Fl.* Burny ; *D.B.* Barn, Beorn, Burn, Bern ; p.n.

BURNSIDE. A loc. n., Westmd.

BURR. From Burgh ; a loc. n., Lincs, Norf. Or Bure, Belg. Prot. ref., Lond. 1687

BURRELL, BURRILL. From Burrell ; a loc. n., Yorks. Or *Fr.* Burel (a little house) ; *G.*, *Dch.*, *Fr.*, *D.B.* Borel ; p.n.

BURRIDGE. A loc. n., Devon

BURRIS. *See* Burrows

BURROWS. A freq. loc. n.

BURSTALL. A loc. n., Suff.

BURT. *N.-Fr.* Berte ; a p.n.
Rot. Hund. 1272. *See* Bird.

BURTENSHAW. *See* Birkenshaw

BURTHNOT. *See* Arbuthnot

BURTON. A freq. loc. n.

BURWASH. A loc. n., Derbysh., Suss.

BURY. A loc. n., Belg., Lancs, Suff. Or Bourry, Norm.

BUSBY. A loc. n., Yorks

BUSCALL. From Buscel ; a loc. n., Normandy ; *D.B.* Buissell ; a p.n.
Bushell in Roll of Battell Abbey.

BUSFIELD. *See* Bousfield

BUSH. Bosch, now Bois; a loc. n., Fland. *S.* Busck ; *D.*, *G.* Busch, Busk ; *Fl.* Bosch ; p.n.
Bushy in Roll of Battell Abbey. De Bosch, tenant in chief, and Busch (Hertf.), a Saxon tenant in *D.B.* Robert de Buscy in Rot. Obl. et Fin., K. John. Paul Bushe, Bp. of Bristol, 1542. Prot. ref., Lond. 1618.

BUSHBY. From Bushbury; a loc. n., Staffs.

BUSHELL. *See* Buscall. A Hugt. n., Lond. 1618

BUSICK. From Buseck, a valley of Hesse Darmstadt. A noble German family of great antiquity
There is also a Fr. p.n., Busiquet. Boussac, a Hugt. n., occurs in London in 1685.

BUSKARD. *Fl.* Buysschært; *Dch.* Bosschaart; *Fr.* Boisard; *D.B.* de Boscroard (?); p.n.

BUSS. *D.*, *Dch.*, *Fl.* Bus; a p.n.

BUSSEY. *See* Boosey

BUSZARD. From Buzet; a loc. n. in Flanders. Or *Dch.* Boshart; *Fl.* Bossaert; *Fr.* La Bussate; p.n.
Buzard in Roll of Battell Abbey. Bossard, a Prot. ref., Sandwich, 1622. *See* Buskard.

BUTCHER. *D.*, *G.* Boettcher; *Dch.* Boddekke; *Fl.* Buker, Buscher; *D.B.* Boscher; *Fr.* Boucher, Bucher; p.n. *See* Boucher

BUTLER. From Bottelaere; a loc. n., Flanders. Ireland, *temp.* Hen. II.
Botelere in Roll of Battell Abbey and Lib. Vit. Dur. Hugo Pincerna, 1066.

BUTLIN. *Fr.* Boutevillaine; a p.n.

BUTT, BUTTER. *N.* Buttr (short); *D.* Butho; *Dch.* Buter; *Fr.* Buteau; *G.* Butte, Butter; *D.B.* Buter, Butor; p.n. Or *A.S.* Bothere; a p.n. (warrior - messenger)
Roger But in Rot. Obl. et Fin., K. John.

BUTTANSHAW. *See* Birkenshaw

BUTTERFIELD. From Butterfell; a loc. n., Cumb.

BUTTERICK. *See* Butterwick

BUTTERWICK. A loc. n., Lincs, Yorks

BUTTERWORTH. A loc. n., Lancs

BUTTERY. *N.-Fr.* Boteri; a p.n., 1180
Buteri, Butery, Rot de Lib.

BUTTEVANT. A loc. n., co. Cork

BUTTIFANT. *See* Buttevant

BUTTLE. *See* Buddle. Butel, a Hugt. n., Lond. 1685

BUTTON. *Fr.* Boutin, Bouton, Butant; p.n. *See* Budden

BUTTRUM. *D.B.* de Bertram; a loc. n.
In Roll of Battell Abbey.

BUTTS. *Fl.* Budts, Buedts; p.n. Fam. n. of Budd

BUXTON. A loc. n., Derbysh., Norf.

BUZZARD. *See* Buszard

BYARD. *See* Boyd

BYAS. From Biars; a loc. n., Normandy. Or Biez, Belg.; *Fr.* Bias; a p.n.

BYE. A loc. n., Dorset. Or *see* Bee

BYERS. *See* Byas

BYFIELD. A loc. n., Northants

BYFORD. A loc. n., Heref.

BYGOTT. *Fr.* Bigot; *Dch.* Biko; p.n. *See* Bagot
D.B. Bigot, a tenant in chief. Bigot in Roll of Battell Abbey.

BYGRAVE. A loc. n., Herts

BYLES. From Bueil; a loc. n., France. *G.* Beil; *Fl.* Byl, Buyl; *Dch.* Buijl; p.n. A Hugt. n.

BYNOE. *See* Baines

BYRNE. From the Irish O'Broin; a p.n. *See* Burns

BYRNEY. *See* Birnie

BYROM. From Byram; a loc. n., Yorks

BYRON. From Biron; a loc. n., Guienne, France. Or Buron, Norm.
D.B. de Burun, tenant in chief. Robert de Burun in Rot. Obl. et Fin., K. John. Biroune in Roll of Battell Abbey.

BYRTH. From Berth; a loc. n., Heref. Or *Fl.* Berth; a p.n. Or *see* Byworth

BYWATER
Radulph juxta aquam occurs A.D. 1170, Empingham, Rutl.

BYWORTH. A loc. n., Suss.

C

CABLE. *G.* Kabel; a p.n. *See* Keble

CABORN, CABOURNE. A loc. n., Lincs

CACKETT. *A.S.* Cœc; *Dch.* Cachet; a p.n. Dim. (a key)

CADBURY. A loc. n., Devon

CADDELL. From the Welsh Caddell (warlike). *Fr.* Cadel; a p.n.

CADDICK. From Catwick; a loc. n., Yorks

CADDIE, CADDY, CADE. *A.S.* Cadda, Ceada; *chad*, for *had* (war); *G.* Kade; *S.* Kadier; p.n.; *D.B.* Cœdd; a p.n.; Chad (?). Or *Fr.* Cadet. A Hugt. n., (younger)

CADEBY. A loc. n., Yorks

CADEY, CADY. *See* Caddy

CADGE. *See* Cage

CADOGAN. Welsh Cadwgan (war)

Kydwgan, Lord of Radnor, Hen. I.

CADWELL. *See* Caldwell

CAFFIN. *Fr.* Chaufin; a p.n. *N.-Fr.* Cauvin (a little calf). *See* Choffin

CAFFREY. From the Irish O'Craffrey, M'Caffrey; p.n.

CAGE. *N.* Kaggi, n.n. (a keg); *A.S.* Ceagga; *G.* Kage; *Dch.* Kagie, Keg, Keja; p.n. Or *see* Kay

CAHAN. *See* Caine

CAIGER. *See* Cage

CAIN, CAINE. From Cahaignes; a loc. n., Normandy. *Fr.* Cahen; *D.B.* de Cahainges. Or Irish O'Cathain; p.n.

W. de Kaynes in Rot. Obl. et Fin., K. John.

CAIRNS. From the Irish O'Cairn; a p.n.; *carn* (a heap, a little hill)

CAISEY. From the Irish Macasey; *cathaiseach* (valiant)

CAKE. *See* Keck

CAKEBREAD. Cæcbrid (bright key). Or *N.-Fr.* Calcebued; a p.n.

CALCOTT. A loc. n., Wilts

CALCUTT. A loc. n., Warw.

CALDECOTE. A loc. n., Lincs, Monmouth, Northants, etc.

CALDECOURT. *See* Caldecot

CALDER. A loc. n., Lanark

CALDERBANK. A loc. n., Lanark

CALDERWOOD. A loc. n., East Kilbride, Scotl.

CALDWELL. A loc. n., Derbysh., Yorks, etc. *See* Coldwell

CALEY. *See* Cayley

CALL. From M'Call. *A.S.* Cal, Calla; *F.* Kalle; p.n. (a man)

CALLAGAN. Irish O'Callagan; *colgan* (?) (swordsman)

CALLANDER. A loc. n., Perth

CALLARD. *Fl.* Callaert, Callewaert; p.n.; *A.S. cal - weard* (man warden)

CALLIER. *See* Colyer

CALLIFORD. From Callford; a loc. n., Suff.

CALLIS. From Caleys; a loc. n., Picardy

CALLOW. A loc. n., Worcest.

CALLOWAY. *See* Galloway

CALLUM. *Gael.* (dove)

CALSTOCK. A loc. n., Cornw.

CALTHROP. From Colthrop; a loc. n., Glos. Or Calthorpe

CALTHORPE. A loc. n., Derbysh., Lincs, Norf.

CALVER. *N.* Kálfr (a calf); *G.* Kalfar; *D.B.* Calvus; p.n. Or from Calver (*D.B.* Caluore); a loc. n., Derbysh. Calfe, Flem. ref., Lond. 1618

CALVERLEY. A loc. n., Yorks

CALVERT. From Calbert; a loc. n., Norm. *A.S.* Ceolweard (keel, ship-guard); *Fl.* Callewaert; p.n.

CAMERON. A loc. n., Fife

CAMFIELD. From Camville; a loc. n., Norm.

CAMIDGE, CAMMIDGE. *See* Cammish and Gammage

CAMM. From Cam; a loc. n., Glos. Or Welsh *cam* (crooked)

CAMMELL. From Campell; a loc. n., Norm. Or *see* Gamble

CAMMISH. Manx, Cammaish. From MacHamish (James's son)

CAMP. From Campe; a loc. n., Norm. Or *N.* Kampi; n.n. (a bearded person); *S.* Camp, Kemp; *D.*, *Dch.* Kemp; *G.* Kampe. Or *A.S.* Camp, Cæmpa (champion); p.n. A Hugt. n., Lond. 1618

CAMPAIN. *D.*, *Dch.* Campagne, Campen; p.n. Or *see* Campion

CAMPBELL. *N.-Fr.* de Camville (de Campo Bello). Or *see* Gamble

CAMPION. *N.-Fr.* p.n.
> W. C. in Norm. 1184; Geof. C. in Eng. 1194. Rot. Cur. Reg. Flem. Prot. ref., Norwich, 1622. *See* Champion.

CANDY. From Candé; a loc. n. near Blois, Norm.

CANE, CANEY. *See* Caine

CANHAM. From Cainham; a loc. n., Salop

CANLER. From Cantley (?); a loc. n., Yorks

CANN. From Canne; a loc. n., Belg. Or Can, Norm.; *D.* Kann; *Fl.* Cahn; *G.* Kann; *Dch.* Canne, Kan; p.n.
> W. de Kanne and Ric. de Can in Rot. Obl. et Fin., K. John.

CANNELL. From Chenel; a loc. n., Norm. Also the Manx form of the Celtic MacConaill; Irish M'Connell. Canwell; a loc. n., Staffs

CANNER. *See* Cann

CANNON. *Fr.* Canonne; a p.n.; *N.-Fr. chanoine* (a canon)

CANNOT. *Fl.* Canoodt; *Fr.* Carnot; *N.* Knútr; *D.* Knud, Knuth; p.n. *See* Nutt

CANT. *See* Cannot and Gaunt

CANTER. *N.-Fr.* Cantor; a p.n. (a singer)
> Gaufrid C., Norm. 1180. Christn. le Chaunter, Rot. Hund. 1272.

CANTERFORD. From Kentford; a loc. n., Suff.

CANTLOW. From Canteleu; a loc. n., Normandy
> In Roll of Battell Abbey.

CANTRELL. *N.-Fr.* Cantrel, Chantrell; p.n. Also a Hugt. n., Lond. 1618
> William Chanterell, *temp.* K. John.

CANTWELL. *See* Canwell

CAPEL. From La Chapelle; a loc. n., Norm., Suff., N. Wales, S. Wales. Also a Hugt. n. Lond. 1618

CAPERN. *N.-Fr.* Capron; a p.n.
> Caperoun in Roll of Battell Abbey.

CAPES. *N.-Fr.* Cape, Capes; p.n.
> W. de Capes, 1199.

CAPON. *Fl.* Capon, Capen; *Dch.* Capoen; p.n.

CAPPER. *N.* Kappi; *Fl.* Cappe; *Dch.* Kappers; p.n. (a hero)

CAPPS. *See* Capes

CAPSTICK. From Copestake; a loc. n.

CARD. *A.S.* Carda; a p.n. (guard); *Fr.* Cardes. A Hugt. n., Lond. 1681

CARDELL. *See* Cardwell

CARDEN. From Carwarden; a loc. n., Ches. *D.B.* Cardun. Also *N.-Fr.* Cardon or Cardun; a p.n.

CARDEW. *See* Carthew or Cordeaux. Hugt. n., Lond. 1622

CARDIN. *See* Carden

CARDINAL. *Dch.* Cardinaal; *Fl.* Cardinael, Cardinal; p.n. *See* p. 12

CARDWELL. From Cardeville; a loc. n., Norm.

CARDY. *See* Cardin

CARELESS. From St Karles de Parcy; a loc. n., Norm. *Fr.* Carliez; *Fl.* Carles; *Span.* Carlos; p.n. From Carolus (Charles)

CAREW. A loc. n., Pembrokesh.
CAREY. *See* Carry
CARFRAE. A loc. n., Scotl.
CARGILL. A loc. n., Perth
CARLETON. A loc. n., Lancs, Yorks
CARLEY. *N.* Karli (carle, churl);
D. Carli ; *Dch.* Carlee ; *A.S.*
Carle ; p.n.
CARLILL. From Carlisle
CARLINE. *N.* Kerling (a woman);
S. Carling ; p.n. Or Carling ; a
loc. n., Germ.
CARLYLE. *See* Carlill
CARLYON. A loc. n., Cornw. Also
Carlehon, Bretagne, France
CARMAN. *A.S.* Carman ; *Fr.* Car-
manne ; *garman* (spearman) ; p.n.
CARMICHAEL. A loc. n., Lanark.
Or Cara Michil (a friend of St
Michael)
CARMODY. *See* Kermode
CARNABY. A loc. n., Yorks
CARNE. From Carn ; a loc. n.,
Cornw. Or *N. - Fr.* Caron,
Charun ; p.n.
CARNEGIE. A loc. n., Forfar
CARNELLEY. From Carnelles; a loc.
n., Norm. Or Irish M'Annally ;
a p.n.
CARNSEW, CARNZU. *Fl.* Carnseuw ;
a p.n.
CARON. *Fr.* Hugt. n., Lond. 1687
CARPENTER. *N.-Fr.* Carpentarius ;
a p.n.
Durand C., a t. in chief, *B.D.* Norf.
CARPUE. *Fr.* Carpiaux (young
carp) ; a p.n.
CARR. *N.* Kárr (curly hair) ; *S.*
Karr ; *G.* Karo ; *Dch.* Kar ; p.n.;
A.S. Car. Or *see* Keir
CARRATT, CARRITT, CAROTTE ; *Fr.*
Carette ; a p.n. Dim. of Carr
CARRELL. From Caril ; a loc. n.,
near Lisieux, Norm.
CARRICK. From the Irish *carraice*
(a rock). *See* Creak
CARRINGTON. A loc. n., Notts
CARROLL. From the Irish O'Cearb-
hoil, M'Carroll ; p.n.

CARRON. A loc. n., Stirling
CARRUTHERS. A loc. n., Dumfries
CARRY. *N.* Kári (the god of the
winds) ; *Fr.* Carré, Karré ; p.n.
Or Irish M'Carrie. Hugt. n.,
Lond. 1685. *See* Carr
CARSBOULT. *A.S.* Garbeald ; a
p.n. (spearbold)
CARSLAKE. A loc. n., Somers. Or
Carsac, Norm.
CARSLEY. From Kersley or Curs-
ley ; a loc. n., Warw.
CARSTAIRS. A loc. n., Lanark
CARSTON. *F., Dch.* Karsten; *D.*
Carsten ; p.n. (from Christian).
See Casson
CARSWELL. A loc. n., Berks
CARTER. From the Irish M'Carter,
arta (great), M'Carthur, Mac-
Arthur. Or Castres ; a loc. n.,
France. Or *A.S.* Carda ; a p.n.
(guard) ; *G.* Kartte ; *N.-Fr.* Car-
tier ; p.n. Hugt., Lond. 1618
Ralph C. held a fief from the See of
Worcester, 13th cent. Caretarius
in Winch. *D.B.*
CARTERLEY. From Chartley. *D.B.*
Certelie ; a loc. n., Staffs.
CARTHEW. A loc. n., Cornw. Or
Catheux ; a loc. n., Normandy
CARTHY. From the Irish Mac
Carthaigh ; a p.n. (*Carthac*, the
founder of a city). Or *see* Carter
CARTLEDGE. From Cartlett (?) ; a
loc. n., Glos.
CARTMELL. From Cartmel ; a loc.
n., Lancs
CARTWRIGHT. From Cauterêts ; a
loc. n., Norm. Or Catherick,
Yorks
Cartrait, Cateray in Roll of Battell
Abbey. De Ceterith, a tenant in
chief in *D.B.* De Cartray in Rot.
Obl. et Fin., K. John.
CARVELL. *N.-Fr.* De Carville ; a
p.n.
CARVER. *See* Calver
CARWARDINE. From Carwarden;
a loc. n., Ches.
CARWITHEN. A loc. n., Cornw.

CASBOLT. *See* Carsboult

CASBURN. A loc. n. *See* Chase

CASE. *A.S.* Casa; *D.* Casse, Kasse; *Dch.* Kas, Käss, Caisse; *Fl.* Cas, Casse, Casy; p.n.; De la Case. Hugt. n.

CASEBOW. *Fr.* Cassabois; a p.n. (wood-breaker)

CASEMENT. *Fl.* Casman; a p.n.

CASEY. From the Irish *cathaiseach* (valiant). Or *see* Case

CASHMORE. From Cashmoor; a loc. n., Dorset

CASSELL. A loc. n., Flanders
Hugo de C., Lond. 1130, Pip. Rolls.

CASSIDY. Irish p.n. (treasurer)

CASSON. *F.* Kassen, from Christian; *i.e.*, Kristjan, Kersten, Karsten, Karsen, Kasjen, Kassen; *D.* Kasten; *S.* Cassen; *Dch.* Carsten; *Fl.* Kastan, Casen, Cason; p.n.

CASTLE. *N.* - *Fr.* Castel; a p.n.
Ino. de Castro, 1272, Rot. Hund.

CATCHPOLE, CATCHPOOL. From Cageypole; a loc. n., Dorset. Or Caterpole, Suff.

CATCHSIDE. From Catcherside; a loc. n., Northumbd.

CATER. *Fr.* Cattreux; a p.n.
Walter Cater occurs in a deed A.D. 1076, Harl. MS. John de Catara, Beswick, Yorks, and Walter Catar his nephew in a deed 1 Steph. Chaitres in Roll of Battell Abbey (?).

CATESBY. A loc. n., Northants

CATFORD. A loc. n., Kent

CATHCART. A loc. n., Lanark

CATHEY. From Cathay; a loc. n., S. Wales. Or *see* Caddy

CATLING. *Fl.* Catelin; p.n. *See* Catt. A dim. Or Castelin; a loc. n., Norm.

CATLOW. *Fr.* Cathelineau (?); a p.n.

CATMORE. A loc. n., Berks

CATMUR. From Catmer; a loc. n., Ess. Or *see* Catmore

CATT. *N.* Köttr (a cat), n.n.; *A.S.* Catta; *N.-Fr.* Le Cat; *D.* Kett; *Dch.* Cate, Kat; *G.* Kathe, Katte; p.n.

CATTEE. *G.* Kathe, Kattey; *Fr.* Chaté; p.n. Or Irish M'Atee (high)

CATTEN. *Dch.* Kattan, Ketting; *S.* Kaeding; p.n.; fam. n. of Catt

CATTERALL. A loc. n., Yorks

CATTERMOLE. *N.* - *Fr.* Quatremeulles (?) *Dch.* Cattermolen; p.n.

CATTERSON. From Catherston; a loc. n., Dorset. Or *see* Cater

CATTLE. From Cattall; a loc. n., Yorks. Or *Fr.* Catel, Châtel; *N.-Fr.* Du Chastel; p.n.

CATTLEY. From Chatterley; a loc. n., Staffs

CATTY. *See* Cattee

CAUDLE. A loc. corr. of Caldwell, Derbysh. Also *N.-Fr.* Caldell or Caudel; p.n.
W. C. Camb. 1272, Rot. Hund.

CAULFIELD. *N.-Fr.* de Calvel or Caville; p.n.
Jas. Calfhill, Calvel, or Calfield, Bp. of Worcs. 1506

CAUNT. *See* Gaunt

CAUSTON. A loc. n., Warw.

CAUTLEY. From Caughley; a loc. n., Salop

CAUX. A loc. n., France

CAVE. A loc. n., Yorks.
The family of De Cave was seated here for eleven generations from the Conquest.

CAVELL. *See* Caulfield

CAVENDISH. A loc. n. (a manor), Suff.
It was assumed by the Norman knight, Gernon de Montfichet; *D.B.* Gernon. Gernun in Rot. Obl. et Fin.

CAVILL. From Cavill; a loc. n., Yorks. Or *see* Caulfield

CAWDWELL. *See* Caldwell

CAWKER. *N.* Kolka; a n.n. (coalblack); *D.* Kalckar; *G.* Kalke; *Fl.* Caukens; *Dch.* Kalker; p.n.

CAWLEY. *See* Macaulay

CAWS, CAWSE. *See* Caux
Robert Cause, Gilbert de Cause, John de Cauz in Rot. Obl. et Fin., K. John.

CAWSTON, A loc. n., Norf., Warw.
CAWTHORNE. A loc. n., Yorks
CAXTON. A loc. n., Camb.
CAYLESS. *See* Careless
CAYLEY. From Cailli; a loc. n., Norm. *Fr.* Caillet; a p.n.

> Hugh de Cailly was Lord of Orby, Norf., *temp.* Edw. I. De Cailly in Rot. Obl. et. Fin. A Hugt. n., Sandwich, 1622.

CECIL. *Fr.* Cécile, Secelle; p.n.

> Ancient spelling Sicelle, Cyssel. From St Cécille, or Sysseele, both loc. n. in Flanders.

CHACEMOOR. From Chackmore; a loc. n., Bucks
CHADD. *N.-Fr.* Cadd; *A.S.* Ceadda, Cedda; p.n.; *chad* for *had* (war); Celtic *cath, cad* (battle)
CHADWICK. A loc. n., Lancs
CHAFFE, CHAFFEY, CHAFY. *A.S.* Caefi, Cóifi (active, bold). Or *N.-Fr.* Le Chauve; a p.n. (the bald); *Fr.* Chavée; p.n.; Chavet. Hugt. n., Lond. 1682
CHAFFER, CHAFFERS. From Chevrières; a loc. n., Norm.

> R. de Cheveriis, Norm. 1195; W. de Caveres, Salop, 1272, Rot. Hund.

CHALCRAFT. *See* Calcraft
CHALK. A loc. n., Kent
CHALLACOMBE. A loc. n., Devon
CHALLICE, CHALLIS. *G.* Callas, Kallesse, Kalisch; *Dch.* Kalis; *Fl.* Calis; p.n. *See* Callis
CHALLINGWORTH. A loc. n., Glost.
CHAM. *See* Camp
CHAMBERLAIN. *N.-Fr.* Chambellan, Chamberlein; p.n. Hugt. n., Lond. 1618
CHAMBERS. From Chambray (?); a loc. n., Normandy. Or Camerarius (a chamberlain). A Hugt. n., Lond. A.D. 1618

> De Cambray, De Camera, and Camerarius in Rot. Obl. et Fin., K. John.

CHAMLEY. From Chamilly or Chambly; a loc. n., Normandy

CHAMNEY. From Chamneis or Champneis, the ancient district of Champagne. *D.B.* Chemarnhee

> In Roll of Battell Abbey. Champaney in Rot. Obl. et Fin.

CHAMPION. *Fr.* p.n.; a loc. n., Flanders
CHANCE. *Fr.* Chansay; a p.n.

> W. de Chanes in Rot. Obl. et Fin., K. John.

CHANNON. A loc. n., Devon
CHANTER. *See* Canter
CHANTLE. *See* Gentle
CHAPLIN. *N.-Fr.* Capelen; a p.n.

> W. Capellanus, Norm. 1180. *D.B.* 1086; York, 1202; Sleford, Lincs, 1443.

CHAPMAN. *See* Coopman
CHARD. A loc. n., Somers.
CHARITY. *Fr.* Charité; a p.n.

> De Caritate in Rot. Obl. et Fin.

CHARLES. *Fr.* p.n.
CHARLEY. *Fr.* Charlet, Charlier; p.n.
CHARLTON. A loc. n., Berks, Glos., Kent. Oxf., Salop, Somers, Suss.
CHARNLEY. A loc. n., Leics
CHARRINGTON. From Charentonne; a loc. n., Normandy
CHASE. *D.* Jess; *Fl.* Jesse; *Dch.* Jes; *G.* Jesche; p.n. *See* Cheese
CHASTEN, CHASTENEY, CHASTY. *Fr.* Chastaigner. A Hugt. n., Lond. 1687
CHATBURN. A loc. n., Yorks
CHATER. *See* Chatto
CHATFIELD. A loc. n., Suss.
CHATT. *See* Chadd
CHATTAWAY. From Chitway; a loc. n., Wilts. Or *A.S.* Catwa; a p.n.; *catwig* (victorious in war)
CHATTERIS. A loc. n., Camb.
CHATTERLEY. A loc. n., Staffs
CHATTERTON. From Chadderton; a loc. n., Lancs
CHATTIN. *Fr.* Chattaine. A Hugt. n., Lond. 1618. *See* Chatwin

H

CHATTO. From Chatou; a loc. n., France. *Fr.* Chateau; *Dch.* Katto; *Fl.* Katto; p.n. *See* Chadd

CHATWIN. *See* Chetwynd

CHAYTOR. From Chatres; a loc. n., Norm.

CHEALES. From Cheal; a loc. n., Lincs

CHEAVIN. *See* Sheavyn

CHECKLAND. From Chachland; a loc. n., Scotl.

CHECKLEY. A loc. n., Staffs

CHEEK. *See* Chick

CHEESE. *A.S.* Cissa; *Fr.* Tsjisse; *Dch.* Chijs; p.n.; *gis* (a hostage) Chese in Hund. Rolls.

CHEESMAN. *A.S.* Gislmund; a p.n. (hostage protector)

CHEESWORTH. From Chisworth; a loc. n., Derbysh.

CHEESWRIGHT. *See* Cheesworth

CHEETHAM. From Chidham; a loc. n., Suss.

CHEFFINS. *A.S.* Ceofa; a p.n.; Ciwing; a fam. n. Or *N.-Fr. chevin* (a chub)

CHELL. A loc. n., Staffs. Or Chelles, France

CHENEREY. From St Ceneri; a loc. n., Norm.

CHENEY. Chênée, Chiny; loc. n., Flanders; Quesnay, Norm. *Fr.* Chesnais, Chesnée; *D.B.* Chenisis, Chenin; p.n.
Cheyne, Cheines, Cheyni in Roll of Battell Abbey. Robert de Chesney Bishop of Lincoln, 1147; Richard Cheyney, Bishop of Lincoln, 1562. William de Chesne in Rot. Obl. et Fin., K. John, 1208. *See* Cheyne.

CHERITON. A loc. n., Devon

CHERRY. *N.-Fr.* De Cerisy; a p.n.

CHESELDEN. From Chiseldon; a loc. n., Wilts

CHESLYN. *See* Cheselden

CHESNEY, CHESTNEY. *See* Chasteney

CHESSELL. *G.* Jessel; a p.n. Dim. *See* Cheese

CHESSON. *See* Jesson

CHESTERFIELD. A loc. n., Derbysh.

CHESTERTON. A loc. n., Camb.

CHETEL. *N.* Ketel (a kettle); *D.B.* Chetel; p.n.

CHETWODE. A loc. n. (a manor), Bucks

CHETWYND. A loc. n., Salop Held by De Verlai, 1086.

CHEVELEY. A loc. n., Camb.

CHEVERTON. From Chevington; a loc. n., Northbd., Worcest.

CHEW. A loc. n., Somers. Or *A.S.* Cheawa; a p.n. (chewed) (?)

CHEYNE. *See* Cheney

CHICK. From Chich; a loc n., Ess. Or *A.S.* Cich; a p.n.; *N. gygr* (a giant); *N.-Fr cec, chike*

CHICKALL. From Chicknall; a loc. n., Ess.

CHICKEN. *N.* Kikini (?); a n.n.; *A.S.* Cich; *Old G.* Ghikin; p.n.; *N. gygr* (?) (a giant) W. Chikin in Rot. Obl. et Fin., K. John.

CHIDDICK. *See* Chadwick

CHIDLEY. From Chudleigh; a loc. n., Devon

CHIETHAM. *See* Cheetham

CHILD. From Schilde; a loc. n., Belg. Or *N.* Skjöldr; *D.* Skjold; *D.B.* Cild, Cilt; *Fl.* Child; *G.* Schild; *Dch.* Schilt; p.n (a shield). Or perhaps from *A.S. hild* (war), the aspirate often changing into *c*

CHILDERS. *A.S.* Cildas; fam. or tribal n.; *Dch., Fl.* Schilders; a p.n. *See* Child

CHILDS. *See* Childers

CHILLCOTT. A loc. n., Somers.

CHILLEY. *N.* Gilli; *A.S.* Ghile, Gil, Gilo; *Fr.* Gillé, Gillet, Gilliet; a p.n. (servant)

CHILLINGWORTH. From Kilworth (Killingworth); a loc. n., Leics

CHILLINTON. From Chillington; a loc. n., Somers.

CHILLYSTONE. From Chellaston; a loc. n., Derbysh.

CHILMAID. *A.S.* Ceolmod ; a p.n. (ship courage)

CHILMAN. *A.S.* Ceolmund ; a p.n. (ship protector) ; *G.* Killmann ; *D.* Kielman ; p.n.

CHILTON. A loc. n., Berks, Suff., Somers.

CHILVERS. A loc. n., Warw.

CHIMLEY. *See* Cholmondeley

CHING. *A.S.* Cyne ; a p.n. (royal)

CHINNEREY. *See* Chenerey

CHIPCHACE. A loc. n., Northbd.

CHIPP. *A.S.* Ceapa, Cyppa ; *D.* Kib (?) ; p.n. (a merchant)

CHIPPENDALE. From Chipnall (?) a loc. n., Salop

CHIPPERFIELD. A loc. n., Herts

CHISHOLM. A loc. n., Inverness

CHISNALL. *Fr.* Chesnell (?) ; a p.n. (a caterpillar)

CHISSELL. *Fr.* Choiseuil (?) ; a p.n. (a form of *N. gisl* (a hostage (?)))

CHISWELL. From Chishall (?) ; a loc. n., Ess.

CHITTAM. *See* Cheetham

CHITTENDEN. From Chittingstone; a loc. n., Kent

CHITTOCK. From Chideock ; a loc. n., Dorset

CHITTY. *N.-Fr.* Cette ; *A.S.* Cyddi, Cyta ; a p.n. ; *Dch.* Chits ; *D.B.* Chit ; p.n. (a striver). *See* Kiddy Rot. Hund. 1272.

CHIVERS. From La Chievere ; a loc. n., Norm. Or *see* Chilvers

CHOAT. From Chute ; a loc. n. in Wilts. Or *Fl.* Jot (?) ; a p.n.

CHOFFIN. *Fr.* Chauvin ; a p.n. (bald). A Hugt. n., Lond. 1684. *See* Caffin

CHOLMELEY. *See* Cholmondeley

CHOLMONDELEY. A loc. n. (a manor), Ches. *D.B.* Calmundelai

CHOPE. *See* Jope

CHORLTON. A loc. n., Lancs

CHOULES. *A.S.* Ceola ; *Dch.* Jaulus (?) ; p.n. (ship man)

CHOWLER. *See* Choules

CHREES. From Chris, a dimin. of Christopher (?)

CHRIMES. *See* Grimes

CHRISTIAN. *A.S.* Cristthegn, Christthin ; *Fl.* Christaen ; *Dch.* Christan ; *S.* Christen ; *G.* Christian ; p.n. (a soldier of Christ

CHRISTIE. A p.n. for Christopher or Christian.

CHRISTOPHERSON. *S.* Kristofferson ; a p.n.

CHUBB. *See* Jubb

CHUBBOCK. Dimin. of Chubb

CHUCK. From Choques ; a loc. n., Fland. Or *G.* Schuch ; a p.n. (shy)

CHUDLEIGH. A loc. n., Devon

CHUGG. *A.S.* Cug ; a p.n. *See* Chuck. Or *G.* Schüge ; a p.n. (shy)

CHUMLEY. *See* Cholmondeley

CHURCH. Atte Cherche, Court of Husting, 1258

CHURCHER. From Churcham (?) ; a loc. n., Glost.

CHURCHILL. *N.-Fr.* de Curcelle ; a p.n. From Courcelles ; a loc. n., France and Belg.

De Corcelles, a t. in chief in *D.B.*

CHURTON. A loc. n., Ches.

CHUSEWORTH. *See* Cheesworth

CHUTTER. *A.S.* Cuda, Cuta, Cutha, Guda, Gutha, *gúd* (war) ; *G.* Chudy (?) ; p.n.

CINNAMON. *See* Symonds

CIRCUIT. *See* Sirkett

CIVILL. *Fr.* Civiel ; a p.n. (polite). Or *see* Saville

CLABOD. *Fl.* Clabots ; a p.n. (?)

CLABON. *Fr.* Cléban ; a p.n.

CLACK. *N.* Klökkr (bending, pliable) ; *Dch.* Kloek ; *A.S.* Clac ; p.n.

CLAMP. *See* Clampett

CLAMPETT. From Clampitt ; a loc. n., Cornw.

CLAPCOTT. A loc. n., Berks

CLAPP. *N.* Klápr (?) (a rough box); *D.* Klepsch; *S.* Klop; *Dch.* Klapp; *A.S.* Clapa; p.n.

CLARABUT. *N.-Fr.* Clarebald (brightly - bold); *Fl.* Clairbaut, Clerebaut; p.n. Prot. ref., Sandwich, 1622

CLARE. A loc. n., Cornw., Suff. Or Clères, France. *See* St Clair

CLARICOAT. From Clerewoodcott(?); a loc. n., Hants

CLARIDGE. From Clarach (?); a loc. n., Cardigan

CLARK. *D., Fl.* p.n. (a cleric). Hugt. n., Norwich, 1622

CLATWORTHY. A loc. n., Somers

CLAUGHTON. A loc. n., Lancs

CLAVERING. A loc. n., Ess.

CLAWSON. *See* Closson

CLAXTON. A loc. n., Dur., Leics, Norf.

CLAYBROUGH. From Claybrooke (?); a loc. n., Leics

CLAYDON. A loc. n., Suff.

CLAYE, CLAY. A loc. n., Normandy. Or *D.* Klee; a p.n.
De Clai in Rot. Obl. et Fin.

CLAYPOLE. A loc. n., Lincs

CLAYTON. A loc. n., Lancs., Yorks

CLEAK. *Fr.* Cliquet; a p.n. (mill-clapper)

CLEARE. *See* Clare

CLEARY. From the Irish *Cleireach* (a clerk)

CLEASBY. A loc. n., Yorks

CLEATHER. From Clitheroe; a loc. n., Lancs

CLEAVER. *Fr.* Clavier; *G.* Kliewer; p.n. (key bearer)

CLEEVE. A loc. n., Glos.

CLEGG. A loc. n., Lancs. Or Manx Clague, contracted from Mac-Liaigh (the leech's son)

CLEGHORN. A loc. n. near Carstairs, Scotl.

CLELAND. A loc. n., Lanark. *See* Cleveland

CLEMENTS. *Fl.* Clement; *G.* Clemens; p.n. Prot. ref. n., Lond. 1618

CLEMO, CLEMOW. *Fr.* Clement; a p.n.

CLENDINNING. *See* Glendinning

CLENT. A loc. n., Worcest.

CLERIHEW, CLEROWE. From Clairvaux; a loc. n. Aquitaine
De Clervaus, 1272, Rot. Pip.

CLERY. *See* Cleary

CLERK. *N.-Fr.* Le Clerc; *Dch.* Clerk; p.n.

CLEVELAND CLIFFLAND. A loc. n., Yorks

CLEVELEY. A loc. n., Lancs

CLEVERDON. From Clevedon; a loc. n., Somers. Or Cleverton, Wilts

CLEVERLEY. *See* Cleveley

CLEWER. A loc. n., Berks

CLEWORTH. From Clayworth; a loc. n., Notts, Somers

CLIBRAN. *See* below

CLIBURN. A loc. n., Westmd.

CLICK. *G.* Klick; a p.n. *See* Cleak

CLIFF. A loc. n., Yorks, etc.
De Clif, in Rot. Obl. et Fin.

CLIFFORD. A loc. n., Glos., Heref., Yorks

CLIFT. *D.* Klifoth; a p.n.

CLIFTON. A loc. n., Beds, Derbysh., Lancs, Notts, Somers, Staffs, Warw., Yorks

CLIMANCE. *See* Clements

CLIMO. *A.S.* Clima; a p.n. *See* Clemo

CLIMPSON. (Clementson (?)). *See* Clements

CLINCKETT. *Dch.* Klinkert; a p.n.

CLINGO. *G.* Klinger; *S.* Klinga; p.n. (a ringer, or a swordsman)

CLINTON. From Glinton; a loc. n., Northants

CLIPSTON. A loc. n., Northants, Notts

CLISBY. *See* Cleasby

CLIXBY. A loc. n., Lincs

CLOAKE, CLOAKIE. *Fr.* Cloquet; a p.n. (bell-flower). Clocke, a Hugt. n., Lond. 1618. Or *see* Clack

CLOD, CLODD. From St Claude, near Blois, Norm. Or *A.S.* Hlōd, Hlōth; p.n. (loud, famous)

CLOONEY, CLOWNEY. *See* Clunie.

CLOSE. Prot. ref. n., Lond. 1618. *See* Clowes

CLOSSON. *S.* Klason; *G., Dch.* Clauson; p.n. From Nikolaus. Prot. ref. n., Lond. 1618

CLOTHIER. *A.S.* Hlothhere; *Fr.* Chlother, Clotaire; p.n. Clothar, the name of a Frankish king. *Clod* for *loth* (fame); *hari* (warrior)

CLOUDESLEY. A loc. n., Warw.

CLOUDSDALE. From Clydesdale; a loc. n., Lanark

CLOUGH. A loc. n., Yorks. *N. Klofi,* a cleft or rift in a hill. Or from the Irish *cloch,* a stone

CLOUT. *D.* Kloth; *Dch.* Kloot, Kluit; p.n. *See* Clodd

CLOUTING. *G.* Klatting; *Dch.* Cloetingh; *Fl.* Cloeten; p.n. Descendants of Kloth

CLOVER. *N.* Klaufi (?) (awkward); *Dch.* Kloover; *D.* Klüver; p.n.

CLOW. *See* Cluff

CLOWES. Dimin. of Niklaus; *F.* Klás; *D.* Kloos, Klose; *Fl.* Claus, Cloes, Close; *Dch.* Kloos, Klous; *G.* Klaus, Klaas, Klaws, Klos, Klose; p.n.

CLUBB, CLUBBE. *A.S.* Cloppa; *G.* Kloebb, Klobe, Klober, Klupsch; *Dch.* Clob, Klop; *Fl.* Clop; p.n. (a loud speaker (?))

CLUCAS. From M'Lucas (a Manx name). Celtic MacLucais, the son of Luke

CLUCKIE. From Macluckie. *See* Luckey

CLUER. *See* Clewer

CLUES. *Dch.* Clüjs; a p.n. Or *see* Clowes

CLUFF. *See* Clough

CLULOW. Welsh Lleulu (?) (light)

CLUNE. From Clun; a loc. n., Salop. Or Irish M'Clune, *clones* (meadows)

CLUNIE. A loc. n., Perth

CLUSBY. *See* Gillespie|

CLUSE. *See* Clowes

CLUTTEN. *See* Clutton

CLUTTERBUCK. A Flem. ref. n.; a loc. n. *A.S. hluttor beck*; *G. lauter-bach* (clearbrook)

Cloerterbooke was Sheriff of Glos. in 1586.

CLUTTON. A loc. n., Ches., Somers

CLYMA, CLYMO. *See* Clemo

CLYNE. A loc. n., Scotl. Or *D., G., Dch.* Klein; a p.n. (small)

CLYST. A loc. n., Devon

COACHAFER. *Fl.* Cauchefer; a p.n.; *Fr. cauchevis* (?) (a crested wren)

COATES. A loc. n., Edinbgh., Yorks

COBB. *N.* Kobbi, dimin. of Jakob. *A.S.* Cobba; *S.* Kobbs; *Dch.* Kop; *G.* Kobe, Kober, Kopp, Kopper; p.n.

Cobb in Rot. Obl. et Fin.

COBBETT, COBETT. Dimin. of Kobbi (Jakob); *Dch.* Cobet; *Fl.* Cobbaert; *G.* Kobitz; p.n. Or from Coubet; a loc. n., Norm. *See* Cobb

Hugo Coubite, Norm. 1180; Suff. 1340.

COBBLE, COBLE. *S.* Cobel; *Fl.* Copal; *G.* Kopple; p.n. *See* Cobbold

COBBLEDICK. From Coppledyke or Coupledyke; a loc. n., Lincs. Or Koppeldijk; a *Dch.* loc. n.

Hund. Rolls, Johann de Cupledick, Test. de Nev. Rob. de Cubbledick.

COBBOLD. *A.S.* Godbeald, Godbold, Godebold; p.n. (Goth prince or bold Goth)

COBLEY. A loc. n., Worcest.

COBON. From Coburn, a contraction of Cockburn

COCHRANE. A loc. n., Renfrew

COCK. *D.* Cock; *A.S.* Cocca; *Fr.* Cocq; *Dch.* Kok; *G.* Koch; *S.* Kock; *D.B.* Coc.; p.n.

Cocus in Rot. Obl. et Fin., K. John. As a surname it is frequent in Cornwall, so is probably derived from *B. coch* (red)

COCKAYNE. *See* Cocking. Or *Fr.* Cocagne; *Dch.* Kocken; p.n. Fam. n. of Cock

COCKBURN. A loc. n., Scotl.

COCKEN. *See* Cockayne

COCKER. *A.S.* Cocca; *Fr.* Cocard, Coqueau; p.n. *See* Cock. A Hugt. n., Norwich, 1622

COCKERELL. *Fr.* Cocquerel; a p.n. From Cocherel; a loc. n., Norm. Or Cockerhill, Ches.

Richard Cokerell in Rot. Obl. et Fin.

COCKERHAM. A loc. n., Lancs

COCKERTON. A loc. n., Dur.

COCKETT. *Fl.* Kockaert; a p.n. Dim. of Cock

COCKIE. *See* Cock

COCKING. A loc. n., Suss.

COCKLE. From Cockhill (?); a loc. n., Somers. Or Kochel; a loc. n., Germ. Cokele, a Prot. ref., Norwich, 1622.

COCKRAM. *See* Cockerham

COCKRILL. *See* Cockerell

COCKS. *See* Cox

COCKSEDGE. From Cockhedge; a loc. n., Lancs

COCKSHAW. *See* Cockshott

COCKSHOTT. A loc. n., Salop

CODD. *Dch.* Kode; a p.n.

CODD, CODE. *A.S.* Cod, God; p.n. *See* Goad. *Dch.* Kode; a p.n. Hugt. n., 1618

CODEY, CODY. From Codhay; a loc. n., Devon. Or *see* Codd

CODLING. A loc. n., Dur. Or dim.

CODNER. From Codnor; a loc. n., Derbysh.

CODRINGTON. A loc. n., Glos.

Held by De Cantelupe, 1201.

COE. *Dch.* Coe, Koe; p.n.; *D.* Koe (?) (a cow)

COFFEE, COFFEY. From the Irish Cobhthaigh. Or *A.S.* Coifi, Cufa (bold); *Fr.* Coffé; p.n.

COFFIELD. *See* Corfield

COFFIN. From Couvin; a loc. n., Belg. Or Couvain, Norm. *A.S.* Cofin; a fam. n.; *Fr.* Coffin; a p.n.

COFIELD. *See* Coffield

COGGAN, COGGING. *Fl.* Coghen; Irish Cogan; p.n.

COGGER. *N.* Kuggi (a cog); *G.* Cogho; *Dch.* Kogghee; *A.S.* Cogga; p.n. Coege, a *Fl.* ref., Lond. 1618

COGGINS. *See* Coggan

COGHILL. *See* Cargill

COGHLAN. From the Irish O'Cochlain; a p.n. (hooded man)

COGMAN. *See* Coggan

COGSWELL. From Coggeshall; a loc. n., Ess.

COKE. *See* Cock

COKER. A loc. n., Somers.

Held by De Mandeville, 1203

COLBECK. A loc. n., Lincs. Or Caldebec, Norm.

COLBORNE. *N.* Kolbjörn. *A.S.* Colbeorn; p.n. (helm-bear)

Colebern, a tenant in chief in *D.B.*

COLBRANT. *A.S.* Colbrand; a p.n. (helm-sword)

COLBY. From Coleby; a loc. n., Lincs, Norf.

COLCLOUGH. A loc. n., Staffs

COLCOMBE. From Challacombe; a loc. n., Devon. Or Chalcombe, Northants

COLDHAM. A loc. n., Camb.

COLDRON. *A.S.* Cold, Gold; *Old G.* Goldrun; *Fr.* Caudron; p.n. (gold-mystery)

COLDWELL. A loc. n., Northbd.

John Coldwell, M.D., Bp. of Salisbury, 1575.

COLE. *See* Colls

Richard Cole in Rot. Obl. et Fin., K. John. Also a Fl. ref., Lond., 1618.

COLEMAN. *A.S.* Colman; p.n. (charcoal man). *See* Colman In *D.B.* and Rot. Obl. et Fin. Or from *coll* (a helmet).

COLEMORE. A loc. n., Hants

COLERIDGE. A loc. n., Devon

COLES. *Fl.* Cools; a p.n. *See* Colls

COLGATE. A loc. n., Suss.

COLGAN. From the Irish *colg* (a sword), a swordsman

COLGROVE. A loc. n., Herts

COLK. *Dch.* Kolk *G.* Kalk; p.n. *See* Cawker

COLLACOTT. A loc. n., Devon

COLLAMBELL. From Colomby; a loc. n., Normandy. *D.B.* de Columbels; *Fr.* Colombel; p.n. In Roll of Battell Abbey.

COLLEGE. From Colwich; a loc. n., Staffs. Or *Fr.* Collige; a p.n.

COLLETT. *Fr.* Collette; a p.n. (collar)

COLLIE, COLLEY. From Cuilly; a loc. n., Norm. *Fr.* Colleye. A Hugt. n., Lond. 1618

COLLIER. *See* Colyer

COLLING. A loc. n., Yorks. *A.S.* fam. n.

COLLINGBOURNE. A loc. n., Wilts

COLLINGRIDGE. From Collingham Bridge (?); a loc. n., Yorks

COLLINGTON. A loc. n., Heref.

COLLINGWOOD. From Callingwood; a loc. n., Staffs

COLLINS. *N.-Fr.* De Colince. From Coulonces; a loc. n., Norm. Or *see* Colling

COLLISHAW. *See* Cowlishaw

COLLS. *N.* Kollr and Kolr (the head); also a pet n. ("my boy"); *S.* Kull; *D.* Koelle; *G.* Kolla, Koller, Kolley, Kohl, Kohler; *Dch.* Koll; *D.B.* Col, Cola, Colo, Cols; *Fl.* Colas, Colles, Colle, Culus; p.n.

COLLYNS. *See* Collins

COLMAN. *N.* Kalman; *A.S.* Colman (helmet-man); *Dch.* Koelman; *G.* Kohlmann; p.n. *See* Colls John Coleman in Rot. Obl. et Fin., K. John.

COLMER. *See* Colemore

COLOMB. From St Colomb; a loc. n., Cornw. Or Colombier, France

COLPUS. *N.* Kálfr (a calf); *Fl.* Calphas; *G.* Kalbas; *A.S.* Calpus; p.n.

COLQUHOUN. A loc. n., Dumbarton

COLSON. *Fl.* p.n. *See* Colls

COLTON. A loc. n., Lancs, Staffs Yorks

COLVER. *See* Calver

COLVILLE. From Colleville, near Bayeux Gilb. de C., Suff. 1086.

COLWELL. A loc. n., Northumbd. *See* Colville

COLYER. From Collioure (?); a loc. n., France

COMAN. *Fl.* Coeman; a p.n.

COMBE. A loc. n., Glos.

COMBES, COOMBES. *N.-Fr.* Comes; a p.n. Rot. Hund. 1272

COMERFORD. From Comberford; a loc. n., Staffs

COMFORT. A loc. n., Cornw. Or *see* Comerford

COMLEY. A loc. n., Salop

COMMERELL. From Comberwell (?); a loc. n., Wilts

COMPER. From Champier (?); a loc. n., Norm.

COMPTON. A loc. n., Dorset, Hants, Somers, Staffs, Wilts

COMYNS. From Comines; a loc. n., Flanders

CONDER, CONDY. *N.-Fr.* Condé; a loc. n., Normandy

CONDUIT. *See* Conder

CONE. From Cosne; a loc. n., France. Or *N.* Konr (noble); *Dch.* Con; *Fl.* Coen; p.n. Or Irish M'Cone

CONGDON. A loc. n., Cornw.

CONGRAVE. *See* Congreve

CONGREVE. A loc. n., Staffs

CONINGHAM. *See* Cunningham

CONINGSBY. A loc. n., Lincs

CONISBEE. *See* Coningsby

CONLEY. From Cononley; a loc. n., Yorks. Or *see* Conolly

CONNEL. Irish Connal; a p.n. (chief's courage)

CONNOR. From the Irish O'Conchobhair; a p.n. (endowed with strength)

CONNORTON. From Conderton (?); a loc. n., Glos.

CONOLLY. From the Irish O'Conghaile; a p.n. (chief courage)

CONQUEST. From Conquet; loc. n., Bretagne

CONWAY. A loc. n., N. Wales

CONYERS. From Coignieres, Isle of France

COOCH. *G.* Kütsch; *Fl.* Couche, *Fr.* Gouche; p.n. *See* Gooch

COOK. *A.S.* Cuc, Cucca; p.n. (quick, lively)

COOKSEY. A loc. n., Worcest.

COOMBE. A loc. n., Cornw., Devon, Hants, etc. Or Irish M'Combe

COOPER. From Cupar; a loc. n., Fife. Or *A.S.* Cuppa (a cup); *Fl.* Kupper; *Dch.* Cuyper; *N.-Fr.* De Cuper, Kooper; p.n.
Coup'e in 1327.

COOPMAN. *A.S.* Copman; *Fl.* Coopman; a p.n. (a merchant, dealer)

COOTE. *A.S.* Cut, Cuth; *Fl.* Coet; *Dch.* Koot; *G.* Kutt; p.n. (noted, skilled)

COPE. *N.-Fr.* Coupe; *Dch.* Koop, Kop, Koope; p.n.
Rot. Hund. 1272.

COPESTAKE. From Corpusty (?); a loc. n., Norf. *D.B.* Corpestig

COPESTICK. *See* Copestake

COPEMAN. *See* Coopman

COPLAND, COPELAND. *See* Coupland

COPLESTONE. A loc. n., Devon

COPPERTHWAITE. *See* Cowperthwaite

COPPING, COPPINGER, COPPON. *N.* Kaupungr; n.n.; *D.* Koeppen; *S.* Koppang; *Dch.* Koppen; a p.n. (a merchant). Flem. ref., Lond. 1618

COPSEY. *See* Cobb

CORAH. From Corrar; a loc. n., Salop

CORBET. *Fr.* p.n. (raven)
Corbet, an under-tenant in *D.B.*, and in Rot. Obl. et Fin., K. John.

CORBY. A loc. n., Cumb., Lincs, Northants. Or Corbie, France; Corbais, Belg.

CORBYN. *N.-Fr.* Corbin; a p.n. (crow)
Corbine, in Roll of Battell Abbey, and Corbin under-tenant in *D.B.*

CORCORAN. From the Irish *corcurach* (purple). *See* Cochrane

CORDINGLEY. From Cottingley; a loc. n., Yorks

CORDOCK. *Fr.* Cordeaux; a p.n.

CORDREY. *See* Cowderoy

CORDY. *Fr.* Cordeau; *Dch.* Cordes, Cordia; *G.* Korte; p.n.

CORE. *See* Cory

CORFIELD. A loc. n., Salop *See* Cornfield

CORKE. From Kork; a loc. n., Germ. *D.* Kork; *Dch.* Korch; *Fr.* Corque. Hugt. n., Lond. 1618

CORKHILL. From the Manx Mac-Corkyll derived from the Scandio-Celtic Macþor-Ketill or Þorkell. Or *see* Cargill

CORNELL. *N.-Fr.* Corniola; *Fl.* Cornehl; p.n.

CORNFIELD. *G.* Kornfeld; a p.n.

CORNFOOT, CORNFORD. *See* Cornforth

CORNFORTH. A loc. n., Dur.

CORNISH. From Cornesse; a loc. n., Belg. Or the county of Cornwall

CORNS. From the Irish Curran

CORNWALL. The county n. Or Cornville, Norm.

CORPE. From Corps; a loc. n., Norm.

CORRINGTON. From Corringdon; a loc. n., Dorset

CORSBY. *See* Cosbey

CORSER. *A.S.* Corsa; *N.Fr.* Corvesar; *G.* Korsawe; p.n. (tormentor (?))

CORY. *N.-Fr.* Coriei; *A.S.* Cari; p.n. Or Irish M'Corry

COSBEY. From Cosby; a loc. n., Leics

COSGRAVE. A loc. n., Northants

COSGROVE. *See* Cosgrave

COSHAM. A loc. n., Hants

COSSEY. From Cossy; a loc. n., Norf.; Coussey, France. Or *N.* Kausi; n.n. (a cat); *D.* Koese; *G.* Kose, Kosig; *Dch.* Cossa; *Fl.* Cossé; p.n.

COSSHAM. A loc. n., Hants

COSSINGTON. A loc. n., Somers.

COSSINS. *See* Cozens

COSSTICK. *See* Copestick

COSTELLO. From Mac Ostello, descendants of Hostilio de Angulo, settled in Ireland *temp.* Hen. II. Or *G.* Gostelle; *Old G.* Costila; p.n.

COSTERTON. A loc. n., Scotl.

COTCHEIFER. *See* Coachafer

COTES. A freq. loc. n.

COTESWORTH. From Cottesford; a loc. n., Oxf.

COTHAM. A loc. n., Glos., Yorks

COTHER. *See* Cottew. Or Irish M'Cottar

COTON. A loc. n., Northants, Staffs

COTTAM. A loc. n., Lancs, Notts

COTTERELL, COTTERILL. *N.-Fr.* Coterel; a p.n.

COTTEW. *Fr.* Cotteau; *G.*, *Dch.* Kothe; *A.S.* Cotta; p.n. *See* Gotto

COTTINGHAM. A loc. n., Northants, Yorks

COTTLE. *N.-Fr.* Cotel; *Fr.* Coutelle; a p.n.

COTTON. A loc. n., Camb., Suff.

COTTY. *See* Cottew

COUCH. From Coucy; a loc. n., Norm.

COULLING. *See* Cowling

COULSON. A loc. n., Devon

COULSTON. A loc. n., Wilts

COULTHART. *D.* Coulthardt; *Fl.* Colleart; *Dch.* Collard; *A.S.* Colta, Couta; p.n. Probably from the *N.* Kollotahart, a hart without horns.

COULTON. From Colton; a loc. n., Lancs

COUNSEL. *N.-Fr.* Consel; a p.n.

COUPLAND. A loc. n., Northumbd.

COURAGE. From Curridge; a loc. n., Berks. Or *Fr.* Correges. a Hugt. n.

COURCEY. *Fr.* De Courcy; a p.n.

COURTEEN. From Courtonne, near Caen. Surr. 1130; Ess. 1189

COURTNAY. From Courtenay; a loc. n., France William de Curtenay, *temp.* K. John. Rot. Obl. et Fin.

COUSENS. *See* Cozens

COUTTS. *See* Cutts

COVEL. *Fr.* Chauvel; a p.n.

COVENTRY. A loc. n., Warw.

COVERDALE. A loc. n., N. Yorks

COVERLEY. *Fr.* Coveliers; a p.n.

COVINGTON. A loc. n., Hunts

COW. *Fr.* Cahu (?); a p.n. (owl). Or *see* Cowie

COWARD. *A.S.* Cuhard (strong, noble). Or from La Couarde, near Rochelle. *Fl.* Couard; *Fr.* Chouard; p.n. A Hugt. n., 1688 De Coarda occurs in Norm. 1198; Roger de Cowert, Rot. Hund. 1272.

COWDEROY, COWDRY. From Cordray; a loc. n., Norm. De Codria, 13th century

COWELL. From the Irish Mac Cathmhoil; a p.n. Or *N.-Fr.* Cauvel

COWES. *D.* Koese; *Dch.* Koes, Coes; *Fl.* Couez; *Fr.* Caux (?); p.n. A loc. n., Isle of Wight

COWIE. A loc. n., Kincardine

COWLAND. A loc. n., Edinbgh.

COWLEY. A loc. n., Bucks, Derbysh., Middlsx., Oxf., Staffs

COWLING. A loc. n., Suff., Yorks

COWLISHAW. From Cowlishall; a loc. n., Lancs

COWLS. *See* Colls

COWPERTHWAITE. A loc. n., Westmd.

COX. *Lat.* Cocus; *Fl.* Kockx; *Dch.* Koks, Kokx; p.n. *See* Cock

COXHEAD. From Coxyde; a loc. n., Belg.

COZENS. From Cusances; a loc. n., Norm.; Cosen, Belg. *Fr.* Cousin; *Dch.* Couzijn; p.n. Hugt. n., Lond. 1618

CRAB. *A.S.* Creba; *G.* Krappe; *Dch.* Krabb; *Fl.* Crab, Crabbe; p.n. (a crab)

CRABTREE. A loc. n., Devon

CRACK. *N.* Kráka *D.* Krage; (a crow); a n.n.; *A.S.* Crac; *D.* Krag; *Fl.* Crach; *Dch.* Kraak; p.n.

CRACKENTHORPE. A loc. n., Westmd.

CRACKNALL, CRACKNELL. From Craigneill; a loc. n., Edinbgh.

CRACROFT. A manor in Lancs

CRADDOCK. A loc. n., Devon. Or Cradoc, S. Wales.

It is probably a corruption of Caradoc, which was Latinised to Caractacus. Welsh *caradwg* (beloved).

CRAFER. *G.* Kreifer; *Fl.* Creve, Creyf; p.n.

CRAFT. *D.* Kraft; *Dch.*, *G.* Kraft, Kroft; p.n. (strength)

CRAGG. A loc. n., Yorks. Or *D.* Krag; a p.n. *See* Crack

CRAIG. A loc. n., Forfar

CRAIGIE. A loc. n., Ayrshire

CRAIK. A loc. n., Sutherland

CRAIKE. A loc. n., Dur., Yorks

CRAKE. A loc. n., Norf., Yorks

CRAMPTON. From Crompton; a loc. n., Lancs

CRANAGE. A loc. n., Ches. Or from Cranwich; a loc. n., Norf.

CRANBROOK. A loc. n., Kent

CRANE. From Crehen; a loc. n., Belg. Or Cranne, in Maine; *D.* Krener; *G.* Kren; *Fl.* Craen; p.n.

CRANEY. *See* Crane

CRANG. *See* Cranke

CRANK. A loc. n., Lancs. Or *D.* Kranker, Crenker; *Fl.* Craninck; *G.* Krancke; p.n. (ill)

CRANKSHAW. *See* Cronshaw

CRANMER. A loc. n., Devon; Cranmore, Camb.

CRANNIS. *G.* Krannisch, Krentsch; a p.n. Dim. *See* Crane

CRANSEN. *See* Cranston

CRANSTON. A loc. n., Edinbgh.

CRANWELL. A loc. n., Lincs. Or from Cramanville, Norm.

CRAPP. *See* Crab

CRASKE. *G.* Kraske; p.n. Dimin. of *D.*, *Fl.*, and *Dch.* Crass

CRATE. *A.S.* Creda, Creoda, Grid; *Dch.* Kret; *G.* Kreth; p.n. From *A.S. hræd* (ready, quick)

CRAUFORD. A loc. n., Lanark

CRAVEN. A loc. n., Yorks

CRAW. *A.S.* Crawe; a p.n. The Scottish form of Crow

CRAWFORD. A loc. n., Dorset, Lanark, Lancs

CRAWHALL. From Crakehall (*D.B.* Cracele); a loc. n., Yorks. Or Croxall, Derbysh., and Staffs

CRAWLEY. A loc. n., Bucks, Hants, Suss.

CRAWSHAW. A loc. n., Lancs

CRAZE. *Fr.* Crez; *Dch.* Kress; p.n.; Crest; a loc. n., France

De Cres in Rot. Obl. et Fin.

CREAK. From Creake; a loc. n., Norf.

CREAM. *See* Gream

CREAMER. *Fl.* Cremer, Crimmers; *G.* Kremer; *Dch.* Cramer, Cremer; p.n. *See* Grimmer. Prot. ref. n., Lond. 1618

CREASE. From the Irish M'Creech

CREASEY. *See* Cresey

CREAVEN. *See* Craven

CREECH. From Creich; a loc. n., Sutherld.; Criech, Fife; Crich, Derbysh. *See* Creak

CREED. A loc. n., Cornw. Or *see* Crate

CREEDY. Irish M'Creedy

CREEKE. *See* Creak

CREER. *See* Grier

CREIGHTON. A loc. n., Staffs

CRELLIN. From Crallan ; a loc. n., Norm.

CRESEY. From Crécy ; a loc. n., Norm.
Cressy is on the Roll of Battell Abbey, and a tenant in chief in *D.B.*

CRESSWELL. A loc. n., Northbd., Staffs. Or *N.-Fr.* De Croissiles ; a p.n.

CREW, CREWE. A loc. n., Ches. Or *Fr.* Croux ; a p.n.

CREWDSON. *A.S.* Creoda, Croda, Crud ; *hrod* (glory) ; *Fl.* Crusen, Crutzen ; p.n. *See* Croote

CREYKE. From Crayke ; a loc. n., Yorks

CRIBBIN. From M'Robin

CRICHTON. A loc. n., Edinbgh.

CRICK. A loc. n., Northants. Or *see* Creak

CRICKET. *See* Critchett

CRIGLEY. *See* Critchley

CRINGLE. *N.* Kringla ; a n.n. (a circle)

CRIPPS. From Crispin. *G.* Krips ; a p.n.

CRISELL. *Dch.* Kressel or Kristel ; a p.n. Dim. of Christopher

CRISP, CRISPIN. From St Crispin ; a Norman-French loc. n.
Milo Crispin, a tenant in chief in *D.B.* Also in Rot. Obl. et Fin.

CRITCHETT. *N.-Fr.* Crichet, Cruchet, Criquet ; p.n.

CRITCHFIELD. From Cruickfield (?); a loc. n., Berwick

CRITCHLEY. From Crickley ; a loc. n., Glos.

CRITTENDEN. *See* Cruttenden

CROAGER, CROAKER. *See* Crocker

CROASDALE. From Croixdal ; a loc. n., Normandy. Or Croxdale, Dur.

CROCKER. *N.-Fr.* Le Crochere ; a p.n. (a cross bearer)
In Rot. Obl. et Fin. and Rot. Hund.

CROCKETT, CROCKITT. *N.-Fr.* Crochett ; *Fl.* Crockaert ; *Fr.* Croquet ; p.n.

CROCKFORD. A loc. n., Kirkcudbright

CROCOMBE. From Crowcombe ; a loc. n., Somers

CROFT. A loc. n., Cornw., Glos., Heref., Yorks. Or *Dch.* Kroft ; a p.n. *See* Craft
Bernard de Croft in *D.B.*

CROKE. *See* Crocker

CROLY. *See* Crawley

CROMBIE. A loc. n., Fife

CROMIE, CRUMMIE. *See* Crombie

CROMWELL. A loc. n., Notts

CRONK. *G.* Krancke ; p.n. *See* Cranke

CRONSHAW. From Cranshaws ; a loc. n., Berwick

CROOK. A loc. n., Devon, Westmd., Dur. Or *N.-Fr.* Croc, Croch, Fitz-Croch ; p.n.

CROOKENDEN. From Crookdean ; a loc. n., Northd.

CROOKES. A loc. n., Yorks

CROOMBE. From Croome ; a loc. n., Worcest., Yorks

CROOTE. From Crot ; a loc. n., Norm. Or *A.S.* Creoda, Crud, Cryda ; *Dch.* Kroode ; p.n. *See* Crewdson
Grud, Grut, Grutt, Saxon tenants in *D.B.* R. Grut in Rot. Hund. 1272.

CROPPER. *N.* Kroppr ; n.n. (a hump) ; *A.S.* Croppa ; *S.* Cropps ; *Dch.* Krop ; *G.* Kropp, Kroppe ; p.n.
Crop in Rot. Obl. et Fin. Also *N.-Fr.* S. de Croper, Northants, 1194.

CROSBY. A loc. n., Cumb., Lancs, Lincs, Westmd.

CROSHER. *See* Crocker

CROSLAND. A loc. n., Yorks

CROSS. From St Croix; a loc. n., Norm. *Dch.* Crosse; a p.n.
De St Cruce, Norm. 1180; de Cruce, Eng. 1199. Prot. ref., Croydon, 1618.

CROSSINGHAM. From Cressingham; a loc. n., Norf.

CROSSLEY. From Crosslee, Renfrew; or Crosslegh, Lancs

CROSSTHWAITE. A loc. n., Cumb.

CROSTON. A loc. n., Lancs

CROTHERS. *See* Carruthers

CROUCH. Atte Crouche, Court of Husting, 1258

CROUDACE. *See* Carruthers

CROUGH. *See* Crocker

CROUGHTON. A loc. n., Northants

CROWDER, CROWDY, CROWTHER. *A.S.* Creoda; *hrod* (glory); *Dch.* Kroode; p.n. Or *see* p. 13

CROWDSON. *See* Crewdson

CROWE. *See* Crocker

CROWHURST. A loc. n., Surr.

CROWLEY. From Crulai; a loc. n., France. Or *see* Crawley

CROWSHAW, CROWSHAY. *See* Crawshaw

CROWSON. *See* Crewdson

CROYDEN. *See* Croydon

CROYDON. A loc. n., Surr.

CROYSDALE. *See* Croasdale

CRUDGE. *G.* Crutge; *Dch.* Kruge; p.n. Dimin. of Crud. *See* Croote. Prot. ref., Lond. 1688

CRUDGINGTON. A loc. n., Salop

CRUM, CRUMMEY. *N.* Krumr; *Fr.* Crombey; p.n. (crooked, a cripple)

CRUMMACK. From Crummock; a loc. n., Cumb.

CRUMP. *See* Crum

CRUMPTON. *See* Crompton

CRUNDALL. From Crundale; a loc. n., Kent

CRUSE. From Creusanisy, Norm. *N.-Fr.* De Creus; a p.n.
De Crus in Rot. Obl. et Fin., Devon, 1199.

CRUSO. From Creusot; a loc. n., France. *Fr.* Creuseau; a p.n. Hugt. n., Norwich, 1622

CRUTCHER. *G.* Krutsche; a p.n. (a cross-bearer). Or *see* Crudge

CRUTHE. *See* Croote

CRUTTENDEN. A loc. n. Kent

CRUTWELL. From Crudwell; a loc. n., Wilts

CRYER. *G.* Kreyher; *Dch.* Kreije; p.n.

CUBITT. From Cowbitt; a loc. n., Lincs (*N. kúa-beit*, cow-pasture)
Pronounced locally Cubbitt, and written Cubyt as late as 1410. Or *see* Cobbett.

CUDBAR, CUDBY. *See* Cuthbert

CUDBY. A loc. n.

CUDDEFORD. From Cuttiford; a loc. n., Cornw.

CUDDEN, CUDDING, CUDDON. *D.* Gudden; a fam. n.; *Fl.* Guttin; a p.n.; *D.B.* Cudhen, Gudhen. *See* Goding. Or Irish M'Cudden

CUFF. *A.S.* Coifi, Cuffa; p.n.; *cóf* (active, bold)

CUFFE. *See* Coffee

CUISHEN. *See* Cushion

CULHAM. A loc. n., Berks

CULL. *A.S.* Cula, Culf; *G.* Kulla; p.n. A form of hwulf

CULLEN. A loc. n., Banffs. Or from the Irish O'Coilean; a p.n.; *coilean* (a young warrior)

CULLEY, CULLY. From Couillet; a loc. n., Flanders
Cuilly in Roll of Battell Abbey. Hugo de Cuilly in Rot. Obl. et Fin., K. John. Or Irish M'Cully.

CULLING. *A.S.*; fam. n. of Cull

CULLINGFORD. *See* Cullingworth

CULLINGWORTH. A loc. n., Yorks

CULLYER. *Fr.* Coulier; a p.n. *See* Colyer

CULMER, CULMORE. From Cullamore; a loc. n., Staffs

CULPECK, CULPICK. From Kilpeck; a loc. n., Heref. Or *Fl.* Callepeck; a p.n. Dim. of Calp

CULPERWELL. From Culverwell (?); a loc. n., Devon

CULPIN. From *N.* Kolbeinn (?) (black legs) ; *A.S.* Colben ; p.n.

CULPIT. *Fl.* Calepet (?) ; a p.n.

CULY. *See* Culley

CUMBERBATCH, CUMBERPATCH. From Comberbach ; a loc. n., Ches.

CUMBERLEGE. From Cumberlow ; a loc. n., Herts

CUMBY. *N.* Kumbi ; n.n. (a chopper) ; *Fl.* Combe ; *Fr.* Combet ; p.n.

CUMMINGS. *See* Comyns

CUNDIL. From Cundall ; a loc. n., Yorks

CUNDY. *See* Condy

CUNLIFFE. From Concliffe or Cunliff ; a loc. n., Lancs. *N.* Gunleif ; *A.S.* Gunleof ; p.n. (war love)

CUNNEEN. From the Irish *coinin* (a rabbit)

CUNNINGHAM. A loc. n., Ayrshire

CUNNINGTON. A loc. n., Hunts

CUPISS, CUPPAGE. From Kippax (?) ; a loc. n., Yorks

CUPPER. From Kupp ; a loc. n., Germ. Or *see* Cooper

CURD. *A.S.* Curda (a staff) ; *G.* Kurde ; p.n.

CURE. *N.-Fr.* De la Cour ; a p.n.

John Cure, Rot. Hund. 1272.

CURL. *A.S.* Ceorl ; *D.* Curjel ; *S.* Correll ; *Dch.* Kurrell ; p.n. (a free man)

CURLING. *N.* Karl, Kerling ; *G.* Kerling ; p.n. *See* Curl

CURLY. A loc. n., Norm.

John de Curley in Warwickshire. Rot. Obl. et Fin., K. John.

CURNOCK. From Carnock ; a loc. n., Fife

CURNOW. *N.-Fr.* du Cournau ; a p.n.

CURRAN. Irish Cwaran ; a p.n. (sickleman, farmer)

CURREY, CURRIE. A loc. n., Edinbgh.

CURSHAM. From Corsham ; a loc. n., Wilts

CURSON, CURZON. From Courçon, near Caen.

Curson in Roll of Battell Abbey. De Curcan in *D.B.*

CURTAIN. *Fr.* Courtin ; a p.n. *See* Courteen

CURTIS. From Cortys ; a loc. n., Belg. Or *Fr.* Courtois ; a p.n. (courteous). Hugt., Norwich, 1622

CURTLER. From Curtley ; a loc. n., Northants. Or *G.* Gertler (a girdle-maker) ; a p.n. Curtelow, Fl. ref., Lond. 1618

CURWEN. *A.S.* Garwine ; *Old G.* Gerwin, Caroin ; *Fl.* Carroen ; p.n. (spear friend)

CUSACK. *Fr.* Queyssac ; a p.n. Or *see* Kissack

CUSSICK. *See* Cusack

CUSHING, CUSHION, CUSHON. *N.-Fr.* Le Cuchon ; a p.n.

CUSS. From Gouis or Gouvis ; a loc. n., Norm. *N.-Fr.* De Guz ; a p.n.

W. Cousche, Cust, or Cushe, Camb., 13th cent. Testa de N.

CUSTANCE. From Coutance ; a loc. n., Normandy

CUTBARTH. *See* Cuthbert

CUTCHER. *G.* Kutscher ; a p.n. (a coachman). Or *see* Goodyear

CUTFORTH. From Cuttiford ; a loc. n., Cornw.

CUTHBERT. *A.S.* Cuthbeorht, Cuthbryt (noted brightness). Or Gûðbeorht (war bright) ; *D.B.* Cutbert ; p.n. *See* Gotobed

CUTLACK. *N.* Guðlaug (good play) ; *A.S.* Cuthlac, Guthlac ; *D.B.* Gotlac ; p.n.

CUTLER. *Fl.* Cotteleer ; a p.n.

Gaufrid de Cuteler in Rot. Obl. et Fin., K. John.

CUTMORE. *See* Catmur

CUTTER. *A.S.* Cuthere ; *G.* Kutter ;
Fr. Coudeyre, Cuttier, le Couteur ;
p.n. (good warrior)
CUTTING. *See* Cudden

CUTTLE or CUTHILL.   A loc. n.,
Haddington. Or *see* Cottle
CUTTS. *See* Coote
CYPHER. *See* Sypher

D

DABBS. *G.* Dabisch ; p.n.   *N.-Fr.*
D'Abice ; De Abbacia
Rot. Hund.
DABLE. *Dch.* Debel ; a p.n. *See*
Daplin
DACK. *G.* Dach ; *Fl.* Dache ; *Dch.*
Dake ; p.n.   *See* Day
DADE. *N.* Dadi ; *A.S.* Dadda, Dado ;
N.-Fr. Dade ; *Irish* M'Dade ; *F.*
Datter, Dede ; p.n. (father)
DADFIELD. A loc. n.
DADY. *See* Dade
DAGG. *N.-Fr.* De Augo ; p.n.   *See*
Day. Dague, Hugt. n., Cant. 1622
DAGGET. *A.S.* Dœgheard ; *D.* Dau-
gaard, Doggert ; *Fl.* Degard ; p.n.
(glory - strong).   Dackett, Flem.
ref., Norwich, 1622
DAGLEY. *Fr.* Dachelet ; a p.n. (?)
DAGNALL. From Dagnell ; a loc. n.,
Worcest.
DAGWORTHY. From Dagworth ; a
loc. n., Norf.
DAINES. *N. Fr.* D'Aines ; a p.n.
DAINTREE. From Daventry ; a loc.
n., Northants
DAINTY. *S.* Dente ; *Fr.* Dantée ;
p.n. Or Anthée ; a loc. n., Belg.
DAISLEY. From Disley ; a loc. n.,
Ches.
DAKING. *N.-Fr.* De Akeny. From
Acquigny, Norm. Or *Dch.* Dek-
king ; p.n. *See* Deck
DALBY. A loc. n., Lincs, Yorks
DALE. A contraction of Dalzell.
Or Atte-Dale
DALLAS. A loc. n., Elgin, Moray
DALLEY. *N.-Fr.* D'Ally ; a p.n. From
Ailly, Norm.
DALLINGER. *N.* Dellingr (day-
spring) ; *G.* Döllinger ; *Dch.* Dal-
lings ; p.n.

DALRYMPLE. A loc. n., Ayrshire.
Gaelic *Dail-á-chruim-puill.*
Anciently spelled Dalruimpuill, Dal-
rimpil.
DALTON. A loc. n., Dumfries,
Devon, Dur., Lancs, Yorks
DALY. From the Irish *dal* (blind).
Or from Dailly ; a loc. n., Belg.
and Scotl.
DALZELL. *See* Dalziel
DALZIEL. A loc. n., Lanark
Anciently Dalyell, Dalvell.
DAMANT. *Dch.* and *G.* Diamant ;
p.n. *See* Dimond
DAMER. *A.S.* Dægmær ; a p.n.
(glory famed)
DAMPIER. From Dampierre ; a
loc. n., Normandy
W. de Danpere in Rot. Obl. et Fin.,
K. John.
DAMS. *N.-Fr.* D'Ames ; *G.* Dam-
mas, Damis, Dams ; *Dch.* Dam-
mers ; *Fl.* Dams ; p.n.   Prot. ref.,
Norwich, 1622. *See* Ames
DANBROOK. From Danbury (?) ; a
loc. n., Ess.
DANBY. A loc. n., Yorks
DANCE. From Ans ; a loc. n.,
Belg. ; *G.* Dance ; *Fl.* D'Ans,
Danse ; p.n.
DANCER. *A.S.* Denisheard (strong
Dane). Or *N.-Fr.* D'Ancere ; a
p.n. From Anceres, Norm. ; *Fl.*
Dansaert ; p.n.
DANDRIDGE. From Danebridge ; a
loc. n., Ches.
DANDY. *Fr.* Dandoy ; a p.n.
DANE. *N.* Danir , *S.* Dann ; *D.*
Dehn, Dein ; *G.* Denia, Deny ;
A.S. Dane, Dene, Dena ; p.n.
See Deyne

DANGAR. *A.S.* Denegær, Dengar (Dane-spear); *D.* Dankert; *G.* Danger; *Fr.* Danguet; p.n. Or *N.-Fr.* D'Angers. Prot. ref., Lond. 1618

DANGERFIELD. *N.-Fr.* Dangerville; a p.n.

DANIEL. *Fr.*; p.n. A Hugt. n., Lond. 1618; Norwich, 1622

DANKS. From Henges, near Amiens. De Henges in Rot. Hund.

DANN. *A.S.* Dan, Dene, Tan; *Fr.* Danne; p.n. *See* Dane

DANNAHY, DENNEHEY. *See* Deneher

DANNATT. *Fr.* Dannet; a p.n. Dim. of Dann

DANSIE. *See* Dance

DANSON. *D.* Dan : *S.* Dann ; *Fl.* Danne ; *G.* Dann ; p.n. *See* Dane

DANVERS. From Anvers, La Manche, France
In Roll of Battell Abbey, *D.B.* and Rot. Obl. et Fin., K. John.

DAPLIN. *S.* Döbelin (Dahbelin); a p.n. Dapperling (a dwarf)

DARBEY, DARBY. From Derby; loc. n.
Dyrbye is a loc. and p.n. in Denmark.

DARCY. From de Ardreci, D'Arcie A tenant in chief, *D.B.* (Lincs).

DARE. *A.S.* Deor, Diar, Dyre; *Fl.* Dare; *Dch.* Diere; p.n. *See* Dyer

DARK. *N.-Fr.* D'Arques; a p.n. *See* Arch

DARKIN. *See* Dorking

DARLING. *A.S.* Deorling, Derling; p.n. (beloved)

DARLINGTON. A loc. n., Dur.

DARLOW. From Darly; a loc. n., Derbysh.

DARNELL, DARNILL. *See* Dartnall

DARNTON. *See* Darrington

DARRAH. *See* Darroch

DARRELL. From Airel; a loc. n., Norm.

DARRINGTON. A loc. n., Yorks

DARROCH. From Darragh ; a loc. n., Isle of Man. Irish, *dair* (oak)

DARTNALL. From Darnhall (?); a loc. n., Ches.

DARVALL, DARVELL. DARWALL, *N.-Fr.* D'Orival ; a p.n.

DARWEN. A loc. n., Lancs. From the British Darwenydd, Derguint (Derwent). Or *A.S.* Deorwynn ; a p.n. (dear friend)

DASENT. *Fr.* Dessaint ; a p.n. *See* Sainty

DASH. From Assche ; a loc. n., Belg. *Fr.* D'Assche ; a p.n.
Roger de Asc in Rot. Obl. et Fin., K. John. De Ash, Court of Husting.

DASHPER. *Fl.* Deschepper ; a p.n.

DASHWOOD. A loc. n.

DATE. *A.S.* Dæda ; *Fr.* Dethy ; p.n. *See* Dade

DAUBENY. From Daubigny ; a loc. n., France. *N.-Fr.* D'Albini ; a p.n.

DAUNT. *G.* Dohnt ; a p.n.

DAUNTON. *N.-Fr.* Dantan, De Donton ; p.n.

DAVAGE. *Fr.* Duverger ; a p.n.

DAVENPORT. A loc. n., Ches.

DAVID. *Fr.*, *D.*, *Dch.*, *G.* ; p.n.

DAVIE. *See* Davy

DAVIES, DAVIS. Welsh Ap Dafydd ; Irish M'Daid ; *Fr.* Devis ; p.n.

DAVIN. Irish *Daimh* (a poet). Or *see* Devine

DAVITT. *Dch.* Dawit, Davijt ; p.n.

DAVY. *Fr.* Dévé ; a p.n.

DAW, DAWES. *D.* Daue ; *F.* Dauewes, Douwes ; *G.* Thou, Dohse ; p.n. Daw is also a dimin. of David

DAWBARN, DAWBIN, DAWBORN. *Fr.* Daubin ; a p.n. *See* Daubeny

DAWBER. *A.S.* Dagobert, Dægbeorht ; *Fr.* Daubert ; p.n. (illustrious)

DAWBRY. A loc. n., Derbysh.

DAWDY. *See* Dade

DAWDRY. *See* Dordry

DAWLEY. *See* Daly

DAWKINS. *See* Daw. Dimin.

DAWSON. *See* Daw. Ger. Prot. ref. n., London, 1621

DAY. *N.* Dagr; *A.S.* Dag, Dæg; *S.* Daug; *G.* Dege; *Fl.* Day, Daye; p.n. (day, brightness, glory). Or from St John de Day, near St Lo

DAYNES. *See* Dane

DEACLE. From Achel (?); a loc. n., Belg. Or *see* Tickle

> De Acle occurs in Rot. Obl. et Fin., K. John.

DEACON. le Dekene in 1327

DEADMAN. *N.* Vjoðmar (brave man); *D.* Dettmer; *Dch.* Dettman; *G.* Dittmann, Dittmer, Tiedemann; *A.S.* Dodeman, Dudeman

DEALY. *See* Daly

DEAN, DEANE, DENE. A loc. n., Hants, Northants, Roxburgh, Yorks

DEARDEN. A loc. n., Lancs

DEARING. *N.* Dyri (a deer); *A.S.* Deoring; fam. n.; *Dch.* Dieren; *S.* Dyring; p.n.

DEARSLEY. From Dursley (?); a loc. n., Glost.

DEARTON. From Dearden; a loc. n., Lancs

DEASE. *A.S.* Dis, Tis, Tisa; *Dch.* Dis; p.n. From the Goth. *thius* (a servant)

DEASON. *See* Dyson

DEATH. *Fr.* D'Ath; a p.n. Ath; a loc. n., Flanders

DEAVES, DIVES. A loc. n. in Normandy. *Fr.* Devis; a p.n.

> Devise in Roll of Battell Abbey. *D.B.* de Dive.

DEAVIN. *See* Devine

DEBENHAM. A loc. n., Suff.

DE BURGH. *See* Bourke

DECENT. *See* Dasent

DECK. *G.* Deck, Decke, Decker; *Dch.* Dekker; p.n. *See* Day

DEDMAN. *See* Deadman

DEE. From St Die; a loc. n., France. *Dch.* Die; a p.n.

DEED. *A.S.* Did, Theod; p.n. (people)

DEEDES. *See* Dade

DEEKES. *See* Dicks

DEEKER. *Dch.* Dieker; p.n. *See* Dicks

DEEVES. *See* Deaves

DEEVEY. *See* Davy

DEIGHTON. A loc. n., Yorks

DELACHEROIS. *Fr.* Delacroix; a p.n.

DELAMERE. *Fr.* Delamare; a p.n.

DELANEY. *Fr.* Delanney; a p.n.

DELAROE. *Fr.* Delarue; a p.n.

DELAY. From the *Fr.* De la Haye; a p.n.

DELLAR. *A.S.* Dealla; *G.* Della (eminent); p.n.

DELMEGE. *Fl.* Delmez; a p.n. Or *see* Talmage

DELMER. *See* Delamere

DELOOHERY. Irish form of Delacroix

DELVE. From Delft; a loc. n., Holl. *Fl.* Delf. A Prot. ref. n., Lond. 1618

DEMER. *Fr.* De Meur; a p.n.

DEMPSER. *See* Dempsey

DEMPSEY. From the Irish *diomusach* (arrogant)

DENCH. *Fl.* Dengis; a p.n. *See* Ding, Danche. A Hugt. n., Lond. 1688

DENEHAN. *Fr.* Denain; a p.n.

DENEHER. *Fr.* Denier or Denoyers; p.n.

DENHAM. A loc. n., Beds, Roxburgh, Suff.

DENIFFE. *Fr.* Deneuve; a p.n.

DENLEY. A loc. n.

DENNENT. *Fr.* Denin; p.n. Denain (?)

DENNETT. *N.-Fr.* D'Anet; a p.n.

DENNEY. A loc. n., Stirling. Or Denée; a loc. n., Belg. *Fl.* Denis, Denie, Deny; p.n.

DENNINGTON. A loc. n., Norf., Suff., Yorks

DENNIS. St Denis ; a loc. n., France. *Fr.* Denis ; p.n. Hugt. n., Lond. 1682

DENNISON, DENNISTON. From Denerdiston ; a loc. n., Suff. Or Denston, Staffs

DENNY. *See* Denney

DENSON. *See* Dennison

DENT. A loc. n., Yorks

DENTON. A loc. n., Lincs, Norf., Lancs, Northants, Northbd., etc. (16 places)

DERHAM. *See* Deerham or Durham

DERING. *See* Dearing

DERLYN. *See* Darling. Hugt. n., Norwich, 1622

DEROW. *Fr.* Derrieu ; a p.n.

DERRICK. A contraction of Theo-deric. Or *Fr.* Deryck, D'Eryc, or D'Heriche ; p.n. Hugt. n., Norwich, 1622

DESBOROUGH. A loc. n., Northants

DEVANY. *See* Devine

DEVERELL. Deverill ; a loc. n., Wilts. From Vireville (?) ; a loc. n., Norm. ; Deverall, Cornw. In Roll of Battell Abbey, Wm. de Deverell of Segelawe in Hund. Rolls, Hen. III.

DEVERY. *Fr.* Devereux ; a p.n.

DEVILLE. From Daiville ; a loc. n., Norm. *N.-Fr.* D'Eville ; a p.n. Devile and Doiville are on the Roll of Battell Abbey. Devle is in *D.B.*

DEVINE, DEVINNEY. *Fr.* Desvignes, Devine ; p.n. Hugt. n., Norwich, 1622

DEW. *N.-Fr.* D'Eu ; a p.n. *Lat.* De Augo, from Eu ; a loc. n., Norm.

DEWDNEY. *See* Dudeney

DEWES. *Fl.* Dewys ; a p.n. Hugt. n., Lond. 1618. *See* Dewey

DEWESBURY. From Dewsbury ; a loc. n., Yorks

DEWEY. From Dhuy ; a loc. n., Belg. Prot. ref., Lond. 1618 De Dwai. t. in chief, *D.B.*

I

DEWFALL. *Fr.* Duval. A Hugt. n., Lond. 1687

DEYNE. *D.* Dehn, Dein ; *Dch.* Deen, Deene ; *G.* Dane, Diehne ; p.n. *See* Dane

DEYNES. *Fl.* Daens ; a fam. n. *See* above

DIAPER. From Ipres ; a loc. n., Fland. *N.-Fr.* De Ypre ; a p.n.

DIBALL, DIBBLE. *See* Dipple

DIBBEN. *D.* Dibbern ; a fam. n. of Dibb

DIBBS. *F.* Tibbe ; *G.* Dibus ; p.n. *See* Tipple

DIBDIN. From Dibden ; a loc. n., Hants

DIBLEY. From Dipley ; a loc. n., Hants

DIBOLL. *See* Dipple

DICEY. From Diss ; a loc. n., Norf. It also appears as Disa, Disce, Disse

DICK. *See* Digges. Also a loc. n. From *A.S. dic* ; *Dch. dijk* (a dyke, bank, mound)
    W. de Dyck was Alderman of Edin-burgh, 1296.

DICKENS, DICKMAN. *See* Dicks

DICKS. *F.* Dîko, Dyko ; fam. n., Dîken, Dyken, Dikena ; *G.* Dix, Dieck, Dicke ; *Dch.* Diek, Dieker, Dikkers, Dikken ; p.n. *See* Digges

DIDLICK. From Didling ; a loc. n., Suss.

DIDSBURY. A loc. n., Lancs

DIDWELL. A loc. n.

DIFFEY. *See* Dive

DIGBY. A loc. n., Lincs

DIGGENS, DIGGES, DIGGON. *A.S.* Diga, Dycga (strong) ; *D.* Dige ; p.n. *See* Dicks

DIGGLES. From Diggle ; a loc. n., Yorks. Or Dikele, Fland. ; D'Eagles, from L'Aigle, Norm., has been suggested

DILKE. *See* Tilke

DILL. *A.S.* Dilla (good) ; *Dch.*, *Fl.* Dille ; *G.* Dill ; p.n. *See* Teele

DILLON. From the Irish O'Dilmhain; a p.n. (David)

DILWORTH. A loc. n., Lancs. Or *Fl.* Dielwart; a p.n.

DIMBLEBY. From Thimbleby; a loc. n., Lincs

DIMMER. *See* Dimon

DIMMOCK. From Dymock; a loc. n., Glost.

DIMON, DIMOND. *D.* Demandt; *Dch.* Dieman, Diamant; *G.* Demand, Demant, Diamant; *Fl.* Deman; *Fr.* Diman; *Old G.* Diomund; p.n. (servant-protector)

DIMPLE. A loc. n., Derbysh., Lancs

DIMSDALE. From Dinsdale; a loc. n., Dur.

DING. *N.* Dengir; cogn. *G.* Dinger; *Dch.* Denike, Dinger; *Fl.* Dengis; p.n. (one who whets)

DINGLEY. A loc. n., Northants

DINGWALL. A loc. n., Scotl.

DINHAM. A loc. n., Monmth.

DINNER. From Dinard; a loc. n., France. *Fr.* Diner, Dineur; *Fl.* Dinear; p.n.

DINSDALE. A loc. n., Dur.

DINSMORE. From Dinmore; a loc. n., Heref.

DINWOODIE, DUNWOODIE. A loc. n., Dumfries

DIPPLE. A loc. n., Devon. Or *see* Tipple

DIPROSE. *N.-Fr.* De Preaux; a p.n.

DISART, DISERT. From Izards; a loc. n., Norm. *N.-Fr.* D'Izard
In Roll of Battell Abbey.

DISBROWE. From Desborough; a loc. n., Northants

DISNEY. *N.-Fr.* D'Isigny; a p.n. From Isigny, Norm.

DITCHETT. From Ditcheat; a loc. n., Somers

DITCHFIELD. *G.* Dickfeld; a p.n.

DITCHLEY. A loc. n., Oxf.

DIVE. *Fr.* Dive; a p.n. *See* Deaves

DIVER. *N.-Fr.* Diveres; a p.n.
Rot. Hund. 1272.

DIX. *See* Dicks

DIXIE. *F.* Diko. Dimin. Dikje; p.n. Or *see* Dicey

DOAK, DOAG. *A.S.* Daga, Docca; *Dch.* Dooge; *Fl.* Docq; p.n. (day, *i.e.* bright, glorious)

DOBBIE. Dimin. of Robert. *Fl.* Doby. A Prot. ref. n., Lond. 1618

DOBBIN. *Dch.* Dobben; *G.* Dobin; p.n.; a fam. n.
Hugo Dobin in Rot. Obl. et Fin., K. John.

DOBBS. *See* Dobbie

DOBELL. *D.* Dobel; a p.n. Dim.

DOBNEY. *See* Daubeny

DOCKER. *Fr.* Docquet; a p.n. Or *see* Dockwra

DOCKERILL. A loc. n.

DOCKRAY, DOCKWRA. From Dockwray; a loc. n., Cumb.

DOD, DODD. *F.* Dodo; *A.S.* Dod; *D.* Dodt; *F.* Dodde; *D.B.* Dode; *Fl.* Dod, Dodd; p.n. *See* Dade
In Rot. Obl. et Fin.

DODDERIDGE. A loc. n., Sandford, Devon
Gilbert de Dodarig, A.D. 1218.

DODDING. *A.S.* Doding; a fam. n.; *F.* Doden. *See* Dodd
William Dodin (Worc.) *temp.* K. John.

DODINGTON. A loc. n., Kent, Lincs, Northants, Northbd.

DODSON. *D.B.* Dodesune; a p.n. *See* Dodd

DODSWORTH. *See* Dodworth

DODWELL. A loc. n., Hants, Warw.

DODWORTH. A loc. n., Yorks

DOE. *N.-Fr.* D'O. From the castle of O, Nerm.
J. and W. Doe in Rot. Hund. 1272.

DOGGETT. *N.-Fr.* Doget, Doket, Duket; p.n. Or *see* Dagget
Rot. Hund.

DOGOOD. *See* Toogood

DOIDGE, DOIG. *See* Doak

DOLAMORE. *See* Dolleymore

DOLBEN. From the *N.-Fr.* D'Albini; a p.n.

DOLEMAN. *A.S.* Doleman ; *N.* *dolgr* (foe) ; *D.* Dohlmann ; p.n.
DOLL. *Dch.*, *A.S.*, *G.* Doll ; a p.n. Dole, a Prot. ref., Norwich, 1622
DOLLAR. A loc. n., Clackmannan
DOLLAS. *See* Dallas
DOLLEYMORE. *N.-Fr.* De la Mare ; a p.n.
DOLLING. *G.* Dollen ; a p.n. ; fam. n. of Doll
DOLPHIN. *A.S.* Dolfin ; *N. dolgfinnr* (Finnish foe) ; *Fl.* Dolphin ; p.n. Dolfin, a tenant in chief in *D.B.*
DOMINY, DOMONEY. *G.* Domina ; a p.n. Dominic (Sunday child)
DONINGTON. From Donnington ; a loc. n., Leics
DONISTHORPE. A loc. n., Derbysh.
DONITHORNE. From Dinnethorn ; a loc. n., Devon
DONKIN. *See* Dunkin
DONNE. A loc. n., Perth
DONOGHUE. Irish (brown chief)
DONOUGH. *See* Donoghue
DORBEN. *See* Dawbin
DORDERY, DORDRY. From Audrey or Aldrey, Norm.
DORE. Dore ; a loc. n., Derbysh. Or *A.S.* Dor, Deor (dear) ; *Fr.* Doré ; *Dch.* Dórr, Dorre
DORKING. A loc. n., Surr.
DORMAN. From Dormans ; a loc. n., France. Or *N.* Þormundr (?) (Thor protector) ; *Dch.* Doorman ; p.n.
DORR. Dour ; a loc. n., Belg. Or *see* Dore
DORRELL. *See* Darrell
DORRINGTON. A loc. n., Lincs
DOTT. *D.*, *Dch.* Dodt ; a p.n. *See* Dodd
DOTTRIDGE. *See* Dodderidge
DOUBIKIN. *See* Dowbiggin
DOUBLE. *Dch.* Dubbel, Dubbeld ; *Fl.* Duballe, Dubal ; *G.* Dubiel ; p.n. ; *N. dubba* (to smite)
DOUBLEDAY. *Fr.* Doublet. A Hugt. n., Lond. 1685
DOUDS, DOWDS. *See* Dod

DOUGHTY. *N.-Fr.* De Oughtia (?) ; a p.n. ; *G.* Daute ; *Dch.* Dothée, Daudeij ; *Fr.* Daudé ; *Fl.* Dotheij ; p.n. Hugt. n., Lond. 1687. *See* Dodd
 De Dote in Rot. Hund.
DOUGLAS. A loc. n., Lanark
DOULTON. From Dolton ; a loc. n., Devon
DOUSE. From Ussey ; a loc. n., Norm.
DOUTHWAITE. A loc. n., Cumb., Yorks
DOVE. *N.* Dufan ; *S.* Dufva ; *D.* Duvier ; *Fl.* Dufey ; *Dch.* Douwe ; *G.* Dove ; p.n. *See* Duff
DOW, DOWE. *See* Duff.
 Dow is the Scottish form of Dove.
DOWDESWELL. A loc. n., Glost.
DOWDING. *A.S.* Dud, Thinda, Dudding ; p.n. *See* Deed
DOWDNEY. *See* Dudeney
DOWLEY. From Dowlais ; a loc. n., S. Wales
DOWNES. From Downies ; a loc. n., Kincardinesh.
DOWNING. A loc. n., Worc.
DOWNTON. A loc. n., Hants, Wilts
DOWNWARD. From Downhead (?) ; a loc. n. in Somerset
DOWSING. *D.* Duusen ; a p.n. *See* Dowse
DOWTELL. *Fl.* Dautel ; a p.n.
DOXEY. A loc. n., Staffs
DOY. *Fl.*, *Fr.* Doy. From Douy and Douai ; loc. n. Hugt. Lond. 1618
DOYLE. From Doel ; a loc. n., Belg.
DRABBLE. *N.-Fr.* D'Arables ; a p.n. Norm. 12th cent. In Rot. Hund. 1272.
DRAKE. *N.-Fr.* Fitz Draco, Fitz Drogo ; *A.S.* Draca, Drag, Thrag ; *D.* Dræger, Dracke ; *S.* Draghi, Drake ; *Dch.* Drager ; *Fl.* Draecke ; p.n. (force, strength). Prot. ref. n., Lond. 1618
DRAKEFORD. From Drayford (?) ; a loc. n., E. Worlington, Devon

DRANE. *N.* Þráin; *D.* Trane; *S.* Trana; *G.* Trenner; p.n.; *A.S. thrægian* (to run)

DRAPER. *A.S.* Drabba; *Fr.* Drapier; *Dch.* Draper; p.n. (a slayer). Hugt. n., Dover, 1622

DRAY. *N.-Fr.* Droie, Drey; p.n.

In Rot. Hund.

DRAYTON. A loc. n., Heref.

DREDGE. *See* Drake

DREW. From Dreux; a loc. n., Normandy. *See* Druse. Hugt. n., Norwich, 1622

DREWITT, DRUITT. *See* Drought

DREWRY. From Roueray; a loc. n., Norm. Or *A.S.* Thrudheri; a p.n. (a true warrior); *N.-Fr.* De Rouvray
Sire Niel Drury, Ald. of Lond., 1312.

DRIFFIELD. A loc. n., Yorks

DRING. From Tring; a loc. n., Herts. Or *A.S.* Dreng; a p.n. (a young soldier); *N. drengr* (a youth)

DRINKALL, DRINKHILL. *A.S.* Dringhel; a p.n. (a young soldier)

DRINKWATER. *Dch.* Drinkwaard (?); a p.n.
The warden of the scot-ale or lord's ale. It has been suggested that it is a corruption of Derwentwater, Cumb. At Eustone, Oxon, the earliest spelling is Derwenkwater.

DRIVER. *N.-Fr.* De Rivers; *Dch.* Druyve, Drijver; p.n.

DROOSTEN. *Dch.* Druivestein; a p.n.

DROUGHT. *N.* Þóriða (?); *A.S.* Drud, Druht, Thrud, Thryth; *G.* Drath; *N.-Fr.* Droart, Drouet, Drueth; p.n. (a true friend). A Hugt. n., Lond. 1618
R. D. in Rot. Hund.

DROZIER. *Fl.* Drogeir. Ref., Lond. 1618

DRUCE. *See* Druse

DRUMMOND. A loc. n., Ross, Scotl. Or *A.S.* Thrythmund, Truhmund; p.n. (true protector)

DRURY. *See* Drewry

DRUSE. *D.* Drews; *G.* Drusche; *Dch.* Dros; *D.B.* De Dreuues; p.n. *See* Drew
Herman de Drewes held many manors under the Conqueror in Glost., Heref., Worc., Wilts.

DRY. *See* Dray

DRYDEN. A loc. n., Lasswade

DRYSDALE. A loc. n., Dumfries

DUBBLE. *See* Double

DUBBLEDICK. From Doubledykes, Stonehouse, Lanark

DUBERLEY. *Fr.* Duboulay; a p.n.

DUCAT. *See* Duckett

DUCE, DUCIE. *See* Douse

DUCK. *N.-Fr.* Le Duc; *Dch.*, *Fl.* Duc; *G.* Duch; *S.* Ducke; p.n. *See* Duke

DUCKER. *S.* Ducke, Dücker; *Dch.* Duker; p.n. *See* Tucker

DUCKETT. *N.-Fr.* Duchet; a p.n.

DUCKHAM. A loc. n., Devon

DUCKWORTH. A loc. n., Camb.
Held by D'Abernon. The name was anciently written Dykewarde

DUDD. *N.* Þjóðar; *A.S.* Thiuda, Dudda; *theod* (people); *G.* Duda; p.n.

DUDDERIDGE. A loc. n., near Alwinton, Devon

DUDDING. From Dudden; a loc. n., Ches. Or *A.S.* Duding; a p.n. (descendants of Dod, Dud, Theod)

DUDENEY. *Fr.* Dieudonné; a p.n. (God-given)

DUDGEON. *See* Dodgson
In the north of England Dodgson is frequently so pronounced.

DUERDON. *Fr.* Dourdoigne; a p.n.

DUFF. *N.* Dufan; a p.n. adapted from the Gaelic in the 10th century; Irish *dubh* (black), *dubhoda* (dark)

DUFFETT. *Fr.* Duffaut; a p.n.

DUFFIELD. A loc. n., Derbysh.
DUFFILL. Duffel ; a loc. n., Belg.
Or *see* Duffield
DUFFUS. A loc. n., Elgin
DUFFY. Irish O'Duffy. *See* Duff
DUGDALE. A loc. n., Staffs
DUGGAN. Irish Duibhcenn ; a p.n.
(black head)
DUIGNAN. From the Irish O'Duibh-
gennain (of the family of Black
Gennan)

The O'Duigenans descend from Mainé,
fourth son of Niall of the nine host-
ages, King of Ireland, who died
A.D. 405. They were historians
(Ollamhs) from remote times.
Maelpeter O'D., Archdn. of Briefny,
1296. (Ann. Four Masters).

DUKE. *A.S.* Dug, Tuc, Tucca ;
p.n. From *A.S.* *dugan* (to be
doughty). *See* Duck. Fl. Prot.
ref., Lond. 1618
DUKINFIELD. From Dunkinfield ;
a loc. n., Ches.
DULLEY. *Fr.* D'Ully or Doullé ;
p.n.
DUMBLETON. A loc. n., Glost.
DUNBAR. A loc. n., Haddington-
shire
DUNCAN. Gaelic Donnachu (brown
chief)
DUNCE. From Dunse ; a loc. n.,
Berwick
DUNCOMBE, DUNCUM. From Dun-
comb ; a loc. n., Dur.
DUNDAS. A loc. n., Dalmeny,
Scotl.
DUNDONALD. A loc. n., Ayr
DUNFORD. A loc. n., Yorks
DUNGER. *Dch.* Duncker ; a p.n.
From Dunckhart
DUNGEY. From Dengie ; a loc. n.
in Essex. Or Dangu, a loc. n. in
Normandy
DUNHAM. A loc. n., Norf., Notts
DUNHILL. A loc. n., Waterford
DUNKIN. From Dunnichen (?) ; a
loc. n., Forfar. Or *N.-Fr.* Doni-
can ; a p.n.

DUNKLEY. From Dinkley ; a loc. n.,
Lancs
DUNLOP. A loc. n., Ayr
DUNN. From Dun ; a loc. n.,
Forfar. Or Irish Duine ; *A.S.*,
S., Dch. Dun ; p.n. (brown)
De Dun in Rot. Obl. et Fin.
DUNNETT. A loc. n., Scotl.
DUNNICLIFF. *See* Tunnicliffe
DUNNING. A loc n., Perth. *See*
Dunn
DUNSTALL. A loc. n., Staffs
DUNSTAN. A loc. n., Devon,
Northbd.
DUNTHORN. *See* Donithorne
DUNTHORPE. A loc. n., Oxf.
DURBRIDGE. From Dwrbach (?) ; a
loc. n., Pembroke
DURDEN, DURDON. From Dourdan ;
a loc. n., France
DURIE. *See* Dury
DURNFORD. A loc. n., Wilts
DURRANT. *D.* Durandin ; *Fr.*
Durand, Durant ; p.n. (enduring)
Durand in Roll of Battell Abbey.
D.B. Durand.
DURRELL. *Fr.* Durell. A Hugt. n.,
Lond. 1687. *See* Darrell
DURST. A Germ. p.n. Or *see* Durston
DURSTON. A loc. n., Somers
DURY. From Durie ; a loc. n.,
Fife. Or *Fr.* Duray, Duré ; p.n.
(durable)
DUTHY. *Fr.* Du Thais ; p.n. Or
see Doughty
DUTT. *A.S.* Dud, Thiuda ; p.n.
See Dade
DUTTON. A loc. n., Ches., Lancs
DWIGHT. *N.-Fr.* Doit ; a p.n. Or
see Thwaite
DYAS. *See* Dyce
DYBALL, DYBBELL. *See* Tipple
DYCE. A loc. n., Aberdeen
DYE. *G.* Thei ; p.n. *See* Tye
DYER. *N.* Dýri (a deer) ; Diore ;
D. Dyhr ; *A.S.* Deór, Dyre ;
S. Dyr ; *G.* Dier ; *N.-Fr.* ; p.n.
DYKES. A loc. n., Scotl.
DYMOCK, DYMOKE. A loc. n., Glost.

DYMOTT. *Fr.* Demotte; a p.n.; *N.-Fr.* de la Motte (fosse, moat)
DYOTT. *A.S.* Dœgheard; *Fl.* Dey-aert (glorious strength); p.n.

DYSART. *See* Disart
DYSON. From Dison; a p.n., Belg. *Dch.* Diessen; a p.n.

E

EACHER. *A.S.* Ecga, Egeor (point, edge); *D.* Egger; *Dch.* Eger; p.n.
EACOTT. *A.S.* Ecgheard; *D.* Eckert, Eigaard; *G.* Eckardt; *Fl.* Eekhout; p.n. (strong edge)
EADE. From Ede; a loc. n., Holland. Or *A.S.* Eadd; *F.* Edde; *S.* Ed; *G.* Eader; *Dch.* Ede, Edie, Ide; *Fl.* Ide; *Fr.* Ede; p.n. *See* Addy
EADIE, EADEY. From Eday; a loc. n., Orkney. Or *see* Addy, and Eade

Edie is used in Ireland for Adams.

EAGLE. A loc. n., Lincs; *D.B.* Aycle. Or *see* Diggles
EAGLESHAM. A loc. n., Renfrew
EAGLETON. A loc. n., Rutland
EAGLING. *N.* Egill; *A.S.* Egel (Ethel), Eagling; a fam. n.; *S.* Egelin; *Dch.* Eggeling; p.n. (noble)
EAKEN. *See* Eykin
EALES. *See* Eels
EALY. From Ely; a loc. n., Camb. Or *see* Healy
EAMES. *See* Ames
EARDLEY. From Eardisley; a loc. n., Heref. Or Eardlew, Staffs
EARL. *N.* Erli, dimin. of Erlingr. From *jarl* (an earl); *N.-Fr.* Le Erl; *S.* Erling; *G.* Erle, Erler; *A.S.* Erlechin, Erlenc; p.n.
In Rot. Hund.
EARNSHAW. A loc. n., Lancs. Or Ernsheugh, Berwick
EARP. From Erpe; a loc. n., Belgium. Or *N.* Erpr; *A.S.* Eorp (a wolf); *Dch.* Erp, Herpe; *G.* Erpff; *Fr.* Herpin; p.n.

EARWAKER, EARWICKER. *A.S.* Eurwacer, *efor wacer* (boar watcher), Eureuuacre, Euroac, Euuacre; *G.* Ehrich; *D.* Eyrich; p.n.
EASDALE. *See* Esdaile
EASLEE. From Eastlee; a loc. n., Hants
EAST. *N.-Fr.* D'Est; a p.n.

Rich. de E. Essex, W. Est, 31 Edw. I.

EASTALL. From Eastwell; a loc. n., Kent
EASTER. From L'Estre; a loc. n., Norm. Also a loc. n., Ess.
EASTERBROOK. A loc. n., Devon
EASTGATE. A loc. n., Dur.
EASTHAUGH, EASTO, EASTOE. *See* Easter
EASTLAKE. A loc. n., Devon
EASTON A loc. n., Devon, Ess., Herts, Northants, Yorks
EASTWOOD. A loc. n., Devon, Ess., Notts, Renfrew, Yorks
EASTY. *See* Easter
EASY, EASEY. *Old G.* Eso; *A.S.* Es, Esa, Esi; *F.* Eisse; p.n. *See* Ess
EATWELL. From Etwall; a loc. n., Derbysh.
EAVES, EAVIS. A loc. n., Lancs, Staffs, and other counties. Or *N.-Fr.* Ivas; *D.* Ivers; *Dch.*, *Fl.* Eves, Ivers; p.n.. *See* Eve. Prot. ref., Lond. 1622
EBBAGE. From Abridge (?); a loc. n., Ess.
EBBERN. *See* Hepburn
EBBLETHWAITE. *See* Ablewhite
EBBRELL. *See* Abrahall
EBBS. *A.S.* Eb, Ebba; *F.* Ebbe; *D.* Eber; *Dch.* Ebers; *S.* Ebbes; p.n. *See* Epps (strong wild boar)

EBBUTT. *See* Hebbert

EBDEN. From Hebden; a loc. n., Yorks

EBRIDGE. *See* Ebbage

EBSWORTH. From Ibsworth; a loc. n., Hants

ECCLES. A loc. n., Berwick, Lancs

ECKERSHALL. From Eccleshall; a loc. n., Staff.

ECKERSLEY. *See* Exley

EDDINGTON. A loc. n., Berks, Somers

EDDLESTONE. A loc. n., Peebles

EDDY, EDEY. From Aidie; a loc. n., Normandy. Or *see* Eade

EDEN. A loc. n., Durham

EDGAR. *A.S.* Eadgar; a p.n. (prosperous spear)

EDGCUMBE. A loc. n., Devon

EDGE. A loc. n., Glost., Salop, Yorks

EDGELL. From Edgehill; a loc. n., Somers

EDGELOW. A loc. n. *See* Edgerley

EDGERLEY. A loc. n., Ches., Salop

EDGINTON. *See* Egginton

EDGLEY. A loc. n., Salop

EDGWORTH. A loc. n., Glost., Lancs

EDINTON. A loc. n., Somers, Wilts

EDLESTON. From Egliston (?); a loc. n., Dorset

EDMASTON. From Edmonstone; a loc. n., Edinbgh.

EDMUNDS. *A.S.* Eadmund; *S.* Edman; *N.-Fr.* de St Edmond; p.n. (happy protector) In Rot. Hund.

EDRIDGE. *See* Etridge

EDWARDS. *A.S.* Eadweard; *D.* Edvard, Edwards; *Fr.* Edouard; p.n. (happy guardian)

EELS. *A.S.* Il, Ille; *G.* Ilse; p.n. (a hedgehog)

EGARR. *N.* Heggr (a kind of tree, *prunus padus*); *F.* Egge; *S.* Eger, Eggers; *Dch.* Eggers; *G.* Eger; p.n. Or *A.S.* Egger, Æthelgar (noble spear)

EGERTON. A loc. n., Kent, Lancs

EGGETT. *A.S.* Ecgheard; *G.* Eggert; p.n. (hard edge or point)

EGGINTON. A loc. n., Derbysh.

EGGLETON. A loc. n., Heref.

EGGS. *See* Egarr

EGLETON. A loc. n., Rutland; Egletons, France

EGLIN. *See* Eagling, Egelen; a loc. n., Pruss.

EGLINGTON. From Eggleton (?); a loc. n., Heref.

EGREMONT. A loc. n., Cumb.

EKE. *D.* Ek; *N.* Eik; *Dch.* Eik; *A.S.* Eaca; p.n. (an oak)

EKINS. *See* Eykins

ELAM. *See* Ellam

ELAND. A loc. n., Northbd. Or *Dch.* Elandt; a p.n.

ELBOROUGH, ELBROW, ELBURY. A loc. n., Somers

ELCOAT. From Elcot; a loc. n., Berks, Wilts

ELDERDICE. *See* Allardyce

ELDERSHAW. *See* Oldershaw

ELDERTON. A loc. n., Ross. Or Alderton, Northants

ELDRID. *See* Aldred

ELDRIDGE. From Eldrig; a loc. n., Wigton. Or *see* Aldridge

ELENGER. *N.* Erlinger; a p.n. *See* Earl

ELGAR. *N.* Álfgeirr (elf-spear); *S.* Elg; *D.* Helge; *G.* Elga, Elger; *Dch.* Elgers; p.n.; *D.B.* Elgar, Elfgar, Algar. *See* Algar

ELGEE. *See* Elgar

ELGOOD. *A.S.* Æthelgeard; *D.* Ellegaard; *B.D.* Elgert; p.n. (noble guardian)

ELKINGTON. A loc. n., Lincs, Northants

ELLABY. From Ellerby; a loc. n., Yorks. Or *D.* Elleby; a loc. and p.n.

ELLACOMBE. A loc. n., Devon

ELLAM. From Elham; a loc. n., Berwick, Kent

ELLAND. A loc. n., Yorks

ELLER. *A.S.* Ealhhere; *D.* Eller; p.n. (hall warrior)

ELLERAY. A loc. n., Westmd.

ELLERBECK. A loc. n., Yorks

ELLERD. *A.S.* Ealhweard; a p.n. (palace guard)

ELLERSHAW. From Elishaw; a loc. n., Northbd., Yorks

ELLERTON. A loc. n., Salop, Yorks

ELLICOMBE. From Ellicum; a loc. n., Belg. Or *see* Ellacombe

ELLICOT. From the Irish Mac Elligott; a p.n.; *Scot.* Mac Leod. Or *see* Elcoat

ELLINGHAM. A loc. n., Norf.

ELLINGTON. A loc. n., Hunts

ELLINGWORTH. *See* Illingworth

ELLIOT. *F.* Elle, Eilert; *A.S.* Ailward, Ailuert, Ailiet, Eli, Eliard, Eliert, Eliet; *N.-Fr.* Eliot; p.n. *See* Aylward

ELLIS. From Alis; a loc. n., Norm. Or Welsh Elias, Eliseus; a p.n. Or *A.S.* Elsa, Elsi, Ælfsige; p.n. (elf victory)

ELLISON. *See* Allison or Elliston

ELLISTON. From Elston; a loc. n., Wilts. Or *A.S.* Elstan, Ælfstan; p.n. (elf stone, *i.e.* firm elf)

ELLWICK. From Eldwick; a loc. n., Yorks

ELLWOOD. *Dch.* Elewoud; *Fl.* Elewaut; p.n. *See* Aylward

ELLYARD. *See* Aylward

ELMAR. *N.* Hjálmr (a helmet); *F.* Helmer; *S.* Hjelm; *Dch.* Helmer; *G.* Elmers. Or *A.S.* Elmar, Æthelmær (famous noble)

ELMHIRST. A loc. n., Staffs

ELMY. From Elmley; a loc. n., Kent

ELNAUGH, ELNEY. From Ellenhall; a loc. n., Staffs

ELPHEE. *A.S.* Ælfa; a p.n. (elf)

ELPHIC. *A.S.* Alfeage, Alfec, Ælfheah; p.n. (high elf)

ELPHINSTONE. A loc. n., Haddington

ELSDEN. From Elsdon; a loc. n., Northbd.

ELSE. *See* Ellis. Elys in 1327

ELSLEY. From Allesley; a loc. n., Warw.

ELSMERE. From Ellesmere; a loc. n., Salop

ELSTON. A loc. n., Devon, Yorks

ELSWORTH. A loc. n., Camb.

ELTON. A loc. n., Lancs

ELVEY. From the Irish M'Elvie

ELVIN. *A.S.* Elwi, Eluenc, Alfwin, Elfin; *S.* Elfwin; *Dch.* Elven; p.n. (elf-friend). Or Irish M'Elveen

ELVIS, ELWES. *A.S.* Ælf (elf); *N.-Fr.* Helouis; *S.* Elvers; *D.* Elvius; p.n.

ELWELL. A loc. n., Dorset

ELWYN. *See* Elvin

ELY. *N.-Fr.* Fitz Elie; a p.n. Also a loc. n., Camb.

EMBLETON. A loc. n., Cumb., Dur., Northbd.
Anciently Elmdene, Elmedon, Emeldon, Emleton.

EMBURY. From Emborough; a loc. n., Somers

EMERIDGE. A loc. n., Devon

EMERSON. *See* Ames

EMERTON. A loc. n., Devon

EMERY. *Dch.* Emmerie; *Fl.* Emery. From Emmerich; a loc. n. Hugt. n., Lond. 1685

EMES. *See* Ames

EMLY. From Elmley; a loc. n., Kent

EMMETT. From Amiot; a loc. n., Norm
William A. in Rot. Hund.

EMMS. *See* Ames

EMSDEN. From Elmstone; a loc. n., Kent

ENDACOTT. A loc. n., Devon

ENDERBY. A loc. n., Leics

ENDERWICK. *See* Inderwick

ENDICOTT. A loc. n., Devon

ENEFER, ENNEFER. From Henfynyw; a loc. n.

ENGLAND. *D.* Engelund ; *S.* Englund ; *N.-Fr.* Anglicus ; p.n. *See* Inglis

ENGLEDOW. *See* Ingledew

ENGLEFIELD. A loc. n., Berks

ENGLEHEART. *See* Ingleheart

ENGLISHBY. *See* Ingoldby

ENNIONS. *See* Onions

ENNIS. From Enys ; a loc. n., Cornw.

ENRAGHT. *A.S.* Eanred ; a p.n. ; *a'nræd* (one-minded)

ENSBY. From Ensbury ; a loc. n., Dorset

ENSELL, ENSOLL. From Hensall ; a loc. n., Yorks

ENSOR. From Edensor ; a loc. n., Derbysh.

ENTECOTT. *See* Endicott

ENTICKNAP. From Endikeknap ; a loc. n., Yorks, E.R.

ENTWISTLE. A loc. n., Lancs

EPPS. *A.S.* Eppa, Eappa ; *F.* Ebbo, Eppo ; p.n. *See* Ebbs.

EPTON. From Heppington ; a loc. n., Kent

ERDINGTON. A loc. n., Worcest.

ERLAM. From Earlham ; a loc. n., Suss.

ERRINGTON. From Erringden ; a loc. n., Yorks. Or *see* Harrington

ERSKINE. A loc. n., Renfrew

ERT. *See* Hart

ESAM. From East Ham ; a loc. n., Ess.

ESBALD. *See* Archibald

ESCOTT. A loc. n., Devon

ESDAILE. From Eskdale ; a loc. n., Cumb.

ESHELBY. From Exilby ; a loc. n., Yorks

ESLER. *See* Easlee

ESLING. *S.* Esselin ; a p.n. Or Eastling ; a loc. n., Kent

ESMOND. *See* Osmund

ESPIE. *D.*, *G.* Espe ; a p.n. *See* Hesp

ESPIN. From Hespen ; a loc. n., Belg.

ESPLEY. A loc. n., Northbd.

ESS. *F.* Eisse, Aisse ; *G.*, *D.*, *Fl.* Esser ; *Dch.* Es ; *A.S.* Æs, Æsc (ash) ; p.n.

ESSINGTON. A loc. n., Staffs

ESTCOURT. *See* Escott

ESTWICK. A loc. n., Herts

ETCHELL. From Nechells ; a loc. n., Staffs ; anciently Echeles. Or *see* Edgell

ETCHES. *D.*, *Dch.* Eggers ; *G.* Egers ; p.n. *See* Egar

ETHERIDGE. From Etterick (?) ; a loc n., Selkirk

ETHERINGTON. From Atherington ; a loc. n., Devon

ETRIDGE. *See* Etheridge

ETTLES. From Etal ; a loc. n., Northbd. Étalle, Belg. ; or Etaieles, France

EVANS. Welsh ; *Fl.* Evens ; p.n.

EVE. *A.S.* Æffa, Eafa, Ef, Efe (elf) ; *N.-Fr.* Ive ; *F.* Eve ; p.n. *See* Eaves. Prot. ref., Lond. 1618

EVELEIGH. From Everley ; a loc. n., Wilts

EVELY. From the Irish M'Evely. Or *see* Eveleigh

EVELYN. *Dch.* Evelein ; *N.-Fr.* Ivelyn ; p.n. *See* Aveling

EVENS. *See* Ivens

EVERARD, EVERED, EVERETT, EVERITT. *A.S.* Eoforheard, Eoferard, Efrard, Ebrard (a strong wild boar) ; *Fl.*, *Dch.* Everard ; *Fr.* Evrard ; *S.*, *D.* Evert ; *G.* Eberhardt ; p.n.

In Rot. Hund.

EVERINGHAM. A loc. n., Yorks

EVERS. *See* Ivers

EVERSFIELD. A loc. n.

EVERSHED. From Evershot (?) ; a loc. n., Dorset

EVERSON. *N.* Evarr ; *A.S.* Efer, Eofer (a boar) ; *S.*, *Fl.* Evers ; *D.*, *Dch.* Eversen ; p.n. Prot. ref., Lond. 1618

EVERTON. A loc. n., Beds

EVERY. From Ivry; a loc. n., Norm.

    D.B. de Iveri.

EVILL. From Yville; a loc. n., Normandy

EVINGTON. A loc. n., Glos., Leics

EVISON. *See* Everson

EWAN, EWEN. *A.S.* Euing; *Dch.* Ewing, Euwen; *G.* Euen; *D.B.* Ewen; p.n. Prot. ref., Lond. 1618. Scotch M'Ewen. From *A.S.* Eo, Eowa, Ewa; p.n. (ancient)

EWART. *N.-Fr.* De Huart; a p.n.

EWBANK. From Yewbank. A loc. n., Cumb.

EXELBY. A loc. n., Yorks

EXELL. A loc. n., Belgium. Or from Exwell; a loc. n., Rutland

EXLEY. A loc. n., Yorks

EXON. The ancient name of Exeter

EXTON. A loc. n., Devon, Rutland, Somers

EYES. From Huysse; a loc. n., Belg. *Fl.* Eyers; a p.n. Hies, a Prot. ref., Norwich, 1622

EYKIN. From Iken; a loc. n., Suff. Or *F.* Eke, Eike; *D.* Eiche, Eicken, Eken; *A.S.*, Ecca; *Dch.* Eck, Eik, Eijken; p.n. Also an Irish form of Aitken. Or fam. n. of Eke

EYKINS. *Fl.* Eykens; a p.n. *See* Eykin

EYLES. *See* Eels

EYRE. *See* Ayre

EYTON. A loc. n., Heref., Salop

    Held by Warin, relative of Pantulf, Baron of Wem, *D.B.*

F

FABB. *D.*, *Dch.*, *Fl.*, *G.* Faber; *Fr.* Fabri, Fabry; *D.B.* Faber, Fabri; p.n. (a smith). Fabre, a Hugt. n., Lond. 1678

FACER. *N.-Fr.* Fessart; a p.n.

FACHNEY. *Fr.* Fauconnier; a p.n. (a falconer)

FACON. *Fr.* Facon; a p.n. (falcon)

FADDY. *See* M'Fadden

FAGAN. From St Fagan; a loc. n., Glamorgan. Irish p.n. Or *A.S.* Fagin; a p.n.; *fægen* (joyful)

FAGE, FAGG. *A.S.* Fagg, Fac, Feg; p.n.; *N.-Fr.* De Fago; p.n.

FAIERS. *See* Fayers

FAIL. *D.* Feill; *Fl.*, *Dch.* Weel, Vael; p.n.; *A.S. væl* (good, true). Or *see* Fell

FAILES. *See* Felce

FAINT. *Dch.* Vendt; *Fl.* Vent; *G.* Fende; p.n. *See* Went

FAIRALL, FAIRHALL. *See* O'Ferrall

FAIRBAIRN. From Fairburn; a loc. n., Yorks

FAIRBROTHER. *A.S.* Færbeorht; a p.n. (illustrious traveller). Verbore, Prot. ref., Sandwich, 1622

FAIRCHILD. *Fl.* Verschilde; a p.n.

FAIRCLOTH. *See* Fairclough

FAIRCLOUGH. A loc. n.

FAIRFAX. From Ffairfach; a loc. n., Carmarthen. Or Irish Fearfassa, a form of Francis. *N. fögr-fax*; *A.S. fæger-feax*; means fair mane, but it is in no list of p.n.

FAIRFOOT. From Fairford; a loc. n., Glos.

FAIRHEAD. *Fl.* Verheide; a p.n. Or *A.S. fægr-heófod* (fair head)

FAIRHURST. From Fairest; a loc. n., Yorks

FAIRLEY. *Dch.* Verlee; *Fl.* Verlegh, Verley; p.n. Or *see* Fairlie

FAIRLIE. From Fairlee; a loc. n., Hants. Or Fairlie, Ayrshire

FAIRMAN. *See* Fearman

FAIRS, FAIREE. *See* Fayers

FAIRWAY. From Farway; a loc. n., Devon

FAIRWEATHER. From Fairwater; a loc. n., Glamorgan

FAIRY. From Verrey; a loc. n., France. Or *Fr.* Ferry, Féré; p.n. (shod with iron). Hugt. n., Lond. 1618. Also a loc. n., Scotl.

FAITH. *N.-Fr.* de St Faith. Or *S.* Feith; *D.* Faith; *G.* Veith; p.n.; *A.S. fétha* (a foot soldier). Hugt. n., Lond. 1618

FAKES. *D.* Fack; *D.B.* Fech; *F.* Feyke; *Fl.* Feykens; p.n. *See* Fagg

FALCONER. *See* Faulkner

FALKLAND. A loc. n., Scotl.

FALLE. *N. - Fr.* Falet; a p.n.; Fellie in Rot. Hund; Irish M'Fall

FALLENTIRE. *Dch.* Valender; a p.n. A Prot. ref., Colchester, 1622

FALLICK. *Fl.* Falck; *G.* Falk; p.n. (falcon)

FALLON, FALLOON. From Fologne; a loc. n., Flanders. Or Valognes, France; *Fl.* Falon; a p.n.

FALLOWS. From Falaise; a loc. n., Normandy. Also Fallais, in Flanders; *Fl.* Falise, Falloise; p.n.; *D.B.* de Faleise; p.n.
William de Faleis in Rot. Obl. et Fin., K. John.

FALLS. *See* Fallows

FALLSHAW. From Fullshaw; a loc. n., Ches.

FALVEY. *A.S.* Fealwe (yellow)

FAMIN. *Fl.* Vermin; a p.n. *See* Fearman

FANCOURT. From Falencourt; a loc. n., Normandy

FANE. From Fains or Veynes; loc. n., France; *D.B.* Fenise (?); *F.* Feyen; *Dch.* Feen; *Fr.* Faine; *Fl.* Fayen, Feyens; p.n.
Thomas de Vein held lands in Glost. *temp.* K. John, A.D. 1207. Rot. Obl. et Fin. Sir Francis Fane of Fulbeck, Lincs, and Aston, Yorks, third son of Francis, first Earl of Westmd., made K.B. at coronation of Charles I., Feb. 1, 1625.

FANN, FANNER. *Dch.* Fane; *Fl.* Vane; a p.n. *See* Fagan

FANNING. From Faineant; a loc. n., Norm.

FANSHAWE. A loc. n., Derbysh.

FARADAY. An Irish form of Ferguson. Or from La Ferte; a loc. n., Norm.

FARDELL. A loc. n., Devon
For some time the residence of Sir Walter Raleigh.

FARE. *See* Phair and Fayers

FAREY. *See* Fairy

FARGER, FARGHER. Gael. Fearachur (manly). *See* Fergus. Manx, contracted from Mac Fearghoir; *Ferg.* (brave). *See* Farquhar

FARIS, FARISH. *See* Ferrers

FARJON. *Dch.*, *Fr.* Fargeon; p.n. Hugt., Lond. 1685

FARLER. *See* Farley

FARLEY. A loc. n., Hants, Salop, Staffs, Surr., Wilts

FARLOW. A loc. n., Salop

FARMAN. *See* Fearman. Prot. ref., Colchester, 1605

FARMER. A loc. n., Somers (*D.B.* Ferramere). Or . *Fr.* Fermier; *Dch.* Vahrmeijer; p.n.; *A.S. feormere* (a farmer)

FARNBOROUGH. A loc. n., Berks, Hants

FARNFIELD. From Farnsfield; a loc. n., Notts

FARNHAM. A loc. n., Ess., Hants, Surr., Yorks

FARNINGTON. From Farmington; a loc. n., Glost.

FARNLEY. A loc. n., Yorks

FARQUHAR. Gael. Fearachur (manly)

FARR. A loc. n., Sutherland. Or *see* Fayer

FARRAGUT. *Old G.* Faregaud; *Fr.* Farcot; p.n. (travelled Goth)

FARRALL, FARRELL. Irish Farrall, O'Farrell; Fearghal (?) man of strength)

FARRANCE, FARRANT, FARREN.
N.-Fr. Farrand; *Fl.* Farin; p.n.
FARRAR, FARRER. *D.* Farrer; a
p.n. (a teacher). Or *see* Ferrers
FARRINGTON. A loc. n., Dorset,
Somers, Yorks
FARROW. *A.S.* Fara, Faro; *Dch.*
Faro; p.n. *See* Fayers
FARTHING. *A.S.* Færthegn, Far-
thein; *Dch.* Fardon, Vaarting;
Fl. Verdeyen; *D.B.* Fardan,
Fardein (Saxon tenants); p.n.
See Varden (a traveller Thane)
FARWIG. A loc. n. in Kent
FASHAM. From Faversham; a loc.
n., Kent (?)
FASSETT. *Fl.* Fassaert, Vassart;
p.n. Or *see* Fawcett
FASTNEDGE. A loc. n.
FATHERS. *N.* Fjöder (a feather);
Dch. Vader; *D., G.* Vater; *A.S.*
Fader, Fæder; *N.-Fr.* Le Feut-
rier; p.n.
FATLING. *A.S.* Fad; *Fr.* Vaudelin;
p.n. *See* Fathers
FAUCIT. *See* Fawcett
FAUCUS. *See* Vaux
FAUGHT. *S.* Vought, Fought; *Dch.*
Vogt; *G.* Fauth; p.n.
FAULCONBRIDGE. From Fauquem-
bergues; a loc. n., Normandy
FAULDING. *A.S.* Folthwine, Ful-
doin; p.n.; *feald, fold* (?) (field.
friend). Or the fam. n. of Fold,
Folth
FAULKE. *N.* Fálki (a falcon); *F.*
Fôlerk, Fôke, Fauke; *S.* Falck,
Falk; *D.* Falck; *Dch.* Folkers,
Valk, Fok, Vokke; *Fl.* Volck;
G. Falk, Forcke; *A.S.* Fale, Folc;
N.-Fr. Fulcher, Fulk, Fulco, etc.;
p.n.

Fouke and Fitz Fouk are in the Roll
of Battell Abbey. Fulche, Fulc,
Fulco, tenants in chief in *D.B.*

FAULKNER. *Fr.* Fauconnier; a p.n.
(a falconer); Hugt. n., Lond.
1681
FAUX. *See* Vaux

FAWCETT. From Fossard, France,
Forcett; a loc. n., Yorks. Or
Farcet, Hunts
Gilbert de Forset, in Lib. Vit. Dur.
FAWELL. *See* Fowell and Vowell
FAWN. *See* Vaughan
FAY. From Fay; a loc. n., Norm.
Or *D.* Faye, Feigh; *G.* Fay,
Fei; p.n. (a fairy)
FAYERMAN. *See* Fairman
FAYERS. From Vayres (?); a loc.
n., France. Or *S., D.* Fehr; *G.*
Farr; *Fl.* Feer; *Dch.* Fehrs; *A.S.*
Fara, Fær (traveller); p.n.
FAZACKERLEY. A loc. n., Lancs
FEA. See Fay
FEAKS. *See* Feek
FEAR. *Fr.* Feauer. *See* Fayers.
Hugt. n., Lond. 1618
FEAREY. *See* Fairy
FEARMAN. *S.* Fehrman; *G.* Fuhr-
mann; *A.S.* Faraman; p.n.
(carter, traveller)
FEARNCOMBE. From Farncombe;
a loc. n., Surr.
FEARNE. A loc. n., Ross. Or
A.S. Forn; a p.n.; *fearn* (fern)
FEARNHEAD. A loc. n., Lancs
FEARNLEY. From Fernilee; a loc.
n., Derbysh.
FEARNSIDE. A loc. n.
FEARON. *N.-Fr.* Feron; a p.n.
Ferun in Rot. Hund.
FEASEY. *See* Veasey
FEAST. *Fr.* Fisette; a p.n.
FEATES. *See* Fetch
FEATHERSTONE. A loc. n. in Yorks
FEATHERSTONEHAUGH. A loc. n.,
Northumbd.
FEAVERYEAR, FEAVIOUR, FEAVYER.
From Favières; a loc. n., France.
Fr. Favière; a p.n.
Richard Feverer in Rot. Obl. et Fin.,
K. John. Also Hugt. n.
FEEK. From Vicques; a loc. n.,
Norm. Or *A.S.* Fec, Feg, Fig;
S., D. Fick; *Dch.* Ficke; *F.*
Feyke, Fekke; p.n.
FEEN. *See* Fane

FEENEY. *See* Finney

FEETHAM, FEETUM. A loc. n., Yorks

FELCE. *A.S.* Wælisc (?); *Dch.* Fels, Velse; *G.* Felsch; p.n. Felles, Hugt. n., Lond. 1687. *See* Wallis

FELDWICK. *Dch.* Veldwijk; a loc. and p.n.

FELGATE. From Fellgate; a loc. n., Westmd.

FELL. *N.-Fr.* Faiel; *D.* Fjel; *Dch.* Vel, Velde, Veldt, Wel; *G.* Feldt, Feleer; *Fl.*, *Fr.* Velle; p.n.; *A.S. feld* (field)

Richard de-la-Felda occurs in Rot. Obl. et Fin., K. John, A.D. 1201 (Yorks). W. de Fall, Rot. Hund. 1272.

FELLOWES. *See* Felce

FELTHAM. A loc. n., Middlx., Dorset

FELTON. A loc. n., Northbd., Somers

FELTWELL. A loc. n., Norf.

FENDER. *A.S.* Wenda; *G.*; p.n. (a Vandal)

FENN. *See* Fane. Fene, a Hugt. n., Norwich, 1622

In Rot. Hund.

FENNELL. *Fr.* Venelle; a p.n.

FENNELLY. *See* Finlay

FENNER. From Feneur; a loc. n., Belg. *See* Venner

FENNIMORE. From Fennemere; a loc. n., Salop. Or Fenemere or Finmere, Oxon

Gilbert de Finemere held lands there in Oxon, A.D. 1208.

FENSHAM, FENSOM. From Vinchem; a loc. n., Fland.

FENTHAM, FENTUM. *See* Phantom

FENTON. A loc. n., Cornw., Lincs, Notts, Yorks

FENWICK. A loc. n., Ayrshire, Yorks

FENWRICK. *D.* Wendrick; *G.* Fenrich; *Dch.* Vendrik; *A.S.* Wenric; p.n. (wend-ruler)

FEREDAY. *See* Faraday

FERGUS. Scot., Celt. Fearghus (man of strength)

FERGUSON. *See* Fergus

FERNIE. *N.-Fr.* Vernie; a p.n. From Vernai; a loc. n., Norm.

FERNIHOUGH. From Fernihalgh; a loc. n., Lancs

FERNLEY. *See* Farnley

FERRABY, FERREBO. From Ferriby; a loc. n., Lincs, Yorks

FERRETT. *A.S.* Færheard; *Fl.* Feraert; *Fr.* Ferrett; *G.* Fereth; p.n. (strong traveller). Hugt. n., Dover, 1622

FERRIE. *See* Fairy

FERRIER. From Ferrières; a loc. n., Norm. and Fland.; *Fl.* Ferier; a p.n.

FERRIES, FERRIS. *Fl.* Verraes; a p.n. *See* Faris

FERRIMAN. *See* Fearman

FERRY. *See* Fairy

FERTEL. *G.* Virtel; a p.n. Dim. of Wird; a p.n. (fate)

FESSENDEN. A loc. n.

FESSEY. *See* Veasey

FETCH. From Vietz; a p.n., Germ. Or Fesches, France; *G.* Vietsch, Fietz, Fitza; *D.* Fitzer; p.n.; *N.-Fr.* Fitz; *Fl.* Vits; *D.B.* Fitheus (?); p.n. *See* p. 8, footnote

FEW. *See* Pugh

FEWKES. *G.* Fuchs; a p.n. (a fox). Or *see* Foggo

FEWSTER. *Fl.* Deveuster and Devuyster; p.n.

William Fuster in Rot. Obl. et Fin., K. John.

FEWTRELL. *N.-Fr.* Vautrel; a p.n. (a hunter)

Ralph Futerel, Herts, 1198. Rot. Cur. Reg.

FFOLKES. *See* Faulke

FFOOKS. *See* Fewkes

FFYTCHE. *See* Fetch

FICKLING. *N.-Fr.* de Wyclyne; a p.n.

FIDDAMAN, FIDDEMAN. *See* Fiddyman

FIDDES, FIDDY. *N.-Fr.* St Fides
FIDDYMAN. *D.*, *G.* Wiedemann ;
S., *Dch.* Wideman ; *Fl.* Widmer,
Wydeman ; p.n. *See* Fiddy
FIDDYMONT. From Wideumont ;
a loc. n., Fland.
FIDGEON. An Irish form of
Pidgeon. Or *Dch.* Viegen ; *Fl.*
Vigen ; p.n.
FIDGETT. From *Fr.* Fichet ; a p.n.
Dim. of Fig. *See* Feek
    In Roll of Battell Abbey. Perhaps
    from the loc. n. Vichte, Belg.
FIDLER. Le Fidelaire ; a loc. n.,
Norm. Or *A.S.* Fitela ; *G.* Fiedler ;
p.n. (a fiddler). *See* Vidler
FIDOE. *See* Fiddy
FIELD. *D.* Fjelde ; a p.n. *See*
Fell
FIELDING. *S.* Felldin ; *Dch.* Vel-
den ; p.n. ; fam. n. *See* Faulding
FIEN, FIENNES. *See* Fane
FIFETT, FIFOOT. *Fr.* Fivet ; a p.n.
FIFIELD. A loc. n., Ess., Hants,
Wilts
FIGGINS. *Dch.* Viegen ; *Fl.* Vigen ;
p.n.
FIGGIS. *Fl.* Figeys ; a p.n. *See*
Feek
FIGURES. *See* Vigors
FILBERT. From St Philbert ; a
loc. n., France. Or *A.S.* Fil-
brith ; *D.* Filbert ; p.n. (fully
bright, illustrious). Also *Fr.*
Philibert ; *A.S.* Wilbeorht ; *Old*
G. Willibert (resolute brightness)
FILGATE. From Villegats ; a loc.
n., Normandy
FILL. *A.S.* Fili ; *G.* Filla ; *Fr.*
Ville ; p.n. Or dimin. of Philip (?)
FILLINGER. *N.* Veljungr (?) ; a n.n.
(a wailing child) ; *D.* Felling ;
Dch. Fellinger ; *D.B.* Felaga ;
p.n.
FILLINGHAM. A loc. n., Lincs
FILLISTON. A loc. n. Or *Dch.*
Vilsteren (?) ; a p.n. (?)
FILLMORE, FILMER, FILMORE. *See*
Phillemore

FINBOW. From Finborough (?) ; a
loc. n., Suff. Or Irish Finbo ;
N. Finnbogi ; p.n. (white bow)
FINCH. From Vynkt ; a loc. n., Belg.
De Vinck, Prot. ref., 1622. *Fl.*
Finch, Vinck ; *G.*, *Dch.* Finke ;
p.n. ; *A.S. finc* (a linnet)
FINCHAM. A loc. n., Norf. ; Finchém,
Belg.
FINCHETT. *Fr.* Vinçotte (?) ; a
p.n. Or dim. of Finch
FINDLATER. A loc. n., Banff
FINELLY. *See* Finlay
FINIGAN. From the Irish O'Finne-
gan ; a p.n. (fair)
FINKELL. *Dch.* Finkel, Vinkel.
See Winkel
FINLAY. Celtic Fionnlaoch (white
soldier)
FINNEMORE. *See* Fenimore
FINNEY. *N.* Finni ; *A.S.* Fin ;
D. Finne ; *Fl.* Finné ; *S.* Finn ;
p.n. (a Finn) ; Celtic (fair)
FINNIS. *See* Fiennes. Ulf Finisc ;
a p.n. in *D.B.*
FIRBANK. A loc. n., Westmd.
FIRK, FIRKINS. *A.S.* Furic ; a
p.n. Dim. of *fýr* (fire). Or
fircynu (race of men)
FIRMAN. *Dch.* Ferman ; a p.n.
See Fearman
FIRMIN. *Fl.* Vermin ; a p.n. *See*
Fearman
FIRMINGER. *Fl.* Verminger ; a p.n.
FIRMSTONE. A loc. n.
FIRTH. A loc. n., Scotl.
FISH. *D.*, *S.*, *G.* Fisch ; a p.n.
See Fiske
FISHBOURNE. A loc. n., Dur.,
Suss.
FISHENDEN. A loc. n.
FISHER. *G.* Fischer ; *D.* Fisker ;
Dch., *Fl.* Visscher ; p.n. ; *A.S.*
fiscere (a fisher)
FISHWICK. A loc. n., Lancs. A
hamlet in the creek of the Ribble.
D.B. Fiscuic
    Johannes de Fyschwyke in Lib. Vit.
    Dur.

FISHLOCK. From Fishlake ; a loc. n., Yorks

FISHPOOL. A loc. n., Lancs, Notts

FISKE. *S.* Fiske ; *D.* Fisker; *G.* Fisch ; *Fl.* Fisco ; *D.B.* Fisc ; p.n. (fish)

FITCH. *See* Fetch

FITCHEW. Fitz Hugh (?)

FITHIAN. *See* Vythian

FITT. *Dch.* Vieth ; a p.n. *See* Fiddy

FITZPATRICK. *See* Patrickson

FIVASH. A loc. n. Or *see* Vivish

FIX. *D., Fr.* ; p.n. ; *A.S.* Fex, Feax ; p.n. (hairy)

FLACK. *See* Flagg

FLADGATE. A loc. n.

FLAGG. *G.* Flach, Flack ; *Dch.* Vlak ; p.n. *See* Flegg

FLAMANK. *Fl.* Flamand, Flament, Vleminck ; p.n. (a Fleming)

FLAMSTEAD. A loc. n., Herts

FLANDERS. The country of the Flemings

FLANNAGAN. Irish. Young Flann (ruddy)

FLATHER. *A.S.* Flæda ; *G.* Flauder, Flatau ; p.n. *See* Flatt

FLATLEY. From the Irish Flattley and Flattholy

FLATMAN. *A.S.* Floteman ; *Dch.* Flotman ; *G.* Flottmann ; p.n. (a shipman (?)). Or *see* Flatt

FLATT. *A.S.* Flad, Flæd, Flod ; *G.* Flatt ; p.n. ; *N. fliôd; Old G. flat* (beauty). Or *N.-Fr.* Floet ; a p.n. From La Flotte, near Rochelle

FLAVELL. *N.-Fr., Lat.* Flavilla (yellow)

FLAXMAN. *Dch.* Vlasman ; a p.n.

FLECK. Or Affleck. *See* Flegg

FLEECE. *Dch.* Vlies ; *G.* Fleege ; p.n. (a fly)

FLEET. A loc. n., Lincs. Or *Dch.* Vliet ; a p.n.

FLEETWOOD. A loc. n., Lancs

FLEWELLEN. *See* Llewellyn

FLEGG. *N.* Flóki (hairy, woolly) ; *D.* Vlak, Fleck ; *Dch.* Vleck ; *G.* Fleck, Fleger ; p.n. Or *N. fláki* (?) (flat moorland)
G. and W. Flegg are hundreds in Norf.

FLEMING. *S.* Flemming ; *Dch.* Vlaming ; *Fl.* Vleminck ; *G.* Flemming ; *D.B.* Flamand, Flandren ; p.n.
William le Fleming received the Manor of Aldingham, Lancs, from the Conqueror. Also a Prot. ref. n., Sandwich, 1622.

FLETCHER. *N.-Fr.* Le Flechier ; a p.n. (arrow-maker)

FLEURY. *Fr.* Fleury ; p.n. (florid). Hugt. n., 1687

FLEWITT. *See* Floyd.

FLEY. From Fly, Norm. *Dch.* Vlie ; *D.* Flye ; p.n.

FLICK. *Dch.* Flick ; *D.* Flig ; p.n. (a patch). Or *see* Flegg

FLIGHT. *D.* Flycht ; *Dch.* Vliet ; p.n. ; *A.S. flit* (?) (strife)

FLIN. *See* Flynn

FLINDERS. *See* Flanders

FLINT. A loc. n., Wales. Or *D.* Flindt, Flint ; p.n. (a fire-lock)

FLITT. From Fleet ; a loc. n., Hants, Lincs. Or *see* Flight

FLITTEN. *See* Flitton

FLITTON. A loc. n., Beds

FLOGDELL. A loc. n.

FLOOD. Atte Flode, Court of Hustings 1258. Or *see* Flatt. *A.S., S.* Flod ; *D.* Flott ; *G.* Flöte, Fluder ; p.n.

FLOOK. *N.* Flóki ; *D.* Floecke ; p.n. *See* Flegg

FLOOKS. *See* Flux

FLORY, FLOREE. A loc. n., Flanders ; *Fl.* Flory ; *Fr.* Floris ; p.n. A Hugt. n., Cant. 1622

FLOWERS. From Fleurus ; a loc. n., Flanders ; *Fl.* Floris, Vloors ; *Dch.* Florus ; p.n. Hugt. n., Lond. 1618
Elyas Flur in Rot. Obl. et Fin., K. John.

FLOWERDAY, FLOWERDEW. *Fr.*
Fleureau (?) ; a p.n. (flowery)
FLOYD. *See* Lloyd
FLUCK. *See* Flook
FLUDE. *See* Flood
FLURRY. *See* Flory
FLUTTER. *A.S.* Flodhere, Floter ;
G. Fluder ; *Fr.* Floutier ; p.n. (sea
warrior)
FLUX. *G.* ; p.n. Floques ; a loc.
n., Normandy
FLY. *See* Fley
FLYNN. Irish O'Flynn ; *N.* Fleinn ;
a p.n.
FOALE. *See* Fowell
FODDY. From the Irish *Fodha*,
the equivalent of Long
FOGARTY. The Irish equivalent of
Swift ; a p.n.
FOGG. *N. fok* (flight). *See* Foggo
FOGGIN. *Dch.* Focken, Vogin ; p.n.;
fam. n.
FOGGO. A loc. n., Scotl. Or
A.S. Focco, Focga ; *N.* Foka ;
fok (flight) ; *F.* Fokke, Fokko ;
p.n. ; *G.* Fökke, Vocke ; *S.*
Fock ; *D.* Fog ; p.n. ; *Fr.* Fou-
caut. Hugt. n., Lond. 1685
FOGWELL. From Vogwell ; a loc. n.,
Devon
FOISTER. *See* Fewster
FOL, FOLEY. From La Folie, Norm.;
Fr. Folie ; *D.B.* Folet ; p.n.
Folet in Rot. Obl. et Fin., K. John.
FOLJAMBE. From Fulgent ; a loc.
n., Norm.
In Hund. Roll.
FOLKARD. *A.S.* Folcheard (Falc
the strong) ; *Fl.* Volckaert ; *G.*
Folkert ; p.n.
FOLLETT. *Fr.* ; p.n. *See* Foley
FOLLIOTT. *N.-Fr.* Foliot ; a p.n.
In Roll of Battell Abbey and Rot.
Obl. et Fin., K. John.
FOLLOWES. *F.* Fôlers ; a p.n. Or
see Fallows
FOLLY. *See* Foley
FOLTROP. From Felthorpe ; a loc.
n., Norf.

FOOKS. *See* Fewkes
FOOT. *Dch.* Wout ; *G.* Wuthe ;
S. Futy ; *D.B.* Fot ; p.n. ; *A.S.*
fôte (nimble(?)))
FOOTER. *Dch.* Wouter ; a p.n. *See*
Foot
FOOTMAN. *A.S.* Wudeman ; *Dch.*
Woutman ; p.n. (woodman). *See*
Foot
FOOTTIT. *N.-Fr.* Fotet ; a p.n.
FORBES. A loc. n., Aberdeensh.
FORD. A loc. n., Devon, Dur.,
Salops, Staffs, Voorde, Fland.
De Ford in Rot. Obl. et Fin.
FORDER. A loc. n., Devon. Or
A.S. Forthere ; a p.n. (warrior)
FORDHAM. A loc. n., Ess.
FORDOM. *See* Fordham
FORDYCE. A loc. n., Banff
FORFEITT. *Fl.* Forfert ; a p.n.
(fault)
FORGAN. A loc. n., Fife
FORGE. *N.-Fr.* ; p.n. (smithy) ;
Forges ; a loc. n., France
and Flanders
FORKER. *See* Farquhar
FORKES. *See* Faulke
FORMAN, FORMON. *D.* Formann ;
Dch. Foreman ; *Fr.* Formont ;
p.n. Hugt. n., Lond. 1618. *See*
Farman
FORMBY. A loc. n., Lancs
FORMES. *G.* ; p.n. Contr. of *A.S.*
Formannus. *See* Fearman
FORREST. A loc. n., Cornw., Norm.,
Salop
FORRESTER. From Forestarius ; an
officer of feudal times
FORSAITH. A loc. n., Scotl.
FORSBREY. *See* Fosbery
FORSBROOK. A loc. n., Staffs ;
D.B. Fotesbroc
Osbert de Focebroc was living 3 John,
A.D. 1201. Pipe Roll, under Staf-
fordshire. Effigy of John de Fosse-
broke, Cranford Ch., Northants,
A.D. 1418.
FORSCUTT. A loc. n., Somers. Or
see Foscote

FORSDICK. *See* Fosdyke
FORSGATE. A loc. n.
FORSHAM. From Fosham ; a loc. n., Yorks
FORSHAW. From Faugeres ; a loc. n., France. Or *D.* Fourchou ; a p.n. From *N. Fagriskógr* (Fairwood) ; a loc. n. Or *Fr.* Faucheur, Fauchois ; p.n. (a mower, reaper)
FORSYTH. *See* Forsaith
FORT, FORTY. *N.-Fr.* le Forte. Or *A.S.* Forth, or Ford ; *Dch.* Voort ; p.n. *See* Fought
FORWARD. *See* Forwood
FORWOOD. A loc. n., Glost.
FOSBERRY, FOSBERY. From Fosbury ; a loc. n., Berks, Wilts
FOSBROOKE. *See* Forsbrook
FOSCOTE. A loc. n., Bucks
FOSDYKE. A loc. n., Lincs
FOSSETT. *See* Fawcett
FOSTER. *Dch.*, *G.* Forster ; *Fl.* Fostier ; *D.B.* Forst ; p.n. (a forester)
FOTHERBY. A loc. n., Lincs
FOTHERGILL. A loc. n.
FOTHERINGHAM. A loc. n., Inverarity, Scotl.
FOULE. *N.* Fugl ; *A.S.* Fugel, Ful. ; p.n. (a fowl)
FOULIS. A loc. n., Perthsh.
FOULGER. *See* Fulcher
FOULSHAM. A loc. n., Norf.
FOUNTAIN. *Fr.* Fontaine. A Hugt. n., Lond. 1688. A loc. n., Norm.
FOURACRE. A loc. n., Devon
FOWELL, FOWLE. *See* Foule
FOWERAKER. *See* Fouracre
FOWKES. *See* Folkes, or Vaux
Faucus in 1327.
FOWLER. *A. S.* Fula ; *G.* Vogler ; *Dch.* Vogelaar ; p.n. Or Foula ; a loc. n., Scotl. *Fr.* Fouiller ; a p.n. (a bird-catcher). *See* Fuller
Le Fowelere in Rot. Hund., Ess., Oxon ; le Feulere in 1327.

K

FOX. *Fl.* Fockx ; a p.n. ; fam. n. of Fokko
H. Fox in Rot. Obl. et Fin., K. John. A Prot. ref. n., Lond. 1618 ; Norwich, 1622. The old English broadsword was called a fox. *See* Vaux and Foggo.
FOXALL, FOXHALL. A loc. n., Suff.
FOXCROFT. A loc. n.
FOXLEY. A loc. n., Devon, Hants, Norf., Staff.
FOXTON. A loc. n., Camb.
FOXWELL. A loc. n., Devon
FOY. From Foye ; a loc. n., Heref. Also a Hugt. n. *See* Faith
FOYSON. *See* Fyson
FOYSTER. *See* Fewster
FRADGLEY. From Fradley ; a loc. n., Staff.
FRAKES. *See* Freeke
FRAME. *A.S.* Fram ; *Dch.* Vreem ; *D.* Frahm ; *N.-Fr.* Fitz Fram ; p.n ; *N. fram* (?) (forward)
FRAMPTON. A loc. n., Dorset, Lincs
FRANCIS. *Fr.* ; p.n.
R. le Franceis in Rot. Obl. et Fin., K. John.
FRANE. From Fresnes ; a loc. n., France
FRANKLAND. A loc. n., Devon
FRANKLANDS. A loc. n., Cumb.
FRANKS. *Fl.* Francus, Francx, Vranckx ; p.n. (free)
Francus in 1327.
FRAREY. *See* Freer
FRASER. Fraize ; a loc. n., France. *Fr.* Fraiseur ; a p.n. From *fraiser*, to plait or to fortify with stakes. Or fraisier (a strawberry)
FRAY. *See* Fry
FRAYLLE. From Fresles ; a loc. n., Normandy. Hugt. n.
FREARSON. *N.* Freyer (the god Freyr) ; *S.* Fria ; *G.* Freier ; *Fl.* Frey ; p.n.
FRECKLETON. A loc. n., Yorks
FREEBODY. *Old G.* Frithubodo ; a p.n. (peaceful messenger)

FREEBORN. *A.S.* Freobeorn, Frebern (free bear) ; *G.* Frieben ; p.n.

FREEKE. *A.S.* Fric ; *Fr.* Friche, Fricot ; *Fl.* Frick ; *G.*, *D.* Frich, Fricke ; p.n. (fresh, lusty, bold)

FREELOVE. *N.* Freyleif or Friðleifr ; *A.S.* Frealaf, Frithulaf ; p.n. (peaceful love)

FREEMAN. *A.S.* Freoman ; *D.* Frieman ; *S.* Friman ; *G.* Friedemann ; *Fl.* Freyman ; p.n. Prot. ref., Norwich, 1622

FREEMANTLE. From Fromanteau ; a loc. n., France. Nigel de Fremantel ; Northants, 1216 ; a loc. n., Hants

FREEN. From Vrigne ; a loc. n., France

FREER. *See* Frere

FREMONT. *N.* Friðmund ; *A.S.* Frithumund ; *Fr.* Frémont ; p.n. (peaceful director)

FRENCH. *Fl.* Frentz ; *Dch.* Fransche ; p.n.

FRERE. Fraire ; a loc. n., Flanders. Or *N.*, *S.*, *D.*, *Dch.* Freyr ; *G.* Freier ; *Fr.* Frère ; *Old G.* Friher (free lord) ; *N.-Fr.* Le Frere ; p.n.

FRESHFIELD. A loc. n., Lancs. Or *N.-Fr.* De Freshville ; a p.n.

FRESHWATER. A loc. n., I. of Wight

FRESTON. A loc. n., Lincs, Suff.

FRETWELL. From Freteval ; a loc. n., France

FREUER, FREWER, FREW. From Freux ; a loc. n., Belg. *See* Freer

FREWIN. *A.S.* Freawine, Frithuwine ; p.n. (peaceful friend)

FRICKER. *See* Freeke

FRIGGENS. *A.S.* Frig ; *G.* Frigge ; p.n. (free) ; a fam. n. ; *N.-Fr.* Frigant ; a p.n.

FRIGHT. *S.* Freit ; *G.* Freiheit ; p.n. (freedom)

FRISBY. A loc. n., Leics

FRISWELL. From Freshwell ; a loc. n., Ess. Or *see* Freshfield

FRITCHLEY. A loc. n., Derbysh.

FRITH. *A.S.* Frith ; *D.* Fryd ; p.n. (peace)

FRODSHAM. A loc. n., Ches.

FROGGATT. A loc. n., Derbysh.

FROGLEY. A loc. n.

FROHAWK, FROHOCK. From Frowick (?) ; a loc. n., Ess.

FROMANT, FROMOW. From Froidmont ; a loc. n., Belg. Or *A.S.* Freomund, Fromund (free protector) ; *Fr.* Fromment ; *D.B.* Frumond ; p.n. Fromeau, Hugt., Lond. 1618

FROOM. From Frome ; a loc. n., Somers

FROSDICK. *See* Fosdyke

FROST. A loc. n., Devon. Or *D.*, *G.*, *Dch.* p.n.

FROSTICK. *See* Fosdyke

FROUDE, FROWDE. *N.* Fróði, *fróðr* (clever) ; p.n. ; *D.* Froede ; *S.* Frode ; *A.S.* Froda, Frod ; p.n.

FRUSHER. *A.S.* Frithugeard (peaceguard) ; *Fl.* Fruchart ; *Dch.* Froschart ; *D.B.* Froissart ; p.n. Fruschart, Prot. ref., Lond. 1687

FRY. From Fry ; a loc. n., Normandy. Or Icel. Frey ; a fam. n. ; *Dch.* Vree ; *Fl.* Frey ; *D.* Frey, Freij, Frie ; *D.B.* Vruoi (?) ; *G.* Frei, Frey ; *A.S.* Freâ (a lord) ; p.n.

FRYER. *N.*, *S.*, *D.*, *G.* Freyer (the name of the god Freyr) ; a p.n. *See* Frere

FUDGE, FUGE. From Foug, France ; Fuidge ; a loc. n., Devon. Or Fouches, Belg.

FUDGER. From Fougères ; a loc. n., France

FUGGLE, FUGILL. *A.S.* Fugel ; *N.*, *D.* Fugl ; *S.* Fogel ; *Fl.*, *Dch.*, *G.* Vogel ; p.n. (a fowl, bird)

FULCHER. *A.S.* Fulcherus, Folchere ; p.n. (falcon warrior) ; *G.* Fulge. Or from Fougeres or Fulgiers ; a loc. n., Bretagne.

FULFORD. A loc. n., Devon, Yorks
FULKE. *See* Faulke
FULLAGAR. *See* Fulcher
FULLALOVE. *A.S.* Ful-leof ; *Old G.* Filuliub ; p.n. (very dear)
FULLARTON. A loc. n., Ayr, Hants
FULLBROOK. From Fullerbrook ; a loc. n., Devon
FULLER. *See* Fowler. Or *A.S. fullere* (a bleacher) ; *Fr. fouleur* (a cleanser of cloth). Le Fulere, Rot. Hund.
FULLERTON. *See* Fullarton
FULLMER. A loc. n., Bucks, Devon
FULLWOOD. A loc. n., Lancs, Notts, Yorks
FULSHAW. *See* Fulcher
FULTON. *See* Fullerton
FUNGE. *D., G., S., Fl., Dch.* Funck, Funke ; a p.n. (a spark)
FUNNELL. From Fundenhall ; a loc. n., Norf.
FURBER. *A.S.* Fulbeorht ; a p.n. (very illustrious) ; *Fr.* Foubert ; A Hugt. n., Lond. 1618
FURBY. From Firby ; a loc. n., Kent, Yorks

FURLEY. A loc. n., Devon
FURLONG. A loc. n., Devon
FURNER. *Fr.* Fournier ; a p.n. (oven-keeper, baker)
FURNESS. A loc. n., Flanders, Ess. N. Lancs
FURNISH, FURNISS. *See* Furness
FURSDON. A loc. n., Cornw., Devon
FURSE. A loc. n., Devon. Or *N.-Fr.* Foursey (?) ; a p.n. ; *D.B.* Fursa Forz in Roll of Battell Abbey.
FUSEDALE. A loc. n., Westmd.
FUSSEY. *N.* Fusi. *See* Fyson
FUSSLE. *N.-Fr.* Fuise ; *D., G.* Füssel ; a p.n. Dim.
FUSTLING. *D.* Füsterling ; a p.n.
FUTCHER. *G.* Füger ; a p.n. *See* Fudger
FUTLER. *See* Footer
FYFFE. From Fife, a county in Scotland
FYLER. *A.S.* Fula ; *G.* Feiler ; p.n. *See* Fuller
FYNES. *See* Fiennes
FYSON. *N.* Fusi (dimin. of Vigfús) ; *G.* Fuhs, Fuss ; *Fl.* Fussen ; p.n.

G

GABB, GABE. *N.* Gapi ; a n.n. (heedless) ; *A.S.* Gab ; *N.-Fr.* Gaipi ; *D.* Gabe ; p.n. *See* Gape
GABBESEY. A loc. n., Ess.
GABBETT. *Fr.* Gabet ; a p.n. Hugt. n., Lond. 1688
GABLE. *G.* Gebel ; a p.n. *See* Gabb
GABY. *Fr.* De Gabay. Hugt. n.
GACE. *See* Gaze
GACHES. From Gages ; a loc. n., Flanders. Or *Fr.* Gauchez ; a p.n. Hugt. n., Lond. 1688
GADD. *A.S.* Gad, Gadelo ; *D.* Gad, Gade ; *G.* Gade ; p.n. ; *N. gaddr* ; *A.S. gád* (a goad, spear)
GADNEY. From Gedney ; a loc. n., Lincs

GADSBY. From Gaddesby ; a loc. n., Leics
GADSDEN, GADSDUN. From Gaddesden ; a loc. n., Herts
GADSWORTHY. From Godsworthy ; a loc. n., Devon
GAFF, GAFFER. From Gavre ; a loc. n., Fland. *Fr.* Gaffé ; a p.n.
GAGE. *See* Gaches. *S.* Gagge ; *Fl.* Gegers ; p.n.
GAGEN. *A.S.* Gagan ; a p.n. Or *N. gagn* (gain)
GAIGER. *See* Gage
GAINSFORD, GAISFORD. From Gainford ; a loc. n., Dur., Yorks
GAITSKELL. From Gaitsgill ; a loc. n., Cumb.
GALBRAITH. A loc. n., Scotl.

GALE. A loc. n., Devon, Lancs, Yorks. Or Gheel, Belg.

GALILEE. *Dch.* Gallé, Gallee, Galjee; *Fr.* Gailly, Gailliet, Gailliez, Gaillait; *G.* Galley; p.n. (cheerful)

GALL. *N.-Fr.* Gal; *D.* Gall; *Fr.* Galle; *Fl.* Gal; p.n. (valour). Or Irish M'Gall; Scot. M'Call

GALLAGHER. From Gellygaer; a loc. n., S. Wales; Irish p.n.

GALLAND, GALLANT. *Fr.* Gaillande; *Fl.* Galland; *G.* Gallant; *D.* Galen; p.n. (lively, spirited). A Hugt. n., Lond. 1687

GALLEY. From Gallaix, Belg. *Fr.* Gallais, Gallait, Gallay, Gallet, Gally; p.n. Hugt. n., Lond. 1687

GALLICK. *See* Garlick

GALLIMORE. From Gallemar
A Walloon Hugt. n., *temp.* James I., Canterbury. *Old G.* Gelemir (pledge of fame).

GALLING. *Dch.* Galen; p.n. *See* Gall; fam. n.

GALLOP. *See* Gollop

GALLOWAY. A loc. n., Kirkcudbright

GALLYON. *N.-Fr.* Gaillon; a p.n. A loc. n., Normandy. Hugt. n., Lond. 1618

GALPIN. *Fr.* Galopin; a p.n. Chalopin, a Hugt. n., Lond. 1684. *A.S.* Galba = Abba. *See* Abbs

GALSWORTHY. A loc. n., Devon

GALT. *See* Gault

GALTON. A loc. n., Somers

GAMBLE. *N.* Gamli; *D.* Gamel; *N.-Fr.* le Gemel; *G.* Kammell; *A.S.* Gamel; p.n. (old)

GAMBLING. *Fr.* Gamblin; a p.n.; *N.-Fr.* dim. *See* Gamble

GAME, GAMES. From Cambes; a loc. n., Norm. Or *A.S.* Gamas; *D.* Gemz, Gjems; *G.* Gems; *Fl.* Geemers, Gemers; p.n.

GAMGEE. *See* Gammage

GAMMAGE. From Gamaches; a loc. n., Normandy
Gamages in Roll of Battell Abbey.

GAMMON, GAMON. *N.* Geir-mundr (spear-protector); *F.* Gërman; *G.* Gehrmann; *D.* Garman, Germund; *N.-Fr.* Gamain, Germain; *Fl.* Germon; *A.S.* Garmund; p.n.

GANDY. *N.-Fr.* De Candy; *G.* Gande; p.n.; *Old G.* Ganthar (wolf warrior)

GANE. *Dch.* Geen; a p.n. *See* Gagen

GANLY. From Ganilly; a loc. n., Scilly Isles

GANNAWAY. *See* Knevitt

GANT. *N.-Fr.* De Gand; *Dch.* Gant; p.n. A loc. n., Fland.
De Gand, tenant in chief in *D.B.*

GANTREY. *Old G.* Gendirih; a p.n. (wolf-ruler)

GAPE, GEPP. *A.S.* Gab, Geb, Geppa, Geppo; p.n. *See* Gabb

GAPP. A loc. n., France. Or *see* Gabb

GAPPER. *G.* Gaber; *D.* Gabe; p.n. *See* Gabb

GARD. *See* Garth

GARDEN. A loc. n., Kirkcudbright; Gardonne, France

GARFIT. *See* Garforth

GARFORD. A loc. n., Berks

GARFORTH. A loc. n., Yorks

GARIOCH. A loc. n., Aberdeen

GARLAND. A loc. n., Devon. Or *N.-Fr.* de Garlande; a p.n.

GARLICK. From the Irish M'Gorlick. Or *G.* Gawlick; *Old G.* Gerlac; p.n. (spear-play); *N.-Fr.* Garlayk; a Breton n.

GARMAN. *See* Gamon

GARNER. *A.S.* Garn, Gern, Georn; *D.* Gerner; *N.-Fr.* Garnier; *D.B.* Garner; p.n. (careful warrior)

GARNHAM. A loc. n., Merioneth

GARRARD. Fr. Hugt. n., Lond. 1618. *See* Garrod

GARRETT. *N.-Fr.* Garet

GARRICK. From Gerrick ; a loc. n., Yorks. Or *Fr.* Garrigues ; a p.n.

GARROD. *N.* Geirröðr (spear-warrior) ; *A.S.* Gærheard (firm spear) ; *Dch.* Gerhard, Gerardts, Geraets ; *Fl.* Gheeraerts, Geeraerts, Geerts ; *G.* Gerhard, Gerhardt ; *Fr.* Garet, Garot, Gérard ; p.n.

GARSIDE. A loc. n., Yorks

GARTH. *N.* Garðr ; *A.S.* Gard, Geard ; *S.* Gardt ; *Fl.* Gard ; *G.* Görth ; p.n. A loc. n., S. Wales (a guard, protection)

GARTHWAITE. From Gawthwaite ; a loc. n., Lancs

GARTLEY. A loc. n., Aberdeensh.

GARTON. A loc. n., Yorks

GARWOOD. From Garswood; a loc. n., Lancs

GASCOIN, GASCOYNE. *See* Gaskin

GASELEE. *See* Gazeley

GASKARTH. From Geitaskarth ; a loc. n. in Iceland. Also Cumbd.(?)

GASKELL. From Gaisgill ; a loc. n., Westmd. Or Gascuil, Norm.

GASKIN. *N.-Fr.* De Gascoigne; p.n. (a native of Gascony)

GASS. From Gacé (?) ; a loc. n., France. *Fr.* Gassé ; a p.n. Or *G.* Gasse ; *Dch.* Gase ; p.n.

GASTON. *A.S.* Gest, Gesting ; *Fl.* Gasten; *Fr.* Gaston; p.n.(stranger)

GATAKER. From Goatacre ; a loc. n., Wilts

GATEHOUSE. A loc. n., Kirkcud-bright

GATES. From Geet ; a loc. n., Belg. Or *A.S.* Getius ; *N.-Fr.* de Geyt ; *Fl.* Gets ; p.n. (a Goth)

GATFIELD. A loc. n.

GATH. *D.* ; a p.n. *See* Gadd

GATHERCOLE. *A.S.* Gaddo ; a p.n. ; *gád-col* (a pointed helmet)

GATLAND. From Garthland ; a loc. n., Renfrew

GATTENBY. From Gatenby ; a loc. n., Yorks

GATTY. *Old G.* Gatto ; a p.n. *See* Gadd

GAULT. *N.* Galti (a boar). Or *A.S.* Gald ; *Fr.* Gâlt ; contr. of Garrelt (Gerhold) ; p.n.

GAUNT. *See* Gant

GAVIN. Celtic (hawk of battle) ; *Fr.* Gauvin (?) ; a p.n.

GAWKROGER. A Scot. term for a foolish wanderer
There is also *rodge*, an old word for a small water-fowl. *See* Gowk.

GAWMAN. *See* Gamon

GAWTHORPE. A loc. n., Yorks

GAY. *N.-Fr.* De Gai ; *Fr.*, *Dch.* Gay, Gee ; *G.* Gey ; p.n.

GAYFER. *See* Gayford

GAYFORD. From Gateford; a loc. n., Notts

GAYLEARD. *Fl.* Gellaert ; a p.n.

GAYTHORPE. From Garthorpe ; a loc. n., Lincs

GAYTON. A loc. n., Lincs, Norf., Staffs

GAZE. From Gays ; a loc. n., Devon. Or *see* Gass

GAZELEY. A loc. n., Suff. Gossel-lies ; a loc. n., Belg. Or *Fr.* Gasly ; a p.n.

GEAR. *A.S.* Gær ; *Dch.* Gier ; p.n. (a spear)

GEARING. *See* Guerin

GEARY. From St Géry ; a loc. n., Belg. Or *N.* Geiri (fire) ; *Fr.* Géry ; *D.* Gjeraae ; *Fl.* Giers ; *G.* Gierig (eager) ; *D.B.* Gheri ; p.n.

GEATER. From Guitres ; a loc. n., France

GEDDES. A loc. n., Nairn

GEDGE. *See* Gage

GEE. From Gits ; a loc. n., Belg. *Fr.* Ghys ; Gy, France ; p.n. Or Irish M'Gee

GEEN. From Guines ; a loc. n., France. Or *see* Ginn

GEERS. *N.-Fr.* De Guerres ; a p.n.

GELASPY. *See* Gillespie

GELDART, GILDART. Irish. Servant of Arthur

GELL. *Fr.*, *Fl.* Geill; *Dch.* Geel; p.n. *See* Jelly

GELLATLY. From Gelly-dy (?); a loc. n., Carmarthen

GELSTHORPE. A loc. n., Notts. *D.* Gjelstrup; *Dch.* Geldorp; loc. and p.n.

GELSTON. From Geldeston; a loc. n., Norf.

GEMLEY. From Gembling; a loc. n., Yorks

GEMMILL. *G.* Gemmell; a p.n. *See* Gamble

GENGE. From Genck; a loc. n., Belg. *Fr.* Gence; a p.n. Or *see* Ginger

GENN. *See* Geen

GENNEY. From the Irish Gennach, M'Kenney

GENT. *Dch.* Gendt; a p.n. *See* Gant

GENTLE. From Gentilly; a loc. n., France. *Fr.* Gentil; a p.n.
> In Rot. Obl. et Fin. J. Gentyl, Longdon, Staffs, 1341.

GENTRY. *See* Gantrey

GEOGHEGAN or MACGEOGHAGAN. From the Irish MacEachagain or MacEoghagain (young warrior)
> The MacGeoghagans were hereditary marshalls of Meath.

GERDAN. *See* Jordan

GERLING. *A.S.*, *Dch.* Gerling; a p.n.; fam. n. from *N.* *geirr*; *A.S.* *gár* (a spear)

GERMAN. St Germain; a loc. n. in Normandy and Belgium. *Fr.* Germon. Hugt. n., Lond. 1618. *See* Gamon

GERRISH. *Dch.* Gerrets, Gerrits; p.n. *See* Garrod

GERVASE. *N.* Geirfuss (?); *N.-Fr.* Gervais; p.n. (spear eagerness)

GERY. *See* Gearey

GETGOOD. *A.S.* Geatgod (a Jute Goth)

GETHING. From Geddiug; a loc. n., Suff.; Gedinne; Belg.; or Geithain, Germ. *Fl.* Goetinck; p.n.

GETTEN, GETTING. *See* Gething

GIBBENS, GIBBINGS. Irish M'Gibben. Or *F.* Jibbo, Jibben; *Fl.* Giebens, Gibbs; *Dch.* Gebbing; p.n.

GIBBS. *D.* Gieb; *F.* Gibbs; *Dch.* Gips; p.n.; a contr. of Gilbert. Or *A.S.* Geb, Geppa, Gibbius; p.n.; *geben* (to give)

GIBERNE, GIBBON. *See* Gibbings. *N.-Fr.* Gibon

GIBLET. *N.-Fr.* Gibelot. *See* Gibbs

GIDDENS, GIDDINGS. From Gidding; a loc. n., Hunts. Or *D.* Giede; *Fr.* Guidon; *A.S.* Ghida, Gidding; p.n.
> Guidon in Rot. Obl. et Fin., K. John. Stephen Guitan, a Hugt. n., London, in 1687. *N.* Gydinga (?) (Jew).

GIDLEY. From Gidleigh; a loc. n., Devon

GIDNEY. From Gedney; a loc. n., Lincs

GIEN. *See* Geen

GIFFEN. A loc. n., Ayrsh.

GIFFORD. *A.S.* Gifheard; a p.n. (give hard). Or *N.-Fr.* Giffard; a p.n. (full-cheeked). Or Gifford, a loc. n., Haddington
> Giffard in Roll of Battell Abbey. Gifard, a tenant in chief in *D.B.*

GIGGLE. *See* Jiggle

GILAIN. From St Ghislain; a loc. n., Belg. Or *see* Gilleny

GILBERT. *N.* Gisli-bjártr; *Fl.* Gillebaert; *Fr.* Gibert, Gilbert; *D.B.* Chilbert, Ghilebrid, Giselbert; p.n.; *N.* *gísl* (hostage), *bjártr* (bright)

GILBEY. From Gilby; a loc. n., Lincs

GILBODY. *N.* Gisl-bodi (?) (hostage envoy)

GILCHRIST. From the Irish Giolla Chriosd (the servant of Christ). *A.S.* Gilcrist; *S.* Gillqvist; p.n.

GILDEA. From the Irish *Giolla Dé* (the servant of God)

GILDEN. *Dch.*; p.n.

GILDERSLEEVES. From Geldersleeuw; a loc. n., Holland

GILES. St Gilles; a loc. n., Flanders. *Fl.* Gilis; *Fr.* Gilles; *D.* Giles; p.n. *N. gisl, gils* (a hostage)

GILFILLAN. A loc. n., Wigtownshire. Or servant of St Fillan

GILHAM. From Gillingham; a loc. n., Dorset, Kent. Or *S.* Gilljam; *Fr.* Gillaume; p.n.

GILL. From the Gaelic *giolla* (a servant or disciple). *G.* Gilla; *Fr.* Gille; *S.* Gihl; *D.* Gille; *A.S.* Gilo, Gile, Ghil; p.n.; Irish M'Gill

GILLAM. *See* Gilham

GILLAN, GILLEN, GILLENY. From the Irish M'Gullian, Gillen, Killen; *gill Oin* (the servant of John)

GILLESPIE. From Gillesbie; a loc. n., Dumfries. Or from the Gaelic Gillescop and Gillespie (the bishop's servant)

GILLETT. *Fr.*; p.n. *See* Gillott

GILLFOYLE. From the Irish *Giolla Phoil* (the servant of Paul)

GILLIBRAND. *A.S.* Gislbrand (hostage sword)

GILLINGHAM. A loc. n., Somers;

GILLINGS. *A.S.* Gilling; a fam. n.; *S.* Gillen; *Dch.* Gilling; *Fl.* Gillain; p.n. *See* Gill

GILLINGTON. A loc. n.

GILLITLIE. *See* Gellatly

GILMARTIN. *See* Kilmartin

GILLOT. *Fr.* Huguenot n., Lond. 1618. Dimin. of Gill

GILMORE. A loc. n., Yorks. Or from the Irish Mac Giolla Muire; a p.n. (son of the great servant)

GILMOUR. *See* Gilmore

GILPATRICK or KILPATRICK. *D.B.* Ghilepatric. From the Irish Giolla Padraig; a p.n. (devoted to St Patrick)

GILPIN. *See* Kilpin

GILSON. *Fl.*; p.n. *See* Gill

GILSTRAP. *See* Gelsthorpe

GILYARD. *A.S.* Gislheard (strong hostage); *Fr.* Gilliard; p.n. Goilard, Hugt. n., Lond. 1687

GIMLETT. *Fr.* Gimlette. A Huguenot n., Lond. 1618. Dim. of *Gimm* (gem)

GINDER. *A.S.* Geanthryth (a true giver); *Fl.* Gindra (?); p.n.

GINGEL. *G.* Ginschel; p.n.

GINGER. *A.S.* Geng (traveller); *Dch.* Genger; p.n.

GINN. From the Irish M'Ginn. Or *Fr.* Gynn; *D.* Gihn; *Dch.* Gijn; *G.* Gins; p.n.; *N. ginn* (a jester); *N.-Fr.* Guines W. de Gene, Rot. Hund.

GIPPS. *See* Gibbs

GIRDLER. *See* Curtler

GIRDLESTONE. A loc. n.

GIRLING. *See* Gerling

GISBOURNE. From Gisburne; a loc. n., Yorks

GISBY. From Girsby (?), Lincs; a loc. n.

GISCARD. *A.S.* Gislheard (firm hostage); *Fl.* Gischard; p.n.

GISSING. A loc. n., Norf.

GISSON. *See* Gissing

GITTENS, GITTINGS. *See* Giddings

GITTUS. From Gits; a loc. n., Flanders. *Dch.* Gidts; a p.n.

GIVEEN, GIVEN. *See* Giffen or Gavin

GLADDING. *See* Gladwin

GLADSTONE. *See* Gledstanes

GLADWELL. A loc. n.

GLADWYN. *N.* Glað-vinnr (a gladsome friend); *A.S.* Gladewin, Gladuin, Gledwin; p.n.

GLAISHER. *N.* Glæsir (shining); *D.* Glæser; *G.* Gläser; *Fl.* Glaser; p.n.

GLANVILLE. A loc. n., Norm.

GLASFUIRD. A loc. n., Lanark

GLASS. *Dch., S.* Glas; *D.* Glase, Glass; *G.* Glass, Glees; *Fr.* Glace; p.n.; Celtic (blue). A Hugt. n., Lond. 1618; a loc. n., Scot.

GLASHBY. *See* Gillespie

GLASPY. *See* Gillespie

GLASSCOCK. Dimin. of Glass. Or Glascote ; a loc. n., Staffs

GLASSINGTON. From Glasserton ; a loc. n., Wigtonshire

GLASSON. A loc. n., Lancs. Or Celtic Glasan (blue). *See* Glass

GLASSPOLE, GLASSPOOL. A loc. n. *B. glâs* (grey), *pwll* (a pool)

GLASSUP. *See* Glossop

GLATWORTHY. *See* Clapworthy

GLAZEBROOK. A loc. n., Lancs

GLAZIN. From the Irish M'Glashin ; a p.n. *See* Glass

GLAZZARD. From Glasoed ; a loc. n., Monmouth

GLEAD. *See* Gleed

GLEADAH, GLEADOWE. From Gleadhow ; a loc. n., Yorks

GLEASON. From Gleaston ; a loc. n., Lancs

GLEDSTANES. A loc. n., Scotland

GLEED. *N.* Glædir (a red-hot coal, fiery) ; *D.* Glad ; *G.* Glied ; p.n. ; *A.S.* Glæd (cheerful)

GLENDINNING. A loc. n., Dumfries

GLENHAM. From Glentham ; a loc. n., Lincs

GLENNIE. From the Celtic Gleannau (a little upland glen). Or *see* Glynne

GLEW. Gheluwe, a loc. n., Belg. *D.* Gleu ; *G.* Glauer ; *A.S.* Gleu ; *gleaw* (skilful, wise) ; p.n. Or *see* M'Glew

GLISTER. *D.* Glistrup ; a loc. and p.n.

GLITHROW. *See* Clitheroe

GLOAG. *See* Cloake

GLOSSOP. A loc. n., Derbysh.

GLOVER. *N.-Fr.* Gantier ; a p.n.

GLYDE. *See* Gleed

GLYNNE. A loc. n., Cornw. Ghlin ; a loc. n., Belg. Or *N.* Glenna, n.n. ; *S.* Glenne ; *D.* Glyhn ; *Fr.* Glin ; *Dch.* Glindt ; p.n. ; Irish M'Glynn

GOACHER. *Fr.* Gaucher ; *N.* Valgeir ; *A.S.* Walcher ; p.n. (foreign spear). Hugt. n.

GOAD. *N.* Goddi (dimin. of comp. names, as Guð-run, etc.). Or *S.* Godha Gohde ; *G.* Göde ; *D.* Goth ; *Fl.* Gody, Gœdde ; *Fr.* Godde, Goudé, Got ; *Dch.* Goede, Götte ; *A.S.* Gode, Godde, Gote, *Goda* (a Goth), Goti, Gouti ; p.n.

Walter Gode in Rot. Obl. et Fin. W. Godio in Rot. Hund.

GOADBY. A loc. n., Leics

GOATE. *See* Goad

GOATLEY. From Godeley ; a loc. n., Ches.

GOBBETT. From Gobit ; a loc. n., Worcest. Or *A.S.* Godbeort ; *G.* Gutbier, Göbert ; *Fl.* Gobert, Gobbet ; *Dch.* Gobits ; p.n. *See* Gotobed

GOBBY. *See* Gobbett

GOBLE. *G.* Göbel ; p.n. Or *Fr.* Goupil (a young fox). *See* Godbold

GODBEER, GODBER. *See* Gobbett

GODBOLD, GODBOLT. *N.* Guðbaldr ; *D.B.* Godebold ; p.n. (good-bold)

GODBY. *See* Goadby

GODDARD. *N.* Guð-rödr (good strength) ; *Fl., N.-Fr.* Godart ; *Dch.* Goddard ; *D., G.* Gotthard ; *A.S.* Godard, Godheard ; p.n. Hugt. n., Lond. 1618

GODFREY. *N.* Guðfriðr ; *D.* Godfred ; *A.S.* Godfrith ; *Fr.* Godefroy ; p.n. (good peace). A Hugt. n., Lond. 1681

GODING. *A.S., Dch., Fl.* Godding ; a p.n. *See* Goad. A Prot. ref. n., Lond. 1685

GODLEE, GODLEY. A loc. n., Ches.

GODSON. From Godstone ; a loc. n., Staffs. Or *see* Goad, Goodson

GOE. From Goé ; a loc. n., Belgium. Gouy, a Prot. ref., Lond. 1688. Or *see* Goy

GOFF. *Fl.* Goffe; *G.* Göffi; p.n.; *A.S. geof* (a gift). *See* Gough

GOFFEN, GOFFIN. *Fl.*, *Dch.* Goffin; p.n.

GOFT. *See* Goff

GOGGS. *A.S.* Gogo; *Dch.* Gog, Gokkes; p.n. *See* Coggan

GOLD. *A.S.* Golde; *D.* Gold; *G.* Golde; p.n. (value)

GOLDBY. From Coleby; a loc. n., Kent, Lincs

GOLDING. *G.* Golding; a p.n.

GOLDINGHAM. From Coldingham; a loc. n., Berwick

GOLDRIDGE. From Coleridge (?); a loc. n., Devon

GOLDRING. A *G.* p.n.; *A.S.* Goldewin (valued friend)

GOLDSBURY. From Goldsborough; a loc. n., Yorks

GOLDSWORTHY. A loc. n., Devon

GOLDTHORPE. A loc. n., Yorks

GOLDUP. *See* Goldthorpe

GOLDY. *See* Gold

GOLIGHTLY. *See* Gellatly

GOLL, GOLLE. *A.S.* Gol; *G.* Golla, Golli; p.n.; *N. gull* (gold)

GOLLEDGE. *See* College

GOLLOP. From Gollup; a loc. n., Germ. *G.* Gollob; a p.n.

GOMERY. From the *N.-Fr.* De Cambray

> This family came from Cambray in Normandy, and were tenants in chief (*D.B.*) of eighty-one manors. Comp. Lee Gomery or Legh Combrey, Salop.

GOMM. *G.*; p.n. *See* Game

GONNER. *A.S.* Gonhard, Gonnar, Gonuerd; p.n. (strong soldier). Or *see* Gunn

GOOBY. *See* Guby

GOOCH. *See* Gowk

GOODACRE. *A.S.* Godwacer (?); *D.* Goedecke; *Dch.* Goudecke; p.n. (watchful Goth); *G.* Godeck; p.n. (Goth watcher). Or from Goatacre; a loc. n., Wilts. Or *see* Gataker

GOODA. From Gouda; a loc. n., Holland. *Fr.* Goudeau; a p.n. *See* Goad

GOODALL. *N.-Fr.* Godel; a p.n.

Godhale, 1199; Godehil in Rot Hund.

GOODAY. *D.* Goday; *N.-Fr.* Godet, Goudé; *A.S.* Goda, Godœg; p.n. (illustrious Goth)

GOODBAN. *N.* Guðbrandr (good sword); a p.n.

GOODBARNE. *See* Goodban

GOODBODY. *A.S.* Godbodi (Goth envoy)

GOODCHAP. From Goodcheap; a loc. n., Kent

GOODCHILD. From Goodchill; a loc. n., Westmd. Or *A.S.* Godecild; a p.n. (Goth soldier (?))

GOODDY, GOODE, GOODEY. *See* Gooday

GOODENOUGH. *Fr.* Godineau; a p.n. (deformed)

> Mr Ferguson thinks it comes from an old Frankish Godenulf (Goth wolf).

GOODFELLOW. *N.-Fr.* Bonenfant; *A.S. godfelaw* (?)

GOODGE. *See* Goudge

GOODGER. *See* Goodyer

GOODHART. *See* Goddard

GOODHEW. *A.S.* Godo; *N.-Fr.* Gaudiou; *Fr.* Godeheu, Godeaux; p.n. *See* Goad

GOODING. *See* Goding

GOODLAD. A *Dch.* p.n.

GOODLIFFE. *N.* Guð-leif; *A.S.* Guthlaf; p.n. (good inheritance)

GOODMAN. *N.* Guðmundr; *A.S.* Gudmund; *D.* Gudmann; *F.* Goddeman, Goodman; *G.* Guttmann; *N.-Fr.* Godeman; *D.B.* Godman, Godmund, Gudmund; p.n. (good protector)

GOODRICH. A loc. n., Heref.

GOODRICK. *N.* Guðrikr (good mighty one); *D.B.* Godric; p.n.

GOODRUM. *N.* Guð-ormr (war-serpent); *A.S.* Guthrum; *G.* Gudrum; *Dch.* Gottmer; p.n.

GOODSON. A loc. n., Norf.

GOODWILL. From Goderville; a loc. n., Normandy

GOODWIN. *N.* Guð-vinr; *A.S.* Godwin, Godwine, Guthwine (good friend or battle friend); *Fl.* Goddyn, Goetvinck, Guttin; *N.-Fr.* Godvinne; *Fr.* Goudinne, Godefin; *G.* Guttwein; p.n.
  N.-Fr. Goduin, a tenant in chief; *D.B.* Goduin, Gotwin, under-tenants at time of Survey. Goduin, Saxon tenant, Edw. Conf. Godwine, Rot. Hund. For varieties of spelling *see* Introduction, page 2. Otto Abel thinks it is equivalent to Theophilus.

GOODYER. *A.S.* Godhere (good warrior); *Fr.* Goudier; p.n.

GOOSE. From Goes; a loc. n., Holland. A Hugt. n., Norwich, 1622. *See* Goss

GOOSEY, GOOZEE. From Gozée; a loc. n., Belg.

GOPP. A loc. n., Flint. *See* Guppy

GOPSILL. From Gopsall; a loc. n., Leics

GORDON. A loc. n., Berwick

GORE. From Goor; a loc. n., Holland. *N.* Gorr (gore); *Dch.* Goor; p.n. Or *see* Gower

GORHAM. A loc. n.

GORING. A loc. n., Oxf., Suss.

GORMAN. *Dch.* Gortman; *Fl.* Gouman; *Fr.* Gourmont; p.n. *See* Gamon

GORNALL. A loc. n., Staffs

GORRILL. *D.* Gorell; *G.* Gorille; p.n. Dim. of Gorr. Or Welsh Gwril (lordly)

GORST. From Jort; a loc. n., Norm. Sire de Jort at Hastings

GORTON. A loc. n., Lancs

GOSFORD. A loc. n., Haddingtonshire

GOSLING. *A.S.* Gozlin, Goscelin, Godzelin; *Dch.* Goseling; *N.-Fr.* Gosselin; p.n. Prot. ref., Lond. 1622. *See* Goss

GOSS. *S.* Gooes; *G.* Gosse; *Dch.* Goos, Goes; *Fl.* Gosse, Gossy; *A.S.* Gos; p.n. From *Old G.* Gauzlind; *goz*, a form of *gaud* (Goth), *lind* (gentle)

GOSSETT. *See* Gozzard

GOSTELLOW. *See* Costello

GOSWELL. From Goosewell, Plymstock, Devon

GOTHORP. *See* Gawthorpe

GOTLEY. From Godley; a loc. n., Ches.

GOTLING. *See* Goad

GOTOBED. *N.* Guðbjártr (good-bright); *A.S.* Cuthbert, Godebert, Guthbeorht, Gutbert; p.n.

GOTSON. *See* Goodson

GOTTO, GOTTS. *See* Goad

GOUDGE. *Fr.* Gouge; a p.n.

GOUGH. From the Irish M'Gough; a p.n. (the red)

GOUK. *See* Gowk

GOULBURN. From Goulborn; a loc. n., Ches., Lancs

GOULD. *See* Gold

GOULDER. *See* Gold

GOUNDRY. *N.-Fr.* de Gundres. Or *A.S.* Gundræd (war counsellor); *Fr.*, *Fl.* Gondry; p.n.

GOURLAY, GOURLEY. *See* Curly

GOVANE. A loc. n., Lanark

GOW. Irish Gobha (a smith). Or *Dch.* Gouw; a p.n.

GOWEN. Irish M'Gowan. *See* Gow

GOWER. From Goher; a loc. n., Norm.
  Thomas de Gaweia in Rot. Obl. et Fin., K. John. Gower in Roll of Battell Abbey.

GOWERS. *Dch.* Govers; *Fl.* Govaerts; p.n. Gouers, a Prot. ref., Lond. 1618

GOWING. A loc. n., Devon. Or *see* Gowen

GOWK. *N.* Gaukr; *G.* Gauck; *Fr.* Gouche; p.n. (a cuckoo)
  Couk in Rot. Obl. et Fin.

GOWLAND. *See* Garland

GOWTHORPE. A loc. n., Yorks

GOWTHWAITE. A loc. n., Yorks
GOWTRIDGE. *See* Gutteridge
GOY, GHOY. A loc. n., Belg. *Fl.*
Goye; *Dch.* Goey; *Fr.* Gouy;
p.n. Gouy; a loc. n., Normandy.
Hugt. n., 1687. *See* Goe
GOYDER. *G.* Geuther; *Dch.* Goede;
p.n. *See* Goad or Gwyther
GOYMER. *See* Guymer
GOZZARD. *Old G.* Gozhart (strong
Goth); *N.-Fr.* Gocet, Gozet, Gos-
set; p.n.
GRABHAM. From Graban (?); a
loc. n., Brecon
GRACE. *See* Gracie
GRACEY, GRACIE. *Fr.* Gresy; p.n.
From Graçay; a loc. n., France
GRADDON. *See* Gratton
GRADWELL. A loc. n., Yorks. *D.B.*
Cradeuuelle
GRAFHAM. A loc. n., Hunts
GRAFTON. A loc. n., Warw., Wilts,
Yorks
GRAHAM. From Grantham or
Graham; a loc. n. in Kesteven,
Lincs
  William de Graham settled in Scotland
  in the twelfth century.
GRAIN. *N.-Fr.* De Grana; *Fr.*
Graine; a p.n.
GRAMMER. From Gramat; a loc.
n., France
  Latinised into Grammaticus, Pipe
  Roll., Middleton, Yorks, 1189
GRAND. *Fr.* Grand; a p.n.
  Graunt in Roll of Battell Abbey; Le
  Grant in Rot. Obl. et Fin.
GRANDIGE. *Fr.* Graindorge; a p.n.
GRANDISON, GRANDCHAIN. A loc.
n., France. *Fr.* Grandjean; a
p.n.
  In Roll of Battell Abbey.
GRANGER. *Fr.* Grangé; a p.n.;
N.-Fr. granger (farmer of a
grange)
GRANT. *See* Grand
GRANTHAM. A loc. n., Lincs
GRANTLEY. A loc. n., Yorks
GRANVILLE. *See* Grenville

GRAPES. *N.* Greipr (?); *S.* Grape;
G. Gräber; *Dch.* Graap; *Fl.*
Greps; p.n.; *A.S. græp* (a ditch).
A Prot. ref. n., Lond. 1618
GRASBY. A loc. n., Lincs
GRATTAN. *See* Gratton
GRATTON. A loc. n., Devon
GRATTRIDGE. *See* Greatrex
GRAVATT. *Fl.* Grauwet; *Fr.* Gravet,
Gravot; p.n. Dim. of Grave
GRAVE. *N.-Fr.* De la Gréve; *D.B.*
Greve; p.n.
GRAVENER. From Greven; a loc.
n., Germ. *Fl.* Greven; p.n.
GRAVER. *Dch.* Greve; *Fr.* Gravé;
p.n. *See* Grave
GRAVES. *Fl.* Gravis; a p.n. *See*
Grave
GRAVESTON. A loc. n. *See* Grave
GRAY. A loc. n., Normandy. *Fr.*
Grey; *G.* Graye; *D.B.* De Grai;
p.n.
  De Gray or Grai in Rot. Obl. et Fin.,
  K. John. A Hugt. n., Lond.
  1618.
GRAZEBROOK. From Gresbroke or
Greasbrough; a loc. n., Yorks
GREABY. From Grebby; a loc. n.,
Lincs
GREAGSBY. A loc. n.
GREAM. *D.*, *Dch.* Grim; a p.n.
See Grimmer. A Hugt. n., Nor-
wich, 1622
GREATHEAD. *N.-Fr.* Grosteste; a
p.n.
  In Rot. Hund. 1272. Robt. G., Bp.
  of Linc. Gretheved, Grethed in
  1327.
GREATREX. From Great Rakes;
a loc. n., Cumb., Derbysh., Staffs.
Or Gayteric (Catterick), Yorks
GREBBY. *Dch.* Grebe; a p.n. *See*
Grubb
GREEDAY. *A.S.* Grid; *Dch.* Greede;
p.n. *See* Crate
GREEF. *D.* Greiff; *Dch.* Griev;
G. Grief; p.n.; *A.S. gerefa*
(sheriff)

GREELY, GRELLY. From Gresillé; a loc. n., Anjou.
Sir T. de Grelly, 1307.

GREEN. A freq. loc. n. Or *A.S.* Gron, Grun; *D.* Grün; *Dch.* Grin, Groen; *D.B.* Grene, Greno, Grino; p.n.; Green, in the sense of young, fresh
H. del Grene in Lib. Vit. Dur.; Atte Grene, Court of Hustings, 1258.

GREENAWAY. A loc. n., Devon. Or *N.* Gronveg; *Dch.* Groeneweg; loc. and p.n.

GREENHALGH. A loc. n., Lancs

GREENHOW. A loc. n., Yorks

GREENLAW. A loc. n., Berwick, Kirkcudbright, Edinb.

GREENLEAF. *A.S.* Granulf (?). Perhaps a corruption of the *N.* Grímólf (stern wolf)

GREENLEES. A loc. n., Scotl.

GREENSLADE. A loc. n., Devon

GREENSTREET. From Greenstead; a loc. n., Ess.

GREENWAY. A loc. n., Devon

GREENWELL. A loc. n., Dur., Yorks. Or Grenville

GREENWOOD. A loc. n.

GREER, GREIR. *Dch.* Greijr, Greier, a p.n. Prot. ref., 1687

GREET. A loc. n., Glost., Salop

GREETHAM. A loc. n., Rutland

GREEVES. *See* Grave

GREGG, GREIG. From Gréges; a loc. n.; France, Graig, Monmouth. Or *G.* Kreck, Krex; *Fl.* Greck; p.n.; Celtic *greg* (fierce)

GRENHAM. From Greenham; a loc. n., Berks

GRENTO. *N.-Fr.* De Grento

GRENVILLE. From Greinville; a loc. n., Norm.

GRESHAM. A loc. n., Norf.

GRESLEY. A loc. n., Leics, Notts
Nigel, second son of Nigel de Toigni (afterwards de Stafford), took the name of de Gresley from his lordship of Gresley, Leics. De Grisele in Rot. Obl. et Fin., K. John.

GRESSWELL. *See* Cresswell

GRETTON. A loc. n., Glost., Northants, Salop

GREW. *Fr.* Grieu, Grout; p.n. (a little dog). Or Le Grue (a crane)

GREX. *See* Gregg

GREY. *See* Gray

GRIBBEN. Fam. n. of *A.S.* Grippo; a p.n. (a gripper). Or from M'Robin

GRIBBLE. A loc. n., Devon

GRICE. *N.-Fr.* De Grisy, Grise. Or *D.*, *G.*, *Fl.* Gries, Greis (grizzled, grey); p.n.

GRICKS. *See* Grix

GRIDLEY. A loc. n.

GRIEF. *See* Greef

GRIFFIN. Welsh Gruffin; a p.n. (ruddy)

GRIFFITH. Welsh Gruffydd; a p.n. (ruddy)

GRIGG. *See* Grix

GRIGGS. A loc. n., Cornw. Or *see* Grix

GRIGSBY. *See* Greagsby

GRIGSON. *See* Grigg

GRIMBLE. *N.* Grimbald (stern, fierce, and bold); *A.S.* Grimbeald; *Fr.* Grimoult; p.n.

GRIMDITCH. A loc. n.

GRIME, GRIMER, GRIMES. *See* Grimmer

GRIMLEY. A loc. n., Worcest.

GRIMMER. *N.* Grímr (stern); *D.*, *S.*, *Dch.*, *G.* Grimm, Grimmer; *D.B.* Grim; p.n.

GRIMMETT. *Fr.* dimin. of Grim

GRIMMOND. *N.* Grimmundr; *Fr.* Grimont; *Dch.* Grimmon; p.n. (stern director)

GRIMOLDBY. A loc. n., Lincs

GRIMSDALE. From Grinsdale; a loc. n., Cumb.

GRIMSEY. From Grimsby; a loc. n., Lincs

GRIMSHAW. A loc. n., Yorks

GRIMSON. *N.* Grimssynr; a p.n. Or *see* Grimston

GRIMSTON. A loc. n., Leics, Norf., Yorks

GRIMTHORPE. A loc. n., Yorks
GRIMWADE. *See* Grimwood
GRIMWOOD. A loc. n., Suff.
GRINDLEY. A loc. n., Staffs
GRINDROD. A loc. n., Lancs. Anciently Grenerawde (Fishwick)
GRINHAM. From Grittenham (?); a loc. n. Wilts
GRINLAW. *See* Greenlaw
GRINLING. Dim. of Green
GRINSLADE. From Greenslade; a loc. n., Devon
GRINSTED. From Grinstead; a loc. n., Kent, Suss.
GRINT. *A.S.* Grind; *Fl.* Grinaert; *G.* Grünert; p.n.
GRISENTHWAITE. From Gristwaite; a loc. n., Yorks
GRISKS. *G.* Grischke; a p.n. Dim. of Grice
GRISS. *See* Grice
GRISSAM. *See* Gresham
GRISSELL. *Fr.* Grisel; a p.n.
GRISTOCK. From Greystock; a loc. n., Cumb.
GRISTON. A loc. n., Norf.
GRITTON, GRITTEN. *See* Gretton
GRIX. *Fl.* Krickx; *Dch.* Griek, Kriek; a p.n.; *A.S. grig* (grey)
GRIZEDALE. A loc. n., Lancs, Yorks
GROCOTT, GROWCUTT. *See* Groocock
GROGAN. A loc. n., Queen's Co., Ireland
GROMIT. *See* Groom
GROOCOCK. *G.* Groche; a p.n. *See* Grew
GROOM. *A.S.*, *D.* Grum; *Dch.* Grummer; *Fr.* Grummeau; *G.* Crumm, Grummich; p.n. (fierce, severe)
GROSS. *D.* Gross; *Fl.* Groos, Gros; *Fr.* Grosse; *Dch.* Grosz; *D.B.* Grossus; p.n. (big, tall)
GROSVENOR. *Fr.* Grovenour; a p.n. *Lat.* Grandis Venator (chief huntsman)
GROTE. *See* Croote

GROUND. *S.*, *G.* Grund; a p.n. Or *see* Grand
GROUT. *N.* Graut (groats); *G.* Grutz, Kraut; *Dch.* Groot; *Fl.* Groeters; *D.* Grude; p.n.; *D.B.* Grutt, Grud. *See* Croote
GROVES. *D.* Grove; a p.n.; *grov* (big). Or Atte-groves; a loc. n.
GROWSE. From Graux; a loc. n., Belg. *Dch.* Graus; a p.n.
GRUBB. *D.* Grubb; *G.* Grube; *Dch.* Grob; p.n. Grube; a loc. n., Holstein (a ditch). Or Irish M'Crub. Prot. ref., Lond. 1618.
GRUEL. *D.* Groule; *S.*, *Dch.* Grewell; *Fr.* Gruelle; *G.* Greul, Grüel (fright); *D.B.* Gruel; p.n. Hugt. n., Lond. 1628
    Griuel in Roll of Battell Abbey.
GRUGGEN. *See* Grogan
GRUNDY. *D.* Gruntvig; *S.* Grundin; *G.* Grundey, Grundig; p.n. (solid, well-grounded). Or *see* Goundry
GRYLLS. *S.* Grill; *G.* Griehl; *Fr.* Grille; p.n.; *N. grylla* (?) (dim sight)
GUBBINS. *N.-Fr.* De Gobion; a p.n. Hugt., Lond. 1618
GUBBY. *A.S.* Guba; *G.* Gubig; a p.n. (scarred). *See* Guppy
GUDGE. *See* Gooch
GUDGEON, GUDGIN. *Fl.*; p.n.; *D.* Gude; a p.n. Dimin. Gudchen. *See* Gooda
GUERIN. From Gueron; a loc. n. in Normandy. A Hugt. n., Lond. 1621
    Gurry in Roll of Battell Abbey. Gerin, a tenant in chief in *D.B.*
GUEST. A loc. n., Norm. *Fr.* Guest; *Dch.* Gest. Or *A.S.* Gest; p.n. (a stranger)
GUIHEN. The Irish form of Wynne
GUINNESS or MACGUINNESS. From the Irish Aongusa (excellent virtue)
    Ancient lords of Iveagh, co. Down.

GUIVER. *A.S.* Wigbeorht (?) (illustrious victor) ; *Fr.* Guibert, Quivy (?) ; *D.B.* Guibert ; p.n.
GULL. *N.-Fr.* Goles, Gouel, Gule ; p.n.

In Rot. Hund.

GULLIFORD. A loc. n., Devon
GULLY. From Golley or Golet ; a loc. n., Norm. Or *N.* Guðleifr ; *A.S.* Guthlaf (divine relic) ; *D.* Gulleiv ; *Fr.* Gually, Gulley ; p.n.

W. Gollay in Rot. Hund., 1272.

GUMBLETON. From Gomeldon ; a loc. n., Wilts
GUMLEY. A loc. n., Leics
GUMMER. *D.* Gummer ; *A.S.* Gummœr ; p.n. (excellent, famous)
GUNBY. A loc. n., Yorks
GUNDRY. *See* Goundry
GUNN, GUNNS. *N.-Fr.* Gons, Goun, Gun ; *A.,S.*, *Fl.* Guns, Gun ; p.n. *See* Gunner
GUNNELL. *N.* Gunnólfr (warrior wolf) ; *A.S.* Gunnulf ; p.n.
GUNNER, GUNNERY. *N.* Cunnarr ; *A.S.* Gunhere, Gunner (warrior)
GUNNING. *A.S.* fam. n. *See* Gunn
GUNSON. *S.* Gunnarson ; *D.* Gunarson ; p.n. *See* Gunn
GUNTON. A loc. n., Norf., Suff.
GUPPY. *N.-Fr.* Coupil ; *Fl.* Goupy ; p.n. *See* Gubby

GURLING. *See* Gerling
GURNER. *A.S.* Georngœr ; *D.* Gerner ; *Fl.* Gernet ; *Fr.* Gurnort ; p.n. (eager spear). Hugt. n., Lond. 1618
GURNEY. From Gournai ; a loc. n., Normandy
Hugo de Gurnai, tenant in chief in *D.B.* (Essex). Also a Hugt. n.
GURR. From the Irish M'Girr (short). Or *see* Gower
GURRIN. *See* Guerin
GUSCOTTE. From Goscote ; a loc. n., Staffs
GUSH. *See* Gooch
GUTHRIE. A loc. n., Forfar
GUTTERIDGE. *See* Goodrich
GUTTERY. *See* Guthrie
GUYMER. *A.S.* Widmœr ; Frankish Guidomer ; *Fl.* Ghémer ; p.n. (famous sense)
GWATKIN. The Welsh form of Watkin
GWILLYAM. *Fr.* Guillaume ; p.n. Or the Welsh form of William
GWYTHER. From Gwydyr ; a loc. n., South Wales. *B. gwydden* (a tree), *gwyther* (a dweller in the woods)
GYE. *Dch.* Guye ; *G.* Goy ; *Fr.* Gay ; p.n. Hugt., Lond. 1684. *See* Goy
GYFORD. *See* Gifford
GYTON. *See* Gayton

H

HABERNATHY. *See* Abernethy
HABGOOD. *See* Hopgood
HACKBUT. *N.* Hagbarðr ; *A.S.* Agabeorht, Ecgbert, Hagbert ; p.n. (bright edge)
HACKER. *N.* Hákr ; *A.S.* Hacca ; *S.* Hake ; *D.* Hackhe ; *D.*, *G.* Hacke ; *Fl.* Hacker ; *Dch.* Hakker ; p.n. (a battle-axe wielder). Prot. ref., Norwich, 1622

HACKETT. *N.-Fr.* Haket ; *N.* Haki a myth. p.n. (a hook) ; *D.* Haak ; *G.* Hake ; *Dch.* Hackert ; *Fl.* Acket, Hack ; p.n. Dim. of Haki. *See* Hatchett

Haket in Roll of Battell Abbey and Rot. Obl. et Fin., K. John. W. Achet, 1086, under-tenant of Giffard, Bucks. Bertram Haget founded Helaugh Abbey, York, 1200.

HACKNEY. A loc. n., Devon, Middlx.

HACKSHAW. *See* Hawkshaw

HACKWELL, HACKWILL. A loc. n., Devon

HACKWOOD. A loc. n., Devon

HACKWORTH. *See* Ackworth

HACON. *N.* Hákon (name of a king); *F.* Hagen, Heiko, Heiken ; *Fl.* Haaken ; *Fr.* Hacquin ; *A.S.* Hacon, Haco, Hago ; p.n.

HADDAH. *A.S.* Hadda, Heathu ; *D.* Hader ; *Dch.* Ader ; *S.* Had ders ; *G.* Hader ; p.n. (warrior)

HADDAWAY. *See* Hathaway

HADDEN. *See* Haddon

HADDER. *See* Haddah

HADDESLEY. A loc. n., Yorks

HADDOCK. *See* Adcock

HADDON. A loc. n., Beds, Derbysh., Middlx., Northants.
De H. in Rot. Hund.

HADFIELD. A loc. n., Derbysh.

HADLEY. A loc. n., Herts, Middlx., Staffs

HADLINGTON. *See* Adlington

HADOW, HADDOW. *See* Haddah

HADWIN. *A.S.* Haduuine ; a p.n. (war friend)

HAGG. *See* Aggs

HAGGARD. *A.S.* Ægheard, Ecgheard ; *Old G.* Agihard ; *D.* Aaggaard ; *S.* Hagert ; *Dch.* Hageraats, Hakkert, Hagers, Hagoort, Hagt ; *G.* Hoeger ; *Fl.* Hager ; p.n. (firm edge, *i.e.* of sword or axe)

HAGGER. *See* Haggard

HAGGIE. *F.* Agge ; *D.* Agier ; p.n. *See* Aggs

HAGGIS. *See* Aggs

HAGGIT. *See* Haggard

HAGON. *See* Hacon

HAGRAM. From Hargham (?) ; a loc. n., Norf.

HAGREEN. *See* Haygreen

HAGUE. *A.S.* Hac, Hag ; *Fl.* Haege, Huyghe; *Dch.* Hage ; *Fr.* Hague ; p.n. Le Heegue, Prot. ref., Lond. 1621. *See* Haggard

HAILL. *See* Hale. Or *Fl.* Heyl; a p.n.

HAILSTONE. From Aylestone ; a loc. n., Leics

HAIME. *F.* Eime, Eme ; *Dch.* Hemme ; *A.S.* Eamer ; *G.* Heim ; p.n. *See* Ames

HAINES. *See* Haynes. Or *N.*, *F.*, *G.* Hein, Hain, Heine ; *Dch.* Hens ; *Fl.* Hennes; p.n. Dim. of Heinrich

HAIRS. From Heers (?) ; a loc. n., Belg. *See* Ayers

HAKE. *See* Haycock
De Hake in Rot. Obl. et Fin.

HAKEN. *See* Hacon

HALBROOK. *See* Holbrook

HALCRO. A loc. n., Scotl.

HALDANE. *N.* Hálfdan (name of a king) ; *A.S.* Haldan (half Dane) ; *N.-Fr.* Alden ; p.n. *See* Alldin.

HALE. A loc. n., Ches., Cornw., Hants, Lincs, Somers, Staffs, Yorks. Haisle, Norm.

HALES. A loc. n., Norf. Or *Dch.* Hales ; *D.* Hallas, Halse, Hels ; p.n. ; *A.S.* Hel, *i.e.* Ælf (elf)

HALESTRAP. *D.* Alstrup ; a loc. and p.n.

HALFACRE. A loc. n., Devon. Or *N.* Hálfrekkr ; a p.n. (the champion of King Half)

HALFHEAD. *A.S.* Ælfheard ; *Old G.* Alfaid ; p.n. (strong elf)

HALFNIGHT. *A.S.* Ælfnoth ; *G.* Elvenich (?) ; p.n. (elf-bold)

HALFORD. A loc. n., Devon, Warw.

HALFPENNY. Irish Alpin, Halpin, M'Alpin ; p.n. Or *Dch.* Alphenaar ; a p.n.

HALFYARD. *A.S.* Ælfgeard (elf-protected)

HALKET. A loc. n., Scotl. Or from Halcote, Northants.

HALL. From Hal ; a loc. n., Belg. Or *N.* Hallr (a hill) ; *D.*, *Dch.*, *S.* Hall ; *Fl.* Hal ; p.n. A Prot. ref., Lond. 1899
De Aule and de la Haule in Rot. Obl. et Fin., K. John ; Atte Hall, 1327.

HALLACK. *See* Hollick
HALLETT. A loc. n., Belg. *N.-Fr.* p.n. *See* Allott
HALLIDAY. From Halyday, Norm. *S.* Helleday; a p.n.
In Rot. Obl. et Fin., K. John. De H., Rot. Cur. Reg. 1194.
HALLIFAX. From Halifax; a loc. n., Yorks
HALLIWELL. A loc. n., Lancs
HALLOCK. *See* Hall. Dimin.
HALLSTEAD. From Halstead; a loc. n., Ess., Kent, Leics. *D.* Alsteed; *S.* Hallstedt; loc. and p.n.
HALLUM. From Hallam; a loc. n., Derbysh., Notts, Yorks
HALLWARD. *N.* Hallvarðr (hill-ward); *S.* Hallbahr; *G.* Halfar; *D.* Halvor; *Fl.* Hallart; *Dch.* Haller; *A.S.* Halweard; *D.B.* Alward, Aluert; p.n.
HALLWORTH. From Halworthy; a loc. n., Cornw.
HALLYBONE. *See* Allbone
HALPIN. *See* Halfpenny
HALTON. A loc. n., Bucks
HAM. A loc. n., Belg., Norm., Dorset, Glost., Hants, Somers, Wilts
De H. in Rot. Hund.
HAMAWAY. From Hamoir; a loc. n., Belg.
HAMBLETON. Leics, Lincs, Surr., Yorks
HAMBLETT. *N.* Ambloði (Hamlet), the mythical prince of Denmark; *Fl.* Hamlett; p.n. A Hugt. n., Lond. 1618
HAMBLIN. *A.S.* Hama, Hamelin; *F.* Amel, Amelung (descendants of the mighty one); *Dch.* Hamerling; p.n.
HAMBY. From Hanby; a loc. n., Yorks. *N.-Fr.* De Hambeia
HAMER. A loc. n., Lancs. Or *N.* Heimir (name of a Jarl); *F.* Heimo; *Fl.* Haemer; *D.B.* Haemer, Haimer; p.n. (houselord)

HAMERTON. *See* Hammerton
HAMEY. *Fr.* Ameye, Hamiet; p.n. Dim. of Hama
HAMILTON. A loc. n., Scotl. Or Hambleton, Lincs; Hamelton, Yorks
HAMMACK. *Fl.* Hamecher; *Dch.* Hamacker; p.n. Dim. of Hama
HAMMANT. *See* Hammond
HAMMERSLEY. *D.* Hammerlev; *S.* Hammarlöw; *Dch.* Hamerslag; loc. and p.n.
HAMMERTON. A loc. n., Yorks
HAMMON, HAMMOND, HAMONT. A loc. n., Belg. *N.* Hámundr (high protector); *D.* Hamann; *G.* Hammann; *D.B.* Hame, Hamon, Hamine, Amund; *Dch.* Ormondt; *Fr.* Aumont; p.n.
In Roll of Battell Abbey; under-tenant in *D.B.*
HAMPSON. *D.* Hampe; a p.n.
HAMPTON. A loc. n., Middlx., Warw., Worcest. *N.-Fr.* De Hantona
HAMSHAW, HAMSHIRE. From Hampshire, the county
HANBURY. A loc. n., Staffs, Worcest.
HANCER, HANCHETT. *A.S.* Haneca; *Fl.* Hannecart, Hansett; p.n. *See* Hankey. Hanser, Prot. ref. n., Lond. 1618
HANCOCK. From Hencot or Hengoed; a loc. n., Salop
W. de Sprenchaux, from S. in Burgundy, lord of H., *temp.* K. Steph. (Eyton's, Salop).
HAND. *A.S.* Han, Hand; *G.* Hander; p.n.
HANDFIELD. From Hanningfield; a loc. n., Ess.
HANDFORD. A loc. n., Staffs
HANDLEY. A loc. n., Derbysh., Staffs. Or from Andelys, Norm.
HANDOVER. From Andover; a loc. n., Hants
HANDS. *A.S.* And; a p.n. (against). Or *G.*, *Dch.*, *Fl.* Hans, Hannes; p.n. (Jack)

HANDYSIDE. A loc. n.
HANEY. *See* Heney
HANFORD. A loc. n., Dorset, Staffs
HANHAM. A loc. n., Glost.
HANINGTON. A loc. n., Hants, Wilts
HANKEY. From Anché, in Poitou. Or *see* Hanks
T. de Hanchet, Camb. 1316
HANKINSON. *See* Hanks
HANKS. *F.* Anke ; *Dch.* Hanke ; *Fl.* Hancke, Hancq ; *G.* Hanke, Hanko ; p.n. *See* Hanchett
HANLON. From the Irish O'Hanlon (champion)
HANMER. A loc. n., Flint
HANNAFORD. *See* Hanford
HANNAH. *N.* Hani (a cock) ; n.n. ; *D.* Henne ; *S.* Hane, Hanner ; *A.S.* Hana ; *Fr.* Hany, Hannay ; *G.* Hanner ; p.n. Or *see* Henn
HANNAM. *See* Hanham
HANNANT. *See* Hennant
HANNATH. From Hanworth ; a loc. n., Suff.
HANNATT. *Fl.* Hanart, Hannot ; p.n. Dim. of Hanno. *Old G. ano* (ancestor). Or *see* Hannah
HANNAY, HANNER. *See* Hannah
HANSELL. *S.* Hansell ; a p.n.
HANSOM. *A.S.* Anselm (?) (god's helm) ; *Fr.* Anceaume ; p.n.
HANSON. *D.* Hansen ; *S.* Hanson ; p.n. (Johnson)
HANWELL. A loc. n., Middlx. Or Andeville, Norm.
HARBARD, HARBORD. *N.* Há-bjártr ; *A.S.* Heahbeorht (illustrious chief) ; *Dch.* Harbord ; p.n.
HARBOTTLE. A loc. n., Northbd.
HARBOUR, HARBUTT. *See* Harbard
HARCOURT. A loc. n., Normandy
Harecourt in Roll of Battell Abbey.
HARCUM. From Harcomb ; a loc. n., Devon
HARDACRE. *A.S.* Hardgear ; *G.* Hardtke ; p.n. (strong spear)

L

HARDAWAY. From Hardway ; a loc. n., Hants, Somers
HARDBOARD. *See* Harbard
HARDCASTLE. From Hardencastle (?), Roxburghshire
HARDEN. *See* Horden or Arden
HARDIMENT. *N.* Hjörtmundr (stag protector) ; a p.n. Hartieman, a Fl. Prot. ref., Lond. 1618
HARDING. *N.* Haddingr (a mythical hero) ; *A.S., D.* Harding ; *S.* Hardin ; p.n.
Harding, a tenant in chief in *D.B.*, held lands which he had occupied *temp.* Edw. Conf. in Glost., Somers, Wilts.
HARDMAN. *A.S.* Heardman ; *D.*, *Fl.* Hardman ; *Dch.* Hardeman ; *G.* Hartman ; p.n. (strong man). Prot. ref., Lond. 1618
HARDMEAT. From Hardmead ; a loc. n., Oxf.
HARDWICKE. A loc. n., Camb., Derbysh., Dur., Norf., Northants, Staffs, Warw., Worcest., Yorks
HARDY. *N.-Fr.* Hardi ; p.n. (bold, strong). Hugt. n., Lond. 1684
In Rot. Hund.
HARE. Heer ; a loc. n., Belg. Or *N.-Fr.* Le Hare ; *N.* Hár ; *F.* Hére ; *D.*, *G.* Herr ; *Dch.* Haar ; *Fl.* Hery ; *D.B.* Her, Har ; p.n. (soldier, hero)
HARFORD. A loc. n., Devon, Somers
HARGRAVE. A loc. n., Suff., Northants
HARGREAVES. A loc. n., Lancs
HARIOTT. *See* Herriott
HARKAN. *See* Hacon
HARKER. A loc. n., Cumb. Or *A.S.* Hardgær, Heregær ; p.n. (strong spear)
HARKNESS. From Hackness ; a loc. n., Yorks
HARKORT. *See* Harcourt
HARLAND. A loc. n., Caithness
HARLE. *N.* Erli ; *F.* Harl ; *A.S.* Erle, Hærle, Herle ; *G. Dch.* Harlaar ; *N.-Fr.* Harel ; p.n. *See* Earl

HARLEY. A loc. n., Salop. Or *Fr.* Harlé; a p.n. *See* Hurly
HARLOCK. A loc. n., Lancs
HARLOW. A loc. n., Ess.
HARMAN. *A.S.* Hereman; a p.n. (soldier man)
N.-Fr. Herman in Rot. Hund.
HARMER. *A.S.* Heremær; a p.n. (famous soldier)
HARMSWORTH. *See* Armsworth
HARNAGE. A loc. n., Salop
HARNESS. *G.* Harnisch; a p.n. (armour)
HARNEY. *A.S.* Arnwi, Earne, Earnwíg; *Fr.* Hahné, Hanet; p.n. (war eagle)
HARPER. *N.* Erpr, *harpari* (a harper); *S.* Arpi, Hjerpe; *D.*, *Dch.* Arp; *A.S.* Herp, Herpo, *herpere* (a harper); p.n.
HARPHAM. A loc. n., Yorks
HARPLEY. A loc. n., Norf. and Worcest.
HARR. *A.S.* Har; *F.* Hâre; *Dch.* Haar; p.n. (a soldier)
HARRADEN, HARRADINE. From Harrowden; a loc. n., Northants
HARRALL. *See* Harrald
HARRALD. *N.* Haraldr; *Dch.* Herold; p.n. Harrald; a loc, n., Beds; name of a king (hostwielder, a leader)
HARRINGTON. A loc. n., Cumb., Northants. Anciently Haverington
HARRIS, HARRISON. *N.-Fr.* Heriz, Fitz Herice, Hairez, Harys; *Dch.* Harries; *Fl.* Hariche; p.n.; *A.S.* *harra* (a lord)
HARROD. *See* Harwood. Or *A.S.* Heahred; a p.n. (high counsel)
HARROP. From Harehope; a loc. n., Northbd.
HARRY. *Fr.* Harrye. A Hugt. n., Lond. 1621. *See* Harris
HARSAM. *See* Hearsum
HARSANT. *A.S.* Hærsand; *Old G.* Hersand; *D.* Herschend; *Fl.* Herssen; p.n. (battle envoy)
N.-Fr. Harsent in Rot. Hund.

HARSTON. A loc. n., Cumb., Leics, Northants
HART. *N.* Hjörtr (a hart, stag); *S.* Hjerta; *D.* Harth; *Dch.*, *G.* Hart, Herte; p.n. Or *A.S.* Hart, Heard; p.n. (strong)
HARTCUP. *G.* Hastkopf; p.n. (strong head)
HARTLEY. A loc. n., Kent, Northbd. Or Hardley, Norf.
HARTOPP. From Hartoft; a loc. n., Yorks
HARTSHORNE. A loc. n., Derbysh.
HARTWELL. A loc. n., Bucks, Devon, Northants
HARTWRIGHT. *A.S.* Heardric, Harteric; p.n. (strong ruler)
HARVARD. *See* Harward
HARVEY. From Hervé; a loc. n., Belg. *Fr.* Hervé; p.n. Hugt. n. Lond. 1618
Herveus, a tenant in chief in *D.B.* William Hervei in Rot. Obl. et Fin., K. John.

HARWARD. *A.S.* Hereweard; *S.* Herouard; *Dch.* Herwaarde; p.n. (army warden)
HARWOOD. A loc. n., Lancs and Yorks
HASE. *G.* Hase; *Dch.* Haas; p.n. (a hare). Or *A.S.* Has, Haso (livid)
HASELL. From Hasle; a loc. n., Yorks. Or *see* Hazle
HASKETT. *See* Hesketh
HASLAM. From Asheldam (?); a loc. n., Ess.
HASLEDEN, HASELDINE. From Hazledine; a loc. n., Worcest.
HASLEHAM. *See* Haslam
HASLEWOOD. A loc. n., Yorks
HASLOCK, HASLUCK. From Hassloch; a loc. n., Germ. Or *N.* Asleikr; *A.S.* Oslac; p.n. (god's play)
HASLOP, HASLUP. *See* Heslop
HASSALL. A loc. n., Ches. Hessell, Prot. ref., Sandwich, 1622

HASSARD. *D.* Hassert; *Fl.* Hasaert; *N.-Fr.* Hasart; p.n. (the gods' strong one)

HASSETT. *N.-Fr.* Hassot; a p.n.
Rot. Hund. 1272. Haste and Hest, Norm., 1180.

HASTED. From Ashstead ; a loc. n., Surr. Or Hawstead, Suff.

HASTELOW. A loc. n.

HASTIE. *See* Hassett

HASTING. From an island off the coast of Normandy
In Roll of Battell Abbey. De Hasting in Rot. Obl. et Fin., K. John.

HASTINGS. A loc. n., Suss.
Held by De Venoix in 1086.

HASTWELL. *See* Eastall

HASWELL. A loc. n., Dur.

HATCH. A loc. n., Beds, Kent, Somers
Atte Hach in 1327.

HATCHAM. A loc. n., Middlx.

HATCHER. *G.* Hatscher ; a p.n. (a halberdier). Or *see* Hatchett

HATCHETT. *Fr.* Hachette ; a p.n. *See* Hacket
Achet, under-tenant at survey in *D.B.*

HATE. *A.S.* Hat, Hæth ; *Fl.* Het ; p.n. *See* Hatt

HATFIELD. A loc. n., Ess., Herts, Worcest., Yorks

HATHAWAY. *A.S.* Heathuwig, Heathewi (victory in war)

HATHERLEY. From Hatherleigh ; a loc. n., Devon

HATHORNTHWAITE. A loc. n., Westmd.

HATT. *N.* Höttr (a hood) ; *D.* Hatte ; *F.* Hatto ; *A.S.* Hat, Heathu ; p.n. (war)

HATTEN. *See* Hatting or Hatton

HATTERLEY. A loc. n., Ches.

HATTERSLEY. *See* Haddesley

HATTING. *D.* ; p.n. *See* Atto, Hatt

HATTON. A loc. n., Middlx., Staffs

HAUGHTON. A loc. n., Dur., Staffs

HAVELL, HAVILL. *See* Hovel

HAVELOCK. *N.* Hafleikr ; a p.n. ; *haf* (sea), *leik* (sport)

HAVERS. *N.-Fr.* De Auvere. Or *N.* Hávarr, *há-vörr* (?) (high lip) ; *Dch.* Havers ; *A.S.* Hæfa ; p.n.

HAVILAND. *G.* Haveland ; a p.n. Or Haverland ; a loc. n., Norf.

HAWARD. *N.* Hávarðr ; *A.S.* Haward, Hahweard, Heahweard ; *Fl.* Havaert, Havard, Hauwaert ; *Dch.* Houwaard ; *G.* Hofert, Hoffarth ; p.n. (high warden). Or *see* Hayward
A Saxon tenant in *D.B.*

HAWEIS. *A.S.* Hathewis ; a p.n. Hathwise (war leader)

HAWKE. *A.S.* Hafoc, Heafeca ; *Fl.* Hauke ; p.n. A Prot. ref. n., Norwich, 1622. *See* Auker

HAWKES. From Hawkers ; a loc. n., Northbd. Or *see* Auker

HAWKINS. From Hawking ; a loc. n., Kent
Osbert de Hawking, *temp.* Henry II.

HAWKRIGG. A loc. n., Westmd.

HAWKSHAW. A loc. n., Lancs
Rob' de Hauconesheu in Rot. Obl. et Fin., K. John, A.D. 1199.

HAWKSLEY. A loc. n., Somers. Or Hauxley, Northbd.

HAWKSWORTH. A loc. n., Yorks

HAWLEY. From La Haulle ; a loc. n., Norm.

HAWORTH. A loc. n., Yorks

HAWS. From Hawes ; a loc. n., Yorks

HAWTAYNE. *Fr.* Hautein ; a p.n. From Autigny (?) ; a loc. n., Normandy. Or *N.-Fr.* Le Hautain ; a p.n. (the proud)
In Roll of Battell Abbey.

HAWTHORN. A loc. n., Lincs

HAWTREY. From Hauterive ; a loc. n., Norm.

HAXALL, HAXELL. From Exwell (?) ; a loc. n., Rutl. Hackensall, Lancs

HAY. A loc. n., Cornw., Staffs. *N.-Fr.* De la Haye. A Hugt. n., Dover, 1622.
Atte Hay, Court of Husting, 1258.

HAYCOCK. A hill in Cumb. Or *F.* Heike ; *Fl.* Haeck ; *A.S.* Hecca ; *Dch.* Heek, Haeij-Koch ; p.n. Dim. of *F.* Hayo. *See* Heyhoe

HAYCROFT. A loc. n., Dorset

HAYES. A loc. n., Norm., Salop ; Hees, Belg. *Dch.* Hees ; a p.n. Hugt. n., Lond. 1618

HAYGREEN. A loc. n., Yorks

HAYLES. A freq. loc. n. *See* Hales

HAYLEY. From Haylie ; a loc. n., Largs, Scotl.

HAYLOCK. From Haylake (?) Cheriton Bishop, Devon

HAYMAN. From Heman ; a loc. n., Germany. *Dch.* Heiman ; *Fl.* Heman, Heyman ; p.n. Or *A.S.* Æceman (edge-man)

HAYNES. From Haiene, Norm. ; a loc. n., Beds, Devon. *See* Haines.
Hugh de H., 12th century.

HAYTER, HAYTOR. A loc. n., Derbysh.

HAYWARD. From Hauwert ; a loc. n., Belg. *Fl.* Hauwaert, Heywaert ; p.n. *See* Haward
Hayward in Roll of Battell Abbey. This being a loc. n. is more likely to be the origin of the noble name of Howard than that of a Saxon tenant. The Conqueror had many Flemings in his army.

HAZARD. *See* Hassard

HAZELRIGG. A loc. n., Northbd.

HAZLE. *S.* Hasle ; *D.* Hassel ; *Dch.* Hazel ; *G.* Hessell ; *D.B.* Hezelin ; p.n. *See* Hassall

HAZLETT. *See* Haseldine

HAZZARD. From Hazard ; a loc. n., Devon. *See* Hassard

HEACOCK. *See* Haycock

HEAD. *A.S.* Headda, Hedde ; *G.* Hede ; *D.* Heede ; p.n. (warrior). Prot. ref., Norwich, 1622
Hedde in Rot. Hund.

HEADEACH, HEADECH. *See* Hedach

HEADIN. *S.* Hedin ; *Dch.* Hedden ; *G.* Hedin ; p.n. ; fam. n. of Head

HEADLAM. A loc. n., Dur.

HEADLEY. A loc. n., Hants, Surr., Worcest.

HEAGREEN. *See* Haygreen

HEAL. A loc. n., Surr.

HEALEY. A loc. n., Northbd., Yorks

HEANEY. *See* Henny

HEAP. *A.S.* Ibba, Ippa ; *F.* Ippe ; *G.* Hippe ; *Dch.* Hiep ; p.n. *See* Abbs

HEARD. *See* Ard

HEARNE. From Heron ; a loc. n., Norm. ; a loc. n., Kent, Surr.

HEARSUM. From Hersham ; a loc. n., Surr.

HEASELL. *See* Hasell and Hazle

HEASLIP. *See* Heslop

HEATH. A loc. n., Derbysh., Devon, Yorks, etc.

HEATHCOTE. A loc. n., Derbysh.

HEATHER. A loc. n., Leics

HEATLEY. A loc. n., Staffs

HEATON. A loc. n., Ches., Lancs, Staffs

HEAVEN, HEAVENS. From Heffen(?) ; a loc. n., Belg. Or *see* Evans

HEAVER. *See* Heffer

HEBB. *A.S.* Ebba ; *Fl.* Hebbe ; *F.* Ebbe ; p.n. *See* Abbs

HEBBERT. *N.-Fr.* Hebart ; *A.S.* Hygebeorht ; a p.n. (bright mind). Higbert, bp. of Worcester. Prot. ref., Lond. 1685

HEBBLETHWAITE. *See* Ablewhite

HEBGIN. *F.* Ebo, Ebbo, Ebbe, Ebken ; *S.* Hebbe ; *G.* Ebbeke ; p.n. Dimin. of Hebbe

HECKFORD. From Hackforth ; a loc. n., Yorks. *D.B.* Acheford. Also Hackford ; a loc. n., Norf.
John de Hackford, A.D. 1340 ; Sir W. de Hakeford, *temp.* Hen. I. (Norf.).

HEDACH. *G.* Heyduck, Hedicke ; p.n. Dim. of Head. *See* Hettich

HEDDERLEY. *See* Adderley

HEDDERWICK. From Hedrick (?); a loc. n., Dur.

HEDDLE. *Dch.* Hedel; a p.n. Dim. of Head

HEDERTON. *See* Hetherington

HEDGE. *Dch.*, *G.* Heege; a p.n. Or *see* Edge

HEDGECOCK. *A.S.* Hecca; *G.* Hedtke (?); a p.n.; *ecg* (edge, sword). Dim.

HEDGELAND. *D.* Hegeland, Heggelund; *S.* Hägglund; loc. and p.n.

HEDGES. *See* Etches

HEDLEY. A loc. n., Dur.

HEEPS. *See* Heap

HEFFER. From Hever; a loc. n., Belg. Or *N.* Evarr; *A.S.* Hefa; *F.* Eve; *G.* Heffe; p.n. *See* Havers

HEFFILL. Dim. of Hefa

HEFFORD. *D.* Heerfordt; a p.n.

HEGGS. *D.*, *Dch.* Eggers; a p.n. *See* Eggs

HELLELEY. From Hellingly; a loc. n., Suss.

HELLERAY. *See* Elleray

HELLIER. From St Hellier, near Rouen, Norm.

HELLING. *F.* Elle (strong, brave), Ellen; a fam. n.; *S.* Helin, Helling; *Fl.* Hellin, Hellings; p.n.

HELLINGS. From Helions; a loc. n., Normandy.

Upton Helions, Devon; in old deeds U. Hyllyngs.

HELM. From Helme; a loc. n., Dur. Or Halme, Norm.; *N.* Hjálmr (a helmet), Hjelm; *Fl.*, *G.* Helm; *A.S.* Helm; p.n.

HELMER. *See* Helm

HELMORE. From Elmore; a loc. n., Glost. Or *A.S.* Helmœr; *Fl.*, *S.* Helmer; p.n. (famous helmet)

HELMSLEY. A loc. n., Yorks

HELPS. *N.-Fr.* De Helpe; a p.n.

Helbe in Rot. Hund.

HELSHAM. From Hailsham; a loc. n., Suss.

HELY. *See* Healey

HEMAN. *See* Hayman

HEMANS. *See* Hemmans

HEMERY. *See* Emery

HEMINGWAY. From Hemingby; a loc. n., Lincs

HEMMANS. *N.* Hemingr (an adopted son); a p.n.; *Dch.* Hemminga; *F.* Emmen, Emminga; *Fl.* Heman; *G.* Hemens; *S.* Hemming; p.n.

HEMMANT, HEMMENT. *See* Hammond

HEMMINGTON. From Hemington; a loc. n., Leics, Northants

HEMPSHALL. From Hempshill; a loc. n., Notts

HEMS. *See* Ames

HEMSLEY. *See* Helmsley

HEMSTEAD, HEMSTED. From Hempstead; a loc. n., Ess., Glost.

HEMSWORTH. A loc. n., Yorks

HEMUS. *See* Ames

HENCHMAN. *G.* Heinzmann; a p.n. (a page, footman). Heinz, dimin. of Heinrich

HENDERSON. *See* Hendry

HENDRA, HENDREY, HENDRY. A loc. n., Cornw. Or *N.* Endriði; *A.S.* Henthryth; p.n. (chief rider (?))

HENEY. From Henis; a loc. n., Belg. Or *see* Henny

HENGULF. *N.* Ingolf; *A.S.* Ingulf; p.n. (Ingswolf)

HENN. *F.* Enno; *A.S.* Hen (old, ancestral); *D.* Henne; *Fl.* Hen; p.n.

HENNANT *Dch.* Hent; a p.n.

HENNELL. From Henlle; a loc. n., Salop

HENNESY. From the Irish O'h Aengusa; a p.n. *See* Guinness

HENNIKER. *A.S.* Haneca; a p.n. (ancient spear); *Old G.* Anager, Enegar; p.n.

HENNY. A loc. n., Ess. *See* Henn

HENSHAW. A loc. n., Northbd.
HEPBURN. A loc. n., Northbd.
HEPHER. *See* Heffer
HEPPLESTON. From Eppleton (?) ;
a loc. n., Dur.
HEPPLEWHITE. *See* Ablewhite
HEPTONSTALL. A loc. n., Lancs
HEPWORTH. A loc. n., Suff., Yorks
Stephen de Hepworth, Chancellor of
Cambridge University A. D. 1257-99.
Adam de Heppeworth, Yorks (for-
merly de Belmont) assumed the
name with the manor A.D. 1303.

HERBAGE. From Herbisse ; a loc.
n., France. Or *G.* Herbich, Her-
big ; p.n.
HERBERT. *N.-Fr.* ¹Herbart, Her-
bet ; p.n. ; *A.S.* Hearra - beorht
(bright lord)
D.B. tenant in chief and under-tenant.
Freq. in Rot. Obl. et Fin., K. John.
Hugt. n., Cant. 1622.

HERCY, HERSEE, HERSEY. From
Hericy ; a loc. n., Norm.
In Roll of Battell Abbey. Hugo de
Hersi vel Hersy in Rot. Obl. et
Fin., K. John. Hugh de Hercy,
1135, Wingram, Bucks.

HEREPATH. A loc. n., Devon
HERIOT. A loc. n., Edinburgh.
Or *N.-Fr.* De Ariete ; a p.n.
HERN. *See* Hearne. Or *A.S.*
Arne, Earn ; p.n. (eagle)
HERON. *Fr.* Héron ; a p.n. ; *D.B.*
de Herion. Le Héron ; a loc. n.,
Normandy
In Roll of Battell Abbey.

HERRICK. *N.* Eireker (peaceful
franklin) ; *A. S.* Herric ; *Fr.* Héri-
cher ; p.n.
D.B. Eric, tenant in chief. Heryce
in Roll of Battell Abbey.

HERRING. *D.* Herring ; *Fl.* Her-
inckx ; *Fr.* Herinne ; *G.* Häring ;
p.n. From *N. Hœringr* (hoary
men), Hérinnes ; a loc. n., Belg. ;
Herin, France
HERRIOTT. *See* Heriot
HERSUM. *See* Hearsum
HESELTINE. *See* Haseldine

HESFORD. From Hessenford ; a
a loc. n., Cornw.
HESKETH. A loc. n., Lancs
HESLAM. *See* Haslam
HESLOP. A loc. n., Derbysh.
HESP. *A.S.* Esber, Esbeorn ; *Dch.*
Hesper ; *G.* Espe ; p.n. *See*
Osborne
HETHERINGTON. A loc. n., Cumb.
HETTICH. *See* Headach
HEUGH. *See* Hughes
HEUSTICE. *See* Eustace
HEWARD. *A.S.* Hugihard ; *Old G.*
Hugihart, Hugard ; *Fr.* Houard,
Huard, Huart ; p.n. (firm mind)
Houard and Huard, tenants at Survey
in *D.B.* Prot. ref., Lond. 1618.

HEWES. *See* Hughes
HEWETT. *N.-Fr.* Huet, Huett ;
p.n. (little Hugh). Hugt. n.,
Lond. 1621. Or from Huest or
Huet, near Evreux, Norm.
HEWISH. From Huish ; a loc. n.,
Devon, Somers. Or *Dch.* Huis,
Huysse ; *Fr.* Hugues, Huez ; p.n.
See Hughes
HEWITT. *See* Hewett
HEWKE. *See* Hook
HEWLETT. *See* Hullett
HEWSON. *Dch.* Huessen ; a p.n.
See Hughes
HEXTALL, HEXTELL. A loc. n.,
Staffs
HEY. *See* Hay
HEYCOCK. *See* Haycock
HEYGATE. *A.S.* Heahgyth ; *G.*
Heygütte; *Dch.* Hegt ; p.n. (noble
Goth)
HEYHOE. *A.S.* Heio ; *F.* Hayo,
Heie, Hei ; *S.* Ey ; *Dch.* Heij ;
G. Hey, Heyer ; p.n. (high)
HIBBERT. *See* Hebbert
HIBBINS. *F.* Ibo, Ibe ; fam. n.,
Ibben ; p.n. *See* Abbs
HIBBIT. *See* Hebbert
HIBBLE. *A.S.* Higelbald (bold
mind), Higbald, bp. of Lindis-
farne; *Dch.*Hibbel; *G.*Hiebel;p.n.
HIBGANE. *See* Hebgin

HIBLING. *Dch.* Hibelen

HICHENS. *S.* ; p.n. *See* Higgins

HICK. *F.* Iko, Ike, Iken ; *Dch.* Hikke ; *Fl.* Ickx ; *A.S.* Hicca, Hig ; p.n.

HICKEN. *See* Higgin

HICKEY. *N.-Fr.* Hequet ; a p.n.

HICKLING. A loc. n., Notts

HICKMAN. *See* Higman

HICKORY. *A.S.* Hygehere ; a p.n. (Hugh the warrior)

HICKS, HICKSON. *See* Hick

HIDDELSTON. *See* Huddleston

HIDE, HIDES. From Hyde ; a loc. n., Middlx. ; Heyd, Belg. Or *N.* Heidr ; *D.*, *G.*, *Dch.* Heide, Heyde ; p.n.

HIGGETT. From Highgate (?) ; a loc. n., Lond. Or *see* Huggett

HIGGIN. *A.S.* Hyge ; *F.* Iggs, Iggen ; *N.-Fr.* Hicun ; p.n.

HIGH. From Huy ; a loc. n., Belg. ; or Haigh, Lancs

HIGHAM. A loc. n., Kent, Lancs, Northants, Leics

HIGMAN. *See* Hugman

HIGNETT. *A.S.* Hugon ; *Fr.* Hugnot, Hognet ; p.n. *See* Hughes

HILARD. *See* Hildyard

HILDERSLEY. From Yeldersley ; a loc. n., Derbysh.

HILDYARD. *A.S.* Hildegeard (war-guard) ; *D.* Hilleraad ; *G.* Hilger ; *Fr.* Guillard ; p.n. ; *D.B.* Hildeuert, Guluert, Wielard, Willard

HILES. *F.* Eilerts, Eilts, Eils ; a fam. n. ; *A.S.* Æthelheard ; *D.* Heil ; *Dch.* Heillers ; *Fl.* Heilaerts ; p.n. (strong noble)

HILEY. From Highley ; a loc. n., Salop

HILL. A loc. n., Devon, Germ., Hants, etc. Or *F.*, *D.*, *G.* Hille ; *Fl.* Hil ; p.n. *Dch.* ref. n., Lond. 1618

HILLARY. From St Hilaire ; a loc. n., France

> Stephen de St Hillary in Rot. Obl. et Fin., K. John.

HILLEN. A *Dch.* p.n. *See* Hill

HILLIARD, HILLYARD. *See* Hildyard

HILLYER. *See* Hellier

HILTON. A loc. n., Derbysh., Dorset, Dur., Lancs, Staffs

HIMUS. *See* Ames

HINCHLIFFE. A loc. n., Yorks

HINCKLEY. A loc. n., Leics

HINDE. *Fl.* p.n. Prot. ref., Lond. 1618

HINDLE. *Dch.* Hindael ; a p.n.

HINDLEY. A loc. n., Lancs

HINDRIE. *See* Hendry

HINDSON. *S.* Hinderson ; a p.n.

HINE, HINER. *D.* Hein ; *G.* Heine ; p.n. (Harry). Prot. ref., Lond. 1618

HINGE. From Irish M'Hinch. Or dim. of Hinc ; *G.*, *Dch.* Hinse ; p.n.

HINKS. *A.S.* Hengst ; a p.n. (horse)

HINNEL. *See* Hennell

HIPKIN, HIPPER, HIPPERSON. *F.* Hibbo, Hibbe ; *G.* Hippe, Hipper, Ibich ; *Dch.* Hipken ; *Fl.* Hippert ; *A.S.* Ibbo, Ibi ; p.n. *See* Abbs

HIPSLEY. From Ipsley ; a loc. n., Warw., Worcest.

HIRD. *A.S.* Hirde ; *D.* Herth ; *S.* Hierta ; *Fl.* Herdies ; *Dch.* Heerde ; *G.* Hirt ; p.n. *See* Hart

HISBENT. *D.* Isbrand ; a p.n. (iron sword)

HISCOX. *A.S.* Eisc ; a p.n. (icy)

HISLOP. A loc. n., Scotl.

HITCH, HITCHCOCK. *F.* Hiddo ; *A.S.* Hidda, Hiddi ; akin to *had* (war) ; *Fl.* Hittecher ; a p.n. Dimin.

HIVES. St Ives ; a loc. n., Cornw., Hunts. Or Hives, Belg.

HOADLEY. From Hoathley ; a loc. n., Suss.

HOARE. From Oare ; a loc. n., Kent ; Ore, Suss. Or Aure, Auray, Bretagne

HOBART. *See* Hubbard. Hugt. n.,
Lond. 1618

HOBBES, HOBBS. *See* Hobson

HOBBINS. *Dch.* Obbens; a p.n.
See Hoben

HOBBIS. From Hobbies; a loc. n.,
Norf. Or *Dch.* Obbes; a p.n.

HOBBLE. *D.* Hobolth; *Dch.* Hob-
bel; *Fl.* Houbel; p.n. *See* Hubble. Prot. ref., Sandwich, 1621

HOBEN. *G.* Hoben; *Dch.* Hob-
ben; *Fl.* Hobin, Hœben; p.n.

HOBHOUSE. *See* Hobbis

HOBKIRK. A loc. n., Roxburghsh.

HOBLYN. From Aublain; a loc. n.,
Belg. *Fr.* Houblinne, Oblin; *G.*
Uebelin; p.n.

HOBOURN. From Holborn; a loc.
n., Middlx.

HOBSON. *A.S.* Oba; *N.* Ubbi (?)
(wild); *D.* Obbe; p.n.
Leuric Hobbesune, a Saxon tenant in
D.B. (Suff.).

HOCKIN. *A.S.* Hoc; a p.n.; Hocing;
a fam. n.; akin to *N.* Hugi; *A.S.*
Hoga; p.n.; *F.* Okko; a p.n.
See Hughes.
Okken, Okking, fam. n., seems to be
derived from Odoko. *See* Oddy.

HOCKLEY. A loc. n., Derbysh.,
Ess.

HODDS. *Dch.* Hoddes; a p.n. Prot.
ref., Lond. 1618

HODDY, HODY. A loc. n., Belg.
Or *N.* Oddi (a leader); *F.* Ode,
Oddo; *D.* Odde, Odder; *N.-Fr.*
Audé; *Fl.* Hody; *A.S.* Oda,
Odda; p.n.
In Rot. Hund.

HODGE, HODGSON. *N.* Hugi; *A.S.*
Hoc, Hoce, Hoga; *Dch.* Hocke;
p.n. (mind). *See* Hogg and
Hughes

HODGERS. *See* Odgers

HODGKIN. *A.S.* Hogcin; a p.n.
Dim. of Hodge. *See* Hughes
and Odger

HODGKINSON. *See* Hodgkin

HODGSON. *D.B.* Odesune; a p.n.
Or *see* Odgers and Hodge

HOFF. *A.S.* Hof, *hófer* (?) (a hump-
back); *S.*, *D.*, *Fl.*, *Dch.*, *G.* Hoff;
p.n.

HOGAN. From the Irish O'h-Ogain;
a p.n. Or *Dch.*, *Fl.* Hoogen; a
p.n. *See* Huggins

HOGARTH. *See* Hoggarth

HOGBEN. *A.S.* Hagbeorn; a p.n.
(clever bear). Or *see* Ogben

HOGG. *N.-Fr.* De Hoga. From La
Hogue, Norm. Or *Dch.* Hog;
Fl. Hogge; *A.S.* Hog, Hoc, *hog*
(prudent); *G.* Hoch, Hocher;
p.n. *See* Hughes

HOGGARTH. *N.* Hofgarðr; *N.-Fr.*
Hogart; *Fl.* Hogger, Hoogaerts;
D. Hofgaard; *A.S.* Hoga; *Fr.*
Hocquart; p.n. (castle warden)

HOGGER. *Fl.*; p.n. *See* Hoggarth

HOGGETT. *N.-Fr.* De la Hoguette,
i.e. Howe. Or *see* Hoggarth

HOGGINS. *See* Huggins

HOLBECHE. From Holbeach; a
loc. n., Lincs. Or *D.* Holbech;
a loc. and p.n.

HOLBECK. A loc. n., Notts

HOLBROOK. A loc. n., Derbysh.,
Yorks

HOLCOMBE. A loc. n., Devon, Dorset, Somers

HOLCROFT. A loc. n., Lancs

HOLDAM. From Oldham; a loc. n.,
Lancs

HOLDAWAY. From Holdawit (?);
a loc. n., Cornw.

HOLDEN. A loc. n., Yorks. Or *S.*
Hollden; *D.* Holten; p.n.

HOLDERNESS. A loc. n., Yorks

HOLDITCH. A loc. n., Devon,
Dorset

HOLDOM. *See* Holdam

HOLDON. *See* Holden

HOLDRON. *See* Oldring

HOLDSWORTH. A loc. n., Yorks

HOLE. A loc. n., Cornw., Devon
Rich. de la Hole in Rot. Hund.

HOLEYMAN. *A.S.* Hallmund; *Dch.*,
Fl. Hollemann; p.n. (hill protector)

HOLEHOUSE. A loc. n., Dumfries
HOLGATE. A loc. n., Lancs, Yorks
HOLKER. A loc. n., Lancs
HOLKHAM. A loc. n., Norf.
HOLL. A loc. n., Germ. Or *A.S.*
Holl; *Dch.* Holl; p.n. *See* Hall
HOLLAND. From Hulland (*D.B.*
Holund); a loc. n., Derbysh.
Or *Dch., Fl.* Holland; a p.n.
HOLLEY. *Fl.* Holle; a p.n. *See*
Holl
HOLLICK. *D.* Holck; *Dch.* Hol-
lak; *G.* Holleck; p.n. Dim. of
Holl
HOLLIDAY. *See* Halliday
HOLLINGHAM. From Holdingham;
a loc. n., Lincs
HOLLINGSHEAD. From Holling-
send; a loc. n., Yorks. Or Hol-
lingside; a loc. n., Dur.
HOLLINGSWORTH. *See* Holling-
worth
HOLLINGWORTH. A loc. n., Lancs
HOLLOMON, HOLLYMAN. *See*
Holeyman
HOLLOWAY. A loc. n., Devon,
Warw.
HOLMES. A loc. n., Lancs, Lincs.;
Atte Holmes. Or *D., S., Dch.,*
G. Holm; *Fl.* Holms; p.n.
From *N. hólmr* (an islet in a lake
or river)
D.B. de Holmo, a tenant in chief.
HOLROYD. Anciently de Howrode;
a loc. n., Yorks
HOLT. A loc. n., Norf.; Atte Holt.
Or *Dch.* Holt; *S.* Holter; *D.*
Holte, Holde; *G.* Holdt; p.n.
(a wood)
De Holt in Rot. Obl. et Fin.
HOLTBY. A loc. n., Yorks
HOLTHOUSE. *Dch.* Holterhuis; *G.*
Holthaus; p.n.
HOLTHUM, HOLTOM. From Hal-
tham; a loc. n., Lincs. Or *D.*
Holtum; a loc. and p.n.
HOLYOAKE. A loc. n., Staffs
HOMBERSLEY. From Ombersley;
A loc. n., Worcest.

HOME. A loc. n., Holland. *See*
Hume
HOMFRAY. *N.* Hólmfríðr, *hólm*
(islet), *friðr* (peace); *G.* Hump-
fer, Humphrey; p.n.
HONE. An Irish form of Owen.
Or from Hogne; a loc. n., Belg.
Also *N.* Aun; *A.S.* Hon, On;
p.n. (old, ancestral)
HONEYBUN. *See* Hunneybun
HONEYCHURCH. A loc. n., Devon
HONSLOWE. From Hounslow; a
loc. n., Middlx. Or *see* Onslow
HONYWILL. From Honeywell; a
loc. n., Devon
HOOD. A loc. n., Devon; Hude,
Germ. Or *N.* Udi; *F.* Udo,
Ude; *D.* Hude; *G.* Hudy; *Dch.*
Ouda; *A.S.* Hud, Hudda, Udi;
p.n. Ude, a Hugt. n., Lond. 1618.
See Hudson
HOOK. A loc. n., Devon, Hants.
Or *A.S.* Huc, Huch, Hyge; *F.*
Uko, Uke (?); *G.* Huck; *S.*
Huch; *Dch.* Hoek; *Fr.* Huc,
Hucq; p.n.
This is one of the French forms of
Hugo. *See* Hughes. A Prot. ref.
n., Lond. 1618.
HOOKER. *A.S.* Hucco; *G.* Hucke;
N.-Fr. Hucherer; p.n. *See* Hook
There is a *N.* n.n. Húkr (one who
sits on his hams), but it hardly ap-
plies. J. Hochard in Rot. Hund.
HOOKWAY. A loc. n., Devon
HOOLE. A loc. n., Lancs
HOOLEY. *Fr* Houllet; a p.n. *See*
Hullett or Howley
HOOPER. A loc. n., Cornw.
HOOPPELL. A Hugt. n., Dover,
1622
HOPE. A loc. n., Derbysh., Salop,
Heref., Yorks, N. Wales
HOPGOOD. *N.* Ubbi (wild); *A.S.*
Ubba; *Old G.* Hopi; p.n.; *gaut*
(a Goth)
HOPKING, HOPKINS. *Dch.* Hoppe,
Hop, Höpken; p.n. Dimin. of
Hob. *See* Hobson
HOPKIRK. *See* Hobkirk

HOPPER. *D.*, *Dch.* Hoppe, Hopper; *G.* Hoppe; p.n. *See* Hobson

HOPPS. *See* Hobbs

HOPSON. *See* Hobson

HOPTON. A loc. n., Yorks

HOPWOOD. A loc. n., Lancs

HORBURY. A loc. n., Yorks

HORDEN. A loc. n. (a manor), Dur.

HORN. *D.*, *S.*, *A.S.*, *Dch.*, *G.* Horn; p.n. (a horn or trumpet)

HORNBLOW, HORNBLOWER. From Hornblotton (?); a loc. n., Somers. Or Horninglow, Derbysh.

HORNBY. A loc. n., Lancs, Yorks

HORNER. *S.* Horner; a p.n. *See* Horn

HORNEY. *S.* Horney; a p.n. *See* Horn

HORNINGHOLD. A loc. n., Rutl.

HORNSBY. *See* Ormsby

HORNSEY. A loc. n., Middlx.

HOROBIN. *N.* Örrabeinn; a n.n. (scar-leg)

HORREX. *N.* Oraekja; *A.S.* Orric; *Dch.*, *Fl.* Horrickx; p.n. Or *N.* Örrek; n.n. (swift driver (?))

HORSEBURGH. A loc. n., Tweeddale

HORSELL. A loc. n., Surr.

HORSENAIL. From Orsmael (?); a loc. n., Belg.

HORSEPOLE. From Herspool; a loc. n., Cornw.

HORSEY. A loc. n., Ess., Norf.

HORSFALL. A loc. n., Yorks, near Hebden Bridge

HORSFIELD. From Hersfeld; a loc. n., Prussia

HORSFORD. A loc. n., Norf.

HORSHAM. A loc. n., Norf., Suss.

HORSINGTON. A loc. n., Lincs, Somers

HORSLEY. A loc. n., Camb., Surr., Yorks

HORSWELL. *See* Horsell

HORTH. From Horwath or Hoath; A loc. n., Kent. Or *See* Hart

HORTON. A loc. n., Devon, Kent, Northants, Surr., Yorks

HORYAN. *Fr.* Horion; a p.n. (a thumb). Also a loc. n., Belg.

HOSGOOD. *N.* Ásgautr (a name of Odin, or divine Goth); *A.S.* Asgot, Osgot, Osgod; p.n. Tenant in chief in *D.B.* Richard Ausgod in Rot. Obl. et Fin., K. John.

HOSKINS, HOSKYNS. *Dch.* Huskens; a p.n. *See* Hodgkinson

HOSTE. *G.* Ost; *Dch.* Haust, Hoost, Oost; *Fl.* Hoste; p.n. Hoost, a Prot. ref., Lond. 1618 The Osti (Estonians) were a people of Germany.

HOTCHKIN. *See* Hodgkinson

HOTCHKISS. *See* Hodgkinson

HOTHAM. A loc. n., Yorks

HOTINE. *Fr.* Autin; a p.n. From Austin, Augustin. Or *see* Hawtayne

HOTSON. From Hoddesdon; a loc. n., Herts. Or *see* Hoddy

HOTTEN. *See* Hotine or Outon

HOUCHEN. *See* Huggin

HOUGH. A loc. n., Ches., Lincs

HOUGHTON. A loc. n., Beds, Dur., Lancs, Norf., Northants

HOULDERSHAW. *See* Oldershaw

HOULGRAVE. From Youlgreave; a loc. n., Derbysh.

HOULSTONE. From Holstone; a loc. n., Devon

HOULTON. *See* Hulton

HOUSTON. A loc. n., Scotl. *See* Owston

HOVELL. From Houville; a loc. n., France. *Dch.* Hoevel; a p.n. In Roll of Battell Abbey. Huwell in Rot. Obl. et Fin.

HOW. *See* Howe

HOWARTH. A loc. n., Lancs

HOWE. A loc. n., Norf., Yorks. From *N.* haugr (a cairn over one dead). Or *D.* Hau, Hou; p.n. Thomas de Hou in Rot. Obl. et Fin., K. John.

HOWARD. *See* Haward and Hayward

This name does not occur in *D.B.* as a tenant in chief. Haward is a Saxon tenant. Houard and Huard are tenants at the Survey, but they may be the *N.-Fr.* forms of Hugihard. *See* Heward. Hayward is in the Roll of Battell Abbey, but neither name appears in Rot. Obl. et Fin., K. John. Burke does not trace Howard farther back than Edw. I. Dugdale suggests that the name took its origin from a high office in Saxon times or from the name of a place.

HOWELL. Name of a Welsh prince in *D.B.* Hoel (lordly). Also a Hugt. n., Lond. 1618

HOWES. From Housse ; a loc. n., Belg. *Dch.* House ; a p.n. Prot. ref. n., Cant. 1622

HOWGHIN. *See* Huggin

HOWITT. From Houyet ; a loc. n., Belg. *D.* Howitz ; *Dch.* Hoet ; p.n. Hugt. n., Cant. 1622. *See* Hewett

A younger branch of Hewet of Killamarsh, Derbysh., acquired Wansley, Notts, and changed the name to Howitt. De Hoet in Rot. Obl. et Fin.

HOWLETT. *See* Hullett

HOWLEY. *N.-Fr.* De Houlei ; a p.n. John Houle in Rot. Hund.

HOWSE. A Cornish form of Haweis. Or *see* Howes

HOWSTON. *See* Owston

HOY. *See* Heyho

HOYLAND. From the Irish Hyland ; a p.n.

HOYNE. An Irish form of Owen

HUARTSON. *See* Heward

HUBBALL, HUBBLE. *A.S.* Hygebeald, Hubald ; p.n. (bold mind, or mind prince)

HUBBARD, HUBERT. *A.S.* Hygebeorht, Hubert ; *G.* Huber, Hubert ; *Fl.* Houba, Houbard ; *N.-Fr.* Houbart ; *Dch.* Huber ; p.n. (bright mind). Hugt. n., Lond. 1618

HUBBLE. *N.* Hugi-baldr (foremost in thought) ; *A.S.* Hygebald ; *Fl.* Houbel ; *G.* Hübel ; *D.B.* Hubald, Hubold ; p.n.

HUBY. *N.* Ubbi ; *F.* Ubbe, Ubbo ; *A.S.* Hubi ; p.n. *See* Hobson

HUCKER. *See* Hooker

HUCKERBY. From Huckaby ; a loc. n., Devon

HUCKLE. From Ughill ; a loc. n., Yorks. Or Uccle, Belg. ; *A.S.* Hicel, a dim. of Hugo ; *N.-Fr.* Hogel, Hockell ; p.n. In Rot. Hund.

HUCKLEBRIDGE. *Fl.* Hucklenbroich; a loc. and p.n.

HUDBUD. *See* Hubbard

HUDD. *See* Hood

HUDDEN. From Houdain; a loc. n., France. Or *Dch.* Uden; *Fl.* Utten; *S.* Udden ; p.n. *See* Hood

HUDDLESTONE. From Huddleston ; a loc. n., Yorks

Nigel de Hudelston was Provost of the Archbishop of York, A.D. 1110. Sir Richard de Hodelston was living at his manor-house of Huddleston in 1262.

HUDGELL. *See* Hugill

HUDSON. *N.* Udr (a son of the night) ; *D.* Hude ; *N.-Fr.* Hudesent ; *F.* Udo, Ude ; *Dch.* Uden, Udsen ; *Fl.* Hudson, Hudsyn ; *A.S.* Hud, Udda, Udi ; p.n.

HUFF. From Hough ; a loc. n., Yorks. Or *A.S.* Hufo (Offa (?)) ; a p.n.

HUFFEN. From the Irish Houghegan, Hogan ; a p.n.

HUGGARD. *See* Hoggarth

HUGGETT. From Huggate ; a loc. n., Yorks. Or *N.-Fr.* Hugot, dim. of Hugo

HUGGINS. *F.* Uken ; *Dch.* Hoogen, Huygens ; *Fl.* Hugens ; p.n.; fam. n. of Hugh

HUGH. *N.* Hugi ; *F.* Uko, Uke ; *G.* Huge, Hugo ; *Fr.* Hue, Hugé; *A.S.* Huc, Hug, Hugi, Hyge ; p.n. (mind, thought)

HUGHES. *D.* Huhs ; *Dch.* Hugues ; p.n. *See* Hugh

HUGHSTON, HUSTON. *See* Houston

HUGILL. A loc. n., Westmd.

HUGMAN. *A.S.* Humman, Hygemund ; *G.* Hieckmann ; *Fr., Dch.* Human ; p.n. (thoughtful protector)

HUKE. *See* Hook

HULKE. *N.* Hugleikr (Hugh the player) ; *A.S.* Hygelac ; *Fr.* Hulek ; *G.* Ulke ; p.n.

HULLAH. From the Irish O'h-Oiliolla ; a p.n. Or *A.S.* Ulla ; a p.n. (wolf)

HULLETT. *Fr.* Houllet, Hulet (owl) ; *D.* Uhlott ; *Dch.* Uloth ; p.n.

HULLEY. *A.S.* Ula ; *G.* Uhle ; *Fr.* Hulet ; p.n.

HULLOCK. *See* Hulke

HULTON. A loc. n., Lancs

Bleythen de Hulton was lord of the manor *temp.* Hen. II. Jorvet de Hulton in Rot. Obl. et Fin., K. John, A.D. 1199.

HULME. A loc. n., Lancs

HULYER. *See* Hildyard

HUMAN. From Humain ; a loc. n., Belg. Or *see* Hugman

HUMBLE. *A.S.* Hunbeald ; *G.* Humbolt (Hun the bold) ; *D.* Humble, Hummel ; *Fr.* Humblet ; p.n.

HUMBY. A loc. n., Lincs

HUME. A loc. n., Berwick

HUMM. *G., Dch.* Humme, p.n. From Humme ; a loc. n. in Hesse Cassel

HUMMERSTON. From Humberstone ; a loc. n., Leics, Lincs

HUMPAGE. From Humphage ; a loc. n., Hants

HUMPHREY. *See* Homfray

HUNN. *A.S.* Hun (a giant), the nation ; *G.* Huhn ; p.n.

HUNNIBELL. From Anneboult ; a loc. n., Norm. Or *D., Fr.* Hannibal ; *Fl.* Hennebel ; p.n. Or *A.S.* Andbeald (bold opponent)

HUNNYBUN. From Honeybourne ; a loc. n., Worcest.

HUNT. *N.* Hundi (a dog) ; *N.-Fr.* le Huant ; *G.* Hund, Hundt ; *Dch.* Hunt ; p.n.

HUNTER. *A.S.* Hunta ; *G.* Hunder ; *Dch.* Hunter ; p.n. (a hunter)

HUNTINGDON. County town, Hunts

HUNTLY. A loc. n., Aberdeensh., Staffs

HUPTON. From Upton ; a loc. n., Devon, Norf., etc.

HURD. *See* Heward

HURLESTONE. A loc. n., Ches.

HURLOCK. From Harlock ; a loc. n., Lancs

HURLOW. *See* Harlow

HURLY. From Hurley ; a loc. n., Berks. Or Irish O'Herlihy

HURN. *See* Hearn and Horn

HURNARD. *Fl.* Arnoeyd ; *Fr.* Arnaud (Arnold) ; p.n.

HURNDALL. *See* Arundel

HURRAN. *See* Uren

HURRELL. *Fr.* Hurel ; a p.n. Dim. of Urr

HURRING. Fam. n. of Urr.

HURSAM. *See* Hearsum

HURST. A freq. loc. n.

De la Hurst in Rot. Obl. et Fin.

HURY. A loc. n., Yorks. Or from Urray ; a loc. n., Ross. Or *Fr.* Huré, Huret, Hurey ; p.n. (boar's head)

HUSBAND. From Husborne (?) ; a loc. n., Beds. Or *N. hús-bóndi* (a house-master)

Simon Huseband in Rot. Obl. et Fin., K. John.

HUSE. *See* Hughes

HUSKISSON. *See* Hodgkinson

HUSON. *See* Hughes

HUSSEY. *Fr.* Houssaye. From *N.-Fr.* de Hossé or de Heuzé ; a p.n. Houssaye ; a loc. n., Norm. Husee in Roll of Battell Abbey.

HUSTHWAITE, HUSTWAIT, HUSTWITT. A loc. n., Yorks

HUTCHINGS, HUTCHINSON. *See* Huggins

HUTH. *A.S.*, *D.*, *Dch.* Huth ; *Fl.* Hutt ; a p.n. (guard, keeper)

HUTHWAITE. A loc. n., Cumb., Notts

HUTT. *See* Huth

HUTTON. A loc. n., Berwick, Dumfries, Somers, Westmd., Yorks

Alan Bussel held it in Yorks in 1153.

HUXFORD. A loc. n., Devon

HUXHAM. A loc. n., Devon

HUXLEY. A loc. n., Ches.

HYAM. From Eyam ; a loc. n., Derbysh. Or *see* Higham

HYATT. From Ayott ; a loc. n., Herts. Or *Fl.* Hyart ; a p.n.

HYE. *See* High

HYLTON. From Hilton ; a loc. n., Dur., Staffs, Suff.

HYMERS, HYMUS. *See* Ames

HYNE. From the Irish O'h-Eidhin ; a p.n. Also Heyne

I

I'ANSON. *See* Johnson

IBBERSON. *A.S.* Ib, Ibba ; *F.* Ibo, Hibbo ; *D.* Ibson ; p.n. *See* Abbs

IBBETSON, IBBOTSON. *See* Hibbert

ICELY. From Isley; a loc. n., Leics

ICKE. *A.S.* Icca, Ycca ; *Dch.* Icke ; *F.* Ikke ; p.n. (sharp-edged)

IDDON. *N.* Iðunn (name of a goddess) ; *S.* Idun ; *F.* Hiddo, Ide, Hidden, Iden ; p.n. Or Iden ; a loc. n., Suss. Hiden, a Prot. ref., Lond. 1618

IDE. A loc. n., Devon. Or *F.*, *D.*, *Dch.* ; p.n.

IDLE. A loc. n., Yorks

IFE. *See* Ivy

IGGLESDEN, IGGULDEN. From Ickleton (?) ; a loc. n., Camb. Or Hickleton, Yorks

ILBERRY. From Hilbury ; a loc. n., Ches. Or Hilborough, Norf.

ILDERTON. A loc. n., Northbd.

ILES. *See* Eels

ILETT. *See* Aylett

ILIFF. *See* Ayliffe

ILLING. *A.S.* Illing ; a fam. n. ; *G.* Illing ; *Fl.* Hillen ; p.n. Or *see* Hillen

ILLINGWORTH. A loc. n., Yorks

ILOTT. *See* Alyett

ILSLEY. A loc. n., Berks. Or Hillsley, Glost.

IMAGE. *G.* Immich, Immig ; p.n. ; *A.S.* Imma ; *F.* Immo, Emma ; p.n. *See* Ames

IMLAY. From Himley. A loc. n., Staffs

IMRAY, IMRIE. *See* Emery

INCE. A loc. n., Lancs. Or *see* Innes

INCHBALD. *A.S.* Ingelbald ; a p.n. (Ingel the bold)

INCHBOARD. *A.S.* Ingibeorht ; a p.n. (the bright or illustrious son)

INCKLE. *See* Ingle

INCLEDON. From Ingleton ; a loc. n., Dur., Yorks

IND. *See* Hinde

INDERWICK. From Innerwick ; a loc. n., Haddington

INESON. *A.S.* Hinn, Ina, Inno (domestic (?)) ; *F.* Ino, Ine ; *S.* Hinnerson ; *Fl.* Hinnsen ; p.n.

ING. *N.* Ingi, a contraction of compounds in Ing, as Ingimundr, etc. *A.S.* Ing, Inga ; p.n.

Ing was identical with the god Freyr

INGALL. *See* Ingle

INGAMELLS. From Ingoldmels ; a loc. n., Lincs

INGATE. A loc. n.

INGELOW. From Inchigeelagh ; a loc. n., Cork. Or *S.* Engellau ; a p.n.

INGERSOL. From Inkersall ; a loc. n., Derbysh.

INGLE. *See* Inglis

INGLEDEW. *A.S.* Angêltheow ; a p.n. (Engel-servant)

INGLEHEART. *N.-Fr.* Engeart ; a p.n. (strong angle)
> Ingelard in Rot. Hund.

INGLESANT. *Old G.* Ingilsind ; a p.n. (Angle companion)

INGLESBY. *See* Ingoldby

INGLET. Dim. of Ingle

INGLETON. A loc. n., Dur., Yorks

INGLIS. *A.S.* Angel, Engel, Ingel ; *Fl.* Inghels ; *Dch.* Ingelse, Inckel ; *S.* Ingelson ; p.n.
> One from the country of the Angles, between Flensburg and the Schley, in Denmark.

INGOLDBY. From Ingoldsby ; a loc. n., Lincs

INGPEN. *See* Inkpen

INGRAM. A loc. n., Northbd. Or *A.S.* Ingiram ; a p.n. (Ingsraven) ; *N.-Fr.* Ingelram

INGREY. From Ingrave ; a loc. n., Herts

INKER. *F.* Ino, Ine, Inke ; p.n, *See* Hinks

INKERSOLE. *See* Ingersoll

INKERSON, INKSON. *A.S.* Ingwar (Ing guarded) ; *D.* Ingverson ; *Dch.* Ingwarsen ; p.n.

INKLEY. *See* Hinckley

INKPEN. A loc. n., Bucks

INKSTER. From Ingestre ; a loc. n., Staffs

INMAN. *N.* Ingi-mundr (Freyer's protection) ; *S.* Ingman ; *D.* Ingemann ; *Dch.* Ingerman ; *Fl.* Indeman ; *A.S.* Ingimund ; p.n.

INN. *F.* Ine, Ino ; *A.S.* In, Ina ; p.n.
> *A.S.* king, A.D. 727.

INNES, INNIS, INNS. A barony in Elgin

INNOCENT. *Fr.* Innocent ; *A.S.* Enisan, Enisant ; p.n.; *ean sind* (?) (companion defender)
> Enisant in Rot. Obl. et Fin., K. John.

INSKIP. A loc. n., Lancs

INSLEY. *See* Hingeley

INSOLE. From Inzell (?) ; a loc. n., Germ. Or *see* Ensell

ION. *N.-Fr.* De Aion ; a p.n.
> Ion in Rot. Hund.

IRBY. A loc. n., Lincs. Or Ireby, Cumb.
> Held by De Amondeville.

IREDALE. From Airedale ; a loc. n., Yorks

IRELAND. *N.* Erland ; *Old G.* Heriland ; *Fl.* Irlen ; a p.n. (*er, out* ; the banished man)

IREMONGER, IRONMONGER. *D.* Irminger ; *A.S.* Eormengær ; p.n. (great spear)

IRONS. From Airan ; a loc. n., Norm. *Fr.* Ayrenx ; a p.n.

IRTON or IRETON. From Ireton ; a loc. n., Derbysh. *D.B.* Hiretune, Iretune

IRVIN, IRVING, IRWIN. From Irvine ; a loc. n., Ayr

ISDELL. From Easdale ; a loc. n.

ISHERWOOD. From Ishlawrcoed or Ushlawrcoed ; a loc. n., Monmouth

ISLE. From Isell ; a loc. n., Cumb.

ISLIP. A loc. n., Northants, Oxf.

ISMAY. *See* Ames

ISOM. From Isham ; a loc. n., Northants

ISON. *See* Izon

ISSITT. *See* Izzard

IVATT, IVETT. *Fl.* Heyvaert ; p.n. Dim of Iva

IVENS. Celtic, *Fr.* Yueins ; Breton, Yvain; Irish, Yyon ; Welsh, Ywain ; p.n. (young warrior, archer). *See* M'Ivor and Owen

IVERS. From Iver (?) ; a loc. n., Bucks. Or *see* Ivor

IVES. *See* Hives

IVOR. *N.* Ivarr ; a p.n. (yew warrior, archer)

IVORY. From Ivry ; a loc. n., Normandy

IVY. *A.S.* Ifa, Iffi, Yffi ; *N. yfa* (?) (to rage) ; p.n.

IXER. *See* Ixworth

IXWORTH. A loc. n., Suff.

IZOD. *See* Izzard

IZON. From Isen ; a loc. n., Germ, Esson, Norm. Or *F.* Eisse. ; Eissen ; *D., S.* Eisen ; *A.S.* Isen (iron) ; p.n. *N.-Fr.* De Aison J. De Eisenne in Rot. Hund.

IZZARD. From Essarts ; a loc. n., Norm. Or *A.S.* Isheard, Ishard (iron firm) ; *Fl.* Izouard ; *D.B.* Iseard ; p.n.

J.

JACK. *F.* Jak ; *G.* Jache, Jach ; *Fr.* Jacques ; p.n. ; *Old G.* Jacco, perhaps from *jagon* (to hunt). Or from Jacob
W. Jak in Rot. Hund.
JACKMAN. *G.* Jachmann ; *Fl.* Jacqmain ; *Fr.* Jacquemont ; p.n. Hugt. n., Canterbury, 1622 (huntsman)
JACKSON. *F.* Jak, Jäckchen ; p.n.
JACOB. *N.* Jakob ; *F.* Jakub, Jakup ; *D.* Jacob ; *Fr.* Jacob ; *D.B.* Jacob ; p.n.
JACOBS, JACOBSON. *D., Dch., S., Fl.* ; p.n. *Fl.* Prot. ref., Lond. 1618
JACQUES. *See* Jack
JAFFRAY. *See* Geoffry
JAGGARD. *Fr.* Jacquard ; *G.* Jagode ; *Dch.* Jagt, Jacot ; p.n. (hunt ward)
JAGGERS, JAGGS. *See* Jaggard
JAKES. *See* Jacques
JAKYLL. *See* Jekyll
JALMAN. *S.* Hjelman ; a p.n. *See* Helmer
JAMES. From St James, Norm. *Fl.* James ; *D.B.* James ; p.n. Prot. ref., Lond. 1621
JAMIE, JAMY. From Chimay (?) ; a loc. n., Belg. *F.* Jimme ; *N.-Fr.* Jamet ; *Fr.* Gimai ; p.n. Or dim. of James
JANE. *A.S.* Gen ; *Fl.* Jegn ; *Fr.* Janet, Jean, Jeanne ; p.n. ; *Old Fr. gens* (gentle)
JANES. *N.-Fr.* De Genez or Gennys ; a p.n. ; *Dch.* Janse ; *G.* Jensch ; *Fl.* Jennes, Jeyens ; p.n.
JANNEY. *G.* Jani ; a p.n. *See* Jane
JANNINGS. *S.* Jahn ; *F.* Jan ; *D.* Janniche ; *Dch.* Janning ; *D.B.* Junain (?) ; a p.n. (John's descendants)

JARDINE. *Fr.* Jardin ; a p.n. (garden)
Jarden in Roll of Battell Abbey.
JARMAIN, JARMAN. *Fr.* Germain ; a p.n. *See* Gamon
JARRED. *A.S.* Garheard (firm spear) ; *F.* Gerd, Gerhard ; *G.* Jerathe ; *Dch.* Gerhardt, Gererts ; *D.B.* Girard, Gerard ; p.n. St Gérard ; a loc. n., Belg.
JARROLD. *A.S.* Garweald (spear ruler) ; *F.* Garrett, Gerrelt ; p.n.
JARVIS. *N.-Fr.* Gerveis ; a p.n. ; *N. geir-ves* ; *A.S. gar-was* (spear-keen). Hugt. n., Lond. 1688.
JARY. *F.* Djure ; *G.* Jury, Jurei ; *Fr.* Jarry. *See* Jarrett
JASPER. From Chassepierre (?) ; a loc. n., Belg. *Dch.* Jasper, Jaspers ; *Fl.* Jaspar ; p.n. Or *Fr.* Gaspard (?) (treasure - master). Prot. ref., Lond. 1621
JAWINS. *A.S.* Jouin, in *D.B.* ; *Fr.* Jouen, Jouvin ; p.n.
Jouve is a *Fr.* form of Job, Jopp.
JAY. A loc. n. Heref. Or *F.* Gayo ; *Dch.* Jay, Jehee ; *Fl.* Jeyens ; p.n. *See* Gay and Gee
Jay is in the Roll of Battell Abbey.
JEAFFRESON. *See* Geoffrey
JEAKES. *See* Jacques
JEALOUS. *Dch.* Jaulus ; *G.* Gelse, Jelsch ; p.n.
JEARY. *See* Jary
JECKELL. *See* Jekyll
JECKS. *See* Jacques
JEE. *See* Gee
JEEVES. *See* Jeffs.
Peter de Cheef, Norm. 1180.
JEFFCOCK, *See* Jeffery
JEFFERSON. *See* Jeaffreson

JEFFERY, JEFFREY. *Fr.* Geoffrey, Jaffré; *N.* Guðfriðr; *D.B.* Godefrid; p.n. *See* Godfrey

JEFFS. *See* above

JEKYLL. Jacle (a fief), Normandy. Or *N.* Jökull (an icicle); *D.* Jœkel; *A.S.* Gicel, Jcel; *G.* Jäckel, Jäkel, Jagel; *Dch.* Jeekel; p.n.
Iuichel or Iuikel, a Presbyter (Norf.), a tenant in chief in *D.B.* W. Jackel, 1180; J. Jacel, 1198. Mag. Rot. Scaccarii, Normanniœ. W. and R. de Jakele, Rot. Hund., 1272.

JELF. *See* Jelly

JELLETT. *See* Gillett

JELLICOE. *A.S.* Geleca; *Old G.* Jeliko. Dirhin. of *F.* Jelle; *Dch.* Gellecum; p.n.

JELLY. From Jelliffe, a form of *N.* Eilifr (enduring). *F.* Jelle; *Fl.* Jelley; p.n.

JEMPSON. *See* James

JENEWAY. *Fr.* Genvier; a p.n., From St Geneviève; a loc. n., Normandy

JENKIN, JENKINS. *Dch.* Jenck, Jenk, Jenkens; *G.* Jenke; p.n. (little John)

JENNER. St Genois (?); a loc. n., Flanders. Or *A.S.* Gener; *Old G.* Genear; p.n. (a refuge, protection); *G.* Jenner; *Fl.* Jenar, Jenart; *Dch.* Jener; p.n.

JENNERY. *A.S.* Genere; *Old G.* Ginhari (?); p.n. (protector lord)

JENNEY. *Fl.* Genis; a p.n. *See* Jane

JENNINGS, JENNYNS. *See* Jannings

JENNIS. *See* Janes

JENNISON. *See* Jennis

JEPHSON. *D.* Jeppesen, Jepsen; *S.* Jepsen, Jippson; a p.n. *See* Ibberson

JERAM. *Fr.* Jerome; a p.n. (holy name)

JERDAN. *See* Jordan

JERMY, JERMEY, JERMYN. *See* Jarmain

JERNINGHAM. *N.-Fr.* Jernegan or Fitz-Jarnegan; p.n.
Forestarius in Bretagne, 1083.

JERRETT. *See* Jarred

JERROLD. *See* Jarrold

JERVIS. *See* Gervase

JESSON. From Jessains; a loc. n., France. Or Jessen, Germ.; *D.*, *N.*, *Dch.*, *Fl.* Jessen; p.n. *See* Chase

JESSOP. *D.* Jess; a p.n. Jesshope; a loc. n.

JESTY. *Fr.* Jestin; a p.n. *See* Jewson

JEUNE. *N.-Fr.* Le Jovene; a p.n. In Rot. Hund.

JEVON. Welsh Jevan (young warrior)

JEWELL. *See* Jouel
Juhel, a sub-tenant in *D.B.*

JEWKES. *See* Jukes

JEWSBURY. *See* Dewsbury

JEWSON. *F.* Juist; *Dch.* Joosten; *Fl.* Jossen; *D.* Justesen; *A.S.* Justeign, Justen, Justan, Justin (guest soldier); p.n. *See* Just

JEX. *See* Jacques

JICKLING. *See* Hickling

JIGGENS. *See* Juggins

JIGGLE. *A.S.* Cich; *Old G.* Gigio; *Fl.* Gigault; a p.n.; *N.gygr* (agiant)

JILBERT. *See* Gilbert

JILLINGS. A loc. n., Yorks. *See* Gillings

JOBLIN. From Jublains; a loc. n., France

JOCKEL. *See* Jekyll

JODDRELL. *S.* Jordell (?); a p.n.

JOEL. *See* Jouel

JOHN, JOHNS. *N.* Jón; *F.* Jan; *G.*, *Fl.*, *Dch.*, *D.* Jan, Jans, Jahn, Jahns, Jen, Johan, Johans, John, Johne, Johns, Jons, Jones; *N.-Fr.* Joannes; *Fr.* Jean, Jouan, Jouen; p.n. Contr. of *Lat.* Johannes. *See* St John.
In Rot. Hund.

JOHNSON. *D.* Johannsen, Johanson, Johnssen, Johnson; *S.* Jansen, Johnsson; *Dch.* Jannissen, Jansen, Johannissen, Johanson; p.n.

JOLLIFFE. *N.-Fr.* Giolif, Jolyf; p.n.

JOLLY. Hugt., Lond. 1681. *See* Jouel

JOHNSTONE. A loc. n., Dumfries, Renfrew

JONAS, JONES. *D.*, *Dch.*, *G.*, *S.*; p.n. *See* Johns

JOPE. From St Job; a loc. n., Belg. *D.* Job, Jopp; *Dch.* Job, Joppe; *Fl.* Job, Jobin; p.n.

Adam de Jope in 1334; Walter Joop, reeve of Marlborough, 1388.

JOPLING. *See* Joblin

JORDAN. *D.*, *G.*, *Dch.* Jordan; *Fl.* Jordaen; p.n.

JOSH. From St Josse; a loc. n., Belg. *G.* Josch; a p.n.

JOSSELYN. *See* Goss

JOUEL. *N.* Jólfr (?) (from Jólfuðr, a name of Odin); *A.S.* Ialf, Iaul, Iol, Yol; *D.* Hjul, Juell, Juhl, Juul; *S.* Juel; *Fr.* Juhel; *Dch.* Jolle, Jolly, Joly; *N.-Fr.* Fitz-Juel; *G.* Jouly, Joul; p.n.

Johol de Lincoln, 1068.

JOYCE, JOYES. From Joyeuse; a loc. n., Normandy

Johais in *D.B.* (St Judocus), undertenant. Ric. de Jorz, 1200; Gaufrid de Jorz, 1207, in Rot. Obl. et Fin. (Notts.); Simon de Jorce, John Jorse (Hoton, Leics), Lay Sub. R., 1329; Ranulph de Jorz, Rob. de Jors, Testa de Neville. Also Sim. de Joyce (Wymeswold) held lands. François de Joyeuse was Abbot of Mont-Saint-Michael in 1594.

JOY. From Goi or Gouy; a loc. n. Norm. *Fr.* Joet; a p.n. Hugt., Lond. 1685

JUBB, JUBY, JUBEY. *G.* Jube, Juppe, Jupe; *Fl.* Jubin; *D.* Juby; p.n. *See* Jupp

JUDD. *F.* Udo, Ude; *Dch.* Joode; *Fl.* Jude; *D.* Jud; *A.S.* Jud, Udi; p.n.

JUDGE. *Fr.* Juge (a judge); *G.* Chutsch; p.n.

According to Ferguson, Judge, Jugg, and perhaps Jukes may be possibly deriqed from *Old G.* Jugo, referred by Stark to Gothic *jiukan* (to combat).

JUDKINS, JUDSON. *See* Judd

JUGG. *D.* Joeg; a p.n. *See* Judge

JUGGINS. *D.* Jürgens (?); a p.n.; fam. n. of Jugg

JUKES. From Choques; a loc. n., Fland. Or *see* Judge

JULER. *N.* Jólfr; *G.* Julich, Jouly; *D.* Juhler; *Fr.* Julez; p.n. *See* Jouel

JULIAN. *Fr.* Julien; a p.n.

JULIER. *Fr.* Juliard; a p.n.

JULIET. *Fr.* Hugt. n., Lond. 1618

JUMP. A loc. n., Devon, Yorks

JUNIPER. *Dch.* Jongeboer (?); a p.n. (young rustic)

JUPP. *G.* Jupp; *Fr.* Chupé; p.n. *See* Jubb, Jope, Chope

JURDAN. *See* Jordan

JURY. *See* Jary

JUST. *A.S.* Iust; *D.* Just; *G.* Just; *Dch.* Juist; *Fl.* Juste; p.n. *A.S.* gyst (?) (a guest, or just, right, straight)

K

KAIL. *A.S.* Ceol, Cil; *Fl.* Kuyl; *D.* Keil; *Dch.* Kehl; *G.* Keyl; p.n. (ship)

K A I N E. Irish M'Kain. *See* Caine

KARSLAKE. *See* Carslake

KAVANAGH. From the Irish O'Caomhanach; a p.n. (comely (?))

KAY. *D.B.* Kee; *A.S.* cœg (a key); *D.* Kai; *S.* Key; *Fl.* Kai, Key; *Dch.* Kea; p.n. Or Scot. M'Kay

KAYNES. *See* Keynes

KEABLE. *See* Keble

KEAL. *See* Keel

KEALEY. Manx. Originally Mac Gilla Ceallaigh. *See* Kelly

M

KEAN. *See* Keen

KEAREY. *See* Carew

KEARNEY. *See* Cairns

KEARNS. *See* Cairns

KEAT. *See* Keith

KEATS. From Kitts; a loc. n., Devon. Or *G.* Keitz; a p.n.

KEBLE. *A.S.* Cædbeald; *Fr.* Quibel; *N.-Fr.* Cabal; *G.* Kiebel; p.n. (war bold)

KECK. *A.S.* Cæc; *D.* Keck; *Dch.* Koek; *Fl.* Koecke; p.n.; *cæg* (key). Prot. ref., Norwich, 1622

KEDGE. *See* Gedge

KEDGLEY. *See* Keighley

KEED. *See* Kidd

KEEFE. Irish O'Keefe. Or *D.* Kieffer; p.n. ¦ *D.B.* Chevre; *A.S. ceafor* (a beetle)

KEEL. From Keele; a loc. n., Staffs

KEELER. *A.S.* Ceola; *Dch.* Kiella; *G.* Kieler, Kille; p.n. (a sailor)

KEELEY. *See* Kieley

KEELING. From Killing or Keeling (*D.B.* Chellinge); a loc. n., Yorks

KEEN. *A.S.* Cen, Cyne (noble); *D.* Kiehn; *Fl.* Kien; p.n.

KEEP. *D.B.* Cepe, Ceppa; *Dch.* Kiepe, Kip; p.n.; *A.S. céap* (a merchant). Prot. ref., Lond. 1618

KEEPING. Fam. n. of Keep. Or *see* Kippen. *D.B.* Cheping; a p.n. *See* Chipp

KEER. *See* Keir

KEETLEY. *See* Keightley

KEEVIL. A loc. n., Wilts

KEFFORD. *Fr.* Quifut (?); a p.n. *See* Gifford

KEGGIN. From the Irish Keghan, M'Keogh; p.n.

KEGLEY. *See* Quigley

KEHOE. *Fr.* Cahot, Cahut, Cayeux; p.n. Or *see* Keogh

    W. de Keheu in Rot. Obl. et Fin., K. John.

KEIGHLEY. A loc. n., Lancs, Yorks

KEIGHTLEY. A loc. n., Yorks

KEINCH. *S., D.* Kinch; *Fl.* Kints; *G.* Kensche; p.n. Or Irish M'Kinch. Dim. of Keen

KEIR. A loc. n., Dumfries

KEITH. A loc. n., Elgin

KEKEWICH. From Kekwick; a loc. n., Ches.

KELF. *A.S.* Ceolf, Ceolwalf (ship wolf); *Dch.* Kalff, Kalf, Kelfkins; p.n.

KELK. A loc. n., Yorks

KELL. *A.S.* Cel, Ceol; a p.n. (a keel, ship). *See* Kill

KELLAWAY, KELLEWAY. A loc. n., Wilts

KELLETT. A loc. n., Lancs

KELLIE. A loc. n., Fife

KELLS. A loc. n., Kirkcudbright

KELLY. A loc. n., Renfrew. Or Irish O'Killy-Kelly, Giolla Cheallaigh (the disciple of Ceallach)

KELSEY. A loc. n., Lincs

KEMBLE. A loc. n., Wilts. Or *A.S.* Cynbald; a p.n. (bold noble)

KEMP. *See* Camp

KEMPSON, KEMPSTER. From Kempston; a loc. n., Beds, Norf.

KEMPTHORNE. A loc. n., Devon

KEMPTON. From Kemberton; a loc. n., Salop. Or *see* Kimpton

KEMSHEAD. From Kempshott; a loc. n., Hants

KEMSLEY. A loc. n., Kent

KEMSTEAD. *See* Kemshead

KEN, KENN. A loc. n., Somers

    John and Richard de Ken in Rot. Obl. et Fin., K. John.

KENDRICK. *See* Kenrick

KENISTON. From Kenstone; a loc. n., Salop

KENNARD. From Kennarth; a loc. n., S. Wales. Or *A.S.* Cyneheard; a p.n. (noble strong)

KENNEDY. From the Irish O'Ceannfhada or O'Cinnidh; p.n. Cineadh (a nation). *See* Kenneth

KENNERLEY. From Kennerleigh; a loc. n., Devon

KENNETH. Irish Caoinnach (peaceable man)

KENNEWAY. From Kennoway; a loc. n., Fife. Or *see* Knyvett

KENNEY. Irish M'Kenny. Or *Fr.* Kenis, Kennis; p.n.; *A.S.* Cyne (noble)

KENNION. *See* Kenyon

KENRICK. From Kenwrick; a loc. n., Salop. Or *A.S.* Cynric; *D.B.* Chenric; p.n. *A.S. cyn* (race, tribe), *ríc* (dominion, power)

KENT, KENTISH. The county

KENYON. A loc. n., Lancs

KEOGH. From the Irish MacEochaidh; a p.n. (horseman). *See* Kehoe

KEPPEL. *N.-Fr.* Capel; *Dch.* Keppel; p.n. *See* Capel

KERBY. *See* Kirkby

KERLIN. *See* Carlin

KERMODE. The Manx form of the Celtic MacDiarmaid; Irish M'Dermott; p.n.

KERNS. *See* Cairns

KERR. *See* Carr and Keir

KERSHAW. A loc. n., Lancs. Anciently Kyrkeshagh

KERSWELL. A loc. n., Devon

KESSANLY. From Kessingland (?); a loc. n., Norf.

KESTERTON. From Casterton; a loc. n., Westmd.

KESTEVEN. A loc. n. (tithing), Lincs

KETCHER. *Dch.* Kegge (?); a p.n.

KETLEY. A loc. n., Salop

KETT. *See* Catt

KETTERIDGE. From Catterick; a loc. n., Yorks. Or Irish M'Kitterick

KETTERING. A loc. n., Northants

KETTLE. A loc. n., Fife. Or *N.* Ketill; *Dch.* Ketel; p.n. (the kettle of the gods)

KETTLEBOROUGH. A loc. n., Suff.

KETTLEBY. A loc. n., Yorks

KETTLEWELL. A loc. n., Yorks

KEWLEY. Manx. A contraction of MacAulay, the shortened form of MacAmhlaibh (Aulaf's or Olaf's son)

KEY. From the Irish M'Kee. *See* Kay

KEYLOCK. From Killough; a loc. n., co. Down, Ireland

KEYMER. A loc. n., Ess.
Symon de Kyma in Rot. Obl. et Fin., K. John.

KEYNES. *D.* Kiens; a p.n. Or *see* Caine

KEYWORTH. A loc. n., Notts

KIBBLE. *See* Keable

KIDALL, KIDDELL, KIDDLE. From Kiddall; a loc. n., Yorks

KIDD, KIDDY. *A.S.* Cydd, Cydda, Cyddi; *D.* Kidde; *Dch.* Kidd; p.n. (a striver)
R. Kide in Rot. Obl. et Fin., K. John. Kede in Rot. Hund.

KIDGELL. *G.* Kitschelt; a p.n.

KIDGER. *N.* Kygeir (people's spear); *Dch.* Kigge; *G.* Kitscher; p.n.

KIDNER. From Kitnor (now Culbone); a loc. n., Somers

KIDNEY. From the Irish Kedney; a p.n. Or *see* Gidney

KIELEY. From the Irish O'Caolidh; a p.n.

KIERNAN. From the Irish Kernaghan; a p.n.

KIGHTLY. *See* Keightley

KILBOURN. From Kilburn; a loc. n., Middlx.

KILBRIDE. *D.B.* Ghilbrid. From the Irish Giolla Bridghid (the servant of Bridget)

KILBY. A loc. n., Leics, Lincs

KILL. *A.S.* Ceol (a ship); *G.* Kille; p.n.

KILLEN. From Killin; a loc. n., Perth

KILLICE. From Killisk; a loc. n., Wexford

KILLICK. *See* Kilwick

KILLMAN. *A.S.* Ceolmund; a p.n. (a ship director)

KILMARTIN. A loc. n., Argyll

KILMINSTER. A loc. n., Caithness

KILMISTER. From Kilminster; a loc. n., Caithness

KILNER. A loc. n., Somers

KILPACK. From Kilpeck; a loc. n., Heref.

KILPATRICK. *See* Gilpatrick

KILPIN. A loc. n., Yorks

KILVERT. From the Irish M'Ilrath; a p.n.

KILVINGTON. A loc. n., Yorks

KILWICK. From Kildwick; a loc. n., Yorks

KIMBELL. *See* Kimble

KIMBERLEY. A loc. n., Notts

KIMBLE. A loc. n., Bucks. Or *A.S.* Cinebeald; *G.* Kimbel; *Dch.* Kimpel; *Fl.* Quimbel; p.n. (noble bold)

KIMM. From Kyme; a loc. n., Lincs

KIMPTON. A loc. n., Hants

KINABLE. *A.S.* Cynebil; a p.n. (noble sword). Or Cynebeald (noble bold)

KINCH. Irish M'Kinch; a p.n. (islander)

KINCHIN. *Fl.* Kinkin; *G.* Kinsing; p.n. Dimin. of Cyn

KINCHLEY. *See* Kingerley

KINDRED. *A.S.* Cynered; a p.n. (noble counsel)

KING. *D.* Kinck, Kink; p.n. Dim. of Cyn. Or *A.S. cyng, cyning* (a king). Perhaps from the character in a mediæval play. *See* official names. A Flem. ref. n., Lond. 1618

KINGDOM. From Kingham; a loc. n., Oxf. Or *see* Kingdon

KINGDON. A loc. n., Devon

KINGERLEY. From Kingley; a loc. n., Warw. Or Kinsley, Yorks

KINGSBURY. A loc. n., Warw.

KINGSFORD. A loc. n., Devon, Worcest.

KINGSLEY. A loc. n., Hants, Staffs

KINGSMILL. A loc. n., Hants

KINIPPLE. *Fr.* Kinable; a p.n. *See* Kimble

KINLOCH. A loc. n., Fife

KINNAIRD. A loc. n., Perth, Stirling

KINNAVY. From the Irish *cnamh* (a bone)

KINNISH. *See* Kinch

KINSEY. *A.S.* Chinesi, Cynesige (noble victor); *D.* Kinzi; p.n. Kynsy, Bishop of Lichfield, A.D. 960.

KIPLING. From Kiplin; a loc. n., Yorks. *D.B.* Chipeling

KIPPEN. A loc. n., Stirling

KIRBY. *See* Kirkby

KIRK. From Atte-kirk (at or near the church), 1327, Lay, Sub. R.

KIRKBY. A freq. loc. n.
    One family of this name lived for eighteen generations at the Old Hall, Kirkby in Furness, Lancs.

KIRKCALDY. A loc. n., Scotl.

KIRKLAND. A loc. n., Cumb., Fife, Lancs, Westmd.

KIRKLEY. A loc. n., Suff.

KIRKPATRICK. A loc. n., Dumfries

KIRKUP. From Kirkthorpe; a loc. n., Yorks

KIRKWOOD. A loc. n., Dumfries, Lanark

KIRSHAW. *See* Kershaw

KIRTLAND. *See* Kirkland

KIRTLEY. From Kirtling; a loc. n., Camb.

KIRTON. A loc. n., Lincs, Suff., Devon. Also a loc. corr. of Crediton

KIRWAN. Irish p.n. (dark visaged)

KISBEE. From Kisby; a loc. n., Hunts

KISSACK, KISSICK. Manx; contracted from MacIsaac. Or *Fr.* Queyssac; a p.n.
    De Cussack in Rot. Obl. et Fin., K. John.

KITCAT. From Kitcott; a loc. n., Devon

KITCHEN, KITCHIN. *D.* Ketjen; *S.* Kitzing; *Dch.* Ketjen; *Fl.* Kitson, Kitzen; p.n. A double dimin. of Christopher. *See* Kitt. Or Irish M'Cutcheon, McEachen, Ketchen. Hutcheon, the Gaelic form of Hugon. *See* Hutchings

KITCHINGMAN. *G.* Kitschmann; a p.n.

KITLEY. A loc. n., Devon

KITT. Dimin. of Christopher. *D.B.* Chit; *G.* Kitt; *Dch.* Kits, Chits; p.n. Or *see* Kidd

KITTEBY. *See* Kettleby

KITTERIDGE. *See* Ketteridge

KITTERMASTER. A corruption of Kidderminster; a loc. n.

KITTLE. *See* Kiddle

KNAGGS. *A.S.* Cynech (?); *Fl.* Knage; p.n. Dim. of Cyn (noble)

KNAPP. A loc. n., Devon. Or *N.* Knappi (a knob); *A.S.* Cnapa (a bag); *G.* Knappe; *D.* Knaap; *Fl.* Knapp; p.n. Knaby; a loc. n., Sweden

De la Cnapp in Rot. Obl. et Fin.

KNAPPIT. *See* Knapp. Dim.

KNAPTON. A loc. n., Leics, Norf.

KNEE. *A.S.* Cyne (?) (noble); *G.* Knie; p.n.

KNEEBONE, KNEEBORN. *A.S.* Cynebeorn; a p.n. (noble bear)

KNEVITT, KNYVETT. From St Pierre de Canivet; a loc. n. Norm.,

KNEWSTUBB. From Knostrop; a loc. n., Yorks

KNIBB. *A.S.* Cnebba, Cnibba (neb, beak); it was used of the prow of a vessel, so might mean a sailor; *Dch.* Knibbe; p.n.

KNIFE. *N.* Kneif; a n.n. (nip). Cniva, the n. of a Gothic king, 3rd cent. Perhaps from *A.S.* Cynefar; a p.n. (noble traveller) Knif in Hund. Rolls.

KNIFTON. *See* Kniveton

KNIGHT. *A.S.* Cniht; *Dch.* Knegt; *G.* Knecht (a servant); Irish M'Knight; p.n.

KNIGHTLEY. A loc. n., Staff.

KNIGHTON. A loc. n., Devon, Leics

KNILL. From Knylle or Knill; a loc. n., Heref.

Sir John de Braose received the Manor of Knille, *temp.* K. John.

KNIPE. *See* Knibb. *Dch.* Knip; *D.*, *G.* Kniep; p.n.

KNIVETON. A loc. n., Derbysh.

KNOCK. Knocke, a loc. n., Belg. Or *N.* Knjúkr (a fighter, striker); *G.* Knoch; *Dch.* Knoek; *D.* Knock; p.n. (a knock, stroke)

KNOTT. *N.* Knöttr (a ball, knob); *D.* Knodt; *G.* Knoth; a p.n. *See* Nute

KNOWLE. A freq. loc. n.

De la Cnoll in Rot. Obl. et Fin.

KNOX. A loc. n., Renfrew

KNYVETT. *See* Knevitt

KYBIRD. *A.S.* Cybeorht, Cynebeort; *Dch.* Kiberd; p.n. (illustrious, noble)

KYD. *See* Kidd

KYFFIN. Welsh Cyffin; a p.n.

KYLE. *See* Kail

KYNASTON. A loc. n., Salop, Staffs

KYRLE. From Criol or Crieul, near Eu, Norm.

KYTE. *A.S.* Cyta; *Dch.* Kuyt; *Fl.* Kayaert; p.n. (a kite)

L

LACHLAN. From the Gaelic *laochail* (warlike)

LACK. From Lacq; a loc. n., France

LACY. From Lessay; a loc. n., Normandy. *D.B.* de Laci, a tenant in chief
De Lacy and De Lascy in Rot. Obl. et. Fin., K. John.

LADBROKE, LADBROOKE. From Ladbrook; a loc. n., Warw.

LADBURY. From Ledbury; a loc. n., Heref.

LADD. *A.S.* Lad, Leod; *Dch.* Laddé; p.n. (people)

LADLER, LADLY. *See* Laidlaw

LAFFEATY, LAFFERTY. *See* Laverty

LAIDLAW. A loc. n., Selkirk

LAIDLAY. *See* Laidlaw

LAILEY. *See* Lely

LAING. *See* Leng

LAITY. A loc. n., Cornw. *See* Leuty

LAKE. From St Martin du Lac, Burgundy; a loc. n., Devon, Hunts, Salop, Wilts. Leke; a loc. n., Belg.

LAKIN. From Lacon, Norm.; Laeken, Belg. Or *A.S.* Læcing; a fam. n.; *Dch.* Leyking; p.n.

LALOR. *Fr.* Lalot, Lalou; p.n.

LAMB. *N.* Lambi (a lamb); *S.* Lamby, Lamm; *Dch.* Lam; *Fl.* Lamme; *D.B.* Lambe; p.n.

LAMBERT. From St Lambert; a loc. n., Belg. and France. *A.S.* Lambeorht, Landbeorht; *Fr.* Lambard, Lambert, Lambret; *D.* Lamberth; *Dch.* Lambert, Lambrecht, Lammerts; *G.* Lambart; *D.B.* Lambert, tenant in chief; p.n. (the country's illustrious one). Also a Flem. ref. n., Lond. 1618
Gen. Lambert, Governor of York, A.D. 1531.

LAMBERTH. *See* Lambert

LAMBETH. A loc. n., Surr.

LAMBOURNE, LAMBURN. From Lamborne; a loc. n., Berks, Cornw.

LAMBSON. From Lambston; a loc. n., S. Wales

LAMBTON. A loc. n., Dur.

LAMERTON. A loc. n., Devon

LAMPARD. *Fl.* Lampaert; *G.*, *Dch.* Lampert; p.n. *See* Lambert

LAMPLUGH. A loc. n., Cumb.

LAMPSON. *See* Lambson

LANCASTER. The county town

LANCE. From Lanz; a loc. n., Prussia. *Dch.*, *G.* Lanz; a p.n. Also a dimin. of Lancelot or Laurence

LANCUM. *See* Langham

LAND, LANT. From Landes; a loc. n., Normandy; Land, Devon. Or *A.S.* Land; a p.n. *See* Lound

LANDER. From Landres; a loc. n., Burgundy. Or *D.*, *Dch.*, *G.* p.n.; *A.S.* Landweard; a p.n. (Landwarden)

LANDFEAR. *See* Lanfear

LANE. A loc. n., Devon. Or *D.* Lehn; *Fl.* Leyn; *Dch.* Leijn; p.n. From Laignes; a loc. n., France
In Roll of Battell Abbey.

LANEY. *See* Delaney

LANFEAR. From Llanfair; a loc. n., N. Wales. Or *A.S.* Landfrith; a p.n. (land peace)

LANG. *A.S.*, *D.*, *Dch.*; p.n.

LANGDALE. A loc. n., Cumb.

LANGFORD. A loc. n., Devon, Notts, Somers, Wilts

LANGHAM. A loc. n., Devon, Ess., Norf., Rutld., Suff.

LANGHORNE. *D.* Langhorn; *Dch.* Lankhoorn; a loc. and p.n.

LANGLEY. A loc. n., Derbysh. and other counties

LANGMAID. *See* Langmead

LANGMEAD. A loc. n., Devon

LANGMORE. From Langmere; a loc. n., Norf.

LANGRIDGE. A loc. n., Devon, Somers

LANGSHAW. A loc. n., Dumfries

LANGSTER. *See* Lancaster

LANGSTON. A loc. n., Devon

LANGTON. A loc. n., Devon, Leics, Somers

LANGTREE, LANGTRY. A loc. n., Devon

LANGWORTHY. A loc. n., Devon

LANKESTER. *See* Lancaster

LANSDELL. *See* Lonsdale

LANSDOWNE. A loc. n., Somers

LANYON. A loc. n., Brittany and Cornw.

LAPPER. *See* Lepper

LAPSLEY. From Lapley; a loc. n., Staffs

LAPTHORNE. A loc. n., Devon

LAPWORTH. A loc. n., Warw.

LARCHER. *N.-Fr.* Le Archier; a p.n. (the archer)

LARCHIN. *See* Larkin

LARCOMBE. A loc. n., Devon

LARDER. *See* Lawder

LARGE. *N.-Fr.* De Largo; a p.n. In Rot. Hund.

LARK, LARKE. *A.S.* Leofric, Leoric; *S.* Larka; *G.* Lerch, Lorke; *D.* Larcher; *Fl.* Larock; *D.B.* Lorch; p.n. *See* Laveric

LARKIN. Dim. of Laurence. Or *N.-Fr.* Largan; a p.n.

LARLHAM. From Laleham; a loc. n., Middlx.

LARMETT. *Fr.* Lermytte; a p.n.

LARTER. From Latour; a loc. n., France. *Fr.* Latour; *Fl.* Latteur; p.n. Le Tour, Hugt. n., Lond. 1618

LASCELLES. From Lacelle; a loc. n., Norm. *N.-Fr.* De Lascelles, under-tenant in *D.B.*
In Roll of Battell Abbey and Rot. Obl. et Fin., K. John.

LASHAM. A loc. n., Hants

LASHMAR. *See* Latchmore

LAST. *Dch.*; p.n.

LATCH. *A.S.* Lac, Lec; *G.* Lach, Lache; p.n. (a leech, surgeon)

LATCHFORD. A loc. n., Ches.

LATCHMORE. From Letchmore; a loc. n., Herts

LATER. *See* Larter

LATHAM. From Letham; a loc. n., Fife; Lathom, Lancs; or Laytham, Yorks

LATHBRIDGE, LETHBRIDGE. *See* Lathbury

LATHBURY. A loc. n., Bucks

LATTA, LATTER. *See* Larter

LAUDER. *See* Lawder. Or from the Irish *laidir* (strong)

LAUGHLAND. From Lawkland; a loc. n., Yorks

LAUGHTON. A loc. n., Lincs, Yorks

LAURENCE. *Fr.*; p.n. From *Lat.* Laurentius (crowned with laurel). Hugt., Lond. 1618

LAURIE. *See* Lowry
In Rot. Hund.

LAVENDER. From Lavendon; a loc. n., Bucks. Or *Fr.* Lavandier; a p.n.

LAVER. *See* Leaver

LAVERICK. *Fr.* Levreux (?); a p.n. Or *A.S.* Leofric, Leuuric (?); p.n. (beloved ruler); *laferc* (lark) does not occur as a p.n.

LAVERTON. A loc. n., Somers, Yorks

LAVERTY. From the Irish O'Labhradha; a p.n.

LAVIES. *Fr.* Lavie, La Vie; *Fl.* Lavies; Prot. ref. n., 1683

LAVIN. *Fr.* Lavigne; a p.n. (a vineyard)

LAVINGTON. A loc. n., Wilts

LAW. A loc. n., Dur., Lanark; Lauwe, Belg.

LAWDER. A loc. n., Berwick

LAWFORD. A loc. n., Warw.

LAWLER. *See* Lalor

LAWLESS. From Loulas (?); a loc. n., S. Wales

LAWLEY. A loc. n., Salop

LAWMAN. From the Irish Laman, Lamon, a form of Lamont; p.n. Or *A.S.* Lagman; a p.n. (lawman)

LAWN. *See* Lound

LAWS. From St Lowe (?), Norm.; p.n. Prot. ref., Norwich, 1622

LAWSON. *N.-Fr.* Loison; a p.n.

LAWTON. A loc. n., Salop

LAXTON. A loc. n., Northants, Notts, Yorks

LAY. From Lea, Lee, Leigh; freq. loc. n. Or *D.* Leigh; *Dch.* Lee; *S.* Leja; p.n.

LAYBORN, LAYBOURN. From Labourn; a loc. n., Surr. Or Leybourne, Kent

LAYCOCK. From Laycock; a loc. n., Wilts, Yorks (*D.B.* Lacoc). Or *Fr.* Lecocq; a p.n. La Cock, Hugt. n., Dover, 1622. *See* Cock

LAYLAND. A loc. n., Cornw., Lancs, Somers

LAYMAN. *Fl.* Leman; a p.n. Prot. ref., Lond. 1618. *See* Leman

LAYT. *A.S.* Let, Leod, Leth; p.n. (people)

LAYTON. A loc. n., Ess.

LAZEL. *Fr.* Lasalle; a p.n. *See* Lascelles

LAZENBY. A loc. n., Yorks. Comp. Lazonby, Cumb.

LEA. *See* Lee and Lay

LEACH, LEECH. *A.S.* Laic, Lec; *G.* Liche; a p.n. *A.S. læce* (a healer)

LEACROFT. A loc. n., Staffs

LEADBEATER, LEADBITTER. *See* Lebetter

LEADER. *A.S.* Lida, Leodhere (people's warrior); *G.* Lieder; p.n. *See* Leather

LEAF. *See* Leefe

LEAGE. From Liege; a loc. n., Belg. Hutg. n., Lond. 1687

LEAK. From Leak; a loc. n., Lincs (*D.B.* Leche). Comp. Leek, Staffs

LEAKEY. From Lickey; a loc. n., Worcest. Or Irish p.n.; *G.* Lichey; a p.n.

LEAN. From Ligne; a loc. n., Belg. *Dch.* Lien; a p.n.

LEAPMAN. *D.*, *Dch.* Lipman; *G.* Lipman, Liebermann; p.n. (a goodly man)

LEAR. From Liers; a loc. n., Belg.; or Lyre, Norm. *G.* Liehr; *Dch.*, *D.* Lier; p.n.

LEARNER. *Fr.* Lernoud (?); a p.n.

LEAROYD. A loc. n.

LEARY. Irish O'Leary

LEASE. A loc. n., Devon

LEASK. *G.* Lieske; a p.n. Dim. of *A.S.* Lis, Lissa; p.n.; *liss* (happy)

LEAT. *See* Leete

LEATHER. *A.S.* Leodhere, Leother; *Old G.* Lethar; *G.*, *Dch.* Leder, Lieder; p.n. (people's warrior)

LEATHERDALE. From Leverdale (?); a loc. n., Staffs

LEATHLEY. A loc. n., Yorks

LEATHWAITE. *See* Lewthwaite

LEAVER, LEVER. *A.S.* Leofhere, Lifher; *Dch.* Lever, Liever; p.n. (a deliverer, beloved warrior)

LEAWOOD. A loc. n., Devon

LEBETTER. *Fr.* Lebouteux (?); a p.n.

LECK. A loc. n., Yorks

LECKY. *See* Leakey

LEDGER. From St Legère; a loc. n., Norm. and Belg. Or *A.S.* Leodgœr; a p.n. (people-spear); *Fl.* Leger; p.n.

LEDSON. From Ledstone; a loc. n., Yorks. Or *A.S.* Led, Leod; p.n. (people)

LEDYARD. *N.* Lidvard; *A.S.* Lidgeard; p.n. (gate ward)

LEE. A loc. n., Ess., Kent, etc.

LEEDHAM. *See* Latham

LEEFE. From Liff (?); a loc. n., Forfar. Or Lives, Belg.

LEEMING. A loc. n., Yorks

LEES. A loc. n., Lancs

LEESON. *See* Licence

LEETE. *A.S.* Let; *Dch.* Liet; p.n. *A.S. læt* (a freeman)

LEETHAM. From Leatham; a loc. n., Yorks

LEEVERS. A loc. n., Lincs. Or *Dch.* Lievers; a p.n. *See* Leaver

LEEVERSUCH. *See* Liversage

LEFGOOD. *A.S.* Leofgod; *Dch.* Lievegoed; p.n. (beloved Goth)

LEFTWICH. A loc. n., Ches.

LEGGATT. *N.-Fr.* Legat; a p.n.; *Lat.* Legatus

LEGH. A loc. n., Ches.

LE GRICE. *Fr.* Legris; a p.n. (grey)

LEIGH. A loc. n., Lancs. Or *D.* Leigh; a p.n. *See* Lay

LEIGHTON. A loc. n., Devon

LEITCH. *See* Leech

LELY. *A.S.* Lil, Lilla; *N.-Fr.* Lele, De Lelay; *Dch.* Lely; p.n. (lily)

LEMAN, LEMMON. *A.S.* Leofman, Leman; *G.* Lehman; *D.* Lejman; *Fl.* Leman, Lemmen; *S.* Lemon, Leman; p.n. (beloved man)

LEMPSTER. From Leominster; a loc. n., Heref.

LENDRUM. A loc. n., Aberdeen

LENG. *Dch.* p.n. *See* Lang

LENNEY. From Lennai; a loc. n., Norm.

LENTHALL. From Leinthall; a loc. n., Heref. Or *G.* Leinethall; a loc. and p.n.

LENTRON. From Lentrathen(?); a loc. n., Forfar

LEONARD. From St Leonard; a loc. n., Norm.

LEPPARD. *A.S.* Leofheard, Lipperd; *G.* Liepert; a p.n. (beloved strong)

LEPPER. *N.-Fr.* Lepère; a p.n. Hugt. n., Lond. 1618. *See* Leppard

LESLIE. A loc. n., Aberdeen, Fife, Stirling

LESSELS. *See* Lascelles

LESSEY. Lesee, a Hugt. n., Lond. 1621. *See* Lacy

LESTER. From Leicester; a loc. n.

LESTRANGE. *N.-Fr.* Bretagne

LETCHWORTH. A loc. n., Herts

LETHAM. A loc. n., Fife, Forfar

LETT, LETTY. *Dch.* Leth; *Fl.* Lette; p.n. *See* Layt

LETTIS, LETTS. *G.* Letsch, Lettig; p.n. Dim. of Lett

LEUTY. *A.S.* Leod, Leot; *Dch.* Loeté; a p.n. (people)

LEVENSTON. *See* Livingstone

LEVER. *N.-Fr.* Lievre; a p.n. A loc. n., Lancs

LEVERETT. *A.S.* Liboret, Leofred; *Dch.* Levert; p.n. (beloved counsellor)

LEVERMORE. *See* Livermore

LEVERS. *See* Leevers

LEVERSON. From Levasson; a loc. n., Norm. Or *see* Leaver

LEVERTON. *See* Laverton

LEVETT. From Livet; a loc. n., Norm.

LEWIN. *A.S.* Leofwine, Leowine, Lewin; *Dch.* Leeuwen; p.n. (dear friend)

LEWIS. *N.-Fr.* De Lues, Luiz, Lews, Lewes; p.n. Or *A.S.* Leodwig; *Fr.* Louis; *Lat.* Ludovicus; *G.* Ludwig; p.n. (defender of the people). A Hugt. n., Norwich, 1622

LEWTHWAITE. From Lowthwaite or Lothwaite; a loc. n., Cumb.

LEY. *See* Lee and Lay

LIBBIS, LIBBY. *A.S.* Leof; *Old G.* Liub; *Fl.* Libois; *G.* Libas, Liebes; p.n. (dear)

LIBERTY. A loc. n., Fife. Or *D.* Libbert, Lippert; *N.-Fr.* Livardé; p.n.

LICENCE. *A.S.* Lis; *Fl.* Liessens, Lissens, Lyssens; *G.* Lieson; *Dch.* Leyssens; p.n.; *liss* (happy)

LICKFOLD. A loc. n., Suss.

LICKORISH. From Lickerigg; a loc. n., Galway

LIDDARD, LIDDIARD, LIDIARD, LID-
YARD. From Lydiard; a loc. n.,
Wilts. Or *A.S.* Lidgeard; a p.n.
(people's guard)

LIDDELL. From Lydale; a loc. n.,
Scotl.

LIDDICOTT. From Lidcott; a loc.
n., Cornw.

LIDDON. From Lidden; a loc. n.,
Kent. Or Lidon, Aquitaine

LIDGEY. From Lidsey; a loc. n.,
Suss.

LIDSTONE. A loc. n., Oxf.

LIELL. From Lisle; a loc. n.,
France. *Fr.* Lille; *Dch.* Lil; p.n.

LIGERTWOOD. *See* Lightwood

LIGHTBAND, LIGHTBOWN. From
Lightbounds; a loc. n., Lancs

LIGHTBODY. *A.S.* Liht; a p.n.;
liht-bodi (nimble messenger)

LIGHTFOOT. *Old G.* Lytfuss; *Dch.*
Ligtvoet; p.n.; *A.S. lyt fot*; *F.
ligt fôt* (nimble footed)

LIGHTOLLER, LIGHTOWLER. A loc.
n., Lancs (Fishwick)

LIGHTWOOD. A loc. n., Staffs

LILL. *A.S., Dch.* Lil; p.n. Or *see*
Liell

LILLINGTON. A loc. n., Dorset

LILWALL. A loc. n., Heref.

LILY. From Lilley; a loc. n.,
Berks, Yorks; Lilly, Norm. Or
D. Lillie; *G.* Lilie; *S.* Lilje;
Dch. Lelie, Lelij; p.n. *See* Lely

LILYWHITE. From Liliethwaite or
Littlethwaite; a loc. n.

LIMBY. *See* Limbeer. Or Linby, Notts

LIMEBEER. From Limber; a loc.
n., Lincs

LIMMER. From Limours; a loc. n.,
France. *N.-Fr.* Limers; *G.*
Limer; *Fl.* Lemaire. Or *A.S.*
Lemmer, Leofmær; p.n. (famous
beloved)

Limers in Roll of Battell Abbey;
and Leimar, a tenant in *D.B.* at
the Survey.

LIND. From Lynde; a loc. n.,
Fland.

LINDLEY. A loc. n., Yorks

LINDOW. A loc. n., Ches. Or *G.*
Lindau, Lindow; *S.* Linder, Lindau; *Fl.* Linters; *Fr.* Lintot;
loc. and p.n.

LINDSAY. *See* Linsey

LINE, LINES, LYNES. From Luynes;
a loc. n., Normandy, or Ligne,
Belg.

LINFOOT, LINFORD, LINFORTH.
From Lynford; a loc. n., Norf.

LING. A loc. n. in Norf. Prot.
ref., Lond. 1618

LINGARD. *D.* Lyngaard; a p.n.

LINGFER, LINGFORD. From Linford; a loc. n., Bucks, Leics

LINGHAM. A loc. n., Ches.

LINKLATER. A loc. n., Scotl.

LINNELL. *Fr.*; p.n. From *N.-Fr.
lignel* or *l'isnel* (prompt)

LINNIKER. From Lenacre; a loc.
n., Yorks

LINNINGTON. A loc. n.

LINSCOTT. A loc. n.

LINSDELL. From Linsdale; a loc.
n., Westmd.

LINSELL. From Lindsell; a loc.
n., Ess. Or *Fl.* Linseele. A
Hugt. n., 1618

LINSEY. From Lindsey; a loc. n.,
Ess., Lincs, Norf.

LINSTEAD. A loc. n., Kent

LINTHWAITE. A loc. n., Yorks

LINTON. A loc. n., Camb., Derbysh.,
Devon, Haddington, Heref., Kent,
Peebles, Roxburgh, Yorks

LINTOTT. From Lintot; a loc. n.,
Normandy

LIPPINCOTT. From Luffingcot; a
loc. n., Devon

In ancient documents Loghyncote,
Loffyngcote, Loginggetot, Lough-
wyncote, Loyhingcote, Luffingcott,
Luffyngcote, Lughencot, Leffyng-
cote, Lippingcote. Robert de
Lywenscot, *temp.* Ed. I., A.D.
1296. Lef, Lefa, Liaf, Lib, Lip,
Liob, Lub, Luf are all variations
of the *A.S.*; Leof, a p.n. (beloved);
Leofing is the tribal n.

LIPSCOMBE. A loc. n.
LIPTON. *See* Lupton
LIQUORISH. *See* Lickorish
LISHMAN. *A.S.* Liseman ; a p.n. ; *liss* (happy)
L'ISLE. A loc. n., Vaucluse, France
LISTER. Old Scot. Litster (a dyer)
LISTON. A loc. n., Ess.
LITHERLAND. A loc. n., Lancs
LITTLE. Lutel ; a p.n. in 1327
LITTLEBOY. *Fr.* Lillebois (little wood) ; a loc. n.
LITTLEDALE. A loc. n., Lancs. Or from Liddeldale ; a loc. n., Roxburgh
LITTLEJOHN. From Littlejoy (?) ; a loc. n., Devon. Or *Fr.* Petitjean
LITTLEMORE. A loc. n., Oxf.
LITTLEPROUD. From Littleport (?) ; a loc. n., Camb.
LITTLER. *See* Laidlaw
LITTLETON. A loc. n., Derbysh., Glost., Hampsh., Middlx., Surr., Somers, Suss., Wilts, Worcest.
LITTLEWOOD. A loc. n., Lancs
LIVERMORE. From Livermere ; a loc. n., Suff.
LIVERSAGE, LIVERSIDGE. From Liversedge ; a loc. n., Yorks
LIVESEY. A loc. n., Lancs. Or *A.S.* Leofsi, Lefsi ; *N.-Fr.* Leuveyse ; p.n. (dear victory)
LIVING. *Fl.* Livain ; *A.S.* Leofing, Lifing, Lyfing ; fam. n. of Leof (dear). Or Leaven ; a loc. n., Yorks. A Hugt. n., Norwich, 1622
LIVINGSTONE. A loc. n. near Linlithgow
LIVOCK. *Fl.* Levacq ; *Fr.* Levaque ; *N.-Fr.* *le vaquier* (cowman). Or Levêque ; a p.n. Hugt., Norwich, 1622
LLEWELLYN. Welsh ; p.n. (like a lion, or perhaps lightning sword)
LLOYD. From Welsh *llwyd* (grey)
LOADER, LODER. *N.* Lióði (a singer) ; *G.* Lode ; *D.B.* Lodi, Loda ; *Dch.* Lodder ; p.n.
La Lodere in Rot. Hund.

LOADES. *A.S.* Loding ; a fam. n. ; *Fl.* Lodens ; a p.n. *See* Loader
LOAKE. *See* Lock
LOANE. From Lohne ; a loc. n., Germ. *Dch.* Loon ; a p.n.
LOASBY. From Lowesby ; a loc. n., Leics
LOBB. A loc. n., Devon, Oxf. Lobbes ; a loc. n., Flanders. Or *N.-Fr.* De la Lobe ; *A.S.* Lob ; *Dch.* Lobbe ; *G.* Lobe ; p.n. *A.S.* *lobb* (spider)
LOBBETT. Dimin. of Lobb
LOBLEY. A loc. n.
LOCH, LOCK. A loc. n., Cornw. Loches, Norm. Or *N.* Loki (a giant god) ; *D.B.* Lochi ; p.n.
LOCKER. *A.S.* Locær ; *G.* Locker ; *Dch.* Lokker ; a p.n. Or from Locre ; a loc. n., Belg. *See* above
LOCKETT. *Fr.* Locquet ; a p.n. *See* Lockhart
LOCKHART. *N.* Loki ; a p.n. (a giant god), *hard* (strong) ; *N.-Fr.* Locard ; a p.n.
LOCKWOOD. A loc. n., Yorks
LOCKYER. *See* Locker
LOCOCK. From Lovetot (?), Norm. Or *see* Luccock
LODBROOK. *See* Ludbrook
LODGE. From les Loges ; a loc. n., Normandy. *Fr.* Logé ; a p.n.
De Loges, a tenant in chief, *D.B.*
LOE. *Dch.* Louw ; *Fr.* de Lo ; *G.* Lohe ; p.n. Hugt., Lond. 1618
LOFTE. *See* Lovett
LOFTHOUSE. A loc. n., Yorks. *D.B.* Lofthus
LOFTING. *A.S.* Leofthegn ; a p.n. (dear soldier). A Prot. ref. n., Lond. 1688
LOFTS, LOFTUS. *See* Lofthouse
LOGAN. A loc. n., Scotl. Or from the Irish O'Leochain ; a p.n.
LOGIE. A loc. n., Fife
LOGUE. *See* Logie

LOMAS, LOMAX. *Fr.* Lammas, La- musse; *Fl.* Lammers; *Dch.* Lom- merse; p.n. (time of birth (?)), (famous)
> Lammasse in Rot. Hund. Lamisso, a Lomb; king, 5th century.

LONDY. *See* Lundy

LONG. *N.-Fr.* De Longa, De Longues; p.n. Also Prot. ref., Lond. 1621
> In Rot. Hund.

LONGBOTTOM. From Longbeddom; a loc. n., Dumfries

LONGBOURNE. A loc. n.

LONGCAKE. From Longacre; a loc. n., Somers. Or Lankaker; a loc. n., Westmd.

LONGDEN. A loc. n. Staffs, Worcest.

LONGFELLOW. From Longueville; a loc. n., Normandy. Also Hugt. n., Lond. 1685
> In Roll of Battell Abbey.

LONGFORD. A loc. n., Derbysh., Glost., Salop, Wilts

LONGHURST. A loc. n., Northbd.

LONGLEY. A loc. n., Yorks

LONGMAID. *See* Langmead

LONGMAN. A loc. n., Banff

LONGMIRE. A loc. n., Westmd.

LONGMORE. *See* Longmire

LONGRIDGE. A loc. n., Lancs

LONGSHANKS. From Longchamps; a loc. n., Normandy
> It was a n.n. of Edward I.

LONGSTAFF. From Longstow (?); a loc. n., Camb. Or Longstock, Hants

LONGSTON. A loc. n., Staffs

LONGTON. A loc. n., Lancs, Staffs

LONGWORTH. A loc. n., Berks, Lancs

LONSDALE. A loc. n., Lancs and Westmd.

LOOKER. *See* Locker

LOOMES. *N.-Fr.* Lomme, Lomb; p.n. *See* Lumb

LOOSE. Los, Norm.; Looz, Flan- ders; or a loc. n., Kent. Or *Fr.* Luce; *Dch.* Loose, Loos; *Fl.* Loze, Lus; p.n. Luce, a Prot. ref., Lond. 1618
> Luse in Roll of Battell Abbey. De Lorz in *D.B.* (?).

LORAINE. From Lauraine; a loc. n., Norm.

LORD. *A.S.* Lord, Lorta; *N.-Fr.* le Lavord; p.n.; *hláf-ord* (a lord)
> In Rot. Hund.

LORKIN. *See* Larkin

LOSH. From Loches; a loc. n., France
> Losse in Rot. Hund.

LOTHERINGTON. From Lotherton; a loc. n., Yorks

LOTHIAN. A loc. n., Edinbgh., Haddington, Linlithgow

LOTT. *Fr.* Loth; *G.* Lott; *Fl.* Lotte; p.n. From Loth; a loc. n., Flanders. Or *A.S.* Loth, Hloth; p.n. (spoil, plunder)

LOUCH. *See* Losh

LOUDON. A loc. n., Ayrsh.

LOUGHTON. A loc. n., Salop

LOUND. *N.* Lundr (a grove); *D.* Lundt, Landt; *S.* Lund; *Dch.* Lund, Lonte, Lantz; *A.S.* Lant; *N.-Fr.* de la Lounde; p.n.

LOVAT. A loc. n., Inverness

LOVE. *A.S.* Leof, Lof; *D., Dch.* Luf; *Fl.* Loef; p.n. (dear)

LOVEBOND. John Lovingsbone, Hugt., Lond. 1621

LOVEDAY. From Loudet; a loc. n., Toulouse, France. Or *A.S.* Leof- dæg, Leuedai; p.n. (glorious beloved); *Fl.* Lovatty; p.n.; *Fr.* Lovedain. Hugt., Canter- bury, 1622

LOVEGROVE. A loc. n.

LOVEJOY. *A.S.* Leofgifu, Lifgiue; *Fr.* Laugeois, Lobjois; p.n. (be- loved giver)

LOVELACE, LOVELESS. *See* Lawless

LOVELL. *N.-Fr.* Louvel; *Fr.* Lovel; p.n. Dimin. of Love. A Hugt. n., Lond. 1618
> In Roll of Battell Abbey. Luvel in Rot. Obl. et Fin., K. John.

LOVER. From Louviers; a loc. n., Norm. Or *A.S.* Leofhere; a p.n. (dear warrior)

LOVERIDGE. From Loughrigg; a loc. n., Westmd.

LOVEROCK. *See* Laverick

LOVESEY. *A.S.* Leofsige, Lyfsye; p.n. (dear victory)

LOVETT. *N.-Fr.* Louvet (a young wolf); a p.n.
D.B. tenant in chief. Luvet in Rot. Obl. et Fin., K. John.

LOVEWELL. *See* Lovell

LOVIBOND. *See* Lovebond

LOVICK. From Lowick; a loc. n., Lancs; anciently Lofwic. Or *A.S.* Leofic, Leofwig; p.n. (dear warrior)

LOW. A Prot. ref. n., Lond. 1621. *See* Lowe

LOWDEN. *See* Loudon

LOWE. A loc. n., Salop. Or St Lo, Norm.

LOWELL. *See* Lovell

LOWER. From Lauwe (?); a loc. n., Belg. *Fl.* Lauwers, Louwers; *Dch.* Lauwer, Louwer; *N.-Fr.* De Luera; p.n. Prot. ref., Lond. 1618
In Rot. Hund.

LOWESBY. A loc. n., Leics.

LOWLESS. *See* Lawless

LOWMAN. *A.S.* Lagman (a lawyer); *G.* Lohmann; *Fl.* Loomans; p.n. Or *see* Leman.

LOWNDES, LOWNES. From Lounds; a loc. n., Lincs

LOWRY. From Lurre, Luri, Lury, or Loury; a loc. n., Norm.

LOWTHER. *A.S.* Hlodhere; *G.* Lothar, Luther; *Fr.* Lothaire; p.n. *See* Clothier. A loc. n., Cumb.

LOWTHIAN. *See* Lothian

LOXDALE. A loc. n., Yorks

LOXLEY. A loc. n., Staffs, Warw., Yorks

LOYDELL. *See* Lydal

LUBBOCK. *A.S.* Leof, Lub; *Old G.* Liub; *F.* Lübbo; *G.* Löbe, Löbbecke; *Dch.* Lub, Lubke; *Fl.* Lubcké; p.n. Dimin. (little dear)

LUCAS. *A.S.* Ludgoz; *Old. G.* Luitgoz, Luikoz; *Fr.* Lucas; p.n. (beloved Goth)

LUCCOCK. *Fr.* Lucq; *G.* Lücke; p.n. Dimin. of Lucas

LUCK. *Fl.* Luc; *Fr.* Lucq; p.n.

LUCKETT. A loc. n., Cornw.

LUCKEY, LUCKIE. *A.S.* Yuca; *Fr.* Lucké; *G.* Lücke; p.n. Dim. of Lucas

LUCKHURST. *Fl.* Luckhaus (?); a p.n.

LUCKING. *Dch.*; p.n. (Luck's descendants)

LUCRAFT. *See* Leacroft

LUCY. A loc. n., Normandy. *Fr.* Louiset; *Fl.* Lucie; p.n. Prot. ref., Lond. 1634
Lucy in Roll of Battell Abbey. De Lucy in Rot. Obl. et Fin., K. John.

LUDBROOK. A loc. n., Devon

LUDFORD. A loc. n., Salop

LUDLOW. A loc. n., Salop

LUFF. *See* Love

LUGG. *Old G.* Lugius; *G.* Luge; *Dch.* Lugt; *Fl.* Luig; p.n. *See* Lucas

LULHAM. *See* Larlham

LUMB. A loc. n., Lancs, Yorks. Or *G.* Lumbe; *Old G.* Lumpe; p.n. *See* below and Loomes

LUMBARD. *A.S.* Lunbeorht, Lumpert (poor, bright); *Dch.* Lombart; *Fl.* Lombaert; p.n. Hugt., Lond. 1687

LUMBY. A loc. n., Yorks

LUMLEY. A loc. n., Dur.
Johannes de Lomley in Lib. Vit. Dur.

LUMMIS. *See* Lomas

LUMSDEN. A loc. n., Aberdeen, Berwick

LUNAN. *A.S.* Luning; a fam. n.; *Fl.,Dch.* Loonen; a p.n. *See* Lunn

LUND. A loc. n., Yorks. *See* Lound

LUNDY. From Lundie; a loc. n., Fife, Perth

LUNN. *A.S.* Lun; a p.n. (poor)

LUNNON. *See* Lunan

LUNNY. *See* Lunn

LUNT. A loc. n., Lancs (*D.B.* Lont). *See* Lund

LUPSON. *See* Lubb

LUPTON. A loc. n., Westmd.

LUSBY. *See* Lowesby

LUSCOMBE. A loc. n., Devon

LUSH. *See* Losh

LUSHER. *N.-Fr.* De Lusoris. From Lisores, Norm.

LUSHINGTON. Formerly Lussyntone, Kent; a loc. n.

LUSK. From Lussac (?); a loc. n., France

LUSON. *See* Lusson

LUSTY. *A.S., Fl.* Lust; *G.* Lustig; p.n. (powerful)

LUTLEY. A loc. n., Staffs

LUTRIDGE. From Lutheridge; a loc. n., Glost.

LUTT. *A.S.* Leod, Lud, Lude; p.n.; *Dch.* Lut, Luth; p.n.; *A.S. leod* (people)

LUTTRELL. From Loudervielle; a loc. n., Normandy. *Fr.* Latreille; *N.-Fr.* Lottrel; p.n.
    Lutterell in Rot. Obl. et Fin.

LUXON. A loc. n., Devon

LUXTON. *See* Luxon

LYALL. A loc. n., Scotl.

LYCETT. A loc. n., Staffs

LYDAL, LYDLE. *See* Liddell

LYE. A loc. n., Devon, Worcest.

LYNCH. A loc. n., Devon, Somers, Suss.

LYNDALL. A freq. loc. n., Sweden, Lancs, etc.

LYNE. A loc. n., Peebles

LYNES, LINES. From Luynes; a loc. n., Normandy

LYNN. A loc. n., Norf., Staffs

LYON. From Lions, Norm. *Fr.* Lion, Lyon; a p.n. Prot. ref., Norwich, 1622

LYSACHT. From the Irish Mac-Giolla Josacht; a p.n.

LYSONS. From Lison, Norm. Or *see* Licence

LYTHABY. A loc. n.

LYTTON. From Litton; a loc. n., Yorks

LYWOOD. *See* Leawood or Lythwood, Salop

M

MABB. From Mabe; a loc. n., Cornw. Or *Fl.* Mabbe; p.n.; Welsh *mabb* (?) (a male child)

MABBOTT, MABBUTT. *N.* Módbjartr; *D.B.* Modbert, Motbert; *Fl.* Mabeyt; *Fr.* Maubert; p.n. (bright courage)

MABER. *See* Mabb

MABSON. *Fl.* Mabesoone; *A.S.* Mapeson; p.n.

MACAULAY. From the Irish Mac-Amhailgaidh; a fam. n. Also MacAuley, MacAwley, MacAuliffe, Macgawley (work, labour)

MACBETH. Gael. son of Beth (life)

MACBRIDE. From the Irish McGill Bride; a p.n. *See* Kilbride

MACCHEYNE. Irish MacShane; a p.n. (Jackson, Johnson)

MACCLELLAN. *See* Gilfillan

MACCLOSKEY. From the Irish Mac-Blosgaidh; a p.n.

MACCORMACK. Irish; son of *Corb, i.e.* (charioteer)

MACCULLAGH. From the Irish MacCeallach; a p.n. *See* Kelly

MACDERMOTT. From the Irish MacDiarmada; a p.n. (freeman)

MACDONALD, MACDONNELL. From the Irish MacDomhnaill; a p.n. (great chief)

MACDUFF. *See* Duff

MACE. *F.* Mês or Mewes (contraction of Bartolomæus); *G.* Mais, Mese; *Dch.* Mes, Mees; *Fl.* Maes, Mees; *D.* Maes, Mess; p.n. Or from Meysse; a loc. n., Belg.; Mes, Norm. Hugt. n., Lond. 1618
    In Rot. Hund.

MACER. *A.S.* Mæssa; *G.* Meser; p.n. *See* Mace

MACGILLIAN. Gael. (son of the servant of John)

MACHELL. *A.S.* Mægenweald; *Old G.* Magoald; *F.* Machelt; *S.* Mæchel; *Fl.* Machiels; *Dch.* Mäschel, Machielse; *G.* Machol; *D.B.* Machel; p.n. (power wielder)
Machel held lands at Crackenthorpe, Westmd., *temp.* Edw. Conf. William Mauchel was living *temp.* K. John, A.D. 1201.

MACHREE. Irish; p.n. (king's son)

MACK. *N.* Mögr (boy, brother, kinsman); *A.S.* Mac, Mæg; Gaelic Mac; *G.* Mache, Mack; *D.* Maak; *Dch.* Mack; p.n. Or *see* Madge

MACKAREL. *N.-Fr.* Makerel; *Dch.* Makkreel; p.n.
Makerell in Rot. Obl. et Fin., K. John. Mackrell, Hugt., Norwich, 1622.

MACKARETH. From the Irish Mac-Craith, Macgrath, Magrath; Scot. Macreath; p.n.; *craith* (to weave, the son of a weaver). Or *A.S.* Mægred; a p.n. (strong counsel)

MACKARNESS. *See* Magness and Guinness

MACKENZIE. *See* Kinsey or Kenneth

MACKLEY. Scotch MacLae or Mac-Leay; p.n. Flem. Prot. ref., Lond. 1618

MACKREATH. *See* Mackareth

MACKROFF. *See* Rolf

MACKWORTH. A loc. n., Derbysh.

MACLEAN. From the Gaelic Mac-Gillian; a p.n. (son of the servant of John)

MACNAUGHTON. From the Gaelic McNachtan (strong as a bull)

MACOUN. From the Irish Mac-Gowan; a p.n. Or *see* McKeown

MACRAE. *See* Machree

MACY. *See* Maisey

MCALPIN. *See* Alpin

MCANALLY. From the Irish McInally; a p.n. (teacher's son)

McANDREW. From the Irish Mac-Aindris; a p.n. (the son of Andrew)

McBEAN. Gael. McVean; a p.n. (a hillman)

McCALL. Irish McGall; Scot. McCall; p.n. From *cathal* (battle, valour)

McCALLUM. *See* Callum

McCLAVE. From the Irish *lamh* (a hand)

McCLEVERTY. *See* Laverty

McCLYMONT. *See* Clement

McCOMBIE. *See* Cumby

McCOSH. From the Irish *cos* (a foot)

McCRAITH. *See* Mackareth

McCREEDY. *See* Read

McCROBIE. Robert's son

McCUE. *See* McHugh

McELGUNN. *See* Gunn

McENERY. *See* Hendry

McFADDEN. From the Irish Mac-Paidin; a p.n. (the son of little Patrick)

McFARLANE. Bartholomew's son

McGIRR. From the Irish *gor* (short)

McGLEW. Irish *clow* (?) (wise)

McGOWAN. From the Irish *Gobha* (a smith)

McGREGOR. Gaelic *grig* or *garig* (the fierce)

McHUGH. From the Irish Mac-Aedha; a p.n. (the son of Hugh)

McILVAIN. Irish McGillbain (son of Bain's servant)

McINNES. Gael. Johnson

McINTOSH. Sons of the chief

McINTYRE. From the Irish *Mac-an-t-saoir* (the son of a workman)

McIVOR. *See* Ivor

McKANE. *See* Caine

McKECHNIE. Gael. Euchrain (son of a horseman)

McKEOWN. The son of Eoin, an Irish form of John

McKERROW. *See* Hare

McKILLOP. Philip's son

McKINLAY. *See* Finlay (fair hair)

McKinnon. Gael. Finnan; a p.n. (fair, blonde)

McLarty. *See* Laverty

McLearey. Irish McGill Cabhair (the clerk's servant's son)

McLeod. From the Gaelic *llwyd* (grey or brown). *See* Lloyd

McLure. *See* McLearey

McManus. Irish *manus* (great)

McNab. *See* Abbs

McNair. Gael. Macaire; p.n. (son of the heir)

McNamara. Irish (son of the sea)

McNaught. Gael. McKnight

McNeill. *See* Neale

McPherson. Sons of the parson

McPhin. Gael. (fair)

McQuillan. *See* Wilson

McRannal. *See* Reynolds

McRory. From the Irish Mac-Ruadhri; a p.n. (red)

McShane. From the Irish Mac-Shawn; a p.n. (the son of John)

McTavish. Gael. Thomson

McTeague. *See* Teager

McTear. *See* McIntyre

McVicar. *See* Viccars

McWhannon. *See* Buchanan

Madden. From the Irish O'Mada-dhain (a wolf (?)). Madden; a loc. n., Armagh

Madder. *G*. Mader; p.n. *See* Mather

Maddick. *See* Maddox

Maddin. *See* Madden

Maddison. *D*. Madsen; p.n. *See* Maddy

Maddle. *A.S.* Madal; *Fl.* Mad-yol; *Fr.* Madoulé; p.n.; *mæthel* (speech)

Maddock. *See* Madocks

Maddy, Maddey. *A.S.* Mada; *D*. Madie; *Dch.* Maade, Made; *Fr.* Madou; p.n.; *A.S. mæth* (dignity, authority)

Madell. *See* Maddle

Madewell. From Maidenwell; a loc. n., Dorset, Lincs

Madge. *N.-Fr.* Magis; *A.S.* Mæg, Mecga; *Fr.* Maggi; p.n. (strength)

Madgett. *See* Matchett

Madgin. *A.S.* Mægen; *D*. Magens; *Fl.* Magnin; *Fr.* Magin; p.n.; fam. n. of Mag, Mac

Madocks, Madox, Maddox. From Maddocks; a loc. n., Devon. Or *Fr.* Madoux; *D.B.* Madoc; Welsh Madoch (good); p.n.

Magee. From the Irish O'Maol-gaoithe; a p.n.

Chief of Muintir Maolgaoithe (*gaoth*, wind; pronounced 'ghee').

Mager, Mauger. *N*. Magr; n.n.; *A.S.* Mæghere; *D*., *S*. Mager; p.n. (able warrior)

Maggs. *See* Madge

Maginn. *N. meginn* (strong). Or *see* Guinness

Maginnes. *See* Guinness

Magnac. A loc. n., Upper Vienne, France

Magnay. *Fr*. Magny, Magnée; p.n. Magnée; a loc. n., Belgium

Magness. *N*. Magnús; *A.S.*, *G*. Magnus; *Fr*. Magniers, Magniez; p.n. (great). Or *see* Guinness

Magniac. *See* Magnac

Magrath. *See* Mackareth

Maguire or MacGuire. From the Irish of MacUibhir or Maguibhir, chief of Fermanagh (goat (?)). Also MacIvir, MacIvor

Mahaffy. Irish McGuffee; a p.n. *See* Duffy

Mahon, Mahony, MacMahon. From the Irish MacMathgham-hain; a p.n. (a bear)

Maidwell. *See* Madewell

Mainwaring. From Mesnilwarin or Menil Garin; a loc. n., Norm. In Roll of Battell Abbey.

Maisey. A loc. n., Wilts, or Mezy, France

Maitland. From Maltalent, near Nantes, or Mautland, Scotl. Thomas de Matulant settled in Scotland in 1220.

MAJOR. *N.-Fr.* Major; a p.n. Hugt., Lond. 1688
> Le Magere, Rot. Hund.

MAJORIBANKS. A loc. n., Scotl.
> The barony of Ratho formed the marriage portion of Marjorie, only daughter of Robert Bruce. It was called Terra-de-Marjorie-Banks (Lower).

MALAN. From Malain; a loc. n., France

MALCOLM. From the Gaelic Mac-Gillecalum (the son of the servant of Columba)

MALE. From Melle; a loc. n., Belg. *Dch.* Mell; *Fl.* Mail; *N.-Fr.* De Maisle; a p.n. Hugt. n., Dover, 1622
> Mayle in Rot. Hund.

MALET, MALLET. *N.-Fr.*; a p.n. From Melet (?); a loc. n., Flanders
> The Conquerer, after the battle of Hastings, committed the body of Harold to W. Malet to see it buried. His son Robert was a tenant in chief in *B.D.* (Surr.). He founded the Monastery of Eye. Malet held lands *temp.* K. John.

MALINS. *Fl.* Maelens, Melens; p.n. Mallines and Mellin, Prot. ref. Lond. 1618. From Melin; a loc. n., Fland.

MALLORY. A loc. n., Flanders. *Fr.* Mellery; a p.n.

MALLOWS. *See* Marlow

MALPAS. A loc. n., Ches., Cornw., Flint

MALT. *Dch.* Molt; a p.n. *A.S.* Malte; *Old G.* Magoald (powerful ruler)

MALTBY. A loc. n., Lincs, Yorks

MALTON. A loc. n., Yorks

MAMMATT. *N.-Fr.* Mamignot; a p.n. A fief of Norm.
> Robt. Maminot, Sire de Corbespine, near Bernai, was father of Gilb. M., bp. of Lisieux, and Ralph, de C., of Kent, Willm. I. M., tenant in chief in *D.B.*

MANBY. A loc. n., Lincs

MANCLARKE. *Fr.* Mauclerc (?); a p.n.
> Rot. Obl. et Fin., *temp.* K. John, 1208.

MANDER. *Dch.* Mandere; *Fr.* Mandre; p.n. Manders; a loc. n. in Normandy

MANGAN. From Mannacan; a loc. n., Cornw. Or *N.-Fr.* Mangcant, Mangon; p.n.

MANGER. *A.S.* Mægengær (strong spear); *Fr.* Mangez; p.n. Or *A.S. mangere* (a merchant)

MANHILL. *N.-Fr.* Manneville; a p.n. From Mandeville; a loc. n. in Normandy
> Maundeville or Meneville in Roll of Battell Abbey. Manneville, a tenant in chief in *D.B.*

MANIFOLD. From Mannofield; a loc. n., Aberdeen

MANISTY. *D.* Mannstead; a loc. and p.n.

MANLEY. A loc. n., Devon

MANLOVE. *A.S.* Manleof; a p.n. (man beloved)

MANN. *N.* Manni (a man, manly); *F.* Manne, Manno; *G.* Mann; *D.B.* Man, Manna, Manne, Manus; *D.* Mann; *Dch.* Mahn, Man; p.n.

MANNERING. *See* Mainwaring

MANNERS. From Mesnieres; a loc. n., Norm. Or *Fl.* Mannaers, Mannaerts; p.n. (strong man)

MANNING. *A.S.*; fam. n.; *Dch.* Manen, Mening; p.n. *See* Mann
> In Rot. Hund.

MANSELL. A loc. n., Heref. Or *N.-Fr.* Mancel; a p.n.
> Robert Le Mansel held lands in Leics. *temp.* K. John. *N.-Fr. mancel* (a rural proprietor)

MANSER. *N.-Fr.* Manesier; a p.n. Or *see* Mansergh

MANSERGH. A loc. n. (manor), Westmd.
> Nicholas de M., 12 Ed. I. 1283 (de Banco Rolls). Thomas de M., 12 Edw. II. 1319. John de M. represented Westmd. in Parliament 7 Ric. II. 1384.

N

MANSFIELD. A loc. n., Notts
MANSON. From Manston; a loc. n., Devon, Yorks. Or *A.S.* Mansuna; *Dch.* Manson; p.n. *See* Mann
MANT. *D.* Manthey; *A.S.* Mantat; *G.* Manth; *Dch.* Mandt, Mante; p.n. (tender man (?)). Or from Mantes; a town of Seine and Oise, France. Fr. Prot., Lond. 1618.
MANTELL, MANTLE. From Mantel; a loc. n., Norm. *Fr.* Mantel ; a p.n.

Tenant in chief, *D.B.*

MANTHORPE. A loc. n., Lincs
MANTON. A loc. n., Lincs, Notts, Wilts
MANWARING. *See* Mainwaring
MANWELL. *See* Manhill
MAPLE. From Mepal; a loc. n., Camb; or Meppel, Holland. *See* Maypole
MAPLESTON. From Mapleton; a loc. n., Derbysh.
MAPLEY. From Mapperley; a loc. n., Derbysh.
MAPP. *See* Mabb
MAPPIN. *N.-Fr.* Magnepeine; a p.n.
MARCH. A loc. n., Camb. Or Marché, Norm.
MARCON. *Fr.* Marquant. A Hugt. n., Cant. 1622
MARDEL, MARDLE. *See* Maddle
MARDEN, MARDON. A loc. n., Heref., Suss., Wilts
MARE. From La Mare; a loc. n., Norm.
MAREHAM. A loc. n., Lincs
MARGETTS. *See* Madgett
MARGRIE. *N.-Fr.* De St Marguerie; *Dch.* Magerey; p.n.

In Rot. Hund.

MARIS, MARRIS. *N.-Fr.* Mariess, Maris; p.n. From le Marais; a loc. n., Normandy. Mares, a Hugt. n., Lond. 1682

MARJORAM. From Margam; a loc. n., Glamorgansh.
MARKETT. *A.S.* Mearcweard (a boundary warden); *Fl.* Merkaert; *Fr.* Marquet; p.n.
MARKEY. From the Irish *marcach* (a horseman); hence a synonym for Knight
MARKHAM. A loc. n., Notts
MARKIN. From Marquain; a loc. n., Belg.
MARKWELL. A loc. n., Cornw.
MARLER. *N.-Fr.* le Marler; a p.n. Or *see* Marlow

In Rot. Hund.

MARLEY. From Merlai; a loc. n., Norm.
MARLOW. A loc. n., Herts ; or Marlieux, France
MARMION. *N.-Fr.* ; a p.n.
MARNEY. From Marigny ; a loc. n., Norm. Or *see* Murnane
MARPLE. A loc. n., Ches.
MARQUIS. *Fr.* ; p.n.
MARR. A loc. n., Yorks ; La Mare, Norm. Or *A.S.* Mar, Mær ; *S.* Mars ; *Dch.* Mar; *Fl.* Maere ; *Fr.* Marre ; p.n. (famous). Hugt. n., Lond. 1618
MARRABLE. From Mirabel; a loc. n., Norm.
MARRACK. *Fr.* Marique ; a p.n. Hugt., Lond. 1688. Or *see* Merrick
MARRIAGE. A loc. n., Devon; Merridge, Somers ; Maurage; a loc. n., Belg. Or *Fr.* Mariage; *D.* Mariager ; p.n. (famous spear)
MARRIFIELD. From Merrifield ; a freq. loc. n.
MARRIOTT, MARRITT. From Merriott ; a loc. n., Somers ; or *Fr.* Marriette ; a p.n. Hugt. n., Lond. 1685. Or *see* Marryat
MARRYAT. A loc. n., Yorks
MARSDEN. A loc. n., Lancs, Yorks
MARSH. A loc. n., Devon, Lancs ; Marche ; a loc. n., Belg. *See* March

MARSHALL. Celtic Marchell; *Fl.* Marchal; *Fr.* Maréchal; p.n. (horse servant). Hugt. n. Lond. 1618

MARSHALLSAY. From Marshallsea (near Crewkerne); a loc. n., Wilts

MARSHAM. A loc. n., Norf.

MARSLAND. A loc. n., Cornw.

MARSTON. A loc. n., Ches., Heref., Lincs, Northants, Staffs, Warw., Yorks

MARTER, MARTYR. *N.-Fr.* Le Martre; a p.n.

MARTIN. From St Martin; a loc. n., Norm. Hugt. n., Lond. 1688

MARTINDALE. A loc. n., Lincs

MARTINEAU. *Fr.* Martiny, Martinais, Martinant, Martinet; p.n. From Martigne; a loc. n. of Ille and Vilaine, France

MARVIN. *A.S.* Maruuen, Merefin, Meruin; p.n. (famous friend)

MARWOOD. A loc. n., Devon, Dorset, Dur.

MARYON. From Marines or Marinis; a loc. n., Normandy

> Werricus de Marines in Rot. Obl. et Fin., K. John, A.D. 1205. Hertford. Marwyn in Rot. Hund.

MASE. *See* Mace

MASH. A loc. n., Dur.

MASHAM. A loc. n., Yorks

MASHEDER, MASHITER. From Meschede; a loc. n., Germany. *G.* Meschter; *Fl.* Mestdagh; p.n.

MASKALL, MASKELL. *See* Marshall

MASKELYNE. *Fr.* Masquelin; a p.n. (masking or disguising)

MASKEW. *G.* Maschke; *Fr.* Mascot; p.n. (a masker)

MASKREY. *Fr.* Mascre, Mascrier; p.n.

MASLEN, MASLIN. From Meslin (?); a loc. n., Flanders. *N.-Fr.* Masselin; a p.n.

> In Rot. Hund.

MASSEY. From Macey; a loc. n., Normd. Hugt. Lond. 1684

MASON. *N.-Fr.* Mavesyn, from Malveysin or Malvoisin; a p.n. Or *Fl.* Meessen; *Fr.* Maçon, Le Mazon, Masson; p.n. Hugt., Lond. 1618

MASSINGBERD. From Massingham; a loc. n., Norf.

> In the will of Ælgyfu, A.D. 1012, it is Mæssanwyrð. The ending often occurs as *wurde, vrde.* *A.S.* Mæssing, a fam. n., is freg. in local n. Massenberg is a loc. and p.n. in Germany.
> Alan Massyngberd in Lay Subsidy Roll, Lincoln, 1 Edw. III. Sir Thomas M., Gunby, Lincs, 1405.

MASSINGER. *See* Messenger

MASSINGHAM. A loc. n., Norf. *D.B.* Massingeham, but earlier Mæssanwyrð

MASTERS. *N.-Fr.* le Maystre; p.n.

MASTERTON. From Mastertown; a loc. n., Fife

MATCHAM. From Masham; a loc. n., Yorks.

MATCHETT. *Fr.* Machotte; a p.n. Dimin. of Mag. *See* Madge

MATE. *A.S.* Mæth; *Dch., Fl.* Met; *Fr.* Mette; p.n. (dignity). Hugt., Lond. 1618

MATHER. *A.S.* Mæthhere (revered lord); *D.* Mathe, Mather; p.n. Hugt., Lond. 1618. *See* Madder

MATHEWS. *Dch.* Matthes, Matthies; *Fl.* Mathys; p.n. Hugt., Lond. 1618

MATSELL. From Mattishall; a loc. n., Norf.

MATTISON. *D.* Matteson, Mathiessen; *Dch.* Mathiesen; a p.n.

MATTIX, MATTOCKS. *See* Maddox

MAUDE. *N.-Fr.* De Mouhaut; a p.n.; a loc. n., Aberdeensh; St Mard, Belg.

> John Maud was living *temp.* K. John.

MAUDSLEY. A loc. n., Lancs

MAUGHAM. A loc. n., Monmouth

MAUGHAN. From Mawgan, Cornw. Or Irish Mahon

MAULE. A loc. n., France. Hugt., Lond. 1618. *See* Moll

MAULKIN. An old dimin. of Mary

MAUN. *See* Maughan

MAUNDER. *See* Mander

MAW. From Mawr ; a loc. n., Glamorgan. Or St Maur ; a loc. n., Belg.

MAWBERY. *See* Mowbray

MAWBY. From Moorby ; a loc. n., Lincs. Or Mautby, Norf.

MAWDESLEY. A loc. n., Lancs

MAWLEY. From Mauley, Poitou.

MAXELL. *See* Maxwell

MAXLOW. From Muxloe ; a loc. n., Leics ; or Moxley, Staffs ; formerly Moceslow

MAXSE. From Maxey ; a loc. n., Northants

MAXTON. A loc. n., Roxburgh

MAXWELL. A loc. n., Roxburgh ; anciently Maccusville

MAY, MAYS. A loc. n., France. Or *A.S.* Mæg, Mei (power) ; *Dch.* Maij, Mee, Mei ; *Fl.* Mahy, May ; *D., G., S.* May ; p.n.

MAYALL. Irish Mael ; *Dch.* Meijll ; *D.* Meil ; *Fr.* Meyelle ; p.n. Celtic *mael* (bald, tonsured disciple)

St Mael, Bishop of Ardagh and founder of the monastery there, died *circa* 488.

MAYBERRY. From Mayborough ; a loc. n. Or Mabire, Norm.

MAYCOCK. *F.* Maike ; *G.* Mäcke ; p.n. A dimin. of Mary

MAYDEW. From Meadow ; a loc. n., Surr. Or *A.S.* Mægtheow (strong servant)

MAYER. *See* Myers

MAYGER. *A.S.* Mægenheard ; *Fr.* Mégard ; p.n. (strong power)

MAYHEW. *Fr.* Mahieu, Mayeux ; p.n. Hugt., Norwich, 1622

MAYNE. A loc. n., Scotl. Or from Mayenne, France. Hugt. n., Lond. 1687

MAYNARD. Mainharðt ; a loc. n,. Germ. *D.* Meinert ; *Dch.* Meijnhardt ; *Fl.* Meynaert ; *D.B* Mainard ; *Fr.* Ménard ; p.n. *See* Mayger. Hugt. n., Dover, 1622

Maniard in Roll of Battell Abbey.

MAYO. *N.-Fr.* Maio ; a p.n.

MAYPOLE. From Maybole ; a loc. n., Ayrsh. *See* Maple

MAYS. *See* Mace

MAYSENT. *See* Mason

MEACHAM. From Mitcham ; a loc. n., Surr.

MEACHEN, MEAKIN, MEEKIN. *N.-Fr.* Le Meschin. Or *Dch.* Meegen, Meeken ; *G.* Michan ; p.n. Dimin. of May

MEAD. A loc. n., Somers

MEADOWS. A loc. n., Surr.

MEADWAY, MEDWAY. A river, Kent

MEADWELL. From Meadenwell ; a loc. n., Cornw.

MEALL. *N.* Mjöll (meal) ; *A.S.* Mil, Mul ; *D.* Moyell ; *Fl.* Mylle ; *Fr.* Mille ; p.n. *See* Mayall

MEAN. *See* Meen

MEANS. *Fl.* Minnens ; a p.n. *See* Meen. Prot. ref., Lond. 1687

MEAR. A loc. n., Devon. Or *see* Meer. Hugt. n., Lond. 1618

MEARA. Irish Meaghar ; a p.n.; *mear* (merry)

MEARS. *See* Meers

MEASE. *See* Mace

MEASURES. From Mèzières ; a loc. n., Normandy. Maziers ; a Hugt. n., Lond. 1687

MEATYARD. *N.-Fr.* Le Meiteier ; a p.n.

MEAUX. A loc. n., Belg. Yorks. *See* Mew

MECK. *See* Meek

MECRATE. *See* Mackereth

MEDCALF. *See* Metcalf

MEDE. *See* Mead

MEDEX. *See* Madox

MEDHURST. From Midhurst; a loc. n., Suss.

MEDLEY. A loc. n., Oxon

MEDLICOTT. A loc. n., Salop

MEDLOCK. A loc. n., Lancs

MEDWELL. *See* Meadwell

MEDWIN. *A.S.* Medwine; a p.n. (revered friend). *See* Methven

MEDWORTH. *Dch.* Medevoort; a loc. and p.n.

MEE. From My; a loc. n., Fland. Or *see* May

MEECH, MEEK. *N.* Mikill (much, great); *D.* Micha; *Fr.*, *Dch.* Miche; *G.* Micke; a p.n.

MEEKING. *See* Meachen

MEEN. From Migne; a loc. n., France. Or *A.S.* Min, Minna (love); *Fr.* Minnes; *G.* Miny, Minner; *Dch.* Minne, Mijn; *Fl.* Mine, Minne, Min; p.n. Prot. ref., Lond. 1618

MEER. A loc. n., Wilts

MEERS. A loc. n., Worcest.

MEESON. *See* Mason

MEFFEN. *Fl.* Meeuwens; a p.n.

MEGGATT. A loc. n., Peebles

MEGGINS. *See* Maginns

MEGGS. *See* Maggs

MEINS. *F.* contr. of Meinert

MELBOURNE. A loc. n., Derbysh., Herts

MELDRUM. A loc. n., Aberdeensh.

MELLER. Mellier; a loc. n., Belg. Hugt., Cant. 1622

MELLERSH. *See* Melluish

MELLIN. *See* Malins

MELLIS. A loc. n., Suff.; Melles, Belgium. *Fr.* Mellisse; a p.n.

MELLISH. *See* Melluish

MELLON. From Melon; a loc. n., Norm.

MELLOR. A loc. n., Derbysh., Lancs

MELLOWS. *See* Mellis

MELLUISH. A loc. n., Devon

MELSOM. A loc. n.

MELVILLE. From Malleville; a loc. n., Normandy

MENDS. Mendez, Hugt. n., London, 1682

MENHINNICK. From Menhynnet; a loc. n., Cornw.

MENLOVE. *See* Manlove

MENTEITH. *See* Monteith

MENZIES. A loc. n., Scotl. Anciently de Mengues, *de maneriis*

MERCER. *See* Merser

MERCY. *See* Merser

MEREDITH. From Mirridith; a loc. n., Heref. Or Welsh p.n. (the roaring of the sea)

MEREST. *A.S.* Meresuuet; *Fr.* Merresse (?); p.n. (a sea-guard)

MERRELLS. *N.-Fr.* De Merel; a p.n.

MERRICK. From Marrick; a loc. n., Yorks. Or *see* Meyrick

MERRIDEW. *See* Meredith

MERRINGTON. A loc. n., Dur., Salop

MERRISHAW. *Fr.* Maréchal or Marescot; p.n. *See* Marshall

MERRISON. *Dch.* Merisson; a p.n.

MERRITT. *A.S.* Merehwit; *Fl.* Marit; a p.n. (sea white)

MERRY. *Fr.* Méret, Mery; p.n. Merrey; a loc. n., Normandy

MERRYDEW. *See* Meredith

MERRYFIELD. A loc. n., Devon

MERRYWEATHER. From Mereworth; a loc. n., Kent. *A.S.* Mereweorðig, merewurðe

    Dōms Johannes de Merwrthe in Lib. Vit. Dur.

MERSER. *Fr.* Mercier. Hugt. n., Lond. 1618; Mercere, 1327

MERWYN. *D.B.* Maruen, Maruuen, Merefin, Meruen. Meruin; Saxon tenant. Mereuuin; tenant in chief. Mereuin; under-tenant. *A.S. mæra-wyne* (illustrious friend)

MERYMAN. From Miremont; a loc. n., France

    It is also an Irish form of Marmion.

MESS. From Meese; a loc. n., Staffs. Or *D. F.* Mess; a p.n. *See* Mace

MESSENGER. From Messingham; a loc. n., Lincs. Or *see* Leggatt

MESSETER. *See* Mashiter

METCHIM. *See* Meacham

METFORD. *See* Mitford

METHVEN. A loc. n., Perthsh.

METTAM. From Metham; a loc. n., Yorks

MEW. *Dch.* Mewe; *Fr.* Mieux; p.n. From Meux; a loc. n., Belg.

MEYER. *See* Myers

MEYNELL. From Mesnil; a freq. loc. n. in Normandy

MEYRICK. *Fl.* Meryck; *N.-Fr.* De Meric; a p.n. Prot. ref. Lond. 1621.

MIALL. *See* Mayall

MICHELL. *Fr.*; p.n. Hugt., Lond. 1618

MICKLESON. *S.* Michaelson; *Dch.* Michelson; *D.* Mikelsen; p.n.

MICKLETHWAITE. A loc. n., Yorks

MIDDLEBROOK. A loc. n.

MIDDLEDITCH. A loc. n.

MIDDLEMASS, MIDDLEMISS. From Middlemarsh; a loc. n., Lincs

MIDDLEMORE. A loc. n., Worcest.

MIDDLETON. A loc. n., Derbysh., Edinbgh., Dur., Lancs, Norf., Northants, Yorks

MIDDLEWEEK. From Middlewich; a loc. n., Ches.

MIDGLEY. A loc. n., Yorks

MIDWINTER. Possibly the first to bear the name was born at that time

MIELL. *See* Miall.

MIGEON. *A.S.* Mic; a p.n. (midge); *Fr.* Migeon; p.n.

MIGGS. *N.* Myg; *A.S.* Mæg, Mec, Meg, Mic; p.n.; *N. mý*; *D. myg*; *A.S. mcg* (a gnat, a midge). Or *mæg* (strength, power)

MIGHT. *N.-Fr.* Miette, Myte; p.n. W. Mite in Rot. Hund.

MILBORROW. From Millbrook; a loc. n., Cornw., Hants

MILBOURN, MILBURN. From Milborne; a loc. n., Dorset, Wilts

MILDMAY. *Fr.* Mildmé; a p.n.

MILEHAM. A loc. n., Norf.

MILES. *N.-Fr.* Miles; *Fl.* Milis; p.n.

MILESON. From Milson; a loc. n., Salop. Or *Fr.* Milsan; a p.n.

MILESTONE. *G.* Milostan; a p.n.

MILFORD. A loc. n., Devon, Hants, Salop, Staffs, Surr., S. Wales

MILICAN. A loc. n., Scotl. Or *Dch.* Milligen, Milikan; *Fl.* Milecan; p.n. Dimin. of Miles

MILK. *G.* Milich, Milke; *D.B.* Melc; p.n. Dimin. of Miles

MILL. *See* Miall. Or Atte Mill

MILLER, MILNER. *N.-Fr.* Le Mouner; a p.n.; *Lat.* Molendinarius

MILLERCHIP, MILLERSHIP. From Millichope; a loc. n., Salop

MILLETT. *Fr.*; p.n. Dim. *See* Miall

MILLIGAN, MILLIKIN. *See* Milican

MILLINGER. *See* Mullinger

MILLINGTON. A loc. n., Ches., Yorks

MILLS. A loc. n., Devon. Or *Dch.* Mills; *Fl.* Miles, Millis; *G.* Milisch; *D.B.* Milo, Miles; p.n. Prot. ref., Norwich, 1622. *See* Miles

MILNE. From Millen; a loc. n., Belg.

MILNTHORPE. A loc. n., Westmd.

MILSOM. From Melksham (?); a loc. n., Wilts

MILSON. *See* Mileson

MILTON. A loc. n., Devon, Dorset, Fife, Hants, Kent, Northants, Oxf., Westmd., Yorks, etc.

MILWARD. *D.* Moellgaard; *Fl.* Moulaert; *Fr.* Milliard; p.n. (mill-keeper)

MIMMACK. From the Irish Mimnagh; a p.n.

MIMMS. A loc. n., Herts and Middlx.

MINCHER. *A.S.* Min, Mina; p.n.; *myn* (love, affection); *G.* Minschke; a p.n. Dimin.

MINCHIN. *See* Minnikin

MINES. *See* Meen. Hugt. n., 1688

MINETT. *Fl.* Minnaert; *G.* Minuth; *Fr.* Minet; p.n. Hugt. n., Lond. 1688

MINGAY. *Fr.* Minquet; a p.n.

MINNIKIN. *F.* Menken; *G.* Mennicke; *Fl.* Minique; *Dch.* Mennecken; p.n. *See* Meen. Dim. (little love)

MINNISH. From M'Nish

MINNITT. *See* Minett

MINNS. *See* Mines

MINSHULL. A loc. n., Ches.

MINTER. *G.* Minte; *Fr.* Minder (a minor); p.n. Mint., Prot. ref., Lond. 1618

MINTERN. A loc. n., Dorset

MINTEY. *See* Minter

MINTING. A loc. n., Lincs

MINTON. A loc. n., Salop. Or *Fl.* Minten; a p.n.

MISSEN. *Fl.* Misson; a p.n. Hugt. n., Lond. 1687. Or Misson; a loc. n., Staffs. *See* Mace

MIST. *Dch.* Misset; a p.n. Dim.

MITCHAM. A loc. n., Surr.

MITCHELL. *See* Michel

MITCHINSON. *See* Meachen

MITFORD. A loc. n., Northbd.

MITTON. A loc. n., Staffs, Yorks. *D.B.* Mutone

MOATE. *See* Mott

Mote in Hund. Rolls.

MOBBS. *Fl.* Mobers; a p.n. *See* Mabb

MOBERLEY. From Mobberley; a loc. n., Ches., Staffs

MOCHRIE. From the Irish M'Rae, M'Cree; p.n.

MOCKLER. *A.S.* Mogla (?); *Fr.* Mauclere. A Hugt. n., Lond. 1689

MODGERIDGE, MODGRIDGE, MODRIDGE. From Modrydd; a loc. n., Brecon

MOELLEDON. From Moel-y-don, Menai Straits, N. Wales

MOFFAT. A loc. n., Dumfries

MOGER. *Fr.* Mauger; a p.n. *See* Mogg

MOGG, MOGGS. *N.* Mögr; *D.* Maag; *Dch.* Mock, Mok; *Fl.* Moke; *G.* Moch; p.n. *See* Madge

MOIR. *N.-Fr.* De Moire; a p.n.

MOLD. A loc. n., Flint

MOLDEN. From Malden; a loc. n., Surr. Or Maldon, Ess.

MOLE. *G.* Mohl; *Fr.* Molé; p.n. *See* Moll

MOLESWORTH. A loc. n., Hunts

MOLINEUX. From Moulineaux; a loc. n., Normandy. Moliner, a Hugt., Lond. 1618

MOLL. *A.S.*, *Dch.*, *Fl.*, *G.* Moll; p.n. A loc. n., Norm., Belg.

MOLLET. *Fr.* Mollet; a p.n. Mulet in Rot. Hund.

MONCKTON. A loc. n., Devon, Dorset, Kent, S. Wales, Wilts, Yorks

MONCRIEFF. A hill in Perthsh.

MONCUR. A loc. n., Perth

MONDAY. *See* Mundy

MONEY. *N.-Fr.* Monnaye, Muny; p.n. Mauny, Monnaie; loc. n., Norm. Hugt. n., Lond. 1618

MONEYPENNY. *N.-Fr.* Magnepeine; a p.n.

Roger M., Norm., 1180-95; Hubt. Manipeni, 1272. Rot. Hund.

MONGER. *A.S.* *mongere* (a merchant, dealer). Or Mongour; a loc. n., Kincardine. *See* Manger

MONK. *N.* Munki; n.n. (monk); *D.* Munck; *Dch.* Monch, Monk, Munk; *Fr.* Moncq; p.n. *See* official names, p. 12

MONKHOUSE. A loc. n., Northbd.

MONKSFIELD. A loc. n.

MONKTON. A loc. n., Dur.

MONNINGTON. A loc. n., Heref.

MONSER. Monceau; a loc. n., Belg. Or *see* Mountseer

MONSEY. *See* Mountseer or Mounsey. A Hugt. n., Lond. 1618

MONSON. From Montzen (?); a loc. n., Belg. Or *A.S.* Mon; a p.n. (man)

MONTAGUE. From Montaigu; a loc. n., France, Belg.
In Roll of Battell Abbey. Tenant in chief, *D.B.*

MONTEITH. A loc. n., Perth

MONTFORD. A loc. n., Salop

MONTGOMERY. A loc. n., Norm.
In Roll of Battell Abbey. Tenant in chief in *D.B.*

MONUMENT. From Mornimont (?); a loc. n., Belg.

MOODY. *G.* Mude; *D.* Muthe; *Dch.* Mudde; *A.S.* Mōd; p.n.; *módig* (proud, courageous)

MOON. From Moyon or Mohun; a loc. n., Normandy. Or *Dch.* Moen; *Fl.* Moine; p.n. Hugt. n., Sandwich, 1622

MOONEY. Irish, from Mahoney (?)

MOOR. A freq. loc. n. *N.* Mór (a Moor); *Dch.* Moor; *Fl.* Morre; *G.* Mohr; p.n. Or Celtic Morre. Or Atte-moor. Moer, a loc. n., Fland. More, a Hugt. n., Lond. 1618

MOORBY. A loc. n., Lincs

MOORHOUSE. A loc. n., Dur. Or from Muirhouse; a loc. n., Forfarsh.

MOPPET. *Fr.* Moppert; a p.n. *See* Mabbut

MORAN. From Morannes; a loc. n., France
Tenant in chief and under-tenant in *D.B.*

MORBEY. *See* Mawby

MORCOM. *Fr.* Marcomb; a p.n. Or Morecambe; a loc. n., Lancs

MORDAUNT. *N.-Fr.* Mordant; a p.n.

MORDEY. From Morda (?); a loc. n., Salop

MORELAND. A loc. n., Westmd.

MORELL, MORRELL. *N.-Fr.* Morel; a loc. n., Normandy
In Roll of Battell Abbey. Philip de Morel in Rot. Obl. et Fin., K. John. Also a Hugt. n., Lond. 1618.

MOREWOOD. From Moorwood; a loc. n., Yorks

MORFATT. *See* Moffat

MORGAN. From the Irish O'Muiregain; Welsh Morgwn; p.n. (a mariner, sea-dweller)

MORKHAM. *See* Morcom

MORLEY. A loc. n., Derbysh., Devon, Yorks, etc.; Morlaix, France

MORRALL. *See* Morell

MORRISS. From St Maurice d'Etelan; a loc. n., Normandy. *Fr.* Maurice, Morisse; p.n.; *D.B.* Mauric, tenant in chief. Meurisse, a Hugt. n., Cant. 1622
Morreis in Roll of Battell Abbey; Morice in Rot. Hund.; de Mori s in Rot. Obl. et Fin., K. John. Harvey de Monte Morisco of Beaumaris, nephew to Richard, Earl of Chepstow, commonly called "Strongbow," went with his uncle to Ireland *temp.* Hen. II.

MORSE. A loc. n., Glost. Or *Dch.* Mors; a p.n.

MORTER. Mortier; a loc. n., Belg. Or *Fr.* Mortiaux, Mortier, Mortoire; p.n. Morteaux; a loc. n., Normandy. A Flem. ref. n., Lond. 1622

MORTIMER. From Mortemer; a loc. n., Normandy. *D.B.* De Mortemer, a tenant in chief
In Roll of Battell Abbey, and Rot. Obl. et Fin., K. John.

MORTLOCK. From Mortlach; a loc. n., Banff. Or Mortlake, Surr.

MORTON. A loc. n., Derbysh., Dumfries, Lincs, Northants, Yorks. Mortagne, France

MOSEDALE. A loc. n., Cumb. Also *D.* Mosdal; a loc. and p.n.

MOSELEY. A loc. n., Lancs

MOSER. From Museres; a loc. n., Norm. *See* Mouser

MOSS. *N.-Fr.* De la Mosce; a p.n.

MOSSOP. *Dch.* Masdorp, Massop loc. and p.n.

MOSTYN. A loc. n., N. Wales

MOTHERSIL, MOTHERSOLE. From Mottishall (?); a loc. n., Suff. Or Moddershall, Staffs

MOTION. *N.-Fr.* Moisson; *Fr.* Maussion; a p.n. (little bird)

MOTT. *Fr.* Motte and De la Motte. From Motte, a town of Cotes du Nord, France. A Hugt. n., Lond. 1621

MOTTERWAY. Welsh Mawddwy; a loc. n. Or Mauduit, Norm. Or *A.S.* Modher, Motheri; p.n. (courageous warrior)

Gilbert de M. in Rot. Obl. et Fin.

MOTTON. *See* Mutton

Sir William Moton, knight, was living at Peckleton, Leics, A.D. 1174. Sir Robert Moton was killed at the battle of Evesham, A.D. 1265. Motten, a Prot. ref., Norwich, 1622.

MOTUM. From Mottingham (?); a loc. n., Ess.

MOUAT, MOWAT. From Mouet; a loc. n., Norm.

MOUEL, MOWLE. *See* Mole

MOULD. Moult; a loc. n., Norm. *See* Mold

MOULES. *See* Mole

MOULTON. A loc. n., Norf., Suff.

MOUNSEY. From Monchy; a loc. n., Norm. *Dch.* Monsee; *Fr.* Montoisy (?); p.n. Mountsey, a Hugt., Lond. 1618

MOUNSHER. *See* Mountseer

MOUNT. *N.-Fr.* De Monte; a p.n.

MOUNTAIN. *Fr.* Montaigne. Hugt. n., Lond. 1618

MOUNTSEER. *Fr.* Monseur. Hugt. n., Lond. 1685

MOUSE. *D.* Muus; *G., Dch., Fl.* Maus, Mus; *Fr.* Mousse; p.n.; *Old G.* form Muoza, from *môd* (courage). Moze, a Hugt. n., Lond. 1687

MOUSER, MOUSIR. *Fr.* Moussier; a p.n. *See* Moser

MOW. A loc. n., Roxburgh

MOWBRAY. From Moutbray; a loc. n., Normandy; or Maubray in Flanders

Moribray and Mowbray in Roll of Battell Abbey. William de M. held lands in Notts. Rot. Obl. et Fin.

MOWCHER. From Mouchard; a loc. n., France

MOXEY. *See* Maxse

MOXON. *D.* Mogensen; *Dch.* Mock, Mok; p.n. *See* Mogg

MOY. *N.-Fr.* De Moeia; p.n.

MOYSE, MOYSEY. From Moissac (?); a loc. n., France. *N.-Fr.* Moisy; a p.n.

MOZLEY. From Moseley; a loc. n., Staffs

MUCKALL. *N.* Mikill; *A.S.* Mucel (big); *D.* Muxoll; *S.* Michal; *Fl.* Michils; p.n. Or from Mucholls; a loc. n., Kincardine

MUCKLEBREED. *See* Kilbride

MUCKLESTON. A loc. n., Salop, Staffs

MUCKLOW. From Mucklagh (?); a loc. n., Kerry, Ireland

MUDD. *See* Moody

MUDDLE. From Muthill (?); a loc. n., Perthsh.

MUDGE. *See* Mogg

MUDIE. *See* Moody

MUELUISH. *See* Mellish

MUFFET. *Fl.* Muffat; a p.n. Or *see* Moffat

MUGFORD. From Mogford; a loc. n., Devon

MUGGE, MUGGS. *See* Moggs

MUGGERIDGE, MUGRIDGE. *See* Modridge

MUGGLESTON, MUGLISTON. *See* Mucklestone

MUGGLETON. From Muckleton; a loc. n., Salop

MUIR. A loc. n., Scotl. *See* Moor

MULHOLLAND. From the Irish O'Maolchallain; a p.n. (descendant of the disciple of Caellin)

MULINGER. *See* Molineux. *Fr.* Moulinier (a silk-mill man). A Hugt. n., Lond. 1618

MULLALLY. From the Irish *eala* (a swan)

MULLEN. *Fr.* Moulin; *Dch.* Mullen; *G.* Mühlan; p.n. (a mill). *See* Mullins

MULLEY. *A.S.* Mula; *Fr.* Mullie; p.n. (miller)

MULLIGAN. Irish (servant of the bald-headed man, *i.e.* priest)

MULLINER. *See* Molineux

MULLINS. From Moulins; a loc. n., Normandy

MULLIS. *G.* Mulitz; a p.n.

MUMBY. A loc. n., Lincs

MUMFORD. From Mundford; a loc. n., Suff.

MUMMERY. *Fr.* Momerie; p.n. (masquerade)

MUNCASTER. A loc. n., Cumb.

MUNCH. *G.* Münch, Münich; *D.* Munnich; p.n. *See* Monk

MUNCY. *See* Mounsey

MUNDAY, MUNDY. From Mondée or Mondaye (Mons Dei); a place and abbey in the diocese of Lisieux, parish of Bayeux, Normandy. French Gazeteer, 1791. Or *N.* Mundi; *A.S.* Munda; *Fl.* Mondis, Munday; *G.* Mund, Munder; p.n. (protection). Also Monedy; a loc. n., Perthsh.

Thomas de Mondaye, abbé de Ardenne, 1282; Geoff. de M., abbot of M., 1290; Gilles de M., 23rd abbot, 1477. Robert de Mundeye, 1258, in deed, Balliol Coll. report, Roy. Hist. Com.

MUNGY. From Montjoye; a loc. n., France

MUNN. *A.S.* Mun; *Dch.* Munne; p.n. Or *see* Moon. A Prot. ref., Lond. 1618

MUNNING. Descendants of Munn

MUNT. *Dch.*, *S.* Munthe; *A.S.*, *G.* Mund; p.n. Or from Munte; a loc. n., Flanders

MUNTING. *See* Mountain

MURCH, MURCHIE. From the Gaelic Murdoch (sea power)

MURCHISON. From Merchiston; a loc. n., Edinburghsh.

MURCOTT. A loc. n., Northants, Wilts

MURE. *See* Moor

MURGATROYD. A corruption of Moorgate Road, Yorks

MURLEY. From Moorly; a loc. n., Wilts

MURNANE. From the Irish Marnane, Mournane (Warren); a p.n.

MURPHY. From the Irish MacMurchada; a p.n. MacMorrow, MacMurrogh (sea warrior)

MURR. *See* Moore or Muir

MURRAY. From Moray; a loc. n., Scotl. Or Irish O'Muiredhaigh; a p.n. (sea protector)

MURRELL. *See* Morell

MURROW. A loc. n., Camb. Or see Murphy

MURSELL. From Moorsel; a loc. n., Fland. Prot. ref., Dover, 1622

MURTHWAITE. A loc. n., Westmd.

MUSCHAMP. From Moschaus; a loc. n., Norm.

MUSCHET. *N.-Fr.* de Montfichet; a p.n. *See* Mussett

In Roll ot Battell Abbey.

MUSCOTT. A loc. n., Northants

MUSGRAVE. A loc. n., Cumb., Westmd.

MUSGROVE. From Mucegros; a loc. n., Norm.

MUSK. From Moussac; a loc. n., France. *Dch.*, *Fl.* Musch; *G.* Muske; p.n.

MUSKETT. From Mousquette; a loc. n., France. *Fl.* Musschaert, Musschot; *G.* Muskat; p.n.

In Rot. Hund.

MUSSETT. From Mozet (?); a loc. n., Flanders. *Fr.* Moussett, Musset; *Dch.* Mussert; p.n.

Musett in Roll of Battell Abbey.

MUSSON. From Mouçon; a loc. n., Norm.; Musson, Flanders. Or Muston, Leics, Yorks

MUST. *See* Mussett

MUSTERS. From Moustier; a loc. n., Flanders. *Fr.* Mustière; a p.n.

Robert de Mosters, a tenant in chief in *D.B.* Gaufrid de Musters, *temp.* K. John, Rot. Obl. et Fin.

MUTIMER. *See* Mortimer

MUTTON. From Motons; a loc. n., Norm. *N.-Fr.* Mouton; a p.n. Or *see* Mitton and Motton

Hugo de Mutton, Rot. Obl. et Fin.

MUTTITT. *Fr.* Mottet; a p.n. (a hillock)

MYCOCK. *See* Maycock

MYERS. *Old G.* Magher; *A.S.* Mæghere (valiant warrior); *D.*, *S.* Meyer; *Dch.* Meier; *G.* Mayer, Meyer; *Fl.* Meyers, Miers; p.n.

MYERSCOUGH. A loc. n., Lancs

MYHILL. *See* Miall. Hugt. n., Lond. 1618

MYLCHREEST. The Manx form of the Celtic Mac Giolla Chriosd. *See* Gilchrist

MYLNES. *See* Mullins

MYNOTT. *See* Maynard

N

NADIN. *Fr.* Nadine; a p.n.; Slavonic (hope). Hugt. n.

NAGGS. *N.-Fr.* De Nages; a p.n.

NAGLER. *N.* Nagli (a nail); *A.S.* Nægel; *D.* Nagel; *G.* Niegel; *Fr.* Naglée; p.n. Nagle; a loc. n., Normandy

NAILER. From Nesle (?); a loc. n., France

NAISH. *See* Nash or Neach

NALDRETT, NOLDARITT, NOLDWRITT. From *N.-Fr.* de Maldrett; a p.n.

NALL. *See* Neale

NANCE. *A.S.* Nan, Nansige (doughty victor); *Fr.* Nens; p.n. *See* Nanney

NANGLE. *See* Angle

NANKIVEL. From Nanckivel; a loc. n., Cornw.

NANNEY. *F.* Nanno, Nanne; *A.S.* Nan, Nennius; p.n.; *N. nenna* (energy)

NAPIER. *N.-Fr.* le Naper, le Napier; p.n.

The officer of the, king's household who had charge of the napery or table linen.

NAPKIN. *G.* Knabechen; a p.n. Dim. of Napp

NAPLETON. A loc. n., Worcest.

NAPP. *N.* Knappi (a servant, boy); n.n.; *A.S.* Cnapa; *Old G.* Hnabi; *D.*, *Fl.*, *Dch.* Knapp; *G.* Knapp, Knabe, Knappe, Knaps, Knop; p.n.

NAPPER. *See* Napier

NAPTHEN. From Napton (?); a loc. n., Warwicksh.

NARES. *N.-Fr.* De Neirs; a p.n.

NASH. A loc. n., Heref., Kent

NASLEN. *See* Nesling

NASSAN. *A.S.* Nas, Neri (a protector); *Dch.* Nussen; *D.* Nissen; *Fl.* Niesen; p.n.

NATERS. *See* Nattrass

NATT. *A.S.* Nata; *Dch.* Nat; *G.* Nath; p.n. Contr. of Nadal (needle)

NATTRASS. *Fl.* Nateris, Natris; p.n.

NAUGHTON. A loc. n., Suff.; Nawton, Yorks

NEACH. *A.S.* Nytta; *G.* Nietch, Nische; p.n. Dim. (useful)

NEAGLE. *See* Neale

NEALE. *N.-Fr.* de Neel. Or *N.* Njáll (from the Gaelic); *S.* Nihl; *D.*, *A.S.*, *Dch.* Niel; *Fl.* Niels, Nille; *Fr.* Nesle; p.n. The original meaning is a noble, or *niadh* (champion), but the *N.-Fr.* Latinised it to Nigellus, supposing it to mean black. Niel; a loc. n., Flanders

Neile in Roll of Battell Abbey; and Nigel, a tenant in chief in *D.B.* Also a Hugt. n., Lond. 1688.

NEAME. *A.S.*, *D.* Nim; a p.n. (holder, keeper)

NEARY. *A.S.* Neri; a p.n. (deliverer)

NEATE. *N.-Fr.* De Nits; *A.S.* Nith, Nid, Nytta, Nyding; p.n.; *nyd* (necessity)

NECK. *Dch.*; p.n. *See* Noakes

NEEBE. From Newby; a freq. loc. n. Or *see* Neighbour

NEECH. *See* Neach

NEED, NEEDES. *See* Neate

NEEDELL. *A.S.* Nadal; *D.* Nedahl; *G.* Niedel; *Fr.* Nidoul; p.n.; *nœdel* (needle)

NEEDHAM. A loc. n., Norf.

NEEP. *A.S.* Cnebba, Cnibba; *G.* Kneip; *Dch.*, *Fl.* Knip; p.n. (nipper)

NEEPER, NEIPER, NEPER. Irish forms of Napier

NEESON. *See* Nassan

NEGUS. *G.* Niegisch, Nikish; *Fr.* Nigaise, Nicaise; p.n. Or *see* Naggs

NEIGHBOUR. *D.* Nyeboe; *G.* Neubauer, Neuber, Niebour, Niebuhr; *S.* Neijber, Nieber; *Dch.* Niebuur, Nueboer; p.n.

NELL. *Dch.*; p.n.; *N.* hnalla (to beat). Or *see* Neale

NELSON. *D.* Neilson, Nielson; *S.* Nelson, Nelzon; *Dch.* Nelson, Nielsen; p.n. *See* Neale

NEOBARD. *A.S.* Nithbeorht (bright need); *Fr.* Néaubert; *G.* Neubert; p.n.

NERTIGAN. *Fl.* Neutgens; *Dch.* Neutegem; p.n. Dimin. of Neute. *See* Nute

NESBET. A loc. n., Dur., Northbd.

NESLEN, NESLIN, NESLING. *A.S.* Nesta; a p.n. (a neighbour); *nestling* (?)

NESS. *D.*, *S.*; p.n. Also a loc. n., Ches., Salop, Yorks. Or from Nas; a loc. n., Norm. Hugt. n., Rye, 1622.

De Nes in Rot. Hund.

NETHERCLIFT. From Nethercleugh; a loc. n., Dumfries

NETHERCOTT. A loc. n., Devon, Somers

NETHERSOLE. From Netherseal; a loc. n., Leics

NETTLE. *Fr.* Niatel; a p.n. *See* Needell

NETTLEFOLD, NETTLEFIELD. From Netherfold (?); a loc. n., Yorks. Or from Netreville; a loc. n., Norm.

NETTLETON. A loc. n., Lincs, Wilts

NEVARD. *Fr.* Nivard; a p.n.

NEVAY. A loc. n., Forfar

NEVE. From Nives; a loc. n., Belg. Or *see* Nevison

NEVELL. *See* Neville

NEVILLE. From Néville; a loc. n., Normandy

Nevill in Roll of Battell Abbey and in Rot. Obl. et Fin., K. John.

NEVISON. *N.-Fr.* Le Neve; *D.* Neve; *Dch.* Neef, Neeve, Neff; *Fl.* Neefs, Neave; p.n.

NEWALL. From Newhall; a loc. n., Ches.

NEWARK. A loc. n., Notts

NEWBEGIN. *See* Newbiggin

NEWBERRY. From Newbury; a loc. n., Berks

NEWBIGGIN. A loc. n., Dur., Fife, Forfar, Lanark

NEWBOLT. *See* Newbould

NEWBOULD. From Newbold; a loc. n., Leics, Yorks. Or *A.S.* Nubold, Nybald; p.n. (new, fresh, bold)

NEWBY. A loc. n., Yorks, etc.

NEWCOME. *A.S. niwe-cuma* (a new comer, a stranger); a n.n.

NEWDICK. A loc. n. (?)

NEWDIGATE. A loc. n., Surr.

NEWELL. From Nieul; a loc. n., France. Or *see* Newall

NEWHAM. A freq. loc. n.

NEWITT. *See* Newt

NEWLING. *G.* Neuling; a p.n. Dim. of *nyr* (young)

NEWLOVE. From Newlaw (?); a loc. n., Kirkcudbright

NEWMAN. *G.* Neumann; *Dch.* Nieman, Numan; *S., D.* Nyman; p.n. le Neuman in 1327.

NEWNES. A loc. n., Salop

NEWNHAM. A loc. n., Glost., Hants, Northants., Salop, Warw., Worcest.

NEWNUM. *See* Newnham

NEWPORT. A loc. n., Bucks, Glost., Hants, Montgy, Salop, Somers, S. Wales. Nieuport; a loc. n., Flanders

NEWSAM. *See* Newsome

NEWSOME. A loc. n., Lincs, Yorks

NEWSON. *Dch.* Nussen, Nijssen; p.n. *See* Nassan

NEWSTEAD. A loc. n., Lincs, Notts, Staffs

NEWT, NEWTH. *See* Nute

NEWTON. A freq. loc. n.

NIBBS. *A.S.* Cnibba; *G.* Nibisch; p.n. (a beak)

NIBLET. *See* above

NICE. From Neisse; a loc. n., Germ. *D.* Niss; *Fl.* Neys, Nys; *Dch.* Nies; *G.* Kneis; p.n. Prot. ref., Lond. 1618

NICHOLAS, NICHOLLS, NICHOLS. *See* Nicker

NICHOLSON. *S.* Nicolausson; *D.* Nikelsen; p.n. Prot. ref., Lond. 1618

NICKER, NICKERSON, NICKLESS, NICKOLS, NICOL. *N.* Nikolás; *D.B.* Nicolaus, Nicol; *G.* Nick, Nicke, Nickel; *Fl.* Nicole; *D.* Nickels; *N.-Fr.* Nicholas; p.n.

NICKLIN. Dim. of Nicholas

NIEL. *See* Neale

NIGHTINGALE. *N.-Fr.* Nightyngale; *G.* Nachtigall; *Dch.* Nagtegaal; *Fl.* Nachtergael; p.n. Nytingall, Flem. refugee, Lond. 1618

NIKER. *See* Nicker

NIMMO. *Dch.* Nimmo, Niemer (Nieman); p.n. *See* Newman

NINCE. From Ninnes, Ninnis; loc. n., Cornw. Or *G.* Nintz; a p.n.

NIPPER. *Fl.* Nepper; a p.n. *See* Neeper

NISBET. A loc. n., Berwick, Haddingtonsh., Roxburgh

NIX, NIXON. *See* Nicker

NOAKES, NOAKS. Noke; a loc. n., Oxf. Or from Atten oak; *D.* Knoak; *Dch.* Noack; p.n.

NOAR. *N.-Fr.* De Noa; or *D.* Nohr; p.n.; *Norra* (a Norseman)

NOBBS, NOBES. *N.* Knappi; n.n. (a knob); *G.* Nabe; *Fl., D.* Knop; *Dch.* Knobbe, Noppe; p.n. *See* Napp

NOBLE. *N.-Fr.* le Noble; *D., Dch.* Nobel; *Fl.* Nobels; p.n.

NOCK. *See* Nonkes

NOCKALL, NOCKLES, NOCKOLDS. *Fl.* Nockels; p.n. *See* Noakes

NODDER. *A.S.* Nod, Noth (bold); *Fr.* Nodé; p.n.

NODE, NODES. *N.-Fr.* Node; *A.S.* Nod, Noth; p.n. (daring, bold)

Note in Rot. Hund. Not in Rot. Obl. et Fin.

NOEL. From Noailles; a loc. n., Normandy

NOKES. *See* Noakes

NOLAN. Irish O'Nuallain; a p.n.; *nuala* (fair shoulders)

NOLLOTH. *D.* Nolleroth; *Fr.* Nolleau, Nollett; *G.* Nolte; p.n. Hugt. n., London, 1687

NOON. From Noyon; a loc. n., Norm.

NOOTT　*See* Nute

NOPS.　*See* Nobbs

NORBURY.　A loc. n., Ches., Derbysh., Salop, Staffs

NORDEN.　*D.* Norden; *Dch.* Noorden; p.n. (North)

NORFOR.　*N.* Narfi (the n. of a giant); *G.* Nafe, Nave, Naveau; *D.B.* Novi; *Fl.* Noeve; p.n.

NORKETT.　From Norracott; a loc. n., Devon. Or *see* Northcote

NORMAN.　*S.* Nordman; *G.* Nordmann; *D.*, *N.-Fr.* Norman; *Dch.* Normant; p.n. (Northman)

NORMINGTON.　From Normanton, Derbysh., Leics, Lincs, Wilts, Yorks

NORRINGTON.　A loc. n., Wilts

NORRIS.　*Fr.* Noris; a p.n.

　Norice in Roll of Battell Abbey. Le Norreis, Rot. Obl. et Fin.

NORSWORTHY.　*See* Nosworthy

NORTHCOTE.　A loc. n., Devon. Or Northcott, Somers.

　Held by De Colville.

NORTON.　A freq. loc. n.

NOSWORTHY.　From Knaworthy; a loc. n., Devon

NOTCUTT.　*See* Northcote

NOTLEY.　A loc. n., Ess.

NOTSON.　*Fl.* Knudsen; a p.n. *See* Nott and Nute

NOTT.　*Fr.* Notte; a p.n. *See* Node

NOTTAGE.　A loc. n., S. Wales. Or *Fl.* Notez; *G.* Nöthig (needful); p.n.

NOTTIDGE.　*See* Nottage

NOURSE.　*See* Nowers

NOWELL.　*See* Noel

NOWERS.　From Noyers; a loc. n., Norm.

　De Noiers, de Noies, de Nouuers, tenants at the time of the Survey, *D.B.* Noers is on the Roll of Battell Abbey. Simon de Noers in Rot. Obl. et Fin., K. John. Sir Robert de Nowers was Lord of the Manor of Knossington, Leics, in 1278.

NOY.　*A.S.* Neue; *Dch.* Noy; p.n. (fresh, young)

NOYCE, NOYES.　*G.* Neuss; a loc. and p.n. Or *see* Nowers

NUDD, NUDDS.　*See* Nute

NUELL.　*See* Noel

NUGENT.　From Nogent; a loc. n., Normandy

　De Nugent, Rot. Obl. et Fin.

NUNN.　*A.S.* Nun; *Old.G.* Nunno; *G.* Nunn; p.n. (an orphan)

NUNNELEY.　From Noneley; a loc. n., Salop

NURSE, NURSERY, NURSEY.　*See* Nourse

NUTBEAM, NUTBEAN.　*G.*, *Dch.* Nussbaum; a p.n. (nut tree)

NUTCHER.　*G.* Knutsche; p.n. Dim. of Knut

NUTE, NUTH, NUTT.　*N.* Knútr (a knot, hill); *A.S.* Canud, Cnud, Cnut; *D.* Knudt; *Dch.* Noot, Nut, Knuijt; *G.* Knuth; *Fl.* Cnudde; p.n.

NUTMAN.　*A.S.* Nothmund; *Dch.* Nootman; a p.n. (daring director)

NUTTAL.　From Nuttall; a loc. n., Notts (*D.B.* Notele)

NUTTER.　*See* Nute

NUTTING, NUTTY.　Tribal n. of Cnut

NYE.　*Dch.* Nije, Nuy; p.n. *See* Noy

O

OAFS.　*A.S.* Of, Offa, Wufa; p.n. (n. of a king)

OAK.　A loc. n., Devon, Somers. Or *A.S.* Oc, Oca, Ocg; p.n. *See* Ogg

OAKDEN.　*See* Ogden

OAKES.　A loc. n., Derbysh., Lancs. Atte Oaks (?)

OAKEY.　From Hockai; a loc. n., Belg. *Fr.* Ocket; *Fl.* Ogy; *G.* Ocke; p.n. Oky; Seal, Leics. 1327.

OAKHAM. A loc. n., Notts, Rutland, Warw.

OAKLEY. A loc. n., Beds, Berks, Bucks, Ess., Hants, Northants, Staffs, Suff., Worcest., etc.

OAKSHETTE, OAKSHOTT. From Oxshott; a loc. n., Surr.

OATES. *N.*, *Fl.* Ots; a p.n. *See* Oddy

OATLEY. *See* Ottley

OBBARD. *See* Hobart

OBEE. From Obaix; a loc. n., Belg.

OBORNE. A loc. n., Dorset

O'BRIEN. From the Irish *brian* (strong)

OCLEE. From Ockley; a loc. n. in Surr. Or Oakley, Ess.

ODAM. A manor in Devon

ODAMS. *Dch.* Odems; a p.n.

ODDIN. From Odeigne; a loc. n., Belg. Or *Dch.* Oddinck; a p.n. *See* Oddy

ODDY. *N.* Oddi (a leader); *F.* Ode, Odo; *D.* Odde; *Dch.*, *Fl.* Otte, Hody; *N.-Fr.* Aude; *G.* Otho, Other, Ott, Otte, Otto; *A.S.* Oda, Odda, Odo, Otha; p.n.

ODEL, ODELL. A loc. n., Bucks, Devon. Or *N.* Oddkell or Ottkel (Ketel the leader); *D.B.* Odel, Oudchell, Ouetel; *G.* Hodel; p.n.

ODGER. *N.* Oddgeir (leader spear); *Fl.* Oger; *A.S.* Eadgar; *Fr.* Audiger; p.n. Prot. ref., Lond. 1622

ODLING. *D.B.* Odelin; a p.n. (Saxon tenant); *N.* *öðlingr* (?) (a landowner); *N.-Fr.* Fitz-Odeline

O'DONOGHUE. From the Irish O'Donchada or O'Donchu; p.n. (brown chief)

O'FERRALL. Irish *O'Feargail.* *See* Farrell

OFFIN. From Offagne or Ophain; loc. n., Belg.

OFFLEY. A loc. n., Herts

OFFORD. A loc. n., Hunts

OGBEN. *See* Ogbourne

OGBOURNE. A loc. n., Wilts

OGDEN. A loc. n., Lancs

OGG. *N.* Ögurr (?) (terrible); *A.S.* Og, Ogga; p.n. Or *see* Oak

O'HART. Irish p.n.; *arta* (great). *See* Carter

O'KANE. *See* Caine

OKES. *See* Oakes

OLCOTT. From Holcott; a loc. n., Northants

OLD. A loc. n., Northants. Or *A.S.* Ald, Eald, Old, Weald (rule, power); *Dch.*, *S.* Olde; p.n.

OLDACRE. From Aldecar; a loc. n., Derbysh. Or *A.S.* Ealdgar; a p.n. (ruler spear)

OLDERNESS. From Holderness; a loc. n., Yorks

OLDERSHAW. From Aldersholes; a loc. n., Yorks

OLDFIELD. A loc. n., Worcest.

OLDHAM. A loc. n., Lancs

OLDING. *D.* Olden; a p.n. Fam. n. of Old

OLDMAN. *A.S.* Ealdman; *G.* Ohlmann; *S.* Ollman. *See* Old

OLDRIDGE. A loc. n., Devon

OLDRING. *A.S.* Aldran (old strength); *Dch.* Olderen; p.n.

OLDROYDE. *See* Holroyd. Or *A.S.* Ealdred (ruler counsellor); *Fl.* Oldrade; p.n.

OLET, OLLETT. *Fr.* Oliette; a p.n. *See* Olyott

OLIFFE. *See* Oliver

OLIPHANT. *Dch.* Ollefen; a p.n.

> The Scot. and Old Engl. form of elephant. Chaucer has "Sire Oliphaunt." Old Norse *olifant* was used for the unicorn, but was a foreign word. Olifant in Roll of Battell Abbey.

OLIVER. *N.* Óláfr or Óleifr; *A.S.* Olaf; *S.* Olof; *Dch.* Olfers; *Fl.* Oleff; *Fr.* Olivier; p.n. Hugt., Lond. 1682

> The original form was Anleifr (inheritance of the gods).

OLLAY, OLLE, OLLEY. From Oleye; a loc. n., Flanders. *D.B.* de Ole, de Olgi, Oiley, de Oilli; p.n.; tenants in chief

OLLIFFE. *See* Oliver

OLNEY. A loc. n., Bucks

OLPHERT. *Fr.* Olivert; a p.n.

Olivard in Roll of Battell Abbey. David de Oliphard, Scotl. 1142.

OLYOTT. *A.S.* Olfgeat, Oluiet; *Fl.* Holliette; p.n. *See* Olett (wolfgate (?)

OMANT. *Fr.* Omont; a p.n. *See* Osmund

OMASH. *Fr.* D'Ormasse; a p.n.

OMER. A loc. n., Devon

OMMANEY. A loc. n., Hants

ONES. *A.S.* Ona; *F.* Onno; *Dch.* Onasse; p.n.; fam. n. Or Onehouse; a loc. n., Suff.

ONG. *N.* Ungi (?) (the younger); *F.* Onke, dimin. of Onno; *G.* Unger; *Fi.* Ongers; p.n. Or Ongar; a loc. n., Ess.

ONGLEY. *See* Onley

O'NIELL. *See* Neale

ONIONS. From Angiens (?); a loc. n., Normandy. Or Welsh Eignion (just)

ONLEY. A loc. n., Northants, Staffs

ONSLOW. A loc. n., Salop. *D.B.* Ondeslow

OPENSHAW. A loc. n., Lincs

OPIE. *Fr.* Aupée; a p.n. Or *see* Obee

ORAM. From Owram; a loc. n., Yorks. Or Horham, Suff.

ORBY. From Orbais; a loc. n., Belg.

ORCHARD. A loc. n., Devon, Somers. Or *see* Archard

ORD. A loc. n., Northbd. Or *A.S.* Ord, Weard; *D.* Orth; *Dch.* Oort, Ort; p.n. (guard)

ORDERS. *A.S.* Orde, Ordarus; *F.* Ordgies; p.n. Akin to *A.S. weard* (a guard)

ORFEUR. *N.-Fr.* Orfrere (Aurifaber); a p.n. (a goldsmith)

ORFORD. A loc. n., Lancs, Lincs, Norf., Suff.

ORGILL. A loc. n., Cumb. Or Orguil, Norm.

ORGLES. *See* Argles

ORLEBAR. From Orlingbury (?); a loc. n., Northants. Or *A.S.* Herlebeorht; *Dch.* Haleber; p.n. (illustrious earl)

ORMAN, ORMANDY. *See* Hammond

ORME. *N.* Ormr; a p.n. (snake)

ORMEROD. A loc. n., Lancs

ORMISTON. A loc. n., Edinbgh.

ORMOND. *See* Ormandy

ORMS. From Ormes; a loc. n., Normandy

ORMSBY. A loc. n., Lincs, Norf., Yorks

ORR. *N.* Orri (heathcock), *tetras tetrix*; n.n.; *D.* Orr; *Dch.* Orri; *Fl.* Ories, Orys; *G.* Oehr; *D.B.* Ori; p.n.

ORRELL. A loc. n., Lancs

ORRIDGE. From Horridge; a loc. n., Devon

ORRIS. *See* Orr

ORROCK. A loc. n., Scotl. Or *see* Horrex

ORTH. *See* Ord

ORTHORPE. From Authorpe; a loc. n., Lincs

ORTNER. *A.S.* Ordnoth; a p.n.

ORTON. A loc. n., Cumb., Hunts, Leics, Staffs, Westmd.

ORVIS. From Avize (?); a loc. n., France. *Dch.* Avis; *Fr.* Avice, Avisse; p.n.

OSBALDESTONE. A loc. n., Lancs

OSBASTON. A loc. n., Salop

OSBORNE. *N.* Ás-Björn (the gods' bear); *D.* Osborn; *N.-Fr.* Osbern; p.n.

OSLAR, OSLER. *N.-Fr.* le Oiselor. Or *A.S.* Osla; a p.n. (Oslaf (?), the gods' relict)

OSMAN, OSMENT. *See* Osmund

OSMONT. *See* Osmund

OSMOTHERLEY. A loc. n., Lancs, Yorks

OSMUND. *N.* Ásmundr (under the guardianship of the gods); *A.S., D., Fl.* Osmund; *Dch.* Osseman; *Fr.* Osmont; *G.* Ossmann; p.n.

OSSINGTON. A loc. n., Notts

OSTICK. *Dch., Fl.* Oosterwijk; p.n. Also a loc. n. in Flanders

OSWALD. *N.* Ásvaldr; *Fl., D., G., A.S.* Oswald; p.n. (power of the gods)

OTTAWAY. *A.S.* Othwig, Eadwig (prosperous victory); *G.* Ottawa; *Fl.* Ottevaere; p.n.

OTTLEY. A loc. n., Salop, Suff., Yorks

OTTY. From Othée; a loc. n., Belg. Or *see* Oddy

OTTYWILL. From Outwell (?); a loc. n., Norf.

OTWAY. *See* Ottaway

OULTON. A loc. n., Cumb., Norf., Yorks

OUNSTEAD. From Houndstreet (?); a loc. n., Somers

OURY. *Fr.* Oury; *G.* Ury; p.n. *See* Orr

OUSELEY. A loc. n., Northants

OUSEY. *See* Hussey

OUTHWAITE. *See* Huthwaite

OUTLAW. From Oathlaw; a loc. n., Forfar

OUTON, OUTTAN. *A.S.* Othin; *F.* Otten; *Dch.* Ouden; *Fr.* Othon; p.n. Fam. n. of Oth, Oddy. Or *see* Houghton

OUTRAM. *Old G.* Audram; a p.n. From *aud*, *A.S. eád* (prosperity), *ram* (strong)

OVENS. *A.S.* Offa, Ofing; *S.* Ovens; *Fl.* Ovyn; *Dch.* Oven; p.n. (wolf's descendants)

OVENSTONE. A loc. n., Fife

OVER. A loc. n., Camb.

OVERALL, OVERELL, OVERILL. From Overhill; a loc n., Worc. Or *N.-Fr.* Avril, de Avrilla; p.n.

OVERBURY. A loc. n., Suff., Worcest.

OVEREND. A loc. n., Worcest.

OVERMAN. *N.* Oframemni (a champion); *Dch.* Overman; *D.B.* Offram; p.n.

OVERTON. A loc. n., Ches., Derbysh., Hants, Lancs, Staffs, Wilts, Yorks

OVERY. A loc. n., Oxf. Or *Fr.* Ouvry; a p.n. Hugt. n., Lond. 1618

OVINGTON. A loc. n., Ess., Norf.

OWEN. British p.n. (a prince). Also *D.* Owen; *Fr.* Ouin; *D.B.* Ouen; p.n.

OWERS. A loc. n., Hants

OWGAN. *See* Hogan

OWLES. A loc. n., Suff.

OWSTON. A loc. n., Dur., Leics, Lincs

OWTHWAITE. *See* Huthwaite

OXBORROW. A loc. n., Norf.

OXENHAM. From Oxnam; a loc. n., Roxburghsh.

OXER, OXIER. From Auxerre; a loc. n., France

OXLADE. From Oxlode; a loc. n., Camb.

OXLEY. A loc. n., Lancs, Staffs

OXX. *N.* Oxi; *Dch.* Ox; p.n.

OYLER. *N.-Fr.* Huelier. Or *G.* Eule; a p.n. (an owl). Hugt. n., Lond. 1618

P

PACE, PACEY. A loc. n., Norm.

PACKER. *A.S.* Baghere (a contentious soldier), Bægeras (the Bavarians)

PACKE. *A.S.* Bag, Pæcg, Pag; *Dch.* Pak; *Fl.* Paké; *G.* Pache; p.n. *See* Bagge
In Rot. Obl. et Fin.

o

PACKHAM. A loc. n., Devon

PACKMAN. *Fl.* Packman; *G.* Pachmann; a p.n. (a farmer)

PADBURY. A loc. n., Oxf.

PADDAY. *N.* Pade; *A.S.* Pada, Peada; *D.*, *G.* Pade; p.n. *See* Badcock

PADDON. From Patton; a loc. n., Yorks (*D.B.* Patun). Or *Dch.* Paddingé; a p.n.

PADEY. *See* Padday

PADFIELD. A loc. n., Derbysh.

PADGET. *See* Paget

PADLEY. A loc. n., Derbysh.

PADMORE. From Pedmore; a loc. n., Worcest.

PAFFEY. *See* Pavett

PAGAN. *A.S.* fam. n.; *D.B.* Paganus, Pagen; p.n.
In Rot. Obl. et Fin. *A.S. bagan* (to contend).

PAGE. *Fr.* Page; a Hugt. n., Lond. 1688; *N.-Fr.* Le Page. Or *see* Packe

PAGET. *N.-Fr.* Pachet; a p.n.
In Rot. Hund.

PAGNAM. *See* Pakenham

PAICE. *See* Pace

PAINE, PAYEN. A loc. n., Normandy. Or *A.S.* Pag, Pagan, Pagen; *G.* Pein; *Fr.* Pain; *Fl.* Payen, Pien; *Dch.* Pen, Penn; p.n. Also a Hugt. n., Lond. 1618
Wm. Paen, *temp.* K. John.

PAINELL. *N.-Fr.* Paganel, Paynel; p.n.

PAINTER. *A.S.* Pender, Pendhere; *D.* Penter; *Fl.* Pinter; p.n. (crowned warrior)

PAKE. From Pecq; a loc. n., Flanders. *Dch.* Peek, Pek; p.n.
Pecche in Rot. Obl. et Fin.

PAKENHAM. A loc. n., Suff.

PALETHORPE. From Pallathorp; a loc. n., Yorks. Or Perlethorpe, Notts

PALEY. *Fr.* Pelay, Pelet, Pelez; p.n.; *pelé* (a bald-headed man)

PALGRAVE. A loc. n., Norf., Suff.

PALIN. *A.S.* Palling, Palig; *N.-Fr.* Palain; p.n. *See* Pelling
In Rot. Hund.

PALK. A loc. n., Devon

PALLETT. From Paillette; a loc. n., France. A Hugt. n., Lond. 1688

PALMER. *N.-Fr.* le Paumier; *Fl.* Palmaert; *Dch.* Pallme; *G.* Palmer; p.n. Flem. ref. n., Lond. 1618
Richard Palmer held lands in Worcest. *temp.* K. John.

PALMES. A loc. n., Languedoc

PANCHEN. From Paunchin; a loc. n., Devon. Or *A.S.* Bana (a slayer); *S.* Panchéen; *Fr.* Panquin; p.n. Dim. *See* Banner

PANGBOURNE. A loc. n., Berks

PANK, PANKS. *A.S.* Panga; *D.*, *S.* Pang; *G.* Pancke; p.n. Dim. of Bana

PANKHURST. A loc. n., Suss.

PANNELL. *See* Painell

PANTER, PANTHER. *A.S.* Band, Panti; *Fr.* Pante, Panthou; *Dch.* Pante; *G.* Panter; p.n. *See* Bond

PANTIN. *See* Panton

PANTON. *N.-Fr.* De Panton; a p.n.
In Rot. Hund.

PANTRY. From Penterry; a loc. n., Monmth.

PAPE. *A.S.* Papo; *Fr.* Pepe; a p.n. *See* Poppy. *N. papi* (a priest). Papper, a Prot. ref., Lond. 1618

PAPWORTH. A loc. n., Camb.

PARADISE. *A.S.* Berrardus (?), Bernardus; *Fl.*, *Fr.* Paradis; p.n. *See* Pardoe

PARAMAN. *See* Pearmain

PARAMORE. From Paramé (?); a loc. n., Norm. *N.-Fr.* Paramor

PARCELL. *Fr.* Parisel; a p.n.

PARCHMENT. *G.* Pergament; a p.n.

PARDOE. *A.S.* Beradus; *Old G.* Peradeo; *Fr.* Pardieu; *Dch.* Pardo; *D.* Pardi; p.n. (bear firm)

PARDON. *Fr.* Pardant, Pardon; *Fl.* Pardaen; *G.* Pardon; p.n.

PARFITT. *N.-Fr.* Parfait; a p.n. (perfect)

PARISH. *See* Parritch or Parris

PARK, PARKE, PERCK. A loc. n., Flanders; Parc, near Valognes; *Dch.* Park; *Fr.* Parc; p.n.
Richard de Parco held lands in Lincs, *temp.* K. John.

PARKER. *N.-Fr.* le Parker; *G.* Parke; *Dch.* Parker; p.n.; *Fr. parquer* (a park-keeper)
Parcher, tenant in chief, *D.B.*

PARKES. From Les Perques; a loc. n. near Valognes. *N.-Fr.* Bertram De P.; a p.n.

PARKHOUSE. A loc. n., Northbd.

PARKHURST. A loc. n., I. of Wight

PARKINS, PARKINSON. *Fl.* Parcyns; a p.n. *See* Perkins

PARLET. *See* Pallett

PARLOUR. *G.* Parlow; a p.n.

PARMETER, PARMINTER. *N.-Fr.* Parmentier; a p.n. (a tailor)

PARNELL. From Pernelle; a loc. n., Norm. *Fr.* Purnelle; p.n.

PARR. A loc. n. in Lancs. Or *Dch.* Parre, Paare; p.n. *See* Barr

PARRINGTON. A loc. n., Ess.

PARRIS. *N.-Fr.* Parez, Paresse, de Paris, Parys; p.n. Or Welsh ap Harris

PARRITCH. From Parwich; a loc. n., Derbysh.

PARROT. *See* Perrott

PARRY. *Fr.* Parré; a p.n. Or Welsh Ap Harry. *See* Parris. A Hugt n., Lond. 1687

PARSLEE, PARSLEY, PARSLOW. *See* Purslow

PARSON, PARSONS. *Dch.* Parson, Passen, Passon, Passens; *D.* Pass, Passen; p.n. *See* Parr or Pass
Atte p'sonnes, 1327.

PARSONSON. *See* Parson

PART. *See* Pert

PARTINGTON. A loc. n., Ches.

PARTON. A loc. n., Camb.

PARTRIDGE. From Pettridge (?); a loc. n., Kent. Or *A.S.* Beorhtric; *Old G.* Perhtric; p.n. (illustrious ruler); Partrick de la Lande, Norm.
Partryk in Dur. Liber Vitæ. Partriche in Hund. Rolls. Patrickes in 1327.

PASCOE. *Fr.* Pasque; a p.n. (Easter)

PASH, PAISH. *Dch.* Pashe; *G.* Pasch; p.n. *See* above

PASHLEY. From Pasley, the Irish form of Paisley

PASK, PASKE. *See* Pascoe (time of birth (?))

PASKELL. *Fr.* Pascal; a p.n.; Hugt. n., Lond. 1687
De Peschall in Rot. Obl. et Fin.

PASS. *A.S.* Passa; *D.* Pass; *Fl.* Pas; *S.* Passy; *Dch.*, *G.* Pas, Pass, Passe; p.n. *See* Bass

PASSMORE. From Peasemore; a loc. n., Berks

PATCH. *A.S.* Pecga; *G.* Patsch; p.n.

PATCHING. A loc. n., Suss.

PATCHITT. *See* Paget

PATE. *A.S.* Pade, Pata; *Fl.* Patte, Peet, Piette; *Dch.* Pet, Peet; p.n. Hugt. n., Canterbury, 1622. *See* Badcock

PATERNOSTER. *Dch.*, *Fl.*; p.n.

PATEMAN, PATMAN. *G.* Patermann; a p.n. *See* Badman

PATON. *See* Peyton. Hugt. n., Canterbury, 1622

PATRICK. *Lat.* Patricius; *N.* Patrekr; Irish Padrig; p.n. (a nobleman) Or *see* Partridge

PATTEN, PATTON. A loc. n., Salop, Yorks. *N.-Fr.* Patin, Patun; p.n.
In Rot. Hund.

PATTERSON. *See* Pate

PATTISON. *Fl.* Patte, Petterson, Patesson; p.n. *See* Pate. Flem. ref., Lond. 1618

PATTLE. From Pathull or Pattis-
hall; a loc. n., Staffs

PAUL. *N.-Fr.* de St Paul. Or *N.*
Páll; *D.* Poul, Pauli, Paulin; *Fl.*
Pauwels, Pauly, Poel, Pol, Polet,
Poly, Polyn, Spoel; *Dch.* Pool,
Pouwels, Spall, Spoel; *G.* Pohl,
Pohler, Pollack, Poli, Pohlit, Pol-
lok, Paul; *D.B.* Pauli; p.n. A
Hugt. n., Lond. 1618

PAULETT. From Poolet; a loc. n.,
Somers. Or *Fr.* Poulet; a p.n.
Dim. of Paul. A Hugt. n., Lond.
1687

PAULGER. *A.S.* Polga; *Dch.* Poelje;
a p.n. Dim. of Paul

PAUNCEFOTE. *N.-Fr.* Pancevolt; a
p.n. *See* Penfold

PAUSE, PAUSEY. *G.* Pause; a p.n.
See Poysey

PAVETT. *Fr.* Pavot; *Fl.* Pevaert;
p.n. (a poppy)

PAVEY. *N.-Fr.* Pavie, Peyveye;
p.n.

PAVIS. *Dch.* Pavias, Paviers; p.n.

PAWLETT. *See* Paulett

PAWLEY. *N.-Fr.* Pauly; *D.* Pauli;
p.n. *See* Paul

PAWSEY. *See* Pause

PAWSON. *D.*, *Dch.* Paulsen; a p.n.

PAXTON. A loc. n., Berwick

PAYNE. *See* Paine

PAYTON, PEYTON. From Paythorne;
a loc. n., Yorks. *See* Paton

PEABODY. *See* Peberdy

PEACE. *Dch.* Piesche, Pees; p.n.
See Pace

PEACHE, PEACHEY. *G.* Pietsch; a
p.n.
  N.-Fr. Peche in Roll of Battell
  Abbey; Pecehaie, a tenant in chief,
  in *D.B.*; Peeche in Rot. Obl. et
  Fin.

PEACOCK. From Peakirk (?); a loc.
n., Northants. Or *G.* Piechocki;
a p.n. *See* Peak. Flem. ref. n.,
Lond. 1618

PEAD. *D.* Pied; *Fl.* Piette; p.n.
See Pedder

PEAK. *N.* Pík (a peak (?), pike,
pick, point of a sword, etc.); *Dch.*
Pieck, Piek; *G.* Pick; *D.* Picker;
A.S. Pic; p.n. *See* Pigg

PEALL. *See* Peel

PEAR. From Peer(?); a loc. n., Belg.
Dch. Peer. Or *Fr.* Pièrre; p.n.
Hugt., Lond. 1687

PEARD. *Fr.* Pirard; a p.n.

PEARETH. A loc. corruption of
Penrith; a loc. n., Cumb.

PEARL. From Perl (?); a loc. n.,
Germ. Or *D.* Perle; *G.* Perl,
Pirle; *N.-Fr.* Perol; *A.S.* Perlo;
Dch. Perlee; *Fl.* Perlau; p.n.
(pearl)
  Perles in Rot. Hund.

PEARMAIN, PEARMAN. *Old G.* Ber-
man; *D.* Permin; *S.* Perman;
Fl. Pierman; p.n. (bear man)

PEARS, PEARSE. *Fl.* Piers; *Dch.*
Peere, Pierse; *D.* Pers; *N.-Fr.* De
Piris; p.n. Peres, a Hugt. n.,
Lond. 1688
  Pers in Rot. Hund.

PEARSON. *Dch.*, *Fl.* Pierson, Pir-
son; *D.* Persson; *G.* Person;
Fr. Pierresenné; p.n. Prot. ref.,
Lond.

PEASCOD. Welsh Pyscoed. From
Dinbych-y-Pys-god, the ancient
name of Tenby

PEASE. *See* Peace

PEASGOOD. *See* Peascod

PEASLEY. A loc. n., Lancs

PEBERDY. *N.-Fr.* Pabode or Pap-
pedæ; p.n.
  Dur.. *temp.* Will. I.

PECHEY. *See* Peachey

PECK. *See* Pake

PECKETT. *See* Pickett

PECKHAM. A loc. n., Surr.

PECKOVER. A loc. n.

PEDDER, PEDDIE. *A.S.* Peada; a
p.n. (K. of Mercia, A.D. 640); *S.*,
D. Peder; *Fr.* Pède; *Fl.* Pètte;
p.n. *See* Padday

PEDDLE. From Pedwell ; a loc. n.,
Somers
PEDLAR, PEDLEY. *See* Padley
PEEBLES. A loc. n., Scotl.
PEED. *See* Pead
PEEK. *See* Peak
PEEL. A loc. n., Lancs ; Pyle, Nor-
mandy. Or *A.S.* Pil (pile, dart) ;
S. Piehl, Pihl ; *G.* Piel ; *Dch.*
Piël ; *D.* Pihl, Piell, Pille ; p.n.
PEEN, PEENY. *N.-Fr.* Peigne ; a
p.n. ; *Fr.* Pin ; a p.n.
PEEPS. *See* Pape
PEERLESS. *G.* Pieles (?) ; a p.n.
PEET. *See* Pead and Pitt
PEGG. *A.S.* Pega, Pæga ; *Dch.*
Peck, Pek ; p.n. *See* Pigg
PEGLAR. *S.* Pegelow ; a p.n.
PEILL. *See* Peel
PEIRSON. *See* Pearson
PELGRAM. *A.S.* Pilgrim, Piligrim ;
p.n. (fierce dart) ; *Fl.* Pelgrim ;
p.n.
PELHAM. A loc. n., Herts
PELL. Pael ; a loc. n., Belg. *G.*
Pell ; *Fl.* Pelle ; *Dch.* Pel ; p.n.
PELLEW. From Pelwe ; a loc. n.,
Norm.
PELLING. From Pelyn ; a loc. n.,
Cornw. Or Pellaines, Belg. *See*
Palin
PELLY. *See* Paley
PEMBER. *See* Pembury
PEMBERTON. A loc. n., Lancs
PEMBURY. A loc. n., Kent. Or
from Pehembury, Devon
PENDER. *A.S.* Pendhere ; a p.n.
(a crowned or decorated warrior)
PENDERED. *A.S.* Pendræt ; *Old
G.* Bandrad ; *Dch.* Pendraat ; a
p.n. ; *bend* (chaplet), *rad* (coun-
sellor)
PENDERGAST. *See* Prendergast
PENDERLEIGH. From Plender-
leith (?) ; a loc. n., Scotl.
PENDLEBURY. A loc. n., Lancs
PENDLETON. A loc. n., Lancs
PENDREIGH. From Pendrea ; a loc.
n., Cornw.

PENFOLD. *A.S.* Pendweald, Pen-
weald, Pineweald ; p.n. (crown
ruler)
Penvald, moneyer, K. Offa ; *D.B.*
Pancevold, a tenant in chief; Pance-
folt, under-tenant at Survey.
PENGELLY. A loc. n., Cornw.
PENGLAZE. A loc. n., Cornw.
PENKETT. From Penketh ; a loc.
n., Lancs
PENLEY. From Pendley ; a loc. n.,
Herts. Or Penly, Normandy
PENMAN, PENMAIN. From Pen-
main ; a loc. n., Monm. Or
Penmaen, S. Wales
PENN. A loc. n., Bucks, Staffs ;
Penne, France. Or *see* Paine
PENNEFEATHER. From Pontfathew;
A loc. n., Merioneth
PENNINGTON. A loc. n., Lancs
PENNISTON. From Penistone ; a
loc. n., Yorks
PENNY. *N.* Peini ; n.n. ; *N.-Fr.*
Penné ; *D.* Peine ; *Fl.* Penet ;
Dch. Pen, Penha ; *Fr.* Peigné,
Penna ; p.n. Peno, Prot. ref.,
Norw. 1622
Peny in Rot. Hund.
PENNYCOOK, PENNYCUICK. From
Penicuik ; a loc. n., Edinburgh
PENRHYN. A loc. n., Cornw., N.
Wales
PENRICE. A loc. n., S. Wales
PENROSE. A loc. n., Cornw.
PENSTONE. *See* Penniston
PENTECOST. From Pentecostes-
Castel in Normandy
Roger Pentecost in Rot. Obl. et Fin.,
temp. K. John. Or from time of
birth.
PENTELOW. From Pentlow ; a loc.
n., Ess.
PENTLAND. A loc. n., Edinburgh
PENTON. A loc. n., Hants
PENTREATH. From Pentraeth ; a
loc. n., N. Wales
PENWALL. From Penwell ; a loc.
n., Devon
PENWARNE. A loc. n., Cornw.

PEPLAR, PEPLER, PEPLOE. *See* Peplow

PEPLOW. A loc. n., Lincs, Salop

PEPPER. *A.S.* Pippa; *N.-Fr.* Pipart; *Dch.* Peper; *Fl.* Pepet, Piepers; *S.* Piper; *G.*, *D.* Pieper, Piper; p.n. (a piper)

PEPPERCORN. *Dch.* Peperkoorn; a p.n.

PEPPERDAY. *See* Peberdy

PEPPERELL. From Pepperhill; a loc. n., Salop. Or *Fr.* Piperelle; *D.B.* Piperel; a p.n. Comp. Peverel

PERCY. From Percy; a loc. n., Normandy
In Roll of Battell Abbey; tenant in chief, *D.B.*

PERFECT, PERFETT, PERFITT. *See* Parfitt

PERKINS. *Fl.* Peterkin (little Peter); p.n.

PERKIS, PERKS. *See* Parkes

PERNIE. A loc. n., France

PEROWNE. *Fr.* Peronny; a p.n. From Perronne; a loc. n., France. Or Péronne, Belg. Hugt., Lond. 1618

PERREN, PERRIN, PERRING. *N.-Fr.* Perrin; *G.* Piering; *Dch.* Perrin; p.n.
In Rot. Hund.

PERRIAM. A loc. n., Somers
De Puryham in 1327.

PERROTT. A loc. n., Wilts. Or *A.S.* Pirot; *Fr.* Perot; p.n.

PERRY. *Fr.* Perrée; *Dch.*, *D.* Perry; p.n.
Pery on the Roll of Battell Abbey; and Peret, a tenant in chief in *D.B.*

PERT. *A.S.* Pert, *beorht* (bright); a p.n.

PERTWEE. From Pertuis; a loc. n., France (a defile, narrow pass)

PESCOD. *See* Peascod

PESKETT. *See* Peascod

PESTALL, PESTELL. *Fr.*, *S.*, *Dch.* Pestel; *G.* Pessel; p.n. (a staff of office (?))

PETCH. *G.* Petsch; a p.n. *See* Patch

PETCHELL. *Fr.* Pechell; p.n. (a fishery). Or dim. of Peche

PETEL. *Fr.* Petel, Pettell; p.n.

PETERS. *D.*, *G.* Peters; *Dch.* Peters, Peeters; *Fl.* Peeters; p.n. Prot. ref., Lond. 1618

PETERSON. *S.* Pedersen; p.n. *See* Pattison

PETHERBRIDGE. From Pethybridge; a loc. n., Devon

PETHERHAM. From Petham; a loc. n., Kent

PETHERICK. A loc. n., Cornw.

PETHERIDGE. *See* Partridge

PETHICK. *See* Petherick

PETLEY. From Peterly; a loc. n., Bucks

PETO. From Poitou, Normandy. Or *Fr.* Piteaux (merciful), Pitot; p.n.
Peito in Roll of Battell Abbey.

PETRE. *See* Pate

PETT. A loc. n., Suss. Or *Dch.* Pet; a p.n. *See* Pate

PETTAR, PETTER. From Pettaugh; a loc. n., Suff. *Fr.* Petteau; a p.n. Or *see* Pate

PETTENGILL. From Portingal; an old name for a Portuguese (Lower)

PETTIFER, PETTIFORD. A loc. n., Worc.

PETTIGREW. From Pettigoe (?); a loc. n., Fermanagh

PETTIT. *Fr.* Petit; a p.n. Hugt. n., 1618

PETTY. A loc. n., Inverness. Or *see* Pettit

PEW. *See* Pugh

PEXTON. *See* Paxton

PEYTON. A loc. n., Ess. Or Pieton, Belg.

PHAIR. Gaelic; p.n. (valour)

PHANTAM, VENDOME. A loc. n., France. Or *Fl.* Vandam; a p.n. Prot. ref., Lond. 1618

PHARE. *See* Phair and Fayers

PHARO, PHAROAH. *See* Farrow

PHAYRE, PHEAR. *See* Phair

PHEASANT. From Peissant; a loc. n., Belg. Or *N.-Fr.* le Paisant; *Fr.* Paysan; p.n. (a peasant)
Peysan in Rot. Hund.

PHELPS, PHIBBS. *See* Phillips

PHILBRICK. *A.S.* Fulbric (very bright); a p.n.

PHILCOX. Dimin. of Philip

PHILLIMORE. From Fullamore; a loc. n., Devon. Or *A.S.* Filmær, Filimar; *Old G.* Filomor; p.n.; *N. fylmærr* (full of fame)
Wm. Fylymore, of Dursley, 1460, will proved 1491. The will of Henry Fylymore, of Wickwar, dated 1546, and proved at Glost., 1562, is endorsed Henry Fynymore. In the registers of Cam, Glost., from 1640 to 1680, Phillimore and Phinimore are used interchangeably.

PHILLIPS. *N.* Philippus; *N.-Fr.* Fitz Philip; *Dch.* Philipps, Philipsen; *Fl.* Phlups; *S.* Philp; p.n. Prot. ref., Lond. 1618

PHILPOTT. Dimin. of Phillip

PHIPPS, PHIPSON. *See* Phillips

PHIZACKERLEY. *See* Fasacklea

PHYSICK. From Figeac; a loc. n., France. Or *G.* Fiescheck, Fietzek; p.n. Or *see* Fisk

PICARD. *N.-Fr.* Picard; *Fl.* Pickert; *Dch.* Piekart (strong fighter); p.n. Hugt. n., Lond. 1621. *See* Peake

PICKEL. *A.S.* Püchel; *N.-Fr.* Pigole; *G.* Pickel; p.n. Or from Pickhill; a loc. n., Yorks. *See* Peake
Pikel in Rot. Hund.

PICKEN. The fam. n. of Pic. Or *N.-Fr.* Picon; a p.n.

PICKERING. A loc. n., Yorks

PICKESS. *See* Peake

PICKETT. *A.S.* Picced; *Fr.* Piquet; *Dch.* Piket; *N.-Fr.* Picot; p.n. *See* Pigott

PICKFORD, PICKFORTH. *See* Pitchford

PICKLES. *See* Pickel

PICKUP. A loc. n., Lancs

PICKWICK. A loc. n., Wilts

PICTHALL. A loc. n. Or *A.S.* Pecthœth, Pictel, Picthad; p.n. (war Pict)

PICTHORN. A loc. n., Salop

PICTON. A loc. n., Flint, Yorks

PIDCOCK. From Pittcott (?); a loc. n., Somers

PIDDING. *A.S.* fam. n. From Peada; *D.* Pied; p.n. *See* Pedder

PIDDINGTON. A loc. n., Northants

PIDGEON. *N.-Fr.* Pichon; *Fr.* Pigeon; p.n.
Pigun in Rot. Hund.

PIDWELL. From Piddle; a loc. n., Worc.

PIERSON. *See* Pearson

PIGG. *A.S.* Pic (a slasher), *bichen* (to slash). *See* Peak and Pegg

PIGGIN. *See* Pidgeon

PIGONY. From Picquigny; a loc. n. near Amiens, France. *Fr.* Pichonnier, Pigné, Pigny; p.n.

PIGOTT. *Fr.* Pegeaud, Pegot, Pichot, Picot; *G.* Pigotta; *D.B.* Picot, Pecoe; p.n. *See* Peake or Bygot
Reginald Pigot held lands in Norf. *temp.* K. John. Hugt. n., Lond. 1685.

PIKE. *See* Peake

PIKESLEY. From Pickersleigh; a loc. n., Worcest. Or Pigsley, Devon

PILBOROUGH. From Pulborough; a loc. n., Surr.

PILCH. *S.* Piltz; *G.* Pils, Pilz; p.n.; *A.S. pylce* (a fur garment). Or dim. of Pil

PILE. *See* Peel

PILGRIM. *See* Pelgram

PILKINGTON. A loc. n., Lancs

PILL. A loc. n., Cornw., Glost., Somers. Or *see* Peel

PILLANS. *Fl.* Pilaen; *Fr.* Pillon; p.n. *See* Peel

PILLINGER. From Pillinge; a loc. n., Beds

PILLOW. From Pilhough; a loc. n., Derbysh. Or *N.-Fr.* Pilot; a p.n. Pilloe, a Hugt. n., Colchester, 1622

PILSON. *S.* Pylsson; a p.n. *See* Peel. Pilison, Fl. ref., Lond. 1618

PILTON. A loc. n., Devon, Northants, Rutland, Somers

PIM. *A.S.* Pymma; *G.* Pimmer; p.n. (speckled (?))

PINCH. From Binche (?); a loc. n., Belg. Or dim. of Pinn. *Dch.* Pink, Pinks, Pinkse; *G.* Pintsch

PINCHARD. *Fr.* Pinchart; *Fl.* Pinchaert; p.n. From Pinchardon or Punchardon; loc. n., Normandy

In Roll of Battell Abbey.

PINCHBACK, PINCHBECK. A loc. n., Lincs

PINCHEN. *Fl.* Pingeon, Pinson; *N.-Fr.* Pinçon (finch); *D.B.* Pinc'u'n, Pinchengi; p.n. Pinchon, a Hugt. n., 1622

PINCHES. *G.* Pincus, Pinkas; p.n. *See* Pinch

PINCHING. *See* Pinchen

PINCOMBE. From Pinnacombe; a loc. n., Devon. Or Bincom, Belg.

PINCOTT. *See* Penkett

PINDAR, PINDER. *G.* Pinder; *N.-Fr.* le Pinder; *Fl.* Pinter; p.n. *See* Pender

PINE. *G.* Pein; a p.n. *See* Payne

PINHEY. A loc. n. (?). *See* Paine

PINK. *See* Pinnock or Pinch

PINKERTON. From Pontcardon (?); a loc. n., Norm.

PINKHAM. *See* Pincombe

PINKNEY. A loc. n., Northants, Wilts

PINN. A loc. n., Devon. Or *Fr.* Pin; *G.* Pinn; *D.B.* Pin; p.n. *See* Peen

PINNEGAR. *A.S.* Pinegear = Winegear; *G.* Pinger; p.n. (friendly spear)

PINNER. A loc. n., Middlx. Or *Fr.* Pineur; a p.n. (a painter). Prot. ref., Norwich, 1622

PINNION. From Pignan; a loc. n. in France. *Fl.* Pingeon, Pinon; p.n. Or *see* Binyon

PINNOCK. A loc. n., Glost.

PINSENT, PINSUN. Pinston; a loc. n., Devon. Or *see* Pinchen

PIPE. A loc. n., Heref., Staffs. Or *Fr.* Pipe; a p.n.

PIPER. *See* Pepper

PIPPET. *Fl.* Pipart; a p.n. (strong piper)

PITCAIRN. A loc. n., Perth

PITCHER. *N.-Fr.* Pichere; a p.n.

PITCHES. *See* Peache

PITCHFORD. A loc. n., Salop

PITE. *See* Pitt and Pyatt

PITFIELD. From Petiville; a loc. n., Norm.

PITKIN. Dimin. of Peterkin

PITMAN. *Dch.* Piderman; *G.* Pitschmann; p.n.

Piteman in Rot. Hund.

PITT. A loc. n., Cornw., Devon. Or *Dch.* Piet, Pitt; *Fr.* Pitte; p.n. *See* Pead

PITTOCK. *See* Pidcock

PITTY. *See* Pettit

PIXEL. From Pickshill; a loc. n., Somers. Or Picts-hill, Yorks

PIXLEY. A loc. n., Dur., Heref.

PIZEY, PIZZEY. *G.* Peysey; a p.n. Or *see* Poysey

PLACE, PLAICE. Le Places; loc. n., Norm. *D.* Plees; *G.* Pless; *Fl.* Pleis; *Dch.* Ples; *Fr.* Place; p.n.

PLAMPIN. *Fl.* Blampain; a p.n.

PLANE. From Pleine; a loc. n., Norm. Or *G.* Plener; *D.B.* Pleines; p.n.

PLANK. From le Planquay; a loc. n., Norm. Or *D.* Planck; *Dch.*, *Fl.* Plank; *Fr.* Planche, Planque; p.n. Prot. ref., Dover, 1622

PLANT. *N.-Fr.* De la Plante; a p.n.

PLANTIN. *Dch.* Planten; a p.n.

PLASTOW. From Plaistow; a loc. n., Derbysh., Ess., Kent, Suss.

PLATT. From Plathe; a loc. n., Germ. (a plain). Or *A.S.* Blæd (glory); *G.* Platt; *D., S.* Plaate; *Dch.* Platte; p.n.

PLATTEN. *D., S.* Platen; *Fl.* Plétain, Plettinck; p.n.; fam. n.

PLAW. *See* Plow

PLAYER. *A.S.* Pleghere; *Dch.* Plieger; *Fr.* Plehiers; p.n. (war player)

PLAYFAIR. *G.* Plewa; a p.n.

PLAYFORD. A loc. n., Suff.

PLAYLE. *G.* Pleul; p.n.

PLEASANCE, PLEASANTS. *N.-Fr.* Plaisance; a p.n.

PLEDGER. *See* Player

PLENTY. *G.* Plantier; a p.n.

PLEWS. *Fl.* Pluys; p.n. *See* Plow

PLIMPTON. From Plympton; a loc. n., Devon

PLIMSAUL, PLIMSOLL. From Plemstall or Plemonstall; a loc. n., Ches.

PLOW. From Plau; a loc. n., Germ. Or *D.* Plógr, Ploug; *G.* Plew, Pluge, Plohs; *Dch.* Ploos; *Fl.* Pluys; p.n.

PLOWDEN. A loc. n., Salop

PLOWMAN. *S.* Ploman; p.n.

PLOWRIGHT. From Plougouvert (?); a loc. n., Norm.

PLUCKROSE. *D.* Plockross; a p.n.

PLUM, PLUMB. *D., Fl.* Plum; *N.-Fr.* Plumme; p.n.

PLUMBRIDGE. A loc. n., Kent

PLUME. *See* Plum

PLUMMER. *N.-Fr.* le Plumer, Plumier; p.n. (plume maker). Hugt. n., Lond. 1682

PLUMPTRE. A loc. n., Notts
Originally De Clerfai, from Clarfait, near Avesnes, Fland. Afterwards Fitz William of Plumtre.

PLUMSTEAD. A loc. n., Norf.

PLUNKETT. From Plouquenat, near Rennes, Bretagne. *N.-Fr.* De Plugenet; a p.n.

PLYMSELL. *See* Plimsaul

POATE. *Dch., Fl.* Poot; a p.n.

POBJOY. *See* Popjoy

POCHIN. *N.-Fr.* Pocin; a p.n.

POCKETT. *Fr.* Pauchet, Pochet; p.n. Dim. of Pook

POCKLINGTON. A loc. n., Yorks

POCOCK. *D.* Pock; *G.* Pocha; p.n. *See* Pook. Dim.

PODD. *See* Paddy

PODGER. Welsh Ap Odger; a p.n.

PODMORE. A loc. n., Staffs

POGSON. *See* Pook

POINTER. *Fr.* Pointier; a p.n. (a maker of points). Or *see* Pont

POINTIN. *See* Poynton

POINTS. From Pontoise (?); a loc. n., Norm.

Ponz, under.tenant in *D.B.* Nicholas Puintz held land in Glost. *temp.* K. John.

POLDEN. A loc. n., Somers

POLE. A loc. n., Devon. Also from St Pol de Leon; a loc. n., Norm.; de la Pole. Or *see* Paull

POLES. *See* Paul

POLEY. *D.* Pol, Poli; *Fr.* Pollet; p.n. *See* Paul

POLGLAZE. A loc. n., Cornw.

POLHILL. A loc. n.

POLKINGHORNE. A loc. n., Cornw.

POLL. *See* Pole

POLLARD. *A.S.* Boldheard (?) (bold, strong); *Fl.* Pollaert; *Fr.* Pollard; p.n. *See* Bollard
Gaufrid Pollard on Rot. Obl. et Fin., *temp.* K. John. Also a Hugt. n., Lond. 1618.

POLLITT. *Fr.* Polet, Pollet; *Dch.* Politz; p.n. *See* Paul. A Hugt. n.

POLLOCK. A loc. n., Renfrew. Or *Dch.* Polak; a p.n. *See* Paul

POLLY. *Fr.* Pollet; *Fl.* Polly; *D.* Poli; p.n. *See* Paul

POLLYN. *See* Paul

POLSUE. Cornish p.n.

POLWARTH. A loc. n., Berwick

POLWHELE. A loc. n., Cornw. (*D.B.* Polhel)

POMFREY. A loc. corruption of Pontefract; a loc. n., Yorks. Or *see* Pumphrey

POND. From Pont; a loc. n., Belg., Cornw. *Dch.* Pont; a p.n. Prot. ref., Lond. 1618

PONDER. *N.-Fr.* le Pondere; *D.B.* Ponther; *G.* Punde; p.n.

PONSFORD. A loc. n., Devon. Or Pontesford, Salop

PONSONBY. A loc. n., Cumb.

PONT. *See* Pond

PONTIFEX. *D.* Pontavice; a p.n.

PONTING. *N.-Fr.* De Pontin; a p.n.

PONTON. A loc. n., Lincs

POOK. From Poucques; a loc. n., Fland. Or *N.* Púki (Puck); *D.* Pogge; *A.S.* Pucca, Puch; *G.* Puche; *S.* Puke; p.n. Also a contraction of Pollock

POOLE. A freq. loc. n., Dorset, Yorks, etc. From *N. Pollr*; *B. pwl* (a pool). Or *see* Paul. Poule, a Prot. ref., Lond. 1621

POORE. From Puers (?); a loc. n., Belg. *G.* Pur; *D.B.* Pur; p.n.
John le Poer held lands in Yorks, *temp.* K. John, 1201.

POOS. *A.S.* Bos; *Dch.* Poesse; *Fl.* Pues; p.n. (a stall)

POPE. *N.* Papar; *A.S.* Papo; *F.* Poppe; *D.* Pop; *S.* Pape; *Fl.* Papy, Poppin; *Dch.* Paap, Pop; *G.* Pape, Papke, Poppe, Poper; p.n. (father)
Poppe was the name of a Duke of Friesland, slain in battle by Charles Martel, A.D. 734.

POPHAM. A loc. n., Devon, Hants

POPJOY. *Fl.* Papegaey; a p.n.; *G. papagei* (a parrot)

POPKIN. *See* Pope. Dimin.

POPLE, POPPLE. A loc. n., Belg. *Dch.* Poppel; a p.n.

POPPLETON. A loc. n., Yorks

POPPY. *See* Pope

PORCHER. *N.-Fr.*; p.n. (swine-herd)

PORLEY. *See* Pawley

PORT. Portes; a loc. n., Norm. *Fr.*, *G.* Port; *Dch.* Porth, Porte; p.n.

PORTAL. *Fr.*; p.n. Hugt. n., Lond. 1687

PORTEOUS. From Portways (?); a loc. n., Oxf.

PORTER. *Dch.* Poorter; *Fr.* Portier; p.n. (a door-keeper). Hugt. n., Norwich, 1622
Ad Porta', 1327.

PORTLOCK. From Porlock; a loc. n., Somers

PORTWAY. A loc. n., Worcest.

PORTWINE. *Fr.* Potvin (good-will). Or *A.S.* Peohtwine (Pict-friend); *Dch.* Portheine; p.n.

POSEY. *Fr.* Pousset; a p.n.

POSSELT. *See* Postlethwaite

POSTEL, POSTLE. *N.-Fr.*; p.n.; *petit poteau* (post, stake)
In Rot. Hund.

POSTLETHWAITE. A loc. n. A clearing enclosed with stakes. *D.* Poselt; a p.n.

POSTON. A loc. n., Heref., Salop

POTCHETT. *See* Pockett

POTHECARY. From Apothecary; the occupation
Laurencius Ypotecarius occurs among the tenants of Ipswich Priory in the thirteenth century.

POTT. *Fl.*, *Dch.* Pot; *S.* Pott; p.n. Prot. ref., Lond. 1618. *See* Body

POTTAGE. From Potheridge; a loc. n., Devon

POTTER. *Dch.* Potter, Potters; *Fr.* Potier, Pottier; p.n. (a potter)
Le Potere in Rot. Hund.

POTTINGER. Fam. n. of Pott. *Dch.* Pottinga; a p.n.

POTTON. From Potterne; a loc. n., Wilts

POTTOW. *Fr.* Poteau, Pottaux; p.n. (a post)

POTTS, POTTES. A loc. n., Belg. *Dch.*, *Fl.*; p.n. *See* Pott

POULTER. *G.* Polte; *Fr.* Poultier; p.n. (a poulterer). Hugt. n., Canterbury, Jas. I.
Le Poleter in Rot. Hund.

POULTNEY. A loc. n., Leics. A hamlet of Misterton
  Sir John de Poultney, knight, Lord Mayor of London, bur. St Paul's, 1349.
POULTON. A loc. n., Glost., Kent, Lancs
POUNCEBY. *See* Ponsonby
POUND. A loc. n., Devon
POUNTNEY. A loc. n., Suff.
POWELL. Welsh ab Howell ; *Fr.* Puel ; a p.n. Hugt. n., Lond. 1618
POWER. *Fr.* Pouyer ; a p.n. (grand). *See* Poore
POWLEY. *See* Paul
POWNALL. A loc. n., Ches.
POYNINGS. A loc. n., Surr.
POYNTER. *See* Pointer
POYNTON. A loc. n., Lincs
POYSER. *A.S.* Boso, Busa, Pusa (stall keeper) ; *G.* Peiser, Peuser ; *Fl.* Pizar ; *Dch.* Peyser ; p.n.
POYSEY. From Poissy ; a loc. n., Norm. Hugt. n., Lond. 1681
PRAHL, PRALL. *D.*, *G.*, *Dch.* ; p.n. (bounce, brag). Or Prawle ; a loc. n., Devon
PRAILL. From Presles ; a loc. n., Belg. *Dch.* Prell ; a p.n.
PRATT. A loc. n., France. *N.-Fr.* Du Prat ; *Fr.* Du Pré (meadow), Prat ; *Fl.* Praet. A Hugt. n., Lond. 1687
PRECIOUS. *Dch.* Preussiche (?) ; a p.n. (Prussian)
PREDAM. *Fr.* Predhom ; a p.n. *See* Prodham
PREDDY, PREEDY. *See* Priddy
PREESE. A loc. n., Lancs. Or *see* Price
PRENDERGAST. A loc. n., Pembroke
PRENTICE, PRENTIS. *A.S.* Prentsa or Prentisa (?) ; a p.n. *See* Prince
PRESCOTT. A loc. n., Devon, Lancs, Salop
PRESENT. *Fr.* Présent ; a p.n.
PRESLAND. *Dch.* ; loc. and p.n.

PRESLEY. *See* Priestley
PRESOW. *Fr.* Preseau ; a p.n. Or Presall ; a loc. n., Lancs. Bressoux, Belg.
PRESS. *G.* ; p.n. Or *see* Preece
PRESSEY. From Precy ; a loc. n., France
PREST. *See* Priest
PRESTIGE. From Prestwich ; a loc. n., Lancs
PRESTON. A loc. n., Kent, Lancs, Mid-Lothian, etc.
PRETTEJOHN. *Fr.* Petitjean ; a p.n.
PRETTY. *See* Priddy
PRETYMAN. *A.S.* Beorhtman, Brihtman ; *G.* Brettman ; p.n. (illustrious man)
PREVOST. *Dch.* Prevost ; *Fr.* Prévost ; p.n. (a provost). A Hugt. n., Rye, 1621
PREWETT. *Fr.* Prevet ; a p.n.
PRICE. Welsh Ap Rhys ; a p.n. Prise ; a loc. n., Yorks. Preece, Denbigh
  Roger Preise in Rot. Obl. et Fin., *temp.* K. John.
PRICKETT. *See* Prichard
PRIDDEN. From Priding ; a loc. n., Glost. Welsh Pryddyn (?)
PRIDDY. A loc. n., Somers
PRIDHAM. *See* Predham
PRIDMORE. *A.S.* Beorhtmær (illustrious famous) ; *D.* Bredmore ; p.n.
PRIEST. *A.S.* Preost ; *N.* Prestr ; *Fl.* Prist ; p.n. From the office
PRIESTLEY. From Priestcliffe (?) ; a loc. n., Derbysh.
PRIGG. *A.S.* Bric, Bright ; *Fl.* Prick ; a p.n. (illustrious)
PRIGGENS. *Dch.* Pricken ; a p.n. ; fam. n.
PRIKE. *See* Prigg
PRIM, PRIME. *A.S.* Brým ; *Dch.* Priem ; *D.* Prime ; p.n. (the sea). Hugt. n., Lond. 1618
PRIMROSE. A loc. n., Fife
PRINCE. *Fr.*, *Fl.* Prins ; *Dch.* Prince, Prins ; *G.* Prinz ; p.n. Hugt. n., Lond. 1618. *See* official names

PRING. *N.* Brynki, from Brynjólfr (mailed Jólfr); *G.* Bring; *Dch.* Brink; p.n.

PRINGLE. From Hop-Pringle (?); a loc. n., Scotl. Pringel, a Prot. ref., Lond. 1687

PRINSEP. From Brinsop; a loc. n., Heref. Or Princethorpe; a loc. n., Devon

PRIOR, PRYER. *Fl.* Preier; *Fr.* Prier; *D.* Prior; p.n. (prior, priest)

PRITCHARD. Welsh Ap-Richard

PRITTY. *See* Priddy

PROBART, PROBERT. Welsh Ap-Robert; a p.n.

PROBY, PROBYN. Welsh Ap-Robin

PROCTER. *Lat.* Procurator (an apparitor); *Fr.* Procureur; a p.n.

PRODGERS. Welsh, Ap-Rodgers

PRODHAM. *Fr.* Prodhomme; a p.n. (gallant, brave)

PROFFITT. *G.* Proft, Prophet; *Fr.* Profit; p.n. Or *see* Proudfoot (?)

PROPERT. *See* Probert

PROSSER. *G* Preusser; a p.n.

PROTHEROE. *See* Prydderch

PROUD. *N.* Pruði; *Fr.* Praud; *A.S.* Pruð; p.n.

PROUDFOOT. *N.* Pruði-fótr; *G.* Prowit (stately foot); a n.n.

PROUDHAM. *Fr.* Prudhomme; a p.n. *See* Prodham

PROUDLOVE. *Fr.* Prioleau (?). A Hugt. n.

PROUT. *See* Proud

PROWSE. A loc. n., Devon. Or *G.* Praus; *Dch.* Prousse; p.n.

PRUDAMES. *See* Proudham

PRUDENCE. *Fr.* Prudans; a p.n. (honest)

PRUDHOE. A loc. n., Dur., Northbd.

PRUDHOM. *Fr.* Prudhomme; a p.n. (a skilful man)

PRUE. *Fr.* Preux; a p.n. (brave). Hugt. n., Lond. 1687

PRUEN. *A.S.* Brun, Bryne, Prun (brown); *Dch.* Preün, Prooijen; p.n.

PRUST. *Fl.* Proust; a p.n. *See* Prevost

PRY. A loc. n., Belg. Prey, Norm.

PRYDDERCH, PRYTHERCH. Welsh Ap-Rhydderch, the son of Roderick (the red). *See* Brodrick

PRYKE. *See* Prigg

PUCKETT. *G.* Puchat; a p.n. *See* Pook. Dim.

PUCKEY. From Puchay; a loc. n., Norm. Or *see* Pook

PUCKLE. *G.* Puchelt; *Fl.* Puckle; p.n. (humped (?)). Or dim. of Puck

PUCKRIDGE. A loc. n., Herts

PUDDEFOOT, PUDDEPHATT. From Puddephats; a loc. n., Herts

PUDDICOMBE. From Pudcombe; a loc. n., Devon

PUDNEY. *See* Putney

PUGH. From the Welsh Ap-Hugh (son of Hugh). Or *A.S.* Puh, Puch; p.n. *See* Pook

PUGSLEY. From Puxley; a loc. n., Northants

PULESTON. A loc. n., Heref.

PULFORD. From Pulsford; a loc. n., Devon

PULHAM. A loc. n., Devon, Norf.

PULL. A loc. n., Belg.

De la Pulle in Rot. Obl. et Fin.

PULLBROOK. From Polebrook; a loc. n., Northants. Or Pullabrook, Devon

PULLEIN, PULLYN. *Fr.* Poullain; a p.n. *See* Paul. A Hugt. n., Lond. 1622

PULLEY. From Pullay; a loc. n., Norm. Or *Fr.* Poullet; a p.n.

PULLUM. *See* Pulham

PULVER. *See* Bulwer

PUMFRIT. *See* Pomfrey

PUMPHREY. From the Welsh Ap-Humphrey (?). Or *see* Pomfrey

PUNCH. *N.-Fr.* Pointz, Ponce, Punce; p.n. Or Irish corruption of Ponsonby

PUNCHARD. *Fr.* Ponchaut; a p.n. *See* Pinchard

PUNG. *Dch.* Puncke; a p.n. *A.S.* *pung* (a purse)

PUNNETT. *G.* Pundt; a p.n.

PUNSHON. *Fr.* Ponchon; a p.n.
Puncin in Rot. Obl. et Fin.

PUNT. *A.S.* Punt; *G.* Pundt; p.n.; *pund* (a mole). *See* Pond

PUNTER. *G.* Punte; a p.n.

PURBROOK. A loc. n., Hants

PURCELL. *N.-Fr.* Pourcel; a p.n. (little pig)
Radulph Purcel held land in Bucks, *temp.* K. John.

PURCHAS. *N.-Fr.* Perahgoz (?) (bear-Goth); *Fr.* Pourchez; a p.n. (a poor knight)
Andreas Purchaz held land in Kent, *temp.* K. John.

PURDAY, PURDEY, PURDIE, PURDUE, PURDY. *See* Pardoe

PURDON. From Purton; a loc. n., Glost., Wilts. Or Pirton, Herts, Staffs., Worcest.

PURFITT. *See* Perfitt

PURGOLD. *A.S.* Burgweald, Burwold; p.n. (the castle ruler)

PURITAN. From Puriton; a loc. n., Somers

PURKHAM. From Purcombe; a loc. n., Devon

PURKIS. *See* Purchas or Perkis

PURR. *A.S.* Bur; *G.* Pur; p.n. *See* Poore

PURRIER. *A.S.* Burhicher (secure warrior). Or *Fr.* Perrier; a p.n. (a quarryman (?))

PURSER. *Fr.* Perseau; a p.n. *See* Purss

PURSLEY. *See* Purslow

PURSLOW. A loc. n., Salop

PURSS. *G.* Pursche; a p.n. (sound). Dim. of Pur

PURTON. A loc. n., Glost.

PURVES, PURVIS. A loc. n., Berwick. Pervyse; a loc. n., Flanders

PUSEY. A loc. n., Berks

PUTLEY. From Putloe; a loc. n., Glost.

PUTNAM. From Puttenham; a loc. n., Herts, Surr.

PUTNEY. A loc. n., Surr.

PUTT. A loc. n., Belg. Or *A.S.* Putta; *G.* Puth; *Dch.* Put; p.n. *See* Pott

PUTTERILL. *Fr.* Poutrel (?); a p.n. (a beam); or a loc. n.

PUTTOCK. *A.S.* Puttoc; *G.* Puttke; p.n. Dim. of Putt

PUXON. From Puxton; a loc. n., Somers, Worcest.

PYATT. *See* Pyett

PYBUS. *Dch.* Pijpers; a p.n.; fam. n. *See* Pepper

PYE. From Pois (?); a loc. n., Belg. Or *D.* Pii; *Fl.* Peys, Pye; *G.* Poyer; p.n.

PYEMONT. *Fr.* Pimont; a p.n.

PYETT. *A.S.* Pyht, Peoht (Pict); *Fl.* Piette; p.n.

PYGALL. *G.* Biegal; *Dch.* Biegel; p.n.

PYKE. *Fl.* Pycke; a p.n. *See* Peak

PYLE. A loc. n., Norm. *See* Peel

PYM. *See* Pim

PYMAN. *See* Pyemont

PYMAR, PYMER. From Pyemoor; a loc. n., Camb.

PYNE. *See* Paine

PYTCHES. *See* Peake

PYWELL. From Bywell; a loc. n., Northbd.

Q

QUADLING, QUODLING. Dimin. of *D.* Quaade; a p.n. *See* Wadd

QUAIE. *Fr.*; p.n. Or Irish M'Qua

QUAIL. A Manx contraction of the Irish MacPhail (Paul's son). Or *A.S.* Wealh; *N.-Fr.* Cuala (a stranger); *G.* Quiel; *D.* Quehl; p.n.

QUAIN. *A.S.* Cwen (an inhabitant of Quenland, a vandal); *Fr.* Quenne; *Dch.* Quien; p.n. Or Irish M'Queen

QUAINTANCE. *Fl.* Quintins; a p.n.

QUALTER. From M'Walter

QUANT. *A.S.* Wand, Want; *Dch.* Kwant; *G.* Quandt; p.n. (Wend). Prot. ref., Lond. 1618

QUANTOCK. A loc. n., Somers

QUANTRELL. *See* Cantrell

QUARMAN, QUARMANE. *A.S.* Wærman; *Fr.* Querment; p.n.; *war* (cautious)

QUARMBY. A loc. n., Yorks

QUARRELLE. *See* Carrell

QUARRINGTON. A loc. n., Dur., Lincs

QUARRY. *A.S.* Cwara; *Fr.* Quarré; a p.n. (wary). Or Scotch M'Quarrie

QUARTERMAIN. *A.S.* Weardman; *Fr.* Quatremains; p.n. (guardman)

In Oxon, Rot. Obl. et Fin.

QUARTLEY. A loc. n., Devon

QUASH. *A.S.* Waso, Wassa; *G.* Quass; p.n. (waterman (?))

QUAY. *See* Quaie

QUAYLE. *See* Quail

QUECKETT. A loc. n., Wilts. Or *A.S.* Wigheard (war firm); *G.* Quickert; a p.n.

QUELCH. *See* Welch

QUENBY. A loc. n., Leics

QUESTED. From Quenstadt; a *G.* loc. and p.n.

QUICK. A loc. n., Yorks. Or *A.S.* Cwic; *Fr.* Guiche; *Old Fr.* Guige; *Fl.* Kwick; *S.* Qvick; *Dch.* Kuijk; *G.* Quicker; p.n. (active)

QUIGLEY. From Quedgeley; a loc. n., Glost. Or *Old G.* Wigilo; *A.S.* Wigelin. Dim. of Wig

QUILLAN. From the Irish *cuileann* (holly)

QUILTY. From the Irish *coillte* (woods)

QUINBY. *See* Quenby

QUINCEY. From Quincé; a loc. n., Maine

Quinci in Roll of Battell Abbey. De Quency, Leics, *temp.* K. John.

QUINN. A loc. n., Killaloe, Ireland. Also M'Quin, from the Irish *Con* (the descendant of Con)

QUINNEY. From Queney; a loc. n., Camb. Or Irish M'Quiney; a p.n.

QUINTOCK. *See* Quantock

QUINTON. A loc. n., Glost., Northants, Warw., Worcest.

QUIRK. A Manx contraction of the Irish MacCuirc (Cork's son); a p.n.; *coirce* (oats)

QUIXLEY. *See* Quigley

R

RABAN. *N.-Fr.* De Rabayne. Or *A.S.* Hraban; = *ram* (strong); *Fr.* Raban, Raband; *Dch.* Rabanus; p.n.

RABBETH, RABETT. *A.S.* Radbod; *G.* Rabat; *Dch.* Rappart; p.n. (counsel messenger)

RABBIDGE. *A.S.* Raba; *G.* Rabisch; *N.-Fr.* De Rabes, Rabace; p.n.

RABBITS. D. Rabitz; a p.n. Also a corruption of Roberts. *See* above

RABEY, RABY. From Raby; a loc. n., Ches., Norm. Or Rebaix, Belg.

RABLEY. A loc. n., Herts

RACE. *See* Reece

RACKETT. *See* Reckett

RACKHAM. A loc. n., Suss.

RACKLEY. A loc. n.

RACKSTRAW, RACKSTRAY. *D.* Rockstroh; a p.n.

RADCLIFFE. A loc., n. Notts

RADFORD. A loc. n., Devon, Notts

RADLEY. A loc. n., Notts, Staffs

RADMALL. From Rathmell; a loc. n., Yorks

RADMORE. From Rathmore; a loc. n., Killarney. Redmire, Yorks. Or *A.S.* Rædmær, Rademar; p.n. (famous counsellor)

RADNALL. From Rednal; a loc. n., Worcest.

RADWILL. *A.S.* Rædwealh; a p.n. (a foreign counsellor)

RAE. *See* Ray

RAEBURN. A loc. n., Dumfries

RAFFE. *See* Rolf

RAFFETY. From the Irish O'Rafferty; a p.n.

RAFFLES. *Fl.* Raphaels; a p.n.

RAGG. *N.* Ragi (a king); *A.S.* Rag, Wraca; *D.* Rager; *Dch.* Rack; p.n. (an exile)

RAGGETT. *N.-Fr.* Ragot; *G.* Rackette; p.n. Dim. of Ragg

RAIKES. A loc. n., Lincs

RAILTON. *See* Relton

RAIN. *N.* Hreinn (reindeer); *A.S.* Wrenna; *Fr.* Raine, Reine; *G.* Renn; p.n. *See* Wren

RAINBIRD. *A.S.* Regenbeort, Regenbert (very bright); *G.* Reinbardt; *N.-Fr.* Reinbert; p.n.

RAINBOW. *A.S.* Regenbod; *G.* Reinboth; *N.-Fr.* Rainbaut; p.n. (chief messenger)

RAINEY. A loc. n., France

RAINHAM. A loc. n., Ess.

RAINS, RAINES. A loc. n., Ess.

RAINSFORD. From Rainford; a loc. n., Lancs

RAIT. A loc. n., Perth

RAITHBY. A loc. n., Lincs

RAKE. A loc. n., Devon

RALEIGH. From Rayleigh; a loc. n., Ess. Or *Fr.* Ralet; a p.n.

RALF. *See* Rolfe

RAMAGE. *D.* Rames; *Fl.* Ramuz; p.n. *A.S.* Hranig(?) (a reindeer). Dim. of Hran

RAMM. *N.* Ramr; n.n. (strong); *D.B.* Ram; *D.*, *G.* Ramm; p.n. Rame, Hugt. n., Lond. 1687

RAMPLEN. *Fr.* Rampillon; a p.n.

RAMSAY. A loc. n., Ess., I. of Man, S. Wales

RAMSBOTHAM, RAMSBOTTOM. A loc. n., Lancs. Comp. *Fl.* Ransbotyn; a p.n.

RAMSDEN. A loc. n., Ess., Herts, Oxf.

RAMSHAW. A loc. n., Dur., Northbd.

RAMSHAY. *See* Ramshaw

RAMSTEAD. *D.* Ramstad; a loc. and p.n.

RAMYELL, RANYELL. *N.* Rafnkell; *A.S.* Ramcytel, Ramechil; *Fr.* Ramioul (?); p.n. (Ketel the strong)

RAND. A loc. n., Lincs. Or *A.S.*, *D.* Rand; a p.n. (a shield)

RANDALL. *A.S.* Rendel; *D.*, *G.* Randel; a p.n.; *N.* Röndolfr (shield-wolf). *See* Rendell

RANDOLF. *See* Randulph

RANDS. From Raunds; a loc. n., Northants. Or fam. n. of Rand

RANDSFORD. *See* Rainsford

RANDULPH. *D.* Randulff; *G.*, *S.* Randel; *A.S.* Randolf, Randulf, Randwuff; p.n. (shield-wolf)

RANGER. *A.S.* Regengar; *N.-Fr.* Reignier; *D.* Rannje; p.n. (chief spear)

RANKIN. A loc. n. Scotl. Or *N.-Fr.* Roncin; *Fl.* Renkin; p.n. Dim. of Renn

RANNALS. *See* Reynolds

RANNEY. From Renaix; a loc. n., Fland. *N.* Hrani (a blusterer); *Fr.* René; p.n. Renie, Hugt. n., Lond. 1688

RANSDALE. From Ravensdale (Raunsdale); a loc. n., Derbysh.

RANSLEY. From Ramsley; a loc. n., Devon

RANSOME, RANSON. *N.-Fr.* Rançon; a p.n. (ransomed)

RANSTEAD. A loc. n.

RANT. *Dch.*; p.n. *See* Rand

RANTELL. *See* Randall

RANTON. A loc. n., Staffs

RAPER. *See* Rope

RAPKIN. *G.* Rappke; a p.n. Dimin. of Rapp

RAPP. *A.S.* Raba; *D.*, *Dch.*, *G.* Rapp; *Fl.* Rappe; p.n. (strong). Hugt. n., Lond. 1681

RAPLEY. *Fr.* Raparlier (?); a p.n.
RAPPARD. *See* Rabbeth
RAPSON. *See* Rapp
RARP. *See* Rapp
RASH. *D.* Rask; *Fl.* Rasse; *G.* Rasch; p.n. Dim. of *A.S.* Ras; a p.n. (rash)
RASHLEIGH. A loc. n., Devon
RASP. *A.S.* Rasbeort, Raspert (illustrious assailant); *G.* Rasper; p.n.
RASTALL. From Rusthall (?); a loc. n., Kent
    W. Rastel in Rot. Obl. et Fin.
RATHWELL. *See* Rothwell or Radwill
RATTEE. *A.S.* Rad, Ratho (counsel); *D.* Rathje; *G.* Ratay, Rathay; *Dch.* Ratté; p.n.
RATTRAY. A loc. n., Aberdeensh.
RATTY. An Irish corruption of Ratcliffe. Or *A.S.* Ræd, Rat, Ratho; p.n. (counsel)
RAVEN. *N.* Hræfn; *S.* Ravn; *D.* Rafn, Raun; *Dch.* Raven; *A.S.* Ræfen, Rauen; p.n. (a raven)
RAVENHILL. From Ravenel; a loc. n., Norm.
RAVENSCLIFFE. A loc. n., Staffs
RAVENSCOURT. A loc. n.
RAVENSCROFT. A loc. n., Ches.
RAVENSWORTH. A loc. n., Dur.
RAVEY. *Fr.* Revet; a p.n. *See* Rivett
RAW. *A.S.* Raue, Ræf; p.n. (raven); *D.*, *Fl.*, *G.* Rau; p.n. *See* Roe, Rowe
RAWCLIFF. A loc. n., Yorks, Lancs
RAWDON. A loc. n., Yorks
RAWKINS. *G.*, *Dch.* Rauch, Raucke; p.n. Dim. of Raw
RAWLE, RAWLL. *Dch.* Rohol; a p.n. *See* Rolfe
RAWLENCE. *N.* Hródland (famous land); *A.S.* Rolland; *Fl.* Roulandt; *S.* Roland; *Dch.* Roelants; p.n.
RAWLEY. *See* Raleigh or Rowley

RAWLINGS. *Dch.* Rohling; a p.n. (descendants of Rolfe)
RAWLINSON. *See* Rolfe
RAWSON. *N.* Rauðssynir (children of the "red"); *Fl.* Raussens; p.n.
RAY. *See* Reay
RAYBOULD. *N.* Rögnvaldr (the keeper of the gods); *A.S.* Rainbald; *G.* Rebohl; *N.-Fr.* Ribald; p.n.
RAYCRAFT. *See* Ryecroft
RAYDEN, RAYDON. A loc. n., Suff. Or *Dch.* Reeden; a p.n.
RAYMENT, RAYMOND. *N.* Hrómundr (famous protector); *D.* Reymann; *Dch.* Reiman; *G.* Rehmann; *D.B.* Raimund; p.n.
    Raimond in Roll of Battell Abbey.
RAYNARD. *A.S.* Ragenheard; *D.* Reinhard; *G.* Rennert; *Dch.* Renard; *Fr.* Renaud; p.n. (wise firmness)
RAYNER. *N.* Hreinnarr (reindeer). Or *A.S.* Regenhere (wise warrior); *D.* Reiner; *G.* Renner; *N.-Fr.* Ranier; *Fl.* Rener; *D.B.* Rayner; p.n.
RAYNHAM. A loc. n., Norf.
RAYNOR. *See* Rayner
RAYSON. From Rasen; a loc. n., Lincs. Or *see* Ray
READ. A loc. n., Yorks. Or *see* Reid
READY, RETHY. A loc. n., Belg. *Dch.* Riede; a p.n.
REAM. *N.* Hreimr; n.n. (noisy); *S.* Reimers; *Dch.* Riem, Reimers; p.n.
REAP. *A.S.* Rip; *Dch.* Reep; a p.n. *See* Ribbans
REARDEN. From Ruardean; a loc. n., Glost. Or *see* Riordan
REASLEY. *See* Risley
REASON. From Ressons; a loc. n., France. *Dch.* Riessen; a p.n. De Reasne, a Prot. ref. n., Lond. 1618
    In Rot Hund.
REAVELEY. A loc. n., Northbd.
REAVELL. *See* Revill

REAY. A loc. n., Caithness, Kirkcudbright. Or *D.* Reeh; *S., Dch.* Ree; *Fl.* Rey, Reh; *N.-Fr.* De Rea; *Fr.* Ray, Rayé; p.n. A Hugt. n., Lond. 1688

REBBECK. From Rebecq; a loc. n., Fland. Rebache, Hugt. n., Lond. 1688

RECKITT. *Fr.* Requette; *Dch.* Reket; p.n.; *N.-Fr. requette* (a stick). Or *A.S.* Ricard, Ricart; *Fl.* Reyekeart, Richet; *N.-Fr.* Racate; p.n. (firm rule)

REDAWAY. A loc. n., Devon

REDDAN, REDON. *Fr.* Redant; a p.n. (toothed)

REDDIE, REDDY. *See* Ready

REDDING. From Reading; a loc. n., Berks. Or *see* Reid

REDDISH. A loc. n., Ches. Or Redditch, Worcest.; or *G.* Rettisch; a p.n. *See* Reid

REDFORD. From Retford; a loc. n., Notts

REDGRAVE. A loc. n., Norf., Suff.

REDHEAD. *A.S.* Rædhæard, Rathart; p.n. (strong counsellor)

REDMAN, REDMAINE. *N.* Raðmaðr or Raðmann (counsellor); *D.* Raadman; *Fl.* Redeman; *A.S.* Rædman; *G.* Rathmann; p.n.

REDMOND. *A.S.* Rædmund (counsel protector)

REDPATH. A loc. n, Northbd.

REDWOOD. A loc. n., Devon

REECE, REESE. Welsh Rhys. Or *N.* Hrísi; a n.n. (illegitimate); *D.* Rüs; *Fl.* Reisse; *G.* Riess; *Dch.* Rees; p.n.

REED. A loc. n., Suff. Or *see* Reid

REEDER. *N.* Hreidarr (?) (a wreath); *D.* Redder; *A.S.* Rædhere, Reder; *G.* Reder; *Dch.* Reeder; p.n. (wise warrior)

REEKIE. *A.S.* Ric (rule); *Fr.* Ricquier; *D.* Rieck; *G.* Ricke, Rieck; *Dch.* Rieke; p.n. Rycke; a loc. n., Belg.

REEKS. *Fl.* Rykers; a fam. n.

REEMAN. *Dch.* Rieman; a p.n.

REEVE. *G.* Riewe; *Dch.* Rieuwe; p.n. Rèves; a loc. n., Belg.; Rives, France. Or *A.S. réfa* (a tax gatherer). *See* Sheriff

REFFELL. *Fl.* Revael; a p.n. *See* Revill

REGAN. From Irish O'Regan; a p.n. Royeoghan (Roy's son)

REGESTER. A loc. corruption of Rochester (Lower)

REID. La Reid; a loc. n., Belg. *G.* Ried; *Dch.* Riede; *D.* Read; p.n. Or *A.S.* Ræd (red, also counsel)

REILLY. From the Irish Radheolagh or Raghalach; p.n. Comp. Reuilly; a loc. n., France. *D.B.* Ruhilie; a p.n.

REITH. From Reeth; a loc. n., Yorks

RELPH. *F.* Rôlf; *Dch.* Reelfs; *A.S.* Radulf, Ralf; p.n. *See* Rolfe

RELTON. From Wrelton; a loc. n., Yorks

REMINGTON. *See* Rimmington

REMNANT. *Fr.* Remont (?); a p.n. Remand, a Hugt. n., Lond. 1687

RENDALL, RENDEL. A loc. n., Orkney. Or *see* Randall

RENNALLS. *See* Reynolds

RENNIE. *See* Rainey

RENNISON. *Fl.* Renson; a p.n. *See* Rain

RENSHAW. From Renishaw; a loc. n., Derbysh.

RENTON. A loc. n., Dumbarton. Or Rennington, Northbd.

RENWICK. A loc. n., Camb.

REPINGTON. From Repton; a loc. n., Derbysh. *D.B.* Rapendune

REPUKE. *Dch., G.* Rehbock; *Fr.* Reboux (?), p.n. Or *see* Rebbeck

RESTALL. *See* Rastall

RESTHER. *N.-Fr.* Fitz-Reste; a p.n. Resteau, a Hugt. n., Lond. 1688

RETALLACK, RETALLICK. A loc. n., Cornw.

REVELEY. *See* Reaveley

P

REVEN. *See* Ruthven

REVILL. From Reville; a loc. n., Norm. *Fr.* Revel, Revelle; p.n. Hugt. n., Lond. 1618
Revel in Rot. Obl. et Fin., K. John.

REW. A loc. n., Devon. Rue, Dorset; Rue, France; Roux, Belg.

REYNOLDS. *N.* Rögnvaldr; *A.S.* Regnald; *D., S.* Reinhold; *Dch.* Reinold, Rennel; p.n. (gods' wielder or ruler)

RHIMES. *See* Ream

RHIND. A loc. n., Perth

RHODES. From Rhodez; a loc. n., Aquitaine. A loc. n., Lancs. *N.-Fr.* De Rodes, 1202

RHYS. Welsh p.n. (a warrior)

RIBBANS, RIBBONS. *A.S.* Rip (reaper, also spoiler); *Dch.* Ribbink; *G.* Rippin; p.n. Or *see* Raban

RIBICK. *See* Rebbeck

RICE. *See* Rhys

RICH. From Riche; a loc. n., Lorraine

RICHARDS. *A.S.* Ricard; *Fr.* Richard; *F.* Rikkerd, Rikkert, Rikkerts; *Dch.* Ricard, Richards; p.n. (strong ruler). Contr. of Ricardus

RICHARDSON. *See* Rix

RICHBELL. *A.S.* Ricbeald (bold ruler)

RICHES. *A.S.* Richere, Ricerus; p.n. (ruler-warrior). *See* Rich

RICHFIELD. From Richeville; a loc. n., France

RICHFORD. From Rickford; a loc. n., Somers

RICHMOND. A loc. n., Surr., Yorks

RICKARBY. A loc. n., Cumb.

RICKET. *See* Reckitt. Ricquart, Hugt., Canterbury, 1622

RIDALL, RIDDEL, RIDDLE. A loc. n., Scotl. Or *D.* Riedel; *S.* Rydall; *Fr.* Ridel, Ridelle; a p.n. (wrinkle). Or dim. of Rid
Richard Ridel in Rot. Obl. et Fin., K. John. Also de Ridal.

RIDDETT, RIDET. *N.-Fr.*; p.n. Dim. of Rid (knight)

RIDDLESWORTH. From Roddlesworth; a loc. n., Lancs

RIDER. *See* Ryder

RIDGARD. *See* Rudyard. Or *A.S.* Ricweard; a p.n. (rule protector)

RIDGE. A loc. n., Devon, Glost., Salop, Wilts

RIDGELY. From Rugeley (?); a loc. n., Staffs

RIDGWAY. A loc. n., Devon, Somers

RIDGWELL. A loc. n., Ess.

RIDLEY. A loc. n., Ches., Kent, Northbd.

RIDOUT. *Fr.* Redouté; a p.n. (dreaded)

RIDPATH. *See* Redpath

RIDSDALE. A loc. n., Northbd.

RIGBY. A loc. n., Yorks (*D.B.* Rigbi)

RIGG. A loc. n., Dumfries

RIGGLESWORTH. *See* Riddlesworth

RIGGS. *See* Ridge

RILEY. *See* Reilly

RILLETT. *Fr.* Rouillet (rusty); *Fl.* Rielaert; Rillaert; p.n.

RIMMINGTON. A loc. n., Yorks (*D.B.* Renitone)
William de Rimington was Prior of Sawley Abbey and Chancellor of Oxford, A.D. 1372.

RING. *N.* Hringr (a ring); *Dch.* Ring; *G.* Ring; p.n.

RINGER. *A.S.* Hringware; *Old G.* Rincar; *Dch.* Rincker; *G.* Ringer; p.n. (a warrior defended by ringed or chain mail)

RINGROSE. *N.* Hringr; a p.n. (a ring); *hrós* (praise); *A.S.* Rinc; a p.n. (warrior)
Stephen Ryngros, Chaplain of St Mary's, Scarborough, 1582. York Wills.

RINTOUL. *Dch* Rintel; a p.n. *See* Randall

RION. A loc. n., France. *D.* Ryan; *Fl.* Rion; p.n.

RIORDAN. Irish O'Riordan

RIPLEY. A loc. n., Derbysh., Ess., Surr., Yorks

RIPPER. *Dch.* Rippe; *Fl.* Ripet; p.n. *See* Reap

RIPPIN. *G.* Rippin; *Dch.* Ripping; a p.n.; fam. n. of Rip

RIPPINGILLE. From Rippingale; a loc. n., Lincs

RIPPON. From Ripon; a loc. n., Yorks

RIPSHER. *G.* Rippke; a p.n. Dim. of Rip

RISELEY. A loc. n., Derbysh.

RISING. A loc. n., Norf. Or *S.* Rising; a p.n.

RIST. *N.* Reistr (a twist); *G.* Rister; *D.*, *Fl.*, *Dch.* Rist; p.n.

RITCHIE. *A.S.* Righeah; *Fr.* Richet; p.n. (high ruler)

RITSON. A loc. n., Devon

RIVERS. *Fr.* Rivez; *D.* Rievers; p.n. From Rivière; a loc. n., Belg.

Rivers in Roll of Battell Abbey. *D.B.* Riveire, a tenant in chief.

RIVETT. *N.-Fr.* Rivet; *Fl.* Riffaert; p.n.; *A.S.* Riu; a p.n. Contr. of Riculf (ruler-wolf)

RIVINGTON. A loc. n., Lancs

RIX. *G.* Rietsch; *Dch.* Rikke, Rikkers; *Fl.* Richez; p.n. *See* Riches

ROBB. *Fl.* Robbe; a p.n. *See* Roberts

ROBBINS. *Fl.* Robyns; a p.n.; fam. n.

ROBERTS. *N.* Hró-bjartr; *A.S.* Rodbeort; *Fr.* Robert; *Dch.* Robart, Roberts; p.n. Robert's, for *N.-Fr.* Robertus (illustrious fame). *See* Christian names

ROBEY, ROBY. A loc. n., Derbysh., Lancs, Yorks

ROBIN. *Fr.*; p.n. Robain, Hugt., Lond. 1687

ROBINETT. *Fr.* Robinet. Dimin. of Robin

ROBINSON. *N.* Robbi, from Hró-bjartr (Robert); *Fl.* Robyns, Robson, Robisson; p.n. *See* Roberts. Prot. ref., Lond. 1618

ROBSON. *Fl.*; p.n.

ROCHE. *Fr.*; loc. and p.n. Hugt., Lond. 1687

ROCHEFORT. A loc. n., Belg. and Norm.

ROCKE. *A.S.* Roc; *N.-Fr.* De la Roca; *Dch.*, *G.* Rock; *Fr.* Rocque; p.n. (a rook)
Roger Roc in Rot. Obl. et Fin., K. John; and Rot. Hund.

ROCKETT. From Rogate; a loc. n., Suss. Or *Fr.* Rochette, Roquet; p.n. From Roquette; a loc. n., Normandy

ROCKLEY. A loc. n., Herts, Notts, Wilts. *N.-Fr.* De Rokela; a p.n.

RODD. *A.S.* Rod, Rodda, Hrod, Rud, Rudda; p.n.; *N.* hróð (famous)

RODGERS. *N.* Hróð-geirr; *D.* Roedeger, Rodgers; *Fl.* Roger; *Fr.* Rogier; *G.* Roger; *A.S.* Rodgar, Roger; p.n. (famous spear)

RODNEY. From *N.-Fr.* Reyney or Radenay

RODWELL. *See* Rothwell

ROE. A loc. n., Herts. Or *see* Raw, Rowe

ROEBUCK. *See* Rebbeck

ROFFE. *N.-Fr.* De Rof; a p.n. *See* Rolfe. Hugt., Lond. 1687

ROGERS. *See* Rodgers

ROGERSON. *See* Rodgers. Or from Rogerstone; a loc. n., Monmouth (?)

ROKEBY. A loc. n., Yorks

ROLFE. *N.* Hródólfr, Hrólfr; *A.S.* Rodulf; *G.* Roll, Rolle, Rolof, Roff, Ruff; *D.B.* Ralf, Roulf, Rolf; *F.* Rôlf; *D.* Rohlf; *Fl.*, *Dch.* Roll, Rolff, Rol; p.n. (glorious wolf)

ROLL, ROLLE. Roly; a loc. n., Belg. *N.-Fr.* De Rouel; a p.n.

ROLLES. *See* Rowles

ROLLESTON. A loc. n., Staffs (*D.B.* Roolfeston)

ROLLING. *Fr.* Rollin; a p.n. *See* Rawling

ROLLINSON. *See* Rawlinson

ROLPH. *See* Rolfe

ROMER. From Roumare; a loc. n., Norm. Or *N.* Ramr (strong); *A.S.* Rom; *G.*, *Dch.* Römer; *Fl.* Romer; a p.n.

ROMILLY. A loc. n., Normandy. Romiley; a loc. n., Ches.
William de Romillé was the first Baron of Skipton, Yorks.

ROMNEY. A loc. n., Kent

RONALD. Scot. Ranald; a p.n. (power of judgment)

RONEG. From the Irish Mulrooney; a p.n.

RONEY. *N.-Fr.* De Roenai; a p.n.

ROOFE. *See* Roffe

ROOK. *N.* Hrúkr; p.n. *See* Rocke

ROOM. Rumes; a loc. n., Belg.; Ruoms, France. Or *A.S.* Rom, Rum; *G.* Ruhm; *Fl.* Rooms; p.n.

ROOPE, ROPE. *N.* Hrappr (a yeoman); *G.* Rupp; *A.S.* Hroppa, Rop, Roppa; *D.* Rupe; *Fl.* Roup; *N.-Fr.* de Rupe; p.n.

ROOT. *See* Rutt

ROPER. From Rupiere; a loc. n., Norm.

RORKE. From the Irish O'Rorke; a p.n.

ROSCOE. A loc. n., Yorks

ROSE. From Ros (now Rots); a loc. n., Norm. Or *N.* Hross, *hrósa* (praise); *A.S.* Ros; *D.*, *G.*, *Dch.*, *Fr.* Rose; a p.n. A Hugt. n., Lond. 1684

ROSHER. From Rochers; a loc. n., France. *Fr.* Rocher. Or *Dch.* Rosier; *Fl.* Rosaer; *D.* Roscher; *G.* Roescher; p.n. (praised warrior)

ROSKILL. From Rosskell or Hrosskell; a loc. n., Cumb. Also *N.* Hrosketel; *A.S.* Roschil; p.n. (horse-kettle)

ROSLYN. A loc. n., Edinburgh

ROSS. A loc. n., Heref., Perth, Yorks. *See* Rose

ROSSALL. A loc. n., Lancs, Yorks

ROSSER. *See* Rosher

ROSWELL. *Fr.* Rousselle; a p.n. *See* Russell. Hugt. n., Cant. 1622

ROTH. *See* Routh

ROTHERHAM. A loc. n., Yorks

ROTHWELL. A loc. n., Lincs, Northants, Yorks (*D.B.* Rodowelle)
Held by De Warneville.

ROTTER. *A.S.* Hroth; *Dch.* Rotte; *Fr.* Routier; p.n. (experienced)

ROTTON. *Dch.* Rooten; a p.n.; fam. n. of Rotte. Or *see* Roughton

ROUCH. *See* Rouse

ROUGH. *See* Ruff

ROUGHTON. A loc. n., Lincs, Norf., Salop

ROUNCE, ROUND. *N.-Fr.* Rotundus; a p.n. *See* Rands

ROUNTREE. From Rowantree; a loc. n., Cumb.

ROUPEL. *G.* Ruppel; a p.n.; *A.S.* Rup. Dim. (a tuft of hair)

ROUSBY. A loc. n., Yorks. *D.B.* Rozebi

ROUSE. A loc. n., Cornw.; Roux, Belg. *N.-Fr.* Le Roux; *Dch.* Rous; *G.* Rausch; *Fr.* Rousse, Rouse; p.n. A Hugt. n., Lond. 1618

ROUT. *N.* Rauðr (red); *G.* Rutha, Roth, Rauter; *D.B.* Rot; *D.* Rauth; *Dch.* Root; *Fl.* Rowet; p.n.

ROUTH. A loc. n., Yorks
Held by De Scruteville.

ROUTLEDGE. A loc. n., Cumb.

ROUTLEY. From Rothley; a loc. n., Leics. Or *see* Routledge

Row, Rowe. From Roeux; a loc. n., France; or Roux, Belg. *Fr.* Raux, Réaux; p.n. An Irish p.n.; *ruadh* (red). A loc. n., Dumbarton, Somers, Yorks. *See* Raw, Roe

Rowan, Rowen, Rowing. *Dch.* Rouwen; *Fr.* Rouen; p.n. Hugt., Lond. 1618

Rowarth. A loc. n., Ches.

Rowbotham. From Robotham; a loc. n., Lancs (near Ashton-under-Lyne)

Robert Robotham of Raskyll, Yorks, received a grant of arms Dec. 1560. Compare Rowbarton, Somers.

Rowdon. From Rowden; a loc. n., Devon, Leics

Rowell. A loc. n., Glost. Or from Rouelles, France. A Hugt. n., Lond. 1687

Rowland. A loc. n., Derbysh. Or *see* Rawlence. Hugt., Dover, 1622

Rowlatt. From Rowlett; a loc. n., Kent. Or *Fr.* Roulet; a p.n.

Rowles. From Rolles; a loc. n., Ess. Or Rouelles, France

De Rolles in Rot. Obl. et Fin.

Rowley. From Reuilly; a loc. n., Norm. Also a loc. n., Dur., Staffs, Wilts

Rowling. *See* Rawlinson

Rowney. From Rosny; a loc. n., France. *Fr.* Rouneau; a p.n. Or *see* Roney

Roworth. A loc. n., Derbysh.

Rowsell. *Fl.* Roussel; a p.n. *See* Russell. A Hugt. n., Lond. 1618

Rowson. From Rowston; a loc. n., Lincs

Rowton. A loc. n., Salop, Yorks

Roxburgh. The county town

Roxby. A loc. n., Lincs, Yorks

Roy. From Roye; a loc. n., France. Or *N.* Hroi; *Dch.* Rooij; *Fr.*, *G.* Roy; p.n. A Hugt. n., Lond. 1688. A loc. n., Belg.

Royal, Royle. *Fr.*; p.n. From Roisel; a loc. n., France

Galfrid Roille in Rot. Obl. et Fin., K. John.

Royce. *G.*, *Dch.*, *Fl.* Reuss; a p.n. *See* Rouse

Roycroft. *See* Rycroft

Royston. From Ryston; a loc. n., Herts, Norf., Yorks

Roythorne. From Rowthorne; a loc. n., Derbysh.

Rubery. A loc. n., Worcest.

Rubie. From Roubai; a loc. n., France. *Dch.* Rube; *G.* Rubie; *Fr.* Ruby; p.n. De Rewbay, a Hugt. n., Lond. 1618

Rudall. From Rudhall or Rudhale; a loc. n., Heref.

Rudd. *A.S.*, *D.* Rud; a p.n. Prot. ref., Lond. 1621. *See* Rutt

Ruddle. *See* Rudall

Ruddock. Dimin. of Rud

Rudgard. *See* Rudyard

Rudge. A loc. n., Devon, Somers, Staffs, Wilts

Rudland. From Rutland. Or *see* Rawlence

Rudrum. From Rotherham; a loc. n., Yorks (*D.B.* Rodreham)

Rudyard. A loc. n., Staffs

Ruff. *G.*; p.n.; Ruffus (red). Prot. ref., Lond. 1618

In Rot. Obl. et Fin.

Ruffell, Ruffles. *Fr.* Rouval; *G.* Rouvel; p.n.

Ruffitt. *Fr.* Rouffart; a p.n.

Ruggles. From Rugeley; a loc. n., Staffs. *D.B.* Rugehala, Rugelie. Or it may be from Rugles; a loc. n., Norm.

The final "s" is a recent addition. Members of the family who emigrated to New England, U.S.A., in 1637, spelled the name Ruggle, and their descendants have it both with and without the "s." It occurs also as Rogyll and Ruggelay. The arms of Rugeley and Ruggles are identical.

RULE, RULLES. A loc. n., Belg.;
Rull, Devon. *Fr.* Ruelle; *Dch.*
Rühl; p.n.

RUMBALL. *G.* Rumpel; *Fl.* Rum-
mel; p.n. *See* Rumbold

RUMBELOW, RUMBLOW. From
Tromelow or Rumbelow (Atte-
Trumelow); a loc. n., Wednes-
field, Staffs
Stephen Rummelowe or Rumbilowe
was governor of Nottingham Castle,
A.D. 1369. The sailors' "Heave,
oh, rumbylow" is a coincidence,
and refers probably to the grog in
prospect.

RUMBLE. *See* Rumbold

RUMBOLD. *A.S.* Rumbald, Rum-
beald, Rumbold; p.n.; *D.B.*
under-tenant; *Old G. hrom,
hruam* (glory, praise), *bald* (bold)
Stephanus Rambald in Rot. Obl. et
Fin., K. John, 1207 (Hants).

RUMLEY. From Romilly; a loc.
n., Norm.

RUMMINGS. *Dch.* Roumen; *S.*
Rumin; *Fl.* Rumens, Rummens;
p.n. Rummen; a loc. n., Belg.;
fam. n. of Room

RUMNEY. *Dch.* Rummenie; a p.n.
Or *see* Romney

RUMP. *D.* Rump; *G.* Rumpe,
Rumpf; *Dch.* Rumpff; p.n.
(body)

RUMSEY. From Romsey; a loc. n.,
Ess.

RUNACRES. *A.S.* Runwacer (?)
(running guard); *Fl.* Runacher;
p.n.

RUNDELL, RUNDLE. *S.* Rondahl;
Dch. Rouendal; a loc. and p.n.

RUNHAM. A loc. n., Norf., Kent

RUNNACLES, RUNNECKLES. *G.*
Runkel; *Dch.* Runckel; p.n.
Dim. of *A.S. rynig* (runner)

RUNNALL. From Runhall; a loc.
n., Norf.

RUNNICUS. *See* Runacres

RUNNIFF. *D.* Roennov; a p.n.

RUSBY. *See* Rousby

RUSCOE. *See* Roscoe

RUSE. From Roose; a loc. n.,
Lancs. Or *see* Rouse

RUSH. A loc. n., Dublin. Or *D.,
G., Dch.* Rusch; a p.n.

RUSHBROOK. A loc. n., Suff.

RUSHBURY. A loc. n., Heref.

RUSHTON. A loc. n., Ches., Dorset,
Northants, Salop, Staffs

RUSHWORTH. From Rishworth; a
loc. n., Yorks

RUSKIN. *A.S.* Ruscing; fam. n.;
Fl. Raskin; *Fr.* Rasquin; p.n.
Or *N. roskinn* (?), met. (vigorous,
doughty, valiant), lit. (ripe,
mature). *See* Rose

RUSS. A loc. n., Germ. *G., Dch.,
Fl.* Russ, Russe; p.n. *See*
Rouse

RUSSELL. From Rosel; a loc. n.,
Norm.
Rushell or Rosel is in the Roll of
Battell Abbey, and Huges de Rozel
occurs as one of the benefactors of
the abbey of St. Étienne at Caen,
founded by William the Conqueror.
Rozel, a tenant in chief in *D.B.*

RUST. *A.S.* Roswith (?) (greatly
praised); *D., G., Dch.*; p.n.

RUSTON. A loc. n., Norf.

RUTH. *See* Routh

RUTHERFORD. A loc. n., Roxburgh. Also Ruddervoorde in
Flanders

RUTHERGLEN. A loc. n., Lanark

RUTHVEN. A loc. n., Perth

RUTLAND. The county

RUTLEY. A loc. n., Worcest.

RUTT. *A.S.* Hrod, Rut; *Dch.*
Ruth (famous); p.n. *See* Rudd.
Rutes, Hugt. n., Lond. 1618

RUTTEN. *Dch.*; p.n.; fam. n. of
Rutt

RUTTER. *N.* Hrútr (a ram); *Dch.*
Rutter; p.n. Prot. ref., Lond.
1618

RUTTLEGE. *See* Routledge

RUTTY. *Fr.* Routier; a p.n. *See*
Rutter

RYALL. A loc. n., Devon. Or
Ryhall, Worcest. *See* Royle

RYAN. From Royan; a loc. n., Normandy; or Ruyen, Flanders. *D.* Ryan; *Fr.* Royon; p.n.

RYDER. From Ryther; a loc. n., Yorks. Or *N.* Hreidarr; *A.S.* Rid, Rida; *G.* Reuter, Reiter; *D.* Ryder; *Dch.* Ruijter; p.n. (horse soldier, knight)

RYE. A loc. n., Suss. Or Rie, Norm.

RYECROFT. A loc. n., Lancs, Yorks

RYGATE. From Reigate; a loc. n., Surr.

RYHOPE. A loc. n., Dur.

RYLAND. A loc. n., Lincs. Rylands; loc. n., Notts

RYLE. A loc. n., Northbd. *See* Royle

RYMAN. *See* Raymond

RYMER. A loc. n., Suff. Or *G.* Reimer; a p.n.

S

SABERTON. From Sapperton; a loc., Derbysh. Or Soberton, Hants

SABEY. *N.-Fr.* Saba, Sabe; *A.S.* Saba, Sæba, Sæbeorht; *Fr.* Sabbe; *D.* Saaby; p.n. (sea illustrious). *See* Sebright

SABIN. *Fl.* Saapin; a p.n.; fam. n.

SACH. *N.* Saxi (Saxon); *G.* Sacha, Sack; *Dch.* Saacke, Sak; *D.* Sack; *N.-Fr.*, *Dch.* Sac; *Fl.* Seck; p.n. Prot. ref., Lond. 1618

SACKVILLE. From Sacquenville; a loc. n., Normandy
De Sacheuilla in *D.B.* Sechevill, Sekeville in Rot. Obl. et Fin., K. John.

SACRET. *Fr.* Secret; a p.n.; *sakeret* (a hawk)

SACRISTAN. From Sacriston; a loc. n., Dur.

SADD. A loc. n., Devon

SADDINGTON. A loc. n., Leics

SADDLE. A loc. n., Argyll

SADGROVE. *See* Sitgreaves

SADLER. *G.* Sattler; a p.n.

SAFFELL. *See* Saville

SAFFERY. *See* Savery

SAFFORD. From Salford; a loc. n., Lancs

SAGE. *N.-Fr.* le Sage (Sapiens); a p.n.

SAGGERS. *A.S.* Sægær, Sagar; *Fl.* Sagaer, Segers, Sager; p.n. (sea spear)

SAINSBURY. From Saintbury; a loc. n., Worcest.

ST AUBYN. From St Albino, near Evreux, Norm.
Granted tithes to St Taurin, Evr. 980. Witness found. chart. Barnstaple Abbey, *temp.* Will. I.

ST CLAIR. A loc. n., Normandy
Sent Clere in Roll of Battell Abbey. *D.B.* de Sent Cler.

ST GEORGE. From St Georges; a loc. n., Norm. and Belg.
In Roll of Battell Abbey.

ST JOHN. *Fr.* Seuntjens; *Fl.* Vansintjan; a p.n.
Three local names in Flanders are Saint Jean (lez-Ypres), Saint-Jean-Geest, Saint-Jean-in-Erems. Sent John in Roll of Battell Abbey.

ST LEGER. From Saint-Léger; a loc. n., Norm.
Sent Legere in Roll of Battell Abbey.

ST QUINTIN. A loc. n., Norm.
Sent Quintin in Roll of Battell Abbey and *D.B.*

SAINTY, SAINTES. A loc. n., Brabant. *Dch.* Sante; *Fl.* Senty; *Fr.* Saintais; p.n.

SAIR, SAIRS. *See* Sayer

SAITE. *A.S.* Sæta; *N.-Fr.* Saiete; *Fr.* Sethe; p.n. (a settler)
Seyot in Rot. Hund.

SALE. *N.-Fr.* De Salle; a p.n. A loc. n., Ches.; Zele, Belg.

SALES. From Seilles; a loc. n., Belg.

SALINGER. *N.* Sælinger ; a n.n. (a wealthy man) ; *G.* ; p.n. Prot. ref., Lond. 1618

SALISBURY. The city of that name

SALKELD. A loc. n., Cumb.

SALL. *A.S.* Sal, Sele ; *Fr.* Salles ; p.n. *See* Sale

SALLIS. From Sallys ; a loc. n., Heref. Or *Dch.* Salis ; *Fr.* Salles ; p.n. Salles ; a loc. n., Belg.

SALLOWS. From Sallowes ; a loc. n., Norf.

SALMON. *N.* Sölmundr (sallow protector) ; *Fl.* Salman, Salmain, Solmon ; *G.* Sallmann ; Scot. Salmond ; *A.S.* Salomon ; *N.-Fr.* Salmon ; p.n.

SALT. A loc. n., Staffs. Or *Dch.* Solt ; a p.n.

SALTER. *N.-Fr.* le Salter ; *S.* Solter ; *Dch.* Selter ; p.n.

SALTHOUSE. A loc. n., Lancs, Norf.

SALTWELL. A loc. n., Lincs

SALVIDGE. *A.S.* Selewig ; *D.* Selvig ; *N.-Fr.* Salvage ; p.n. (dark, swarthy)

SAMBRIDGE. *See* Sambrook

SAMBROOK. A loc. n., Salop

SAME. From Seaham ; a loc. n., Dur.

SAMERS. *See* Sammars

SAMES, SAMS. From Seames ; a loc. n., Yorks. Or *D.* ; p.n.

SAMMARS. From Samarés ; a loc. n., Jersey

SAMMON. *See* Salmon or Seaman

SAMPLE. *See* Sempill

SAMPSON. From St S. ; a loc. n., Norm.

SANDAY. From St Die, France ; or Sandy ; a loc. n., Beds. Or *see* Sandys

SANDBACH. A loc. n., Ches. Or *D.* Sandbech ; a loc. and p.n.

SANDBROOK. *See* Sandbach

SANDELL. From Sendall ; a loc. n., Yorks. Or *D.*, *S.* Sandell ; a p.n.

SANDEMAN. *Dch.* Sandman ; a p.n. *See* Sandys

SANDERSON. *S.* Sanderson. *See* Sandys

SANDFORD. A loc n., Devon, Lanark, Salop, Somers, Westmd.

SANDHALL. *See* Sandell

SANDHAM. From Sandholme ; a loc n., Lincs, Yorks

SANDIFER. From Sandiford ; a loc. n., Staffs

SANDILANDS. A loc. n., Lanark

SANDLANT. *S.* Sandlund ; a loc. and p.n.

SANDS. *See* Sandys

SANDWELL. A loc. n., Devon, etc.

SANDWITH. A loc. n., Cumb.

SANDYS. *N.* Sandi ; n.n. ; *G.*, *D.*, *S.* Sand, Sander ; *Dch.* Sande, Sanders ; *Fl.* Sannes, Sanders ; *A.S.* Sand, Sanda, Sendi ; p.n. (a messenger)

SANGER. *A.S.* Sangere (a singer) ; *Fr.* Sangier ; *Dch.* Sanger ; p.n.

SANGSTER. *Dch.* Sangstier ; a p.n. ; *A.S.* Sangstere (a female singer)

SANKEY. A loc. n., Lancs. Or *Fl.* Sancke ; *Fr.* Sanchez ; *Dch.* Sanches ; p.n. Dim. of Sand.

SANN. *See* Sandys

SANQUHAR. A loc. n., Dumfries

SANSOM. *Fr.* Sanson ; *D.B.* Sanson and de St Sansone ; p.n.

SANXTER. *See* Sangster

SAPEY. From Cepie ; a loc. n., France. Or *see* Seapey

SAPSED, SAPSEID. From Shepshed ; a loc. n., Leics

SAPSWORTH. *See* Sopworth

SAPWELL. From Sopewell ; a loc. n., Herts

SARE. From Sarre ; a loc. n., Kent. *See* Sayer

SARLL. *See* Serle

SARSON. A loc. n., Hants. Or *N.-Fr.* Sarazin ; a p.n.

SARTAIN. *Fr.* Sarton ; a p.n.

SARTORIS or SARTRES. *Fl.* Sartorius ; a p.n. A Hugt. n., Lond. 1684

SASSE. *A.S.* Sas, Sahs, Sæx; *N.-Fr.* De Sace; *D.* Sass; p.n. (a Saxon)

SATCHELL, SATCHWELL. A loc. n., Hants. *See* Setchell

SATTERLEIGH. A loc. n., Devon

SATTERTHWAITE. A loc. n., Lancs

SATTLEY. *See* Satterleigh

SAUCHIE. A loc. n., Perth

SAUL. From Saughall; a loc. n., Ches. Saul; a loc. n., Glost. Or *N.* Sjölfr, contr. of Sæ-úlfr (sea-wolf); *G.* Saul, Sauler; *D.B.* Saulf, Seulf, Saul; *Dch.* Scholl, Saul; *Fl.* Swolf, Soualle; p.n.

SAUMAREZ. *See* Sammars

SAUNDERS. *See* Sandys

SAURY. *See* Sawrey

SAVAGE. *Fr.* Sauvage; a p.n. *See* Salvidge

Le Sauvage in Rot. Obl. et Fin., K. John. A Hugt. n., Lond. 1687.

SAVERY. *Fr.* Savary, Sevrey. From Sivry; a loc. n., Belg. De Savary, a Hugt. n., Lond. 1687

SAVILLE. *N.-Fr.* De Sevele, De Sayville; *D.* Sevel; p.n. From Serville (?); a loc. n., Belg.

SAVORY. *See* Savery

SAW. *Fr.* Saut; a p.n. (a leap). Or *A.S.* Sawata; a p.n. (sower)

SAWBRIDGE. A loc. n., Warw., Westmd.

SAWER. *See* Sawyer

SAWREY. A loc. n., Lancs. Sorée, Belg.

SAWYER, SOHIER. A loc. n., Belg. *Fr.* Soyer; a p.n.

SAWYERS. A loc. n. in Essex. Or Sahurs, Norm.

SAXBY. A loc. n., Leics, Lincs

SAXELBY. A loc. n., Leics

SAXTON. A loc. n., Yorks

SAY. Séez; a loc. n., Norm. Or *A.S.* Se, Sæ, Sig (victory); *Fr.* Saye; *Fl.* Saey; *Dch.* See; p.n.

SAYCE. *Fr.* Sayes; *Dch.* Seys; p.n.

SAYER. *A.S.* Sihar (victorious warrior); *G.* Sehr; *Old G.* Sigheri; *Fl.* Sehier; *D.*, *Fr.* Seyer; p.n. Or St Saire; a loc. n., Norm. Serre, Hugt. n.

SAYLE. *See* Sale

SAYMER. *A.S.* Sigemær (victory famous), or Sæmœr (sea-famous); *D.B.* Semar, Samar; *Dch.* Seemer, or St Maur (?); p.n. Simore, Hugt. 1618

SCADDING. *D.* Schad, Skade; p.n.

SCAGELL. *See* Scargill

SCAIFE. *N.* Skeifr; a n.n. (askew); *Fl.* Scaff; *G.* Skiefe; *D.* Skife; p.n. Skive; a loc. n., Den.

SCALES. A loc. n., Lancs

Or from Hardwin de Scalers or D'Echellers, a follower of the Conqueror, and tenant in chief in *D.B.* William de Escales in Rot. Obl. et Fin., K. John.

SCAMBLER. *G.* Schammler; a p.n. *See* Scammell

SCAMMELL. *N.* Skam-háls; a n.n. (short neck). Or dim. of *N.* Skammi; *A.S.* Scamma (the short); *G.* Schammel; a p.n.

SCANES. *A.S.* Scan; a p.n. (shiny); *Dch.* Schans; a fam. n.

SCARBOROUGH. A loc. n., Yorks

SCARCE. From Skears; a loc. n., Dur. Or *see* Shears

SCARD. *See* Scarth

SCARE. *G.* Schar; *Dch.* Schier; p.n.; *N. sker*; *A.S. scear* (share)

SCARFE. *A.S.* Sceorf; *G.*, *D.*, *Dch.* Scharf; a p.n. (sharp). *See* Sharpen

SCARLES. *See* Scarll

SCARLETT. From Escarlat; a loc. n., Norm. *G.* Scharlot; a p.n.

SCARLL. From Scarle; a loc. n., Notts

SCARSBROOK. From Scarisbrick; a loc. n., Lancs

SCARTH. A loc. n. (a mountain pass). Or *N.* Scarði; n.n. (hare-lip); *D.* Scard; *G.* Scharte; p.n.

SCARVELL. From Escardeville; a loc. n., Norm.

SCATTERGOOD. *See* Shadgot

Schatregod, Rot. Hund. 1273; Scatergude, Test. Ebor. 1481.

SCHICKLE. *N.* Skekill (shank); *G.* Schichel; p.n.

SCHOFIELD. From Scholefield; a loc. n., Lancs. Or Escoville, Norm.

SCHOLES. A loc. n., Yorks. Or *Fl.* Schoels; a p.n. *See* Scully

SCHOLEY. *See* Scully

SCHOOBERT. *G.* Schubart; a p.n.

SCHUSTER. *D.* Schuster; a p.n. (a shoe-mender)

SCOBEL. A loc. n., Devon

SCOGGINS. *N.* Skaggi; a p.n. (skew); *A.S.* Scacca; *D.* Schackinger; *Dch.* Schokking; *Fl.* Schaekens, Shoukens; fam. n.

SCOONES. *Dch.* Schoen; a p.n.

SCOPES. *A.S.* Scop (a poet, minstrel); *G.* Schoppe; p.n.

SCORER. From Scorrer; a loc. n., Cornw. Or *A.S.* Scorra; a p.n. (scarred)

SCOTCHER. *A.S.* Scot (an arrow); *Dch.* Schotse; p.n. Dim of Scot

SCOTCHMER. *A.S.* Scotmær (famous archer); *Dch.* Schottemeijer; p.n.

SCOTT. *N.* Skati (a lordly man), or Skotti (archer); n.n.; *G.* Schotte; *Dch.* Schot; *Fr.* Scotti; *S.*, *D.* Skotte; p.n.

Jordan Scot in Rot. Obl. et. Fin., K. John.

SCOTTER. A loc. n., Lincs

SCOTTOW. A loc. n., Norf.

SCOURFIELD. *See* Schofield

SCOVELL. From Escoville (now Ecoville); a loc. n., Normandy

Radulph de Scovill held land in Wilts, *temp.* K. John.

SCRACE. *See* Scrase

SCRAFIELD. From Scrayfield; a loc. n., Lincs

SCRAGGS. *See* Scroggs

SCRAGIE. *See* Scroggie

SCRASE. *A.S.* Scræwa; a p.n (a shrewmouse). Or *N.* Skreyja; a n.n. (a boaster); *Fl.* Schreyers (?); a fam. n.

SCREETON. From Screveton; a loc. n., Notts; locally pron. Screeton

Scrime. *N.* Skrymir (n. of a giant); *G.* Schrimmer; p.n.

SCRIMGEOUR. A loc. n., Scotl.

SCRIMSHAW, SCRIMSHIRE. *See* Skrymsher

SCRIVEN. A loc. n., Yorks

SCRIVENER. Belonging to Scriven. Or a law-writer

SCROGGIE. From Scrogie; a loc. n., Perth

SCROGGS. A loc. n., Cumb., Dumfries

SCROGHAM. A loc. n.

SCROTTOW. A loc. n.

SCRUBY. From Scrooby; a loc. n., Lincs, Yorks

SCRUTON, SCRUTTON. A loc. n., Yorks

SCRYMGEOUR. *See* Skrimgeour

SCUDAMORE. From Escudimore; a loc. n., Norm.

Sent Scudamore in Roll of Battell Abbey. It is not in *D.B.*, unless Scudet, a tenant in chief, be the same.

SCULLY. *N.-Fr.* De Scoleio. Or *N.* Skuli (a protector); *G.* Schylla; *A.S.* Scule, Scula; p.n.

SCUPHAM. From Scupholme; a loc. n., Lincs

SCURLL. *N.* Skirvill (?) (the name of a dwarf); *G.* Skeurell; p.n. Or *see* Scarll

SCURRAH, SCURRY. *See* Scorer

SCUTT. *D.* Skytt; *Dch.* Schutt; p.n. *See* Skeat. Hugt. n., Lond. 1687

SEABER. *Fr.* Sibert; a p.n. *See* Seabright

SEABOURNE. *N.* Sæbjörn; *A.S.* Sigbeorn; a p.n. (victorious bear)

SEABRIGHT. *A.S.* Sæbeorht ; *G.* Seibert, Siebert ; p.n. (sea-illustrious)

SEABROOK. A loc. n., Kent

SEABURY. *A.S.* Sæburh ; a p.n. (sea-protection)

SEADON. *Fr.* Sidon ; a p.n.

SEAFORD. A loc. n., Suss.

SEAGER, SEAGO. *N.* Siggi, dimin. of Sigurðr ; *A.S.* Secgga, Sigar ; *Dch.* Segar, Seger, Sieger ; *F.* Sikke ; *D.* Sekker, Seeger ; *S.* Seger ; *Fl.* Segher ; *G.* Sieg ; p.n. (victory spear)

SEAGRAVE. A loc. n., Leics, Northants

SEAKER. *See* Seager

SEAL. A loc. n., Kent, Leics, Surr. Or *see* Sill

SEALBY. From Selby ; a loc. n., Yorks

SEALEY. *See* Seeley

SEAMAN, SEAMON. *A.S.* Sæmann ; *Dch.* Seeman ; p.n. (a sailor)

SEAPEY. *N.* Sibbi, pet n. of Sigbaldr (foremost in victory) ; *F.* Sebo, Sibo ; *A.S.* Sibba, Sibbi, Sibold ; *G.* Siber, Seppe ; *Dch.* Siep, Sepp, Seepe ; p.n. *See* Sapey

SEAR, SEARS, SEEAR, SEER. From Cire ; a loc. n., France. *G.* Zier ; a p.n. Or *see* Sayer

SEARBY. A loc. n., Lincs

SEARCH, SERWECH. *N.-Fr.* De Cherches. Or *A.S.* Siric, Sigeric ; *Dch.* Sierich ; p.n. (victorious ruler)

SEARLE. *See* Serle

SEARY. From Cirey ; a loc. n., France

SEATLE. A loc. n., Lancs

SEATON. A loc. n., Cumb., Devon, Dur., Nairn, Northbd., Ross, Yorks. *D.B.* Seton

SEAVERS. *Dch.* Sieverts ; *D., G.* Sievers ; *Fl.* Severs, Seyffers ; p.n. *See* Seward

SEAWARD. *A.S.* Sæweard ; a p.n. (sea warden). Or *see* Seward

SECCOMBE. A loc. n., Devon. Or Seacombe, Ches.

SECKER. *See* Seager. Prot. ref., Lond. 1618

SEDDING. *A.S.* Sidewine (?) ; *Fr.* Sedyn ; p.n. (a great friend)

SEDDON. *See* Sedding

SEDGER. *Fr.* Segers ; a p.n. *See* Seager

SEE. *See* Say

SEELEY. From Sillé ; a loc. n., Normandy ; Silly ; a loc. n., Belg. Or *G.* Siele, Sille ; *Fr.* Sillyé ; p.n. *See* Sill. Hugt., Lond. 1621

SEEVILL. *See* Civill

SEFTON. From Sephton ; a loc. n., Lancs

SEGON. *A.S.* Segen, Segwine, Sigen, Sigewine ; *Fl.* Seghin ; p.n. (victorious friend). Seguin, Hugt. n., Lond. 1688

SEGRAVE. *See* Seagrave

SEGRE. *A.S.* Sigar ; a p.n. *See* Segon

SEILY. From Zele ; a loc. n., Belg. Or *see* Seeley

SELBY. A loc. n., Yorks

SELDEN. From Seldon ; a loc. n., Devon

SELF. *N.* Sjölfr, a contr. of Sæ-ulfr (sea-wolf) ; *Fl.* Swolf ; *A.S.* Seolf, Seulf ; p.n.

SELKIRK. A loc. n., Scotl.

SELL. From Celles ; a loc. n., Belg. *Dch., G.* Selle ; *Fl.* Sell ; p.n.

SELLERS. *Dch.* Zeller ; *Fl.* Selders ; *N.-Fr.* Selchar ; *Old G.* Salahar. Or *A.S.* Sellier (dark warrior) ; *Fr.* Sellau ; p.n.

SELLEY. *Fr.* Sailly ; a p.n. Or from Selly ; a loc. n., Salop

SELLICK. From Sellack ; a loc. n., Heref. Or Zellick, Belg.

SELLINGER. *See* St Leger

SELWY, SELWYN. *A.S.* Selui, Selwine ; *Fl.* Sallewyn ; p.n. (dark friend)

Saxon tenant in *D.B.* William Selveyn held land in Oxon, *temp.* K. John.

SEMAIN, SEMMENCE, SEMMENS, SEMON. *Fr.* Sement; a p.n. *See* Symonds. Hugt., Lond. 1618

SEMPER. *G.*; p.n. Or *Fr.*· Saint-Pierre

SEMPILL, SEMPLE. A loc. n., Scotl. Or *Fl.* Sempels; a p.n.
Robert de Sempill, of Renfrew, *temp.* Alex. III., Scotl.

SENDALL. *D.* Sandell; *Fl.* Sendall; p.n.

SENIOR. From Signau (?); a loc. n., Switz.

SENNETT, SENNITT. From St Neot; a loc. n., Cornw.

SENTANCE. From St Anne's; a loc. n., Cornw. Or *Fr.* Seuntjens; a p.n. *See* St John

SEPPINGS. *See* Seapey

SERJEANT. *Fr.* Sergeant; a p.n.; *Lat.* Servientem

SERLE. *A.S.* Særle; *Fr.* Serlé, Serlui; *D.B.* Serlo; *Dch.* Sarlie; *S.* Serling; p.n. (a suit of armour)
Magister Serlo in Rot. Obl. et Fin., K. John (Devon), A.D. 1205.

SERMON. *Fr.* Serment; Hugt. p.n. Also Sermain; *A.S.* Saraman; *N.-Fr.* Sireman; p.n. (armour man)

SERRES. From Serez; a loc. n., Norm. *N.-Fr.* De Siry; *Fr.* Serès; *Fl.* Serruys; p.n. A Hugt. n., Lond. 1622

SERVANT. *Fr.* Serviant; a p.n. *See* Serjeant

SERVICE, St Servais; a loc. n., Belg. *Fr.* Servais; a p.n.

SESSENS. *See* Sisson

SETCHELL. From Setchell; a loc. n., Camb. Or Sachville, Norm.

SETON. *See* Seaton

SETTERINGTON. A loc. n., Yorks

SETTLE. A loc. n., Yorks

SEWARD. *N.* Sigvatr (bold in victory), a name of Odin; *D.* Sivert; *S.* Sivard; *G.* Sievert, Siewert; *Fl.* Siffert; *Dch.* Sieuwerts; *D.B.* Siward, Seward, Suert; p.n.

SEWILL, SEWELL. *A.S.* Sæweald (sea ruler). *See* Saville

SEXTON. *See* Saxton

SEYMOUR. From St Maur; a loc. n., Norm. Or *see* Saymer
In Roll of Battell Abbey.

SHACKLE. *Dch.* Schakel; a p.n.; *A.S.* sceacul (a shackle)

SHACKLETON. From Shakerton (?); a loc. n., Dur.

SHACKSBEE. From Skegby (?) (*D.B.* Schegebi); a loc. n., Notts. *D.* Schacke; *A.S.* Scœcca; p.n.; *bær* or *byr* a (dwelling). Comp. Shakerly, Shackerston, Exbear, Ailsbeare, Shebbeare, etc.
In Rot. Obl. et Fin. it is Scheggeby. Shacksbee is a p.n. in Mass., U.S.A.

SHACKSON. *D.* Schacke; *Dch.* Schaik, Schake; *G.* Schach; *Fl.* Schack, Schaeck, Schaek; p.n. *A.S.* Sceacca (brandisher)

SHADBOLT. *A.S.* Cædbeald; a p.n. (war prince, or bold in war)

SHADDICK, SHADDOCK. *G.* Schadeck; p.n. Dim. of Chad

SHADE. *See* Sheedy

SHADFORD. From Shadforth; a loc. n., Dur.

SHADGOT. *Old G.* Hadugot; *Fr.* Chagot; p.n.; *A.S.* Ceaddagod, Chadgod (war Goth)

SHADRAKE. *A.S.* Ceadric; *Old G.* Chadric; *G.* Schadrich; p.n. (war ruler)

SHADWELL. A loc. n., Middlx., Salop, Yorks

SHAFT. *N.* Skapti (a shaft-maker); *A.S.* Sceaft; *D.* Skafte; *G.* Schaffert; p.n.

SHAFTO. From Shaftoe; a loc. n., Northbd. Or *see* above

SHAKERLEY. A loc. n., Lancs, Salop

SHAKESPEARE. *See* Shacksbee
Or *N.-Fr.* Saquespée; a p.n., from *saquer* (to shake), *spée* (a lance.) *Lat. spatha* (a long sword.) Hence the personal name Saquespée or Sache-Espée.

SHAKESPEARE—*continued*

A.S. *scæccaspeare* means one who shakes or brandishes a spear, but there is no such personal name in any known list.

The *N.-Fr.* form, however, appears in the Norman records.

In 1195 Roger Sakespee paid a fine of 10s. in the bailifry of the Caux near Lillebonne. In 1198 William Sakespee occurs in the same bailifry. In 1195 William Sakespee owed two marks as security for Reginald le Blaier in the bailifry of Hiesmes. In 1203 Roger Sacespee paid a fine in the bailifry of Coutances, and Godfrey Sacespee another fine at the same time and place. (Great Rolls of the Exchequer, Normandy.) The Archives du Calvados relate a donation made in 1241, by Roger de Rupiere, to the Abbey of Villers-Canivet of all the land which Thomas Sach - Espée held of him in Grenteville. Another gift is recorded, made in 1250, to the Abbey of Troarn, by Robert, called Saquespée, of certain rights in corn in the parish of Touffréville. Again, Robert Saquespée, in 1257, sells to Troarn divers rents, and a sale is made in 1294 by Raoul de Noerville to Master Philippe Saquespée of a rent.

M. Jal, in his *Glossaire nautique*, mentions one Robin Saque-Espée, a pilot of a galliot (Anthoine-Nègre), and in the *Memorial de la Chambre des Comptes* of Paris, 1424, Ducange refers to a canon bearing the name of Jacob Saque-espée. Lastly, it occurs as a local name. There is a gorge or defile in la Manche, near Mortain called " Pertuis de Saque-spée," which, according to an ancient tradition, was the scene of a battle ; and there is also another place of the name in the commune of Cérences, in the same department. (Moisy, *Glossaire Anglo-Normand.*)

The question arises—did a branch of the Norman family return to Normandy after acquiring the English local name ?

SHALDERS. *N.* Skjöldr ; *A.S.* Scald, Sceald (a shield) ; *Fl.* Scholders ; p.n. *See* Skelt

SHALE. *See* Skeels

SHALLESS. *Dch.* Schallies ; *G.* Schallisch ; p.n. *See* Callis

SHAMBROOK. *See* Sambrook

SHAND, SHANDY. From Chanday ; a loc. n., Normandy

SHANKS. *D.*, *Dch.* Schank ; *Fl.* Schangh ; p.n. ; *sceanca* (leg)

SHANNON. Irish Shanahan ; a p.n. (a fox)

SHAPCOTT. A loc. n., Devon

SHAPLAND. From Shopland ; a loc. n., Ess.

SHARDALOW, SHARDLOW. A loc. n., Derbysh.

SHARLAND. From Shirland ; a loc. n., Derbysh. (?)

SHARMAN. From Charmont (?) ; a loc. n., France. Or *G.* Scharmann ; *Dch.* Schürman ; *D.* Schauman ; *D.B.* Sceman (?) ; p.n. (Shearman). *See* trade names, p. 13

SHARP. *A.S.* Scearp, Scerp ; *N.-Fr.* Poinant ; *Dch.* Scharp ; p.n. (sharp, quick, skilful)
Scarp in Rot. Hund.

SHARPEN, SHARPINS. *N.* Skarpheðinn, Skarpin (dried goat-skin coat) ; *G.* Scharf, Scharfen ; p.n. ; *A.S.* Scerphuin

SHARPUS. *Dch.* Schaapes ; a p.n.

SHARR. *See* Shaw

SHARWOOD. *See* Sherwood

SHATTICK, SHATTOCK. *G.* Schattke ; a p.n. *See* Shaddick

SHATTON. A loc. n., Derbysh.

SHAUL. From Shawell ; a loc. n., Leics

SHAVE. From Chièvres (?) ; a loc. n., Belg. Or *D.* Schevers ; *Fl.* Schaeff ; *G.* Schäfer ; p.n. *See* Chafy
Chievre, tenant in chief, *D.B.*

SHAW. A loc. n., Lancs, Oxf., Wilts. From *N.* Skógr (a wood). Or *S.* Skog ; *D.* Schau, Shaw ; *Dch.* Schouw, Schowe ; *Fl.* Schaugh ; p.n. Sceaux ; a loc. n., France

SHAWFIELD. A loc. n., Lancs

SHAWNEY. *See* Shorney

SHEAR. From Shere; a loc. n., Surr. Or *see* Shears

SHEARER. *A.S.* Scira; a p.n. *See* Shires

SHEARHOD. *A.S.* Scirhód; a p.n. (bright hood)

SHEARS. *A.S.* Scir; *Dch.* Schier; *G.* Schierse; p.n. (glorious)

SHEAVYN. *A.S.* Sceafwine (sheaf friend); *S.* Schevin; *Fl.* Scheyvin; a p.n.

SHEEDY. From the Irish *sioda* (silk). *N.* Skíði (a kind of bird); *G.* Schiedeck; *Dch.* Scheijde; *D.* Scythe; p.n.

SHEEKEL. *See* Shickle

SHELDON. A loc. n., Derbysh., Devon

SHELDRACK, SHELDRAKE, SHELD-RICK. *A.S.* Scealdric; a p.n. (shield ruler)

SHELFORD. A loc. n., Warw.

SHELL. An Irish corruption of Shields, Shiel

SHELLEY. A loc. n., Yorks

SHELTON. From Skelton; a loc. n., Yorks (*D.B.* Scheltun). Or Shelton, Beds, Norf.

SHEMMILL. From Chemille; a loc. n., France

SHENSTONE. A loc. n., Staffs

SHEPHERD, SHEPPARD. From Chebbard; a loc. n., Dorset. Or *Dch.* Schappert; a p.n. *A.S. scephyrde* (a shepherd)

SHEPPEY. A loc. n., Kent

SHERATON. A loc. n., Dur.

SHERBORNE. A loc. n., Devon, Dorset, Glost., Hants, Somers

SHERBROOKE. From Shirebrook; a loc. n., Derbysh.

SHERIDAN. From Shrawardine; a loc. n., Salop. Or *A.S.* Scerda; *S.* Scherdin; p.n.

SHERIFF. *N.* Greifi; n.n. *A.S.* Geréfa; *Engl.* Reeve, Shire-reeve; *G.* Schriefer; *D.* Schreve; p.n.; the office

SHERINGHAM. A loc. n., Norf.

SHERINGTON. A loc. n., Wilts

SHERLOCK. From Shurlach; a loc. n., Ches.

SHERRARD, SHERRATT. From Cheratte; a loc. n., Belg. Or *A.S.* Scirheard; *N.-Fr.* Sirart, Scirat (clever, firmness), Gerhard; *Fr.* Gerard; p.n. (firm spear). Sheraret, Flemish Prot. ref., Lond. 1618

SHERREN, SHERRIN. *See* Sherwin

SHERRINGTON. A loc. n., Bucks, Wilts

SHERRY. *See* Serres

SHERSBY. From Shearsby; a loc. n., Leics

SHERT. *See* Sherrard
In old documents Short is sometimes spelled Shert.

SHERVIL. From Sherwill; a loc. n., Devon

SHERWIN. *A.S.* Sceorfwine, Scorphuin; *D.* Scherwin; *Fl.* Scheyvin; *Dch.* Scherren; *G.* Scherwing; p.n. (clever friend)

SHERWOOD. A loc. n., Notts

SHEW. *See* Shaw

SHEWILL. *Dch.* Schewel; a p.n.

SHEWRING. From Shering; a loc. n., Ess. Or *Dch.* Schuring; a p.n.

SHICKLE. *G.* Schickel; a p.n.

SHICLE. *See* Shickle

SHIELDS, SHIELLS. From Shields; a loc. n., Dur.

SHILDRICK. *See* Sheldrick

SHILLAKER. From Shellacres; a loc. n., Northbd.

SHILLCOCK. *G.* Schilke; a p.n. Dim of *A.S.* Scel, Sceld; p.n.

SHILLING. A loc. n., Dorset. Or *A.S.* Scilling, Scylding; *D.*, *G.*, *Dch.* Schilling; p.n. Descendants of Scyld (shield)

SHILLINGFORD. A loc. n., Devon

SHILLITOE. *A.S.* Scealda; *Dch.* Schilte; *G.* Schilter; p.n. (shield bearer). Or *Ital.* Sillito (?)

SHILTON. A loc. n., Northants, Oxf., Worcest.

SHIMMIN. *D.* Schieman ; a p.n. *See* Skey

SHINGLE. *Dch.* Schenkel ; a p.n.

SHINGLETON. *See* Singleton

SHINN, SHINNER. From the Irish Shinan, originally O'Shanahan ; a p.n. (Lower). Or *A.S.* Sin ; a p.n. = *sig* (victory)

SHIPP. *A.S.* Scepi ; *D.* Schipke ; *Dch.* Schipper ; a p.n. (a sailor)

SHIPPARD. *See* Sheppard

SHIPPEY. From Shiphay ; a loc. n., Devon

SHIPPING. From Shippon ; a loc. n., Oxf. Or fam. n. of Shipp

SHIPLEY. A loc. n., Derbysh., Salop, Yorks

SHIPSIDES. From Shepshed (?) ; a loc. n., Leics

SHIPTON. A loc. n., Glost., Oxf., Salop, Yorks

SHIPWASH. From Sheepwash ; a loc. n., Devon, Northbd.

SHIPWAY. *See* Shippey

SHIRES. *A.S.* Scir ; a p.n. ; *Fl.* Scheyers ; a fam. n. (sheer, bright)

SHIRLEY. A loc. n., Derbysh., Hants, Kent, Surr., Worcest.

SHIRT. *See* Sherrard

SHIRTCLIFFE. *See* Sutcliffe

SHIVES. A loc. n., Scotl.

SHOEBRIDGE, SHOOBRIDGE. From Shewbridge ; a loc. n., Lancs

SHOESMITH, SHOOSMITH. A shovel or spade-maker

SHOLL. *N.* Skjöldr ; *A.S.* Scald (shield) ; *G.*, *Dch.* Scholl ; a p.n.

SHONE. *Dch.* Schoen ; a p.n. ; *A.S.* *scóne* (beautiful)

SHOOLBRED. From Shulbred ; a loc. n., Suss.

SHOPPEE. *A.S.* Scop ; *D.* Schoppe ; p.n. (a minstrel) ; *Fr.* Shoppée. Hugt. n.

SHORE. From Shoore ; a loc. n., Fland. *Dch.* Schoor ; a p.n.

SHOREY. *Fr.* Chourrier (?) ; a p.n.

SHORING. *See* Shewring

SHORLAND. A loc. n., Devon

SHORMAN. *See* Sharman

SHORNEY. *Fl.* Schournoy ; a p.n.

SHORROCK. *A.S.* Særic, Saric, Seric ; p.n. ; *serc* ; Scot. *sark* (a shirt of mail)

SHORT, SHORTER. *A.S.* Scorta ; *D.* Schorti ; *G.* Scharte, Schorter ; p.n. (short)

SHORTEN, SHORTING, SHORTINS. *Fl.* Scharten ; fam. n. of Short

SHORTRIDGE. From Shortbridge ; a loc. n., Suss.

SHOTBOLT. *See* Shadbolt

SHOTLIFF. *See* Shirtcliffe

SHOTTER. From Shothaugh ; a loc. n., Northbd. Or *G.*, *Dch.* Schotte ; a p.n. *See* Scott

SHOTTIN. From Shotten ; a loc. n., Dur. Or Shooten ; a loc. n., Belg.

SHOUT. *Dch.* Schout ; a p.n. ; *Fl.* ; p.n. *See* Skeat

SHOVE. From Echauffour ; a loc. n., France. Or *A.S.* Scuff, Scuffa (a shover) ; *Fr.* Chauveau (?) (bald) ; *Dch.* Schouw, Schuver ; *D.* Schow ; p.n.

SHOVELLER, SHOWLER. *See* Shuffle

SHOWEL. *See* Shuffle

SHOWERING. *See* Shewring

SHOYE. Irish form of Joyce

SHREEVE. *See* Sheriff

SHRIGLEY. A loc. n., Ches.

SHRIMPLING. *G.* Schrempel ; a p.n. ; *schrumpel* (a wrinkle)

SHRIMPTON. A loc. n.

SHROSBREE. From Shrewsbury ; a loc. n., Salop

SHRUBSOLE. A loc. n., Staffs

SHUBROOK. From Shobrook ; a loc. n., Devon

SHUCKBURGH. A loc. n., Warw.

SHUDD. *See* Scutt

SHUELL. *See* Sewill

SHUFFLE. *Dch.* Schewel ; *Fr.* Chauvel, Chouville, Chaville ; p.n.

SHUFFREY. *Fr.* Chaufouraux (?); a p.n.

SHUGAR. *See* Seager

SHUM. *A.S.* Sceomma; *G.* Schumm; p.n. (bashful, modest)

SHURMAR. *G.* Schirmer; *Dch.* Schermer; p.n. (protector, screener)

SHURY. *See* Shorey

SHUTE. A loc. n., Devon. Or *A.S.* Sceot; *Dch.* Schoot, Schut; *G.* Schütt; *D.* Skytte; p.n. *See* Skeat

SHUTER. *A.S.* Scytta; *Dch* Schuter; p.n. *See* Skeat

SHUTLER. *G.* Schüttler; a p.n. (shaker)

SHUTTLEWORTH. A loc. n., Yorks. *D.B.* Scitelesuuorde

SIBBERIN. *Fr.* Sibron, Sibrin. A Hugt. n., 1681

SIBBETT, SIBBIT. *Dch.*, *G.* Siebert; p.n. *See* Sigbert

SIBEL. *N.* Sig-baldr (foremost in victory); *A.S.* Sibba, Sibi, Sibbold, Sigbeald; *F.* Sibo; *G.* Sibe, Siebe, Sieber, Siebler, Seppelt, Sebald; *Dch.* Sibbelee; *Fl.* Siebels, Sibille; p.n.

SIBERT. *See* Sibbett

SIBLEY. From Sible; a loc. n., Ess. Or *Dch.* Sibbelee; a p.n.

SIBTHORPE. A loc. n., Notts

SIBUN. *A.S.* Sibban; *Fl.* Sibon; p.n.

SICH. *See* Sitch

SICKLEMORE. From Sicklemere; a loc. n., Suff.

SICKLIN. *See* Suckling

SIDDALL. A loc. n., Lancs. Or *see* Sydal

SIDDERS. *Dch.* Sieders; a fam. n. (Side)

SIDDON. *See* Seadon and Seaton

SIDE. A loc. n., Glost. Or *A.S.* Sida; *G.* Seite; p.n. (broad, great)

SIDEBOTTOM. A loc. n.

SIDEWAY. From Sidway; a loc. n., Staffs

SIDLE. *See* Sydal

SIDNEY. From St Denis (?); a loc. n., France. A loc. n., Suss. Originally Sithney

SIDWELL. A loc. n., St Sativola

SIELEY. *See* Seeley

SIEVEWRIGHT. *A.S.* Sefrith, Sœfrid, Sefred; p.n. (sea peace)

SIGBERT. *N.* Sigbjartr; *A.S.* Sigbeorht, Sigibert; p.n. (victory bright)

SIGGE, SIGGERS. *N.* Sig-urðr (fated to victory); *D.* Seyghers; *Dch.* Seegers; p.n. *See* Segon

SIGGINS. *See* Segon

SILCOCK. *Dch.* Sielcken; a p.n. Dim. of Sill. *See* Silk

SILENCE, SILLENCE. *D.* Seiling, Sillin; *A.S.* Sœling; p.n.

SILITOE. *See* Shillitoe

SILK. *A.S.* Sigelac, Silac, Sylc; p.n. (victory sport). *See* Silcock

SILL. *A.S.* Sil; *D.* Sillo; *S.* Sillow; *Fl.* Siegel; *G.* Siele, Sille; *Dch.* Siehl; p.n. *Sigel* (the sun)

SILLETT. *See* Sillitoe

SILLIS. From Seilles; a loc. n., Belg. *Dch.* Silles; p.n.

SILVER. *N.* Silfra (silver, greyhaired); n.n.; *D.* Silfver; *Dch.* Silva; *Fl.* Silver; p.n.

SILVERLOCK. *D.* Silberloh; a p.n.

SILVERSIDE. A loc. n.

SILVERSTONE. A loc. n., Northants

SILVERTON. A loc. n., Devon

SILVERTOWN. A loc. n., Ess.

SILVESTER. From St Sylvestre; a loc. n., Norm. *Fl.*, *G.* Silvester; *Fr.* Silvestre; p.n.

SILVEY. *See* Silver

SIMCOCK, SIMCOE, SIMKIN. Dimin. of Simmund, Simmon, Simon. From *N.* Sigmundr; a p.n. (victorious protector)

SIMMENS, SIMMONS, SIMMS. *See* Symonds

SIMPER. *G.* Semper, Simba; a p.n. Or from St Pierre

SIMPLE. *G.* Zimpel; a p.n. Or *see* Semple

SIMPSON, SIMSON. *N.* Simba, dim. of Sigmundr; *G.* Simba, Simm; *D.* Simeson; *S.* Simson; p.n. *See* Symonds

SIMVIL. *See* Somerville

SINCLAIR. *See* St Clair

SINEMON. *See* Symonds

SINGER. *Dch.*, *Fl.*; p.n.; *A.S.* Isenger (?) (iron spear); *singere* (singer)

   N.-Fr. Le Chaunter in Rot. Hund.

SINGLEHURST. *See* Swindlehurst

SINGLETON. A loc. n., Yorks

SIRER. *Fr.* Sirier; a p.n. (lordship)

SIRGOOD. *See* Sirkett

SIRKETT. From Cercottes; a loc. n., France. A Hugt. n., Lond. 1688

SIRR. From Seurre; a loc. n., France. *Dch.* Suur; a p.n.

SISLEY. From Sysseele; a loc. n., Fland. *Dch.* Sisselar; a p.n. *See* Cecil

SISON. From Syston; a loc. n., Leics

SISSENS, SISSON. From Siston; a loc. n., Glost.; Seesen (?); a loc. n., Germ. *Fl.* Sisen; *Dch.* Sisseren; p.n.

SITCH. From Sytch; a loc. n., Salop

SITDOWN. From Seatown; a loc. n., Dorset. Or *see* Seadon

SITGREAVES. From Seagrave; a loc. n., Leics. *D.B.* Satgrave

SITWELL. *See* Sidwell

SIVIL. *See* Civill

SKAE. *Dch.* Schee; a p.n.

SKAIFE. *See* Scaife

SKAKEL. *See* Shackle

SKAYMAN. *D.*, *Dch.*, *G.* Schiemann; a p.n.

SKEAT, SKEET. *N.* Skyti; *A.S.* Scytta, Scet; *D.* Skytte (archer); p.n. (a shooter, marksman). Scate, a Dch. Prot. ref., Lond., 1621

SKEDGE. *See* Skegg

SKEELS, SKELLS. From Schelle; a loc. n., Belg. *D.* Skeel; *Dch.* Schell; *Fl.* Schoels (shell); p.n. Or *A.S. scel*

SKEEN. *See* Skene

SKEFFINGTON. A loc. n., Leics

SKEGG. *N.* Skaggi; *A.S.* Scæcca, Scacca; *D.* Schek; *Dch.* Scheick; *G.* Schech; *Fl.* Schaek; p.n. (a shaker, brandisher)

SKELT. *Dch.* Scheltes; a p.n. *See* Child

SKELTON. A loc. n., Cumb., Yorks

SKENE. A loc. n., Aberdeen

SKERRITT. From Skirrid; a loc. n., Monmouth; Skerwith, Cumb.

SKERRY. A loc. n., Antrim. Or *see* Skerritt

SKETCHLEY. A loc. n., Leics

SKETT. *See* Skeat

SKEVINGTON. *See* Skeffington

SKEWES. A loc. n. (manor), Cornw. Or *Dch.* Schüss; a p.n.

SKEY. From Scy; a loc. n., Belg. *Dch.* Schey, Schie; p.n.

SKIDMORE. *See* Scudamore

SKIFFENS. *A.S.* Scefing; a fam. n.; *Dch.* Schiewink; *G.* Skiefe; p.n. (sheaf)

SKILBECK. From Skellbeck; a loc. n., Yorks

SKILES. *See* Skoyles

SKILLINGTON. A loc. n., Lincs

SKILLITO. *See* Shillitoe

SKILTON. *See* Skelton

SKINNER. *A.S.* Scinna, Scyn (bright, splendid)

SKIPPER. *Dch.* Schipper; a p.n.

SKIPPINS. *A.S.* Scepi (a sailor); *G.* Skiba, Skiebe; *D.* Schipke; p.n.

SKIPTON. A loc. n., Yorks

SKIPWITH. A loc. n., Yorks

SKIPWORTH. *See* Skipwith

SKIRLING. A loc. n., Peebles

SKIRROW. *See* Scorer

SKITT. *See* Skeat

SKITTERY. *A.S.* Sceotheri, Scyttaheri; *Dch.* Schutterij; p.n. (shooter, archer-warrior)

SKONE. *See* Scone

SKOULDING. *Dch.* Scholten. *See* Skelt

SKOYLES. *Fl.* Schoels; *Dch.* Schuil; a p.n. *See* Skeels

SKRINE. From Skreen; a loc. n., Sligo

SKRYMSHER. *G.* Schremser; a p.n. Or *see* Scrime

SKUCE. *See* Skewes

SKUDDER. *See* Shutter

SKULL. *N.* Skuli (from *skjol*, a shelter, protector); *Dch.* Schule; *Fl.* Schul; *D.B.* Scule; p.n.

SKULTHORPE. A loc. n., Norf.

SKUSE. *See* Skewes

SKY. *See* Skey

SLACK. A loc. n., Derbysh., Yorks

SLADDEN, SLADEN. *A.S.* Sledda; a p.n. (a dweller in the plain (?)). Or from Slaidburn; a loc. n., Yorks

SLADE. A loc. n., Devon, Suff. Or from Slad; a loc. n., Glost.

SLAPP. *N.* Slappi (a lump-fish); *G.* Schlappe; p.n.

SLARK. *G.* Slach; a p.n. *See* Slack

SLATCHER. *See* Slaughter

SLATER. *D.* Schlytter; *Dch.* Schlette, Sluyter, Sluiter; p.n. (striker)

SLATFORD. From Slaughterford; a loc. n., Wilts

SLATTER. *See* Slaughter

SLAUGHTER. A loc. n., near Sherborne, Glost. Or *G.* Slotta; *Dch.* Slooter; *Fl.* Slotte; p.n. (a privileged hunter)

SLEDDALE. A loc. n., Yorks

SLEEP. From Sleepe; a loc. n., Heref.; Sleap, Salop; or Slepe, Dorset. Or *Dch.* Schlipp, Sloep; *Fl.* Sleyp; *D.* Schlippe; a p.n. Slype; a loc. n., Flanders. *See* Slipper

SLEIGH. *D.* Schlie; *Dch.* Sluy; p.n.; *A.S. slýh* (a slayer)

SLEIGHT. A loc. n., Wilts

SLINGSBY. A loc. n., Yorks

SLIPPER. *N.* Sleppi; n.n. (one who lets slip); *D.* Schlippe; *G.* Schleppe; *Dch.* Schleper; p.n. Or an inhabitant of Slype. *See* Sleep
Ric. Sliper in Rot. Obl. et Fin., K. John.

SLOCOMBE. A loc. n., Devon

SLOGG, SLOGGER. *See* Slugg

SLOPER. *Dch.* Sloeper; a p.n. (a sleeper)

SLOUGH. A loc. n., Berks

SLOW. From Sloo; a loc. n., Devon. Or *see* Slough
Atte-Slo, Court of Husting.

SLOWMAN. *D.* Slomann; a p.n.; *N. slá-mann* (?) (a slayer, fighting man)
Lower thinks this is a disguise of the Jewish name Solomon.

SLUCE. *Fl.* Sloos, Sluys; p.n. Prot. ref., Lond. 1618

SLUGG. *Dch.* Sloog; a p.n. (slayer)

SLY. *See* Sleigh

SLYPER. *See* Slipper

SMAIL, SMALE. From Esmael (?); a loc. n., Belg. Or *A.S.* Smala; *Fl.* Smal; *Dch.* Smale; *G.* Schmehl; p.n. *A.S. smæl* (small, slender). Hugt. n., Lond. 1618

SMAILHOLM. A loc. n., Roxburgh

SMALLBONE. *N. smá-beinn*; *A.S. smœl-bán* (dwarfish)

SMALLEY. A loc. n., Derbysh.

SMALLFIELD. A loc. n., Yorks

SMALLMAN. *A.S.* Smaleman; a p.n.; *N. smá-menn* (mannikin)

SMALLPAGE. *See* Smallpiece

SMALLPIECE. *See* Malpas
Francis Smalpece, Mayor of Norwich, 1622.

SMALLWOOD. A loc. n., Ches., Staffs

SMART. *D.* Smart; *A.S.* Smert; p.n. (pain). Hugt. n.

SMEATON. A loc. n., Inverness, Cornw., Yorks

SMEDDLES. *See* Smethills

SMEE. *G.* Smy; a p.n.
SMELLIE. From Smeley; a loc. n., Ess. Or Semilly, Norm. *See* Smail
SMELT. *A.S.*, *Dch.*; p.n. (mild). Prot. ref., Lond. 1618
SMETHILLS. A loc. n., Lancs
SMETHURST. A loc. n.
SMILES. *See* Smail
SMILEY. *See* Smellie
SMIRKE. *Fl.* Smerche ; a p.n.; *A.S.* *smœrc* (a smile)
SMITH. *N.* Smiðr; *D.* Schmidt, Schmith, Smidt, Smidth, Smit, Smith; *Dch.* Smid, Smiet, Smith, Smitt ; *Fl.* Smet, Smit ; *G.* Schmidt, Schmitt; p.n.
John ye Smyth on a brass at Brightwell Baldwin, Oxon, A.D. 1400.
SMITHERS. *See* Smithies
SMITHIES. A loc. n., Yorks. Or *Dch.* Smithuis ; a p.n.
SMITHSON. A loc. n., Devon
SMOUT. *Fl.* ; p.n. (smooth)
SMURTHWAITE. From Smirthwaite ; a loc. n., Cumb.
SNADHORST. From Snadhurst; a loc. n., Kent
SNAGGE. *A.S.* Snoc; *D.* Schnack ; p.n. (a snake)
SNAITH. A loc. n., Yorks
SNAPE. A loc. n., Devon, Norf., Suff., Yorks. Or *Dch.* Sneep; *Fl.* Schnepp; p.n. (a peak)
SNAPPER. *Dch.* ; p.n.; *N.* Sneypir (?) (a snipper)
SNARE. *N.* Snori; *D.* Snaaijer; *D.B.* Snerri ; *G.* Schnier; *Dch.* Snoer, Schnaar; *Fl.* Sneyers; p.n. (active, quick)
SNART. A local corruption of Snargate, Kent. Or *A.S.* Snahard; *N.-Fr.* Senart; p.n. (snow firm); *N. snart* (swift, keen)
SNASDALL. A loc. n.
SNAZLE. From Snedshill; a loc. n., Salop
SNEAD. A loc. n., Worcest.
SNEATH. *See* Snaith

SNEE. *A.S.* Snæ; *G.* Snay; p.n. (snow)
SNEEZUM. From Snettisham; a loc. n., Norf.
SNELGROVE. A loc. n.
SNELL. *N.* Snjallr; n.n.; *A.S.*, *Dch.* Snel ; *G.* Schnell, Schnelle; p.n. (swift, courageous)
SNEPP. *See* Snape
SNEYD. A loc. n., Staffs, Worcest. Or Snaith, Yorks
SNOAD. *A.S.* Snod ; a p.n. (a cap, hood)
SNODDON. *See* Snowdon. Or *A.S.* Snoding ; a p.n. (descendants of Snod)
SNODGRASS. A loc. n., Scotl.
SNOOK. *N.* Snákr; n.n.; *A.S.* Snoc; *D.* Snog; *Dch.* Schnücke; *Fl.* Snoek; *D.B.* Snoch; p.n. (a snake)
SNOOKS. A loc. n., Devon. Or *Fl.* Snoeckx; a fam. n. of Snook
Lower thinks it is a corruption of Sevenoaks, Kent.
SNORE. *See* Snare
SNORING. A loc. n., Norf.
SNOWDEN. A loc n., Yorks
SNOWDON. A loc. n., Staffs, Wales
SNOXALL, SNOXELL. A loc. n.
SNUGGS. *See* Snooks
SNUSHALL. From Snowshill; a loc. n., Somers
SOAM. From Soham; a loc. n., Camb.
SOAMES. *See* Somers
SOANE. *A.S.* Son; *G.* Sohn; *Dch.* Son; p.n.
SOANES. *G.* Sohns; *Fl.* Soons; p.n.
SOAR. From Sore; a loc. n., France. Or *N. Sárr* (a wound); *Dch.* Soer; *G.* Sohr; p.n.
Sor in Rot. Obl. et Fin.
SOBEY. From Soubie; a loc. n., France. Or *N.* Sópi; a n.n. (a sweep); *A.S.* Sop; *Dch.* Sobbe; p.n.
SODDY. *See* Soder

SODEN. *Dch.* Soeding; a fam. n.
SODER. *A.S.* Sodda; *Fr.* Sodeau; *Dch.* Soede; p.n. (truthful)
SOFFE. *Fr.* Soffie; a p.n.
SOFLEY, SOFTEY, SOFTLEY. A loc. n., Dur.
SOLE. *N.-Fr.* De Sola; a p.n. In Rot. Hund.
SOMERFIELD. *D., S., G.* Sommerfeld; a p.n. *See* Summerville
SOMERFORD. A loc. n., Hants, Wilts
SOMERS, SOMES. From Sommeri; a loc. n., Norm. Or *A.S.* Som, Somar; *Fl.* Somme, Somers; *N. Sômi* (honour); p.n.
SOMERSET. The county
SOOBY. *See* Sobey
SOOLE. *See* Sole
SOONS. *See* Soanes
SOPER, SOPPER. From Sober; a loc. n., Yorks. Or *A.S.* Soppa; *G.* Sober; *Fl.* Sopers; p.n. *See* Sobey
SOPPET, SOPWITH. From Sopworth; a loc. n., Wilts
SORBEY, SORBY. A loc. n., Yorks
SORE. *See* Soar
SOREL. *N.-Fr.*; p.n. (yellow) In Rot. Hund.
SOTHAM. From Southam; a loc. n., Warw.
SOTHEBY. From Sotby; a loc. n., Lincs
SOTHERN. From Sotherton; a loc. n., Suff.
SOTHERS. From Southease; a loc. n., Suss.
SOUL. *See* Sole
SOULBY. A loc. n., Westmd.
SOULSBY. *See* Soulby
SOUNDY. *See* Sanday. Or *N.* Sjaundi; a p.n. (the seventh child)
SOUPER. *See* Soper
SOUTH. Hugt. n., Lond. 1618
SOUTHALL. A loc. n., Middlx.
SOUTHAM. A loc. n., Glost., Warw.
SOUTHARD. *See* Southward

SOUTHBY. *See* Sotheby
SOUTHCOMBE. A loc. n., Devon
SOUTHCOTT. A loc. n., Cornw., Devon. Or from Southcote; a loc. n., Devon, Yorks
Michael S., of S., Devon, 27 Hen. III. (1242); Will. S., of S., 19 Ed. III. (1345), Harl. MSS.
SOUTHERN. From Southton; a loc. n., Wilts
SOUTHERWOOD. *See* Southwood
SOUTHEY. A loc. n., Devon. Or *Fr.* Souday; a p.n.
SOUTHGATE. A loc. n., Middlx.
SOUTHWARD. From Southworth; a loc. n., Lancs. Or *see* Southwood
SOUTHWELL. A loc. n., Dorset, Notts
SOUTHWOOD. A loc. n., Somers
SOUTTARR. *See* Sowter
SOWARD. *See* Southward
SOWELS. *See* Saul
SOWERBUTTS. A loc. n., Lancs. Or *A.S.* Sarabeorht, Sarbert; p.n. (bright armour)
SOWERBY. A loc. n., Lancs, Yorks. *D.B.* Sorebi
SOWLER. From Soliers; a loc. n., Norm.
SOWTER. From Sautour (?); a loc. n., Belg. *A.S.* Sota; *G.* Sotta, Sauter; *Dch.* Soeter, Souter; *Fl.* Suttor; *Fr.* Sutter; p.n. Or *A.S. sutere* (a shoemaker). Sotteau, Hugt., Cant. 1622
SOWTON. A loc. n., Devon
SPAIN. *N.-Fr.* De l'Espagne; *Dch.* Spaan; p.n.
SPALDING. A loc. n., Lincs
SPALL. From Sporle; a loc. n., Norf. Or *Dch.* Spall, Spoel; p.n. *See* Paul
SPANKIE. *Fl.* Spanoghe; or *G.* Spanger; p.n. (a buckle-maker); *A.S. spange* (a clasp)
SPANSWICK. A loc. n.
SPANTON. From Spaunton; a loc. n., Yorks
SPARHAM. A loc. n., Norf.

SPARKE. *A.S.* Spearhafoc, Sperauoc; *Dch.* Sporck; p.n. (spar-hawk)

SPARROW. *A.S.* Spar; *S.* Sparre; p.n. *See* Spurr

SPARSHOTT. From Sparsholt; a loc. n., Hants

SPAULL. *See* Spall

SPEAIGHT. *See* Speight

SPEAK, SPECK, SPEKE. From Speke; a loc. n., Lancs. Or *N.-Fr.* Espec; a p.n.

Le Spec in Rot. Obl. et Fin.

SPEAKMAN. *Dch.* Spiekerman; a p.n. (a spikeman)

SPEAR, SPEER, SPEIR. *A.S.* Spar, Sper; *Fl.* Spiers (small); *G.* Speer; *Dch.* Spier; p.n. Prot. ref. n., Lond. 1622

SPEARING. *Dch.* Spiering; a fam. n.

SPEARMAN. It is said to be a corruption of Aspromont

Surtees, Hist. Dur., vol. i. p. 94. Aspermound in Roll of Battell Abbey.

SPEECHLY. From Spetchley; a loc. n., Worcest.

SPEED, SPEEDY. *N.-Fr.* De Spada; a p.n.

Sped in Rot. Hund.

SPEIGHT. *A.S.* Spieta; *Old G.* Spiz; *G.* Spiess (spear); *S.* Spethz, Spitz; *D.* Speich; *Dch.* Spigt; *Fl.* Specht; p.n.

SPELLER, SPELLS. *Fl., Dch.* Spellers; a p.n. (speaker)

SPELLMAN. *Dch.* Speelman; *G.* Spielmann; *Fl.* Spelmans; p.n. (a musician)

SPENCE, SPENCER. From Despenser (*Lat.* Dispensator); a steward

Dispensator, a tenant in chief in *D.B.*

SPENCELEY. A loc. n.

SPENDLOVE. *A.S.* span - leof (?) (alluring dear)

SPERLING. *G.*; p.n. Dimin. a young sparrow. *See* Spurr

SPICE, SPICER. *Old Fr.* Espicier (?); *G.* Spiess; p.n.

Benedict le Spicer in Rot. Obl. et Fin., K. John.

SPIKINGS. *Old G. spiz* (a spear). *See* Speight. Dimin. *A.S. spicyng* (a nail)

SPILL. *Dch.*; p.n. (a spoiler (?))

SPILLANE. *See* Spilling

SPILLER. *G.*; p.n. *See* above

SPILLING. *D.* Spelling; a p.n.

SPILSBURY. A loc. n., Worcest.

SPINK. *S., D.* Spincke; *Dch.* Spaink; *Fl.* Spinnock; p.n. (a fieldfare)

SPITE. *See* Speight

SPITTA. *See* Speight

SPITTAL. A loc. n., Derbysh., Ess., Lincs, Northbd., S. Wales, Yorks

SPITTLE. A loc. n., Yorks

SPITTY. A British loc. n., Spyddid or Spytty. From the Latin *hospitium*, a hospital, as in Yspytty Ystwith (Card.) and Llan-spyddid (Brecons). Or *see* Speedy

SPLAINE. *See* Spillane

SPOER. *See* Spurr

SPOFFORD. *See* Spofforth

SPOFFORTH. A loc. n., Yorks

SPOKES. *Dch.* Spook; a p.n.; *N. spakr* (?) (wise)

SPON. A loc. n., Staffs.

SPONG. *D.* Sponneck (?); a p.n.; *N. spöng* (spangle)

SPOONER. *G.* Sponer; a p.n.; *N. Spánn* (?) (a Spaniard)

SPORE, SPOURS, SPOUS. *See* Spurr

SPORLE. A loc. n., Norf.

SPORTON. From Sproughton (?); a loc. n., Suff.

SPOTTISWOODE. A loc. n., Berwick

SPRAGG, SPRAGUE. *See* Sprake

SPRAGGETT. *See* Sprake

SPRAKE. *A.S.* Sperauc; a p.n. (sparrow-hawk). Or *N. sprakr* (active, sprightly); or *A.S. spræca* (a speaker, counsellor)

SPRANGE. *Dch.* Sprang; a p.n.; *N. spranga* (sprightly)

SPRATLEY. From Sproatley; a loc. n., Yorks

SPRATLING. *A.S.* Spræcaling; a p.n.; *N. sprakr* (active)

SPRATT. *Dch.* Spruit; *G.* Sprotte; p.n. *See* Sprott

SPRAY. *See* Spry

SPRECKLEY. *N.* Spræklegr; *A.S.* Spræcaling (sprightly); *D.* Spechler; p.n.

SPRIGGINS, SPRIGGS. *A.S.* Spræca (a speaker); *Dch.* Sprik; p.n.

SPRING. *G., Dch., D.* Springer; a p.n. (a leaper). Prot. ref., Dover, 1622

SPRINGALL, SPRINGHALL. From Springhill; a loc. n., Lancs. Or *Fl.* Springael; a p.n.; *A.S. springlíc* (lively)

SPRINGBELT, SPRINGETT. *Dch.* Springveldt; a p.n.

SPRINGTHORPE. A loc. n., Lincs

SPRINKS. *G.* Springst; a p.n. *See* Spring

SPROAT, SPROD. *See* Sprott

SPROSTON. A loc. n., Ches.

SPROTT. *A.S.* Sprat, Sprot (a stick, spear), Spretman (a spearman); *G.* Sprotte; p.n.

SPRUCE. *Dch.* Spross; *G.* Sprosse; p.n. (a sprout)

Hence the old term Prussian or spruce beer, made from pine sprouts.

SPRULES. From Spreull; a loc. n., Scotl.

SPRY. *Dch.* Spree; *G.* Spreu; p.n. (chaff (?))

SPUNNER. *See* Spooner

SPURGE, SPURGEON, SPURGIN. Dim. of Sporre (Spörrechen). *See* Spurr

SPURR. *N.* Spörr; n.n. (a sparrow); *D.* Sporré; *Dch.* Spoor; *D.B.* Spur, Sperri, Sporri; p.n.

SPURRELL. From Spurwell; a loc. n., Devon. Or *G.* Spörel; a p.n. *See* Spurr

SPYER. Spy; a loc. n., Belg. *G.* Speier; *Dch.* Spijer; p.n. Belonging to Spy

SQUANCE. *G.* Schwanitz; a p.n. (tail)

SQUARE, SQUAREY, SQUIRE. *Fr.* Esquier; a p.n.

John le Squier in Rot. Obl. et Fin., K. John. Also a Huguenot n.

SQUIRELL. *A.S.* Scirweald, Scirold, Scirrell; p.n. (bright ruler) glittering, as applied to armour

SQUIRL. *See* Squirell

STABLE. From Staple; a loc. n., Devon, Kent. Or *see* Steble

Alex. de Stapele, Worcs., in Rot. Obl. et Fin., K. John.

STABLEFORD. A loc. n., Salop, Staffs

STACEY. *Fr.* St Eustace; a loc. n.

STACPOOLE. A loc. n., Pembrokesh.

STADDON, STADEN. A loc. n., Devon; also a loc. n., Flanders. *Dch.* Staden; a p.n.

STAFF. Stave; a loc. n., Belg. Or *D.* Staw; *S.* Staaf; *G., Fl., Dch.* Staff; p.n.

STAFFORD. The county town

STAGG. *D.* Stage; *Fl.* Stache; *G.* Stach; p.n.; *A.S. stác-a* (a stake)

STAGOLL. *See* Steggall

STAIGHT. *See* Stead

STAINER. Steener; a loc. n., Flanders. Or *N.* Steinnar; *A.S.* Stenhere; *Fl.* Stanier; *G.* Steiner; p.n. (firm warrior). Prot. ref., Lond. 1618

STAINES. A loc. n., Middlx.

STAINNS. *See* Staines

STAINTON. A loc. n., Cumb., Dur., Lancs, Yorks

STAIR. A loc. n., Ayrsh. Or *A.S.* Ster; *D.* Stæhr, Sthyr; *G.* Stähr, Stehr; p.n.; *A.S. stær* (a starling)

STALEY. A loc. n., Ches.

STALKER. *Dch.* Stolker, Stolkert; p.n.; *N. stál-görr* (?) (made of steel)

STALLABRASS, STALLEBRASS. From Stallingbusk (?); a loc. n., Yorks. Or *N. stál-brass* (hardened steel)

STALLARD, STALLER. *Fl.* Stallaert; *Dch.* Staller; p.n.; *A.S. steallere* (a steward); *Fr.* de Stailleurs. Hugt. n., Lond. 1618

STALLION. *S.* Stahlin; *Fl.* Staelens; *G.*, *Dch.*, Stalling; *Fr.* Stalin; p.n.

STALLWOOD, STALLWORTHY. Loc. n. (?)

STAMER, STAMMERS. *D.B.* Stam; *G.* Stammer; *Dch.* Staamer; p.n. (family, race). Or *A.S. stamor* (stammering)

STAMFORD. A loc. n., Lincs

STAMP. From *N.-Fr.* D'Estampes; a p.n.; Stampes, a ville, Norm. Or *D.*, *G.* Stampe; p.n. (a stamper). Prot. ref., Lond. 1622

STAMPER. Stembert; a loc. n., Belg. Or *Dch.* Stamperius; *Fl.* Stampaert; p.n.

STANBOROUGH. From Stainborough; a loc. n., Yorks

STANBRIDGE. A loc. n., Beds, Dorset, Ess., Yorks; Steenbrugge, Fland.

STANBURY. A loc. n., Devon, Yorks

STANCLIFFE. From Staincliffe; a loc. n., Yorks

STANCOMBE. A loc. n., Devon, Dorset

STANDEN. A loc. n., Wilts

STANDIDGE. A loc. n., Yorks

STANDISH. A loc. n., Glost., Lancs

STANDFAST. *G.* Standfuss; a p.n.

STANESBY, STANSBY. From Stonesby; a loc. n., Leics

STANFORD. A loc. n., Norf.

STANGER. *D.*, *G.* Stanger; *S.* Stange; p.n. Or a loc. n., Cumb. (a pole, stake)

STANHAM. *See* Stoneham

STANHOPE. A loc. n., Dur.

STANIFORD. A loc. n., Devon, Salop

STANIFORTH. From Stainforth (*D.B.* Stenforde); a loc. n., Yorks

STANILAND. From Stainland; a loc. n., Yorks

STANLEY. A loc. n., Staffs, Dur., Glost., Lancs, Lincs, Yorks
The name of this manor was assumed by the Norman knight Valescherville. *D.B.* de Valuille.

STANNARD. *N.* Steinröðr (stone, *i.e.* firm glory); *G.* Steinert, Steinhardt, Stanner; *Fl.* Standaert; *D.B.* Stanard, Stanart, Stanhert; p.n.

STANNERS, STANNETT. *See* Stannard

STANPFLY. From Stanfree (?); a loc. n., Derbysh.

STANSFIELD, STANFIELD. A loc. n., Camb., Lancs, Suff., Yorks. *D.B.* Stanesfelt

STANSHAW. A loc. n. Or *see* Stanger

STANTON. A loc. n., Derbysh., Heref., Salop, Somers, Wilts

STANWAY. A loc. n., Ess., Glost., Salop

STANWELL. A loc. n., Middlx.

STANYON. A loc. n., Northants

STAP. *A.S.* Steapa; *Fl.* Staps; *Dch.* Stappes; p.n. *See* Staff
R. Stape in Rot. Obl. et Fin.

STAPLES. From Staplers; a loc. n., Hants. Or Staple, Devon. *See* Stable

STAPLETON. A loc. n., Glost., Salop, Somers, Wilts

STAPLEY. A loc. n., Ches., Devon

STARBUCK. From Starbeck; a loc. n., Yorks. Or Stabroeck, Sterrebeek; loc. n., Flanders

STAREY. *See* Sterry

STARK. *N.* Starkaðr; a p.n. *Sterk-Höðr* (strong warrior), a mythical Danish hero; *A.S.* Starc; *D.* Starck; *G.* Stark; *Fl.* Starck, Sterck, Storck; *Dch.* Stark, Sterk, Stork, Sturk; *D.B.* Stercher, Stergar; p.n.

STARKEY. *See* Stark

STARLEY. From Stawley (?); a loc. n., Somers

STARLING. Dimin. *D.B.* Saxon tenant. Or Easterling. *See* Starr

STARNE. *N.* Stjárn (a star); *G., D., Fl., Dch.* Stern; p.n.

STARR. *N.* Starri (starling); *D.B.* Stari, Stori, Stare; *Dch.* Storre, Starre; *G.* Stöhr, Stör, Stahr; *S.* Stahre, Star, Stare; *D.* Stahr; p.n.

START. A loc. n., Devon

STARTIN. From Starton; a loc. n., Warw.

STARTUP. *D.*; loc. and p.n.

STATHAM. A loc. n., Ches.

STATHER. *See* Stathern

STATHERN. A loc. n.

STATTER. *See* Stather

ST AUBYN. From St Aubin; a loc. n., Normandy

STAUNTON. A loc. n., Glost., Heref., Leics, Worcest.

STAVELEY. A loc. n., Derbysh., Yorks, Westmd.; also Flanders

STEABBEN. From Stebbing; a loc. n., Ess.

STEAD, STEED. From Stidd; a loc. n., Lancs. Or Stydd, Derbysh. *See* Studd

STEAMSON. *See* Stephenson

STEANE. A loc. n., Belg., Northants

STEARN. *See* Starne

STEBBENS, STEBBINGS. *See* Steabben

STEBLE. *N.* Styr-baldr; *S.* Stiebel; *D.* Stabel, Stibolt; *Dch.* Stapel; *D.B.* Stable; *G.* Stebel, Stiebahl; a p.n. (war bold, or battle prince)

STED. *See* Stead

STEDALL. *G.* Steidel; a p.n.

STEED. *See* Stead

STEELE. A loc. n., Northbd., Salop. *Dch., G.* Stiel; a p.n.

STEER. *N.* Styrr (battle); *D.* Stühr, Stæhr; *S.* Stühr; *G.* Steer, Stehr, Stier; *Fl.* Stiers; *Dch.* Steer; *A.S.* Ster, Sterr, Stir, Stur, Styr; p.n.

Styr, a thane at the court of Ethelred II., mentioned in Royal Letters Patent. Also in Hardicanute's reign.

STEGGALL, STEGGLES, STEGGOLD. *N.* Stag-näl (?); n.n. (a darning-needle); *S.* Stagnell; *G.* Steckel; *Dch.* Stechel, Stiggel; p.n.

STEMBRIDGE. A loc. n., Somers, S. Wales

STENHOUSE. A loc. n., Stirling. Also Steenhuyze; a loc. n., Flanders

STENSON. A loc. n., Derbysh. Or *D.* Stensen; *S.* Stennsson. From Stephenson; p.n.

STENT. *See* Stunt

STEPHENS. Hugt. n., Lond. 1618

STEPTOE. *A.S.* Stepiot; *G., Fl.* Steppe, Stiphoudt; a p.n. *See* Stibbard

STERLING, STIRLING. A loc. n., Scotl.

STERRY. *See* Steer

STEVENSON. *See* Stiffin

STEWARD, STEWART. *D.* Stigaard (war guard); *S., Dch.* Stuart; *Fl.* Steyaert, Stuywaert; p.n. Or *A.S. stiweard* (steward)

The descendant of Alanus Dapifer, son of the Norman Fitzalan, styled himself *Senescellus Scotiæ* from the hereditary office. Q. Mary first spelled the name Stuart, *temp.* David I.

STIBBARD. *A.S.* Stithbeorht; *Dch.* Stibbe, Stiphout; *G.* Stibor; p.n. (firm illustrious)

STIBBON. *N.* Styr-björn; *D.* Stybe; *G.* Stibane; p.n. (war-bear)

STICHBURY. *See* Stutchbury

STICHLEY. From Stirchley; a loc. n., Salop

STICHLING. From Stickillin; a loc. n., co. Louth. Or *D.* Stick; *G.* Stich; a p.n. Prot. ref., Norwich, 1622

STICKLAND. A loc. n., Dorset

STIFF. *S.* Styffe; *G.* Steffe, Stief; *Dch.* Stiev, Stiffij; *Fl.* Steuve; *D.B.* Stefan; p.n. *See* Stiffin

In the Midland counties Stiff is used as a contraction for Stephen.

STIFFIN. *D.* Steffens, Steffin; *Dch.* Stieven; a p.n. *See* Stephens

STIGGANT. *N.* Stigandi; n.n. (a stepper); *A.S.* Stigand; a p.n.

STIGGINS. Stekene; a loc. n., Fland. Or *N.* Stigandi; n.n; *D.* Stikken; *Fl.* Stickens; p.n.

STIGGLE, STIGGLES, STIGLE. *See* Steggall

STILES, STYLE, STOYLE. From Styal; a loc. n., Ches. Or *G.* Steil; a p.n.

STILL. *G.*, *Dch.* Stille; a p.n. (quiet)

STILLINGFLEET. A loc. n., Yorks

STILWELL. A loc. n. (manor), Surrey. Stilewell, Styelwell

STIMSON. *See* Stephens

STINSON. *See* Stenson

STIRK. *Dch.* Sterk; *Fl.* Sterck; *G.* Stercke; p.n.; *N.* *sterkr*; *A.S.* *stearc* (strong)

STIRRUP. From Styrrup; a loc. n., Notts. Or *D.* Stürup; a p.n. *See* Steer

Stürup is the Danish form of Styrthorp, a loc. n.

STIVELEY. *See* Staveley

STOBBS. A barony in Roxburgh. *See* Stubbs

STOCK, STOCKS. A loc. n., Salop. *D.*, *Fl.*, *G.* Stock; *Dch.* Stok; *D.B.* Stochi, Stoches; p.n.

De Stok and De Stokes occur several times in Rot. Obl. et Fin., K. John.

STOCKBRIDGE. A loc. n., Dorset, Hants

STOCKDALE. A loc. n., Cumb.

STOCKEN. *See* Stocking

STOCKER. *Fl.* Stocquart; *G.* Stöcker; *D.* Stoker, Stokker; p.n.; *A.S.* *stocc* (a trumpet), *stoccheard* (?) (strong trumpeter)

STOCKFORD. From Stokeford; a loc. n., Dorset

STOCKHAM. A loc. n., Ches., Devon; Stockhem, Belg.

STOCKING, STOCKINGS. A loc. n., Herts. Or *Dch.* Stokkink; p.n.; fam. n. of Stock. Prot. ref., Norwich, 1622

STOCKTON. A loc. n., Dur., Salop, Warw., Worcest.

STOCKWELL. A loc. n., Devon, Surr.

STOFER. *A.S.* Stuf; *Fl.* Stoove, Stouffe; *Dch.* Stoffers, Stöver; *G.* Stöffer; p.n.; *A.S.* *stof* (a club, stake)

STOKE. A loc. n., Ches., Devon, Heref., Kent, Northants, Salop, Somers, Staffs, Surr.

STOKELY. A loc. n., Cornw.

STOKER, STOKEY, STOKOE. *See* Stocker. Hugt. n.

STOKES. A loc. n., Devon

STOLLERY. *G.* Stolareyck (?); a p.n.

STONARD. *See* Stannard

STONE. A loc. n., Kent, Staffs, etc. Or *N.* Steinn; *D.* Steen; p.n.

STONEHAM. A loc. n., Hants. Or Stonham, Suff.

STONEHOUSE. A loc. n., Devon, Hants, Glost.

STONELAKE. From Stoneleigh; a loc. n., Warw.

STONELEY. A loc. n., Hunts, Warw.

STONES. *D.* Steen; *S.* Stein; *N.* Steinn (stone); *A.S.* Stan, Sten; *Fl.* Steens; p.n. A freq. loc. n. Atte Stunnes, 1327.

STONEX. From Stanwix; a loc. n., Chesh.

STONEY. A loc. n., Warw.

STOOP, STOPP. *See* Stubbs

STOPFORD. A loc. n.

STOPHER. *See* Stofer

STOPS. From Stopes; a loc. n., Lancs

STOREY. *Fl.* Storie, Story; *Fr.* Stora; *A.S.* Stori; p.n. (sturdy)

STORK. A loc. n., Yorks. *D.B.* Estorch

STORMONT. From Stoumont; a loc. n., Belg. *Fl.* Stoumon; a p.n.

STORR. *D.* Stahr; *Dch.* Stor; p.n. *See* Starr

STORRS. A loc. n.,Westmd.

STORRY. *See* Storey

STOTE. *Fl.* Stoht; *Dch.* Stout; p.n. *See* Stott

STOTESBURY. From Stottersbury; a loc. n., Northants

STOTHERS. From *G.* Stoddart; a p.n.

STOTT. *N.* Stóti (a bull); *A.S.* Stotte; *Dch.* Stoete; p.n.

STOURTON. A loc. n., Wilts

STOUT. A loc. n., Devon, Somers. Or *Dch.* Stout; *G.* Staudte; p.n. *See* Stott

STOVELL. *See* Stowell

STOVING. From Stoven; a loc. n., Suff.

STOW. A loc. n., Ess., Northants, Salop, Staffs

STOWELL. A loc. n., Glost., Somers, Wilts

STOWER. A loc. n., Dorset. Or *Dch.* Stower; a p.n.

STOWERS. *See* Stower

STRACHAN, STRAHAN. A loc. n., Kincardine

STRAKER. *A.S.* Starc, Strac; *Dch.* Stracke; p.n. (straight, erect). *See* Stark

STRANG. *A.S.*, *N.* Strangr (strong); *Dch.* Strange; p.n. Streing, Hugt. n., Lond. 1688
John le Strange held land in Staffs, *temp.* K. John.

STRANGE. *N.-Fr.* L'Estrange; a p.n.

STRANGER. *A.S.* Strangher (strong hero)

STRANGWAYS. A loc. n., Lancs

STRANGWICH. *See* Strangways

STRAPP. *D.* Starup; or *Dch.* Straub; p.n.

STRATFOLD. From Stratfield; a loc. n., Hants

STRATFORD. A loc. n., Oxf., Suff., Warw., Wilts

STRAWBRIDGE. A loc. n., Somers

STRAWSON. *D.B.* Struostun; a p.n.

STREATFIELD. *N.-Fr.* De Stratavilla or Estreville; a p.n. Or Stratfield, Hants

STRECKLE. *G.* Streckel; a p.n. *See* Straker. Dim.

STREDWICK. *See* Strudwick

STREET. A loc. n., Devon, Hants, Somers, Suss.

STREETER. *A.S.* Struth; *Old G.* Striter; *D.* Stræter; *G.* Streda; p.n. (a fighter, warrior)

STREETON, STRETTON. A loc. n., Derbysh., Staffs, Warw., etc.

STRELLEY. A loc. n., Notts. *D.B.* Strahlei
Walter de Straley in Rot. Obl. et Fin., K. John.

STRETCH. *G.* Streich; a p.n.; Stric in *D.B.*; *N.* strjúka; *D.* stryge; *A.S.* strica (a stroke)

STRIBLING, STRIPLING. Dimin. of Stripp

STRICKLAND. A loc. n., Cumb.

STRICKSON. From Strixton; a loc. n., Northants. Or *see* Stretch

STRICKSTOCK. A loc. n.

STRIDE. *G.* Streit; a p.n.; *A.S.* strið (strife)

STRINGER. *Dch.* Strenger; *G.* Stringer; p.n. (strict, vigorous, firm, brave). *See* Stranger

STRIP, STRIPP. *D.* Stripp; *Dch.* Streep; p.n.; *N.* stripr (a stripling, youth)

STRODE. *See* Stroud

STRONG. *See* Strange

STRONGITHARM. *See* Armstrong

STROTHERS. A loc. n., Dur.

STROUD. A loc. n., Dorset, Glost., Hants, Middlx.

STROVER. *G.* Struwe; *Dch.* Stroeve, Struwer; p.n.; *Fl.* struve; *Goth.* struban (proud)

STROWGER, STROWYER. *D.* Stroeyer; *Fl.* Strohouwer; p.n. (strewer (?))

STRUDWICK. *Dch.* Strodijk; a p.n.

STRUMPSHAW. A loc. n., Norf.

STRUTHERS. A loc. n., Scotl.

STRUTT. *A.S.* Struth ; *Fl.* Stroot ; p.n. (strife, battle) ; hence *G.* Struttmann ; a p.n. (a fighting man, a spoiler)

> In the pedigree of Baron Rayleigh Burke derives this name from Godfrid Strutz de Hinkelred of Unterwalden in Switzerland.

STUART. *See* Stewart

STUBBINGS. A loc. n., Berks

STUBBS. A loc. n., Yorks (*D.B.* Stubuzan, Stubbsham). Or *N.* Stubbi ; n.n. ; *D.B.* Stubart ; *G.* Stöbe ; *D.* Stüb ; *Dch.* Stoop, Stübbe ; p.n. (branch) of lineage (?)

> Adam de Stubber in Rot. Obl. et Fin., K. John.

STUCK, STUCKEY. *A.S.* Stuca ; *Dch.* Stucki ; p.n. (a pikeman (?))

STUCKBERY. *See* Stutchbury

STUDD. *A.S.* Stedda, Stid, Stith, Stut ; *D.* Stuhde ; *G.* Studer, Studt ; p.n. *stíð* (firm)

STUDHOLME. From Studham ; a loc. n., Herts

STUKELEY. From Stewkley ; a loc. n., Bucks, Hunts

STUMORE. *See* Sturmer

STUNT. *G.* Zunz ; a p.n.

STURCH, STURGE, STURGES. From Sturridge ; a loc. n., Devon. Or *A.S.* Styrgar ; a p.n. (battle spear)

STURGEON. *Fr.* Lestourgeon ; a p.n. Hugt. n., Lond. 1683

STURMER. *N.* Styrmir ; *A.S.* Styrmær (famous fighter) ; *G.* Stürmer ; p.n.

STURROCK. *Dch.* Sturk ; a p.n. *See* Stark

STURT. *See* Stuart

STUTCHBURY. A loc. n., Northants

STUTFIELD. From Estouteville (?) ; a loc. n. near Yvetot, Norm.

STUTTER. *A.S.* Stuthere ; *G.* Stutzer ; p.n. (firm warrior). *See* Studd

STUTTLE. *See* Stutfield

STYAN. *N.* Steinn (stone, firm) ; a p.n.

STYGLE. *See* Steggall

STYTH. *See* Studd

SUART. *See* Seward

SUCKER. *G.* ; p.n. *See* Sugg

SUCKLING. *F.* Sikke, Sikko ; *A.S.* Sycling ; *S.* Syk ; *Dch.* Suchtelen, Sukkel ; *G.* Suche, Suckel ; p.n. *See* Sugg

SUDBURY. A loc. n., Middlx., Suff.

SUDLOW. From Sudeley, Glost.

SUEL. *See* Sewill

SUFFELL, SUFFIELD. A loc. n., Norf., Yorks

SUFFLING. *A.S.* Swefling ; a p.n. *Swæf* (Suabian)

SUGARS. *See* Sugg. Fl. ref., Lond. 1618

SUGDEN. A loc. n., Salop

SUGG. *A.S.* Sucga, Suga, Sig, Syg ; *G.* Suge ; p.n. (victory)

SUGGATE, SUGGETT, SUGGITT. From Southgate ; a loc. n., Derbysh., Middlx.

SULLIVAN. Irish O'Suillobhean (the one-eyed man)

SULLOCK. *See* Sellick

SULLY. A loc. n., S. Wales. Or *Fr.* Soulé ; a p.n.

SUMERIL. *See* Somerville

SUMMERBEE. From Somerby ; a loc. n., Lincs

SUMMERFIELD. *See* Somerfield

SUMMERS. A loc. n., Ess. Or *N.* Sumarliði ; *A.S.* Somar (summer sailor) ; *Fl.* Somers ; p.n. Prot. ref., Lond. 1618

SUMMERSBY. *See* Summerbee

SUMMERSUN. From Somersham ; a loc. n., Hants. *D.B.* Summersham

SUMMERVILLE. From Sommerville ; now Sommervieux, Norm.

SUMNER. An apparitor, a summoner

> Halliwell, quoting Nominale MS. Nomina dignitatum clericorum, gives "*Aparator* (a summunder)."

SUMPTER. From Sometour, a sumpterman

SUMPTON. From Summerton; a loc. n., Camb., Norf., Oxf., Somers. Sommethone; a loc. n., Belg.

SUNMAN. *A.S.* Suneman (sunman); *Dch.*; p.n.

SURFLIN. *See* Suffling

SURREY. The county. Or *Fr.* Surée, Sury; p.n. Sury; a loc. n.

SURRIDGE. A loc. n., Devon

SURTEES. A loc. n., derived from the river Tees, Durham

The name of an ancient family which long resided there. Dominus Thomas Suyrtayse *miles*, in Lib. Vit. Dur.

SUSSENS. *See* Sisson

SUTCH. *G.* Suche; a p.n. *See* Zouch

SUTER, SUTRE. *See* Sowter

SUTHERLAND. The county

SUTLIFF. From Southcliffe; a loc. n., Lincs, Yorks

SUTTABY. *See* Sutterby

SUTTERBY. A loc. n., Lincs

SUTTLE. From Southill; a loc. n., Beds. Or *see* Southwell

SUTTON. A loc. n., Ches., Devon, Lancs, Notts, Yorks, etc.

SWABY. A loc. n., Lincs

SWAIN. *N.* Sveinn (a boy); *Dch.* Swen; *D.* Svenne; *Fr.* Suin; *Fl.* Svenne; *A.S.* Swegen, Swen, Swain; p.n.

SWAINSON. *S.* Svenson; *D.* Svenssen; p.n. *See* Swain

SWALLOW. A loc. n., Lincs

SWALLWELL. A loc. n., Dur.

SWAN. *N.* Svanr (a swan); *D.* Swane, Svane; *D.B.* Suuan, Suan; *Dch.* Swaan; *S.* Svan; p.n.

SWANSTON. A loc. n., Edinburgh

SWASH. *N.* Svasi (n. of a giant); *A.S.* Suauis; *G.* Swazina; p.n.

SWAYNE. *See* Swain

SWEARS. *A.S.* Swar; a p.n.; *Old G. suari* (important); *Gothic swers* (honourable). Or *see* Swyre

SWEENEY. A loc. n., Salop

SWEET. *A.S.* Suid, Suith, Swet, Swid, Swith, *swið* (strong, powerful, great); *Dch.* Swidde; p.n.

SWEETAPPLE. *Dch.* Zoetappel is the corresponding word, but there is not the certainty of its being a p.n.

SWEETING. *Dch.* Swieten; *A.S.* Sweting; p.n. *See* Sweet

SWEETLAND. A loc. n., Devon. Comp. Swithland

SWEETMAN. *A.S.* Suetman, Swetman; *Dch.* Soetman; p.n. *See* Sweet

SWEETSER. *G.* Schweitzer; *Fl.* Switser; p.n. (a Swiss). Swiss ref., Lond. 1618

SWEPSTONE. A loc. n., Leics

SWETENHAM. From Swettenham; a loc. n., Ches.

SWIFT. *A.S.*; p.n. (swift, nimble)

SWINBORNE. *See* Swinburn

SWINBURN. A loc. n., Northbd. Or *N.* Sveinbjörn; a p.n. (boybear)

SWINDELL. From Swindale; a loc. n., Cumb.

SWINDLEHURST. From Windlehurst; a loc. n., Ches.

SWINDLEY. *See* Swindell

SWINEY. *See* Sweeney

SWINFEN. A loc. n., Staffs

SWINGER. *G.* Schwinger; a p.n. (a brandisher)

SWINGLEHURST. *See* Swindlehurst

SWINGLER. *G.* Schwingel; a p.n.

SWINHOE. From Swinhope; a loc. n., Lincs

SWINNARD. From Swynearde; a loc. n., Fland.

SWINNERTON. From Swynnerton; a loc. n., Staffs

SWINSON. *See* Swainson

SWINSTEAD. A loc. n., Cumb., Lincs

SWINTON. A loc n., Berwick

SWIRE. *See* Swyre

SWITHINBANK. A loc. n.

SWORD. *A.S.* Sward, Sweart, Swert, (black); or *sweord* (sword); *N.* Svertingr; *F.* Sweerd; *Dch.* Sweertz; *Fr.* Sourdes; p.n. Fl. ref., Lond. 1618

SWORN. *See* Swan

SWYRE. A loc. n., Dorset

SYDAL. *A.S.* Sidel; *D.* Seidel; *G.* Siedel; p.n. Dim. of Side

SYDENHAM. A loc. n., Devon, Kent

SYDER. *See* Side

SYER. *See* Sayer

SYFERT. *N.* Sighvatr; *A.S.* Sigweard; *D.* Sievert; *G.* Seiffert, Seyffert; *Fl.* Seyffers; *Dch.* Seyffardt; p.n. *See* Seward

SYKES. A loc. n., Yorks. Also Fl. ref., Lond. 1618

SYME, SYMES, SYMS. *Dch.* Seijm; a p.n. *See* Simms

SYMINGTON. A loc. n., Ayrsh.

SYMONDS. *N.* Sigmundr; *A.S.* Sigemund, Simond (victorious protector),; *G.* Siegmund, Siegmann, Siemens, Siemon, Siems, Simmon; *N.-Fr.* Fitz-Simon; *Dch.* Semeins; *Fl.* Symon; p.n. Hugt., Lond. 1618

SYPHER. *See* Syfert

SYRES. *See* Sayer. Or St Cyres; a loc. n., Devon

SYRETT. From Sarratt; a loc. n., Herts

T

TABB. *A.S.* Tæbba; *F.* Tebbe; *Dch.* Tappe; *G.* Taube (?); p.n.; *N.* *táp* (?) (brave)

TABBERER. *N.* Tabarðr (a tabard, a herald's coat); *N.-Fr.* Taborer; p.n.; Tabourier (a tambouriner). Ref. n., Lond. 1678

TABER, TABOR. *Fr.* Tabur; a p.n. *See* Tabberer

TABERNACLE. *Dch.* Tabbernal; a p.n.
> In old records *tabernaculum* (a public inn).

TABNER, TABINER. *Lat. tabernarius* (a tavern-keeper); *N.-Fr.* Tabernar; a p.n.

TABRAM. A loc. n.

TABRAR. *See* Tabberer
> Scholars in Queen's Coll., Oxon, were called Tabardiers, from Tabard, a short gown which they wore.

TACK. *S.*, *D.*, *Fl.* Tack; *Dch.* Tak; *N.-Fr.* Tac, Tagg; p.n.; *A.S.* *tácn* (?) (a standard)

TACKLEY. A loc. n., Lancs. Or Takeley, Ess.

TACON. *Dch.* Takken; a p.n. *See* Tack

TADD, TADDY. *A.S.* Tad, Tadda; *F.* Tade; *Fr.* Thadée; p.n. from Thaddeus. Or Goth. *thiuda* (father)

TADHUNTER. Scot. a foxhunter

TAFF. A loc. n., S. Wales. Also Welsh dim. of David, and used as a dim. of Theophilus

TAGART. From Scot. McTaggart; p.n. Or *A.S.* Dægweard; *Old G.* Taganwart (day guard)

TAGG. *See* Tack

TAHOURDIN. Fr. Hugt. n., Lond. 1685

TAILBY. *N.-Fr.* Taille-bois; *Fl.* Talgebosch; *D.B.* Tailgebosc, Talliebosc; p.n. (wood-cutter)

TALBOT. *Fr.* Talbot; *Fl.* Talabot; *D.B.* Talebot; p.n. (a dog with a turned-up tail)
> In Roll of Battell Abbey. The *A.S.* form would be Talbot (speech or tale envoy), but there is no such name recorded. It is more likely to be from *A.S.* Dallbeorht or Tallbeorht, *Old G.* Dalbert (illustrious), the badge or cognisance being assumed later.

TALER, TALL. *A.S.* Tella; *F.* Tale; *Dch.* Tal, Tall; p.n. (a reckoner)

TALLACK. From Tallach; a loc. n., Scotl.

TALLBOYS. *See* Tailby

TALLEMACH. *See* Tollemache

TALLENT. From Talland; a loc. n., Cornw.

TALLON. *A.S.* Tæling; *S.* Talén; *Fr.* Talon; p.n.; fam. n. of Tall

TALMADGE, TALMAGE, TALMIDGE. *See* Tollemache

TAMBLYN, TAMLYN. *Fr.* Tamberlain; a p.n. *See* Tombling

TAME. From Thame; a loc. n., Oxf.

TAMMADGE, TAMMAGE. *See* Tollemache

TAMPEN, TAMPIN, TAMPLIN. *See* Tamblyn

TANCRED. *N.* Þakk-raðr (grateful counsel); *D.* Tanggaard; *D.B.* Torncrd; *G.* Tancred; *Dch.* Tanker (?); p.n.
Latinised in Norman times into Tancredus.

TANDY. *Fr.* Tantais; a p.n. (dyed)

TANEY. From Tany; a loc. n., Norm.

TANGYE, TANK. *N.* Þenja (?); n.n. (an axe); *D.* Tang, Tange, Teng; *Dch.* Tang, Tenger, Tinga, Tinke; *Fl.* Tanghe; *Fr.* Tanguy; p.n.

TANKARD. *See* Tancred

TANKLIN. Dimin. of *D.* Tang; a p.n.

TANN. From Thann; a loc. n., France. Or *N.* Tanni (toothed); *F.* Tanno; *G.* Tanne; *Fr.* Tanne; p.n.

TANNER. *G.* Tanner; p.n.
Le Tanur in Rot. Obl. et Fin.

TANSLEY. A loc. n., Derbysh.

TAPHOUSE. A loc. n., Devon

TAPLEY. A loc. n., Devon

TAPLIN. *N.-Fr.* Topelin; a p.n.

TAPLOW. A loc. n., Bucks.

TAPP. *See* Tabb

TAPPER. *A.S.* Teappa, Tapa (a vintner); *Dch.* Tappé; *D.* Tappert; *G.* Tapper; p.n.

TAPPIN. Fam. n. of Tapp

TAPSCOTT. A loc. n.

TAPSFIELD. From Toppesfield; a loc. n., Ess.

TAPSON. *N.-Fr.* D'Abison (?); a p.n.

TAPSTER. The Scot. and N. Engl. form of Tapper. *A.S.* tæppestre (a female tapper)

TARBART, TARBET, TARBUTT. From Tarbat; a loc. n., Ross

TARDY. *Fr.*; p.n. (slow). Hugt., Lond. 1688

TARGETT. *N.* Þorgautr; *A.S.* Turgot; p.n. (Thor's Goth). Hugt. n., Lond. 1681

TARLTON. A loc. n., Glost.

TARN. From Thearne; a loc. n., Yorks. *N.-Fr.* Taurne; a p.n.

TARPEY. From the Irish Torpey; a p.n.

TARR. A loc. n., Somers

TARRANT. A loc. n., Dorset

TARRAS, TARRIS. *G.* Tarras; a p.n.

TARRY. *See* Terry

TARTAR, TARTE. *Fr.* Thard; a p.n.

TARVER. *N.* Þorvarðr (Thor's guard); *D.B.* Toruerd, Toruert, Torht; p.n. Or from Torver; a loc. n., Lancs

TASH. *A.S.* Tæsa; *Fr.* Tassy; *G.* Tasche; *Fl.* Tesch; p.n. (kind)

TASKER. *N.-Fr.* Taskier; *Dch.* Teske; a p.n.

TASSELL. From St German de Tassell, Norm. *Fr.* Tassel; *D.B.* de Taissel; p.n.
Tassilo, n. of a Bavarian k., 6th century.

TASWELL. A loc. n.

TATE. *N.-Fr.* Teste (Tête); a p.n.

TATHAM. A loc. n., Yorks

TATTENHALL. A loc. n., Staffs

TATTERSHALL. A loc. n., Lincs

TATTON. A loc. n., Ches.

TAUNTON. A loc. n., Somers

TAVERNER, TAVINER, TAVNER. *N.-Fr.* Tavernier; *Dch.* Taverne; p.n. Hugt., Lond. 1622

TAY. *N.-Fr.* De Toie; *Fl.* Tay; *Fr.* Téhy; p.n.

TAYLOR. *N.-Fr.* le Telier; *Fr.* Tailleau, le Tailleur, Taillir; p.n. Or *A.S.* Telia; a p.n. (a dealer, divider). Or *see* Tyler
Silvester Taillor in Rot. Obl. et Fin., K. John.

TAYNTON. A loc. n., Glost.

TEAGER. Irish McTeague. Or *G.* Tiecke; *Dch.* Tieger, Tieke, Tiggers; *S.* Tiger; *A.S.* Tic, Tig, Tiger, Tigga; *Fr.* Tigé; p.n. (secure, fast)

TEAGLE. *G.* Tiegel; a p.n. *See* Tickle

TEAGUE. Irish McTeague. Tadhg (a poet)

TEAKLE. *See* Tickle

TEALE. From Theale; a loc. n., Somers. Or *see* Teele

TEAPE. *A.S.* Tib; *Dch.* Teepe, Tip; p.n. (timid)

TEAR, TEER. From Thiers; a loc. n., France. *Fr.* Thier, Thiers; *Dch.* Thier; p.n. Or *A.S.* Tir; a p.n. (a leader)

TEARLE. *Dch.* Terlet; a p.n.

TEASDALE. A loc. n., Dur.

TEASDELL, TEASDILL. *See* Teasdale

TEASEL. *G.* Tiesler; *D.* Thysel; *S.* Tisell; *Dch.* Tessel; p.n. *See* Tash

TEATHER. *See* Tedder

TEAZE. *See* Tice

TEBAY. A loc. n., Westmd.

TEBB, TEBBS. *F.* Tebbe; a p.n. *See* Tibbetts

TEBBATTS, TEBBITT, TEBBUT. *A.S.* Tatbeorht, Tedbert; *Fl.* Tybaert; *Fr.* Thibaut; p.n. (illustrious Tad)

TEDDER. *A.S.* Tathere; a p.n. (Tad the warrior). *See* Tate

TEDDY. *See* Tedder

TEE. *See* Tye. Or *Fr.* Thys; *D.* Thye; p.n.

TEECE. *See* Tice

TEED. *See* Tidd and Tate

TEELE. From Thiel (?); a loc. n., France. Or *A.S.* Thyle, Tilla, Dil, Til; *G.* Tille, Tylle; *D.B.* Tihel, Tehel; *Dch.* Tiele, Til; *Fr.* Thil; p.n. (good)

TEEVAN. *See* Tiffen

TEGART. *See* Taggart

TEGG. *Dch.*; p.n. *See* Day

TELFER. *N.-Fr.* Taillefer, Tailfer; a p.n. (iron-worker)

TELFORD. A loc. n., Kent

TELLET. *See* Tillett

TELLING. Tellin; a loc. n., Belg. *Fl.* Telen, Tellin; *D., Dch.* Telling; p.n.

TEMME. *G.* Themme; a p.n. Or *see* Tame

TEMPANY. *D.* Tempenau (?); a p.n.

TEMPERLEY. From Timperley; a loc. n., Ches.

TEMPEST. *Fl.* Tempst; a p.n.

TEMPLE. A loc. n. near Caen, Norm. *Dch., G.* Tempel; *Fl.* Tempels; p.n.

TEMPLETON. A loc. n., Devon

TENCH. *Dch.* Tenge; a p.n. *See* Tangye

TENNENT. Dinant; a loc. n., Belg. *G.* Thenen; a p.n.

TENNET. *See* Dennett

TEPPER. *A.S.* Teppa; *Dch.* Tepe; *G.* Tepfer; p.n. (brave). *See* Tabb

TERRELL. *See* Tyrrell

TERRINGTON. A loc. n., Norf.

TERRY. *A.S.* Theoderic; *F.* Tiaderik (people's ruler); *Fr.* Terris, Therry, Thery, Thierry; p.n. Hugt., Lond. 1618

TESTER. *Fl.* Testaert, Testar, Teste; p.n. (a test, witness, will; also a head-piece). Testard, Hugt. n.

TETLEY, TETLOW. *See* Titley

TETSALL. *See* Tattersall

TETT. *See* Tate

TEULON. From Toulon ; a loc. n., France

TEVERSON. From Teversham ; a loc. n., Camb.

TEWELS. *Fl.* Tevels ; a p.n.

TEWKESBURY. A loc. n., Glost.

TEWSON. *See* Tyson

TEXTOR. *Dch.* ; p.n. *See* Thatcher

THACKER. *A.S.* Dæcca, Dæghere ; *Fl.* Dacker ; *Dch.* Dekker ; p.n. (glorious warrior)

THACKERAY, THACKWRAY. *See* Tancred

THAIN. *N.* Þegn (a thane); *D.* Thiene ; *Fl.* Thein ; *Dch.* Theyn ; *G.* Thien, Thenen ; *D.B.* Tain, Taini, Teini, Teigni ; p.n.

THAIRLWALL. *See* Thirlwall

THAKE. *See* Thacker

THANE, THAYNE. *See* Thain

THARP. *See* Thorpe

THATCHER, THAXTER. *See* Thacker

THEAKSTON. A loc. n., Yorks

THEED. *See* Tidd

THELWALL. A loc. n., Ches.

THEOBALDS. *See* Tipple

THEW. From Thieu ; a loc. n., Belg. Or *A.S.* Þeow (a serf)

THEXTON. *See* Theakston

THICK. *G.* Dicke ; a p.n. (stout)

THICKBROOM. A loc. n., Staffs

THICKNESSE. *Fr.* Xhignesse ; a p.n.

Robert Thicknesse was lord of Balterley, Staffs, Ed. I. 1274. Also said to be derived from Thickens, *Gent's. Mag.*, Nov. 1809.

THIN. Thynes ; a loc. n., Belg. *A.S.* Dynne, Thynne ; a p.n. (thin, lean), Dux, Kent ; *Dch.* Thijn ; *D.*, *G.* Thien ; *Fr.* Thin ; p.n.

Burke states that "John Boteville, *temp.* K. John, resided in one of the Inns of Court, and was styled John o' th' inne." De Thain in Rot. Obl. et Fin.

THING. *A.S.* Thing ; a p.n. ; perhaps Thingman (a Danish soldier)

THIRGOOD. *See* Toogood

THIRKETEL, THIRKETTLE, THIRTLE. *N.* Þórketell (Thor's kettle) ; *D.B.* Torchetel, Torchil, Turchil ; *S.* Torkels ; *D.* Therchil, Terkel, Thorkel ; *N.-Fr.* Fitz Turquetil ; p.n.

THIRLWALL. A loc. n., Northbd.

THIRST. *G.* Durst ; a p.n. (thirst); probably a contr. of *N.* Þorsteinn; *A.S.* Thurstan (Thor's stone)

THISTLE. *D.* Thysel ; *S.* Thiesel ; *Dch.* Dissel ; p.n.

THISTLETHWAITE. A loc. n.

THISTLETON. A loc. n., Cumb ; Lincs, Rutland

THODAY. *D.* Thode ; a p.n. *See* Todd

THOM, THOMPSON. *N.* Tumi (pet name for Thomas); *S.* Tomasson; *D.* Thomassen ; *Dch.* Thomson ; *D.B.* Tumi, Tumme, Tombi., p.n. Prot. ref., Lond. 1618

THORBURN. *N.* Þór-björn (Thor's bear) ; *S.* Torbiörn ; *D.* Thorbjoern ; *A.S.* Thurbeorn, Torbern ; p.n.

THORLEY. A loc. n., Dorset, Hants, Herts

THORNBER. *See* Thornborough

THORNBOROUGH. A loc. n., Cumb., Northbd., Oxf., Yorks

THORNE. A loc. n., Devon, Yorks, Suff. *D.B.* Torn. Or *N.* Thórny (a thorn) ; *D.* Thorning ; *Dch.* Thorn ; p.n.

THORNHILL. A loc. n., Derbysh., Dorset, Wilts, Yorks

THORNICROFT. A loc. n., Ches.

THORNLEY. A loc. n., Dur., Lancs

THORNS. *See* Thorne

THORNTON. A loc. n., Devon, Lancs, Leics, Yorks

THORNTOUN. A loc. n., Edinburgh

THOROLD. *N.* Þóraldr (Thor's ruler) ; *D.B.* Tored, Torold, Tori, Torol, Toi, Thori ; *Fr.* Thorel, p.n.

THOROUGHGOOD. *See* Toogood

THORPE. A freq. loc. n., Lincs, Yorks, etc.

THORRINGTON. A loc. n., Ess.

THOULESS. *See* Thurlows

THOYTS. *See* Thwaites or Toats

THRASHER, THRESHER. *D.* Drescher; a p.n.

THREADGALE, THREADKELL, THREADKILL. *See* Trudgil

THRELFAL. From Threlfield; a loc. n., Yorks. *D.B.* Threlfeld, Trelefelt

THRESH. *G.* Drescher; a p.n.

THRIDGOLD, THRIDGOULD. *See* Trudgil

THRIFT. *Dch.* Drift; a p.n.

THRING. *D.*, *S.* Thorin; *Fl.* Thurin; *G.* Thöring; p.n.; fam. n. of Thor. Or. *A.S.* Dreng; a p.n. (soldier, guard)

THRIPP. *See* Thrupp

THROCKMORTON. A loc. n., Warw.

THROOP. A loc. n., Dorset, Hants, Somers, Wilts

THROSSEL. *G.* Drossel; a p.n; *A.S.* þrostle (a thrush)

THROWER. *See* Trower

THRUPP. A loc. n., Glost., Northants

THUNDER. *A.S.* Thunar; *Fl.* Tunder; p.n.

THURBURN. *See* Thorburn

THURGAR, THURGUR. *N.* Þorgeirr (Thor's spear); *A.S.* Thurgar; p.n.

THURKETTLE, THURKLE. *See* Thirkettle

THURLAND. From Thurgoland; a loc. n., Yorks

THURLES. *See* Thurlows

THURLEY. From Thurleigh; a loc. n., Beds

THURLOW, THURLOWS. A loc. n., Suff.

THURRELL. *Fr.* Thorel; a p.n. *See* Thirkettle

THURSBY. A loc. n., Cumb.

THURSFIELD. A loc. n., Staffs

THURSTON. A loc. n., Lancs, Norf., Suff. Or. *N.* Þorsteinn; a p.n.

THURTELL. *See* Thirketel

THURWOOD. *N.* Þorvarðr; *A.S.* Thurweard; *G.* Thorwardt; p.n. (Thor-protector)

THWAITES. A loc. n., Cumb., Yorks

THWING. A loc. n., Yorks

THYER. *N.* þýr; *A.S.* þeowa (a bond-woman); *D.* Thyre; p.n. Or *A.S.* Thyrra; a p.n. (withered (?))

THYNNE. *See* Thin

TIARKO, TIARKS. *F.*; p.n. Perhaps from *N. jarki, jaðrki*, metaph. (the highest, best)

TIBB, TIBBS, TIBBY. *A.S.* Tib, Tibba; p.n. *See* Tipple

TIBBALD. *See* Tipple. Hugt. n., Lond. 1688

TIBBETTS, TIBBITTS, TIBBITT. *Dch.* Dibbetts; p.n. *See* Tebbut

TIBBLES. *See* Tipple. Tiboles, Hugt., Lond. 1618

TIBNAM. From Tibbenham; a loc. n., Norf.

TICE. *Fl.* Thyes; *Dch.* Theijs; *Fr.* Thiess; *G.* Thys; p.n. A contr. of Mathias. Prot ref., Lond. 1618
    Teice in Rot. Obl. et Fin.

TICHBON. *See* Tichborne

TICHBORNE. A loc. n., Hants (formerly Itchenborne)

TICK. *See* Tigg

TICKELL. *See* Tickle

TICKETT. From Tecket; a loc. n., Northbd.

TICKLE. From Dickele; a loc. n., Fland.; Tickhill; a loc. n., Yorks. *Dch.* Tikkel; p.n.

TICKLEPENNY. From Dickelvenne (?); a loc. n., Fland. Or Gaelic (overhanging hill)

TICKNER, TICKNOR. From Ticknall; a loc. n., Derbysh.

TIDBALL. *See* Tibbald

TIDBURY. A loc. n., Hants

R

TIDD. A loc. n., Camb., Lincs. Or *see* Tidder

TIDDER, TIDDY, TIDEY, TIDY. From Tydee; a loc. n., Monmouth. Or *F.* Tide; *A.S.* Tida; *theod* (people); p.n.

TIDMAN. *A.S.* Theodman, Tidman (people's man); *D.* Thideman; *G.* Thiedemann; *Dch.* Tiedeman; p.n.

TIDSWELL. From Tideswell; a loc. n., Derbysh.

TIERNAY. Irish Tighearnach; a p.n.; *tighearn* (a king)

TIFFEN. *Fr.* Thifane, Tiphaigne, Typhaigne; *N.-Fr.* Epiphany. Hugt., Lond. 1618

TIGG. *A.S.* Tic, Ticca; *N.-Fr.* Tike; p.n.
Tig in Rot. Hund.

TIGHE. *See* Teager or Tye

TIGHT. Irish Tuite; *G.* Ticht; *Dch.* Tuit; *D.* Teitge; p.n. *See* Tite

TIGWELL. *See* Tugwell

TILBROOK. *See* Tilbury

TILBURY. A loc. n., Ess.

TILDESLEY. From Tyldesley; a loc. n., Lancs

TILKE. *D.* Tillge; *A.S.* Tilluc; *G.* Tilke; p.n. Dimin. of Till

TILL. *See* Teele

TILLARD, TILLEARD. *D.* Theilgaard, Theilade; *G.* Tillert; *Dch.* Tillaard; *Fr.* Thillard; p.n. (good protection)

TILLCOCK. *See* Teale. Dimin.

TILLETT. A loc. n., Belg. *Fr.* Tillot; a p.n. Or dim. of Till

TILLEY. A loc. n., Somers. Or *see* Tilly

TILLING. *A.S.* p.n.; fam. n. of Till; *Fl.* Thielen; a loc. and p.n.

TILLS. *See* Teele

TILLY. From Tilly; a loc. n., Belg. *Fr.* Thillais, Tilley; p.n. Or *see* Teele
Geoffroy de Tilly occurs as one of the benefactors of the abbey of St Étienne, Caen, Normandy, founded by William I. Henry de Tilly held Marshwood, Somers, *temp.* K. John.

TILLYER, TILYARD. *See* Tilleard

TILNEY. A loc. n., Norf.

TILSON. From Dilsen; a loc. n., Belg. Or *see* Teele

TIMBERLAKE. From Timperley (?); a loc. n., Ches.

TIMBERS. *A.S.* Tima; a p.n.; *Dch.* Timmers; a fam. n.; *A.S. tyma* (a leader)

TIMBRELL. From Timble; a loc. n., Yorks

TIMBS, TIMES, TIMMS. *See* Tims

TIMEWELL. A loc. n., Devon

TIMGATE. A loc. n.

TIMS. *D., S.* Thim, Timm; *Dch.* Tim, Tims; *G.* Thimm; p.n. *See* Timbers

TINCKHAM. *See* Tingcombe

TINDALL, TINDALE, TINDELL. *Dch.* Tindal; *S.* Tengdahl (?); a loc. and p.n.

TINGCOMBE. From Teigncombe; a loc. n., Devon

TINGEY. *See* Tangye

TINGLE. A loc. n., Yorks

TINHAM. A loc. n.

TINK, TINKER. From Dinker; a loc. n., Germ. *Dch.* Tinke, Tuinker; p.n. Or *see* Tangye

TINKLER. From Dinklar; a loc. n., Germ. *Dch.* Dinkelaar; a p.n.

TINKLEY. From Dingley; a loc. n., Northants

TINN. *Fl.* Tinne; *Dch.* Tijn; *Fr.* Thin; p.n. *See* Thin

TINNEY. *Fl.* Tinne; a p.n. *See* Thin

TINSLEY. A loc. n., Yorks

TINWORTH. From Timworth; a loc. n., Suff.

TIPP, TIPPELL, TIPPER. A loc. n., Kildare. Or *A.S.* Tibba; a p.n. *See* Tibb, Tipple

TIPPETT, TIPPETTS. *See* Tibbitt

TIPPING. *Dch.* Tieben, Tippen; a p.n. Fam. n. of Tib

TIPPLE, TIPLER. *A.S.* Theodbald; *D.* Theobald; *Fl.* Thiebauld; *Fr.* Thibault; *G.* Thepold, Tiepolt, Thiebau; *D.B.* Tidbold, Tebald; p.n. (people's prince). *See* Tibbles

TIPTAFT, TIPTOFT. *See* Tiptod

TIPTOD. From Thibtot; a loc. n., Norm.

Tibtote in Roll of Battell Abbey.

TIREBUCK. *G.* Tirbach; a loc. and p.n.

TISSINGTON. A loc. n., Derbysh.

TITCHEN. *G.* Titsche; *Dch.* Titsingh; p.n. Dim. of Tide, Tidy

TITCHMARSH. A loc. n., Northants

TITCOMB. A loc. n., Wilts

TITE. From Thuit; a loc. n., Norm. *N.-Fr.* Tiet, Titte; *Fl.*, *Dch.* Tuyt; p.n. *See* Tight

De Tuit in Rot. Obl. et Fin.

TITFORD. From Thetford; a loc. n., Camb., Norf.

TITLEY. A loc. n., Heref.

TITLOW. *See* above

TITMAS. From Tidmarsh; a loc. n., Oxf. Or *see* Titchmarsh

TITT. *A.S.* Tid, Tit; *D.* Thiede; *G.* Tita; *Dch.* Tiedt, Tito; *Fl.* Tits; p.n. *See* Tiddy and Tite

TITTERTON. From Titterstone; a loc. n., Salop

TITTLE. *A.S.* Titel; *G.* Tietel, Tittel; p.n. Dim. of Tid

TIVEY. Irish Tavey, McEtavey; p.n.

TOALE. *See* Toghill or Toll

TOAS. *See* Tosar

TOATS. *D.* Thott; *Fl.* Toto; *D.B.* Toti; p.n. *See* Dodd

TOBIN. *See* St Aubyn

TOBY. *Fr.* Tobie, Toby; *Dch.* Tobi, Tobé; p.n. From Tobias

TOCK. *See* Tooke

TODD. *N.* Tjod; *F.* Todo; *G.*, *Dch.* Tode; *D.* Thode; *D.B.* Dodd, Toda, Todi, Tot; p.n. Or *A.S.* Theod; Goth. *thiuda* (people's ruler). *See* Dodd

Todd is the Scottish for a fox; but *A.S.* Dod seems to be the original form of the name.

TODHUNTER. *See* Tadhunter

TOFTS. A. freq. loc. n. *See* Tuffs

TOGHILL. From Taghill; a loc. n., Derbysh. Or *see* below

TOGWELL. From Touqueville; a loc. n., Norm.

TOINTON. From Torrington; a loc. n., Devon, Lincs

TOLD. *D.*; p.n. (toll)

TOLER, TOLLER. *G.*; p.n. Or from Toller; a loc. n., Dorset. *A.S. tólere* (a tax gatherer)

TOLFREE, TOLFREY. From Tollervey (?); a Cornish p.n. Or *A.S. tól-fréo* (toll free)

TOLL. *A.S.* Thola, Tol, Tola, Thol; *Dch.*, *D.*, *S.*, *G.* Toll; p.n. *A.S. tól*; *N. tollr*; *D. told* (tax); or *þól* (patient)

TOLLADY. From Tolladine (?); a loc. n., Worcest. *N.-Fr.* De Toleta; *Dch.* Toledo; p.n.

TOLLEMACHE, TOLMASH. *Fr.* Toulmouche; a p.n. Or from Tollmarsh; a loc. n., Buckfastleigh, Devon; Toulemer, Norm.

Tollemach in Roll of Battell Abbey. Richard Talamag, Talamasch, or Talemasch, held lands in Ess. and Oxon, *temp.* K. John, Rot. Obl. et Fin. Talmach, a benefactor to Ipswich Priory, 13th century.

TOLLINGTON. From Tallington; a loc. n., Lincs

TOLVER. *Fr.* Tolleve. Hugt. n., Norwich, 1622

TOMBE. *See* Toombs

TOMBLESON, TOMBLIN, TOMLINE, TOMLINSON. *See* Tombling

TOMBLING. From Tomblain; a loc. n., Norm.

TOMPKINS. *See* Toombs

TONGUE. A loc. n., Sutherland. Or Tonge, Leics; Tong, Yorks

TONKIN, TONKS. Dim. of Antonius. *F.* Tönjes; p.n. *See* Town

TONSON. *See* Townson

TOOBY. *See* Tubby

TOOGOOD. *N.* Þorgautr (Thor's Goth); *D.* Thuge; *Fl.* Tycknert; *G.* Tückert; *Dch.* Tuke; *D.B.* Thurgod, Turgot; p.n.

TOOHEY. Irish Tuohig, Tuohy, Tooey; *Dch.* Tahey, Tooy; p.n. *See* Toy

TOOKE. *N.* Tóki (foolish, simple); *D.* Tyge or Thuge; *Lat.* Tycho; *G.* Tuch; *Dch.* Tuck, Tuk, Tuke, Tukker; *A.S.* Tochi, Toc, Tuc; *Fr.* Touq; p.n. Or from Touques; a loc. n., Norm.

Touke in Roll of Battell Abbey. De Toke in Rot. Obl. et Fin.

TOOLE, TOOLEY. From the Irish O'Tuathail; a p.n. (lordly). *A.S.* Tula (a bard). Or *D.* Thule; *Dch.* Tulle; *S.* Tul; *Fl.* Toullet; p.n.

TOOMBS. *A.S.* Tomus; *Dch.* Toom, Thoms; *D.* Thom; *G.* Thomas, Tomisch; p.n.

TOOMEY. *N.* Tumi (pet n. for Thomas); *D.B.* Tumie, Tumme, Tombi; p.n.

TOONE. From Thuin; a loc. n., Belg. Or *Dch.* Tuin; *D.* Thun; p.n. *See* Town

TOOP. *See* Topp

TOOSEY. From Thuisy; a loc. n., France. *Fr.* Touzé, Touzet; p.n. Tuse, Prot. ref., Lond. 1622

TOOT, TOOTH. From Tot, a fief in Norm. Or *N.* Toti; n.n.; *Fr.* Touté; *A.S.* Tota, Toti; p.n.

Tut in Rot. Hund.

TOOTAL, TOOTEL, TOOTLE. *See* Tuthill

TOOVEY. *N.* Dufva; *S.* Thufva; *Fl.* Dufey; *Fr.* Tuvée, Tuffay; *A.S.* Tof, Tuffa; p.n.; *D. tove* (a dove)

TOP. *See* Topp

TOPHAM. From Topsham; a loc. n., Devon

TOPLER, TOPLEY. From Topcliffe (?); a loc. n., Salop, Yorks

TOPLIS. From *G.* Toplitz; a loc. and p.n.

TOPP. *Dch.*, *Fl.* Top; *S.*, *D.* Topp; *A.S.* Tope, Topp; p.n.; *top* (a tuft)

Top in Rot. Obl. et Fin.

TOPPING. A descendant of Topp. Or *Fr.* Taupin; a p.n. (tawny)

In Rot. Hund.

TOPPLE. *See* Topley

TOPPS. *Dch.* Tops; a p.n. *See* Topp

TOPSOM. From Topsham; a loc. n., Devon

TORBET, TORBITT. *A.S.* Thurbeorht, Torbert; *G.* Taubert; p.n. (Thor bright, illustrious)

TORR. A loc. n., Cornw., Devon. Or *A.S.* Thor, Tor; p.n. (the god)

TORRANCE. A loc. n., Stirling

TORRENS. *Dch.*; p.n. Or *see* Torrance

TORRINGTON. A loc. n., Devon

TORROP. *D.* Thorup, Torup; loc. and p.n.

TORRY, TORRIE, TORREY, TORY. *N.* Þóri; a n.n. (a young bull); *A.S.* Thorri; *Fl.* Thorez; *Fr.* Thouret; p.n. Prot. ref., Lond. 1618. Turry, a castle and barony, Norm.

TOSAR. *Dch.* Tuser; *D.B.* Tosard; p.n. *See* Toosey

TOSH. *N.-Fr.* De Tosca; a p.n. Or McIntosh

TOSSELL. *See* Tassell

TOSSELYN. *D.B.* Tascelin, Tezelin; *Dch.* Teeseling; p.n. *See* Teasel

TOSWILL. *See* Tassell

TOTHERICK. From Todridge; a loc. n., Northbd.

TOTHILL. A loc. n., Lincs

TOTTENHAM. A loc. n., Middlx.

TOTMAN. *A.S.* Dodman; a p.n. (the people's man)
TOTTERDELL. A loc. n.
TOTTLE. *See* Tothill
TOUCH. *G.* Tusch; *Fr.* la Touche; p.n. *See* Took
TOUGH. A loc. n., Aberdeen. Or *Dch.*, *A.S.* Tof, Tofig, Tou, Tuff, Touw; p.n.
TOULD. *D.B.* Torold, Touilt; p.n. *See* Thorold
TOULMIN. *Fl.* Tolleman; a p.n. (tax, toll, or customs officer)
TOVELL. *N.-Fr.* Tavel; a p.n.
TOVEY. *See* Toovey
TOW. From Thou; a loc. n., Normandy. Or *N.* Tofi, Toui; *Dch.* Touw; *G.* Thau, Toui, Tou; p.n. Or *see* Thew
TOWELL. A loc. n., Devon. Or *see* Tovell
TOWERS. From Tours; a loc. n., Normandy
> W. de Tours had the manor of Lowick or Lofwick, Lancs, from W. de Taillebois, baron of Kendal, after the Conquest, and assumed the name of de Lofwick.

TOWLER. *See* Toler
TOWN. *N.* Tónn; n.n. (a tune); *D.* Tonn; *S.* Tuné; *Dch.* Tuin; *A.S.* Ton, Tone, Toni; p.n. Or *Dch.* Toon, dimin. of Anthony; a p.n.
TOWNDROW. From Town Row (?); a loc. n., Sussex
TOWNS. *Fl.* Teuns; a p.n. *See* Toone
TOWNSEND. A loc. n., Devon
> Atte Tounesende, 1327.

TOWNSON. *N.-Fr.* Tunçon; *D.* Tonnesen; p.n. *See* Town
TOWSE, TOWSEY. *See* Toosey
TOY, TOYE. *See* Tye
TOZE, TOZER. *See* Tosar
TRACEY. From Tracy, a barony near Vire, Norm.
> Tracy in Roll of Battell Abbey. De Traci and de Trascy in Rot. Obl. et Fin.

TRAFFORD. A loc. n., Lancs
TRAILL. *See* Tyrrell
TRAIN. From Treignes (?); a loc. n., Belg. *N.-Fr.* Traine; a p.n. *See* Drane
> Simon T. in Rot. Hund.

TRAINER, TRAYNER. Irish Tremfear (strong man). Or *see* Treanor
TRAISE. *See* Tracey
TRAPP. From Trappes; a loc. n., France. Or *Fl.*, *D.*, *Dch.*, *S.*, *G.*; p.n. (a bustard)
TRAQUAIR. A loc. n., Peebles
TRASK. *G.* Treske; a p.n. Dim. of Trass
TRASS. *N.*]'rasi; *Dch.* Traus; p.n. (pugnacious)
TRATT. *See* Troutt
TRAVELL, TRAVIL. From Traffell; a loc. n., Cornw.
TRAVERS. From Trevieres; a loc. n., Norm.
TRAVIS. *See* Travers
TREACHER. *See* Treasure
TREADGOLD. From Tregolds; a loc. n., Cornw. Or *see* Thridgold
TREADWELL. From Tredgarville; a loc. n., S. Wales
TREANOR. From Trenear or Trenower; loc. names, Cornw.
TREASURE. *G.* Tresser; p.n.; *tressor* (treasure). Or *see* Thrasher
TREBECK. *Dch.* Traarbach; a p.n.
TREBLE. A loc. n., Devon. Or *N.-Fr.* Trepel; a p.n.
TREBY. From Trebigh; a loc. n., Cornw.
TREDGETT. From Treguth (?); a loc. n., Cornw.
TREE. *Dch.* Tree; *Fr.* Tré; p.n. Prot. ref. n., Lond. 1618. *See* Drake
TREEBY. *See* Treby
TREEN. A loc. n., Cornw.
TREETON. A loc. n., Yorks
TREFFRY. A loc. n., Cornw.
TREFUSIS. *Fr.* Tréfousse (?); a p.n.
TREGARTHEN. A loc. n., Cornw.
TREGEAR. A loc. n., Cornw.

TREGELLAS. A loc. n., Cornw.

TREGENZA. From Tregenna; a loc. n., Cornw.

TREGIDGO. From Tregidhoe; a loc. n., Cornw.

TREGO. From Tregue; a loc. n., Cornw.

TREGONING. A loc. n., Cornw.

TREGURTHA. From Tregotha; a loc. n., Cornw.

TREHARNE, TREHEARNE, TRE-HERNE. From Trehane; a loc. n., Cornw.

TREINEN, TRINEN. From Trinent; a loc. n., Monm̂.

TRELAWNY. A loc. n., Cornw.

TRELEASE. A loc. n., Cornw.

TRELEAVEN. From Trelaven; a loc. n., Cornw.

TRELIVING. *See* Treleaven

TRELOAR. From Trelow; a loc. n., Cornw.

TREMAIN, TREMAYNE. A loc. n., Cornw.

TREMBETH. From Trembath; a loc. n., Cornw.

TREMBLE. *Fr.* Tremblay; a p.n. From le Tremblay; a loc. n., Norm.; or Trembleur; a loc. n., Belg. Or *see* Turnbull

TREMELLEN. From Tremellin; a loc. n., Cornw. (the mill-town)

TREMENHEERE. A loc. n., Cornw.

TREMLETT. From Trembleth; a loc. n., Cornw.

TRENAM. *See* Trenaman

TRENAMAN. From Trenmaen; a loc. n., Cornw.

TRENBATH. From Trembath; a loc. n., Cornw.

TRENCH. From La Trenche; a seigneurie in Poitou, France. A loc. n., Salop
Trencheville in Roll of Battell Abbey.

TRENDELL. From Trendeal; a loc. n., Cornw.

TRENGROUSE. A loc. n., Cornw.

TRENGROVE. A loc. n., Cornw.

TRENNER. *See* Treanor

TRENOW. From Trenower; a loc. n., Cornw.

TRENT. A loc. n., Somers. *D.B.* Trend, Trent; p.n.

TRENTHAM. A loc. n., Staffs

TRENWITH. A loc. n., Cornw.

TREPESS. A loc. n., Cornw.

TRESHAM. A loc. n., Glost.

TRESIDDER. From Tresaddern; a loc. n., Cornw.

TRESIZE. From Tresayes; a loc. n., Cornw.

TRETHEWY. A loc. n., Cornw.

TRETT. *Fr.* Tréhet; a p.n.

TREVALDWYN. A loc. n., Wales. Baldwin's dwelling

TREVALLION. *See* Trevelyan

TREVASKIS. A loc. n., Cornw.

TREVATT. From Trevarth; a loc. n., Cornw. Or *see* Trevitt

TREVELYAN, TREVILLION. From Trevelgen or Trevellan; loc. n., Cornw.

TREVENEN. From Trevennen; a loc. n., Cornw.

TREVERTON. *See* Trevethan

TREVETHAN. A loc. n., Cornw.

TREVETT, TREVITT. *Fr.* Trevette; a p.n. *See* Truwhitt
Trivet in Roll of Battell Abbey.

TREVOR. A loc. n., N. Wales; or Trevoux, France

TREW. From Trou; a loc. n., Norm. Or *see* Trow

TREWBY. *See* Treby

TREWINNARD. From Trewinard; a loc. n., Cornw.

TREWREN. From Trewern, N. Wales. Or Truren; a loc. n., Cornw.

TRIA. *Dch.* Trier; a p.n. Trier, the *G.* n. for Trèves

TRIAIRE. From Trehire; a loc. n., Cornw.

TRIBE. *Dch.* Treub; *G.* Treiber; p.n. (a driver)

TRICK, TRICKER, TRICKETT, TRICKEY. *N.-Fr.* Trichet; *Fr.* Triquet; p.n. (a small club, bat)

TRIFFITT. *See* Trevitt
TRIGG. *D.* Thrige, Trygg; *Dch.* Tright; *D.B.* Trec; p.n. *See* Trigger
TRIGGER. *N.* Tryggvi (faithful, true); *D.* Trygg, Træger; *A.S.* Tricga; *Dch.* Drieger; *Fl.* Trigot; *G.* Troeger; *S.* Trygger; p.n. Or Trigueres; a loc. n., France
TRIM. *Dch.*; p.n.; *A.S.* Trum. *See* Trumm
TRIMER, TRIMMER. From Tremeer; a loc. n., Cornw. Or *A.S.* Trumhere; a p.n. (firm warrior)
TRIMMING. *See* Trim
TRINDER. A Cornish p.n.
TRINGALL. *See* Drinkall
TRINGHAM. From Trimingham; a loc. n., Norf.
TRIPLOW. A loc. n., Camb.
TRIPP. *Dch.* Trip, Triep; p.n.
TRISTRAM. *N.-Fr.* Tristan, from the Celtic Trystan; a p.n. (herald)

In Rot. Hund.

TRITTON. *Dch.* Tritten; a p.n. Or *see* Treeton. Prot. ref., Lond. 1687
TRIXON. *See* Trigg
TROLLOP. A loc. n.
TROMP. *Dch.*; p.n. *See* Trumm
TROOD. *A.S.* Drud, Druht, Trud, Thryth; *Dch.* Traude; *Fl.* Truyt; *Fr.* Troude; p.n. (true)
TROST. *G.* Trost; *Dch.*, *Fl.* Troost; a p.n. (comfort)
TROTMAN. *G.* Trautmann; a p.n. *See* Trood
TROTT. *A.S.* Trot; *Dch.* Trots; *S.* Trotz; p.n. *See* Trood
TROTTER. *A.S.* Trothere (true warrior); *Dch.* Trottier; p.n.
TROUBRIDGE. *See* Trowbridge
TROUGHTON. From Trohoughton; a loc. n., Dumfries. Compare Trawden, Lancs; Treodythin, Llandaff; Trotton, Suss.
TROUNCE. *Fl.* Truyens; a p.n. *See* Trew

TROUP. A loc. n., Banffsh. Or *see* Throop
TROUSDALE. A loc. n., Yorks
TROUTBECK. A loc. n., Westmd.
TROUTT. *See* Trood
TROW. *See* Trew
TROWBRIDGE. A loc. n., Wilts
TROWELL. A loc. n., Notts
TROWER. From Troars or Troarn; a loc. n., Norm. Or *N.-Fr.* Trouvère; a p.n. (a troubadour)
TROWSE. *G.* Trautsch (?); *Fr.* Troussé; a p.n. (well-shaped)
TROY. *G.* Treu; a p.n. (true)
TRUDGETT. *Fr.* Trugard (?); a p.n. Or *see* Tredgett
TRUDGILL. *A.S.* Thrythgild or Thrythhild; a p.n. (true value)
TRUE. *A.S.* Thruth, Thryth; *G.* Treu, Trew; *Dch.* Trouw; *D.* Thrue, Thrye; p.n. *A.S.* treów (trust, faith), trýw (true). Or *see* Trew, Trow
TRUEFITT. *N.* Þorvið; *D.* Turvid; p.n. (Thor's wood). Or *see* Truwhitt
TRUELL. From Trull; a loc. n., Somers. Or *see* Trowell
TRUELOVE. A loc. n., Devon
TRUETT. *See* Trood and Truwhitt
TRUMAN. *A.S.* Thrythman, Trutman; *Dch.* Trijman; *G.* Trauman; *D.B.* Trumin; p.n. (true man)
TRUMBALL, TRUMBLE. *A.S.* Trumbald; a p.n. (strong, bold); *Fl.* Trumpel; p.n.
TRUMM. From Drum; a loc. n., Aberdeen. Or *A.S.* Trum; *Dch.* Tromm; p.n. (firm, strong)
TRUMMER. *A.S.* Trumhere; a p.n. (strong warrior)
TRUMPER, TRUMPLER. *Fl.* Trumper; *Dch.* Trompee; *G.* Trümper; p.n. (a trumpeter). Or *A.S.* Trumbeort; a p.n. (firm bright)
TRUMPET. A loc. n., Heref.
TRUMPP. A loc. n., Glost. Or *see* Trumm

TRUNDEL. *N.* Trandill (a trundle); p.n.; *S.* Tranell; *Fl.* Trentels; a p.n.

TRUNDLEY. A loc. n.

TRUSCOTT. From Trescott; a loc. n., Staffs. Or Tresscoit, a manor in St Mabin, Cornw.

TRUSLER, TRUSLOW. From Trusley; a loc. n., Derbysh.

TRUSSON. *S.* Trysen; a p.n. *See* Try

TRUST. *Dch.* Troost; a p.n.

TRUSWELL. From Tresawell; a loc. n., Cornw.

TRUWHITT. From Trewhitt; a loc. n., Northbd. Or *see* Tyrwhitt and Trood

TRY. From Trie; a loc. n., Norm.

TRYON. *Fr.* Trion. Hugt. n., Broad Street, London, 1618

TUBB, TUBBS, TUBBY. Tubize (?); a loc. n., Belg. Or *A.S.* Dub, Tubba, Tube; *G.* Dube; *Dch.* Tubbing, Tupkin; *Fr.* Toubeau; p.n.; *N. dubba* (to smite)

TUBMAN. *G.* Taubmann; a p.n.

TUCK, TUCKEY. *See* Tooke

TUCKER. *A.S.* Dug, Tuc, Tucca; *Dch.* Tukker; p.n.; *A.S. dugan* (to be doughty). *See* Tooke

TUCKETT. *A.S.* Tuc, Tuca; *Fr.* Toquet; *G.* Tuckert; *Fl.* Tyckaert; p.n. *See* Tooke and Tuttiett

TUCKNESS. *See* Thicknesse

TUCKWELL. *See* Tugwell

TUDBALL. *See* Theobald

TUDDENHAM. A loc. n., Suff.

TUDGE. *See* Touch

TUDHOPE. From Tudhoe; a loc. n., Dur.

TUDOR. The Welsh form of Theodore. *A.S.* Theodhere; a p.n. (the people's warrior)

TUFF. *Dch.* Duif, Toff; p.n. *See* Toovey

TUFFEN, TUFFIN. *N.* Dufan (from the Gaelic); *S.* Dufven; p.n. Or *see* Tiffen

TUFFIL. *See* Duffill.

TUFFLEY. A loc. n., Glost.

TUFFNELL. *N.* Dufnial (from the Gaelic); *N.-Fr.* Tafernel; p.n.

TUFFS. *See* Tuff or Tufts

TUFNAIL. *See* Tuffnell

TUFTON. A loc. n., Hants

TUFTS. From Tofts; a loc. n., Norf.

TUGWELL. *See* Togwell

TUKE. *See* Tooke

TULEY, TULLEY, TULLY. *N.-Fr.* Tuelou, Tulye; p.n. Hugt. n., Lond. 1618

TULL. *See* Toole

TULLETT. From Tult; a loc. n., Devon. Or *Fr.* Toullet; a p.n.

TULLIDGE, TULLIS. From Tullich; a loc. n., Aberdeen

TULLOCH. A loc. n., Perth

TULLOCK. *See* Tulloch

TUMPENNY. *See* Tempany

TUNALEY. *See* Tunley

TUNBRIDGE. A loc. n., Kent

TUNGATE. From Tundergarth (?); a loc. n., Dumfries

TUNKIN, TUNKS. *See* Tonkin

TUNLEY. A loc. n., Somers

TUNMER. *See* Tunmore

TUNMORE. A loc. n. Eight places in Ireland and Scotland

TUNNEY. From Toesni; a loc. n., Norm.

TUNNICLIFFE. From Tonnacliff; a loc. n., Lancs

TUNSTALL. A loc. n., Dur., Kent, Staffs, Suff.

TUPHOLME. A loc. n., Lincs

TUPMAN. *See* Tubman

TUPP, TUPPER. *A.S.* Tub, Dub, Tubba (a striker (?)); *G.* Töpper (a potter); p.n. Or *see* Tubb

TUPPING. *Dch.* Tubbing; a p.n.; fam. n. of Tubb

TUR. *See* Torr

TURBAND. *N.* Þorbrandr; *D.B.* Torbrand, Turbrand (Thor's sword); *G.* Turbin; p.n.

TURBEFIELD. From Turberville or Troubleville; a loc. n., Norm.

TURBETT. *See* Torbet

TURBEY. *G.* Turbe; a p.n. *See* Thorburn

TURK. *A.S.* Turca; *N.-Fr.* Turkeis; *Fl.* Turck; *Dch.* Turk; *D.* Türck; *G.* Tourke, Türk; p.n. Dim. of Thor (?)

TURNADGE. *See* Turnidge

TURNBULL. From Tournebu; a barony in Norm.

TURNER. *Fr.* Tournaire, Tourneur, Turnier; *Fl.* Turner; p.n.

> *N.-Fr.* From the *tourn*, or feudal court, from attending which the tenant's deputy was styled an attorney. Turnerus, capellanus, in a grant to Croyland, A.D. 1051. Reginald le Turnur held land in Oxon *temp*. K. John.

TURNEY. From Tournay; a loc. n., France. *D.B.* de Torny; a p.n.

TURNHAM. A loc. n., Devon, Middlx.

> De Garlande held it.

TURNIDGE. From Turnditch; a loc. n., Derbysh.

TURPIN. From Turpin au Bois; a loc. n., Norm. *G.* Turbin; *Dch.* Torbein; *Fr.* Turpin; p.n.

> Walter Turpin held lands in Dorset *temp*. K. John, 1202.

TURRELL *N.-Fr.* Turel; a p.n.

TURTLE, TURTILL. *See* Thirketel

TURTON. A loc. n., Lancs

TURVEY. A loc. n., Beds

TURVILLE. A loc. n., Bucks. Or Tourville, Normandy

TUSHAW. *G.* Tusche; a p.n.

TUSON. *See* Tyson. Prot. ref., Lond. 1688

TUSTIN. *N.-Fr.* Fitz Tustin; *N.* Þorsteinn; *A.S.* Thorstan, Thurstan, Tustain, Tusten; p.n. (Thor's stone); or *A.S.* Thurstegn (Thor's soldier)

TUTCHER. *Fr.* Tousjours (?); a p.n.

TUTE, TUTT. *See* Tooth

TUTHILL, TUTILL, TUTTELL, TUTTLE. From Toothill; a loc. n., Hants, Lincs

TUTING. From Tooting; a loc. n., Surr.

TUTTIETT. From Touchet, near Mortaine, Norm.; a baronial n. Cephas Tutet, Hugt., Lond. 1681

> Ursin de T., 1082, Norm. Jocelin T., Ches., *temp*. W. I., Lords Audley, Earls of Castlehaven. Toget, Tuchet in Roll of Battell Abbey.

TWADELL. *See* Tweddel

TWAITS. *See* Thwaites

TWAMLEY. From Twemlow; a loc. n., Ches.

TWEDDEL. From Tweed-dale; a loc. n.

TWEED, TWEEDIE. *N.* Þveit; *D.* Tvede; p.n. *See* Thwaites

> At first a local n. (a piece of land cut off or reclaimed, *A.S. thwitan* (to cut)), it became a p.n.

TWEEN. Thuin; a loc. n., Belg. *N.-Fr.* Tuinc; *Dch.* Tuijn, Tuyn; p.n.

> Twin in Rot. Hund.

TWELLS. Originally Atte-Wells

TWIDDY. *See* Tweedie

TWIGG. *A.S.* Twicga; a p.n.; *tweg* (two, twin (?))

TWIGHT. *See* Twite

TWINBERROW. A loc. n., Worcest.

TWINER, TWINN. *See* Tween

TWINING. *See* Twyning

TWISDEN. From Twisten; a loc. n., Lancs

> Twisten was called Twysilton *temp*. K. John, at which period the family of that name were owners there.

TWISLETON. A loc. n., Yorks

TWISS. *Dch.*; p.n.; *Old G.* Zuiso; p.n.; *A.S. twis* (twin)

TWITCHELL. *See* Twitchwell

TWITCHIN, TWITCHING. From Twitchen; a loc. n., Devon, Norf.

TWITCHWELL. From Titchwell; a loc. n., Norf.

TWITE. From Thwaite; a loc. n., Norf., Yorks. Or *Dch.* Tuit; a p.n.

TWOGOOD. *See* Toogood

TWOO. *See* Tow or Thew

TWYCROSS. A loc. n., Leics

TWYDELL. *See* Tweddle

TWYFORD. A loc. n., Derbysh., Hants, Lincs, Norf., Salop

TWYNAM. From Twineham; a loc. n., Salop

TWYNING. A loc. n., Glost.

TWYSDEN. A loc. n., Kent. Formerly Twysenden

TYACK. *Fr.* ,Taiche; p.n. *See* Teager

TYARS, TYAS, TYCE. *See* Tice

TYDEMAN. *Dch.* Tydeman; a p.n. *See* Tidman

TYE. From Teigh; a loc. n., Rutld.; or Thy, Thys, Belg. *D.* Thye; a p.n. *See* Dye

TYERMAN. *Dch.* Tieman; a p.n.

TYLECOTE. From Tulket; a loc. n. on the Ribble, near Preston, Lancs (Brit. Tylcoed (?)). Or Holecote, Ullcote, Northants

Philip de Ulecot and Hugh de Bailiol, in 1216, sided with King John against his brother Richard. Persons

TYLECOTE—*continued*
of the name of Talkatt, Tallcot, Taylcote, Taylcott were living at Braintree, Essex, in 1623. John Tallcott occurs in a list of emigrants to America in 1632.

TYLER. From Tilers, a fief and castle in Norm. *N.-Fr.* De Telieres; a p.n.

De Tilere in Rot. Hund.

TYNDALE, TYNDALL. *See* Tindal

TYRER. *N.-Fr.* Terrer; a p.n.

TYRIE. A loc. n., Aberdeen

TYRRELL. A loc. n., Norm. *D.* Turrell; *Fr.* Thirel, Tirel; p.n.; *N.-Fr.* a little castle or tower

Tirell in Roll of Battell Abbey; and de Tirel, under-tenant, in *D.B.*

TYRWHITT. From Tywardreth; a loc. n., Cornw. Or *see* Truwhitt

TYSON, TYSSEN. *D.* Thuessen, Thyssen; *Dch.* Thijssen, Tijssen; *Fl.* Tison, Tyssen; *N.-Fr.* Tison, Tisun; p.n.

Gislebert Tison, a tenant in chief, *D.B.* (Notts, Yorks, Lincs), had twenty-nine manors forfeited upon the ravaging of Yorks by William I. Teison or Thisun in Rot. Obl. et Fin.

U

UBANK. *See* Ewbank

UDALL. *Fr.* Oudalle; a p.n. From Ouvedale; a loc. n., Norm.

UDEN. *N.* Uðr; *A.S.* Ud, Uda; *F.* Uda, Udden; *Dch.* Uden; *S.* Uddén; p.n. Trib. n. of Udo (the prosperous)

UDNEY. A loc. n., Aberdeen

UFF. *A.S.* Uffa, Wuffa; *D.* Uffe; p.n. *See* E. Angl. king (an owl, vulture)

UFFINDEL. A loc. n. Wo Uffendale

UGLOW. *S.* Uggla (?); a p.n.

ULLATHORNE. A loc. n.

ULLETT. *See* Hullett

ULLMER. *A.S.* Ulfmær, Ulmer; *D.*, *Dch.* Ulmer; p.n. (famous wolf)

ULP, ULPH. *N.* Ulfarr or Ulfr (wolf); *F.* Ulferd; *D.B.* Ulf, Ulfere, Ulfii; *G.* Uhl, Uhlfig, Ulfert; p.n.

ULYATT. *See* Ullett

UNCLE. A loc. n., Holland and Germ. *Dch.* Unkel; a p.n.

UNDERDOWN. A loc. n., Cornw.

UNDERHAY. From Underheugh; a loc. n., Cumb.

UNDERHILL. A loc. n., Devon

UNDERWOOD. A loc. n., Derbysh., Devon, Notts

UNGOOD. From Hengoed; a loc. n., Salop

UNITE. From Unity; a loc. n., Cumb.

UNSWORTH. A loc. n., Lancs

UNTHANK. A loc. n., Cumb. and Northbd.

UNWIN. *N.* Aun; *A.S.* Onwine, Unwen, Unwinus (friend of the gods); *Fl.* Unwin; p.n.

UPCHER. *See* Upsher

UPCOTT. A loc. n., Devon, Somers

UPFILL. From Uphill (?); a loc. n., Devon

UPHAM. A loc. n., Hants

UPJOHN. Welsh Apjohn (?); a p.n. (Johnson)

UPPERTON. A loc. n., Devon

UPSALL. A loc. n., Yorks

UPSDALL. From Upsall (?); a loc. n., Yorks

UPSHER. From Upshire; a loc. n., Ess.

UPSOM. A loc. n.

UPTON. A loc. n., Berks, Cornw., Devon, Dorset, Hants, Kent, Lancs, Northants, Somers, Wilts, Yorks

UPWARD. *See* Upwood

UPWOOD. A loc. n., Hunts

URE. From Urr; a loc. n., Kirkcudbright. Or *A.S.* Ur; *N.* Úrr; p.n. (wild ox)

UREN. A contr. of Trewren; a loc. n., Cornw.; or Welsh Urien (heavenly). St Urien; a loc. n., Norm.

URIE. A loc. n., Inverness

URMSTON. A loc. n., Lancs

URQUHART. A loc. n., Elgin

URRY. *See* Hurry

URWICK. From Urswick; a loc. n., Lancs

Adam de Urswick, 6 Edw. III. (1332), was chief forester of Bowland. Sir Robert, knight of the shire, 5 to 20 Rich. II., and 1 and 2 Henry IV. Sir John de Urswick, 14 Rich. II., sheriff. Christopher, chaplain to Henry VII., the "Sir Christopher" of Rich. III., Act V. § 5, buried in Hackney Church.

USBORNE. From Husborne; a loc. n., Beds. Or *see* Osborne

USHER. From Ushaw; a loc. n., Dur. Or *A.S.* Hoshere, Oshere; p.n. (the gods' warrior)

The family of De Neville assumed the name of Le Uschere or Le Huissier, from the office granted to them by K. John.

USHERWOOD. *See* Isherwood

USILL. From Ussel or Uzel; loc. n., France. *Dch.* Husel; a p.n.

UTTERMARE. From Udimore; a loc. n., Kent

UTTERTON. From Otterton; a loc. n., Devon

UTTING. *N.* Udr; *F.* Udo, Ude, Uden; *G.* Otte, Oettinger; *Dch.* Ouden; *Fl.* Utten; *S.* Udden; *D.B.* Eudo, Udi, Othingar; p.n. Prot. ref., Sandwich, 1622. *See* Udden

UWINS. *See* Ewens

UZZELL. *See* Usill

V

VACHELL. From Vaucelles; a loc. n., Fland.

VAGG. *See* Wagg

VAIL. *See* Vale

VAISEY, VAIZEY. *See* Veasey

VALE. *N.-Fr.* De Vetula or De Veel; a p.n.

VALENTINE. *Fr.* Valentin; *Dch.* Valentien; p.n. Hugt. n., 1618

VALIANT. *Fr.* Vaillant; a p.n. Hugt. n., Lond. 1681

VALLER. From Valeres; a loc. n., Norm.

VALLANCE. From Valence; a loc. n., Norm.

VALLINGS. *A.S.* Wealing; a fam. n.; *D.B.* Wellen (strangers, foreigners); *D.* Wahlin, Wallin; *Dch.* Walen; *Fl.* Wallens; p.n.

VALPY. From *D.* Valby; a loc. n.

VANCE. A loc. n., Belg.

VANDELEUR. *Fl.* Vande Laer, Vanderloo; p.n. Theodorus Vanderlaugh, gent., Prot. ref., Lond. 1618

VANE. *See* Fane

VANNE. From Van; a loc. n., Glamorgan. Or *Dch.* Vane; a p.n.

VANNECK. *Fl.* Van Eck, Vanneck; p.n. Dch. ref., Lond. 1618

VARDEN. *A.S.* Weording; a fam. n.; *D.* Warding; *G.* Wardein; *Dch.* Vaarting; *Fl.* Verdeyen; *D.B.* Werden; p.n. Or *see* Verdon

VARDIGANS. *See* Vertigan

VARDY. *N.-Fr.* La Ferté; a loc. n. (barony), Norm., near Evreux

VARGUS. *See* Fergus

VARLEY. A loc. n., Ess. Also *Fr.* Varlez; a p.n.
R. de Verli, Norf. 1086.

VARLO. *See* Varley

VARNAM. *See* Farnham

VARNELL. From Verneuil (?); a loc. n., Norm. Or *Fl.* Fannell; a p.n.

VARNEY. *Fl.* Warny; a p.n.

VARNHAM. *See* Farnham

VARVILL. From Varaville; a loc. n., Norm. *Fr.* Vauville; a p.n.
Varuurile in Roll of Battell Abbey. De Warwell in *D.B.*

VASEY. *See* Veasey

VASS. *A.S.* Was; *Dch.* Vas, Vasse, Vassy; *Fl.* Fas; p.n. (water)

VASSAR. *Fr.* Vasseur; *Fl.* Vassert; *G.* Wasser; *A.S.* Waso; p.n.; *N.-Fr.* Levasseur (a vassal)

VATCHER. *N.-Fr.* Vachier; a p.n. (cow-keeper)

VAUGHT. *See* Faught

VAUS, VAUSE, VAWSE. *See* Vaux

VAUX. A loc. n., Belg. and Norm.

VAVASSOUR. *Fr.* Vavasseur, Le Vavasseur; p.n. *See* official names

VAWDREY. From Valdaré or Vaudaré; a loc. n., Norm.; or Waudrez, Belg. *N.-Fr.* De Valdairie: a p.n. Hugt. n., Norwich, 1622

VAWSER. *See* Vassar

VEAL. From Ville; a loc. n., Belg. *See* Viall

VEAR. *See* Vere

VEARS. *A.S.* Wær (wary); *Dch.* Weers; p.n.

VEASEY. *N.-Fr.* De Vaacy; a p.n.; *D.B.* de Veci
Vessay or de Vesci in Roll of Battell Abbey and in Rot. Obl. et Fin., K. John.

VEITCH. *See* Fetch

VELLUM. *See* Welham

VENABLES. A loc. n., Norm.
D.B. Gislebert de V., an under-tenant (Ches.), 1086. Richard de V. in Rot. Obl. et Fin. The barony of Kinderton continued in this family till 1676.

VENESS. *Fl.* Van Esse, Vanesse; a p.n. Or *N.-Fr.* De Venis; a p.n.

VENIMORE. *See* Fennimore

VENN. A loc. n., Cornw., Devon

VENNING. *See* Fane

VENTRIS. *N.-Fr.* Ventras or Vintras; a p.n.
Ralph de Vintyr in Rot. Hund.

VERDON. From Verdun; a loc. n. in France
Verdoune in Roll of Battell Abbey. Bertram de Verdun, a tenant in chief in *D.B.* (Staffs). In 1273 John de Verdun held lands in Belton, Leics. Bertram de Verdun founded Croxden Abbey, 23 Henry II., 1176.

VERE. From Ver; a loc. n., Norm. *D.B.* de Ver; a p.n.
In Roll of Battell Abbey and Rot. Obl. et Fin.

VERLANDER. *Fl.*, *Dch.* Verlant, Verlinde; p.n.

VERLEY. *See* Varley

VERNEY. *See* Fernie

VERNON. From Vernon; a loc. n., Norm. Hugt. n., Lond. 1618

Vernoun in Roll of Battell Abbey; *D.B.* de Vernon, tenant in chief.

VERRY. From Viry or Verrey; a loc. n., Norm. *Fr.* Wéry; *Fl.* Werry; *Dch.* Verre; p.n.

VERSCHOYLE. From Vascœuil; a loc. n., Norm. *Fl.* Veerschuijl; a p.n.

VERTIGAN. *B.* Vortigern (?) (great king)

VERTUE. *See* Virtue

VERVILL. *See* Varvill

VESEY. *See* Veasey

VESPER. *Dch.* Weesper; a p.n.

VESTEY. *A.S.* West; *D.* Westi; a p.n. *See* West

VIALL. From Vile or Vielles; a loc. n., Norm. *See* Veal. Viel, a Hugt. n., Lond. 1864

Vile and De Vile are in the Roll of Battell Abbey.

VIAN. A loc. n., Fland. and Norm. *Fr.* Viane; a p.n.

VIBERT. *A.S.* Wigbeorht; *Old G.* Wigbert, Wibert; p.n. (war famous)

VICARAGE. *A.S.* Wigric; *Old G.* Wigirich (war rule); *Fl.* Wichterich; p.n.

VICARY. From La Vacherie; a loc. n., Norm.

R. de Vickery in Rot. Hund.

VICKERMAN. *D.* Wickman; a\p.n.

VICKERS. *N.* Víkarr (a viking (?)); *D.* Wick, Vickers; *Fl.* Wyckaerts; *Dch.* Wichers, Wiggers; *G.* Wickert; p.n.

VIDLER, VIDLOW. From Vis-de-lou, Norm. Or *see* Fidler

Vis-de-Lew, tenant in chief, *D.B.*, Berks.

VIGORS. From St Vigor; a loc. n., Norm. *Fr.* Vigor. *See* Wigger

Viger in Rot. Obl. et Fin.

VILLIERS. From Villiers; a loc. n., Belg. and Norm. *Fl.* Villers; *D.* Willer; *Dch.* Willaars; p.n.

VIMER. *D.B.* Wimer; *G.* Wimmer; p.n. *See* Wyman

VINCE. *A.S.* Winsi (Winsige); *Fl.* Vinche, Wyns; *Dch.* Wins; *G.* Vins; p.n. (victorious friend). Or from *N.-Fr.* De Vinas; a p.n.

VINCENT. *N.-Fr.* St Vincent; a loc. n., Norm. Hugt., Lond. 1618

VINE, VINN. From Veynes; a loc. n., France. *Fr.* Vin; *Fl.* Wion, Wyn; *Dch.* Vinne; p.n.

VINEY. From Vinhay; a loc. n., Devon; Vinney, Somers; or Vignie, Norm.

VINNECOMBE. From Venycombe; a loc. n., Hants

VINRACE. *See* Wainwright

VINT. *Fl.* Windt; *D.* Wind; p.n.

VIPOND, VIPONT, VIPAND. *N.-Fr.* De Vieuxpont; a p.n. (barons of Westmd.)

Thomas Vipont, Bishop of Carlisle, 1255.

VIRGIN. From Verchin; a loc. n., France. Or *S.* Virgin; *Fl.* Wirtgen (dimin. of *F.* Wêert); p.n.

VIRGO, VIRGOE. *Fl.* Vergote; *D.* Vergo; *Dch.* Vergouw; p.n.; *A.S. wær-gota* (?) (war Goth)

VIRTUE. From Vertou; a loc. n., France

R. de la Vertu, 1180.

VISE. *See* Wise

VISGERS. *Fl.* Visschers; a p.n. *See* Whisker

VISICK. *See* Physic

VITTERY. From Vitry; a loc. n., Belg. and France. *Fr.* Vitré and de Vitré; p.n.

VIVEASH, VIVISH. *Fr.* Fievez; a p.n.

VIZARD, VIZER. *Fr.* Visart, Viseur; *Dch.* Visser; p.n. (a vizard or vizor; a mask for the face, attached to a helmet)

VOISEY. *Fr.* Voisin; a p.n. (neighbour)

VOKES. *See* Vaux

VORES. *G.* Voras; a p.n. *See* Vears

VOS, VOSE. *D.*, *Dch.*, *Fl.*, *G.* Voss; a p.n. *See* Vass

VOWEL. *See* Fowell

VOWLES. *See* Foule

VOYCE. *Dch.* Voijs; a p.n. De Voyce, Hugt. n., Cant. 1618

VYE. *Fr.* Vuy, Vuye; p.n. De la Fuyé, Hugt. n., Lond. 1683

VYNER. *A.S.* Winehere (friend-soldier); a p.n.

VYSE. *See* Wise

W

WABE. *A.S.* Wæba; a p.n. (a weaver)

WACE, WACEY. *A.S.* Was, Wass, Wassa (water (?)); *G.* Weese, Wehse; *Dch.* Wees; *N.-Fr.* De Wasa; p.n.
In Rot. Obl. et Fin. and Rot. Hund.

WACKETT. *See* Waggett

WADD. *N.* Vaði (a wader); *D.* Wad; *A.S.* Wada, Wade, Wado; p.n.

WADDELL. A loc. n., Scotl. Or *A.S.*, *D.* Wadel; *S.* Wadell; p.n. Dim. of Wad

WADDELOW. *See* Vidler. Wadelo; a p.n. in *D.B.*

WADDESLEY. From Wadsley; a loc. n., Yorks

WADDILOVE. *See* Waddelow

WADDING. *See* Woodin

WADDINGTON. A loc. n., Devon, Lincs, Yorks

WADDUP. From Whadub; a loc. n., Cumb.

WADDY. *See* Wadd

WADE. A loc. n., Hants
De W. in Rot. Hund. In Rot. Obl. et Fin.

WADHAM. From Waddingham; a loc. n., Lincs. Or *Dch.* Wadum; a p.n.

WADLEY. A loc. n., Berks, Devon

WADMAN. *S.*; p.n.

WADSWORTH. A loc. n.; Lancs, Yorks

WAGER. *A.S.* Wæghere (sea warrior); *G.* Wager; p.n.

WAGG. A loc. n., Somers. Or *N.* Vágr; *A.S.* Wag; *D.* Waage; *Dch.* Waag; *D.B.* Waga; p.n. (wave, sea; or in the sense of waving, *i.e.* brandishing a sword)

WAGGETT. *G.* Weckert; *S.* Vagt; p.n. Dim. of Wagg

WAGGON. *N.* Vagn; *A.S.* Wagan; *Fl.* Wagon; p.n.; fam. n. of Wagg (?)

WAIGHT. *See* Waite

WAILING. *See* Vallings

WAIN. *D.* Wain; *G.* Wehn; p.n. *See* Waggon

WAINER. *G.* Wehner; a p.n.

WAINWRIGHT. *D.* Weinrich; *G.* Weinerich; *A.S.* Wineric; p.n. (friendly ruler)

WAITE. *A.S.* Wet, Wetta, Hwæt; *D.* Vet, Wiet; *Fl.* Vets; *F.* Wêt, Wiet; *G.* Weth; p.n. (sharp, keen)

WAKE. *A.S.* Wac, Wacar; *D.* Weeke; *G.* Weck; *Fl.* Weeck; p.n. (watchful)
In Rot. Obl. et Fin.

WAKEFIELD. A loc. n., Northants, Yorks

WAKEFORD. A loc. n.

WAKEHAM. A loc. n., Dorset

WAKELIN, WAKELING. *N.-Fr.* Walchelin; *S.* Wacklin; p.n.

WAKELY, WAKLEY. A loc. n., Herts

WALCOTT. A loc. n., Lincs, Norf., Salop, Worcest.

WALDEGRAVE. From Walgrave; a loc. n., Northants; anciently Waldegrave

Held by De Maloure of Bretagne.

WALDEN. A loc. n., Yorks

WALDON. *See* Walden

WALDRON. A loc. n., Suss. Or *A.S.* Waleran; *Dch.* Woelderen; p.n. (powerful raven)

WALDUCK. *Dch., G.* Waldeck; a loc. and p.n. (forest oak)

WALE. *A.S.* Wale, Wealh, Wel; *D.* Wehl; *Fl.* Weyll; p.n. (stranger, foreigner)

WALES, WAILES, WAYLES. From Wales; a loc. n., Yorks (*D.B.* Walise). Or *G.* Wels; a p.n.

WALESBY. A loc. n., Lincs, Notts

WALEY. *See* Whalley

WALFORD. A loc. n., Staffs

WALKDEN. A loc. n., Lancs

WALKER. *N.* Valka (a foreigner); *Dch.* Walkart, Walker; *Fl.* Walckiers; *G.* Walke, Walker; *A.S.* Walcher, Wealhere; p.n. (a stranger soldier)

It is a very old n. The tribe of Wealceringas was among the early settlers. *A.S. wealcere* (a fuller) is not so likely a derivation.

WALKERLEY. From Walkley; a loc. n., Yorks

WALKINGSHAW. A loc. n., Renfrew

WALL. A loc. n., Staffs. Or *A.S.* Wal, Weal; p.n. (a stranger)

WALLACE or WALLIS. *N.* Valir; *A.S.* Valas or Wealas (the Welsh, *i.e.* foreigners or strangers); *A.S.* Wealhisc; *Dch.* Walsch; *Fl.* Wallays; p.n.

There was an influx of Anglo-Normans into Scotland in the reign of David I. Among these was Richard Waleys, the ancestor of the great Wallace. He has left his name at Richardtun in Ayrshire. Valers is in the Roll of Battell Abbey; and de

WALLACE or WALLIS—*continued*

Vals, de Wals, Walo, Walise, Walscin are in *D.B.* The north-western part of France was called by the Norsemen Walland.

WALLACH, WALLEDGE. *Dch., D.* Wallich; a p.n. *See* above

WALLBRIDGE. A loc. n., Glost.

WALLER. *A.S.* Wealhere; *S., Dch., Fl.* Waller; p.n. (a stranger warrior)

WALLETT. From Waillet; a loc. n., Belg. *Dch.* Walet; a p.n.

WALLING. *D.* Wallin; *S.* Wallen; p.n.; descendant of Wall

WALLINGTON. A loc. n., Hants, Norf., Surr.

WALLIS. *See* Wallace

WALLMAN. *See* Whall

WALLOP. A loc. n., Hants

WALMSLEY. A loc. n., Lancs, Staffs

WALPOLE. A loc. n., Norf., Somers, Suff.

WALRON. *N.-Fr.* Waleran; a p.n. *See* Waldron

WALSH. From Wallash; a loc. n., Staffs. Or *see* Wallach

WALSHAM. A loc. n., Norf., Suff.

WALSINGHAM. A loc. n., Norf.

WALSOM. *Dch.* Walsem; a p.n. Or *see* Walsham

WALTERS. *A.S.* Walder, Walter, Wealdhere; *Dch.* Wolters; *Fl.* Wauters, Wouters; p.n. (ruler-warrior); a contr. of Walterus. Prot. ref., Lond. 1621

WALTHEW. *N.* Valþjóf (a foreign servant); *G., Dch.* Walther; *A.S.* Wealtheow; *D.B.* Wallef, Waltef; p.n.

WALTON. A loc. n., Berks, Derbysh., Herts, Lancs, Norf., Somers, Staffs, Suff.

WAND. From Wandre; a loc. n., Belg. *D.B.* Wand; *G.* Wander; p.n. *See* Want

WANKLYN. *A.S.* Wan, Wana; *S.* Wancke; *D.* Wang; p.n. A dim. (pale)

WANNOP. From Wandhope; a loc. n., Cumb.

WANSBOROUGH. From Wanborough; a loc. n., Surr., Wilts

WANT. From Wanz; a loc. n., Belg. Or *N.* Vandráðr; *D.B.* Wand, Wanz, Wants; *G.* Wander; *Dch.* Wandt; *Fl.* Wanet; p.n. (zealous counsellor)

WARBEY, WARBY. From Warboys; a loc. n., Hunts. Or Verbois, Norm.

WARBRICK. From Warbreck; a loc. n., Lancs

WARBURTON. A loc. n., Ches.

WARD. A loc. n., Devon. Or *A.S.* Ward, Weard (guard); *Dch.* Waard. Warde; p.n. Garde; a loc. n., I. of France

WARDALE, WARDELL. *See* Wardle

WARDEN. A loc. n., Kent, Northants, Northbd. Wardin, Belg.

WARDLAW. A loc. n., Inverness

WARDLE. A loc. n., Lancs

WARDLEY. A loc. n., Rutland. Or Weardley, Yorks

WARE. A loc. n., Devon, Herts

WAREHAM. A loc. n., Dorset

WARFORD. *See* Walford

WARHURST. *D.* Warhus; *Fl.* Verhust; p.n. (wood warden)

WARING. *See* Wearing

WARLAND. *Fl.*; p.n.

WARLEIGH. A loc. n., Somers

WARLOW. From Wardlow; a loc. n., Derbysh.

WARMAN. *A.S.* Wearman (warman; or cautious, wary); *D.* Warming; p.n.

WARMER. *A.S.* Wærmær; *G.* Warmer (war famous). Or Walmer; a loc. n., Kent

WARMINGTON. A loc. n., Northants, Warw.

WARN, WARNE. From Waghen or Wawne; a loc. n., Yorks. Or *see* Wearing

WARNEFORD. A loc. n., Hants

WARNER. *A.S.* Warner, Wernhere; *N.-Fr.* le Warner; p.n.

WARNES. *A.S.* Warinus; *D.* Warns; p.n.

WARR. *A.S.* War, Wær; *D.* Warrer; p.n. (cautious warrior) Le Warre in Rot. Obl. et Fin.

WARRAM. From Warham; a loc. n., Norf.
Held by De Vere.

WARREN. *N.-Fr.* Warin, Verenne; p.n. *See* Wearing
Gundred de Warren or Warrenna held lands in Wilts *temp.* K. John, 1201.

WARRENER. From Garenne; a loc. n., Norm.
W. de W., 1066; Earl of Surrey, 1089.

WARRINGTON. A loc. n., Ches.

WARRY. *See* Warr

WARSAP. *See* Worsop

WARTER. A loc. n., Yorks

WARTH. *See* Ward or Worth

WARWICK. A loc. n., Cumb., Hants, and the county town

WASE, WASEY. *See* Wace, Wasce (Wascheham (?))
In Rot. Obl. et. Fin.

WASHBOURN. A loc. n., Devon

WASHINGTON. A loc. n., Dur., Suss.

WASPE. *See* Warsap

WASTELL. A loc. n., Worcest.

WATCHAM. From Watchcombe; a loc. n., Devon

WATERALL. From Waterfall; a loc. n., Staffs

WATERFIELD. From Waterville; a loc. n., Norm.

WATERHOUSE. A loc. n., Staffs

WATERLOW. *Fl.* Waterloos; a loc. and p.n. Or *see* Waddelow

WATERS, WATERSON. *See* Walters. Prot. ref. n., Lond. 1618

WATERSTONE. A loc. n., Pembroke

WATFORD. A loc. n., Derbysh., Herts, Northants

WATKINS. *See* Watts

WATLER. *Fr.* Watelet; a p.n.

WATLING. *A.S.*; fam. n.

WATLOW. *See* Waterlow

WATMORE. *See* Whitmore

WATTON. A loc. n., Norf.

WATTS. *N.* Hvati (active); *A.S.* Wat; *D.* Watt; p.n. *See* Wait
WAUCHOPE. From Warcop (?); a loc. n., Westmd.
WAUD. *See* Wadd
WAUGH. *See* Wagg. Or from the Irish McWhaugh
WAUGHN, WAWN. *G.* Wahn; *Dch.* Waan; *D.* Wohn; p.n. *See* Waggon
WAVELL. *See* Weevill
WAY. A loc. n., Devon, Kent. Or *see* Wagg
WAYBORN. From Waybourne; a loc. n., Norf.
WAYCOTT. *See* Waygood
WAYGOOD. *A.S.* Wigod, Wigot; *Old G.* Wihgoz; p.n. (war Goth)
WAYHAM. A loc. n.
WAYLAND. A loc. n., Dorset. Or *Fl.* Weyland; a p.n.
WAYLES. *See* Wales
WAYMAN. *See* Wyman
WAYMOUTH. *See* Weymouth
WEAGER. *See* Widger
WEAKLEY, WEAKLIN. *See* Wakelin
WEAL. *A.S.* Wil; *Old G.* Willo; *Dch.*, *Fl.* Wiel; *G.* Wiehl; p.n. (resolution)
WEARE. A loc. n., Somers
WEARING. *N.* Væringi; the name of the Warings or northern warriors who served as body-guards to the Byzantine Emperors; *A.S.* Wæring; a fam. n.; *Fl.* Vering; *D.B.* Warenger, Werinc, Wareng, Warinc, Warin; p.n.
The Varangian Guard was originally composed of this Scandinavian tribe, but was afterwards recruited from Northern Europe and England. There is a Varengafjord in Norway.
WEATHERALL. A loc. n., Camb. *See* Wetherall
WEATHERBURNE. *See* Wedderburn
WEATHERLEY. A loc. n., Warw. From Wetherley; a loc. n., Camb.
WEATHERS. *See* Withers
WEATHERSTONE. From Withersden; a loc. n., Kent

WEAVER. A loc. n., Ches., Devon. *N.-Fr.* De Wevre; a p.n. Or *D.* Wæver; a p.n (a weaver)
WEAVING. *Dch.* Wieffering; a fam. n.
WEBB, WEBBER. *Fl.* Webb; *D.*, *Dch.*, *G.* Weber (a weaver)
WEBSDALE. A loc. n.
WEBSTER. The Scot. and N. Engl. form of *D.*, *G.*, *Dch.* Weber (a weaver)
WEDD. *See* Weed
WEDDERBURN. A loc. n., Berwick
WEDDERSPOON, WITHERSPOON. *See* Wotherspon
WEDDING. *D.* Weden; *S.* Wedin; p.n; fam. n. of Weed
WEDDUP. A loc. n.
WEDGEWOOD. A loc. n., Staffs
WEDLAKE, WEDLOCK. *See* Widlake
WEDMORE. A loc. n., Somers
WEEDE. *D.* Wied; *A.S.* Wid, Widda; *Fl.* Widy; *S.* Wid; p.n. (famous)
WEEDEN. From Weedon; a loc. n., Northants
WEEDING. From Weeting; a loc. n., Norf. Or *see* Weeden
WEEDS. *F.* Wiets; *D.B.* Widius; p.n. *See* Weed
WEEKS. A loc. n., Ess.
WEEVILL. From Wauville; a loc. n., Norm.; Wyvill, Lincs. Or *N.* Vífill (a beetle); *D.* Wivel; *D.B.* Wifle; *Dch.* Wiwel; p.n. *See* p. 2
Viville, Wyville, Wivel, in Roll of Battell Abbey. Richard de Wyvill held lands in Yorks *temp.* K. John, A.D. 1200.
WEGG. *Dch.* Wegge; *D.B.* Wege, Weghe; p.n. Prot. ref., Sandwich, 1622. *See* Wagg
WEIGHTMAN. *A.S.* Wetman; a p.n. *See* Waite
WEIR. Scot. form of *N.-Fr.* de Vere
WELBORE. From Wellebue; a loc. n., Norm. *See* Wildbore

WELBORN. A loc. n., Lincs, Norf. Or *A.S.* Wilbeorn (resolute bear); *G.* Wilborn; a p.n.

WELCHER. *See* Wilscher

WELDON. A loc. n., Northants

WELFORD. A loc. n., Berks, Glost., Northants, Warw.

WELHAM. A loc. n.

WELLAND. A loc. n., Devon, Worcest.

WELLBY. A loc. n., Leics, Lincs

WELLINGHAM. A loc. n., Norf.

WELLINGTON. A loc. n., Salop, Somers

WELLS. A loc. n., Norf., Somers

WELLSPRING. A loc. n., Devon

WELLSTEAD. A loc. n. (?). Or *A.S.* Wealhstod; a p.n. (an interpreter)

WELLUM. *See* Welham

WELTON. A loc. n., Lincs, Northants, Somers, Staffs, Yorks

WEMBORN. From Wimborne; a loc. n., Dorset

WEMYS. A loc. n., Fife

WENBORN. *See* Wemborn

WENDEN. A loc. n., Ess.

WENHAM. A loc. n., Suff.

WENLOCK. A loc. n., Salop

WENT. *D., G., S.* Wendt; *Fl.* Vent; *Dch.* Went; p.n. (a vandal; a native of Jutland)

WENTWORTH. A loc. n., Camb., Yorks

Held by De Oissy.

WESLEY. *N.* Vestliði (a western sailor); *S.* Westlau, Wessling; *Dch.* Wesler, Wesseling; *G.* Wesely; *Fl.* Wesly; p.n. Or from the Irish MacUaislaidh; a p.n. *See* Westley

WEST. *N.* Vestarr (a western man); *D., Dch., Fl.* West; *D.B.* Westre; p.n. Prot. ref., Lond. 1621

WESTACOTT. A loc. n., Devon

WESTBEAR, WESTBEER. A loc. n., Devon, Kent

WESTBROOK. A loc. n., Berks, Norf., Wilts

WESTCOTT. A loc. n., Devon, Warw.

WESTERBY. *D.* ; loc. and p.n.

WESTGATE. A loc. n., Yorks, Dur. Kent

WESTHORPE. A loc. n., Lincs, Northants, Notts, Suff.

WESTLEY. A loc. n., Camb., Salop, Suff.

De Westle in Rot. Hund.

WESTON. A loc. n., Herts, Northants, Staffs, Suff., Yorks

WESTRAY. A loc. n., Orkney. Or *N.* Vestarr, Vestre; *D.S.* Wester; *Dch.* Westra; *D.B.* Westre (Saxon tenant); p.n. *See* West

WESTREPT. From Westhorpe; a loc. n., Norf. *See* Westrop

WESTROP. A loc. n., Wilts. *D.* Westrup; a loc. and p.n.

WESTWATER. From Wastwater, Cumb.

WESTWOOD. A loc. n., Dur., Devon, Kent, Notts, Wilts, Yorks

WETHERALL. A loc. n., Cumb.

WETHERLEY. From Wetherby (?); a loc. n., Yorks

WETHERSETT. *S.* Wetterstedt; a loc. and p.n.

WETMORE. *See* Whetmore

WETTERN. *Dch.* Wetten, Wetteren; p.n.

WETTERTON. From Wetherden; a loc. n., Suff.

WEY. From Ways; a loc. n., Belg. Or *N.* Véi or Vé-geirr (woe-spear); *D.* Weyhe; *D.B.* Weghe, Wege, Waih; *Fl.* Wey; *Dch.* Weih; p.n. Or *See* Wagg

WEYMOUTH. A loc. n., Dorset

WHADCOAT. *See* Whatcott

WHAITES. From Weeze (?); a loc. n., Fland. Or *see* Waite

WHALE. *See* Wale

WHALEY. A loc. n., Derbysh., Hants

WHALL. *G.* Walla, Walle; *Dch., S.* Wall; p.n. *See* Wall

WHALLEY. A loc. n., Derbysh., Lancs

WHARMBY. From Warmanbie; a loc. n., Dumfries

WHARNSBY. A loc. n.

WHARTON. A loc. n., Heref., Lancs, Lincs, Westmd.

WHATCOTT. From Whatcote; a loc. n., Warw.

WHATELEY. A loc. n., Warw.

WHATLEY. A loc. n., Somers

WHATLING. *A.S.* Watling; a fam. n. *See* Watts

WHATTON. A loc. n., Leics. Or Whaddon, Camb., Wilts

WHAYMAN. *See* Wyman

WHEALS. From Houilles; a loc. n., France

WHEATBREAD. *See* Whitebread

WHEATCROFT. A loc. n., Derbysh.

WHEATER. *Dch.* Witte; a p.n. *See* White

WHEATLEY. A loc. n., Devon, Dur., Lancs, Notts, Oxf., Yorks

WHEATON. A loc. n., Staffs

WHEATSTONE. From Whetstone; a loc. n., Leics, Middlx.

WHEDDON. From Whaddon; a loc. n., Glost.

WHEELER. *N.* Víl-raðr (confused) (?). Or *Dch.* Wielaerts; *G.* Wiehle; *D.* Vieler; *A.S.* Wilred (resolute counsel); p.n.

WHEEN. *See* Wynn

WHELAN. Irish Phelan. Or *Dch.* Wielen; p.n.

WHELHAM. From Whelnetham; a loc. n., Suff.

WHELPDALE. From Wheldale; a loc. n., Yorks

WHENT. *See* Went

WHERRY. *A.S.* Wær, Wer; *Fl.* Wéry; p.n. (cautious)

WHERWELL. A loc. n., Hants

WHETMORE. From Wetmoor; a loc. n., Staffs

WHETTAM. *Dch.* Wettum; a p.n. Or *see* Whitham

WHEWELL. *See* Weevill

WHIBLEY. From Weobley; a loc. n., Heref.

WHICHCOTE. A loc. n., Salop

WHICHELOW. A loc. n.

WHICHER, WHICKER. *See* Widger

WHIDBORNE. From Whitburn; a loc. n., Heref., Linlithgow

WHIDDEN. From Whiddon; a loc. n., Devon. Or *S.* Widen; a p.n.

WHIDDINGTON. *See* Whittington

WHIFF. *A.S.* Wif; *D.* Wiuff; a p.n. *See* Whipp

WHIFFLE. *See* Whipple

WHIGHAM. From Whickham; a loc. n., Dur.

WHILEY. From Wyley; a loc. n., Ess. ; or Wylye, Wilts. *See* Wayles

WHIMPER. From Whymple; a loc. n. in Devon. Or Wimpole, Camb.

WHIN. Irish Quinn. Or *D.* Wiene; *D.B.* Wine; *Dch.* Win; *Fl.* Wyns; p.n. (a friend)

WHINCOP. A loc. n., Cumb. Or *A.S.* Wincuf; *Dch.* Wincoop; p.n. (strenuous friend)

WHINERAY, WHINNERAH. *A.S.* Wineræd; a p.n. (friendly counsel)

WHINYATES. From Wingates; a a loc. n., Northbd.

WHIPHAM. From Wipham; a loc. n., Suss.

WHIPP, WHIPPS, WHIPPY. *N.* Vippa; n.n. ; *D.B.* Wiber; *G.* Wippert; *A.S.* Wippa (a whip); p.n.

WHIPPLE. *A.S.* Wifel; *N.* Vívill (a beetle); *S.* Wibell; a p.n.

WHISH. *See* Hewish

WHISKER. *A.S.* Wiscar, Wisgar (wise spear); *N.-Fr.* Guiscard; p.n.

WHISSELL. From Oissel; a loc. n., Norm. Or *G.* Wissell; a p.n. Oisel in Rot. Obl. et Fin., K. John.

WHISTLECRAFT. *G.* Wesselhöft; a loc. and p.n.

WHISTLER. *N.-Fr.* Oiselur. Or *Dch.* Wissel, Wisselaar; p.n.; *A.S. hwistlere* (a whistler, piper)

WHISTON. A loc. n., Cornw., Northants, Staffs, Yorks

WHITBREAD. *See* Whitebread

WHITBURN. A loc. n., Dur., Heref.

WHITBY. A loc. n., Yorks

WHITCHER. *See* Widger

WHITCHURCH. From Whitechurch; a loc. n., Yorks

WHITCOMBE. A loc. n., Devon, Dorset, I. of Wight, Somers

WHITE. *N.* Hvítr; *S.* Witt; *Dch.* Witte; *A.S.* Hwitta, Wit, Wita; p.n.

WHITEAR. *See* Whiterod

WHITEBREAD. *A.S.* Wihtbrord; *Fl.* Wittebord; *D.B.* Witbert, Wibert; p.n. (courageous sword). Prot. ref., Norwich, 1622

WHITEHAND. *N. - Fr.* Blanchesmains; a p.n.
    Steph. Blanmong, 1272, Rot. Hund.

WHITEHEAD. *See* Whiterod

WHITEHEART. *A.S.* Wihtheard (strong, courageous)

WHITEHORN. A loc. n., Devon

WHITEHOUSE. A loc. n., Aberdeen. Or *Dch.* Withuis; a p.n.

WHITEHURST. A loc. n., Staffs

WHITELAM. *A.S.* Wihthelm; a p.n. (strong, heavy helmet)

WHITELAW. From Whitlow; a loc. n., Northbd.

WHITELEGGE. *A.S.* Wihtlæg; a p.n. (wise law)

WHITELEY. A loc. n., Devon, Yorks

WHITELOCK, WHITLOCK. *A.S.* Wihtlac; *S.*, *Dch.* Witlok; a p.n. (courageous sword player)

WHITEMAN. *Dch.* Witman; *D.B.* Wihtmar; p.n.

WHITEROD. *A.S.* Wihtræd; *F.* Witerd, Withert; p.n. (courageous counsellor)

WHITESIDE. A loc. n., Cumb.

WHITEWAY. From Whitway; a loc. n., Hants

WHITFIELD. A loc. n., Dorset, Kent, Northants, Salop

WHITHAM, WITHAM, WHITWHAM. From Witham; a loc. n., Ess., Lincs

WHITHARD. *A.S.* Wihtheard; *F.* Witherd; *Dch.* Wittert; p.n. (firm courage)

WHITING, WHITTING. *A.S.* Witting; a fam. n.; *D.* Witten; *S.* Witting; p.n.

WHITLEY. A loc. n., Northbd., Wilts, Yorks

WHITMARSH. From Whitnash; a loc. n., Warw.

WHITMORE. A loc. n., Staffs

WHITNEY. A loc. n., Bucks, Heref.

WHITTAKER. From Whitacre; a loc. n., Worcest.; Wheatacre, Norf. Or *A.S.* Wightgar; a p.n. (strong spear)

WHITTALL. *See* Whittle

WHITTENBURY. From Whittlebury; a loc. n., Heref.

WHITTERIDGE. *See* Witheridge

WHITTET. *See* Whithard

WHITTICK. From Whitwick; a loc. n., Leics

WHITTINGHAM. A loc. n., Haddingtonsh.

WHITTINGTON. A loc. n., Norf., Salop, Staffs, Warw., Worcest.

WHITTLE. From Whittle; a loc. n., Lancs. Or Whitle, Derbysh. *See* Whitwell

WHITTLESEY. A loc. n., Camb.

WHITTOME. From Whittenham; a loc. n., Oxf.

WHITTON. A loc. n., Lincs, Norf., Salop, Staffs, Yorks

WHITRICK. *A.S.* Wihtric; a p.n. (courageous rule). Or *see* Witheridge

WHITWELL. A loc. n., Derbysh., Hants, Herts, Leics, Norf., Yorks

WHITWORTH. A loc. n., Dur., Lancs

WHUR. *See* Wyer

WHYART, WHYATT. *A.S.* Wigheard, Wiard ; *D.* Wiegardt ; *Dch.* Wijaarda, Wyatt ; *F.* Wiaarda ; *Fl.* Wuyts ; p.n. (war strong). Prot. ref., Lond. 1622

WHYBORN. *See* Wayborn

WHYBREW, WHYBROW. From Wyeborough or Wyebrow ; a loc. n. on the Wye. Or *see* Wybrow

WHYLE. *See* Wylie

WHYTLAW. *See* Whitelaw

WIBBERLEY. *See* Whibley

WICK, WICKS. *See* Wigger. Prot. ref. n., Sandwich, 1622

WICKENDEN. From Wichingdine ; a loc. n., Rutland

WICKETT. *A.S.* Wigod ; *Fr.* Wicot ; p.n. (war Goth)

WICKHAM. A loc. n., Berks, Dur., Ess., Hants, Kent, Suff.

WIDDICOMBE. A loc. n., Devon

WIDE. *See* Weed

WIDGER, WIDGERY. *A.S.* Wichere, Wighere ; *Old G.* Wigheri ; p.n. (war soldier)

WIDLAKE. From Widelake ; a loc. n., Cornw.

WIDNALE. From Widdenhall; a loc. n.

WIDNELL. A loc. n.

WIFFIN. *A.S.* Wif, Wifare ; a p.n. ; *Dch.* Wijvering ; a fam. n. ; *wifre* (a weaver)

WIGER. *See* Widger

WIGFALL, WIGFUL. From Wigfield (?) ; a loc. n., Yorks, W.R.

WIGG. *A.S.* Wig ; *G.* Wick ; *D.* Wigh ; *S.* Wik ; p.n. *See* Wigger

WIGGAN. From Wigan ; a loc. n., Lancs

WIGGER. *A.S.* Wigar, Wicgar, Wiga ; *G.* Wicke ; *Dch.* Wiggers; *D.* Wiecke ; p.n. (war-spear)

WIGGETT. *See* Wichett

WIGGIN. *N.* Víkingr (a sea rover) ; *N.-Fr.* Wiguen, Wygeyn ; *S.*, *Fl.* Wiking ; *Dch.* Wijking ; *D.B.* Wicing, Wichin, Wiking ; p.n. Or *A.S.* Wighen, a contr. of Wighelm (war helmet)

WIGGINGTON. A loc. n., Herts, Yorks

WIGHT. *See* Wiggett or White

WIGHTMAN. *See* Whiteman

WIGLEY. A loc. n., Hants

WIGMORE. A loc. n., Heref., Salop

WIGNAL. From Wiggenhall ; a loc. n., Norf.

WIGRAM. *A.S.* (strong in battle)

WILBERFORCE. From Wilberfoss ; a loc. n., Yorks

WILBOURN. *See* Welborn

WILBRAHAM. A loc. n., Camb. ; anciently Wilburgham

WILBY. A loc. n., Norf., Northants, Suff.

WILCH. *See* Wilscher

WILCOCKS. *Fl.* Wilcockx ; *D.B.* Willac ; p.n. Dimin. of Will

WILD. *See* Wildee

WILDBORE. *A.S.* Wilburh ; *Dch.* Wildeboer; p.n. (resolute protection)

WILDEE. *F.* Wildert, Wilt ; *A.S.* Wild ; *G.*, *D.*, *Dch.* Wilde ; p.n. ; *A.S. wyldde* (powerful)

Adam le Wilde in Rot. Obl. et Fin. W. le. W. in Rot. Hund.

WILDGOOSE. *A.S.* Wilgils, Wildgis ; p.n. (resolute hostage). Or *Old G.* Wildigoz (powerful Goth). Joseph Wildigos, a Prot. ref. n., London, 1688

WILDMAN. *Dch.*, *Fl.* Wildeman ; a p.n. (a verderer, or powerful man)

WILDONE. From Wilden ; a loc. n., Beds

WILEMAR. *N.* Víl-Hjálmr (resolute helmet) ; *F.* Wilhelm, Wilm ; *D.B.* Wilmar, Willelm, Wilelmus, Willa ; *G.* Wilhelm ; *Dch.* Willemar ; p.n.

WILES. *Fl.* Weyllas ; a p.n. *See* Wales

WILFORD. A loc. n., Notts. Or Williford, Staffs

WILGOSS. *See* Wildgoose

WILGRESS. *N.* Vilgeirr (resolute spear); *A.S.* Wilga; *Dch.* Willekes, Willigers; *G.* Williger, Williges; p.n.

WILKE. *F.* Wilko, Wilke; fam. n. of Wilken; *Dch.* Wilke, Wilkes; p.n. Dimin. of Will

WILKEN, WILKENS. *D.*, *Dch.* Wilken, Wilkens; *Fl.* Wilkain; p.n.
Wileken in Rot. Obl. et Fin.

WILKERSON, WILKIE. *See* Wilke

WILKINS, WILKINSON. *See* Wilkens

WILLEMENT. *N.* Vil-mundr (resolute protector); *A.S.* Wilmund; *G.* Willigmann, Willman; *Dch.* Willeman; p.n.

WILLES, WILLIS, WILLS. From Wellis, a fief in Norm.
John de W. and R. W. in Rot. Hund.

WILLESEE. From Wilsey; a loc. n., Suff.

WILLETT. Dimin. of Will

WILLEY. A loc. n., Devon, Lancs; Velly, Norm. Or *D.* Wille, Willig; *Fl.* Wyllie; *G.* Wiehle, Wille, Willich; *Dch.* Wiele, Wille, Wijle; p.n.
In Rot. Hund.

WILLIAMS, WILLIAMSON. *See* Wilemar. Flem. ref., Lond. 1618

WILLIMONT. *See* Willement

WILLIMOT. *See* Wilmot

WILLING. *Dch.* Willing; a fam. n.

WILLOUGHBY. A loc. n., Leics, Lincs, Notts, Warw.
De Wilgeby in Rot. Obl. et Fin. Muschamp held it.

WILMOT. *Old G.* Wilmod; *Fl.* Wilmart, Wilmet; *Fr.* Wilmotte; p.n. (resolute courage)

WILMSHURST. A loc. n., Suss.

WILSCHER. *See* Wilsher

WILSDON. From Willesden; a loc. n., Middlx.

WILSHAK. *G.* Wilschek; a p.n. Dim. Or Wilsick; a loc. n., Yorks

WILSHEE, WILSHER. From Wilshaw; a loc. n., Staffs, Yorks. Or Wiltshire

WILSON. *D.* Will, Wilson; p.n. Prot. ref., Lond. 1622

WILTON. A loc. n., Cornw., Norf., Northants, Somers, Wilts, Yorks

WILTSHEAR, WILTSHIRE. The county

WIMBLE. From Wimpole; a loc. n., Camb. Or *A.S.* Winebeald; a p.n. (a strong friend)

WIMBUSH. From Wimbish; a loc. n., Ess.

WIMHURST. *See* Wilmhurst

WINCE, WINCH. A loc. n., Norf. Or *A.S.* Winc, Wing; *S.*, *D.* Winge; *Dch.* Wins; p.n. Dim. of Winger (a friendly spear)

WINCHCOMBE. A loc. n., Glost.

WINCKELS. *See* Winkel

WINCKLEY. From Winkleigh; a loc. n., Devon

WINCKWORTH. From Wingerworth; a loc. n., Derbysh.

WINCOP, WINCUP. *See* Whincop

WINCOTT. A loc. n.

WINDALL. *S.* Windahl; a loc. and p.n. Or *see* Windle

WINDER. *A.S.* Windhere, Winidhere; *D.* Winder; p.n. (a wend warrior)

WINDISH. *A.S.* Windæg, Windig; *G.* Windisch; p.n. (glorious friend)

WINDLE. A loc. n., Lancs

WINDLEY. A loc. n., Derbysh.

WINDOVER. From Wendover; a p.n., Hants

WINDSOR. A loc. n., Berks, Dorset

WINDUS, WINDUST. From Windrush (?); a loc. n., Glost. Or *see* Windish

WINDYBANK. A loc. n., Lancs

WINEARL. *See* Winnall

WINFIELD. *See* Wingfield

WING. A loc. n., Rutl. Or *see* Winch

WINGATE. A loc. n., Dur.

WINGFIELD. A loc. n., Derbysh., Suff.
Held by De Braiose.

WINGROVE. From Wingrave; a loc. n., Bucks

WINKEL, WINKLE. From Wynkel; a loc. n., Fland. *Dch.* Winkel; a p.n.

WINKFIELD. *See* Wingfield

WINKUP. *See* Whincop

WINMILL. A loc. n., Devon

WINN. *See* Whin and Wynne

WINNALL. A loc. n., Warw.

WINNINGTON. A loc. n., Ches.

WINSER, WINZAR. *See* Winsor

WINSLOW. A loc. n., Bucks, Heref., Yorks

WINSON. *See* Winston

WINSOR. A loc. n., Cornw., Hants. Or *see* Windsor

WINSPEAR. From Winceby (?); a loc. n., Lincs. *D.B.* Winzebi. *See* Shakespeare

> Winsbær or Winsbyr is the Danish form.

WINSTANLEY. A loc. n., Lancs

WINSTON. A loc. n., Dur., Suff.

WINTER. *A.S.*, *D.*, *S.*, *Dch.*, *Fl.*, *G.* Winter; a p.n. *See* Winder

WINTERBORN, WINTERBOURNE. A loc. n., Glost.

WINTERBOTHAM, WINTERBOTTAM. *See* Winterbourne (?)

WINTERTON. A loc. n., Lincs, Norf.

WINTHORP. A loc. n., Lincs

WINTLE. *See* Windle

WIRE. *See* Wyer

WISBY. From Wiseby; a loc. n., Lincs

WISDEN. From Wissendine (?); a loc. n., Rutl.

WISDOM. *D.* Wisbom (?); a p.n.

WISE. *A.S.* Wis; *G.* Weis, Weiss; p.n. (wise)

WISEDALE. A loc. n.

WISEMANN. *Dch.* Wiseman, Wisman; *G.* Weissmann; p.n. (sage, philosopher)

WISKER. *See* Whisker

WISSON. *See* Whiston

WHITCOMB. A loc. n., Somers

WITFORD. A loc. n., N. Wales

WITH. From Withy; a loc. n., Somers. Or *see* Withers

WITHALL. *See* Whittall. Or from Withiel; a loc. n., Cornw.

WITHERBY. A loc. n., Worcest.

WITHERIDGE. A loc. n., Devon

WITHERINGTON, WITHRINGTON. From Widdrington; a loc. n., Northbd.

WITHERN. A loc. n., Lincs

WITHERS. *N.* Viðarr (name of a god); *F.* Withers; *N.-Fr.* Witer; *G.* Wieder; *A.S.* Wider, Wihthere; p.n. (courageous warrior)

WITHNELL. *See* Widnell

WITT. A Dch. p.n. *See* White

WITTON. *See* Whitton

WITTY. *Fl.* Wittigh; a p.n. (wise)

WIX. A loc. n., Ess.

WIXLEY. From Whixley; a loc. n., Yorks

WOAKES. *A.S.* Woc; *D.* Woges; p.n. (watchful)

WOBBE. *F.* Wobbo, Wobbe; *Dch.* Wubbe; p.n. (a weaver)

WOLLARD. *A.S.* Wolfhard; a p.n. (strong wolf)

WOLNO. *See* Woolnough

WOLSELEY. A loc. n., Staffs

WOLSEY. *See* Wolseley

WOLSTENCROFT. A loc. n.

WOLSTENHOLME. A loc. n., Lancs

WOLTON. *See* Walton

WOLVERIDGE. *See* Woolrych

WOLVERTON. A loc. n., Hants, Kent, Wilts

WOMACK. *A.S.* Wigmearc, Wihomarc, Wimarc; p.n. (a Mercian warrior)

WOMBWELL. A loc. n., Yorks

WONNACOTT. From Onecote; a loc. n., Staffs

WOOD. *A.S.* Wuda; a p.n. Or from Atte-wood; a loc. n. Fl. ref., Lond. 1618. *See* Uden

WOODALL. From Woodhall; a loc. n., Lincs, Worcest., Yorks

WOODARD. *A.S.* Wadweard; *D.* Wodder; *Fr.* Oudard, Oudart; *D.B.* Wadard; p.n.; *A.S. wuduweard* (a wood ward), or *wádweard* (ford guard)

  Waudard in Rot. Obl. et Fin., K. John (Warwick), A.D. 1200.

WOODBERRY. *See* Woodbury

WOODBRIDGE. A loc. n., Camb., Suff.

WOODBURN. A loc. n., Northbd.

WOODBURY. A loc. n., Cornw., Devon, Hants

WOODCOCK. Dimin. of *F.* Ude (Udke). Or *A.S. wudu-coc* (the bird)

WOODEND. A loc. n., Staffs, and other counties

WOODERSON, WOODESON. *See* Woodard

WOODERSPOON. *See* Wotherspon

WOODFALL. A loc. n., Kent, Wilts

WOODFIELD. A loc. n., Dur.

WOODFORD. A loc. n., Ess., Glost., Northants, Somers

WOODGATE. A loc. n., Lancs, Staffs

WOODGER. *See* Woodard

WOODHAM. A loc. n., Ess.

WOODHEAD. A loc. n., Ches., Northbd.

WOODHOUSE. A loc. n., Derbysh., Hants, Lancs, Staffs, Somers

WOODIN, WOODING. *A.S.* Woden; *N.-Fr.* Waudin; *Dch.* Wouden; *Fl.* Wodon; p.n.

  It is doubtful if this is the god Odin or Woden. It is more likely from *N.* Auðunn; a p.n. (charitable or prosperous friend).

WOODLAND. A loc. n., Devon, Lancs

WOODLEY. A loc. n., Devon, Hants

WOODMASON. From Woodmanstone; a loc. n., Surr.

WOODROFFE, WOODRUFF. *See* Woodrow

WOODROW. A loc. n., Dorset

WOODSTOCK. A loc. n., Oxf.

WOODTHORPE. A loc. n., Derbysh., Lincs, Oxf., Yorks

WOODWARD, WOODYARD. *See* Woodard

WOOF. *See* Uff

WOOKEY. A loc. n., Somers

WOOL. A loc. n., Dorset. Or *G.* Wolle; *D.* Uhl, Woll; p.n. (wolf)

WOOLAGE. From Woolwich; a loc. n.

WOOLARD, WOOLLARD. *A.S.* Wulfheard; *S.* Wollert; p.n. (strong wolf)

WOOLASTON. A loc. n., Heref., Northants, Salop, Staffs, Worcest.

WOOLCOCK. *G.* Wolke; a p.n. Dim. of Wulf

WOOLCOTT. From Woolscott; a loc. n., Staffs

WOOLDRIDGE. *See* Worledge

WOOLERSON. From Woolverstone; a loc. n., Norf. Or *see* Woolaston

WOOLFENDEN. A loc. n.

WOOLISCROFT. From Woolescroft; a loc. n., Staffs

WOOLLATT, WOOLLETT. *A.S.* Wulfhat; a p.n. (war wolf); *Fr.* Volett. Hugt. n., Dover, 1622

WOOLLEY. A loc. n., Derbysh.

WOOLMAN. *A.S.* Wulfman; *D.* Vollmann; *G.* Wollmann; p.n.

WOOLMER. A loc. n., Hants. Or *A.S.* Wulfmær; *D.* Vollmer; p.n. (famous wolf)

WOOLNOUGH. *N.* Ulf-njótr; *A.S.* Ulnod, Ulnoth, Wulfnoth; p.n. (bold wolf)

WOOLRYCH. *A.S.* Wulfric; a p.n. (wolf ruler)

WOOLSTON. A loc. n., Hants, Oxf.

WOON. A loc. n., Cornw.

WOOR. *See* Whur

WOOSNAM. *See* Wolstenholme

WOOSTER. From Worcester; the county town

WOOTON. *See* Wootton

WOOTTEN. A loc. n., Suff.

WOOTTON. A loc. n., Hants, Heref., Northants, Salop, Somers

WORBOYS. A loc. n., Camb., Hunts

WORBY. *See* Worboys

WORD. A loc. n., Kent, Suss.

WORDLEY. From Wordsley; a loc. n., Staffs

WORDSWORTH. From Wardysworth or Wadysworth, W.R., Yorks
    Held by De Tilly.

WORLAND. A loc. n.

WORLEDGE, WORLLEDGE. From Warlage; a loc. n., Northbd.

WORLEY. *See* Whalley

WORM. *N.* Ormr; *A.S.* Orm, Ormar; *D.* Worm; *Dch.* Wormer; *G.* Wormt, Wurm; p.n. (a snake)

WORMALD. *A.S.* Wurmbeald; a p.n. (bold snake)

WORMER. *See* Warmer or Worm

WORMSLEY. A loc. n., Heref.

WORMULL. From Wormhill; a loc. n., Derbysh. Or *see* Wormald

WORN. *See* Warne

WORNER. *See* Warner

WORNUM. From Warnham; a loc. n., Suss.

WORPOLE. From Warpole; a loc. n., Devon

WORRALL. A loc. n., Yorks

WORROW. *A.S.* Worr; *D.* Worre; p.n. (defence)

WORSDELL. From Worsall; a loc. n., Yorks

WORSEY. *D.* Worsaae; a p.n. (victorious defender (?))

WORSFIELD. A loc. n.

WORSFOLD. A loc. n.

WORSHIP. From Warsop; a loc. n., Notts. Or *see* Wauchope

WORSLEY. A loc. n., Lancs

WORSSAM. A loc. n.

WORSTER. From Worstead; a loc. n., Norf. Or from Worcester

WORTH. A loc. n., Ches., Suss., Yorks. Also a Germ. loc. n.

WORTHAM. A loc. n., Suff.

WORTHING. A loc. n., Suss.

WORTHINGTON. A loc. n., Lancs, Leics

WORTLEY. A loc. n., Glost., Yorks

WORTON. A loc. n., Middlx.

WOSTENHOLME. *See* Wolstenholme

WOTHERSPON. A loc. n., Scotl.

WOTTON. A loc. n., Glost.

WRAGG. From Wragoe; a loc. n., Lincs. Or *see* Ragg

WRANGHAM. From Wrangham or Wrangholm; a loc. n., Lammermoor, Scotland
    Radus de Wrengham in Rot. Hund., p. 198. Thos. Wrangh'm, 1565, York Wills.

WRATE. *D.* Wriedt; *S.* Wrede, Wret; p.n. *See* Wright

WRATTEN. From Wratting; a loc. n., Camb., Norf., Suff.

WREFORD. From Wreyford; a loc. n., Devon

WREN. From Rennes; a loc. n., France. Or *see* Rain

WRENCH. *G.* Wrensch; a p.n. Dim. of Wren. Or *see* Renishaw

WRENFORD. From Rainford; a loc. n., Lancs

WRENTMORE. A loc. n.

WRETHAM. A loc. n., Norf.

WRIGHT. *D.* Wright; a p.n.; *A.S.* *wyrhta* (a wright). Or Wryde; a loc. n., Camb.

WRIGLEY. A loc. n.

WRINCH. *See* Wrench

WRING. *See* Ring

WRISTBRIDGE. *D.* Wrisberg (?); a p.n.

WRITER. *G.* Reiter; a p.n. *See* Ryder

WRODT. A loc. n., Lincs

WROTTESLEY. A loc. n., Staffs

WURR. *See* Worrow

WYAND. *Dch.* Weijand; a p.n.

WYARD, WYATT. *See* Whyart

WYBROW. *A.S.* Wigburh; *D.* Wibroe; p.n. (war protection). *See* Whybrow

WYBURN. *A.S.* Wigbeorn, Wibern; p.n. (war bear). Or *see* Wayborn

WYCHE. A loc. n., Lincs

WYER. From Weyer; a loc. n., Belg. Or *A.S.* Wighere; *Old G.* Wiher (warrior); *Dch.* Weijer; *G.* Wier; p.n. Prot. ref., Lond. 1618

WYETH. *See* Wythe

WYGARD. *See* Wigger and Whyart

WYKE. A loc. n., Yorks

WYKEHAM. A loc. n., Hants, Lincs, Northants, Yorks

WYKES. A loc. n., Northants, Salop Surr.
De Wikes in Rot. Obl. et Fin.

WYLDE. *See* Wildee

WYLIE. *See* Whiley

WYMAN. *N.* Vémundr (temple protector); *D.B.* Wimund, Wimer; *Dch.* Weyman, Wijmen; *G.* Wim-

WYMAN—*continued*
mer, Weiman; *S.* Weman; *Fl.* Wyman; Weman; p.n. Or *A.S.* Wigman (war-man)

WYNDHAM. From Windham; a loc. n., Norf. Or Wymondham, Leics

WYNEKEN. *A.S.* Wineca; *Fl.* Vinken, Wynesken; p.n. Dim. of *wine* (friend)

WYNNE. *Welsh* Gwynn (white)

WYNYARD. *A.S.* Winegeard; *Fl.* Wyngaard; *Dch.* Wijngaart; p.n. (friendly protector)

WYON. *Fl.* Wion; a p.n. *See* Vian

WYRE. *See* Wyer

WYTHE. *D.* Wiethe; a p.n. *See* White

WYTTON. *D.* Witten; a p.n.

WYVILL. A loc. n., Lincs. *See* Weevill

Y

YALDEN. From Yalding; a loc. n., Kent. Or *A.S.* Ealdwine; a p.n. (old friend)

YALE. *F.* Jelle; *S.* Yell; *Fl.* Jell; p.n. *See* Jelly

YALLOP. *N.* Hjálp (help); *G.* Hallupp, Halop; p.n. *See* Gallop

YAPP. *A.S.* Gab, Geb; *F.* Jabbo, Jabbe; *G.* Jaap; *Fl.* Jabé; *D.* Jappe; p.n. *See* Gibbs

YARDE. A loc. n., Somers. *See* Youard

YARDLEY. A loc. n., Northants, Worcest.

YARHAM. From Yarm; a loc. n., Yorks

YARINGTON. A loc. n.

YARKER. *See* Tiarko
Jarkir is on a runic inscription quoted by Stevens.

YARLEY. *See* Yardley

YARMUTH. A loc. n., I. of Wight, Norf.

YARNALL, YARNEL. *A.S.* Iarna; *G.* Janel; p.n. Dim. *N. járn* (iron), *járna* (mailed)

YARR. From Yarrow; a loc. n., Somers

YARRAD. *See* Jarred

YARRANTON. From Yarnton; a loc. n., Oxf.

YARROD. *See* Jarred

YARROW. A loc. n., Scotl., Somers. Also Jarrow, Dur.

YATE. A loc. n., Glost.

YATES. *See* Gates

YAXLEY. A loc. n., Camb., Norf., Suff. From *F.* Jak

YEAMES. *See* James

YEAMON. *Fl.* Jemayne; a p.n. *See* Yeoman

YEARSLEY. A loc. n., Yorks

YEILDING. A loc. n., Worcest.

YELD. From Yelt; a loc. n., Cornw.

YELDHAM. A loc. n., Ess.

YELL. *See* Jelly, Yale

YELLAND. From Yealand; a loc. n., Lancs

YELLOLY, YELLOWLEE, YELLOWLEES. A loc. n., Scotl.

YELLON. From Yelling; a loc. n., Hunts. Or fam. n. of Yell

YELLOPP. *See* Yallop

YELVERTON. A loc. n., Norf.

YENDON. A loc. n., Staffs (Endon)

YEO. From Yea, *i.e. A.S. ea* (water). Or *see* Ewen.

> Galfrida de la Ya held lands in Devon *temp.* Hen. III. It has been written Ya, Yaa, Yae, Yea, Yeo, and pronounced yaw.

YEOMAN. *G.* Jochmann; a p.n. (a bowman). Or *A.S.* Eomund; a p.n. (ancient protector)

YEOWELL. From Yeovil; a loc. n., Somers. Or *see* Jouel

YEREURY. From Yearby; a loc. n., Yorks

YERLING. *See* Yirling

YETTON. *See* Yatton

YEULETT. *See* Ullett

YEVES. *See* Jeeves

YEWDALL. From Yewdale; a loc. n., Lancs. Or *see* Udall

YEWENS. *Fl.* Juveyns; a p.n. *See* Ewen

YEXLEY. *See* Yaxley

YIRLING. *N.* Erlingr; *S.* Gjerling; *D.B.* Erlenc; a p.n. *See* Earl

YONGE. *D., Dch., Fl., G.* Jong, Jung, Junger; p.n. (young)

YORK. The city of that n.

YORSTON. From Yorton; a loc. n., Salop

YORWARTH. From Yoadwath; a loc. n., Yorks

YOUARD, YOUART. *See* Heward

YOUD. *See* Judd

YOUELL, YOUELS, YOUHILL, YOUILL. *See* Jouel

YOUENS. *See* Yewens

YOULDEN. *See* Youlton

YOULES. *See* Jouel

YOULTON. A. loc. n., Yorks

YOUNG. *See* Yonge

YOUNGER. *D.* Junker; a p.n.

YOUNGHUSBAND. *N.* Ungi-Ásbjorn (?); a p.n. Osborn the younger. *See* Osborne

YOUNGMAN. *D., Dch., G.* Jungman; a p.n.

YOUNGS. *Fl.* Junges; a p.n.

YOXALL. A loc. n., Staffs

YOXLEY. *See* Yaxley

YULE, YULL. *See* Jouel

Z

ZOUCH. From Sauchay (?); a loc. n., Normandy; or Jauche, Belg.

Souch in Roll of Battell Abbey. De la Zuche in Rot. Obl. et Fin., K. John.

APPENDIX

THE following names are under consideration. Many of them are local names, but as they cannot be found in any existing gazetteer or county directory, they are very likely those of manors, which are not necessarily parishes, or small estates situated in different parts of the country.

Any information respecting them will be thankfully received by the author, as will any other suggestions for the improvement of this work in a future edition, should such be called for.

Alefounder, Allshorn, Artingstall, Ashmole, Ayerst.

Banthorpe, Bearcroft, Beardshaw, Bestman, Bidmead, Blackbeard, Brasnett, Broadbent, Budibent, Bulport.

Challingsworth, Corbishley, Cragild, Crickmer, Cruickshank, Cudby, Culpeper.

Dadfield, Dashwood. Densley, Dewsnap, Dibley, Dockerill, Drakeford, Drakeyoung, Dryland.

Everest, Eversfield.

Fairservice, Faithful, Fastnedge, Faulding, Faultless, Fessenden, Firmstone, Fishenden, Fladgate, Flear, Flindall, Flinders, Flintoff, Flogdell, Fothergill, Foxcroft, Fripp, Frogley, Furlo, Furmstone.

Gadum, Gallafent, Gatfield, Getcliffe, Gillington, Girdham, Girdlestone, Gisby, Gladwell, Gorham, Goswell, Greagsby, Greensmith, Gridley, Grigsby, Grimsdick, Grindrod, Grinham, Grinslade.

Hadgraft, Hainbon, Handyside, Harkaway, Havergal, Haylock, Heavyside, Hebditch, Helpman, Heritage, Hignell, Hobday, Hogsflesh, Hoodless, Horlack, Horlick, Hostome, Hulcup, Huxtable.

Jeffcoat, Joyner.

Kenningham, Kethro, Kinglake, Kinstruck, Kirty, Kistrick, Knew.

Lamplin, Lasken, Lattey, Lealoyd, Leatherburrow, Lilliecrap, Lin-

285

nington, Linscott, Lipscombe, Littlechild, Longbourne, Lovecraft, Lovegrove, Lovelady, Lovelock, Lushington, Lythaby.

Maidment, Mainprice, Makemade, Manchip, Marrable, Melsom, Metcalf, Middlebrook, Middleditch, Monksfield, Mothersdill, Mottershead, Munnion.

Nall, Narraway, Nettleship, Nind, Norcross.

Orbell, Oxtoby.

Pagriff, Pedgrift, Penlington, Pieby, Pimlot, Popplewell, Prebble, Pummel, Pythian.

Rackley, Ranstead, Ravenscliffe, Ravenscourt, Reith, Remblance, Reside, Resther, Rexworthy, Ridler, Robjent, Rubrum.

Sculpher, Searson, Shalders, Shoard, Shrapnell, Shrimpton, Sidebottom, Silverside, Singlehurst, Sloggett, Slorach, Smethurst, Snelgrove, Snoxall, Snoxell, Spanswick, Spearpoint, Spenceley, Sperring, Sporton, Spyver, Squibb, Standeven, Stent, Stentiford, Stopford, Stradling, Strickstock, Strudger, Struggler, Stunt, Sturdy, Sunnuck, Supple, Swarbrick, Sweetapple, Swithinbank, Swivel.

Taffinder, Tapscott, Tarling, Tartelling, Taswell, Thickbroom, Timgate, Timlet, Tinham, Tinson, Tiplady, Todkill, Tofield, Tolhurst, Toplady, Totterdell, Trant, Tranter, Trapnell, Trimming, Trimy, Trinder, Triphook, Tripper, Trollope, Trubshaw, Truckle, Truelock, Trundley, Tumblety, Twelvetrees, Twentyman, Twisaday, Twyman.

Uffindel, Ullathorne, Umphleby, Uniacke, Ungless, Upsdall, Upsom.

Vamplew, Verity, Vousden.

Wagstaff, Wakeford, Wapshere, Warlock, Waterfield, Wayham, Waylet, Wellbeloved, Wharnsby, Whichelow, Widnell, Wimperis, Wildash, Wimpey, Wimpory, Wincott, Winship, Wisden, Wisedell, Wolstencroft, Wolveridge, Worland, Worsfield, Worssam, Wrentmore, Wrigley.

Yabsley, Yarnall, Yarnel, Yearren, Yeatman, Yendon, Yetman, Yeves, Yockney, Yount.